A Basic Introduction to Criminal Justice

A Basic Introduction to Criminal Justice

Sue Titus Reid, J.D., Ph.D.

Askew School of Public Administration and Policy
Florida State University

ASPEN PUBLISHING

Cover image: iStock/wragg Stock photo ID: 185120019

To contact Customer Service, e-mail customer.service@aspenpublishing.com,
call 1-800-950-5259, or mail correspondence to:

Aspen Publishing
Attn: Order Department
PO Box 990
Frederick, MD 21705

Printed in the United States of America.

1 2 3 4 5 6 7 8 9 0

ISBN 978-1-5438-0022-7

Library of Congress Cataloging-in-Publication Data application is in process.

About Aspen Publishing

Aspen Publishing is a leading provider of educational content and digital learning solutions to law schools in the U.S. and around the world. Aspen provides best-in-class solutions for legal education through authoritative textbooks, written by renowned authors, and breakthrough products such as Connected eBooks, Connected Quizzing, and PracticePerfect.

The Aspen Casebook Series (famously known among law faculty and students as the "red and black" casebooks) encompasses hundreds of highly regarded textbooks in more than eighty disciplines, from large enrollment courses, such as Torts and Contracts to emerging electives such as Sustainability and the Law of Policing. Study aids such as the *Examples & Explanations* and the *Emanuel Law Outlines* series, both highly popular collections, help law students master complex subject matter.

Major products, programs, and initiatives include:

- **Connected eBooks** are enhanced digital textbooks and study aids that come with a suite of online content and learning tools designed to maximize student success. Designed in collaboration with hundreds of faculty and students, the Connected eBook is a significant leap forward in the legal education learning tools available to students.
- **Connected Quizzing** is an easy-to-use formative assessment tool that tests law students' understanding and provides timely feedback to improve learning outcomes. Delivered through CasebookConnect.com, the learning platform already used by students to access their Aspen casebooks, Connected Quizzing is simple to implement and integrates seamlessly with law school course curricula.
- **PracticePerfect** is a visually engaging, interactive study aid to explain commonly encountered legal doctrines through easy-to-understand animated videos, illustrative examples, and numerous practice questions. Developed by a team of experts, PracticePerfect is the ideal study companion for today's law students.
- The **Aspen Learning Library** enables law schools to provide their students with access to the most popular study aids on the market across all of their courses. Available through an annual subscription, the online library consists of study aids in e-book, audio, and video formats with full text search, note-taking, and highlighting capabilities.
- Aspen's **Digital Bookshelf** is an institutional-level online education bookshelf, consolidating everything students and professors need to ensure success. This program ensures that every student has access to affordable course materials from day one.
- **Leading Edge** is a community centered on thinking differently about legal education and putting those thoughts into actionable strategies. At the core of the program is the Leading Edge Conference, an annual gathering of legal education thought leaders looking to pool ideas and identify promising directions of exploration.

In loving memory of my cousin
Elizabeth ("Beth") Blosser Weisinger
October 29, 1952–September 14, 2018

Brief Contents

Brief Contents

Contents

Chapter 2: Crime, Offenders, and Victims 23

Part II Entry into Criminal Justice Systems: Policing 47

Part III Processing a Criminal Case: Criminal Court Systems 123

Chapter 6: Criminal Court Systems 125

Chapter 7: Prosecution, Defense, and Pretrial Procedures 145

Preface

One of the most serious domestic problems in the United States is crime. Despite a downturn in estimated serious crimes as reported by the FBI in recent years, U.S. crime and incarceration rates are among the highest in the world, and the country faces immense problems associated with criminal activity. The concern for crime extends beyond the nature and frequency of occurrence to include official and unofficial reactions to crimes. Criminal justice systems appear inadequate to prevent crime and are questionable systems for coping with crimes that do occur.

Some react with bitter criticism of U.S. criminal justice systems but offer no meaningful suggestions for improvement. Others take the law into their own hands and fight back, wounding, and in some cases killing, those who attempt to victimize them. Still others take a close look at the systems with the hope of retaining the best parts and changing those that need improvement.

The latter view is taken in this text, which also considers the interrelationships of the various parts of criminal justice systems, for it is important to understand that a change in one area of a criminal justice system may and usually does have a significant impact on other areas of that system.

Significant changes were made in previous editions of this text, with the number of chapters being reduced from 18 to 14 and then to 12. The 12-chapter format was well received and has been continued in this edition.

This edition retains the author's reputation for including the most recent information on topics discussed. All topics have been checked for the latest information available at the time the manuscript left the author's hands. All legal citations, including cases and statutes, were checked to determine whether they had been altered or overruled by subsequent legislation or court decisions. Where possible, issues are illustrated with recent cases, although some older cases are presented because they are *classic* statements on the law and are still in effect, or because they represent the latest U.S. Supreme Court decisions on these issues.

Along with recent scholarly research in the social sciences, this edition retains the practice of using current events from popular sources to illustrate what is happening in criminal justice. These events were updated to the latest point in the book's publication.

Significant changes were made in the production of this edition, and they are noted in the next section. The major change, however, is that the text has been significantly shortened, but deleted and additional materials are presented in a Supplement, which is available to faculty who adopt and to students who purchase the text. This approach has been used in the author's other texts and has been well received.

Chapter Format

Each chapter begins with a list of learning objectives, which are designed to suggest to students what they should be learning during their progression through the chapter; an outline of the chapter's content; and an overview. Combined with end-of-chapter study questions and a summary, these features provide an excellent study guide for each chapter. Key terms are boldfaced within each chapter and defined in the Glossary at the end of the text. Key terms are also listed alphabetically at the end of each chapter with the pages on which they appear in the text. Material within the chapters is illustrated and emphasized further by tables, figures, photographs, and spotlights. Each chapter includes an insert on a particular professional opportunity, designed to enlighten those students who seek careers in criminal justice, and an insert on a particular dilemma faced by criminal justice systems pertaining to topics discussed in that chapter. Some chapters also contain excerpts from the appellate opinions of the U.S. Supreme Court or lower courts, although many of those excerpts, along with recently decided cases, were moved to the Supplement.

Organization of the Text and Important Content Information

The text is divided into five parts. Part I, "Introduction to Criminal Justice Systems," contains two chapters. The first, "Criminal Justice: An Overview," covers issues regarding punishment, criminal law, the concept of crime, and the purposes and reach of the criminal law. The chapter's topics are illustrated with references to recent crimes and discussion of issues raised by courts in recent cases, such as those involving whether police should be permitted to seize and search the cell phones of those they arrest, which is discussed in the Supplement with the cases of *United States v. Wurie* and *Carpenter v. United States*. The issue of whether the criminal law should be used to sanction pregnant women who give birth to drug dependent babies is discussed. The 2014 death of a young woman who chose to die by physician assisted suicide (PAS) rather than live a life of pain is discussed, and recent legal changes in PAS are noted.

Chapter 2, "Crimes, Offenders, and Victims," focuses on the 2017 FBI crime data, the latest available for this text. The data discussion in Chapter 2 emphasizes crimes, offenders, and victims, along with the interrelationships between the latter two. The chapter's discussion of rape, which includes date rape and marital rape, notes the recent changes in the FBI's definition of the crime. The chapter includes the definitions of what the FBI refers to as lesser crimes; includes a section on hate crimes; and touches on focus crimes, including child abuse, stalking, cybercrime, the new and fast growing body of criminal law in the area of animal rights, and human trafficking. The Supplement covers the special areas of terrorism and white collar crime, as well as a focus on the federal stalking statute.

Chapter 2's discussion of hate crimes illustrates this edition's inclusion of recent examples as it discusses the crimes that occurred in Charlottesville, Virginia in 2017 and at the Tree of Life Synagogue outside Pittsburgh, Pennsylvania in January 2019.

Part II, "Entry into Criminal Justice Systems: Policing," contains three chapters. Chapter 3, "The Emergence and Structure of Police Systems," covers the history of policing, including English policing. The problems resulting from illegal immigration and the policies regarding such are noted, along with allegations of racism among police. The changes in administration at the Federal Bureau of Investigation are discussed, noting the firing of FBI director James B. Comey and the appointment and confirmation of Christopher A. Wray as the new FBI director. Significant attention is given in both the text and the Supplement to the recent developments in the area of immigration.

Crimes on U.S. campuses and universities are under investigation amid allegations that officials do not properly investigate sex crimes; those are discussed. Attention is given to the conviction and sentencing of former Penn State President Graham B. Spanier and two aides for failure to report campus sexual assaults, and to the demotion of Baylor University president Ken Starr and the firing of that university's football coach for their handling of sexual assault cases on that campus. The discussion of private security was updated, as were the discussions on broken windows and zero tolerance policing.

Chapter 4, "Policing in a Modern Society," explores the structure and function of policing, featuring additional information on the recruitment, training, and education of police, some of which is in the Supplement. Prominently featured are the general requirements for entering policing, and all data concerning policing are updated. The latest data on police behavior during traffic stops are noted. The material on racial profiling is updated both in the text and in the material moved to the Supplement.

Chapter 4 features an extensive discussion of home searches. *Fernandez v. California* raises the issue of whether police can seize evidence from a home in the absence of a nonconsenting resident when consent was given by another resident. *Florida v. Jardines*, which involves the use of a drug-sniffing dog on a front porch of a home to gather evidence, is analyzed. A 2013 case, *Florida v. Harris*, involving a dog search of a vehicle, is included, along with a 2012 case involving the use of a GPS to search a vehicle: *United States v. Jones*. The 2016 case of *Birchfield v. North Dakota*, which discusses the criminalizing of a refusal to submit to a blood test when suspected of driving while intoxicated, is noted. Spotlight 4.4 covers the May 2018 motor vehicle search cases decided by the United States Supreme Court: *Byrd v. United States* and *Collins v. Virginia*.

The search and seizure issue as it pertains to searching a high school student for drugs, the focus of *Safford Unified School District #1 v. Redding*, is retained in the text, although the case excerpt was moved to the Supplement.

This edition includes a decision made in January 2019, by the U.S. Supreme Court, to hear an appeal from a Wisconsin case, *State v. Mitchell*, in which the defendant was convicted of operating a motor vehicle while intoxicated. His blood was drawn without a warrant

while he was unconscious. On appeal, the defendant claimed that the warrantless blood draw violated his Fourth Amendment rights to be free of an unreasonable search and seizure. The Wisconsin Supreme court held that the blood draw was reasonable under the state statute concerning implied consent when operating a motor vehicle. The case was not decided in time for the decision to be included within the text, but the Supreme Court's decision in *Mitchell v. Wisconsin* is included in the Supplement, with a notation to that effect in the text.

Chapter 5, "Problems and Issues in Policing," includes updated sections on evidence-based policing and policing "hot spots," with the latter referencing the 2018 August Vollmer address by Professor David Weisburd before the annual meeting of the American Society of Criminology.

A new Spotlight (5.2) presents the mission statement of the Police Officers' Lives Matter and well as that of Black Life Matters. The sections on stress among police as well as police subcultures were moved to the Supplement, but the text contains a new discussion on policing and mental health. A new law to encourage lawyers to devote pro bono time to domestic violence victims, the Pro bono Work to Empower and Represent Act of 2018 (known as the POWER Act), signed into law by President Trump in September 2018, is noted in the section on policing and domestic violence. Some of the major provisions of that statute are included in the Supplement.

The section on police misconduct, which features a discussion of the impact of illegal drugs on the subject, is followed by notations of misconduct in the use of deadly force. A 2018 case concerning police use of force, *Kisela v. Hughes*, is noted, and Supplement 5.8 excerpts Justice Sotomayor's dissent, in which she argued that the Court's decision permits police to "shoot first and think later." Some vehicle pursuit and search cases were moved to Supplement 5.9, but a 2015 case on the topic, *Mullenix v. Luna*, is referenced in the text. Violence against police includes updated data regarding police killed in the line of duty and notes some of the recent shootings by police.

The discussion on the control of policing includes regulation by police departments, by federal regulations, courts, and community relations. This section is updated with a discussion of the recent findings of the Department of Justice with reference to policing in Baltimore, Maryland.

Finally, the latest decisions on affirmative action as they might relate to policing are noted in Supplement 9.11.

The three chapters in Part III, "Processing a Criminal Case: Criminal Court Systems," explore the procedures and issues that arise from arrest through sentencing and appeals. Chapter 6, "Criminal Court Systems," sets the stage for this discussion with an overview of court systems. Supplement 6.3 features the first Latina on the U.S. Supreme Court, Associate Justice Sonia Sotomayor, and Spotlight 6.1 features an outstanding Florida judge in the context of judicial control through issuing contempt orders.

The text discusses the problems with President Barack Obama's unsuccessful attempt to have Chief Judge Merrick B. Garland of the District of Columbia Court of Appeals appointed to the U.S. Supreme Court, as well as the two successful nominations by President Donald J. Trump: Judges Neil M. Gorsuch and Brett J. Kavanaugh. Special attention was paid to the controversy surrounding the nomination of Judge Kavanaugh.

Finally, the text discusses the recall vote in the case of a California judge who sentenced a Stanford University swimmer to a very short sentence in a highly publicized sexual assault case.

Chapter 7, "Prosecution, Defense, and Pretrial Procedures," begins with an analysis of the role of lawyers in criminal court systems and proceeds through the pretrial procedures. It examines the roles of prosecutors and defense attorneys historically and currently, paying close attention to the modern problems of providing an adequate defense for indigent defendants. The discussion of the prosecutor's role includes cases of innocent defendants who were convicted and served time.

Some of the U.S. Supreme Court cases on ineffective assistance of counsel discussed in the previous edition were moved to the Supplement, but the text introduces a 2018 case, *Wessinger v. Vannoy*, in which Justice Sonia Sotomayor dissented from the Court's refusal to hear a case involving the neglect of defense counsel to present evidence of mitigating circumstances at sentencing in a capital case. The text also features information from another 2018 case, *McCoy v. Louisiana*, which raised the issue of ineffective assistance of counsel when the defense attorney, against his client's wishes, told the jury that his client was guilty of the three murders for which he was charged. The attorney apparently thought that his client's admitting guilt would diminish the chances he would be given the death penalty.

Chapter 7 contains considerable updating of indigent defense issues and recent cases. Recent bail reform laws, such as those in California, the first state to abolish cash bail, are noted. Also noted is a decision by the U.S. Supreme Court in April 2019 to refuse to hear and decide the issue of bail that does not consider a defendant's ability to pay. *Walker v. City of Calhoun, Ga.* involved a pedestrian who was arrested for being under the influence of alcohol in violation of a state statute. The statute provided only for a fine upon conviction, but the defendant was held in jail because he was detained pending a bail hearing and could not pay the standard $160 cash bond required for persons charged under the statute. The American Bar Association had filed a "friend of the court" brief urging the Supreme Court to hear the case and reverse the lower appellate court's upholding the city's practice of utilizing a fixed-bail policy to hold a defendant prior to a bail hearing without any consideration of a person's ability to pay. According to the ABA, jailing defendants who cannot pay bail is a violation of the equal protections clause of the Fourteenth Amendment.

Chapter 7 also includes a 2019 case, *Garza v. Idaho* decided by a 6-3 vote in February, in which the U.S. Supreme Court ruled that even though the defendant had signed appeal waivers in his plea agreements, he was entitled to a presumption that he was prejudiced when his attorney declined to file an appeal despite being told to do so by his client on several occasions after his sentencing. Earlier recent plea bargaining decisions that are noted in Chapter 7 include *Lee v. United States*, involving a deportation issue decided by the U.S. Supreme Court and the cases involving Dylann Roof, who murdered nine parishioners at a Charleston, South Carolina historically black church in 2015, and a light penalty given to a former fraternity president at Baylor University who was charged with rape.

Chapter 8, "Trial, Sentencing, and Appeal," describes the basic procedures involved in the trial, sentencing, and appeal phases of criminal cases. This edition features the 2014 decision by the Ninth Circuit, *SmithKline Beecham v. Abbott Laboratories*, holding that sexual orientation cannot be a reason for excluding a juror.

The case of Jeffrey Skilling, CEO of Enron, who won some concessions on appeal, was updated in the previous edition to show his new sentence: 14 years (down from 24 years). This edition further updates that case in the Supplement: Skilling was released from prison. The text also updates the latest sentencing changes embraced by the Trump administration. The discussion on capital punishment is updated to the date of release of this manuscript by the author. A 2018 report citing the declining support for the death penalty in the United States is noted, along with specific data on the number of executions of persons with mental illnesses, intellectual disability, or brain damage.

Chapter 8 notes the 2018 decision of the U.S. Supreme Court in *Flowers v. Kentucky* a death penalty case, in which the Court agreed to hear another case involving the issue of whether the *Batson* rule was applied correctly. The chapter also discusses the controversial pardons by then-California Governor Jerry Brown on Christmas Eve, 2018, when he issued 143 pardons and 131 commutations. It adds a 2019 capital punishment case in the Supplement and notes the 2018 execution by electric chair in Tennessee in the case of *Zagorski v. Haslam*, in which the U.S. Supreme Court refused a stay of execution.

The issue of racial prejudice in sentencing was updated in the discussion of a 2017 U.S. Supreme Court case, *Buck v. Davis*, in which the defendant's trial attorney introduced an expert who testified that statistically, the defendant would likely be dangerous in the future because he is black. The text introduced a 2016 case, *Elmore v. Holbrook*, in which Justice Sonia Sotomayor, joined by Justice Ginsburg, dissented from the decision of the U.S. Supreme Court not to hear the case, which involved a defendant whose attorney had never before tried a capital case and who failed to introduce evidence that his client might be brain damaged.

The text includes the capital punishment case of *Moore v. Texas*, decided by the U.S. Supreme Court in 2017, but again before the Court, which issued a decision in February 2019. Finally, the text contains discussion of the bipartisan bill on criminal justice reform that passed the Congress and was signed by President Trump in late 2018. Finally, the text contains discussion of the bipartisan bill on criminal justice reform that passed the Congress and was signed by President Trump in late 2018.

Part IV, "Confinement and Corrections," focuses on corrections, with three chapters examining the methods of confining offenders in total institutions or of placing them in the community under supervision. The discussion begins in Chapter 9, "The History and Structure of Confinement," with a look at the history of prisons and jails and a discussion of the federal and state prison systems. Prison and jail population data are updated. Considerably more information on women in prison is included, and the chapter contains an enhanced discussion of the children of inmates. Specifically, the California prison population issue, discussed in the previous edition, is updated with an inclusion of the October 2018 report by the state to the federal three-judge panel, as required, noting that the state's population numbers were in compliance with the panel's orders.

The chapter increased and updated the coverage on private prisons, noting that former President Barack Obama's DOJ was planning to phase out the use of private prisons in the federal system, but that President Trump quickly reversed that position with an executive order shortly after he took office. The text cited the example of the closing of one prison that was declared by a federal judge to be a place of "horror and corruption."

Chapter 10, "Life in Prison," discusses inmates and correctional officers and the interactions between them. It explains the legal issues involved in prison administration, looks at inmate rights versus privileges, and explores First Amendment issues. The discussion of prison administration includes the roles of correctional officers, both male and female. Particular attention is given to the methods of social control that involve inmates and officers. The chapter examines how inmates cope with the pains of imprisonment and distinguishes between the types of adjustments of female compared to male inmates. Special attention is given to the growing problems of dealing with elderly inmates, as well as those who are physically or mentally challenged. The chapter notes the special problems of female inmates (such as their unique medical needs) and those of the children of inmates.

The most recent changes in prison life as decided by courts are illustrated by two examples. A federal judge in California issued a temporary injunction in a case in which female inmates alleged that breakfast at 4 a.m. and pill call at 2:30 a.m., as well as maintenance during the night constitutes cruel and unusual punishment. Supplement 10.3 updates a discussion of the Department of Justice investigation into conditions in the Alabama men's prisons to include the findings of that investigation published in April 2019.

The chapter updates the discussion on New York's Rikers Island, noting in the Supplement that in 2017, the city's mayor announced plans to replace the detention facility with smaller institutions within the city. In August 2018, the mayor announced plans for four detention facilities and described the benefits they would provide.

The last part of the chapter focuses on six areas of prison issues. It begins with a section on solitary confinement, one of the most talked-about issues today and one that features statutory changes in two states: Colorado and New York. The discussion includes a look at an inmate who spent 41 years in solitary confinement. Supplement 10.9 contains a statement by Justice Sonia Sotomayor, who joined in the U.S. Supreme Court's refusal to hear two cases from Colorado on the issue of solitary confinement in prison. She nevertheless stated her concerns about the impact of solitary confinement on inmates. The Supplement includes a summary of the settlement in California concerning the issue of solitary confinement.

The second focus is on visitation in prison and introduces the new practice of video visitations, which in some institutions are replacing in-person visitations. The third focus, inmate sexual behavior, notes differences between male and female inmates in this regard. The fourth focus introduces significant new information on elderly inmates, as well as those who are physically and mentally challenged. A 2019 article from the American Bar Association describing the increased use of prisons and jails to house mentally challenged persons who have not been charged with crimes is noted. Criminal Justice Systems Dilemma 10.1 is updated with the decision of the court in the case of a deaf inmate who successfully sued under the Americans with Disabilities Act and won a judgment of $400,000 plus fees and costs.

The fifth focus is on prison work programs and the importance of providing educational opportunities for inmates. The sixth and final focus is on prison violence. Chapter 10's long-standing discussion of prison riots has been revised, updated, and moved to the Supplement. This discussion includes the 2017 South Carolina uprising in which seven inmates were killed and 17 were seriously injured. The discussion also includes the 2016 prison uprisings in Alabama and the April 2019 announcement by the U.S. Department of Justice concerning its conclusions in the investigation into the Alabama men's prisons and notes the execution in 2019 of another of the Texas 7 escape inmates.

Finally, Chapter 10 discusses the California federal judge's issuing of a temporary injunction in the case in which female inmates alleged that breakfast at 4 a.m. and pill call at 2:30 a.m., as well as maintenance noise during the nights constitutes cruel in unusual punishment.

Part IV closes with Chapter 11, "Community Corrections, Probation, and Parole," which examines the preparation of inmates for release, problems they face upon release, and the supervision of offenders in the community. The chapter contains a section on the diversion of nonviolent drug offenders and another on mentally challenged inmates. Data on confined inmates are updated.

Data on parole and probation are updated, including data on medical parole, as well as data on the registration of convicted sex offenders and constitutional issues concerning the incarceration and release of such offenders. The Supplement includes the most recent U.S. Supreme Court decisions on legal issues concerning the treatment of registered sex offenders, covering the June 2019 decisions, *United States v. Haymond* and *Gundy v. United States*. Chapter 11 also considers the civil commitment of sex offenders who are legally eligible for release from incarceration.

Chapter 11 also updates the discussion of drug laws involving state marijuana through May 2019, including mention of the proposed changes in federal laws: the Ending Federal Marijuana Prohibition Act of 2019.

The final part of the text, Part V, "Juvenile Justice: A Special Case," contains one chapter on juvenile justice systems, a special approach that was developed for the processing of juveniles who get into trouble with the law or who are in need of supervision or care because of neglectful parents or other guardians. Chapter 12, entitled "Juvenile Justice Systems," explains juvenile justice systems, contrasts those systems with adult criminal court systems, and considers the changes in juvenile justice systems that have resulted from decisions of the U.S. Supreme Court, as well as those of lower courts.

Chapter 12 contains a spotlight explaining the recent statutory change in one state, New Hampshire, that increased the age of the courts' jurisdiction from 17 to 18. New information is presented on other issues regarding juvenile justice and how those are viewed. The trial of juvenile cases in adult criminal courts, an issue that has come under scrutiny recently, is illustrated with one of the latest school shooting cases, which occurred in the Highlands High School in Colorado (near Denver) in May 2019.

The 2012 decision in *Miller v. Alabama* adds to the U.S. Supreme Court's earlier decision on the capital punishment of juveniles in the Court's reasons for its holding concerning life without parole. In 2016, in *Montgomery v. Louisiana*, the Court applied *Miller* retroactively. Cases involving *de facto* life without parole sentences are noted as illustrating the problems in sentencing juveniles who are convicted of serious crimes. The relevance of sex offender registration laws to juveniles is noted in the Supplement. The text discussed the 2018 passage of the reauthorization of the Juvenile Justice and Delinquency Prevention Act, which was signed by President Trump.

Considerable new information on juvenile correctional facilities is included, showing the continued trend toward deinstitutionalization. However, the mistreatment of juveniles within institutions continues and is noted in light of recent legal efforts to combat that practice. The text discusses a class action lawsuit brought by juveniles housed in prisons with adults in Michigan. The case was argued in December 2018 before the Sixth Circuit Court of Appeal and was not decided as of the date of publication.

A brief assessment section closes Chapter 12 with a message about the future.

Two appendices assist the reader with legal issues. Appendix A reprints the amendments to the U.S. Constitution, many of which are cited throughout the text. Appendix B explains the abbreviations and references that are used in legal case citations. Individual indexes assist the reader who desires quick access to names, subjects, and legal cases cited in the text.

Additional resources for students and instructors are available at the companion website that accompanies the text at https://www.AspenPublishing.com/.

Acknowledgments

Throughout my writing career, special friends and colleagues have been supportive and encouraging, and to them I give my unconditional thanks. My college roommate and friend of over 50 years, Heidi van Hulst, continues to support my writing habit with understanding and humor. Heidi's frequent e-mails never fail to contain some message asking about how the manuscript is progressing. Also e-mailing with frequent comments is Deborah DeFforge. Kerri Mohar, my former student, former Delta flight attendant, and friend, not only e-mails encouragement about the manuscript but about the perils and the joys of flying. My dear cousin and close friend, Gay Blosser, whose mother and stepfather took me in at age 12 when my family was homeless, is a frequent correspondent concerning the progress on the revision. During the revision, Gay's oldest child, Beth Weinsinger, passed away, and this edition is dedicated to her memory. Beth, an avid reader, was assigned my criminology text when she was a first-year college student. After graduation she served as a probation officer briefly until she married and worked with her husband in their successful electrical business.

My weekly trips to Florida ceased for this edition as I moved from Texas back to my New Hampshire home where I am spending a sabbatical year and enjoying a return to piano lessons and practice. My teacher, Ellen Schwindt, has reintroduced me to the rigors and joys of the instrument that was such a big part of my childhood and teen years. My long-time friend Sandy Louis, who looked after my New Hampshire home during the six years I lived in Texas, continues to check on me and the cats for whom she serves as the "cat nanny" when I travel. "Delta" (yes, she is named after the airline on which I have logged over 2 million miles) and "Jackson PD" (yes, he is named after the local police department, in which I am an honorary officer) have adjusted to their new home after their first (and hopefully last) very long hours in airports and on flights. They were both model passengers! Both they and I miss their Texas professional pet sitter and my close friend Nancy Burris, who traveled with me to help move them to New Hampshire. Special thanks to George Burris, who continues to handle all of my computer problems and to Eileen Hamilton, master stylist and skin care specialist, whose weekly treatments eased my stress. My Delta Airline friends continue to keep in contact despite my reduced travel. In particular I am grateful to Atlanta-based agents Jeffrey P. Penzkowski, Libby Hunt, and Steve Garrett, who always ensured that my layovers in the world's largest airport were as nonstressful as possible.

To my students at Florida State University's Askew School of Public Administration and Policy, who challenge and enlighten me, and to the school's director, Keon-Hyung Lee, who supported my request for the sabbatical, I am grateful. I will return to FSU with enthusiasm in the fall of 2019.

Finally, I want to thank my family for years of support of my writing endeavors: my sister and her husband, Jill and Roger Pickett, my niece and her husband, Rhonda Sue and John Santoyo, and my nephew and his wife, Clint and Stephanie Pickett. The children of our small family, Cherith Pickett and Eli and Jack Santoyo, are delights. May these precious children never experience the topics about which I write!

The production of a text requires the infinite patience and expertise of a professional production staff. My thanks to my acquisitions editor, David Herzig, who signed this book and the fifteenth edition of my criminology text. Betsy Kenny, who continued her excellent work from the criminology text, took care of the initial stages of placing the manuscript into production by obtaining and placing photos and converting the manuscript into the publisher's required format.

My special thanks go to my production manager, Paul Sobel at The Froebe Group, who guided the manuscript through my proofing and correcting of the copyedited and final page proofs, and to Renee Cote, copyeditor. These processes occurred during busy and difficult times for me, and I am grateful to all who eased my burdens.

Sue Titus Reid, J.D., Ph.D
Professor
Askew School of Public Administration and Policy
Florida State University
Tallahassee, Florida

About the Author

Sue Titus Reid, a professor in the Reubin O'D. Askew School of Public Administration and Policy at Florida State University, Tallahassee, has taught law students, graduate students, and undergraduate students in many states. She has served on the board of the Midwest Sociological Society and the executive staff of the American Sociological Association. She has been a chairperson, associate dean, and dean. In 1977, she was a distinguished visiting professor of law and sociology at the University of Tulsa. In 1985, she held the prestigious George Beto Chair in criminal justice at the Criminal Justice Center, Sam Houston State University, Huntsville, Texas.

Dr. Reid's formal training in criminology began in graduate school, but her interest in the field dates back to her early childhood. She was strongly influenced in her career by her father, who was born in the jail where his father, the under sheriff of a small east Texas county, lived with his family. Her grandmother prepared the inmates' meals. As a child, she helped her father in his grocery store and was quite disturbed when, on three separate occasions, he was victimized by criminals, one an armed robber. In each instance, the offender took all the cash and checks; no one was ever apprehended.

Dr. Reid graduated with honor from Texas Woman's University in 1960 and received graduate degrees in sociology (M.A. in 1962 and Ph.D. in 1965) from the University of Missouri-Columbia. In 1972, she graduated with distinction from the University of Iowa College of Law. She was admitted to the Iowa Bar that year and later to the District of Columbia Court of Appeals. She has also been admitted to practice before the U.S. Supreme Court.

Dr. Reid is unique among authors in the criminal justice field because of her distinguished qualifications in both law and the social sciences. She launched her text publishing career with *Crime and Criminology* in 1976, and that text, now in its fifteenth edition, has been widely adopted throughout the United States and in foreign countries. Dr. Reid's other titles include *Criminal Justice*, ninth edition; *Criminal Law*, ninth edition; *Criminal Law: The Essentials*, third edition; *The Correctional System: An Introduction*; and *Population Crisis: An Interdisciplinary Perspective* (with David L. Lyon). She has contributed articles to the *Encyclopedia of Crime and Justice* and the *Encyclopedia of American Prisons*, as well as to other books, in addition to publishing scholarly articles in both law and sociology.

Dr. Reid's contributions to her profession have been widely recognized nationally and abroad in both law and the social sciences. In 2018, she was elected to Lawyers of Distinction, for "Recognizing Excellence in Professor Teaching Law to Undergraduates." In August 2010, the Commission on Physical and Mental Disabilities of the 400,000-member American Bar Association featured Dr. Reid as its monthly spotlight on lawyers and judges who, despite disabilities, have made significant contributions to the legal profession. In 2019, Marquis Who's Who included her in its Lifetime Achievement Award and its Who's Who in the World. In 1982, the American Society of Criminology elected her a fellow "for outstanding contributions to the field of Criminology." Other national honors include the following: Who's Who Among Women; Who's Who in America; Who's Who in American Education; Who's Who in Criminal Law; 2,000 Notable Women (Hall of Fame for Outstanding Contributions to Criminal Law, 1990); Personalities of America; and Most Admired Woman of the Decade, 1992.

Her international honors include numerous recognitions from the International Biographical Centre (IBC), Cambridge, England, including the prestigious International Order of Merit. The IBC named Dr. Reid an inaugural member as one of the Top 100 Educators–2008, an honor limited by the IBC "to those individuals who, in our belief, have made a significant enough contribution in their field to engender influence on a local, national or international basis." Among the other international honors received by Dr. Reid are the following: International Woman of the Year, 1991-1992; International Who's Who of Intellectuals; International Who's Who of Professionals; International Who's Who of Professional and Business Women; International Order of Merit, 1993; Who's Who in the World; International Biographical Centre, England, Marquis Who's Who in the World; and the Manchester Who's Who Among Executive and Professional Women.

In 1979, Dr. Reid received the Distinguished Alumna Award from Texas Woman's University, one of the youngest graduates to be awarded that honor; in 2000, she received a university teaching award from Florida State University.

Dr. Reid has traveled extensively to widen her knowledge of criminal justice systems in the United States and in other countries. In 1982, she was a member of the Eisenhower Foundation–sponsored People-to-People Crime Prevention delegation to the People's Republic of China. Her several trips to Europe included a three-month study and lecture tour of ten countries in 1985. She is a member of the American Bar Association, the American Association for Justice, and the American Society of Criminology which recognized her in 2019 as one of the Golden Members—members who have belonged to the professional organization for over 50 years.

About the Author

Sue Titus Reid, a professor in the Reubin O'D. Askew School of Public Administration and Policy at Florida State University, Tallahassee, has taught law students, graduate students, and undergraduate students in many states. She has served on the board of the Midwest Sociological Society and the executive staff of the American Sociological Association. She has been a chairperson, associate dean, and dean. In 1977, she was a distinguished visiting professor of law and sociology at the University of Tulsa. In 1985, she held the prestigious George Beto Chair in criminal justice at the Criminal Justice Center, Sam Houston State University, Huntsville, Texas.

Dr. Reid's formal training in criminology began in graduate school, but her interest in the field dates back to her early childhood. She was strongly influenced in her career by her father, who was born in the jail where his father, the under sheriff of a small east Texas county, lived with his family. Her grandmother prepared the inmates' meals. As a child, she helped her father in his grocery store and was quite disturbed when, on three separate occasions, he was victimized by criminals, one an armed robber. In each instance, the offender took all the cash and checks; no one was ever apprehended.

Dr. Reid graduated with honor from Texas Woman's University in 1960 and received graduate degrees in sociology (M.A. in 1962 and Ph.D. in 1965) from the University of Missouri-Columbia. In 1972, she graduated with distinction from the University of Iowa College of Law. She was admitted to the Iowa Bar that year and later to the District of Columbia Court of Appeals. She has also been admitted to practice before the U.S. Supreme Court.

Dr. Reid is unique among authors in the criminal justice field because of her distinguished qualifications in both law and the social sciences. She launched her text publishing career with *Crime and Criminology* in 1976, and that text, now in its fifteenth edition, has been widely adopted throughout the United States and in foreign countries. Dr. Reid's other titles include *Criminal Justice*, ninth edition; *Criminal Law*, ninth edition; *Criminal Law: The Essentials*, third edition; *The Correctional System: An Introduction*; and *Population Crisis: An Interdisciplinary Perspective* (with David L. Lyon). She has contributed articles to the *Encyclopedia of Crime and Justice* and the *Encyclopedia of American Prisons*, as well as to other books, in addition to publishing scholarly articles in both law and sociology.

Dr. Reid's contributions to her profession have been widely recognized nationally and abroad in both law and the social sciences. In 2018, she was elected to Lawyers of Distinction, for "Recognizing Excellence in Professor Teaching Law to Undergraduates." In August 2010, the Commission on Physical and Mental Disabilities of the 400,000-member American Bar Association featured Dr. Reid as its monthly spotlight on lawyers and judges who, despite disabilities, have made significant contributions to the legal profession. In 2019, Marquis Who's Who included her in its Lifetime Achievement Award and its Who's Who in the World. In 1982, the American Society of Criminology elected her a fellow "for outstanding contributions to the field of Criminology." Other national honors include the following: Who's Who Among Women; Who's Who in America; Who's Who in American Education; Who's Who in Criminal Law; 2,000 Notable Women (Hall of Fame for Outstanding Contributions to Criminal Law, 1990); Personalities of America; and Most Admired Woman of the Decade, 1992.

Her international honors include numerous recognitions from the International Biographical Centre (IBC), Cambridge, England, including the prestigious International Order of Merit. The IBC named Dr. Reid an inaugural member as one of the Top 100 Educators–2008, an honor limited by the IBC "to those individuals who, in our belief, have made a significant enough contribution in their field to engender influence on a local, national or international basis." Among the other international honors received by Dr. Reid are the following: International Woman of the Year, 1991-1992; International Who's Who of Intellectuals; International Who's Who of Professionals; International Who's Who of Professional and Business Women; International Order of Merit, 1993; Who's Who in the World; International Biographical Centre, England, Marquis Who's Who in the World; and the Manchester Who's Who Among Executive and Professional Women.

In 1979, Dr. Reid received the Distinguished Alumna Award from Texas Woman's University, one of the youngest graduates to be awarded that honor; in 2000, she received a university teaching award from Florida State University.

Dr. Reid has traveled extensively to widen her knowledge of criminal justice systems in the United States and in other countries. In 1982, she was a member of the Eisenhower Foundation–sponsored People-to-People Crime Prevention delegation to the People's Republic of China. Her several trips to Europe included a three-month study and lecture tour of ten countries in 1985. She is a member of the American Bar Association, the American Association for Justice, and the American Society of Criminology which recognized her in 2019 as one of the Golden Members—members who have belonged to the professional organization for over 50 years.

Part I

Introduction to Criminal Justice Systems

Criminal justice systems throughout the world vary considerably, and within the United States there are differences among the various state systems. The federal system also has unique features. All criminal justice systems, however, face common issues, such as developing a punishment philosophy, defining the conduct to be included in criminal law, defining the elements of the included crimes, collecting crime data, enforcing and adjudicating crimes, processing crime suspects, and so on. Criminal justice professionals must also decide how to respond to crime victims.

Part I of this text features U.S. criminal justice systems. The first chapter presents an overview of the punishment philosophies on which these systems are based and explores the reality of how they work. Chapter 1 also contains an overview of criminal law, beginning with the nature and philosophical bases of punishment. It mentions the components of criminal justice systems, and it discusses the meaning of criminal law as compared with civil law, the sources of criminal law within the context of the adversary system, and the constitutional limits of criminal law. The latter includes the U.S. Supreme Court cases requiring search warrants for searching cell phones of arrestees. The concept of crime is explored, with consideration given to the elements of crimes. The final section analyzes the reach of criminal law, which begins with a section on physician assisted suicide (PAS) and then looks at crimes against private sexual behavior and illegal drug abuse.

Chapter 2 discusses the methods for securing and analyzing crime and victimization data and looks at the most serious violent and property crimes as well as at less serious crimes, with special attention to hate crimes and includes an analysis of characteristics of offenders and of victims. It focuses on the specific crimes of child abuse, stalking, cybercrime, animal cruelty, and human trafficking.

The chapters in Part I set the stage for the subsequent and more extensive analyses of the basic parts of criminal justice systems—police, prosecution and defense, courts, and corrections—that constitute the remainder of the text.

1

Criminal Justice: An Overview

Chapter Outline

Learning Objectives

After reading this chapter, you should be able to do the following:

- List, define, and illustrate the major punishment philosophies
- Discuss the importance and impact of discretion in criminal justice systems
- List and describe briefly the major components of criminal justice systems
- Explain the difference between *civil law* and *criminal law*
- Contrast the *inquisitory* and the *adversary* systems
- Define *equal protection* and *due process*
- Explain what is meant by constitutional limits on criminal law
- List and analyze the sources of criminal law
- Define *crime*, explain how crimes are classified, and discuss the general elements of a crime
- Explain criminal *defenses*
- Comment on the meaning and current legal status of physician assisted suicide (PAS)
- Explain the pros and cons of including private, consensual sexual behavior, and the use of marijuana for medicinal purposes within the criminal law

Throughout the United States in recent years, serious property and violent crimes have occurred, challenging criminal justice systems and shocking the residents of small villages as well as large cities. Numerous individuals have been attacked in their neighborhoods, in shopping malls, and on school, college, and university campuses. Some of the more extensive and publicized school shootings were the killing of 17 students and staff at the 3,000-student Marjory Stoneman Douglas High School in Parkland, Florida, in February 2018; the April 2007 killings at Virginia Tech University, the scene of the largest mass murder in U.S. history when a lone gunman killed 32 fellow students on the university's campus in Blacksburg, Virginia; and the 2012 killing of 20 children and 6 adult staff members at Sandy Hook Elementary School in Connecticut by a gunman who killed his own mother just prior to opening fire on the grade school campus. In July 2018, shooters opened fire on a street in New Orleans, and in April of that year, four people lost their lives in a restaurant shooting in Nashville, Tennessee.

School crossing guard Wendy Behrend lights a candle at a memorial outside Marjory Stoneman Douglas High School during the one-year anniversary of the school shooting, Thursday, Feb. 14, 2019, in Parkland Fla. On that date in 2018, 14 students and three staff members were killed when a gunman opened fire at the high school.

Law enforcement officials have been killed in the line of duty; and law enforcement officials have killed suspects, often minorities, in situations that have led many to accuse them of racial targeting. These and other crimes remind us of our vulnerability to violent crime, such as the acts of September 11, 2001, when terrorists overpowered the crew of four U.S. commercial aircraft, flying two of them into the Twin Towers of the World Trade Center in New York City; another into the Pentagon in Washington, D.C.; and a fourth into a field in Shanksville, Pennsylvania. Approximately 3,000 people lost their lives; the World Trade Center was demolished; the Pentagon was damaged; and untold numbers of persons lost money or jobs as a result of the economic effects of these unbelievable terrorist acts.

Serious property crimes, were also in the news as we were all warned to be cautious of fraud through cyber attacks and phone calls. The declining data were of little comfort to those who were victimized or who feared becoming victims.

This chapter analyzes some of the issues regarding the imposition of punishment in criminal courts before looking briefly at the systems that impose that punishment and the criminal law on which punishment is based. Emphasis on careers is included, too, as noted in Professions 1.1. The chapters of the text also include references to the online supplement that is available to faculty who adopt the book and students who purchase the text. The entries in the supplement add additional information while enabling the author to reduce the length of the text.

The chapter begins with a look at the nature and meaning of punishment, along with the historical and current philosophies underlying punishment. But in reality, societies punish for other reasons, some of which are illegal. It is important to understand the reality of any criminal justice system, and this chapter looks at the wide discretion of decision making in criminal justice systems.

The chapter briefly describes the basic components of criminal justice systems—police, prosecution, courts, and corrections. An overview of criminal law follows, with an examination of the distinction between criminal and civil law, an exploration of the adversary system, and a brief explanation of the constitutional limitations on criminal law. The sources of criminal law are mentioned briefly. The concept of crime is analyzed in terms of the ways in which crimes are classified and the basic elements of a crime. Brief attention is given to defenses to criminal cases. The chapter contains a discussion of how far the criminal law should reach in its efforts to control behavior, such as physician assisted suicide (PAS), consensual sexual behavior by adults in private, and the use of substances (such as marijuana) thought by some not to be harmful.

Professions 1.1

Criminal Justice Careers

Each chapter in this text includes a "Professions" box that focuses on careers. Although it is not possible to discuss all of the careers available in criminal justice or to prepare students for applying for specific jobs, exposure to job possibilities is always beneficial. This "Professions" box presents a brief overview of criminal justice careers.

Careers in criminal justice encompass a wide range of activities, from custodial services to high levels of administrative and professional positions, such as that of a U.S. Supreme Court justice. They include professions in law, psychology, criminology, sociology and other social sciences, architecture, accounting, forensics, physical sciences, and many other fields. Persons in criminal justice may investigate criminal activities on the streets or in the labs, engage in administrative activities in a wide variety of settings, counsel adult or juvenile offenders, design prisons or jails, supervise persons on parole or probation, train correctional officers or other personnel, supervise shop or other job assignments or train inmates in correctional facilities, teach college students in criminal justice courses, or engage in many more activities. These and other positions require training and education ranging from a high school education and on-the-job training to a Ph.D. or a law degree, perhaps with experience.

This text introduces you to criminal justice systems and their functions. Not all of you will become employed in the field, but even for those who do not, the information should be of general usefulness in related professions.

Enjoy your excursion through one of the most important and challenging areas of employment.

Criminal Justice Systems Dilemma focus boxes are included throughout the text. To illustrate their purpose, consider the two cases described in Criminal Justice Systems Dilemma 1.1, which illustrates one of the issues faced in criminal justice systems: whom to prosecute and for which crime(s). This focus box presents cases that could be considered murder. Most people have no difficulty contrasting the cases of Henry Brisbon and Hans Florian, in view of the number and nature of the killings Brisbon committed. But there is a strong argument that the legal elements of first-degree murder were present in both cases.

In the case of Hans Florian, the grand jury refused to indict. Similar cases have resulted in indictments, trials, convictions, and incarcerations. For example, in 1990, Florida officials approved the release from prison of Roswell Gilbert, age 81, who was incarcerated for murdering his ailing wife in what he called a mercy killing. Gilbert was convicted of first-degree murder and sentenced to 25 years to life in prison. He served several years before his release for health reasons. Should Gilbert have been convicted of first-degree murder on facts similar to those of Florian and others? All these persons claimed that they acted out of love when they killed their terminally ill spouses, who begged to be relieved of their suffering. If Gilbert deserved to serve time in prison, why should he have been released for medical reasons?[1] Gilbert died in 1994.

THE NATURE AND PHILOSOPHICAL BASES OF PUNISHMENT

A **criminal justice system** is designed to prevent people from violating its rules and to **sanction**, or impose legal punishments, on those who do. Issues arise, however, regarding the behavior that should be covered by **criminal** punishments, who should be sanctioned, and which sanctions should be applied. These issues are discussed in various chapters throughout the text, but at this point, we look at the philosophical bases for punishment.

The cases discussed in Criminal Justice Systems Dilemma 1.1, along with other criminal cases, may be analyzed in terms of four objectives recognized historically as bases for punishment: **incapacitation, retribution, deterrence,** and **rehabilitation**. The debate over which of these objectives *should* be the basis for punishment continues. Each objective deserves brief attention.

First is *incapacitation,* which may be employed to make it impossible for offenders to offend again. In the

Criminal Justice Systems Dilemma 1.1

Two Cases of Murder?

One element of a crime in all U.S. criminal justice systems is an intent, but its presence does not ensure a conviction in all cases that could be considered murder. Analyze the following cases, both of which apparently involved an intent to kill. Do you think the offenders should have been treated alike? Would the death penalty be an appropriate punishment for either or both of them?

In the first case, a young woman driving a Chevrolet Caprice along Interstate 57 in southern Cook County, Illinois, on the night of June 3, 1973, was forced off the highway by a car occupied by four men. With one of the men pointing a gun at her, she was ordered to remove her clothing and climb through a barbed-wire fence at the side of the road. Henry Brisbon Jr. responded to her pleas for her life by thrusting a shotgun into her vagina and firing. She was in agony for several minutes before her assailant fired the fatal shot at her throat.

In less than an hour, Brisbon had committed two more murders. Brisbon's next victims, also riding in their car along Interstate 57, were planning to be married in six months. When they pleaded for their lives to be spared, Brisbon told them to lie on the ground and "kiss your last kiss," after which he shot each in the back. Brisbon took $54 in cash, two watches, an engagement ring, and a wedding band from his victims. He was arrested and convicted of these crimes, but because the death penalty in Illinois had been invalidated, he was given a term of 1,000 to 3,000 years. While serving that term, he killed an inmate and was sentenced to death under the state's new death penalty statute.

During an earlier incarceration, Brisbon had been involved in 15 attacks on correctional officers and inmates and was responsible for beginning at least one prison riot. He had hit a warden with a broom handle and trashed a courtroom during a trial. Despite these acts of violence, Brisbon said, "I'm no bad dude . . . just an antisocial individual." He blamed his problems on the strict upbringing by his Muslim father, who taught him to dislike white people. The result: "I didn't like nobody." How did he feel about his victims? "All this talk about victims' rights and restitution gets me. What about my family? I'm a victim of a crooked criminal system. Isn't my family entitled to something?"[1]

In February 2003, noted lawyer and best-selling novelist Scott Turow was interviewed on National Public Radio about the death penalty and specifically about Brisbon. Turow had just published *Reversible Errors*, his novel about a lawyer who was trying to free a man facing imminent execution. Turow had visited Brisbon in the supermax prison in Thames, Illinois. Turow described Henry Brisbon as the "poster child for capital punishment in Illinois," suggesting that for "incredible monsters" like Brisbon, the death penalty may appear to be just. But the critical issue "is whether a system of justice can be constructed that reaches only the rare, right cases, without also occasionally condemning the innocent or the undeserving." Turow pointed out that dangerous persons such as Brisbon evoke little if any sympathy, but it is the most atrocious cases that are most likely to produce mistakes in prosecution, leading to the conviction of the innocent. This is because of the enormous public pressure on law enforcement officials to obtain convictions in these cases. In Turow's judgment, supermax prisons, such as the one in which Brisbon was incarcerated, are sufficiently secure to mitigate the possibility that he will kill again.[2]

Brisbon's death sentence, along with the death sentences of over 150 other inmates, was commuted to life without parole by the state's governor, George Ryan, who placed a moratorium on the death penalty in that state in 2003 after he received the report of a commission he appointed to study the use of the death penalty in Illinois. Based on that report, Governor Ryan concluded that the death penalty should not be utilized until the state could guarantee that innocent persons would not be executed. Subsequently, the Illinois General Assembly passed a bill to abolish the death penalty in that state, and it was signed by Governor Pat Quinn in 2011.

In contrast to the case of Brisbon is that of Hans Florian. In March 1983, Florian, age 79, went to the hospital to visit his wife of 51 years, who was suffering from a disease that eventually would make her senile and helpless. Florian had placed his wife in a nursing home because he was unable to care for her, but when she became too ill for that facility, she was hospitalized.

Florian visited his ailing wife daily. During each visit, he placed her in a wheelchair and pushed her around the floor of the hospital to give her a change of scenery. On the day in question, he wheeled her into a stairwell and shot her in the head, ending her life quickly. Friends claimed that Florian was not a murderer. He killed his wife because he loved her so much that he wanted her to be free of her suffering.[3]

Florian was charged with first-degree murder. Should he have been convicted of that charge? Apparently, his act was premeditated and without legal justification. If convicted, should he have been sentenced to death? The text contains more information on this and a related case.

1. "An Eye for an Eye," *Time* (January 24, 1983), p. 30.
2. "Scott Turow Discusses the Death Penalty," Show: *Fresh Air* (National Public Radio, February 18, 2003), 12 Noon; Anne Stephenson, "New and Notable," *Arizona Republic* (Phoenix) (September 28, 2003), p. 4E.
3. "When Is Killing Not a Crime?," *Washington Post* (April 14, 1983), p. 23.

past (and in some countries today), the hands of a thief were amputated; the eyes of a spy were gouged; rapists were castrated; prostitutes were disfigured to make them unattractive. Another form of incapacitation was to brand the offender with a letter symbolizing the crime; thus, an adulteress was branded with the letter *A*, a thief with the letter *T*. The assumption was that, if people knew the nature of offenders' crimes, they would avoid those persons. Today, incapacitation is accomplished primarily through incarceration in a penal institution or through home confinement or other similar methods.

The second philosophy is that of *retribution* (also called *revenge*). Historically, revenge was one of the most important justifications for punishment. The philosophy of revenge, or retribution, is the eye-for-an-eye doctrine, which can be traced back for centuries. Revenge was acceptable, and the victim (or the victim's family) was expected to avenge the offense. Later, private revenge was replaced by official government punishment, and today the philosophy of revenge has been replaced by that of *retribution*, which is widely recognized as an appropriate reason for punishment. The earlier eye-for-an-eye approach is not recognized legally today, but in 1976, in *Gregg v. Georgia*,[2] the U.S. Supreme Court approved retribution as a basis for punishment, even for capital punishment. **Supplement 1.1** discusses the Court's consideration of the punishment concepts of both retribution and deterrence (discussed next) in imposing capital punishment.

The main punishment philosophies in vogue in the past century were deterrence and rehabilitation. Both continue to influence legislation and court decisions.

Deterrence includes *individual deterrence*, which refers to preventing the apprehended offender from committing additional criminal acts, and *general deterrence*, which assumes that punishing that offender will keep others from engaging in criminal acts because potential offenders will refrain from criminal behavior after seeing the punishment imposed on actual offenders. **Supplement 1.2** discusses the issue of deterrence as it might apply to college students.[3] **Supplement 1.3** discusses whether there is empirical evidence for the effectiveness of deterrence theory.

Rehabilitation has been described as the *rehabilitative ideal*, which is based on the premise that human behavior is the result of antecedent causes that may be known by objective analysis and that permit scientific control. The assumption is that offenders, especially younger ones, should be treated, not punished. In the mid-1900s, social scientists endorsed the rehabilitative ideal and began developing treatment programs for institutionalized inmates. The ideal was incorporated into some statutes, proclaimed by courts, and supported by presidential crime commissions.

The demise of the rehabilitative ideal was emphasized in a 1982 magazine headline: "What Are Prisons For? No Longer Rehabilitation, but to Punish and to Lock the Worst Away." The article referred briefly to the original purpose of U.S. prisons: not only to punish but also to transform criminals "from idlers and hooligans into good, industrious citizens." It concluded, however, that "no other country was so seduced for so long by that ambitious charter."[4]

The simple fact is that prisons did not work as intended. The result was a movement toward more severe and definite sentences. California, a state that used the rehabilitation philosophy, led the way in returning to a punitive philosophy by declaring in its statutory changes in 1976 (to become effective the following year) that "the purpose of imprisonment for crime is punishment."[5] At the federal level, the U.S. Congress eliminated rehabilitation as a goal in its correctional system.[6]

Recent evidence suggests a movement back to rehabilitation. California changed the name of its department of corrections to the California Department

Spotlight 1.1

Treatment Rather Than Punishment for Substance Abuse

The Alcoholism and Intoxication Treatment Act[1] of the state of Idaho provides the following declaration of policy:

> **It is the policy of this state that alcoholics, intoxicated persons or drug addicts may not be subjected to criminal prosecution or incarceration solely because of their consumption of alcoholic beverages or addiction to drugs but rather should be afforded treatment in order that they may lead normal lives as productive members of society.**
>
> **The legislature hereby finds and declares that it is essential to the health and welfare of the people of this state that action be taken by state government to effectively and economically utilize federal and state funds for alcoholism and drug addiction research, and the prevention and for the treatment and rehabilitation of alcoholics or drug addicts. To achieve this, it is necessary that existing fragmented, uncoordinated and duplicative alcoholism and drug treatment programs be merged into a comprehensive and integrated system for the prevention, treatment and rehabilitation of alcoholics.**
>
> **The legislature continues to recognize the need for criminal sanctions for those who violate the provisions of the uniform controlled substances act.[1]**

1. Idaho Code, Chapter 3, Section 39-301 (2018).

of Corrections and Rehabilitation, and since 2001, California law has provided treatment rather than incarceration for nonviolent drug offenders convicted of first or second offenses. However, California had the most stringent three-strikes statute in the country, which resulted in serious prison overcrowding issues and a corrections system under federal court monitoring. The California system is discussed in detail later in the text. For now, Spotlight 1.1 features an Idaho statute that provides for treatment rather than criminal prosecution for some cases of substance abuse.[7]

Finally, the philosophies of deterrence and retribution are sometimes combined to form the **just deserts** model,[8] which may be viewed as a reaction against the perceived ineffectiveness of rehabilitation. Under the justice model, an incarcerated person should be allowed to choose whether to participate in rehabilitation programs. The only purpose of incarceration is to confine for a specified period of time, not to rehabilitate the criminal. The offender receives only the sentence he or she deserves, and that sentence is implemented according to fair principles.

The justice model sounds good. People should be punished in accordance with what they deserve. But try applying it to the cases discussed in Criminal Justice Systems Dilemma 1.1 and the accompanying text. Which, if any, of the offenders *deserve* to be executed? Would the refusal to execute Henry Brisbon Jr. result in more people committing atrocious murders such as those he committed? Would his execution cause those who contemplate such murders to refrain from committing them? How about mercy killing? Did incarcerating a Florida mercy killer deter others from such acts? Would incarceration have deterred Hans Florian from committing that offense again, or was imprisonment unnecessary for specific deterrence in his case? Or is it possible that, regardless of the stated underlying punishment philosophies accepted by a society, the reality is that particular decisions are sometimes made for other reasons? Is it also possible that reactions to crime are due to other reasons, such as politics?

THE ROLE OF DISCRETION IN PUNISHMENT

It is characteristic of criminal justice systems throughout the world that decisions may be made for political reasons that have little, if anything, to do with the issues. A large body of scholarship has developed in an attempt to explain criminal justice systems as an area where critical decisions are made by those in power for the purpose of maintaining control over those not in power. It is alleged, for example, that in the United States, women, racial and ethnic minorities, and the poor can expect the blunt end of justice, whereas white men make most of the important decisions legislatively, administratively, and judicially and receive better treatment in criminal justice systems.

Others disagree with this position, and the conflict may be expected to continue. But as long as **discretion** is possible, decisions may be made for political and other extrajudicial reasons. *Discretion* means that individuals may use their own judgment to make decisions. The text discussion of Criminal Justice Systems Dilemma 1.1 provides examples of the exercise of discretion. Hans Florian was not tried for the murder of his wife, but Roswell Gilbert, who took his wife's life under similar circumstances, was convicted and served prison time. The jury could have chosen not to convict him, as has often happened in similar cases. Thus, the jury had considerable discretion. In Gilbert's case, the governor exercised his discretion in releasing Gilbert before he completed his sentence.

Various persons within criminal justice systems, including police, prosecutors, judges or justices, correctional officials, and paroling authorities, may exercise discretion. In addition, defense attorneys exercise discretion in determining which defenses to advance at trial. Defense attorneys and prosecutors exercise discretion in plea bargaining.

Discretion is inevitable within criminal justice systems, although the degree to which it is permitted varies. Discretion may be abused, but it is not necessarily a negative aspect of the system. It is possible to establish guidelines for the exercise of discretion, but it is not possible to eliminate it completely. In addition, attempts to abolish discretion in one area of the system may increase it in others. Thus, for example, if longer sentences are instituted to control crime but jurors perceive these sentences as being too harsh, they might acquit rather than convict persons whom they believe to be guilty. In such cases, the system would have no alternative but to free the accused. On the other hand, conviction of more offenders with longer sentences has clogged courts and prisons, creating serious overcrowding in both areas.

COMPONENTS OF CRIMINAL JUSTICE SYSTEMS

Criminal justice systems are made up of several components and processes, and they differ throughout the world. Figure 1.1 diagrams the most common model in the United States, although states organize and operate their systems in different ways. The federal system also has some unique features. The various criminal justice systems have many common features, which are emphasized throughout this text.

In the United States, the most common organization of criminal justice systems consists of four institutions: police, prosecution, courts, and corrections (noted at the top of Figure 1.1). The different stages are discussed in more detail where appropriate throughout the text.

A case may enter the system when a crime is reported to the police or when police observe behavior that appears to be criminal. After a crime has been reported, police may conduct a preliminary investigation to determine whether there is sufficient evidence that a crime was committed. If so and the suspect is a juvenile, he or she may be processed through the juvenile rather than the adult division of the system. Juveniles may also be transferred to adult criminal courts.

Not all arrested suspects proceed to the end of criminal justice systems. In fact, most cases do not go that far, for a number of reasons. Police may decide that no crime has been committed or that a crime has been committed but that there is not enough evidence on which to arrest a suspect. A suspect may be arrested but released quickly for lack of evidence. Persons who remain suspects through booking, the initial appearance, and the preliminary hearing may be dismissed, or the charges may be dropped at any of those stages. These decisions may be made for lack of evidence or other reasons, some of them highly controversial, such as political pressures. Even after formal charges have been made against the accused, they may be dropped or reduced.

Suspects who proceed to trial may not be convicted. Despite strong evidence against them, they may be acquitted. They may be convicted but placed on probation, fined, or sentenced to work in the community rather than confined in a jail or a prison. Those sent to jails or prisons may be released prior to serving their full terms. This decrease in cases between initial apprehension and exiting the system is diagrammed in Figure 1.2, which shows that of every 100 persons charged with a felony in the 75 counties surveyed, only 68 were convicted (and for 11 of those, the conviction was for a misdemeanor, not a felony), and only 24 actually went to prison and 24 to jail.

Criminal justice systems involve processes as well as stages, and many factors affect how a suspect experiences the system. Those factors are considered throughout the text, but first, we look at the basis of criminal justice systems—criminal law.

Figure 1.1

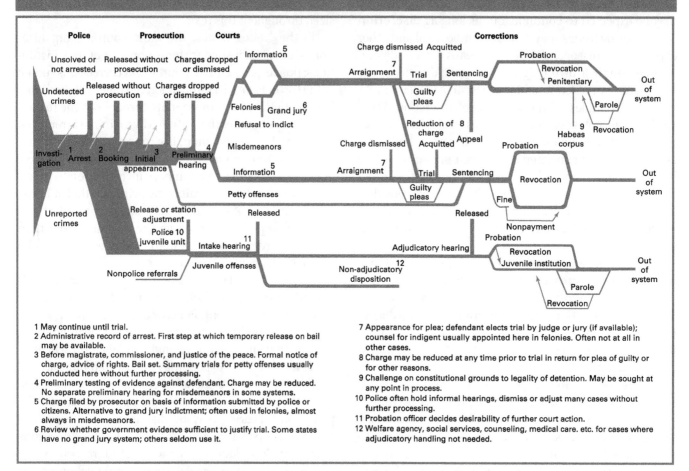

Institutions and Stages in American Criminal Justice Systems

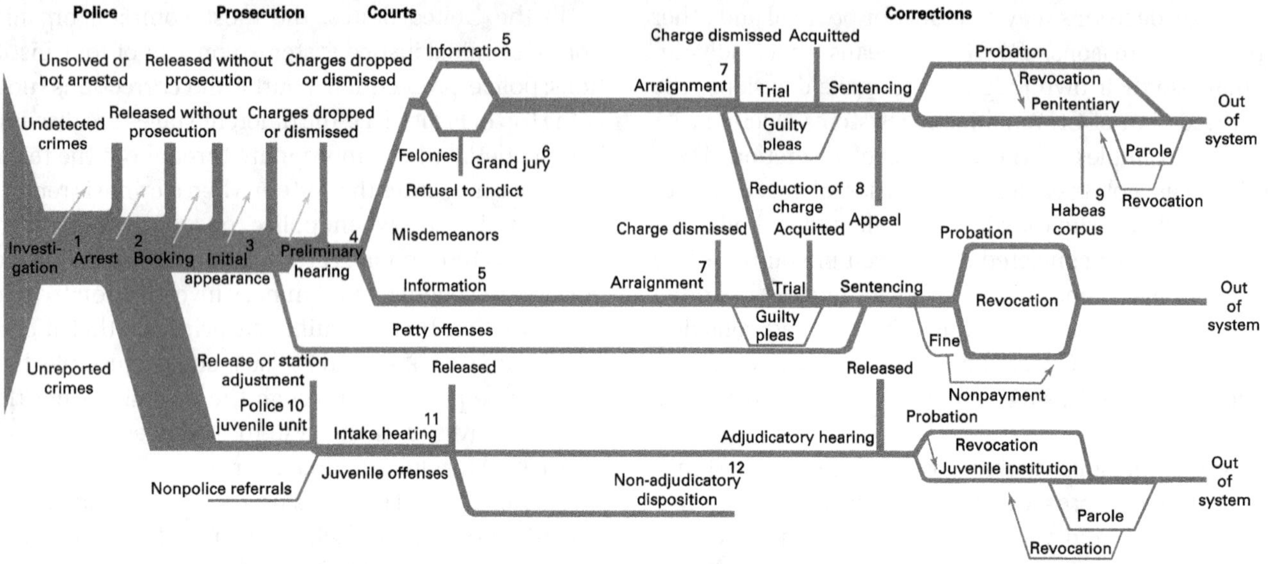

1 May continue until trial.
2 Administrative record of arrest. First step at which temporary release on bail may be available.
3 Before magistrate, commissioner, and justice of the peace. Formal notice of charge, advice of rights. Bail set. Summary trials for petty offenses usually conducted here without further processing.
4 Preliminary testing of evidence against defendant. Charge may be reduced. No separate preliminary hearing for misdemeanors in some systems.
5 Charge filed by prosecutor on basis of information submitted by police or citizens. Alternative to grand jury indictment; often used in felonies, almost always in misdemeanors.
6 Review whether government evidence sufficient to justify trial. Some states have no grand jury system; others seldom use it.
7 Appearance for plea; defendant elects trial by judge or jury (if available); counsel for indigent usually appointed here in felonies. Often not at all in other cases.
8 Charge may be reduced at any time prior to trial in return for plea of guilty or for other reasons.
9 Challenge on constitutional grounds to legality of detention. May be sought at any point in process.
10 Police often hold informal hearings, dismiss or adjust many cases without further processing.
11 Probation officer decides desirability of further court action.
12 Welfare agency, social services, counseling, medical care. etc. for cases where adjudicatory handling not needed.

Source: President's Commission on Law Enforcement and Administration of Justice, *The Challenge of Crime in a Free Society* (Washington, D.C.: U.S. Government Printing Office, 1967), pp. 8-9.

CRIMINAL LAW: AN OVERVIEW

This overview begins with the differences between **criminal law** and **civil law**. The two differ in significant ways, but they also have similarities.

Criminal and Civil Law Distinguished

Criminal laws provide the basis for the actions that take place in criminal justice systems. These laws define acts that are so threatening to society (not just to individual victims) that they require the government to prosecute offenders. Criminal laws list and define the punishments that may be imposed for each criminal offense once there is a conviction.

Civil laws provide a vehicle for legal redress for those who are harmed by others. They are used to uphold certain institutions, such as the family. Civil laws regulate marriage and divorce or dissolution, the handling of dependent and neglected children, and the inheritance of property. They protect legal and political systems, organize power relationships, and establish who is superordinate and who is subordinate in given situations.

Civil and criminal cases are governed by different procedural rules; there are differences in the evidence that may be presented and in the extent of proof each system requires. Whether the action is civil or criminal may determine the type of court in which the case is processed. In some cases, the act may not be considered a crime the first time it occurs. For example, a first offense for driving while intoxicated is considered a traffic violation and not a crime in some **jurisdictions**, but a subsequent offense may be a crime. In some jurisdictions, the first offense might be considered a crime if it results in a death.

The distinction between a civil and a criminal violation is also important to the offender. The repercussions of being accused of violating a criminal law are more serious than those for violating a civil law. In addition to the possibility of a prison sentence (or capital punishment, in the case of first-degree murder), persons accused of a crime may experience social repercussions even if they are acquitted. They may lose their jobs as soon as they are charged with a crime, particularly when it involves allegations of sexual offenses. Criminal law should not be taken lightly, and the term *criminal* should be used only in referring to people who have been convicted of a *criminal* offense.

Because of the serious impact of a criminal conviction, the law provides greater safeguards for those accused of crimes than for those facing civil suits. The most important safeguards are embodied in the concept of the **adversary system**.

The Adversary System

U.S. criminal justice systems are adversarial, in contrast to the **inquisitory system**, which is characteristic of some other countries. The two approaches may be distinguished in several ways. The adversary approach presumes that accused defendants are innocent. They do not have to prove their innocence; rather, the state (or the federal government if it is a federal trial) must prove their guilt. In contrast, in the inquisitory system, the accused are presumed guilty, and they are required to prove that they are innocent. This difference between the two approaches is related to another basic contrast: The inquisitory approach places a greater emphasis on

Figure 1.2

Typical Outcome of 100 Felony Defendants Arraigned in State Courts in the 75 Largest Counties

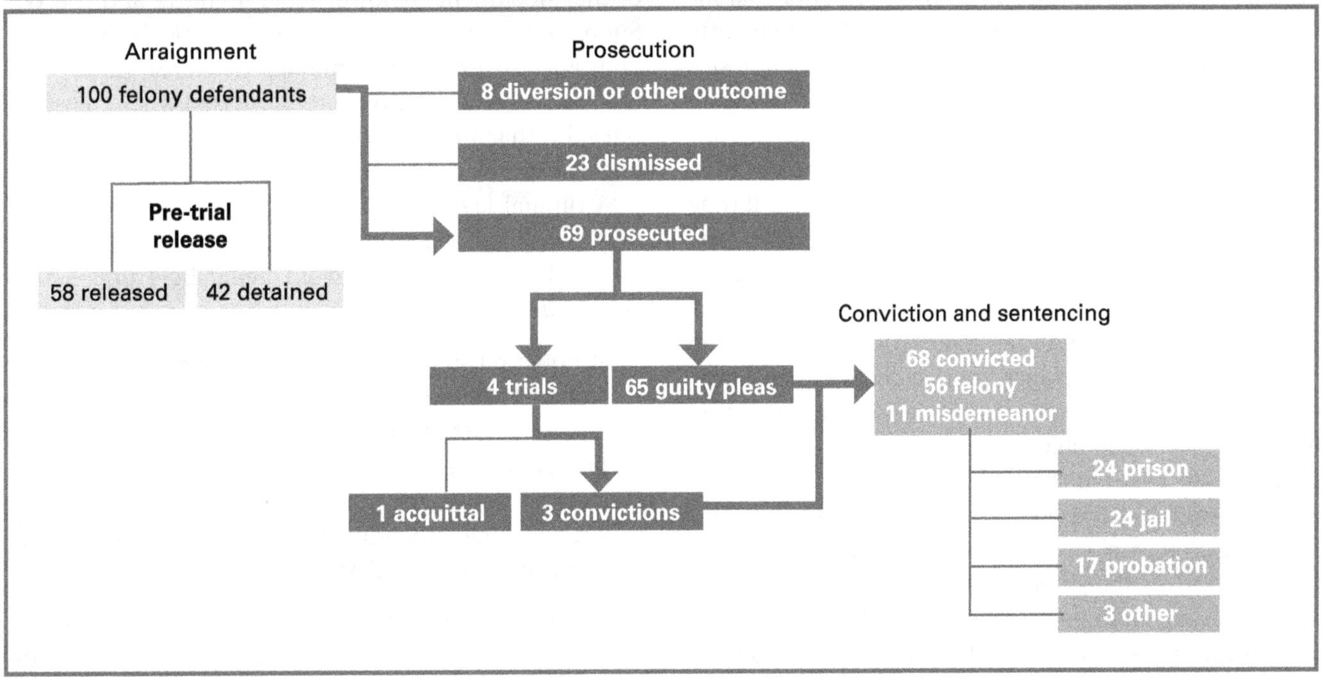

Source: Thomas H. Cohen and Tracey Kyckelhahn, Bureau of Justice Statistics, *Felony Defendants in Large Urban Counties, 2006* (May 2010; revised July 15, 2010), p. 1, https://www.bjs.gov/content/pub/pdf/fdluc06.pdf, accessed August 1, 2018.

conviction than on the *process* by which that conviction is secured.

The adversary approach requires following proper procedures designed to protect the rights of the accused. Those procedures are guided by two important principles: **due process** and **equal protection**, concepts considered necessary to create a system in which the accused has a fair chance against the tremendous powers of prosecutors and the resources of the government. Theoretically, constitutional protections prevent prosecutors from obtaining guilty verdicts against innocent defendants. In reality, justice does not always prevail.

Among other provisions, the U.S. Constitution's Fifth Amendment prohibits the government from depriving any person of "life, liberty, or property, without due process of law." This amendment, along with the rest of the Bill of Rights, which consists of the first ten amendments, was held to apply only to the federal government, but it has been applied to the states through the Fourteenth Amendment (see Appendix A), which adds the concept of equal protection. The U.S. Supreme Court has decided numerous cases in which it has been argued that the due process or equal protection rights of individuals have been violated. It would take an extensive course in constitutional law to explore these concepts adequately, but we can look at them briefly. They are explained in more detail where relevant in subsequent chapters.

The concept of *due process* means that those who are accused of crimes and processed through U.S. criminal justice systems must be given their basic rights guaranteed by the U.S. Constitution. For example, defendants may not be subjected to unreasonable searches and seizures. When questioned by police about acts that, upon conviction, may involve a jail or prison term, they are not required to answer until they have an attorney. If they do not wish to talk then, they may remain silent. If they cannot afford an attorney, the state must provide one for them. They may not be compelled to testify at trial. Certain rules of evidence must be followed during trials.

Defendants may not be tried twice for the same offense; once a judge or jury has decided that the defendant is not guilty, the state (or federal government) may not bring the same charges again in an effort to wear down the accused. In short, the state must conduct the criminal trial and the processes preceding, during, and following that trial by the rules embodied in the U.S. Constitution, as interpreted by the U.S. Supreme Court, and according to the established procedural statutes of the relevant jurisdiction. State trials must also follow the procedural safeguards established by their respective state constitutions and legislatures, as interpreted by their state courts.

Equal protection means that, in general, the government may not infringe on the rights of persons solely because of characteristics such as race, age, national origin, ethnicity, religion, or gender. Some jurisdictions have added disability and sexual orientation or identification by statute, constitutional amendment, or judicial decisions. Some have also added homelessness.

Constitutional Limitations on Criminal Law: A Brief Look

There is no question that observation of defendants' due process, equal protection, and other constitutional rights creates obstacles for law enforcement. If authorities could accuse anyone of a crime regardless of available evidence, search and seize at will, interrogate suspects for unlimited periods of time when those suspects do not have attorneys, coerce confessions physically and psychologically, and so on, there would be more convictions, but the resulting loss of individual freedom and liberty, along with wrongful convictions, would not be tolerable in U.S. criminal justice systems.

In addition to the constitutional limits of due process and equal protection, state legislatures and Congress are limited by the federal Constitution (and interpretations of that document by lower federal courts and the U.S. Supreme Court) in how they may define criminal law. They are also limited in criminal procedures. Throughout the text, these limitations are discussed where relevant, but a few that are of importance to a general understanding of criminal law are noted here.

Criminal laws cannot be vague or too broad. Laws may not specify everything that is prohibited; they must be flexible. However, to avoid being held unconstitutional due to vagueness,

1. statutes must give notice or warning to all who are subject to them;
2. statutes must protect against arbitrary and discriminatory enforcement; and
3. statutes must not unreasonably deny other rights, such as First Amendment rights of free speech, religion, and so on (see Appendix A).

With regard to breadth, a statute should not "sweep within its ambit other activities that constitute an exercise" of other constitutional rights.[9]

Another constitutional limitation of particular importance in federal criminal justice systems is the Eighth Amendment's prohibition against **cruel and unusual punishment** (see Appendix A; this amendment is applied to the states through the Fourteenth Amendment). The issue arises frequently in capital punishment cases, and although the U.S. Supreme Court has ruled that capital punishment per se is not unconstitutional, it may be so if applied arbitrarily and capriciously.[10]

One critical limitation on criminal justice systems, the right to privacy, has been the focus of many U.S. Supreme Court decisions. In a unanimous decision in June 2014, the Court held that when police arrest, they may not examine all of the aspects of a suspect's cell phone without first obtaining a search warrant. Spotlight 1.2 contains a brief statement about that case, which is excerpted in **Supplement 1.4**, and a more recent case involving privacy and cell phones, *United States v. Carpenter*, decided in 2018,[11] which is excerpted in **Supplement 1.5**.

The right to privacy and other constitutional limitations are noted where relevant throughout this text.

SOURCES OF CRIMINAL LAW

Laws come from three sources: constitutions, statutes, and court decisions. In addition to the federal Constitution, each state has a constitution. State legislatures also enact statutes that apply to actions in their respective states. Congress enacts statutes that apply to the federal government as well as to the District of Columbia. These statutes are called **statutory law**. They apply only to the jurisdiction in which they are passed, with the exception that no state may enforce statutes conflicting with the rights guaranteed by the U.S. Constitution or federal laws.

Statutes also define the procedures that are appropriate for law enforcement. These are called **procedural laws**. Others define the elements that are necessary for an act to constitute a violation of the civil or criminal law. They are called **substantive laws**. For example, a statute may define *murder* as the killing by one human being of another with malice aforethought. Convicting a person under that statute requires proof of these elements: that a person was killed, that the person was killed by the accused, and that the killing involved malice aforethought, which refers to the requirement of an intent to kill and the absence of any legal justification for that killing. But if the statute does not define that element, then court decisions, another source of law, may be used for a definition.

Law that comes from court decisions is called **case law**. Much U.S. case law is derived from or influenced by **common law**, which consists of those customs, traditions, judicial decisions, and other materials that guide courts in decision making but that have not been enacted by legislatures into statutes or embodied in constitutions.

Another source that is important to an understanding of criminal law is **administrative law**. State legislatures and Congress delegate rule-making power to state and federal administrative agencies. For example, prison officials are given authority to make rules that regulate the daily operations of their institutions. The Federal Bureau of Investigation (FBI) is granted power to make rules governing the enforcement of laws under its jurisdiction. Such rules must be made according to specific procedures and guidelines. Administrative rules are important, but normally, the violation of them is not viewed as criminal although they may become criminal under some circumstances.

THE CONCEPT OF CRIME

A **crime** may be defined as an "act or omission prohibited by law for the protection of the public, the violation of which is prosecuted by the state in its own name and punishable by incarceration."[12] Some jurisdictions define certain acts as *violations* or *infractions*. Those acts may be subject to fines or other minor penalties in criminal law or to civil penalties, but the commission of those acts is not considered criminal under most circumstances. When an act is not defined or processed as a crime, it should not be labeled as a crime.

Classification of Crimes

Crimes are classified according to the seriousness of the offense. A **misdemeanor** is a less serious offense; a **felony** is a more serious one. Generally, misdemeanors are punishable by a short jail term, fine, probation, or a combination of these or other penalties that do not involve incarceration in a prison. Felonies are normally punishable by more than a year in jail, **incarceration** in a prison, or capital punishment, although in some cases they, too, involve alternative punishments, such as community service, house arrest, a fine, or probation

Spotlight 1.2

The Right to Privacy

The U.S. Constitution does not contain the word *privacy*, but over the years the U.S. Supreme Court has interpreted various Amendments in the Bill of Rights (as applied to the states through the Fourteenth Amendment) as implying a right to privacy. In June 2014, the U.S. Supreme Court held that when police arrest a suspect, they must obtain a search warrant before they examine information on that person's cell phone. Two cases were combined in this decision, an unusual unanimous one, and the Court's actions reaffirmed the right to privacy in this country. The case is very important in that the right to privacy is key to many constitutional rights. Excerpts of the case are presented in **Supplement 1.4.** In that excerpt, the Court explains why cell phones are different from other possessions a suspect might have on his or her person at the time of arrest. The facts and the holding illustrate how interpretations of the U.S. Constitution must change as conditions change. The decision involved the search of a smart phone in one case and a flip phone in the other, with both yielding information (and photos) that led police to the evidence used in both trials, resulting in convictions of both appellants.[1]

At the end of its 2017-2018 term, the U.S. Supreme Court decided another important cell phone case involving the right to privacy. In *Carpenter v. United States*,[2] in the words of Chief Justice John Roberts, who wrote the opinion, the Court considered "the question of whether the Government conducts a search under the Fourth Amendment when it accesses historical cell phone records that provide a comprehensive chronicle of the user's past movements." Justice Roberts continued with an explanation of the extent of information that may be obtained from such records and followed with the Court's holding. **Supplement 1.5** presents an excerpt from his opinion.

In Carpenter v. United States, *the U.S. Supreme Court held that when police arrest a person, they must secure a search warrant before they seize digital information from that person's smart phone. The decision was a unanimous affirmation of the previously recognized right to privacy.*

1. *Riley v. California; United States v. Wurie*, 573 U.S. 373 (2014).
2. *Carpenter v. United States*, 138 S. Ct. 2210 (2018).

or some combination of these or other penalties. In some jurisdictions, *violations* constitute a third category and consist of offenses that are less serious than misdemeanors.

Crimes may also be classified as ***mala in se*** or ***mala prohibita***. *Mala in se* refers to acts that are considered criminal in nature, such as murder and rape. *Mala prohibita* refers to acts that are not universally regarded as criminal; they are criminal because the legislature has designated them as crimes. Violations of laws regulating the private, consensual sexual conduct of adults, the use of some drugs, and the use of alcohol by certain age groups are examples of *mala prohibita* crimes.

Elements of a Crime

Certain elements must be proved before a person can be convicted of a crime. These vary from crime to crime and from jurisdiction to jurisdiction, but some common elements distinguish crime from noncrime.

An Act

In U.S. criminal justice systems, a person may not be punished for his or her thoughts; there must be an act of commission or omission, although some crimes do not require an act in the traditional definition of the term. For example, in the crime of conspiracy, which involves an agreement between two or more people to commit an illegal (or, in some jurisdictions, an unlawful) act, the *agreement* constitutes the act. Two parties may be convicted of conspiracy to commit a crime, even though only one (or neither) is convicted of the crime for which they conspired, such as murder. In addition, a crime may be committed when a person plays a role in assisting another person to commit a crime.

A crime may be committed when a person has made an **attempt** to commit—but has not committed—an act defined as a crime. The person must have made a substantial attempt to commit the crime.[13] Failure to act may also constitute a crime but only when a person has a **legal duty** to act. If a child is drowning and two people watch without making any effort to rescue the child, the lack of action of one may be a crime, whereas that of the other might not meet the requirements of a criminal act of omission. In the first instance, the observer is a parent with a legal duty to aid the drowning child. Conversely, if the other person is not a close relative, has no contractual obligation to the child, and has not placed the child in that position of peril, he or she may not have a legal duty to come to the child's aid. Failure to do so does not constitute a crime, no matter how reprehensible the lack of action may be from a moral point of view.

For an act to be criminal, it must be voluntary. A driver who has a sudden epileptic seizure, loses control of the car, strikes another car, and injures or kills another human being, has not necessarily committed a crime. But a driver who has had prior attacks of a similar nature might be found guilty of a crime for recklessly creating a situation of danger to others by driving a car when he or she knows such attacks may occur.

An Unlawful Act

A crime is an act prohibited by criminal law, which must be reasonably clear. A statute will be declared void when "men of common intelligence must necessarily guess at its meaning and differ as to its application."[14]

An Intent

For an act to be a crime, the law requires the element of intent, or ***mens rea***, a guilty mind. This is to distinguish those acts that may be harmful to others but for which the actor had no immoral or wrongful purpose. **Negligence** can cause harm to others, who may recover damages in a civil suit, but with the exceptions noted below, the law requires a guilty or an immoral mind for acts to be considered criminal. Former U.S. Supreme Court Justice Oliver Wendell Holmes Jr. described the meaning of this distinction when he said, "Even a dog distinguishes between being stumbled over and being kicked."[15]

The intent requirement is complex. Neither court decisions nor scholarly legal writings provide an easily understood meaning. The requirement may vary from crime to crime. In simple terms, an intent to do something means that the actor meant to bring about the consequences of his or her actions or engaged in acts that were reasonably certain to bring about those consequences. The actor is not required to intend the *specific* result that occurs. A person who fires a gun into a crowd intending to kill a specific person but who misses and kills another person could be convicted of murder. In this example, the intent comes from the evidence that the individual *purposely* and *knowingly* took the action that resulted in the death of another. Usually, this is the easiest kind of case in which to prove intent, but the required intent need not be that obvious. Criminal intent may be found in cases in which the action is extremely reckless or grossly negligent. The Texas Penal Code, reproduced in part in Spotlight 1.3, is an example of one state's approach to defining criminal culpability.[16] **Supplement 1.6** contains more information on the issue of establishing intent.

The Concurrence of Act and Intent

For an act to be a crime, the act and intent must occur together. It is not sufficient to have a criminal intent one day but not commit the act until another day.

Causation

The final element of all crimes is that there must be proof that the result is *caused* by the act. **Causation** in criminal law is intricate and complex, but legal cause is a crucial element that must be proved before a person is convicted of a crime.

Attendant Circumstances

In addition to proving an act, an intent, concurrence of the act and the intent, and causation, for some crimes the prosecution must prove the existence of **attendant circumstances**, which are facts surrounding an act. For example, a statute may provide a higher penalty for crimes that are committed against law enforcement officers, in which case the prosecution would have to prove that the victim was an officer, and, in some jurisdictions, that the perpetrator knew or should have known that fact.

Defenses to Crimes

The prosecution may prove all of the elements of a criminal offense beyond a reasonable doubt, but U.S. criminal justice systems will not hold a suspect responsible for a crime if certain **defenses** are proved. Defenses to criminal culpability have varied over the years, and like all areas of law, this one is in transition, with new attempts at criminal defenses occurring often, although some defenses have been traditional in many societies.[17]

THE REACH OF CRIMINAL LAW

Historically, the reach of criminal law has been the subject of extensive debate. Some people argue that only clearly *criminal* acts should be included and that criminal law should not be used to try to control behavior that many people do not consider wrong. Others take the position that criminal law is the most effective method of social control and therefore should embrace even those acts that some consider to be *mala prohibita* rather than *mala in se*.

The discussion begins by analyzing to what, if any, extent the criminal law should be used to cover what some people think of as **euthanasia** or mercy killing. Criminal Justice Systems Dilemma 1.1 noted the example of a Florida man who killed his wife, allegedly at her request. This section raises the issue in general of whether anyone should ever be permitted to do this without being charged with a crime. In particular, it discusses whether physicians should be charged with a crime if they assist persons to die.

Physician Assisted Suicide (PAS)

The U.S. Supreme Court recognizes the right to die with dignity but, in 1997, the Court upheld the Washington and New York statutes that criminalized the act of a physician's aiding or abetting a suicide.[18] However, the Court left open the right of states to permit such actions, thus giving legal recognition to **physician assisted suicide (PAS)**. Oregon had already authorized PAS by voter referendum; in November 2008, voters in the state of Washington voted to permit it.[19] In the fall of 2008, the Montana Supreme Court held that under a Montana statute, a patient's *consent* to the assistance of a physician for purposes of ending life is a defense to a homicide charge against the assisting physician.[20] PAS is also legal in Vermont, Hawaii, Colorado, and California, and in April 2019, the New Jersey governor signed PAS into law in that state, and in June 2019, the Maine governor signed PAS into law in that state.

The legal recognition of PAS may be expected to continue gaining support in the United States as medicine prolongs the lives of many individuals. The issues surrounding the practice received attention in November 2014, when Brittany Maynard, 29, took her life. Maynard, who said she did not want to die the death she faced with an inoperable brain tumor, moved from California to Oregon to establish residency in a state that permits PAS. Her death was met with praise and criticism. Subsequently, California adopted the practice.

Sexual Behavior

Another area of criminalization that is questioned involves sexual behavior between consenting adults in private. In recent years, many states have repealed criminal statutes that proscribe this behavior. They have limited criminal statutes to covering sexual behavior that is the result of force against any person, that is engaged in without force but with an underage or a mentally or physically incompetent person, or that is committed in public. Some states have retained the common law approach, however, and provide criminal penalties for adult consensual sexual behavior that is considered deviant by some members of the population.

In the controversial 1986 *Bowers v. Hardwick* decision, the U.S. Supreme Court upheld the right of a state to criminalize consensual sex between two men in the privacy of their Georgia home, where police had gone for legal reasons. In 1998, the Georgia Supreme Court held that the state's statute on which the case was based violated the Georgia constitution.[21]

In 2003, the U.S. Supreme Court decided *Lawrence v. Texas*, involving the issue of private and consenting sexual behavior between same-gender persons; in that case, the Supreme Court specifically overruled *Bowers v. Hardwick*, holding that the case "was not correct when it was decided, and it is not correct today." The

Spotlight 1.3

General Requirements of Culpability

TEXAS PENAL CODE, CHAPTER 6 (2017)

Section 6.02. Requirement of Culpability.

(a) Except as provided in Subsection (b), a person does not commit an offense unless he intentionally, knowingly, recklessly, or with criminal negligence engages in conduct as the definition of the offense requires.

(b) If the definition of an offense does not prescribe a culpable mental state, a culpable mental state is nevertheless required unless the definition plainly dispenses with any mental element....

(d) Culpable mental states are classified according to relative degrees, from highest to lowest, as follows:

(1) intentional;
(2) knowing;
(3) reckless;
(4) criminal negligence....

Section 6.03. Definitions of Culpable Mental States.

(a) A person acts intentionally, or with intent, with respect to the nature of his conduct or to a result of his conduct when it is his conscious objective or desire to engage in the conduct or cause the result.

(b) A person acts knowingly, or with knowledge, with respect to the nature of his conduct or to circumstances surrounding his conduct when he is aware of the nature of his conduct or that the circumstances exist. A person acts knowingly, or with knowledge, with respect to a result of his conduct when he is aware that his conduct is reasonably certain to cause the result.

(c) A person acts recklessly, or is reckless, with respect to circumstances surrounding his conduct or the result of his conduct when he is aware of but consciously disregards a substantial and unjustifiable risk that the circumstances exist or the result will occur. The risk must be of such a nature and degree that its disregard constitutes a gross deviation from the standard of care that an ordinary person would exercise under all the circumstances as viewed from the actor's standpoint.

(d) A person acts with criminal negligence, or is criminally negligent, with respect to circumstances surrounding his conduct or the result of his conduct when he ought to be aware of a substantial and unjustifiable risk that the circumstances exist or the result will occur. The risk must be of such a nature and degree that the failure to perceive it constitutes a gross deviation from the standard of care that an ordinary person would exercise under all the circumstances as viewed from the actor's standpoint.

Court also invalidated a Texas statute providing that "[a] person commits an offense if he engages in deviate sexual intercourse with another individual of the same sex." The statute defined deviate sexual intercourse to include oral and anal sex, but such acts were considered criminal only if engaged in by two persons of the same gender.[22]

Illegal Drug Abuse

Another use of the criminal law to control behavior to which many people object involves laws prohibiting the use of drugs. We look first at the growing, distributing, and prescribing of marijuana for medicinal reasons. The sale and possession of marijuana for any reason is a serious offense, with long penalties in many states. In the federal system, the use of marijuana is not permitted for any reason other than federally approved research. However, in California and a growing number of other jurisdictions, *state* law allows the use of marijuana for medicinal reasons with a prescription from a physician.[23] The drug relieves pain and other symptoms in some diseases and is tolerated by some patients who do not respond well to other medications.

Federal authorities have taken the position that the prescription of marijuana for medicinal reasons violates the federal Controlled Substances Act (CSA) and, during the Bush administration, focused on prosecuting those in California who violated this statute. They had some success, with the U.S. Supreme Court ruling that the *necessity defense* is not available to a defendant who grows marijuana for medicinal reasons. That means that the defendant charged with violating the federal CSA by growing marijuana could not put forth a defense that this was done because the drug is necessary for medical treatment. However, federal prosecutors wanted to avoid the harsh penalties of the federal statute and thus petitioned the California court to issue an **injunction** prohibiting anyone from providing marijuana for medical reasons. The state court did so, and that permitted federal prosecutors to process through the civil rather than the criminal court anyone who grows, sells, or uses marijuana for medicinal purposes.[24]

Angel Raich, who suffered severe pain from a brain tumor and other physical conditions, found some relief from the medicinal use of marijuana. She and her husband, an attorney, launched an unsuccessful attempt to secure marijuana legally for pain control. Many states have legalized such use, but it is illegal in the federal system.

In 2005, the U.S. Supreme Court decided a case involving the use of marijuana for medical reasons. The two plaintiffs in *Gonzales v. Raich*[25] were using marijuana to ease the pain from their respective diseases; no other medications had given them relief. The Supreme Court held that the federal statute was within the proper exercise of federal power "even as applied to the troubling facts of this case." Advocates of the medical use of marijuana must now convince Congress to change the federal statute. There is no evidence that this is likely to happen even though an increasing number of jurisdictions have also approved the purchase of small amounts of marijuana for recreational purposes.

Conclusion on the Reach of Criminal Law

Even if we decide that all of the acts discussed in this section of the chapter should be included within criminal law, we should consider carefully what penalties to assess. For example, what is accomplished by incarcerating a dying person who uses marijuana for medicinal purposes? And how long should we incarcerate a physician who prescribed the drug?

This discussion of criminalizing acts some consider private matters raises the issue of whether criminal law is used too extensively and therefore goes beyond the purpose of protecting the public's safety and welfare and interferes unreasonably with the behavior of private persons. Those who take this position argue that criminal law is being used to encompass acts without victims. They assert that the results are harmful in the long run: Police may invade personal privacy rights to enforce the law; minorities and other marginalized groups may be harassed; courts, jails, and prisons may be overcrowded as a result of processing these people through criminal justice systems; underground markets may develop to supply prohibited products, such as marijuana; and attempts to enforce unpopular and unsupported criminal statutes may create disrespect for the law. Critical police resources may be diverted from more important functions.

Supporters argue that criminal law is a necessary symbol of morality and that the removal of *mala prohibita* acts from the criminal law would place society's stamp of approval on the behaviors in question. Resolution of these two positions regarding the use of criminal law to control morality involves religious, moral, and ethical considerations, as well as legal and empirical issues. In the final analysis, the answer may be a personal one. But it is clear that, whatever position is taken, it will have important repercussions on criminal justice systems.

Summary

This chapter presented an overview of criminal justice systems and criminal law. Although the systems differ, all may be analyzed in terms of punishment philosophies: incapacitation, retribution, rehabilitation, deterrence, and reparation or restitution. Today in the United States, the philosophies of deterrence and retribution, often combined in the just deserts approach, are dominant. Just a short time ago, U.S. systems were dominated by the philosophy of rehabilitation, and today some efforts are being made to bring back that emphasis and with some success.

The role of discretion in punishment is crucial to criminal justice systems. It exists at all levels and cannot be eliminated, but it can be controlled by some measures. If left unchecked, discretion can result in unfairness to defendants.

After an overview of discretion, this chapter looked briefly at the components of criminal justice systems, using a diagram of general U.S. approaches for illustrative purposes. All of the elements of the systems are discussed in more detail throughout the text.

Crucial to all criminal justice systems is the basis for those systems, criminal law. A criminal justice system is based on a society's willingness to grant legal authority to some individuals to impose punishment. Criminal law provides that basis in modern societies, and this chapter began its overview of criminal law by distinguishing between criminal and civil law. Criminal law has existed for centuries, predating and forming the basis for much of our civil law.

Criminal justice systems may be based on either the adversary or the inquisitory model. U.S. systems follow the adversary model, in which all accused persons are presumed innocent and the state must prove their guilt beyond a reasonable doubt. In contrast is the inquisitory system, in which the accused are presumed guilty and must prove their innocence. The adversary system is characterized by due process and equal protection. Other constitutional limitations include the prohibition of statutes that are vague or too broad as well as the prohibition of cruel and unusual punishment. The concept of privacy is also an important limitation; it was discussed highlighting the requirement that a search warrant be obtained before police may search the cell phones of arrested persons.

Criminal law emerges from statutes enacted by the legislative branches of government, administrative rules and regulations, constitutions, and court decisions. All of these are important sources of law.

Criminal law is based on the concept of *crime*, which must be defined legally to fall within criminal justice systems. Crimes are classified as serious (felonies) or less serious (misdemeanors). Crimes may be classified as *mala prohibita*, criminal because they are so designated by society, or *mala in se*, criminal per se. Crimes have elements that must be proved before a person is convicted. Those elements include an illegal act that concurs with a guilty mind, causation, and for some crimes, attendant circumstances. Some acts that fit these elements may not be considered criminal because the accused has an acceptable defense.

Scholars, politicians, and the general public continue to debate what the reach of criminal law should be. This chapter considered first whether physician assisted suicide (PAS) should be permitted for terminally ill patients who wish to die with dignity. It then discussed the use of the criminal law to control private consensual sexual behavior between adults. Finally, the chapter looked at using criminal law to control the possession of illegal narcotics and closed with a brief conclusion on the reach of the criminal law.

This overview chapter on criminal justice systems and criminal law sets the stage for more detailed analyses of the components of the systems. The next chapter focuses on another foundation important to the understanding of criminal justice systems—the collection and analysis of data on crime, offenders, and crime victims.

Key Terms

administrative law 13
adversary system 11
attempt 15
attendant circumstances 15
case law 13
causation 15
civil law 10
common law 13
crime 13
criminal 5
criminal justice systems 5
criminal law 10
cruel and unusual punishment 13
defenses 16
deterrence 5
discretion 9
due process 12
equal protection 12
euthanasia 16
felony 13
incapacitation 5
incarceration 13
injunction 18
inquisitory system 11
jurisdiction 11
just deserts 8
legal duty 15
mala in se 14
mala prohibita 14
mens rea 15
misdemeanor 13
negligence 15
physician assisted suicide (PAS) 16
procedural laws 13
rehabilitation 5
retribution 5
sanction 5
statutory law 13
substantive law 13

Study Questions

1. Briefly summarize some violent crimes that have occurred on U.S. soil recently.
2. Explain and distinguish among deterrence, rehabilitation, incapacitation, and retribution. Explain how these punishment and sentencing philosophies relate to the justice model of punishment.
3. Discuss the punishment implications of the examples discussed in Criminal Justice Systems Dilemma 1.1.
4. How do you think discretion should be regulated in criminal justice systems? Discuss the process in terms of specific personnel, such as police, prosecutors, judges, and juries. Consider your answer at the end of the course to determine whether your views have changed.
5. Contrast civil and criminal law.
6. Distinguish between the adversary and inquisitory systems of criminal justice.
7. Explain the meaning of due process and equal protection. What other constitutional limitations are placed on criminal law and included in this chapter?
8. Do you think capital punishment is cruel and unusual punishment? How about a life sentence without parole for drug possession? For drug sales? Would your answer to the last two questions depend on the amount of drugs?
9. List and discuss the sources of criminal law.
10. How are crimes classified?
11. Discuss the basic elements of a crime.
12. What are criminal defenses?
13. Explain what is meant by physician assisted suicide (PAS) and analyze the current legal status of this practice.
14. Should the criminal law be used to control any or all of the following: premarital sex, extramarital sex, same-gender sex?
15. What position should criminal law take on the use of marijuana for medicinal purposes?

Notes

1. See "Clemency Granted to a Mercy Killer," *New York Times* (August 2, 1990), p. 9.
2. See *Gregg v. Georgia*, 428 U.S. 153, 183-185 (1976).
3. For a discussion of the role of fear in deterrence, see the recent article by Justin T. Pickett et al., "Toward a Bifurcated Theory of Emotional Deterrence," *Criminology* 56(1) (February 2018): 27-58.
4. "What Are Prisons For? No Longer Rehabilitation, but to Punish—and to Lock the Worst Away," *Time* (September 13, 1982), p. 38.
5. Cal. Penal Code, Article 1, Section 1170 (2018).
6. USCS, Article 28, Section 994(k) (2019).
7. See Cal. Penal Code, Section 1210.1 (2014); Idaho Code, Section 39-301 (2018). For a discussion of rehabilitation historically, see Doris Layton MacKenzie and Pamela K. Lattimore, "President's Crime Commission: Past and Future: To Rehabilitate or Not to Rehabilitate: That Is the Question for Corrections," *Criminology & Public Policy* 17(2) (May 2018): 355-377.
8. See, for example, Ernest van den Haag, *Punishing Criminals: Concerning a Very Old and Painful Question* (New York: Basic Books, 1975); and David Fogel, *We Are the Living Proof: The Justice Model for Corrections* (Cincinnati, OH: Anderson, 1975).
9. *Thornhill v. Alabama*, 310 U.S. 88, 97 (1940).
10. See *Furman v. Georgia*, 408 U.S. 238 (1972).
11. *Riley v. California; United States v. Wurie*, 573 U.S. 373 (2014); *Carpenter v. United States*, 138 S. Ct. 2210 (2018).
12. Model Penal Code, Section 1.104(1).
13. See, for example, *Rex v. Scofield*, Cald. 397, 400 (1784).
14. *Connally v. General Construction Company*, 269 U.S. 385, 391 (1926).
15. Oliver Wendell Holmes Jr., *The Common Law*, as cited in *Morissette v. United States*, 342 U.S. 246, 252 (1952).
16. Tex. Penal Code, Chapter 6, Sections 6.02-6.03 (2017).
17. For more details on defenses, see Sue Titus Reid, *Criminal Law: The Essentials*, 3d ed. (New York: Oxford University Press, 2017), pp. 65-97.
18. See *Washington v. Glucksberg*, 521 U.S. 702 (1997), and *Vacco v. Quill*, 521 U.S. 793 (1997).
19. See Oregon's Death with Dignity Act, Or. Rev. Stat., Section 127.880 et seq. (2009). The Washington statute that prohibited physician assisted suicide, Wash. Rev. Code, Section 70.122.100 (2008), was rewritten by Initiative Measure 1000, adopted at the November 4, 2008 election, and now permits the practice, effective March 5, 2009. See Wash. Rev. Code, Section 70.245.901, 904 (2014).
20. "World Sunflashes Column," *Toronto Sun* (December 7, 2008), p. 42. The case is *Baxter v. State*, 2008 Mont. Dist. LEXIS 482 (December 5, 2008), *aff'd in part and rev'd in part, vacated, in part*, 224 P.3d 1211 (Mont. 2009). The statute is Mont. Code Ann., Section 45-2-211 (2013).
21. *Bowers v. Hardwick*, 478 U.S. 186 (1986), *overruled by Lawrence v. Texas*, 539 U.S. 558 (2003). See also *Powell v. State*, 510 S.E.2d 18 (Ga. 1998).
22. *Lawrence v. Texas*, 539 U.S. 558 (2003).
23. The California statute is the Compassionate Use Act of 1996, Cal. Health & Safety Code, Section 11362.5 (2018).
24. *United States v. Oakland Cannabis Buyers' Cooperative*, 532 U.S. 483 (2001).
25. *Gonzales v. Raich*, 545 U.S. 1 (2005).

2

Crime, Offenders, and Victims

Chapter Outline

Learning Objectives

After reading this chapter, you should be able to do the following:

- List and evaluate the major sources of crime and victimization data
- Recognize the importance of misdemeanors in criminal justice systems
- List and explain the reasons that crime data may not be accurate
- Discuss reasons for the nonreporting of crime by victims
- List and define the eight serious crimes as categorized by the Federal Bureau of Investigation
- Analyze and summarize recent crime data
- Explain the meaning of *hate crime*, and analyze the U.S. Supreme Court decision regarding cross burning
- Detail the demographic characteristics of offenders and victims
- Define *victimology* and describe and criticize the sources of victimization data
- List the major variables used to analyze victimization data and explain the meaning of each
- Explain the relationship between victims and offenders
- Discuss and evaluate the ways in which criminal justice systems have attempted to respond to the needs of victims
- Discuss at least three types of crimes beyond those included among the eight serious crimes as recorded by the FBI

Each year, usually in September, the **Federal Bureau of Investigation (FBI)** releases the official crime data reported to that agency. Specific data are examined later in this chapter, but it is important first to consider some factors that might influence the reporting, collection, and analysis of data on crime and victims, both of which are featured in this chapter.

The major source of crime data, the FBI, emphasizes that data should be analyzed carefully in light of changing demographics and other variables, such as those presented by the FBI and reproduced in Spotlight 2.1. As a result of these factors, and perhaps others, the collection of crime data is not as precise as some would have us believe. Not all crimes are reported to the police. Not all reported crimes are cleared by arrest; fewer still are cleared by conviction. In addition, politics may enter into the reporting and interpreting of data. As the president of the American Society of Criminology pointed out in his 2017 presidential address, quoting Daniel Patrick Moynihan, "You are entitled to your own opinion, but you are not entitled to your own facts."[1] All of these factors mean that no data source is complete in its measure of criminal activity. Additional problems exist when comparisons are made among jurisdictions and methods of data collection.

Despite the impossibility of detecting all criminal activity or prosecuting and convicting all guilty parties who are detected, crime data serve an important function. Official agencies need the data to determine policies and budgets. Police officials use the data to determine the best use of their limited resources. Crime data may also be used by private citizens who are determined to make their communities safer for all who live there. Social scientists who study criminal behavior use crime data, both official and unofficial, in their analyses of why and under what circumstances people commit criminal acts. Crime data may also be used for political reasons in an effort to convince voters of the success or failure of crime prevention efforts. The point is not to dismiss crime data because of problems of inaccuracy but, rather, to consider carefully the various sources of data and to determine which are best for a particular purpose.

This chapter examines, analyzes, and compares the most common methods for collecting crime data. Data are then examined by the two major categories of serious crimes recorded by the FBI: violent crimes and property crimes. The FBI's category of less serious crimes is examined, with special attention given to hate crimes. The chapter analyzes the characteristics of criminal offenders and crime victims, before considering the relationships, if any, between them. The chapter concludes with a special focus on the specific crimes of child abuse, stalking, cybercrime, animal cruelty, and human trafficking, just a few of the crimes to which attention has been given only in recent years.

SOURCES OF CRIME DATA

There are many sources of crime data, but official crime data come primarily from the sources discussed in this section, with the FBI reporting systems being the most frequent source.

The Uniform Crime Reports (UCR)

The ***Uniform Crime Reports (UCR)*** consists of crime data collected by the FBI. Originally, seven crimes were selected, because of their seriousness and frequency, to constitute the *UCR* crime index. Known as Part I, or **index offenses**, they include murder and nonnegligent manslaughter, forcible rape, robbery, aggravated assault, burglary, larceny-theft, and motor vehicle theft. Congress added arson to the crime index in 1979 and referred to the crime index as the *modified crime index*.

In June 2004, the FBI ceased using the concept of *index offenses* for reporting data because of the agency's concern that this category was misleading. For example, overall, most serious crimes are property crimes, with larceny-theft constituting over 70 percent of serious crimes. Thus, if one jurisdiction had a large increase in larceny-theft, that could raise its overall crime index offense data significantly even though it had an insignificant increase in serious violent crimes.

Each month, law enforcement agencies report the number of **crimes known to the police**, that is, the number of Part I offenses verified by police investigation of complaints. A crime known to the police is counted even if no suspect is arrested and no prosecution occurs. If a criminal activity involves several different crimes, only the most serious one is reported as a Part I, or serious, offense. Thus, if a victim is raped, robbed, and murdered, only the murder is counted in the *UCR*. Nor do offenses known to police show how many persons were involved in a particular reported crime.

The *UCR* data are used to calculate a **crime rate**. The national crime rate is calculated by dividing the number of Part I reported crimes by the number of people in the

Spotlight 2.1

Factors Affecting Crime Data

According to the Federal Bureau of Investigation (FBI) any or all of the following factors might affect crime data.

- "Population density and degree of urbanization.
- Variations in composition of the population, particularly youth concentration.
- Stability of the population with respect to residents; mobility, commuting patterns, and transient factors.
- Economic conditions, including median income, poverty level, and job availability.
- Modes of transportation and highway systems.
- Cultural factors and educational, recreational, and religious characteristics.
- Family conditions with respect to divorce and family cohesiveness.
- Climate.
- Effective strength of law enforcement agencies.
- Administrative and investigative emphases of law enforcement.
- Policies of other components of the criminal justice system (i.e., prosecutorial, judicial, correctional, and probational).
- Citizens' attitudes toward crime.
- Crime reporting practices of the citizenry."

Source: Federal Bureau of Investigation, *Uniform Crime Reporting Statistics: Their Proper Use,* https://www.fbi.gov/ucr-statistics-their-proper-use, accessed August 3, 2018.

country (data obtained from census reports). The result is expressed as a rate of crimes per 100,000 persons.

The *UCR* also reports the number of Part I offenses that are cleared. Offenses are cleared in two ways: (1) when a suspect is arrested, charged, and turned over to the judicial system for prosecution; and (2) by circumstances beyond the control of the police. For example, a suspect's death or a victim's refusal to press charges may signal the end of police involvement in a reported crime. Crimes are considered cleared whether or not the suspect is convicted.

Several persons may be arrested and one crime cleared, or one person may be arrested and many crimes cleared. The *clearance rate* is the number of crimes solved, expressed as a percentage of the total number of crimes reported to the police. The clearance rate is critical in policy decisions because it is one measure used to evaluate police departments. The higher the number of crimes solved by arrest, the better the police force looks in the eyes of the public.

Violent crimes are more likely than property crimes to be cleared by arrest. This is because victims (or families, in the case of murder) are more likely to report (and to report more quickly) violent crimes than property crimes. Victims of personal violence, as compared with victims of property crimes, are more likely to be able to give police pertinent information that might lead to an arrest. Murder is the crime most likely to be cleared by arrest; burglary is least likely, but motor vehicle theft and larceny-theft also have low clearance rates.

Arrest information in the *UCR* is presented in two forms: (1) the total estimated numbers of arrests by crime for each of the recorded offenses; and (2) the number of arrests made during one year for each of the serious offenses per 100,000 persons. The *UCR* does not report the number of persons arrested each year because some individuals are arrested more than once during the year. The actual number of arrested persons, therefore, is likely to be smaller than the total number of arrests.

In addition to data on crimes reported and arrest information for Part I offenses, the *UCR* publishes the number of arrests but not the volume of offenses for less serious crimes, known as *Part II offenses,* which are discussed later.

Despite its place as the major source of crime data, the *UCR* has significant limitations. The most serious and obvious one is that the source does not include all crimes that are committed. This is true for several reasons.

First, not all crimes are reported; in fact, most crimes are not reported to police. There are many reasons for not reporting a crime. Some victims think police will not do anything. Others are embarrassed or believe they will be blamed for the crime. For example, sex crime victims may think that they will be suspected of encouraging the crime, particularly if the offense was committed by a relative or an acquaintance. Sex crime victims may not want to go through a trial in which they must face the alleged offender and submit to detailed and embarrassing questions by the defendant's attorney.

A second factor affecting crime data is the delay in reporting crimes. Delay may be caused by an inability to decide whether to report the crime. There are three reasons for this indecisiveness: Some individuals want to verify that a crime has occurred. Others take some actions to cope with the crime before calling the police. Still others experience conflict about calling the police, so they try to avoid making a quick decision. Once the decision to call the police has been made, there may be further delays. A phone may not be available. The caller may not know the police number. The caller may have difficulty communicating with the police department dispatcher.[2]

Police decisions also affect *UCR* crime data. Crimes are included in the *UCR* only if the police decide there is sufficient evidence to believe that a crime has been committed. Police have wide discretion in making that determination, and factors such as the seriousness of the crime, the relationship between the complainant and the alleged offender, the desire for informal disposition of the case, and deference shown the police may influence police decisions regarding arrest.

Police individually, or as a department, may want to downplay the amount of crime in their areas. Consequently, they may not record all reported crimes, even when there is sufficient evidence that a crime has been committed. To illustrate, criminologists who surveyed hundreds of retired high-ranking members of the New York Police Department (NYPD) found that some of them distorted crime data because of the pressure to reduce crime. The city's mayor admitted that some fudging might occur, but insisted that the NYPD officials took the matter of crime data quite seriously.[3]

UCR crime data are also affected by the fact that some crimes are not included within the list of crimes for which data are collected. This includes crimes that, for example, may involve significant financial loss but do not fit into traditional crime categories and are handled informally or by administrative agencies rather than by criminal courts and thus are not counted as crimes. The FBI recognized these and other limitations of the *UCR* and instituted a new program to enhance its collection of crime data.

The National Incident-Based Reporting System (NIBRS)

In 1988, the FBI published details of its proposed **National Incident-Based Reporting System (NIBRS)**. The NIBRS views crime, along with all its components, as an *incident* and recognizes that the data constituting those components should be collected and organized for purposes of analysis. The NIBRS collects data on additional crime categories beyond those included in the *UCR*. It includes 46 specific crimes in 22 offense categories. Those offenses are listed in **Supplement 2.1**. The data are collected by computer, and each reporting agency may individualize its system to suit its unique needs. Through the use of NIBRS, which is still being developed, agencies may collect more data than is possible through the summary system of the *UCR*, discussed earlier. The FBI plans to transition to NIBRS only by 2021. Recent NBRS data include the data on the crimes of animal cruelty, identity theft, and hacking/computer invasion.[4]

National Crime Victimization Survey (NCVS)

The existence of unreported crime, often called the *dark figure of crime*, which never becomes part of official crime data, led to the establishment of another method of measuring crime. It was thought that, if victims do not report crimes to the police, perhaps they will do so on questionnaires submitted to samples of the general population.

Victimization surveys conducted by the **Bureau of Justice Statistics (BJS)** are called the **National Crime Victimization Survey (NCVS)**. The NCVS is based on the results of interviews conducted yearly with a representative sample of 76,000 households. Residents ages 12 or older are questioned about whether they have been the victims of rape, robbery, assault, household burglary, personal and household larceny, or motor vehicle theft. As noted earlier, murder is not included. In addition, the NCVS conducts research on large samples in 20 of the largest cities in the country, along with 8 impact cities. These surveys include questions on business as well as personal victimizations. In 2006, some methodological changes were made in the NCVS, which led the organization to conclude that 2006 data were not comparable to data of previous years.

The NCVS is a valuable supplement to the *UCR*. In addition to disclosing some crimes that are not reported

Spotlight 2.2

The NCVS and the UCR Compared

"Because the NCVS and UCR measure an overlapping, but not identical, set of offenses and use different methodologies, congruity between the estimates is not expected between estimates from these two data sources. Restricting the NCVS to serious violence reported to police keeps the measures as similar as possible. However, significant methodological and definitional differences remain between serious violent crimes in the NCVS and the UCR:

- **The UCR includes homicide and commercial crimes, while the NCVS excludes these crime types.**
- **The UCR excludes sexual assault, while the NCVS includes it.**
- **NCVS estimates are based on interviews with a nationally representative sample of persons in U.S. households. UCR estimates data are based on counts of crimes reported by an incomplete census of law enforcement agencies and are weighted to compensate for the incomplete reporting.**
- **The NCVS excludes crimes against children age 11 or younger and persons in institutions (e.g., nursing homes and correctional institutions). It may also exclude highly mobile populations and persons who are homeless. Victimizations against these persons are included in the UCR.**

Given these differences, the two measures of crime should be compared but should be viewed as complementary sources, which together provide a more comprehensive picture of crime in the United States."

Source: **Rachel E. Morgan and Grace Kena, Bureau of Justice Statistics, *Criminal Victimization, 2016* (December 2017), p. 6, https://www.bjs.gov/content/pub/pdf/cv16.pdf, accessed August 3, 2018.**

to police, these surveys relate the reasons people give for not reporting crimes. However, the data are dependent on victim recall and perception, which may not be accurate. Despite this problem, victimization studies add to our knowledge of criminal activity.

Spotlight 2.2 compares the *UCR* and the NCVS.

Self-Report Data (SRD)

In addition to the *UCR* data and surveys of the population that report how many people have been victimized, self-report studies are used to gather data on the extent and nature of criminal activity. **Self-report data (SRD)** are acquired by two methods: (1) an interview, in which a person is asked questions about illegal activities; and (2) a questionnaire, usually anonymous. Initially, self-report studies were conducted mainly with juveniles, but increasingly, the method is also being used to study adult career criminals.

SRD have been criticized on several grounds. The first problem is that of accuracy. Some respondents, especially juveniles, overreport their involvement in illegal activities, whereas others do not report some or all of their criminal activities. Other criticisms of SRD are that the surveys include too many trivial offenses and sometimes omit serious crimes, such as burglary, robbery, and sexual assault. Furthermore, self-report studies include too few minorities.

Taken together, these criticisms raise serious questions. White respondents tend to report greater involvement in less serious crimes that occur more frequently, and African Americans tend to report illegal acts that are less frequent but more serious. One study found that African American male offenders fail to report known offenses three times more often than white male offenders.[5]

Differences by gender have also been reported. Such findings do not invalidate the use of self-reports, but they do suggest that it may be necessary to compare these results with other measures and to develop more sophisticated methods for data analysis.

Crime Data: An Analysis

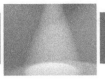

All methods of counting and compiling crimes have problems. How crime is defined and how crimes are counted affect the results of all the methods. Crime is recorded and counted according to the policy used to determine whether one or more crimes occurred during the interaction between the offender and his or her victim. Frequently, the issue arises in sex crimes. For example, in one case, a defendant was convicted of three counts of forcible genital penetration. The defendant argued that he should have been convicted of only one count because each act lasted only a few seconds and all three occurred during a brief period, 7 to 10 minutes. The court disagreed, stating that the statute's prohibition of "penetration, however slight, of the genital or anal openings of another person by any foreign object, substance, instrument, or device" against the victim's will means that *each penetration* is a separate act. A "violation is *complete* the moment such 'penetration' occurs." The court emphasized that the purpose of the statute is to punish those who commit the "outrage to the person and [violate] feelings of the victim" and that this outrage occurs "each time the victim endures a new, unconsented sexual insertion."[6]

A crime that meets the definition of a serious violent or property crime might be charged as a **lesser included offense**, which means that the charged crime is related to the major crime but is less serious. For example, second-degree murder is a lesser included offense in murder; so one who is thought to have committed first-degree or even capital murder might be charged with second-degree murder. Or a person alleged to have committed a sexual crime might be charged with lewd behavior.

A serious factor is reporting of crimes by victims. The BJS reported in December 2018 that in 2017, victims reported only 45 percent of violent crimes to police although the percentage was higher for some individual offenses. Specifically, crime victims reported 49 percent of robberies (down from 57 percent in 2016) and 57.2 percent of aggravated assaults (compared to only 41.3 percent of simple assaults). Victim reporting of rape/sexual assaults was 40.4 percent, a significant increase from 23.2 percent in 2016. In 2017, victims reported 47.5 percent of **intimate partner violence (IPV)** assaults. Property crime victims reported 35.7 percent overall, with 79.0 percent reporting motor vehicle thefts, 49.1 percent reporting household burglaries, and 30.2 percent reporting thefts.[7]

SERIOUS CRIMES: PART I OFFENSES

With these caveats, we will look at crime data using the FBI's official categories. The FBI divides crimes into Part I and Part II offenses. Part I offenses are divided into two categories: **violent crimes** and **property crimes**. That division is used here for further analysis of crime data.

Violent Crimes

The four serious violent crimes included in the FBI's *Uniform Crime Reports* are listed and defined in Spotlight 2.3. The latest available *UCR* data for serious violent crimes overall, graphed in Figure 2.1, shows a decrease of 0.2 percent between 2016 and 2017. The estimates for 2017 were 10.6 percent below those for 2008 but 6.8 percent above the estimates for 2013. The rate of violent crime in 2017 was approximately 0.9 percent below the 2016 estimated rate and 16.5 percent below that of 2008.[8]

Murder and Nonnegligent Manslaughter

Of the four serious violent crimes, **murder** and **nonnegligent manslaughter** are the most serious but least frequently committed (1.2 percent of the serious crimes reported in 2017). It was estimated that in 2017, 17,284 murders were committed, representing a 0.2 percent decrease over the 2016 estimate and a 20.7 increase over the 2013 estimate. The 2017 rate of murders was 1.4 percent lower than the 2016 rate but 17.3 percent higher than the 2013 rate.[9]

Figure 2.1

Trends in U.S. Serious Violent Crimes, 2013-2017

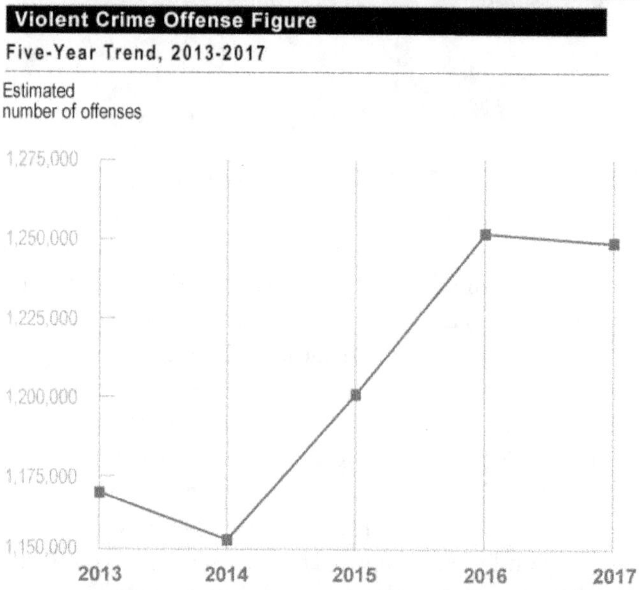

Source: Federal Bureau of Investigation, *Crime in the United States, Uniform Crime Reports 2017*, "Violent Crime," (September 2018), https://www.fbi.gov/, accessed February 11, 2019.

Spotlight 2.3

UCR Definitions of Serious Violent Crimes

Murder and nonnegligent manslaughter: "the willful (nonnegligent) killing of one human being by another."

Rape: "the penetration, no matter how slight, of the vagina or anus with any body part or object, or oral penetration by a sex organ of another person, without the consent of the victim."*

Robbery: "the taking or attempting to take anything of value from the care, custody, or control of a person or persons by force or threat of force or violence and/or by putting the victim in fear."

Aggravated assault: "an unlawful attack by one person upon another for the purpose of inflicting severe or aggravated bodily injury. . . . [T]his type of assault is usually accompanied by the use of a weapon or by other means likely to produce death or great bodily harm."

* Until 2013, the FBI referred to the crime of *forcible rape*, defined as "the carnal knowledge of a female forcibly and against her will. Attempts or assault to commit rape by force or threat of force are also included; however, statutory rape (without force) and other sexual offenses are excluded." The use of the word *forcible* was dropped in 2013.

Source: Federal Bureau of Investigation, *Crime in the United States: Uniform Crime Reports, 2017* (September 2018), https://www.fbi.gov/, accessed September 30, 2018.

Rape

The least frequently committed of the four serious crimes is **rape**. As Spotlight 2.3 notes, the FBI changed its definition of *rape*, with the new definition, noted in that spotlight, first used in 2013. The crime of rape can include the rape of a spouse, referred to as **marital rape**. It also includes rape committed in courtship situations, often referred to as **date rape** and, unfortunately, thought by some to be a lesser crime or not a crime at all. Sexual assaults with male victims are counted as assaults or sex offenses, depending on the circumstances. The FBI reported an estimated 135,755 rapes in 2017, representing a 2.5 percent increase from 2016 and a 19.4 percent increase from estimated rapes in 2013.[10]

Robbery

In terms of frequency, **robbery** ranks second among the four serious violent crimes as recorded and reported by the FBI. A word of explanation is in order. The crime of robbery is, unfortunately, frequently used to refer to an act that constitutes theft rather than robbery. Robbery involves the same elements as theft (discussed below with other property crimes) but adds two elements that make it a violent crime: (1) taking the property from the person or in the presence of the person; *and* (2) using force or threatening to use force. An estimated 319,356 robberies were reported in 2017, representing a 4.0 percent increase from 2016 and a 7.5 percent decrease from the 2013 estimate. Firearms were used in 40.6 percent of the 2017 robberies, and strong-arm tactics were used in 41.5 percent. Collectively, the 2017 estimated robberies cost an estimated $438 million.[11]

Aggravated Assault

The most frequently committed of the four serious violent crimes according to UCR data is **aggravated assault**, which constituted 65.0 percent of the serious violent crimes reported to the FBI in 2017. The number of aggravated assaults, estimated at 810,825 in 2017, represented a 1 percent increase from 2016 and a 3.9 percent decrease from the 2008 estimated figures.[12]

Property Crimes

Most of the serious crimes committed in the United States are not violent personal crimes; they are **property crimes**. These crimes involve taking money, property, or other items of value that belong to others, in which no force is used against the victims. The four crimes included in the FBI's serious property crimes are listed and defined in Spotlight 2.4.

Spotlight 2.4

UCR Definitions of Serious Property Crimes

Burglary (breaking or entering): "The unlawful entry of a structure to commit a felony or a theft." The crime includes attempted forcible entry.

Larceny-theft (except motor vehicle theft): "The unlawful taking, carrying, leading, or riding away of property from the possession or constructive possession of another. Examples are thefts of bicycles, motor vehicle parts and accessories, shoplifting, pocket-picking, or the stealing of any property or article that is not taken by force and violence or by fraud. Attempted larcenies are included. Embezzlement, confidence games, forgery, check fraud, etc., are excluded."

Motor vehicle theft: "The theft or attempted theft of a motor vehicle.... [A] motor vehicle is a self-propelled vehicle that runs on land surfaces and not on rails. Examples of motor vehicles include sport utility vehicles, automobiles, trucks, buses, motorcycles, motor scooters, all-terrain vehicles, and snowmobiles. Motor vehicle theft does not include farm equipment, bulldozers, airplanes, construction equipment, or water craft such as motorboats, sailboats, houseboats, or jet skis. The taking of a motor vehicle for temporary use by persons having lawful access is excluded from this definition."

Arson: "Any willful or malicious burning or attempt to burn, with or without intent to defraud, a dwelling house, public building, motor vehicle or aircraft, personal property of another, etc."

Source: Federal Bureau of Investigation, *Crime in the United States: Uniform Crime Reports, 2017* (September 2018), https://www.fbi.gov/, accessed September 30, 2018.

The FBI data reveal an estimated 8,832,512 property offenses in 2013, representing a 4.1 percent decline from 2012 and a 16.3 percent decline from the 2004 estimates. Figure 2.2 graphs the trends in U.S. serious property crime between 2013 and 2017.[13]

Burglary

The crime of **burglary** has three categories: forcible entry, unlawful entry where no force is used, and attempted forcible entry. For 2017, the FBI reported an estimated 1,401,840 burglary offenses, representing a 7.6 percent decrease from 2016, a 27.4 percent decrease from 2013, and a 37.1 percent decrease from 2008. In 2017, burglary accounted for 18.2 percent of all estimated serious property crimes, with 57.5 percent of the burglaries involving forcible entries, 36.2 percent involving unlawful entries without force, and 6.3 percent classified as attempted forcible entry. Residential dwellings were the targets of 67.2 percent of the 2017 estimated burglaries. The average loss per burglary in 2017 was $2,416.[14]

Larceny-Theft

The most frequently committed property offense is **larceny-theft**, which accounted for 71.7 percent of all serious property crimes in 2017. Larceny-theft includes

Figure 2.2

Trends in U.S. Serious Property Crimes, 2013-2017

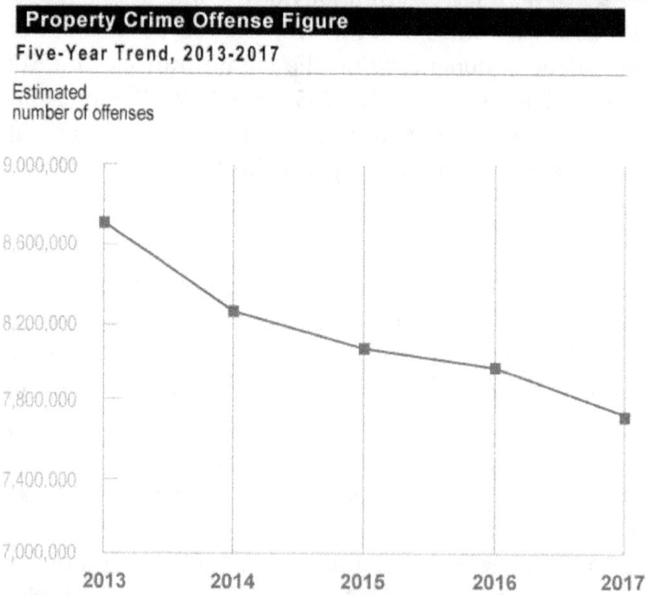

Source: Federal Bureau of Investigation, *Crime in the United States: Uniform Crime Reports, 2017* (September 2018), https://www.fbi.gov/, accessed February 22, 2019.

theft from motor vehicles, shoplifting, picking pockets, snatching purses, thefts of motor vehicle parts and accessories, bicycle thefts, or any other property item in which there is no use of force, violence, or fraud. Attempted larcenies are included within the *UCR*'s larceny-theft category, but crimes such as embezzlement, confidence games, forgery, check fraud, etc., are not included. The number of estimated larceny-thefts in the United States in 2017 was 5,519,107, representing a decline of 2.2 percent from 2016, an 8.3 percent decline from 2013, and a 16.2 percent decrease from 2008. In 2017, the estimated cost of larceny-thefts per victim was $1,007, and the estimated total loss to all larceny-theft victims was $5.6 billion.[15]

Motor Vehicle Theft

The third serious property offense is **motor vehicle theft**. Note that the definition of this crime (see again Spotlight 2.4) does not include taking a vehicle for a joyride or stealing motor vehicle parts. It also does not include stealing items from a vehicle.

Most motor vehicle thefts involve an automobile as the target (75.4 percent in 2017). According to the FBI data, an estimated 773,139 motor vehicle thefts occurred in 2017, representing a 0.8 percent increase over the 2016 data, a 10.4 percent increase from 2013, but a 19.4 percent decrease from the 2008 estimates. The 2017 motor vehicle thefts cost an average of $7,708 loss per offense and a total of $6 billion for all.[16]

Arson

The final serious property crime is **arson**. The FBI excludes from its arson estimates fires of suspicious or unknown origin but includes fires that are determined to have been willfully or maliciously set. Arson did not become a Part I offense until 1979; thus, only limited trend data are available for this crime. Data are also not available for all reporting agencies, and the FBI warns that, as a result, caution must be used in interpreting arson data. During 2017, an estimated 41,171 arson offenses were committed, representing a decrease of 1.7 percent from 2016. The average loss per offense was $15,517.[17]

LESS SERIOUS CRIMES: PART II OFFENSES

In addition to the eight serious crimes categorized as Part I offenses, the FBI collects data on Part II offenses, which are considered the less serious crimes. Those offenses are listed and defined in **Supplement 2.2**. Unlike Part I offenses, for which the FBI collects data on crimes known to the police, for Part II offenses, the agency only collects arrest data. Other agencies collect data on the frequency of some of the Part II offenses, as are noted in subsequent discussions of crime victims.

There is obvious overlap in some of the Part II offenses, and some acts that could be classified as Part II offenses are similar to those classified as Part I offenses. For example, if the act is serious enough, a person who hits (batters) his or her spouse could be charged with aggravated assault, a Part I offense. This perpetrator could also be charged with the Part II offense of simple assault.

The offense categories listed as Part II offenses may be more serious than Part I offenses, depending on how one defines *serious*. For example, one who commits the crimes of fraud or embezzlement may cost a victim far more in financial loss than an offender who commits larceny-theft. To complicate the picture further, other agencies, social scientists, and anyone else who studies criminal behavior may use different classifications, such as **domestic violence**, a category that may include rape, **incest**, elder abuse, child pornography, simple assault, and so on. Consequently, definitions of crimes, along with the interpretations of the meaning of all of the elements of those crimes, must be examined carefully. Some of the categories of Part I and Part II offenses will surface in discussions throughout this text.

HATE CRIMES

The category of hate crimes is frequently in the national news and singled out by federal law for data collection. On April 23, 1990, the U.S. Congress passed the Hate Crime Statistics Act, which requires the U.S. attorney general to collect and publish yearly data on crimes that

> manifest evidence of prejudice based on race, gender and gender identity, religion, disability, sexual orientation, or ethnicity, including where appropriate the crimes of murder; non-negligent manslaughter; forcible rape; aggravated assault; simple assault; intimidation; arson; and destruction, damage or vandalism of property.[18]

All of these target categories were not included in the original act. For example, *disability* was added in 1994; thus, data on disability bias are not available prior to that date. Gender and gender identity were added as a result of the Matthew Shepard and James Byrd Jr. Hate Crimes Prevention Act of 2009. Both Shepard and Byrd were **hate crime** victims. The 2009 Act also added to the Hate Crime Statistics Act the requirement to collect data on crimes that are "committed by, and crimes directed against juveniles."[19]

The Matthew Shepard and James Byrd, Jr., Hate Crimes Prevention Act was named for two hate crime victims. Byrd was killed when he was chained to the back of a pickup truck and dragged through the streets of a small Texas town in 1998. In this photo, his sister Betty Byrd Boatner mourns at his gravesite.

All of the acts listed in the definition of hate crime are covered by state statutes. Thus, some argued, there was no need for a federal hate crime statute. But Congress recognized the seriousness of hate crimes and sought to prevent and punish them under a *federal* statute. The assumption is that the ability to prosecute under a federal statute provides additional assurance that offenders will be convicted and punished. The punishment for a hate crime might also be more severe than that provided for the traditional crime, such as aggravated assault. States may also have hate crime statutes, and many do. They may or may not cover all of the specifics of the federal statutes; they could add more (e.g., a state might include the category of homelessness).

The attorney general delegated to the FBI the responsibility of designing a program and collecting the data. The FBI's first publication under the Hate Crime Statistics Act was *Hate Crime Statistics, 1990: A Resource Book*. The FBI now publishes annually its data on hate crimes or, as they are also called, *bias* offenses, which are divided into five categories: racial bias, religious bias, sexual-orientation bias, ethnicity/national origin bias, and disability bias. Law enforcement must indicate one of these categories for each reported bias offense. The FBI defines a *single-bias incident* as "an incident in which one or more offense types are motivated by the same bias." It defines a *multiple-bias incident* as "an incident in which more than one offense type occurs and at least two offense types are motivated by different biases." In 2018, the FBI released hate crime data for 2017, and those figures are contained in **Supplement 2.3**.

Numerous examples of alleged hate crimes have been the focus of media attention recently. In March 2019, James Alex Fields, Jr., who drove his car into a crowd of protestors at a white nationalist rally in Charlottesville, Virginia, in August 2017, resulting in the death of a paralegal and injuries to others, entered guilty pleas to federal hate crimes, a plea that will subject him to a life sentence. The prosecutor agreed to drop a charge carrying the death penalty. Fields had already been convicted of a state murder charge and sentenced to life in prison.

In January 2019, federal authorities added 19 hate crime charges to other charges against Robert Bowers, who was quoted as yelling "all Jews must die" when he entered the Tree of Life Synagogue outside Pittsburgh, Pennsylvania, on October 27, 2018, during religious services, opened fire, and killed 11 congregants and wounded two congregants and five police officers. The federal charges were under the Matthew Shepard and James Byrd, Jr., Hate Crimes Prevention Act, mentioned above, and counts for discharging a firearm during his rampage. Bowers had already entered not guilty pleas to 44 state charges in the shooting that occurred on October 27, 2018.

The U.S. Supreme Court has decided cases involving hate crime statutes. One, in which the Court dealt with the characterization of an act as a hate crime or an expression of free speech, is the subject of Criminal Justice Systems Dilemma 2.1. The case of *Virginia v. Black* demonstrates one of the dilemmas criminal justice systems face: the balancing of individual constitutional rights against the government's interest in and right to protect society. Hate crimes are serious crimes that may lead to mental and physical injury or even death. In *Black*, the Court considered whether burning a cross is ***prima facie* evidence** of an intent to commit a hate crime or whether further evidence is required to support the intent element of a hate crime.

As mentioned earlier, the FBI reports information on persons who are arrested for crimes; from these data, we glean information on the characteristics of offenders.

CRIMINAL OFFENDERS

Earlier discussions in this chapter noted that the FBI does not report the number of persons arrested; rather, the agency reports the number of offenses cleared or closed, which can be done by arrest or by exceptional means, which were explained in the previous discussion. Violent crimes are more frequently cleared than are property crimes. Murder and nonnegligent manslaughter lead the percentage of clearances, while the lowest rates for clearances are motor vehicle theft and burglary. Those data are presented in **Supplement 2.4**.

In 2017, the FBI data estimated 10,544,995 arrests (518,617 for the four serious violent crimes and 1,249,757 for the four serious property crimes). The highest number of arrests for any category of offenses was for drug violations, with an estimated 1,632,921 arrests. As **Supplement 2.5** shows, the majority of drug abuse arrests were for possession, not the sale or manufacturing of drugs, and marijuana led the arrests for possession of illegal drugs, representing 36.7 percent of all arrests for drug possession and 3.7 percent of arrests for drug sales/manufacture.[20]

Most of the arrests in 2017 were of adults, with juveniles (persons under age 18) constituting 10.1 percent of all arrests for the four serious violent crimes and 13.4 percent of all arrests for the four serious property crimes. Arrests of juveniles in 2017 were 4.5 percent lower than in 2016. In 2017, 68.9 percent of arrestees were white; 27.2 percent were African American, although African Americans accounted for 54.3 percent of arrests for robbery and 53.1 percent for murder and nonnegligent manslaughter.

In terms of gender, most arrests were males (73 percent compared to 27 percent for females). Men constituted 79.5 percent of arrestees for violent crimes and 64.2 percent of all arrests for property crimes.

The differences between the crime rates of men and women and of African Americans and whites do not mean that gender or race *causes* the criminal activity or the reaction to that activity. There is some evidence that it is not age, race, or gender that influences official reaction to the alleged offender but, rather, the seriousness of the offense committed and the degree of the offender's involvement in that offense. There is evidence, too, that the differences in crime rates between the SRD and *UCR* data may be explained by the fact that only a small number of African Americans are sampled in the self-report studies. Furthermore, some studies show that African Americans and whites differ in their tendencies to report certain crimes, but it may also be argued that the differences in crime rates by race are too great to be explained in any way other than discrimination.[21]

CRIME VICTIMS

Historically, the study of crime victims was not an important focus among social scientists. This has changed in recent years, with more attention being given to studying the characteristics and problems of victims, as well as to improving the responses of criminal justice systems to victims' needs and legal rights. Professional societies such as the National Organization for Victim Assistance (NOVA) have been instrumental in passing federal and state legislation to provide resources for victims at the state and national levels. Workshops on **victimology** have increased our knowledge and understanding of the problems victims face. Job opportunities have been developed in victimology, as illustrated by Professions 2.1 (see p. 35).

Concern with victims' rights and needs has led to national legislation on their behalf. In response to the federal Victim and Witness Protection Act of 1982,[22] the U.S. attorney general's office issued detailed guidelines concerning the treatment of crime victims and witnesses by prosecutors and investigators in the U.S. Department of Justice. These guidelines are designed to protect the privacy of victims and witnesses and to provide medical, social, and counseling services. Notification of court proceedings, **restitution**, and other programs available for the assistance of victims and witnesses are also provided. Some states have gone beyond the federal provisions and have enacted additional legislation to aid victims, and in the 1994 crime bill, Congress included some provisions to enhance victims' rights, with a major focus on domestic violence victims.[23]

Special legislation was provided to compensate the victims of the 9/11 terrorist attacks. Within 11 days of the attacks, Congress enacted the Air Transportation Safety

Criminal Justice Systems Dilemma 2.1

Hate Crime versus Free Speech

One of the most difficult and serious dilemmas facing criminal justice systems is balancing the various rights afforded by the U.S. Constitution. The First Amendment right to free speech (see Appendix A) is one of our most precious rights. The right may not be regulated by the government unless it can show a compelling interest in doing so, along with other stringent tests, including a very strong burden of proof on the part of the government. The case of *Virginia v. Black*, decided in 2003 by the U.S. Supreme Court, balanced the right to use symbolic speech (such as cross burning) and the right of the government to maintain order and prevent, in this case, hate crimes.

The case involved a Virginia statute that provided: "It shall be unlawful for any person or persons, with the intent of intimidating any person or group of persons, to burn, or cause to be burned, a cross on the property of another, a highway, or other public place." The second part of that statute provided that "[a]ny such burning of a cross shall be *prima facie* evidence of an intent to intimidate a person or group of persons." Three separate cases were joined for purposes of the appeal. The facts are as follows:

Barry Black led a Ku Klux Klan rally, in which 25 to 30 people gathered on private property, talked about their beliefs, made negative comments about African Americans and Mexicans, and burned a cross. Black was tried before a jury that was instructed that the prosecution must prove that the defendant intended to intimidate, which means to put in fear, but that the intent could be *inferred* by the fact of cross burning.

In a separate incident, Richard Elliott and Jonathan O'Mara, along with another individual, attempted to burn a cross on the yard of an African American, James Jubilee. Jubilee, who lived next door to Elliott, had inquired of Elliott's mother about shots that were fired from behind the Elliott home. Elliott's mother responded that her son shot firearms as a hobby and that he did so in his backyard. In an apparent attempt to "get back" at Jubilee for his complaint about the firearms, Elliott and O'Mara drove a truck onto Jubilee's property, planted a cross, and attempted to burn it. Jubilee saw the partially burned cross the next morning. He said he was "very nervous" because "a cross burned in your yard . . . tells you that it's just the first round."

In considering these cases, the justices of the U.S. Supreme Court were not in agreement on several of the issues, some of which are procedural and beyond the scope of this text. Relevant here is that a majority of the Court held that it is not unconstitutional to ban cross burning with the intent to intimidate, but for a conviction to be upheld under this statute, prosecutors must prove beyond a reasonable doubt that the cross burning was for the purpose of intimidation rather than as an expression of *symbolic* speech, which is included within the First Amendment right to free speech. That intent may not be inferred from the act of cross burning.

Justice Clarence Thomas wrote a scathing dissent, in which he characterized cross burning as a unique symbol of racial hatred and discrimination. He argued that the act of cross burning is evidence of an intent to intimidate; thus, the statute was constitutional.

Source: Virginia v. Black, 538 U.S. 343 (2003).

and System Stabilization Act of 2001 to provide financial compensation for victims who agreed not to sue the airlines or others for negligence.[24]

Other victims' rights issues with regard to 9/11 are those of the injured workers who toiled in the debris, many without adequate respirators. Some grew sick; others worried about future illness as a result of being in that environment for extended periods. A settlement was reached between those workers and New York City, as well as contractors, and subcontractors.[25] Changes have also been made by states (such as New York) to accommodate sex abuse victims by lengthening the statute of limitations for filing abuse claims.

Victim compensation programs do not solve all of the problems of victims. Many of these programs are not adequately funded and thus do not provide sufficient money to satisfy reasonable claims. Furthermore, such programs place heavy burdens on prosecutors, who are primarily responsible for the implementation of these programs. Prosecutorial offices must hire additional staff

Professions 2.1

Careers in Victimology

In recent years, Congress and most states have enacted legislation to provide assistance to crime victims, creating numerous job opportunities in victimology. Provisions for financial assistance require qualified persons to administer the programs. Counseling of crime victims necessitates providing specialized training, especially in the treatment of victims of rape and other sex crimes. Many jurisdictions have established rape crisis centers, whereas others have concentrated on training police and prosecutors to understand the trauma suffered by sex crime victims. Schoolteachers must be informed regarding what to expect from children who are crime victims.

Background checks for employees in many jobs are important to avoid the negligent hiring of persons who might victimize those with whom they come into contact during work. All individuals who work with victims must be sensitized to the privacy requirements regarding those victims. Preparing victim impact statements for courts is a crucial area of administrative work required of probation officers and others. Requirements that victims be notified of pending court and other important hearings create jobs for persons charged with these responsibilities.

Although we have a long way to go before victims receive sufficient assistance in our criminal justice systems, we have made progress at the national, state, and local levels, and interesting and challenging job opportunities exist for those who wish to work with crime victims.

For more information, visit the web page of the American Society of Victimology, http://www.american-society-victimology.us, accessed August 3, 2018.

and develop policies and programs that require financial and other resources. In the case of the 9/11 victims, fees paid to lawyers and to administrators consumed a significant portion of the funding. Finally, some of the compensation laws are not written clearly or are not enforced widely.

The National Crime Victimization Survey (NCVS) of the Bureau of Justice Statistics (BJS) publishes information on reported crime victimizations. The data published in December 2017 and concerning 2016 data, involved a methodological redesign, resulting in problems comparing 2016 data with previous years. In 2016, the BJS introduced a methodological redesign, resulting in problems comparing 2016 data with previous years. The 2017 data showed that violent crimes remained relatively stable between 2016 and 2017. Reporting of crime victimizations to police remained at a relatively low level (45 percent of violent victimizations and 35.7 percent of property crimes). Victims were more likely to report aggravated assaults and robbery than to report simple assault. Property crime victims were most likely to report motor vehicle thefts (79 percent).[26]

The NCVS also provides data on the demographic characteristics of crime victims. Young people, men (except for rape and sexual assault), African Americans, Hispanics, divorced or separated people, the unemployed, the poor, and residents of central cities are the most frequent violent crime victims. Persons from the ages of 12 to 17 and those between the ages of 18 and 24 are the most frequent victims of violent crime. The lowest rates of violent crime and serious violent crime victimizations are among those who are 65 or older. Most of the crimes against the elderly are property crimes, and they are disproportionately victimized by property crimes.[27] Approximately 59 percent of the time, those crimes occur at or close to their homes. The elderly are less likely than younger victims to suffer personal injury when those property crimes are committed. In **identity theft** crimes, persons 65 and older are more frequently victimized (5 percent) than are victims ages 16 to 24 (3.8 percent) but less frequently victimized compared to persons ages 25 to 49 (7.9 percent). Elderly victims are more likely than victims in the age group 12 to 25 to report violent crimes to the police.[28]

The elderly may be abused by families and strangers, and although data are scarce, the Centers for Disease Control estimate that as many as one in ten elderly persons suffer emotional, physical, or sexual abuse or potential abuse.[29] **Elder abuse** occurs in the form of neglect in nursing homes, sexual and physical abuse, and fraud schemes. Congress sought to target some of these abuses when it passed the Elder Justice Act in 2011 as part of the controversial health care bill, the Patient Protection and Affordable Care Act.[30]

The elderly are frequently targeted for fraud crimes. Richard Guthrie, 92, was defrauded of funds from his bank account with Wachovia Corporation. The bank subsequently agreed to a $10 million fine, to pay $8.9 million for consumer education, and to pay up to $125 million in restitution to persons victimized as a result of the bank's negligence. The corporation was accused of engaging in unsafe practices that permitted telemarketers to use customer accounts to steal money. Guthrie died before he received full restitution.

Another important demographic with regard to crime victimization is race. Victimization data show that African Americans suffer higher rates of violent and household crime victimizations than do whites, and violent crimes against African Americans generally are more serious than those committed against whites. Offenders who victimize African Americans are more likely to use weapons; violent crimes against African Americans involve a gun in twice as many cases compared with whites. African American victims are more likely than whites to be attacked physically during the crime's commission.[31]

Black/African American victims constitute only 13 percent of the total U.S. population, yet they constitute almost one-half of all homicide victims. Black/African Americans have higher victimization rates than whites for all violent crimes that the NCVS measures, with the exception of simple assault. The violent crime victimization rates of blacks are also generally higher than those of other racial groups, although there are some differences for Hispanics. In general, non-Hispanics have higher violent crime rates than Hispanics, primarily because they have a higher rate of simple assaults. Hispanics are more likely than non-Hispanics to be robbery victims.[32]

Gender is another important demographic in crime victimization. Overall, men are more likely than women to be victimized by crime, especially serious violent crime, although trend data show that the rates are getting closer. Women have higher violent crime victimization rates than men in only the categories of rape and other sexual assaults. Even though men are much more likely than women to be violent crime victims, research discloses that the fear of violent crime is greater among women, mainly because of the fear of rape.[33]

A new category of victimization data was added by the Crime Victims with Disabilities Awareness Act,[34] which requires that the BJS collect annual data on victims with disabilities, categorized by these six types:

- Sensory
- Physical
- Cognitive functioning
- Self-care
- Go-outside-home
- Employment

The BJS defines *disability* as "a sensory, physical, mental, or emotional condition lasting 6 months or longer that makes it difficult for a person to perform activities of daily living."[35]

In July 2017, the BJS released data on crimes against persons with disabilities between 2009 and 2015. The data analysis took into consideration age-adjusted rates, as persons with disabilities are generally older than those without disabilities. Among other findings, the report noted that the "rate of violent victimizations against persons with disabilities . . . was 2.5 times the rate for persons without disabilities" and that was true for both males and females. The differences among races were not statistically significant. Among disability types, the highest rates of violent crimes were among persons with cognitive disabilities.[36]

RELATIONSHIP BETWEEN VICTIMS AND OFFENDERS

Social interaction between offenders and their victims is an important factor in some crimes. Normally, violence in the form of assault or murder is preceded by social interaction, and physical violence is more likely if both the offender and the victim define the situation as one calling for violence. If only one person is prone to physical violence, the altercation generally will not become a physical one. In this sense, the victim may contribute to his or her own injury or death, but that does not mean the victim *caused* or is responsible for the crime.

The extent of violence committed by those who know each other, especially within the domestic setting, is difficult to estimate. These crimes may not be reported by the victims or by other family members because of fear or embarrassment, or for other reasons, such as a hope that the situation will improve. Many violent crime victims, especially murder victims, know their assailants, but recent data reveal a decline in **intimate partner violence (IPV)** although that decline is not as sharp as the decline in overall violence. Significantly more women than men are IPV victims. IPV (also called *courtship violence*) is more common among college and university students than it is among noncollege students. It is estimated that each year over 97,000 college and university students between the ages of 18 and 24 are victims of sexual assault or date rape, mostly in alcohol-related situations.[37] In recent years, the U.S. Department of Justice has been investigating numerous college and universities with regard to their policies and actions concerning reported sexual assaults on campuses throughout the United States.

Despite the frequent interaction between victims and their assailants, there is also an element of fear of random violence among potential victims, as noted in the discussion in **Supplement 2.6**.

CRIMINAL JUSTICE SYSTEMS AND CRIME VICTIMS

Research in the 1980s and 1990s provided information on how victims react to crime. The findings of this research led to significant changes in criminal justice systems. It has not been an easy journey for crime victims; nor are all of their problems solved. Victim reaction, however, has been a key factor in these changes.

In 1982, President Ronald Reagan established the President's Task Force on Victims, which was followed in 1984 by the Attorney General's Task Force on Family Violence. Both commissions interviewed crime victims and others. Most of the victims spoke negatively about their treatment in criminal justice systems.

The criminal justice systems' reaction to some crime victims means that they are victimized twice: once by the criminal and once by the system in a variety of ways. First, the victim may be blamed for the crime. Particularly in the case of sexual assault, the response of the system may be that the victim asked for it by being in a questionable place, such as a bar; by hitchhiking; by having a questionable reputation; or by wearing provocative clothing. This is referred to as **victim precipitation**.

In addition to being blamed for the crime, victims may perceive that police and others will not be sympathetic to crimes committed by persons known to the alleged victim—that they view those actions as domestic problems, not violence. Some rape victims have complained about the reactions of police and prosecutors, alleging that they have not tried to understand the problems suffered by the victims.

Third, some victims (and others) complain that U.S. criminal justice systems favor defendants over victims. This response should be analyzed in light of later discussions in this text of defendants' rights, but basically the position is that criminal justice systems have gone too far in protecting defendants to the exclusion of victims.

Some changes designed to benefit victims have been made within criminal justice systems. Many departments now train police and prosecutors to be sensitive to the needs of adult rape and domestic violence victims, as well as young children who are abused in any way by their families, their friends, or strangers. Other departments have special units of officers designated to handle allegations by these or other types of victims. The rise of the #MeToo movement in recent years has resulted in more awareness of sexual harassment and sexual assaults in the workplace, leading to required sensitivity training sessions and the reassignment, demonstration, firing, or forced resignation of known offenders, some in very high places within businesses and other places.

Police departments have changed their arrest policies in response to victims who have complained that often police do not arrest offenders, and when they do, some prosecutors will not file charges. Police response to that complaint has been that most victims will not cooperate, and without their cooperation, most prosecutions of domestic violence cases will not be successful. Victims respond that they are afraid that, if they cooperate, the alleged offenders will retaliate.

In an attempt to remove the responsibility (and thus the increased chances of retaliation by the accused) from the victim, some police departments have instituted a policy of mandatory arrests in domestic battery cases. Mandatory arrests remove from police the discretion to avoid the situation, mediate, or recommend civil action only. If called to the scene of a domestic battering, police must arrest if they have probable cause to believe that battering has occurred.

Legislative and administrative changes in the roles of prosecutors and judges have also been made. Training programs for prosecutors have given them greater understanding of the unique problems suffered by rape, domestic abuse, and child abuse victims. The provision of counseling services for victims; court-ordered counseling for those found guilty of rape, domestic violence, or child abuse; greater restrictions on pretrial release of suspects; and many other changes have occurred. Significant changes have been made in research on and the teaching of victimology and victims' rights.[38]

Earlier in this chapter, we mentioned that some criminal justice systems have responded to victims' needs by establishing victim compensation programs, but some jurisdictions have also enacted legislation to benefit witnesses, and some legislation is designed to benefit both crime victims and witnesses. Congress passed a victim compensation bill that applies to victims and witnesses involved in federal crimes—the Victim and Witness Protection Act of 1982 (VWPA), which has been amended subsequently. The act contains various provisions designed to prevent harassment of victims and witnesses. It establishes guidelines for fair treatment of crime victims and witnesses in criminal justice systems. It requires victim impact statements at sentencing, contains more stringent bail requirements, and provides that the sentencing judge must order defendants to pay restitution to victims or state reasons for not doing so.[39]

Congress also passed the Victims of Crime Act (VOCA) of 1984, which authorizes that federal funds be distributed by the Office of Justice Programs through its Office for Victims of Crime and Bureau of Justice Statistics for state victim compensation and assistance programs. VOCA originally provided that federal funds would stop after September 30, 1988, but Congress reauthorized the program to continue. The money for the fund comes from fines, penalties, and the sale of forfeited goods. The fund is distributed to local agencies and has been used for hiring counselors to work with victims, to compensate victims, and even for technology, such as computers, used to assist victims.[40]

In recent years, additional attempts have been made to compensate victims and to increase their participation in criminal justice systems. Although a proposed amendment to the U.S. Constitution was withdrawn by its sponsors, who stated that they knew they could not get the necessary support for passage, a federal bill was passed by the U.S. Congress and signed by President George W. Bush in 2004. In part, the Crime Victims' Rights Act provides the following:

> (1) The right to be reasonably protected from the accused.
>
> (2) The right to reasonable, accurate, and timely notice of any public court proceeding, or any parole proceeding, involving the crime or of any release or escape of the accused.
>
> (3) The right not to be excluded from any such public court proceeding, unless the court, after receiving clear and convincing evidence, determines that testimony by the victim would be materially altered if the victim heard other testimony at that proceeding.
>
> (4) The right to be reasonably heard at any public proceeding in the district court involving release, plea, sentencing, or any parole proceeding.
>
> (5) The reasonable right to confer with the attorney for the Government in the case.
>
> (6) The right to full and timely restitution as provided in law.
>
> (7) The right to proceedings free from unreasonable delay.
>
> (8) The right to be treated with fairness and with respect for the victim's dignity and privacy.[41]

SPECIAL FOCUS ON SPECIFIC CRIMES

This chapter has discussed crime data in terms of the eight serious violent and property crimes as recorded by the FBI and the data collected by the BJS. Those eight crimes, however, constitute only a small percentage of all crimes committed in the United States, and many would argue that they are not more serious than some other crimes. Mention was made of the lesser offenses recorded by the FBI. This section focuses on a select number of crimes that are not included as such within the FBI's serious crimes (although they may overlap with some of them, such as assault and battery). Some of these occur frequently; others do not. All are important and many are controversial. No attempt is made to suggest which are more important, or for that matter, more extensive. Nor is any attempt made to categorize the crimes. They are, however, crimes that either are frequently in the news or noted because the acts have only recently been designated as criminal. **Supplement 2.7** discusses terrorism; **Supplement 2.8** discusses **white collar crime**. This section briefly discusses child abuse, stalking, cybercrime, animal cruelty, and human trafficking.

Child Abuse

The abuse of children takes many forms, and while some would not consider **fetal abuse** to fall within the category of child abuse, it is important and involves criminal activity—the killing of a fetus. Fetal abuse may involve physical abuse, but in some cases it results in the death of a fetus caused by a pregnant woman who uses alcohol and other drugs.

There is sufficient evidence that consumption of alcohol and other drugs by pregnant women may cause harm to their fetuses that warnings are widely given (for example, in bars) and, in some jurisdictions, criminal sanctions are imposed. Such statutes are not common, but South Carolina convicted a woman of murder after she gave birth to a stillborn fetus that, the state alleged, resulted from her substance abuse during pregnancy. The conviction was upheld by the South Carolina Supreme Court, and the U.S. Supreme Court refused to hear the case on appeal.[42] The U.S. Supreme Court has, however, held that a state may not force pregnant women suspected of drug abuse to be drug tested involuntarily if the primary purpose of the test is to report their actions to the police.[43]

In contrast, a Missouri court refused to permit charging a pregnant woman with child endangerment after she and her child tested positive for drugs. The court noted that, of the 15 state legislatures that considered the issue, only South Carolina enacted a statute that, in effect, provides for a charge of homicide by child abuse against a pregnant woman whose act or omission causes the death of a fetus. The Missouri court concluded that a better approach than the criminal law for such situations is to utilize social service agencies. And the Kentucky Supreme Court has held that it was unconstitutional under that state's law to prosecute a pregnant woman for wanton endangerment in the first degree because she ingested drugs during her pregnancy (at birth the child tested positive for cocaine).[44]

Injury to a pregnant woman that leads to the death of her fetus is now covered by some statutes, such as the California murder statute, which previously defined murder as "the unlawful killing of a human being with malice aforethought" and now contains the words *or a fetus* after the words *human being*.[45] The statute has an exclusion for death to a fetus resulting from a legal abortion. Congress enacted the Unborn Victims of Violence Act of 2004 to change the federal criminal code and that of the military code to protect unborn children from assault and murder.[46]

In recent years, many jurisdictions have enacted **Baby Moses laws**, which make provisions for protecting mothers (or fathers) who abandon their newborn children in ways that will protect those infants.

Children beyond the fetus stage are also frequent crime victims, and those victimizations are not included in the NCVS. **Child abuse** is a broad term, which is defined by the Federal Child Abuse Prevention and Treatment Act (CAPTA) as at a minimum:

> Any recent act or failure to act on the part of a parent or caretaker which results in death, serious physical or emotional harm, sexual abuse or exploitation; or
> An act or failure to act which presents an imminent risk of serious harm. . . .[47]

Child abuse may also include **kidnapping** and **parental kidnapping**, with the latter occurring when the parent without legal custody takes the child from the other parent (or from a school or other place in which the child is located) in violation of the legal custody agreement and refuses to return the child when requested to do so. Child abuse includes **statutory rape** (sex with an underage person even if no force is involved) and incest (sex with a family member or a person too closely related to marry). It includes the exploitation of children through pornography.

Child abuse data are not complete, but the Centers for Disease Control and Prevention in 2018 published 2016 data indicating that 676,000 children were victims of abuse and neglect and that about 1,750 children died of abuse or neglect.[48]

Stalking

The BJS defines the term **stalking** as "a course of conduct directed at a specified person that would cause a reasonable person to feel fear." Included within this definition are the following behaviors:

- "making unwanted phone calls
- sending unsolicited or unwanted letters or e-mails
- following or spying on the victim
- showing up at places without a legitimate reason
- waiting at places for the victim
- leaving unwanted items, presents, or flowers
- posting information or spreading rumors about the victim on the internet, in a public place, or by word of mouth."[49]

The last item on the list is referred to as **cyberstalking**, which is a form of stalking that involves the Internet, e-mail, or some other form of electronic communication to harass or otherwise threaten another. Women are more likely to be targeted for stalking than men, and approximately one of every four stalking victims experiences some type of cyberstalking, such as e-mail (83 percent) or instant messaging (35 percent). Most victims know their offenders.[50]

Anti-stalking statutes are relatively new, with the first state statute enacted in California in 1990. The federal statute, the Interstate Stalking Punishment and Prevention Act, was enacted in the fall of 1996. This statute is aimed at stalking on federal property or across state lines. It is reproduced in **Supplement 2.9.**[51] Stalking on college and university campuses is discussed in **Supplement 2.10**.

Cybercrime

Although stalking and other crimes do not require the Internet, the Internet is used to facilitate the growing number of **cybercrimes.** In particular, this section looks at the need to protect children from cybercrime. The U.S. Department of Justice (DOJ) emphasizes that online threats to children are expanding and becoming more sophisticated, and it is increasingly difficult to assess the threats. Clearly, though, there has been an increase in the detected use of the Internet for child pornography and for enticing children. The DOJ estimates that 200 new images of child pornography are placed on the Internet daily and that the annual income from these crimes may exceed $20 billion. Children and teens who run away from home are enticed into prostitution, with the number of such complaints made to the Internet Crimes Against Children (ICAC) Task Forces increasing by 914 percent between 2004 and 2008.[52]

Another way that children and teens become cybercrime victims is through online bullying, which has become so pervasive that the U.S. Department of Education held a Bullying Summit in Washington, D.C. The participants heard a member of the DOJ present cases of bullying and emphasize the far-reaching effect that is the result of online posting. In particular, children and teens were advised not to engage in *sexting*. Some of the advice given by the FBI with regard to this activity is presented in Spotlight 2.5.

The FBI places a high priority on preventing cybercrime. In 2000, the agency established the Internet Crime Complaint Center (IC3) "as a partnership between the FBI and the National White Collar Crime Center (NW3C) to serve as a means to receive Internet criminal complaints and to further research, develop, and refer" those complaints to the appropriate local, state, or federal agency. Congress enacted statutes to combat cybercrimes, which are punishable by a fine of up to $250,000 and up to five years in prison.

Animal Cruelty

Cruelty against animals is a relatively recent addition to criminal law, and it is not widely covered in criminal law books and almost never in undergraduate texts. Legislation is spreading, however, and enforcements are more likely. According to the American Bar Association, animal abuse law is "one of the fast-growing—and more emotional—niches" in U.S. criminal law.[53]

Concerned with animal abuse and its potential relationship to crime, some states have enacted legislation requiring counseling for those who abuse animals. Texas, for example, provides that when a child violates the state's animal abuse statutes, "the juvenile court shall order the child to participate in psychological counseling for a period to be determined by the court."[54]

In 2016, Connecticut became the first state to enact legislation to permit judges to appoint lawyers and law students to serve as advocates for abused and neglected animals. The law was viewed as necessary because prosecutors are too overburdened with other cases to prosecute animal abuse cases, with as many as 47 percent of reported cases falling into that category.[55] In addition, some jurisdictions are considering awarding civil damages to abused animals. Consider the case of Justice, an abused 8-year-old quarter horse, whose owner pled guilty to criminal neglect. Justice sued that former owner for neglect, requesting at least $100,000 for veterinary care plus damages for pain and suffering. Permitting an animal to sue is unusual; this case, in Oregon, one of the most progressive states in the area of animal cruelty, was dismissed in 2018 by a judge who ruled that "non-human animals are incapable of accepting legal responsibilities." In January 2019, the horse's attorney appealed that dismissal.[56]

In 2016, the FBI for the first time included data on animal cruelty in its NIBRS crime data. Prior to that time, offenses against animals were included in the category of "all other offenses." By including animal cruelty within NIBRS, the FBI hopes to get a better picture of the nature of cruelty and its potential relationship to cruelty against humans. The National Sheriffs' Association was a leader

Spotlight 2.5

Sexting: Advice to Young People

In an article on sexting posted on the FBI website, two authors presented data and examples of this risky practice, which, they stated, is engaged in by 22 percent of female teens and 18 percent of teen boys. The authors discussed the widespread impact of these postings, the dangers to the targeted victims, and the repercussions to the senders. They also analyzed the issues for law enforcement, especially concerning how to react to sexting from young teens or children, ranging from no response to prosecution with the eventual requirement that the individual register for life as a sex offender.

The advice presented was as follows:

Advice for Young People

"*Think about the consequences* of taking, sending, or forwarding a sexual picture of yourself or someone else underage. You could get kicked off of sports teams, face humiliation, lose educational opportunities, and even get in trouble with the law.

Never take images of yourself that you wouldn't want everyone—your classmates, your teachers, your family, or your employers—to see.

Before hitting send, remember that you cannot control where this image may travel. What you send to a boyfriend or girlfriend easily could end up with their friends, and their friends, and their friends.

If you forward a sexual picture of someone underage, you are as responsible for this image as the original sender. You could face child pornography charges, go to jail, and have to register as a sex offender.

Report any nude pictures you receive on your cell phone to an adult you trust. Do not delete the message. Instead, get your parents or guardians, teachers, and school counselors involved immediately."

Source: Art Bowker and Michael Sullivan, "Risky Actions and Overreactions," Federal Bureau of Investigation, "Tips to Prevent Sexting," http://www.fbi.gov/stats-services/publications/law-enforcementbulletin/july-2010/sexting, originally published on the National Center for Missing and Exploited Children, accessed January 10, 2015.

---

in this movement, citing evidence of animal cruelty by such noted criminals as Ted Bundy, Jeffrey Dahmer, and the "Son of Sam" killer David Berkowitz. The organization points to the "overlap animal abuse has with domestic violence and child abuse." It will be a few years before the data show meaningful patterns.[57]

Human Trafficking

The previous discussion of cybercrime mentioned the illegal use of children in pornography as well as the online efforts to entice them to engage in sexual activity online. In May 2006, the U.S. Department of Justice launched Project Safe Childhood in an effort to locate and prosecute those who use the Internet to exploit children, as well as to rescue child victims. The children may be further victimized by human trafficking, which also victimizes adults and may include labor as well as sexual victimization. *Human trafficking* (also referred to as modern-day slavery) is defined in various ways, but essentially it refers to the recruiting, soliciting, harboring, transporting, or transferring human beings by use of threats, abduction, force, fraud, coercion, or deceit for the purposes of exploitation for sex, labor, or domestic servitude. The FBI announced in a January 2018 news release that January was National Slavery and Human Trafficking Prevention Month. "The FBI works human trafficking investigations through its task forces, operations, and initiatives—all of which take a victim-centered approach." In 2018, the FBI was in its fifth year of collecting data on offenses and arrests for this crime, and reports can be secured from the agency's website.[58]

The seriousness of human trafficking, especially sex trafficking of children, is illustrated by the life sentence handed down to Demarcus Davis, aka "Zigg," 26, in August 2018. The defendant was a co-conspirator with two others, all of whom were found guilty of conspiracy to commit sex trafficking of underage girls.[59]

Summary

This chapter presented an overview of data on crime, offenders, and crime victims, and discussed how those data are secured. The three basic methods for collecting crime data were described and analyzed. The official data of the *Uniform Crime Reports (UCR)* report the amount of crime as recorded by police departments and reported to the FBI.

In recent years, the FBI has recognized the limitations of its method of collecting and recording crime data. Its most significant change, the National Incident-Based Reporting System (NIBRS), is in operation in many states. NIBRS views crime as an incident that involves many elements, including alcohol and drug abuse; the types of victims, weapons, and criminal activity; the victim's and arrestee's residency; the relationship between victims and offenders; and a description of property and property values. The collection of these additional elements of criminal acts will significantly enhance our ability to analyze crime.

The second source of crime data is the National Crime Victimization Survey (NCVS). It is valuable because it reveals that many victims do not report their victimizations to the police. The NCVS provides data on why people do not report victimizations. It does not give any information on arrests, and it is dependent on the accuracy of perception and reporting of crime victims.

The third major source of crime data—self-report data (SRD)—provides information not secured by either of the official methods on characteristics of people who say they have committed crimes. SRD provide valuable data for social scientists who study why crimes are committed, as well as for officials who must make decisions concerning the use of resources aimed at crime control and prevention. SRD allow the study of repeat offenders. The major problem with this approach is that respondents may underreport or overreport crimes.

All the data sources can be used to analyze the nature and extent of crime, but it is important to analyze carefully the time periods and the definitions of crimes being measured before comparing data from the various sources. Data in this chapter come primarily from the *UCR*, with victimization data coming from the NCVS.

Following the look at data, this chapter explored the recently developed and rapidly expanding study of victimology. It discussed the characteristics of crime victims, along with the problems those victims face in criminal justice systems.

The chapter summarized some of the specific problems crime victims face within criminal justice systems, including efforts to assist crime victims, and it mentioned such measures as victim compensation, revised court procedures, and victim participation in criminal justice processes.

Like most changes in the system, recognizing the rights of victims creates other needs, such as training programs for professionals within the system and financial backing for those programs as well as for victim compensation plans. Furthermore, victims' rights and defendants' rights may come into conflict. Nevertheless, changes made in the system to help victims may produce positive results, such as increased crime reporting and more arrests and convictions. But what appear to be positive results could create problems for the system and society because of the increased need for jails and prisons. Thus, a study of crime victims provides another example of the need to assess the effect that changes in one aspect of the system have on the rest of the system and on society.

The chapter closed with a brief look at specific areas of crime that are increasingly studied and recognized but are not included in the FBI's eight most serious crimes: child abuse, stalking, cybercrime, animal cruelty, and human trafficking.

This completes the introductory chapters. We turn now to a look at policing, the criminal justice component through which many people enter criminal justice system processing.

Key Terms

Aggravated assault 29
Arson 31
Baby Moses laws 39
Bureau of Justice Statistics (BJS) 26
Burglary 30
Child abuse 39
Crime rate 24
Crimes known to the police 24
Cybercrime 40
Cyberstalking 40
Date rape 28
Domestic violence 31
Elder abuse 34
Federal Bureau of Investigation (FBI) 24
Fetal abuse 39
Hate crime 32
Identity theft 34
Incest 31
Index offenses 24
Intimate partner violence (IPV) 28
Kidnapping 39
Larceny-theft 30
Lesser included offense 28
Manslaughter 28
Marital rape 28
Motor vehicle theft 31
Murder 28
National Crime Victimization Survey (NCVS) 26
National Incident-Based Reporting System (NIBRS) 26
Nonnegligent manslaughter 28
Parental kidnapping 39
Prima facie evidence 33
Property crimes 29
Rape 28
Robbery 28
Self-report data (SRD) 27
Stalking 39
Statutory rape 39
Uniform Crime Reports (UCR) 24
Victim compensation programs 34
Victimology 33
Violent crimes 28
White collar crime 39

Study Questions

1. Describe and contrast the major sources of crime data.
2. Why should attention be paid to misdemeanors?
3. What are the limitations of the *UCR*?
4. Explain and evaluate the FBI's NIBRS system of data reporting.
5. Why are some crimes not reported by victims? If you were a crime victim, would you call the police? Would it depend on the nature of the crime?
6. What are the advantages and disadvantages of self-report studies?
7. What are the major differences between serious violent crimes and serious property crimes? List and define the four crimes in each of these categories.
8. Explain the FBI's definitions of *rape*.
9. What is a *hate crime*? Discuss. How does the U.S. Supreme Court case on cross burning relate to hate crimes?
10. What progress has been made recently in the study of victims?
11. Discuss the characteristics of crime victims.
12. What lifestyle changes might you consider because of the risk of crime?
13. What changes have been made in recent legislation to improve the plight of crime victims?
14. Define *fetal abuse* and *Baby Moses laws*.
15. Explain what is meant by cybercrime.
16. What is *stalking* and why is it an important crime to study?
17. Why do you think animal cruelty is gaining recognition as a crime?
18. What is human trafficking?

Notes

1. Quoted in James Lynch, "2017 Presidential Address to the American Society of Criminology: Not Even Our Own Facts: Criminology in the Era of Big Data," *Criminology* 56(3) (August 2018): 437-454; quotation is on p. 437.
2. William Spelman and Dale K. Brown, *Calling the Police: Citizen Reporting of Serious Crime* (Washington, D.C.: National Institute of Justice, October 1984), pp. xxiv-xxvii.
3. "Crime Survey Raises Questions About Data-Driven Policy," *New York Times* (February 9, 2010), p. 20.
4. Federal Bureau of Investigation, "FBI Releases 2016 NIBRS Crime Statistics in Report and CED, Promotes Transition of Agencies," https://ucr.fbi.gov, accessed August 4, 2018.
5. Michael J. Hindelang et al., "Correlates of Delinquency: The Illusion of Discrepancy Between Self-Report and Official Measures," *American Sociological Review* 44 (December 1979): 995-1014.
6. *People v. Harrison*, 768 P.2d 1078, 1081, 1082 (Cal. 1989).
7. Rachel E. Morgan and Jennifer L. Truman, Bureau of Justice Statistics, *Criminal Victimization, 2017* (December 2018), p. 7, https://www.bjs.gov/content/pub/pdf/cv17.pdf, accessed April, 11, 2019.
8. Federal Bureau of Investigation, *Crime in the United States, Uniform Crime Reports 2017, "Violent Crimes,"* (September 2018), https://www.fbi.gov, accessed February 11, 2019.
9. Ibid.
10. Ibid.
11. Ibid.
12. Ibid.
13. Ibid.
14. Ibid.
15. Ibid.
16. Ibid.
17. Ibid.
18. Hate Crime Statistics Act, USCS, Title 28, Section 534 (2019).
19. The 1994 act is the Violent Crime Control and Law Enforcement Act of 1994, USCS, Title 28, Section 994. The Matthew Shepard and James Byrd, Jr., Hate Crime Statistics Act is codified at USCS, Title 18, Section 249 (2019).
20. All of the arrest data are from the FBI's *Uniform Crime Reports, Crime in the United States, 2017* (September 2028), https://ucr.fbi.gov, accessed November 30, 2018.
21. See, for example, William Wilbanks, *The Myth of a Racist Criminal Justice System* (Monterey, CA: Brooks/Cole, 1987) and Joan Petersilia et al., *Racial Equity in Sentencing* (Santa Monica, CA: Rand, February 1988).
22. USCS, Title 18, Section 3663 (2019).
23. See, for example, Title IV, Violence against Women, of the Violent Crime Control and Law Enforcement Act of 1994, Public Law 103-322 (September 13, 1994).
24. The Air Transportation Safety and System Stabilization Act of 2001, as amended in 2002, Public Law 107-72 (2011).
25. "City Settles with WTC Rescue Workers," *The Star-Ledger* (Newark, NJ) (March 12, 2010), p. 1.
26. Morgan and Truman, *Criminal Victimization, 2017*, pp. 1, 4, 7.
27. Ibid., p. 9.
28. Rachel E. Morgan and Britney J. Mason, Bureau of Justice Statistics, *Crimes Against the Elderly, 2003-2013* (November 2014), pp. 1, 2, https://www.bjs.gov/content/pub/pdf/cae0313.pdf, accessed August 7, 2018.
29. "Understanding Elder Abuse," Centers for Disease Control and Prevention, https://www.cdc.gov/violenceprevention/pdf/em-factsheet-a.pdf, accessed August 7, 2018.
30. Patient Protection and Affordable Care Pact, Public Law 111-148 (2011).
31. Erika Harrell, Bureau of Justice Statistics, *Black Victims of Violent Crime* (August 2007), p. 1, https://www.bjs.gov/content/pub/pdf/bvvc.pdf, accessed August 7, 2018.
32. Ibid. See also, Morgan and Truman, "Criminal Victimizations, 2017," p. 9.
33. Ibid. See also, for example, Bonnie S. Fisher and John J. Sloan III, "Unraveling Fear of Victimization Among College Women: Is the 'Shadow of Sexual Assault Hypothesis' Supported?," *Justice Quarterly* 20(3) (September 2003): 633-659.
34. Crime Victims with Disabilities Awareness Act, Public Law 105-301 (1998).
35. Erika Harrell and Michael R. Rand, Bureau of Justice Statistics, National Crime Victimization Survey, 2008, *Crime Against People with Disabilities, 2008* (December 2010), p. 1, https://bjs.ojp.usdoj.gov/content/pub/pdf/capd08.pdf, accessed March 2, 2011.
36. Erika Harrell, Bureau of Justice Statistics, "Crime Against Persons with Disabilities, 2009-2015—Statistical Tables" (July 2017), pp. 1, 3, 4; https://ww.bjs.gov, accessed August 7, 2018.
37. National Institute on Alcohol Abuse and Alcoholism (NIAAA), "College Drinking," http://pubs.niaaa.nih.gov/publications/CollegeFactSheet/CollegeFactSheet.pdf, accessed August 7, 2018.
38. For an excellent series of articles on victims and victimology, see the *Journal of Criminal Justice Education* 25 (4) (December 2014).
39. USCS, Title 18, Section 3663 (2019).
40. USCS, Title 42, Section 10601 et seq. (2019).
41. Crime Victims' Rights Act, USCS, Title 18, Section 3771(a)(1)-(8) (2019).
42. *State v. McKnight*, 576 S.E.2d 168 (S.C. 2003), *cert. denied; McKnight v. South Carolina*, 540 U.S. 819 (2003). The South Carolina statute, which is entitled Homicide by Child Abuse, is codified at S.C. Code Ann., Title 16, Section 16-3-85 (2018).
43. *Ferguson v. Charleston*, 532 U.S. 67 (2001).
44. "Missouri Court of Appeals Western District Case Summaries," *Missouri Lawyers Weekly* (September 17, 2007). The Missouri case is *State v. Wade*, 232 S.W.3d 663 (Mo. Ct. App. 2007). The Kentucky case is *Cochran v. Commonwealth*, 315 S.W.3d 325 (Ky. 2010). The Kentucky statute is Ky. Rev. Stat., Section 508.060 (2018).
45. Cal. Penal Code, Section 187(a)(b)(2018).
46. Unborn Victims of Violence Act of 2004, USCS, Title 18, Section 1841 (2018).
47. Federal Child Abuse Prevention and Treatment Act (CAPTA), USCS, Title 42, Section 5106g (2018), as amended by the Keeping Children and Families Safe Act of 2003, as revised by the CAPTA Reauthorization Act of 2010.

48. Centers for Disease Control and Prevention, "Child Abuse and Neglect Prevention," https://www.cdc.gov/violenceprevention/childabuseandneglect/index.html, accessed August 7, 2018.
49. Shannan Catalano, Bureau of Justice Statistics, *Stalking Victims in the United States—Revised* (September 2012), p. 1, https://www.bjs.gov/content/pub/pdf/svus_rev.pdf, accessed August 8, 2018.
50. Ibid.
51. Public Law 104-201 (1997); USCS, Title 18, Section 2261 (2011).
52. U.S. Department of Justice, "Protecting Our Children from Crimes Online" (May 11, 2010), http://blogs.usdoj.gov/blog/archives/792, accessed March 2, 2011.
53. Terry Carter, "Beat Practices," *American Bar Association Journal* 93 (November 2007): 39.
54. Tex. Fam. Code, Title 3, Chapter 54, Section 54.0407 (2017).
55. Rick Rojas, "Abused Dogs and Cats Now Have a (Human) Voice in Connecticut Courts," *New York Times*, https://www.nytimes.com/2017/08/27/nyregion/animal-abuse-connecticut-court-advocates.html, accessed August 14, 2018.
56. Karin Brulliard, "Seeking Justice for Justice the Horse," *The Washington Post* (August 13, 2018), https://www.washingtonpost.com, accessed August 13, 2018; "Lawyers Appeal Dismissal of Lawsuit Filed on Horse's Behalf," *The Today File* (January 23, 2019).
57. Federal Bureau of Investigation, "Tracking Animal Cruelty: FBI Collecting Data on Crimes against Animals" (February 1, 2016), https://www.fbi.gov/stories/-tracking-animal-cruelty, accessed December 1, 2018.
58. "FBI, This Week: National Slavery and Human Trafficking Prevention Month" (January 10, 2018), https://www.fbi.gov/audio-repository/ftw-podcast-human-trafficking-month-011018.mp3/view, accessed August 14, 2018. For an overview of human trafficking, see Jeffrey W. Goltz et al., *Human Trafficking: A Systemwide Public Safety and Community Approach* (St. Paul, MN: West Academic Publishing, 2017).
59. The United States Attorney's Office, Northern District of Texas, "Fort Worth Man Sentenced to Life in Prison for His Role in Sex Trafficking of Children," https://www.justice.gov/usao-ndtx/pr/fort-worth-man-sentenced-life-prison-his-role-sex-trafficking-children-0, accessed August 13, 2018.

Part II

Entry into Criminal Justice Systems: Policing

Law enforcement officers occupy the front line in our continuing struggle to combat terrorism and other crimes. Our ability to do what we want, free from the fear of crime, depends on them. But, despite the responsibilities and powers granted to these important persons, they cannot deal effectively with crime without the assistance of victims and witnesses, and that cooperation is not always given. Yet law enforcement officers are often blamed if crime rates increase and if reported crimes are not solved.

Part II explores the nature, organization, function, and problems of policing. Chapter 3 covers the history of policing and explains how formal police systems emerged. It differentiates the levels of public police systems in the United States, looks briefly at international policing, and reviews the nature and problems of private policing. The organization and administration of police systems is considered, with a focus on problem-oriented and community-oriented policing. The chapter concludes with a discussion of police strategies and crime reduction.

Chapter 4 describes what police actually do, ranging from performing many services within the community to engaging in the dangerous job of apprehending criminals. Police functions are discussed in the context of legal requirements and empirical social science research. Part II closes with Chapter 5, which focuses on the major problems and issues in policing.

3

The Emergence and Structure of Police Systems

Chapter Outline

Learning Objectives

After reading this chapter, you should be able to do the following:

- Discuss the history of U.S. policing, paying special attention to the contributions of British policing
- Explain the meaning of decentralized policing in the United States
- Distinguish among local, state, and federal policing systems
- State and evaluate the role and function of the Federal Bureau of Investigation (FBI)
- Comment on federal legislation and the development of agencies designed to combat terrorism
- Discuss the nature and purpose of the Department of Homeland Security (DHS)
- Become familiar with current issues of policing immigration
- Give an overview of campus policing
- Explain the difference between private and public policing, and discuss their comparative growth and importance
- Note early reform efforts in the organization and administration of policing systems
- Explain what is meant by a professional model of policing
- Discuss what is meant by a problem-oriented approach to policing
- Analyze community-oriented policing
- Explain and evaluate COMPSTAT and discuss the relationship of the concept of "broken windows" to crime reduction

Policing is one of the most important functions in criminal justice systems. As stated by a noted expert on policing: "The strength of a democracy and the quality of life enjoyed by its citizens are determined in large measure by the ability of the police to discharge their duties."[1] The ability of U.S. police to function effectively and properly, however, has come into serious question in recent years. Chapters 3, 4, and 5 explore some of the reasons for this, as they examine the past, present, and future of policing in the United States.

This chapter begins with a history of policing to explain the reason for the formal systems of present-day public policing. The history is traced from policing's informal beginnings in other countries to today's formal systems in the United States. The decentralized systems of U.S. policing are examined by their major categories: local, state, and federal policing systems.

This chapter features a special focus on immigration and one on campus security and then discusses the role of private policing and private security in comparison to public policing. Brief attention is given to international policing before the chapter focuses on the organization, administration, and management of police departments. After a brief look at early reform efforts, attention is given to policing models, including the professional, problem-oriented, and community-oriented approaches. The chapter closes with a discussion of **police** strategies for crime reduction.

THE HISTORY OF POLICING

Although formal policing is a relatively modern development, some form of policing has existed for centuries. When societies were small and cohesive, with most members sharing goals and activities, it was usually possible to keep order without a formal police structure. The rules and regulations of the society were taught to new members as they were socialized, and most people observed the rules. Others could be coerced into observing those rules by informal techniques of social control. If that did not work and the rules were violated, crime victims might have handled the situation informally. The victim might also have been permitted to take private revenge against the offender.

In some countries, informal policing was organized beyond the immediate family or individual concerned. England had the **frankpledge system**, in which families were organized into a **tithing** (10 families) and a **hundred** (10 tithings) for purposes of protecting each other and enforcing laws. The frankpledge was a system of mutual pledge or mutual help, with all adult members responsible for their own conduct and that of others in the system. If the group failed to apprehend a lawbreaker, the English Crown fined all of the group members.

Individual private policing had its limits, however, and as societies grew in size and complexity, public policing was needed. The appointment of constables in England in the twelfth century signaled the beginning of public policing in that country. An unpaid **constable** was responsible for taking care of the weapons and the equipment of the hundred, as well as for keeping the peace by enforcing laws.

A second kind of police officer emerged when hundreds were combined to form **shires**, which were analogous to today's counties. The king appointed a shire-reeve to supervise each shire. The position of shire-reeve was the forerunner to that of the **sheriff**. Originally, the shire-reeve was responsible only for ensuring that citizens performed their law enforcement functions adequately, but later, the duties were expanded to include apprehending law violators. The shire-reeve, the only paid official, was assisted in his duties by constables.

During the reign of Edward I (1272-1307), the **watch system**, the immediate forerunner of modern police systems, emerged in England. The watch system was developed as a means of protecting property against fire and for guarding the walls and gates of the cities. Watchmen were responsible for maintaining order and monitoring public behavior and manners. The London watchmen carried clubs and swords. They did not wear uniforms and could be distinguished from other citizens only by the lanterns and staffs they carried. Originally, they were to patrol the streets at specified intervals during the night, announcing that all was well. As the city grew, a day shift was added. **Supplement 3.1** contains more details about the early English police systems, noting some of the reasons England moved toward a more formal policing system. In addition, the rise of industrialization in England contributed to the need for a formal police force. As more people moved to cities and life became more complex, maintaining law and order was increasingly difficult, and the less formal system of policing was no longer sufficient.

Modern Policing: The London Beginning

Although scholars debate how and why formal police systems emerged, usually the beginning is traced to

England, where Londoners protested the ineffectiveness of the watch system and agitated for a formal police force. Some believed that a police force constantly patrolling the town would reduce and eventually eliminate street crime. Others feared that the concentration of power necessary for a formal police force would lead to abuses, especially if the force were a national one. Eventually, the tension between these two positions was resolved by the establishment of local police systems.

Dissatisfaction with the constable system led the English to experiment with other systems. In the mid-eighteenth century, John Fielding and Henry Fielding, London **magistrates**, instituted a system called the **Bow Street Runners**. The Fieldings selected constables with a year of experience and gave them police investigation and arrest powers. The constables were given training and paid a portion of the fines in the cases they prosecuted successfully.

Increased concern about safety and security in London led citizens to pressure for improved police protection. Between 1770 and 1828, a total of six commissions appointed by the English Parliament investigated policing and made suggestions, but an attempt in 1785 to establish a metropolitan police force was defeated by the opposition of powerful commercial interests. None of the English efforts were successful in establishing a satisfactory police force until 1829.[2]

In 1829, the first modern police force, the Metropolitan Police, was founded in London by Sir Robert Peel. The men employed by the force were called *Peelers* or *Bobbies* after the founder. Working full time and wearing special uniforms, the officers' primary function was to prevent crime. They were organized by territories, and they reported to a central government. Candidates had to meet high standards to qualify for a job as a police officer in London. The system has been described as follows:

> Peel divided London into divisions, then into "beats." The headquarters for the police commissioners looked out upon a courtyard that had been the site of a residence used by the Kings of Scotland and was, therefore, called "Scotland Yard." . . . [I]n 1856 Parliament required every borough and county to have a police force similar to London's.[3]

London set the example; the rest of England was slow to follow, but other countries began establishing modern, formal police systems. Some countries developed a centralized police system, but a decentralized system developed in the United States. Most European countries followed the British practice of not arming the police, but the amount of violence led the British to change that tradition in 1994, when some specially trained Bobbies began carrying guns.

Despite its historical reputation for professional and successful policing, Scotland Yard faced a crisis in 1999, when an investigation concluded that it was infected with institutional racism. The force had a poor record of minority recruitment, hiring, retention, and promotion. Only 3 percent of London's officers were minority compared to 25 percent of the city's ethnic population. Police were criticized for their overall investigation of the slaying of an 18-year-old black man, Stephen Lawrence, who was stabbed to death at a bus stop in South London by a group of whites in 1993. According to the report, police were insensitive to minorities' rights, including the rights of minorities who worked within the department. The police were ordered to recruit one-fourth of their new officers from ethnic and racial minorities by 2009.[4]

Police in London are called Bobbies, and historically they have commanded widespread respect. In recent years, however, a London commission charged them with institutional racism characterized by a poor record of recruiting, hiring, and training minority officers.

Despite the efforts of British officials to combat racism, the five men who were accused of murdering Lawrence were not convicted, and in April 2006, Scotland

Yard confirmed that the special team that was investigating the case had been disbanded, although the department would investigate any new leads brought to their attention.[5] Another policing incident that occurred in 2005 led to increased criticism of the British police. That incident is discussed briefly in **Supplement 3.2**.

Allegations of racism among British police, citing the number of black people killed while in police custody,[6] led in 2018 to the resignation of Amber Rudd, Secretary in the British Home Office. British authorities were also accused of violating human rights, in particular with regard to immigration.[7]

The Emergence of Policing in the United States

People in the United States saw a variety of policing systems in the early days. Immigrants brought many aspects of the English system to this country. The constable was in charge of towns, and the sheriff had jurisdiction over policing counties. Before the American Revolution, these positions were filled by governors appointed by the British Crown, but subsequently most constables and sheriffs obtained their positions by popular elections.

Many of the colonies adopted the English watch system. The New York City system was said to be an example. Bellmen walked throughout the city, ringing bells and providing police services. Later, they were replaced by a permanent watch of citizens and, still later, by paid constables.

One of the most familiar kinds of policing, still in use in some rural areas today, was the **posse**. Under the posse system, a sheriff could call into action any number of citizens over a certain age if they were needed to assist in law enforcement.

In some early U.S. systems, law enforcement officials were paid by local government. Others were paid by private individuals. "By the early nineteenth century, American law enforcement had become a hodgepodge of small jurisdictions staffed by various officials with different powers, responsibilities, and legal standing. There was no system, although there were ample precedents for public policing."[8]

It did not take long, however, for Americans to realize that these methods of policing did not produce the efficiency and expertise necessary to control the urban riots and increasing rates of crime and violence that accompanied the industrialization, increased complexity, and growth of American cities. A professional police system was needed, and by the late 1880s most American cities had established municipal police forces, although the county sheriff system continued to provide policing services in rural areas. State police systems were added gradually, followed by the federal system. The state and federal systems, however, were not to supersede the local systems.[9]

One final type of policing that should be mentioned is **vigilantism**, which refers to the acts of a person who is alert, cautious, suspicious, and ready to take action to maintain and preserve peace. Vigilantism is based on the belief that laws aid persons who are vigilant and who do not sleep on their rights. In colonial days, people (usually only men) formed vigilante committees to stop rebellions and other problems and to catch and punish criminals. These groups operated outside the law but apparently viewed themselves as preserving law.

Vigilante committees and groups continue to operate within the United States and often aim their efforts at the suppression of racial and other minority groups, thus constituting a serious threat to the rights of these people. They may, however, also be very helpful, as indicated in **Supplement 3.3**, which relates the events during an attempted terrorist act on an airplane.

DECENTRALIZED POLICING: U.S. SYSTEMS

In the United States, formal police systems are decentralized, operating at local, state, and federal levels.

Local Policing

Local policing includes police agencies at the rural, county, and municipal levels. Most studies of police focus on municipal policing. Few criminal justice texts discuss rural policing, and usually only slight attention is given to county police systems, leaving the impression that these levels of policing are not important. This conclusion is erroneous because local and county levels of policing cover significant geographical areas of the country. In fact, the majority of police agencies in the United States are located in small towns, villages, or boroughs.

Throughout the United States, but particularly in southern and western regions, many towns and villages are too small to support a police department. Some of these areas depend on the county police system for protection. Others have their own systems, usually consisting of an elected official. This official, who may be called a *constable*, has policing duties similar to those of the county sheriff. Constables might not be trained in law or policing. However, they have the power to enforce laws, to arrest, to maintain order, and to execute processes from the magistrate's courts, which are courts of limited jurisdiction, often called *justice of the peace courts.*

Rural policing is very important but often plagued with financial and personnel problems. One officer cannot police even a small area for 24 hours a day; police officers may be overworked; and in many jurisdictions, funds are not available for the support services, such as office assistance, necessary for adequate policing.

Many rural officers do not have sufficient resources for investigating criminal activity. They are more isolated than urban officers. Quick backup services from other officers may be a scarce luxury rather than a daily reality. Working conditions of rural police may be less desirable than those of police officers at other levels. Most salaries are low and not necessarily compensated for by a lower cost of living. Initial training may not be geared to the unique problems of rural policing. Most officers must train in urban settings because in many areas there are not enough rural police to justify separate training centers. As a result, those officers may have unrealistic expectations of rural policing. In addition, rural officers may not have opportunities for continuing education and training.

Budget planning and other activities concerning policing in rural areas might be town projects, with police officers involved in heated discussions from which their urban counterparts might be shielded by police administrators. This high visibility and total immersion in local problems and politics might affect the social life of the officer, who may find it impossible to go anywhere in the area without being viewed as a police officer. For rural officers, long periods of inactivity may lead to boredom. In comparison with urban police, rural police may face greater citizen expectations for a variety of services not connected with law enforcement.

On the positive side, some rural officers enjoy their involvement in community activities with local citizens. The lower crime rates, particularly the lower rates of violence, may increase police security. The lack of complexity in the police system might be seen as a positive rather than a negative factor. Problems associated with a lack of security, when only one officer is assigned to an area, might be eliminated or greatly reduced by cooperation from the next level—county policing.

In some rural jurisdictions, officers may follow a case from beginning to end. They arrest, investigate, send evidence to labs, file all reports, and attend court hearings on a given case. When arrestees are thought to be under the influence of alcohol or other drugs, it is the arresting officer who transports the suspect to the local hospital to have blood drawn. In some cases, the officer will detain the suspect in the lockdown located in the police offices. Despite the lower volume of cases, some rural police view their positions as more expansive than those of urban or state police and, in some cases, more challenging. For example, in some rural villages the police may be charged with prosecuting misdemeanors.

Some county police agencies are rural, but the county system is larger and usually employs a sheriff as the primary law enforcement officer. The county sheriff may have numerous other functions unrelated to law enforcement, such as acting as the coroner, collecting taxes, or supervising any number of government activities. If the department is large enough, the county police department might have a deputy sheriff and law enforcement officers assigned to patrol the county and enforce order.

The sheriff is considered the most important law enforcement officer in the county, but in practice, the functions of the sheriff's office are usually limited to the unincorporated areas of the county, with law enforcement in the incorporated areas handled by the municipal police in the larger cities.

Most sheriffs are elected officials. Previously, most sheriffs served for very long periods but, for political and other reasons, it is becoming difficult, if not impossible, for long sheriff tenures. In many jurisdictions, political activists have been successful in unseating sheriffs who have served for years.

Larger county police departments may contract their services to smaller county or rural departments. The county department may employ a county **marshal**, a sworn officer whose primary function is to perform civil duties for the courts, such as delivering papers to initiate civil proceedings or serving papers for the arrest of criminal suspects.

Larger county police departments have investigative units that service the district attorneys who bring the prosecutions in the county. These departments are staffed by sworn officers and support personnel. Departments too small for investigative units may contract for such services from the municipal or urban police departments in the area or from the Federal Bureau of Investigation (FBI), discussed later in this chapter.

Municipal police departments differ from other local police agencies mainly in their size, organization, complexity, and services. Although they may service smaller geographical areas than rural or county systems, most municipal police systems have more employees and provide more extended services. The complexity of the departments leads to greater problems in staffing, organization, and fulfillment of the public's needs. Many municipal departments have more resources, which may be shared with rural and county systems on a contract basis. On the other hand, citizens' expectations for services from municipal police departments may be greater than expectations at the rural or county level, where the department's mandate may be less defined and more open-ended.

Municipal departments, in contrast to departments at other levels, may encounter more difficult political problems with their governing bodies. The municipal police department competes with other agencies for funding. The costs of policing are highest in urban areas, where population changes may present more problems. Many large cities have experienced significant changes in population numbers, compared with the number of people who commute daily to work. The residential tax base goes down as the need for services, order maintenance, and law enforcement increases.

Generally, crime rates are much higher in urban than in rural or county areas. The composition of an urban population may present greater policing problems. Urban areas have a more heterogeneous population, as well as a greater number of unemployed people, transients, and those who have been in trouble with the law.

The final type of local policing involves police who patrol highways and regulate traffic. They have the primary responsibility for enforcing some state laws and for providing services such as a system of criminal identification, police training programs, and a communications system for local law enforcement officials. The organization and services provided by state patrol vary from state to state. This lack of centralization stems from the historic distrust of national police systems, as well as from the different law enforcement needs of the individual states, as illustrated by the discussion of the Texas Rangers in **Supplement 3.4**.

State Policing

The industrialization and expansion of the country led to many problems that could not be handled adequately at the local level, and although Texas had the first state police agency, Pennsylvania's system became the early model for state police in the United States. In the late 1870s, a powerful secret organization, the **Molly Maguires**, responded to anti-Irish riots in Pennsylvania by forming Irish labor unions, which used violence to terrorize the state's coal-producing regions. The Molly Maguires controlled all hiring and firing. Some employers who ignored their mandates were killed. The terrorists threatened the growing Pennsylvania economy, which was heavily dependent on mineral wealth. The state was sparsely settled, and local police authorities could not control the Molly Maguires. "The Pinkerton Detective Agency, a private national organization, was eventually brought in to infiltrate the Molly Maguires, and 20 of its members were convicted of murder and other crimes."[10]

In 1905, Pennsylvania's governor succeeded in convincing that state's legislature to appropriate funds for a constabulary to help prevent future disasters, such as those caused by the Molly Maguires. The movement toward state policing did not happen quickly, however, for many still feared that the next step would be national police and political repression. But the use of automobiles and increased problems with traffic on state roads and highways in the twentieth century created an obvious need for state police.

State police are similar to the state patrol. Both have uniformed, sworn officers who carry weapons. They differ primarily in their law enforcement powers. Most state patrol officers engage primarily in traffic control. Although they may be empowered to enforce criminal laws violated in their presence, on the highway, or within sight of or adjacent to the highway, they do not have general powers of law enforcement for all state laws, as state police have. State police, in contrast to state patrol, may have their own investigative units as well as a forensic science laboratory.

State police and state patrol also differ in that many state police systems include specialized forms of policing, such as control over fishing and gaming laws, regulation of gambling and horse racing, and regulation of alcohol sales. The Alcohol Board of Control is a state agency responsible for investigating requests for liquor licenses and has the power to establish rules concerning the conditions under which liquor is sold. This board is in charge of enforcing state laws enacted to regulate the sale of dangerous drugs.

Federal Policing

Historically, enforcement of criminal laws in the United States has been viewed as the function of states, although

Professions 3.1

U.S. Marshals Service

The U.S. Marshals Service, located within the U.S. Department of Justice, is the oldest (operating since 1789) and most versatile federal law enforcement agency. The service consists of one U.S. marshal in each of the 94 federal court districts. These marshals are appointed by the U.S. president, with the advice and consent of the Senate. They are assisted by U.S. deputy marshals and criminal investigators (3,571 in 2018).

The primary function of U.S. marshals is to transport federal inmates between prison and court and to escort them to homes or jobs when they have temporary leaves. The marshals provide protection for federal jurors, judges, prosecutors, attorneys, and witnesses. They are in charge of seizing and auctioning property that has been taken by officers under federal court orders. As sworn police officers, U.S. marshals may make arrests for federal offenses and perform other police functions such as controlling riots and executing federal fugitive warrants. In 2017, U.S. marshals closed 101,167 warrants by arrest of fugitives and arrested 12,859 sex offenders.

U.S. marshals carry out special missions and programs and are responsible for the federal Witness Security Program. They protect individuals who are in high-threat situations during all actions related to judicial proceedings. They also transport prisoners internationally, house and supervise federal detainees daily, and handle asset forfeitures.

Minimum qualifications for the position of deputy U.S. marshal are as follows:

"Must be a U.S. citizen

Must be between the ages of 21 and 36 (must be appointed before 37th birthday)

Must have a bachelor's degree, 1 year of specialized experience, or a combination of education and experience equivalent to the GL-07 level

Must have a valid driver's license in good standing

Must successfully complete a structured interview and other assessments

Must successfully complete a background investigation

Must meet medical qualifications

Must be in excellent physical condition

Must undergo a rigorous 21½ week basic training program at the United States Marshals Service Training Academy in Glynco, GA"

Source: U.S. Department of Justice, U.S. Marshals Service, https://www.usmarshals.gov, accessed August 22, 2018.

---

states may and do delegate some of their powers to local police agencies. The U.S. Constitution does not provide for a central police agency. It gives the federal government specific power to enforce only a limited number of crimes. The Constitution also provides that all powers not delegated to the federal government are reserved to the states. It gives Congress the power to pass laws that are "necessary and proper" for the exercise of congressional powers. Over the years, Congress has enacted legislation establishing federal crimes, such as hate crimes.

Federal law enforcement includes federal prosecutors and federal police agencies. The federal policing level is complex and encompasses more than 50 enforcement agencies, which are located within various departments. Professions 3.1 examines one of the federal police agencies—the U.S. Marshals Service—and also shows how agencies at various levels can and do cooperate to solve crime.

The U.S. Marshals Service is located in the U.S. Department of Justice (DOJ), which, in addition to its own criminal division, encompasses other major criminal investigative agencies, such as the Bureau of Alcohol, Tobacco, Firearms and Explosives (ATF), the Drug Enforcement Administration (DEA), and the Federal Bureau of Investigation (FBI). The DOJ also includes administrative agencies related to criminal activity (e.g., the federal Bureau of Prisons) and many other functions and agencies. The largest and best known, however, is the FBI.

The Federal Bureau of Investigation (FBI)

On July 26, 1908, President Theodore Roosevelt directed the U.S. attorney general to issue an order creating the agency now known as the **Federal Bureau of Investigation (FBI)**. In 1924, J. Edgar Hoover was appointed director of the organization and remained in that position until his death in May 1972. The FBI is the primary governmental agency charged with enforcing all federal laws not assigned to other special agencies. FBI headquarters are located in Washington, D.C. Field officers are located in major cities throughout the United States and in San Juan, Puerto Rico. The director of the FBI is appointed by the president of the United States, by and with the consent of the U.S. Senate. The FBI is not a national police force. Primarily, it is an investigative agency. FBI agents may investigate crimes over which the federal government has jurisdiction by statute; they may investigate state and local crimes when requested to do so.

The investigative work of the FBI is performed by special agents, who are trained at the FBI Academy, located on the U.S. Marine Corps base in Quantico, Virginia. In addition to special agents, the FBI employs individuals who perform such investigative functions as fingerprint examinations, clerical and receptionist duties, computer programming, and laboratory work. Attorneys, accountants, and other professionals are also employed by the agency.

The training facilities of the FBI Academy are also used by other agencies for training law enforcement officers; some foreign officers are accepted into the program. The academy also provides continuing education and training for officers. Another important function of the FBI, discussed in Chapter 2, is the collection of crime data.

Throughout its history, particularly during the long years it was headed by J. Edgar Hoover, the FBI was severely criticized as well as highly praised. During most of its existence, the FBI has had only loose directives from Congress. A strong leader such as Hoover was able to take advantage of that situation and build a powerful, extremely influential organization, which allegedly held extensive control even over the presidents under whom Hoover served.

Among recent directors, Judge Louis J. Freeh was appointed by President Bill Clinton and confirmed in 1993 after Director William Sessions resigned. In the summer of 2001, Robert S. Mueller III was confirmed as FBI director and was in office until July 2013, when President Barack Obama's nominee, James B. Comey, was confirmed. In his announcement of the nomination, President Obama stated his belief that Comey is a man of "fierce independence and deep integrity."[11] Comey was fired by President Donald J. Trump in May 2017. President Trump nominated Christopher A. Wray, who was previously in charge of the DOJ's criminal division; Wray was confirmed.

Prior to the 9/11 terrorist attacks, the FBI had experienced charges of scandals, corruption, favoritism, discrimination against minorities and women, sexual harassment, and other problems. In July 2001, Vermont Senator Patrick J. Leahy commented, "There are some very, very serious management problems at the FBI."[12]

In the fall of 2001, the Bush administration announced its plan to revamp the FBI, focusing the agency's efforts on counterterrorism, which would require a deemphasis on some of the agency's traditional targets, such as drug enforcement, bank robbery, and some violent crime investigations. In fact, within hours after the 9/11 terrorist attacks, thousands of FBI agents were reassigned to counterterrorism.

Significant changes were made in the FBI, and the June 2003 reports of two investigative groups, constituting the most thorough recent study of the FBI, gave encouraging but cautious comments. The reports stated that the FBI had made significant progress in its reorganization efforts but that important challenges remained. Specifically, the reports considered the efforts of the FBI to update its technology systems, develop programs for sharing intelligence information with other government agencies, and maintain full law enforcement in traditional areas (such as drug trafficking), while focusing on counterterrorism. In particular, the GAO report noted an approximate 15 percent decrease in drug trafficking referrals made by the FBI, compared with the previous year. Approximately 400 FBI agents were transferred from units investigating illegal drugs to units concerned with terrorism. Another concern was the lack of independence of the newly created Terrorism Threat Integration Center. The purpose of this agency is to filter intelligence information concerning terrorism across government agencies, but several lawmakers to whom the reports were presented noted that the Central Intelligence Agency (CIA) runs the Terrorism Threat Integration Center. Some feared that the CIA would not be willing to share some of the terrorism information with other agencies.[13]

The 9/11 Commission Report, the *Final Report of the National Commission on Terrorist Attacks upon the United States* (the commission was established by the U.S.

Congress and President George W. Bush in November 2002), was critical of the FBI. Consider, for example, the following statement from that report:

> Responsibility for domestic intelligence gathering on terrorism was vested solely in the FBI, yet during almost all of the Clinton administration the relationship between the FBI director and the President was nearly nonexistent. The FBI director would not communicate directly with the president. His key personnel shared very little information with the National Security Council and the rest of the national security community. As a consequence, one of the critical working relationships in the counterterrorism effort was broken.[14]

The chair of the commission said that reports of the FBI's work both before and after the 9/11 attacks was an "indictment of the FBI. It failed and it failed and it failed and it failed. . . . This is an agency that does not work. It makes you angry. And I don't know how to fix it."[15]

Some changes in the FBI were made in 2005. The bureau, under pressure from the Bush White House, agreed to accept some of the recommendations of a presidential commission. Specifically, the FBI agreed to permit the newly appointed and first director of national intelligence, John D. Negroponte, to assist in the selection of the FBI's intelligence chief, the third-ranking official of the FBI. It was the first time in history that the FBI gave an outsider a significant role in the selection of one of its top officials.

In 2006, the FBI director told the Senate Judiciary Committee, "[T]his year will mark the five-year anniversary of September 11th, and the FBI has changed dramatically since the terrorist attacks of that day. And we will continue to evolve to meet the emerging threats to our country."[16] That the agency had not evolved sufficiently is evidenced by the oversight conclusions of the Office of the Inspector General (OIG), which are noted, in part, in Spotlight 3.1. That spotlight also updates the recent changes in the leadership at the FBI.

The FBI, like other federal law enforcement agencies, should be viewed as a supplement to, not a replacement of, state and local agencies. The bureau is assisted by other federal agencies; all are aided by recent legislative enactments. A small sample are included in the next section.

Recent Federal Legislative Enactments

After the 9/11 terrorist attacks, President George W. Bush proposed and Congress enacted several pieces of legislation to create new federal agencies and to empower those agencies and others in the fight against terrorism. The **USA Patriot Act** (Uniting and Strengthening America by Providing Appropriate Tools Required to Intercept and Obstruct Terrorism Act of 2001) was passed by Congress and signed by President Bush in the fall of 2001. The act expanded the powers of the federal government to deal with terrorism. Some of those powers involve the expansion of wiretaps on terrorist suspects' e-mail, telephone conversations, and use of the Internet. Tighter controls were placed on immigration and on money laundering.[17]

One of the major enactments of Congress after the 9/11 terrorist attacks was the creation of the **Department of Homeland Security (DHS)**. The creation of the DHS, a presidential cabinet level agency, constituted the most extensive federal government reorganization in 50 years. The new agency combines 22 former federal agencies. The components of the DHS are listed and described in **Supplement 3.5**. All of these components are important, but the one that has been the subject of the most attention and controversy in recent years is the U.S. Immigration and Customs Enforcement (ICE), dealing with immigration.

Special Focus: Immigration

One of the most controversial issues in current times, both in the United States and some other countries, is immigration. This text cannot explore all of the ramifications, many of which are highly political, but this special focus summarizes some of the recent problems associated with immigration. Arizona's attempt to control immigration into that state is explained in **Supplement 3.6**.

On November 20, 2014, President Barack Obama, who said he was frustrated by the lack of congressional action on immigration, used his executive power to permit approximately 5 million undocumented immigrants to remain in the United States. Republicans argued that the president went beyond his power in this order. A Texas district court judge issued a stay on Obama's orders, and a panel of that court declined to lift the stay.[18] In June 2016, the U.S. Supreme Court affirmed "by an equally divided court."[19]

The issue of illegal immigration escalated after the election of Donald J. Trump as president in 2016. During the presidential campaign, Trump called for building a wall to separate the United States from Mexico, and he made comments, such as "banning all Muslims," that

Spotlight 3.1

Focus on the Federal Bureau of Investigation

Since the 9/11 terrorist attacks, the Federal Bureau of Investigation (FBI) has been closely scrutinized, with some arguing that the country's major law enforcement agency should have been more vigilant in detecting terrorism. Significant changes, some of which are detailed in this text, have been and continue to be made in the agency. This spotlight highlights a portion of the testimony of the Honorable Glenn A. Fine, inspector general of the U.S. Department of Justice, in a testimony before the Senate Judiciary Committee. The Office of Inspector General (OIG) is charged with overseeing the operations of the FBI. Some of the conclusions of the OIG's recent evaluation of the FBI are summarized here.

The FBI had made significant changes and progress since 9/11, but there were areas in which improvement needed to continue. First, the FBI needed a modern, effective case management and records system. The agency spent millions of dollars developing one system, the Virtual Case File, only to have it collapse. It was replaced with a system called the Sentinel Project. Senator Patrick Leahy, ranking member of the Senate Judiciary Committee, emphasized the importance of the FBI's having an effective informational technology (IT) infrastructure, stating, "The Bureau's effectiveness hangs in the balance, and the American people cannot afford another fiasco."[1] The OIG found that the FBI had made progress in its ability to develop and manage a major IT project, but the agency still had some concerns. For example, the OIG expressed concern about Sentinel's "ability to connect with external systems in other Department of Justice components, the Department of Homeland Security, and other intelligence community agencies." If the FBI is not able to do that, the other agencies might be forced to spend large sums to alter their communication systems. The OIG also found that the FBI had problems in the area of civil rights and civil liberties, with violations of one or more of the attorney general guidelines in 87 percent of the confidential informant files that the office examined. The OIG found significant difficulties in the ability of the FBI to recruit, train, and retain employees in some areas of expertise within the agency. In addition, the OIG noted that information sharing remains a problem and that the FBI needs to improve its work in this area. In short, the inspector general testified that, although the FBI had made some improvements since 9/11, "more progress is clearly needed."[2]

In May 2009, FBI director Robert S. Mueller III testified before the House Judiciary Committee, emphasizing that the agency's top priority since 9/11 was counterterrorism, followed by counterintelligence and cyber security. Mueller's September 2009 testimony before the Senate Judiciary Committee stated that the FBI's agents had developed the intelligence the country needed to fight terrorism. But after the November 2009 shootings at Fort Hood, Texas, Mueller's conclusions were questioned. Major Nidal Malik Hasan, an army psychiatrist, was charged with murdering 13 people and wounding 32 others at the base that day, leading Mueller to issue this press statement: "It is essential to determine whether there are improvements to our current practices or other authorities that could make us all safer in the future."[3]

Major Hasan was convicted and sentenced to death, but in April 2014, Army Spc. Ivan Lopez shot and killed 3 soldiers and wounded 16 others at Ft. Hood before committing suicide. Again, the FBI's ability to prevent such crimes came into question as it did in 2013 with respect to the Boston Marathon bombing. Later that year, the FBI announced that its own investigation concluded that there was nothing the agency could have done to prevent that bombing even though in 2011, a Russian intelligence agency had asked the FBI to investigate one of the two suspects, Tamerlan Tsarnaev, who may have become radicalized while in the United States.[4]

Mueller left office in 2013, and on September 4, 2013, James B. Comey was sworn in as director of the FBI. Comey came under fire in 2016 when he concluded that there was insufficient evidence to charge Democratic presidential candidate Hillary Clinton for her use of a private e-mail server. In May 2017, President Donald J. Trump fired Director Comey, an act that was highly controversial. The president's nominee to replace Comey, Christopher A. Wray, was confirmed and remained in office as of this writing.

Former FBI director Mueller became the special prosecutor to investigate whether the Trump administration engaged in any illegal activities during the election in which he was a successful candidate. That investigation was completed in the spring of 2019.

Attorney General Barr released a four-page summary. A redacted version of the full report was released on April 16, 2019.

1. "FBI Oversight," testimony by Patrick Leahy, ranking member, Senate Judiciary Committee, Capitol Hill Hearing Testimony, *Federal Document Clearing House Congressional Testimony* (May 2, 2006), n.p.

2. "FBI Oversight," testimony by Glenn A. Fine, inspector general, United States Department of Justice, Capitol Hill Hearing Testimony, *Federal Document Clearing House Congressional Testimony* (May 2, 2006), n.p.

3. Federal Bureau of Investigation Press Release, "Director Asks Judge Webster to Conduct Independent Review" (December 8, 2009), http://www.fbi.gov/pressrel, accessed March 3, 2011.

4. "F.B.I. Said to Find It Could Not Have Averted Boston Attack," *New York Times* (August 2, 2013), p. 13.

suggested religious and other types of discrimination in immigration procedures. His views were controversial, but he was elected, and on January 27, 2018, President Trump signed Executive Order No. 13769, Protecting the Nation From Foreign Terrorist Entry Into the United States. That order was quickly challenged in courts. The government responded with a second order on March 6, 2017, and that order was also challenged successfully in lower federal courts. The government appealed on several issues.

In June 2017, the U.S. Supreme Court responded to the president's revised immigration plan (which banned new visas for 90 days for travelers to the United States from Iran, Libya, Somalia, Sudan, Syria, and Yemen). The Court agreed to hear the government's petitions and consolidate the cases for argument in the first session of the next Court term. The Court lifted injunctions imposed by the Fourth Circuit Court of Appeals and the Ninth Circuit Court of Appeals "to the extent the injunctions prevent enforcement of [the ban] with respect to foreign nationals who lack any bona fide relationship with a person or entity in the United States."[20]

On October 10, 2017, the U.S. Supreme Court vacated its decision to hear the case because no case or controversy existed. The executive order concerning "the temporary suspension of entry of aliens abroad" expired on September 24, 2017. The case was remanded to the Fourth Circuit "with instructions to dismiss as moot the challenge to Executive Order No. 13,780." The Supreme Court stated that it did not express any view on the merits of the order.[21]

President Trump issued subsequent orders and stated that people who enter the United States illegally should be deported without a hearing. On May 7, 2018, Attorney General Jeff Sessions issued a statement that the Department of Justice would follow a zero tolerance policy "for illegal entry on our Southwest border. If you cross this border unlawfully, then we will prosecute you. It is that simple." In addition, "If you are smuggling a child, then we will prosecute and that child will be separated from you as required by law."[22] That policy was changed on June 20 to an executive order requiring that families be kept together during immigration and criminal proceedings to the extent permitted by law, and subsequently efforts were made to reunite parents with the children from whom they had been separated. In late August, a federal judge barred separating children from their parents at the border; the DOJ planned to appeal. At that time, the legal consensus was that parents detained at the border could decide whether they wanted their children to be detained with them or placed in youth shelters until they could be placed with sponsors.[23]

January 10, 2019: Mexico, Tijuana: U.S. Customs and Border Guard officials take part in an exercise at the San Ysidro border crossing between the U.S.A. and Mexico and close the crossings as part of the exercise. Actions at such borders have become the focus of intense political disagreements in the United States.

Reaction to the May 7 announcement was swift, including public demonstrations and lawsuits. U.S. law firms called for an "army of lawyers" to work pro bono to assist immigrants in their efforts to remain in the country, and many responded, spending their own time and resources to represent immigrants detained in U.S. facilities and threatened with deportation. The American Bar Association expressed its "strong opposition to

Criminal Justice Systems Dilemma 3.1

Illegal Immigration: Difficult Solutions

An estimated 11.4 million illegal immigrants were in the United States in 2014, with the country facing an influx of hundreds of children, many coming alone into the country through its southern borders. The 2014 figure compares to an estimated 3.5 million illegal immigrants in 1990, 8.6 million in 2000, and 11.3 million (including approximately 5 million children) in 2010. Many persons were concerned with the increasing number of illegal immigrants, but some authorities believed that from 27 to 57 percent of the illegal immigrants, at least until recently, entered the country legally but remained beyond their permitted time period, thus becoming illegal immigrants. Others disputed that and maintained that efforts should be made to stop the flow of illegal immigrants.[1]

The dilemma faced by the border states is a sensitive one: keeping the border safe from the various problems associated with illegal immigration without offending or violating the civil rights of legal immigrants or infringing on the federal government's power to control the border. The issue of unaccompanied children is particularly sensitive, and Texas responded by requesting that lawyers be trained to assist those children with their legal issues regarding immigration. Hundreds of lawyers signed up for the pro bono work.[3]

1. Pew Hispanic Center, "Unauthorized Immigrant Populations: Stable for Half a Decade," http://pewhispanic.org, accessed August 27, 2018.
2. "Amid Influx of Migrants, Obama to Skip Border Visit on Texas Trip," *New York Times* (July 4, 2014), p. 12; "Fierce Debate Expected," *Dallas Morning News* (July 4, 2014), p. 1B.
3. "Lawyers Line Up to Help Flood of Young Migrants," *Dallas Morning News* (July 28, 2014), p. 1.

recent actions by the Department of Justice and the Department of Homeland Security that have resulted in a drastic increase in the separation of children from their parents when arriving at the southern border. . . . [T]he policy appears particularly unfair, inhumane, and, in the end, ineffective. . . . We urge you to rescind the 'zero tolerance' policy and refrain from criminally prosecuting those who are seeking asylum in the United States."[24]

In the fall of 2018, President Trump sent U.S. troops to the southern borders after a caravan of people began its trip to those borders for the purpose of entering the United States. As of this writing, President Trump and Congress continued to disagree on how to police the border, and a revised immigration policy had not been enacted. Criminal Justice Systems Dilemma 3.1 contains more information about the issue of children who enter the country illegally, many of them unaccompanied by parents or guardians.

Special Focus: Campus Policing

The security of college and university campuses has become a major policing issue in recent years, especially after shooting rampages such as the one that occurred at Virginia Tech University in April 2007, when a student killed 32 plus himself and wounded others. These and other crimes in recent decades have led to the presence of law enforcement officials on college and university campuses as well as at elementary and secondary schools. A publication by the Bureau of Justice Statistics (BJS) highlights its analysis of campus law enforcement findings, noted in Spotlight 3.2.[25]

Federal law known as the Campus Crime Security Act (also referred to as The Clery Act), which became law in 1994 and has been amended subsequently, requires colleges and universities that receive federal funds to have in place a program that collects and discloses crimes that occur on those campuses. The major requirements of that act are as follows:

- Publish annually (by October 1) a report that documents the previous three years of crimes on campus and in nearby areas, such as fraternity and sorority houses. This report must be made available to current and prospective students and employees.
- Maintain a public log of all crimes reported or otherwise known to campus law enforcement officials.

Spotlight 3.2

Highlights: Campus Law Enforcement, 2011-2012

"Among 4-year institutions enrolling 2,500 or more students during the 2011-12 school year—

- About 75% of the campuses were using armed officers, compared to 60% during the 2004-05 school year.
- About 9 in 10 public campuses used sworn police officers (92%), compared to about 4 in 10 private campuses (38%).
- Most sworn campus police officers were authorized to use a sidearm (94%), chemical or pepper spray (94%), and a baton (93%).
- Most sworn campus police officers had arrest (86%) and patrol (81%) jurisdictions that extended beyond campus boundaries.
- About 7 in 10 campus law enforcement agencies had a memorandum of understanding or other formal written agreement with outside law enforcement agencies.
- Most campus law enforcement agencies serving 5,000 or more students had personnel designated to address general crime prevention (91%), rape prevention (86%), drug education (79%), alcohol education (78%), stalking (75%), victim assistance (72%), and intimate partner violence (69%).
- Compared to private campuses, a higher percentage of campus law enforcement agencies on public campuses met regularly with special interest groups, such as advocacy groups (64% public compared to 43% private) and groups seeking to prevent domestic violence (69% compared to 48%) or sexual violence (76% compared to 58%).
- Nearly all campuses had a mass notification system that used email, text messages, and other methods to alert and instruct students, faculty, and staff in emergency situations."

Source: Brian A. Reaves, Bureau of Justice Statistics, Special Report, *Campus Law Enforcement, 2011-12* (January 2015), p. 1, https://www.bjs.gov/content/pub/pdf/clc1112.pdf, accessed August 27, 2018.

This report must be available to the public during regular business hours.

- Institutions must give timely warning of crimes that represent a threat to student or employee safety.[26]

In the spring of 2014, in response to what appeared to be a growing number of allegations of sexual assaults on college and university campuses, the Obama administration made recommendations and suggested guidelines (based on the report of a task force appointed by the White House) that the educational institutions should follow. The White House listed 55 colleges and universities that were under federal investigation for questionable handling of sexual assault allegations. One of those 55, Harvard University, quickly announced that it would hire a special team of trained investigators to handle sexual assault complaints rather than leave such matters to individual departments and schools.[27] Other colleges and universities have subsequently taken similar action.

Colleges and universities have also taken steps to discipline or fire faculty, coaches, administrators, and staff who do not follow guidelines on reporting crimes, especially sexual assaults. In 2016, Baylor University demoted President Ken Starr and fired its football coach Art Briles for their handling of sexual assault cases. In 2017, former Pennsylvania State University president Graham B. Spanier was found guilty of child endangerment for his role in the Jerry Sandusky case. Sandusky, a former assistant football coach, was found guilty of sexual assault and sentenced to prison. Spanier was sentenced to two months in jail, two months on house arrest, fined $7,500, and ordered to perform 200 hours of community service. Two aides were also sentenced to jail and house arrest.

Finally, recent court decisions are requiring universities to hold due process hearings in cases involving alleged violations of their sexual assault policies and of statutes. It appears that in future allegations of sexual assaults on campus, universities will not be permitted to deny such hearings, at least in some jurisdictions.[28]

PRIVATE POLICE AND SECURITY FORCES

An important development all over the world is the growth of private policing. Retail businesses employ security guards to protect their premises from shoplifting and to secure the personal safety of employees and shoppers. Security guards are employed to escort female employees from their places of work to their automobiles at night, particularly in high-crime areas. College and university campuses employ persons to escort students, especially during the night hours. Apartment owners and neighborhood associations have increased their use of **private security forces**. Increasingly common are guard gates, at which drivers entering an association's area are required to stop and present adequate identification before being granted permission to enter the premises.

In many large cities, private security officers are hired to patrol housing and business areas. Private security services may be customized to meet the individual needs of customers. The demand for private security has risen as citizens have felt a lack of sufficient security provided by public police. The types of private security systems are discussed in **Supplement 3.7**.

There are problems with private security, however. Despite recent legislation, some states still do not have licensing requirements for private security. In those jurisdictions, there are few, if any, checks on the quality of security services or on the recruitment or training of security personnel.

Some states have enacted statutes providing for the regulation of private security, but issues remain, such as statutes that are not broad enough to include all types of private security. Increased reliance on private security forces also raises the moral and ethical question of whether society can afford to have a system in which necessary police protection is available only to those who can pay for it.

INTERNATIONAL POLICING

The functions that federal agencies may provide for local and state police are illustrated by the participation of the federal government in the International Criminal Police Organization, commonly known as **INTERPOL**, the world's largest international police organization, with 192 member countries. INTERPOL was established to promote cooperation among nations involved in common police problems. The organization was founded in 1923 but did not function actively until after its reorganization in 1946. The United States became a member in 1938. Any member of INTERPOL may initiate requests for assistance.[29]

The INTERPOL website states the following:

> At INTERPOL we aim to facilitate international police cooperation even where diplomatic relations do not exist between particular countries. Action is taken within the limits of existing laws in different countries and in the spirit of the Universal Declaration of Human Rights. Our constitution prohibits "any intervention or activities of a political, military, religious, or racial character."[30]

The importance of international cooperation through INTERPOL was emphasized in recent years, when a picture of a suspected pedophile, whose image had been altered digitally, was posted on the Internet sexually abusing children. INTERPOL agents and other experts, utilizing approximately 350 tips, unscrambled the maze and posted an identifiable image, leading to the suspect's arrest. Christopher Paul Neil, a 32-year-old school teacher at the time of his arrest in 2007, was captured in Thailand. Neil was convicted and sentenced to prison for sexually abusing young boys.[31]

THE ORGANIZATION, ADMINISTRATION, AND MANAGEMENT OF POLICE SYSTEMS

The organization, administration, and management of any large agency presents numerous challenges and problems, but these may be particularly acute in publicly supported police departments. The police department is the largest and most complex agency in many criminal justice systems, with patrol officers exercising immense authority. The functions performed by these people are varied and complex, although the training for the job is focused primarily on only one of those functions: law enforcement.

Despite the importance of police administration, until recently little attention was given to the issues and problems of organization or administration. Indeed, in contrast to the well-planned development of the English police system, the development of U.S. policing was preceded by little planning because of a basic mistrust of a professional police force. Early systems were characterized by corruption and inefficiency.[32]

Widespread corruption, inefficiency, and a realization of the often negative impact of partisan politics on police systems gave rise in the early 1900s to a study of the role of organization and administration in improving the quality of policing and to the increased use of private security officers. These early reform efforts were assisted by the work of August Vollmer, often referred to as the father of modern police management systems or the dean of American chiefs of police. As chief of the Berkeley, California, police department, Vollmer instituted a summer program in criminology at the University of California at Berkeley and began an emphasis on the importance of formally educating police.

In 1931, the School of Criminology was founded at Berkeley. In 1933, it granted the first police degree, an AB degree with a minor in criminology. In 1930, the first two-year college police program was begun at the San Jose (California) Junior College, but the first grants to such programs were not offered until 1966. These programs comprised courses in liberal arts, behavioral sciences, public administration, law, and government. Many changes have occurred in criminal justice education, with other programs developing and some, such as Berkeley's School of Criminology, being abolished.

Others who were influential in the development of earlier criminal justice programs were Bruce Smith, who contributed to police professionalism through his writings and as a police consultant, and O. W. Wilson. Wilson was an influential police chief in the late 1920s who emphasized advanced training for law enforcement officers in Wichita, Kansas. He was dean of the School of Criminology at Berkeley and authored a widely acclaimed text on police administration. He is perhaps best known for his contributions in the 1960s as Chicago's police superintendent.

Vollmer, Smith, and Wilson influenced the emergence of a professional model for policing, which included not only the use of management skills at the administrative levels of policing but also the application of modern technology in improving police work. The result was a model characterized by

> a tight quasi-military organization; rigorous discipline; a streamlined chain of command; higher recruitment standards; a lengthy period of preservice training; the allocation of available personnel according to demonstrated need; and extensive use of vehicles, communications, and computer technology.[33]

Policing Models

The organization and management of police departments received considerable attention from the President's Commission on Law Enforcement and Administration of Justice (hereafter referred to as the President's Commission), appointed by President Lyndon Johnson in 1965. Some of the commission's conclusions, stated in its 1967 report on police, were the lack of qualified leadership; resistance to change; the lack of trained personnel in research and planning, law, business administration, and computer analysis; the inefficient use of personnel; and departmental organization that did not incorporate "well-established principles of modern business management."[34]

A Professional Model of Policing

The President's Commission graphed one model of departmental organization—the traditional, or professional, model—characterized by a hierarchical structure, with the police chief as the central authority in the organization. The chain of command in the professional model is clear: Heads of departments such as internal investigation, community relations, administration bureau, operations bureau, and services bureau, report directly to the chief and each of these heads has subordinate administrators reporting directly to him or her. Under this model, the police department is organized around specialized functions, such as patrol, traffic, personnel and training, and data processing, all of which are subunits of the major divisions of administration, operations, and services. This model has major units concerned with internal investigations and community relations. Some departments have a unit specializing in crime prevention.

The professional model involves many rules and regulations, with little input from subordinates in developing them. It may be a very efficient model for making quick decisions, prescribing safety measures, and internally controlling subordinates. In fact, the professional model often results in high production output.

The professional model of policing gained momentum with the reports of the 1967 President's Commission and the 1973 National Advisory Commission on Criminal Justice Standards and Goals. According to the 1981 report of the U.S. Commission on Civil Rights: "These two commissions, in particular, gave added impetus to some specific suggestions, such as the more effective use of police personnel and, most emphatically, the requirement that police officers have some college education."[35]

The need for professional police systems became obvious in the 1960s, when television brought into American homes the violent clashes between police and minorities, including the young as well as racial and ethnic groups. The urban riots of the 1960s demonstrated the need to train police in handling orderly protests as well as violence and law enforcement.

During the 1960s, the federal government focused attention on policing and other elements of criminal justice systems. The President's Commission issued several reports in 1967. In 1965, Congress established the Office of Law Enforcement Assistance and, in 1968, the **Law Enforcement Assistance Administration (LEAA)**. Until its demise in 1982, the LEAA provided over $7 billion for research, development, and evaluation of various programs in criminal justice, some of which went for hardware in police departments (a source of criticism of the LEAA). Money was provided for police education through the **Law Enforcement Education Program (LEEP)**. The result was the development of criminal justice departments throughout the country. Most of them focused on police education or training, discussed in Chapter 4.

The professional model is criticized for being too authoritarian and for establishing policing units that are too specialized. For example, if a police officer assigned to the patrol division encounters a problem with a juvenile, under the professional model, the youth should be turned over to the juvenile division, even though the patrol officer in that district may have more knowledge of the individual and his or her background. Controlling traffic and issuing traffic citations are the specialty of the officers in the traffic division; they should be called for handling these problems in the patrol officer's district. The officer may arrest a suspect for violating a crime, but the investigation of that crime will be conducted by a detective in another division. There may be overlap in the recordkeeping of these various divisions, in addition to the obvious fragmentation of functions.

Problem-Oriented Policing

Dissatisfaction with the professional model led to an emphasis on an approach to policing that focuses on *problems* rather than *incidents*. Problems consist of incidents that are in some way related—for example, they all occur in the same area of the city—or they are thought to have the same underlying causes. The problem-solving nature of this approach focuses on a less extensive division of labor, fewer rules and regulations, and fewer levels of authority. The emphasis is on solving problems, and power comes from the ability of employees to succeed in that goal, not from the titles of their positions. Its emphasis is on gaining knowledge and using that knowledge to adapt to new situations. This model provides greater flexibility, which may be necessary for some decisions, while permitting more involvement of subordinates in the police force. It is based on the belief that police effectiveness may be increased if the expertise and creativity of line officers are utilized to develop innovative methods for solving the underlying problems that cause or influence criminal behavior.

Since much of police work requires officers to make on-the-spot decisions, the problem-oriented model may be more effective than the professional model in developing the ability to make decisions effectively. Problem-oriented policing can focus on underlying problems in any or all of the three traditional areas of policing: order maintenance, law enforcement, and community service (all discussed in Chapter 4). It is designed to enhance the effectiveness of policing by identifying underlying problems and attempting to solve them.

The problem-solving approach to policing was emphasized in the writings of Herman Goldstein, who developed his earlier published ideas in a 1990 book. Among other examples, Goldstein discussed a Philadelphia case involving a police sergeant who noted that many noise complaints (505 separate calls in a six-month period) about the same bar had been made to police, who responded to all of the complaints. The officers did not find the noise to be in violation of the city ordinance. After some time, however, officers discovered that the noise about which the neighbors complained was coming from the vibration of the jukebox located at the common wall. The jukebox was moved to another wall, and the noise complaints stopped.[36]

A focus on problem-oriented policing does not mean that police will not respond to calls for service, but the demands created by these calls may lead administrators to rationalize that they do not have the personnel to engage in innovative policing, such as problem-solving approaches. It is necessary to integrate the traditional calls for service with problem-solving policing, and this cannot be done without better management of police time.

Goldstein responded to the time issue by stating:

> A common reaction to problem oriented policing is that the agency has no time available for it.... This type of reaction assumes that problem oriented policing is an add-on. It fails to recognize that the concept raises fundamental questions about how police currently spend their time, both in responding to calls for assistance and in the intervals between calls.[37]

It is argued that the time that police may waste in patrol under the professional policing model can be used more effectively if the police are involved in problem-solving approaches. For example, they can be given daily assessments of specific problems in their patrol areas and be permitted to work on those problems. Problem-oriented policing is based on the concept that officers should become less anonymous and more integrated into the communities they patrol. Returning to foot patrol or using horses or bicycles assists officers in this effort. There are research publications reporting evidence that foot patrol is a reasonable way to prevent crime as well as reduce fear.[38] Police become more visible and accountable to the public, and they are encouraged to view citizens as partners in crime prevention. Furthermore, more decision making at the patrol level means that those who are best informed of the problems in the community are the ones making important policing decisions.

The problem-solving approach to policing requires that police assume a **proactive** rather than a **reactive** role. That is, police should take the initiative in preventing crime rather than waiting for others to call in complaints.

The stage for the problem-solving approach was set by the emphasis on returning to foot patrol articulated in a 1982 article, "Police and Neighborhood Safety: Broken Windows," written by James Q. Wilson and George L. Kelling. The broken windows concept embodies the belief that minor offenders who disrupt the quality of life should be controlled, thus making neighborhoods safer, resulting in a reduction of fear and of crime. The concept was illustrated by a "Safe and Clean Neighborhoods Program" that began in New Jersey (primarily in Newark) in the mid-1970s and involved putting police back on foot patrol. An evaluation of foot patrol programs by the Police Foundation concluded that the programs did not result in a reduction in crime but that residents *felt* safer within their neighborhoods and *felt* that crime had been reduced. In addition, the officers on foot patrol had "higher morale, greater job satisfaction, and a more favorable attitude toward citizens in their neighborhood" than did their counterparts in patrol cars. Wilson and Kelling concluded that, despite the fact that the overall crime rate did not go down, there were advantages to foot patrol in Newark. The residents of that city were correct in believing that their neighborhoods were safer because the presence of the police did maintain order in the neighborhoods.[39]

Criminologists have analyzed problem-oriented policing and some have concluded, that, compared to other approaches to policing, "problem-oriented policing offers the most targeted, analytical and in-depth approach."[40]

Community-Oriented Policing

The influence of problem-oriented policing is seen in the federal development of the Community Oriented Policing Services (COPS), established by the Violent Crime Control and Enforcement Act of 1994.[41] COPS, located within the Department of Justice (DOJ), defines *community-oriented policing* as a policing philosophy that "promotes and supports organizational strategies to address the causes and reduce the fear of crime and social disorder."[42] The organization follows that definition with reference to the work of Herman Goldstein, an early founder of the problem-oriented approach to policing whose work is cited earlier in this chapter.

COPS provides grants to local, tribal, and state law enforcement agencies for hiring and training community policing professionals. An additional mission of COPS is to develop and test innovative policing strategies and to acquire and utilize new techniques for preventing and fighting crime. Some focus topics for which COPS has provided assistance to local law enforcement offices are domestic violence, gang violence, youth firearms violence, and school-based programs.

COPS has also assisted local law enforcement agencies to put more police on the streets, but funding has been an issue for the program. Some Washington, D.C.-based economists, however, estimated that significant funding of the COPS program would actually save the federal government money and that COPS appeared to be "one of the most cost-effective options available for fighting crime" in a society in which crime costs could be as high as $2 trillion.[43] This analysis was supported in part by criminologists who found that COPS programs resulted in a significant reduction in property crimes within cities of 100,000 or more, although it had no significant effect in smaller cities.[44] Others concluded that COPS funding had done little to reduce crime.[45]

Police Strategies and Crime Reduction

Have the changes in police management and procedures made a difference in crime rates? Perhaps it was inevitable that politicians would claim all of the credit for the crime reductions in their cities during the 1990s. Here we will look at New York City's approach.

Significant attention has been given to the crime reduction in New York City in the 1990s during the administrations of Mayor Rudolph Giuliani and his police commissioner William J. Bratton, who took office in 1994. The program introduced by Bratton and subsequently adopted in police departments throughout the country, is called **COMPSTAT**. COMPSTAT is described as "a goal-oriented strategic management process that uses computer technology, operational strategy and managerial accountability to structure the manner in which a police department provides crime-control services." The process has been acclaimed by the Ford Foundation and the John F. Kennedy School of Government at Harvard University and its implementation credited with the decreases in crime in New York City.[46]

It is maintained that since the return to foot patrol in the 1980s, police departments have been going through a process of "examination, reflection, and experimentation that involves a variety of managerial and operational strategies."[47] At the center of the COMPSTAT approach is the computerization of information about crime. Crime data are processed, mapped, and analyzed, and the results are sent on a regular basis to operational managers, who have the power and the responsibility to discuss the information with their subunits. They are held accountable for appropriate problem-solving responses.[48] However, the process is not a quick fix to lower crime rates. It requires major changes in organizational structure and thinking, and we do not yet know whether its use will have long-term success in reducing crime.[49]

The broken windows concept, introduced earlier in this chapter, was key to New York's approach to the use of COMPSTAT. The emphasis was on cleaning up the streets: arresting minor offenders whose presence may suggest that the police are not in control. Administrators took pride in their claims that New York City has become a cleaner and, consequently, a safer place to live as the police have taken back the streets. Not all criminologists agree that the police were responsible for these positive changes, and some insist that more careful and scientific evaluations are necessary before such conclusions of police success can be accepted.[50]

One example was the increased arrests for the crime of smoking marijuana in public view (MPV) in New York City, an increase of over 2,670 percent between 1989 and 2000. Researchers found that African Americans and Hispanics were disproportionately represented in these arrests and there was no significant evidence that the arrests resulted in crime reduction. To the contrary, there was evidence that the arrests had the reverse effect. Furthermore, the initiative was very expensive and, according to the researchers, constituted "an extremely poor trade-off of scarce law enforcement resources."[51]

In January 2014, Bratton was back in the position as New York City's police commissioner, and the broken windows concept was again featured. During the first two months of 2014, police arrests of peddlers and panhandlers in the city's subway systems were over three times as high as during that period in 2013. Arrests had declined in recent years, partly as the result of charges of illegal frisking and racial profiling in that city. That subject is discussed in a subsequent chapter of this text. But Chief Bratton announced that under his direction, police would be aggressive against low-level infractions and misdemeanors to maintain order but also because he believed such broken windows infractions could lead to more serious acts. "If you take care of the little things, then you can prevent a lot of the big things."[52]

William J. Bratton, who began his career as New York City's police commissioner in 1994, served in that capacity in Boston and as police chief in Los Angeles before returning to the position in New York City in 2014 and remaining until 2016. Bratton was widely recognized for his support of the "broken windows" concept of policing, which, he argued, contributes to lowering the crime rate by keeping a city's streets and neighborhoods clean and organized.

The mayor and the police commissioner faced serious criticism and the broken windows concept came under new and intense scrutiny, especially after Bratton retired as New York's police commissioner in 2016. He was succeeded by James P. O'Neill, at which time the city's major, Bill de Blasio, stated that especially in predominantly minority areas, where tensions between the police and residents were high, the emphasis would be on neighborhood policing. By 2017, the zero tolerance policy was less of an emphasis, leading to the dismissal by August of 644,000 arrest warrants for minor offenses such as riding a bicycle on a city street or drinking alcohol in public.[53]

Studies showed the negative effects of zero tolerance on cities and on targets, citing, for example, an incident in which a young black male in Baltimore was arrested for loitering in front of the house in which he resided.[54] Social scientists questioned some policing practices, noting the increased tensions between the police and the public.[55] More attention is given to this topic in subsequent chapters.

Summary

This chapter described the emerging need for formal police systems. It examined the history of informal and formal policing methods in England and the United States. Many factors contributed to the need for formal policing, but in both countries, the increasing complexity that resulted when society became industrialized was crucial. The rising levels of criminal activity, public unrest, and riots that accompanied industrialization demonstrated the inability of informal methods of policing to provide adequate protection.

The formal system of policing that has evolved in the United States—a decentralized system having local, state, and federal levels—results in overlaps and gaps among levels. It also permits states and localities to experiment with methods that might be effective in light of the problems that distinguish their policing needs from those of the federal government. The various levels of policing cooperate in some functions, such as investigation and training. Numerous law enforcement agencies exist at the federal level, and they are available to assist states and local agencies as well. These federal agencies have undergone dramatic changes in recent years, especially since the 9/11 terrorist attacks on U.S. soil. The changes have not been without controversy, and neither has the legislation that created and empowered them.

Formal, public policing systems have been the object of criticism for a long time; some citizens have reacted by employing private police or by having security devices installed in their homes or businesses. Conflict between public and private policing developed and continues, although there is some evidence of cooperation between the two. Some states have established minimum requirements for licensing private security firms.

The type of police organization and administration may have a significant effect on policing. This chapter discussed early reform efforts in police organization and administration and then focused on differentiating policing models: the professional model, problem-oriented policing, and community-oriented policing. The chapter closed with a look at police strategies for crime reduction, noting the emphasis on "broken windows" and the return of William J. Bratton as police commissioner in New York City, from which he retired in 2016.

This chapter provided a framework within which to examine the nature and functioning of policing, the focus of Chapter 4.

Key Terms

Study Questions

1. What is the purpose of a formal system of policing?
2. Explain the significance of the following to the development of modern policing: Bow Street Runners, Peelers or Bobbies, posse, and Molly Maguires.
3. Define *vigilantism*, and discuss its advantages and disadvantages with regard to air travel today.
4. Compare local, state, and federal police systems. What are the advantages and disadvantages of decentralized policing?
5. What are some of the unique problems of rural law enforcement?
6. What is the role of the county sheriff in most jurisdictions?
7. What are the functions of U.S. marshals?
8. Discuss the strengths and weaknesses of the FBI, and comment on the reorganization and reputation of this agency since the 9/11 terrorist attacks.
9. Describe the Department of Homeland Security (DHS).
10. Briefly discuss recent developments in the U.S. system of immigration.
11. What developments have occurred with regard to law enforcement on college and university campuses?
12. What is the role of private police agencies? Evaluate.
13. Explain the meaning of INTERPOL and relate its mission to eradicating the sexual abuse of children.
14. How would you describe the administration of early police systems in the United States?
15. Evaluate the traditional, authoritarian model of organizational structure of police departments.
16. Trace the development of the professional model of policing.
17. Describe and analyze the concepts of problem-oriented and community-oriented policing.
18. Explain what is meant by COMPSTAT, and discuss why it is considered, at least by some, to be effective. Relate this concept to that of "broken windows."

Notes

1. Herman Goldstein, *Policing in a Free Society* (Cambridge, MA: Ballinger, 1977), p. 1.
2. David H. Bayley, "Police: History," in *Encyclopedia of Crime and Justice*, vol. 3, ed. Sanford H. Kadish (New York: Free Press, 1983), pp. 1122-1123.
3. Louis B. Schwartz and Stephen R. Goldstein, *Law Enforcement Handbook for Police* (St. Paul, Minn.: West, 1970), p. 34.
4. "Police Race Bias Moves Blasted," *Daily Star* (August 24, 2004), p. 6.
5. "Police Chief Vows to Bring Racist Killers to Book," *The Guardian* (London) (final edition) (April 27, 2006), p. 6. The information on the Lawrence investigation is from "Lawrence Police Team Disbanded," *Evening Standard* (London) (April 24, 2006), p. 19.
6. "UN Criticises 'Racism' of British Police Forces; Human Rights Experts Condemn Numbers of Deaths in Custody; Warning Puts New Pressure on Beleagured Amber Rudd," *The Independent* (April 28, 2018), p. 1.
7. "'Hostile Environment' Checks Halted Until Ministers Confident Windrush Scandal Solved," *Mirror* (July 12, 2018), p. 1.
8. Bayley, "Police: History," p. 1124.
9. *Ibid.*
10. Robert Borkenstein, "Police: State Police," in *Encyclopedia of Crime and Justice*, vol. 3, ed. Kadish, p. 1133.
11. "2004 Showdown Shaped Reputation of F.B.I. Pick," *New York Times* (June 23, 2013), p. 9.
12. "Senators Criticize F.B.I. for Its Security Failures," *New York Times* (July 19, 2001), p. 16.
13. "F.B.I. Is Retailoring to Meet New Threats but Stretched Thin, Reports Say," *New York Times* (June 19, 2003), p. 15.
14. The 9/11 Commission Report: *Final Report of the National Commission on Terrorist Attacks upon the United States, Authorized Edition* (New York: W.W. Norton & Company, 2004), p. 358.
15. "F.B.I. Is Assailed for Its Handling of Terror Risks," *New York Times* (April 14, 2004), p. 1.
16. Robert S. Mueller III, Director of the Federal Bureau of Investigation, "FBI Oversight," Testimony Before the Senate Judiciary Committee, *Federal News Service* (May 2, 2006), n.p.
17. The USA Patriot Act, as amended, is codified at USCS, Title 18, Section 1229 et seq. (2019).
18. *Texas v. United States* 809 F.3d 134 (5th Cir. 2015). For an analysis of the relationship between immigration and crime, see Kevin A. Wright and Nancy Rodriguez, "A Closer Look at the Paradox: Examining Immigration and Youth Reoffending In Arizona," *Justice Quarterly* 31(5) (October 2014): 882-904.
19. *Texas v. United States*, 809 F.3d 134 (5th Cir. 2015), *aff'd*, *United States v. Texas*, 136 S. Ct. 2271 (2016).
20. *Trump et al. v. International Refugee Assistance Project et al.*, 137 S. Ct. 2080 (2017).
21. Order List, United States Supreme Court (October 10, 2017), https://www.supremecourt.gov, accessed October 14, 2017, regarding 16-1436, *Trump, President of U.S. et al. v. Int'l Refugee Assistance et al.*
22. "Attorney General Sessions Delivers Remarks Discussing the Immigration Enforcement Actions of the Trump Administration," San Diego, CA (May 7, 2018), https://www.justice.gov, accessed August 28, 2018.
23. "US Says It Will Appeal Injunction Barring Separation of Immigrant Families," *American Bar Association Journal* (August 27, 2018), http://www.abajournal.com, accessed August 28, 2018.
24. Letter from the ABA President to the U.S. Attorney General and the Secretary, U.S. Department of Homeland Security (June 12, 2018).
25. Brian A. Reeves, Bureau of Justice Statistics Special Report, *Campus Law Enforcement, 2011-12* (January 2015), p. 1, http://www.bjs.ojp.gov/content/pub/pdf/cle1112.pdf, accessed April 20, 2015.
26. Jeanne Clery Disclosure of Campus Security Policy and Campus Crime Statistics Act, USCS, Title 20, Section 1092(f) (2019).
27. "White House Sets a College Agenda on Sex Assaults," *New York Times* (April 29, 2014), p. 1; "55 Colleges Named in Federal Inquiry Handling of Sexual Assault Cases," *New York Times* (May 2, 2014), p. 13; "Harvard to Bring on Specialists to Examine Sexual Assault Claims," *New York Times* (July 3, 2014), p. 15.
28. See, for example, *Doe v. University of Cincinnati*, 872 F.3d 393 (6th Cir. 2017); "Judges Changing the Way Universities Handle Sexual Assault Investigations," *Detroit Free Press* (August 27, 2018).
29. Michael Fooner, "INTERPOL," in *Encyclopedia of Crime and Justice*, vol. 3, ed. Kadish, p. 912, updated, https://www.interpol.int/About-INTERPOL/Overview, accessed August 28, 2018.
30. INTERPOL, "About Interpol," https://www.interpol.int/Abvout-INTERPOL/Overview, accessed August 28, 2018.
31. "Thailand: More Jail Time," *The Advertiser* (Australia) (November 25, 2008), p. 28.
32. The basis for this discussion is the article by Herman Goldstein, "Police Administration," in *Encyclopedia of Crime and Justice*, vol. 3, ed. Kadish, pp. 1125-1131.
33. Ibid., p. 1126.
34. The President's Commission on Law Enforcement and Administration of Justice, *Task Force on the Police, Task Force Report: The Police* (Washington, D.C.: U.S. Government Printing Office, 1967), p. 44.
35. United States Commission on Civil Rights, *Who Is Guarding the Guardians? A Report on Police Practices* (Washington, D.C.: U.S. Government Printing Office, 1981), p. 6.
36. Herman Goldstein, *Problem Oriented Policing* (New York: McGraw-Hill, 1990), p. 81 (n.6).
37. Ibid., p. 151.
38. Eric L. Piza and Brian A. O'Hara, "Saturation Foot-Patrol in a High-Violence Area: A Wuasi-Experimental Evaluation," *Justice Quarterly* 31(4) (August 2014): 693-718.
39. James Q. Wilson and George L. Kelling, "Police and Neighborhood Safety: Broken Windows," *Atlantic Monthly* 249 (March 1982): 29-38.
40. Gary Cordner and Elizabeth Perkins Biebel, "Problem-Oriented Policing in Practice," *Criminology & Public Policy* 4(2) (May 2005): 155-180, quotation is on p. 158.
41. Violent Crime Control and Law Enforcement Act of 1994, Public Law 103-322 (September 13, 1994).
42. COPS, U.S. Department of Justice, "Solving Crime Problems," http://www.cops.usdoj.gov/, accessed January 5, 2015.
43. "Economists Say More COPS Funding Would Save Government Billions," *Criminal Justice Newsletter* (April 2, 2007), p. 7.

44. Jihong Zhao et al., "Funding Community Policing to Reduce Crime: Have COPS Grants Made a Difference?," *Criminology & Public Policy* 2(1) (November 2002): 7-32.
45. John L. Worrall and Tomislav V. Kovandzic, "COPS Grants and Crime Revisited," *Criminology* 45(1) (February 2007): 159-190.
46. William F. Walsh, "COMPSTAT: An Analysis of an Emerging Police Managerial Paradigm," in *Critical Issues in Policing*, 6th ed., eds. Roger G. Dunham and Geoffrey P. Alpert (Long Grove, IL: Waveland Press, 2010), pp. 197-211; quotation is p. 197.
47. Ibid., p. 198.
48. Ibid., p. 206.
49. Ibid., p. 209.
50. See, for example, Richard Rosenfeld et al., "Did Ceasefire, COMPSTAT, and Exile Reduce Homicide?," *Criminology & Public Policy* 4(3) (August 2005): 419-450; and James J. Willis et al., "COMPSTAT and Bureaucracy: A Case Study of Challenges and Opportunities for Change," *Justice Quarterly* 21(3) (September 2004): 463-496.
51. Bernard E. Harcourt and Jens Ludwig, "Reefer Madness: Broken Windows Policing and Misdemeanor Marijuana Arrests in New York City, 1989-2000," *Criminology & Public Policy* 6(1) (February 2007): 165-181; quotation is on p. 176.
52. "Arrests of Panhandlers and Peddlers on Subways Triple Under Bratton," *New York Times* (March 7, 2014), p. 18. See also "Broken Windows, Broken Parks," *New York Times* (June 29, 2014), p. 28.
53. "NY District Attorneys Get Some 644K Outstanding Warrants for Minor Offenses Dismissed," *American Bar Association Journal* (August 10, 2017), http://www.abajournal.com, accessed August 11, 2017; "Justice Report Cites Discriminatory and Unconstitutional Policing in Baltimore," *American Bar Association Journal*, http://www.abajournal.com, accessed August 11, 2018.
54. Ibid.
55. See, for example, the following journal, which was devoted to articles analyzing the crime drop in New York City: *Justice Quarterly* 31(1) (February 2014).

4

Policing in a Modern Society

Chapter Outline

Learning Objectives

After reading this chapter, you should be able to do the following:

- Describe the issues regarding police recruitment and selection
- Discuss the role (or the lack thereof) of higher education in policing
- Analyze the importance of police training
- Explain the meaning and importance of discretion in policing
- List and discuss the three major areas of police functions
- Discuss recent U.S. Supreme Court decisions regarding traffic stops and searches
- Explain the difference between an investigatory stop and an arrest
- Assess the meaning and importance of racial profiling and how the courts react to allegations of it
- Discuss the meaning of probable cause, and explain the purpose of requiring a warrant for most searches
- Explain what police can and cannot do in searching a home, a vehicle, and a person
- Understand the importance of the prohibition against unreasonable searches and seizures, even in public school settings
- Compare the police role of interrogation with that of investigation
- Explain and evaluate the *Miranda* rule, its exceptions, and updates

Police in the United States are expected to prevent crime, apprehend and arrest criminals, enforce traffic ordinances and laws, maintain order in domestic and other kinds of disputes, control or prevent disturbances, and perform numerous miscellaneous services. Police must perform these functions in the context of political, legal, and societal expectations, which may be unrealistic and conflicting.

Some of the functions assigned to police are shared by other persons or agencies, which often results in conflict concerning police roles. But police are given greater discretion and power in performing their tasks. Why? The possibility that disorder, or even violence, will occur convinces us that the police should handle the situation. Therefore, we are willing to grant police the power to act when intervention is necessary.

This chapter focuses on what police do in a modern society, but those functions should be examined in the context of the extensive discretion police have in performing their jobs. The importance of discretion and the possibility of its abuse require that high standards be maintained by those who occupy policing roles. The chapter's discussion of discretion is thus preceded by a look at preparing for policing.

The discussion of police functions focuses first on order maintenance and community service before devoting substantial coverage to law enforcement, which begins with an overview of constitutional issues. The specifics of law enforcement begin with an analysis of traffic stops and other attempts to enforce traffic ordinances. The investigatory stop by police is examined in terms of **racial profiling** and other issues regarding stop and frisk. The arrest, search, and seizure of suspects is examined by a look at warrants and the meaning of probable cause, along with a summary of the laws regarding home, vehicle, and person searches. The final two sections cover the interrogation and investigation of suspects.

PREPARING FOR POLICING

The importance of policing demands that careful attention be given to the recruitment and selection—as well as the education and training—of persons who will become police officers.

Recruitment and Selection

One difficulty in the recruitment and selection of police is that desirable qualities and characteristics are usually not defined in measurable terms. Perhaps the problem is that, in the past, the focus was on police recruits and their qualities, the assumption being that, if different types of people were attracted to policing, the profession would improve. Some researchers reported that certain types—for example, authoritarian and cynical people—are attracted to policing. Others argued that policing *creates* these personalities.[1]

Good policing requires intelligence and the ability to think independently, perform different roles and functions, comprehend and accept other cultures and subcultures, and understand the importance of freedom and the dangers of abusing authority. It is crucial for police departments to recruit people who have high moral and ethical standards and who have not had serious infractions with the law. Chapter 5 discusses corruption in policing; avoiding that problem requires recruiting persons who will not succumb to the temptations facing law enforcement officers. This is difficult to do, however, as police officials throughout the country have discovered. Officers are recruited from a generation of young people who have grown up in a culture in which it may be considered acceptable to engage in some law violations, such as using illegal drugs. Trying to recruit persons who have never used illegal drugs may be an impossible task. . . . Of course, recruiting ethical candidates for jobs is important in most jobs, but it is particularly crucial in policing.

The success of efforts to recruit persons with high moral and ethical standards into policing and to encourage them to maintain those standards may be analyzed in terms of the subsequent behavior of recruits. In that respect, the New York City Police Department (NYPD) is often the focus of attention. In testimony before the New York City Council, Frank Serpico, a former New York City police officer, stated, "We must create an atmosphere where the crooked cop fears the honest cop, and not the other way around." In the early 1970s, Serpico reported and testified against officers who engaged in corrupt or other forms of illegal behavior. He almost lost his life in his fight against the problems of the NYPD, and his story became a best-selling book and movie, *Serpico*.[2]

Recruiting well-qualified candidates for policing has become a serious problem in some areas. The low salaries and high risk are not attractive to many individuals. At the same time, in some departments the need for recruits has increased as the result of retirements and population growth. Professions 4.1 provides some general information regarding general qualifications that departments seek in all police candidates.

Clearly, salary is an issue in recruiting police. In 2017, for example, the Dallas Police Department was struggling

Professions 4.1

Police Personnel: Recruiting and Hiring

In today's world of extensive media opportunities, police recruiting and hiring differs significantly from past years. Most local police departments have websites that provide photographs, lists, and explanations of the requirements for specific jobs within the department; test schedules; details of job benefits; and so on. This information differs significantly from department to department. Generally, the requirements for becoming a police officer are as follows:

- High school diploma or the equivalent (perhaps some college; a few require a college degree);
- A minimum age of 21 at hiring; may not be hired after age 44;
- United States citizenship;
- Proficiency in speaking and writing in English (additional compensation may be provided for those who are bilingual);
- Honorable discharge if in the military;
- Limitations on law violations (e.g., no convictions of a felony, no convictions within a stated time period, no convictions for crimes involving morals, etc.);
- Good moral character;
- A driver's license and a good driving record;
- The passing of a physical exam, including vision and hearing;
- No addictions to narcotics or habit-forming drugs or excessive alcohol consumption; and
- A good credit rating.

Compensation varies among local departments but generally includes paid holidays, vacation leave, health benefits, incentive pay, life insurance, and death benefits. Many include tuition reimbursement for approved courses and a take home car program. Salaries vary significantly but generally are stated on the department's website and increase with time in service. Following are some general postings from police departments regarding desired characteristics:

- Integrity and humility
- Foresight—visionary, creative, courageous, and decisive
- Shows care and concern for others
- Systems thinker comfortable with complexity
- Ability to influence and motivate others
- Excellent organizational skills
- Demonstrated past achievement
- Strong critical thinking skills
- Skilled communicator
- Perseverance in the face of challenges
- Compassion

All of these (and other) qualities are appropriate for many positions, but one that candidates might not expect showed up on many police department websites—the requirement that any tattoos, body art, branding, or even scarring must not be visible when the officer is in official uniform. Likewise, body piercings are prohibited or limited (example, no pierced ears for men and only one per ear for women).

---

to recruit. The starting salary of $49,207 a year (to rise to $55,288 in 2018) was thousands below the starting salaries in nearby suburbs. Even in the nearby metropolitan area of Fort Worth, the starting salary for a police recruit was $54,312 (up to $61,000 with two to five years of experience).[3]

Supplement 4.1 discusses the importance of hiring female and minority candidates in policing. A July 2016 BJS report indicated that of the recruits entering police basic training between 2011 and 2013, approximately one in seven were women and almost one in three were members of a racial or ethnic minority.[4]

Education

Most would agree that education is important for police officers, but there is disagreement over the amount and type of education that should be required. The dispute over whether any college education should be mandated is significant. As far back as 1917, a college education for police received attention from August Vollmer, when he recruited part-time police officers from students at the University of California. Despite his emphasis on the importance of higher education and his reputation as an outstanding police administrator, Vollmer did not succeed in convincing many police departments to follow his lead. During the Great Depression, when jobs were scarce, police departments recruited college educated men, but that practice ceased with the end of the Depression.

In 1967, when the average police officer had only slightly more than a high school diploma, the President's Commission on Law Enforcement and Administration of Justice (hereafter referred to as the President's Commission) recommended that the "ultimate aim of all police departments should be that personnel with general enforcement powers have baccalaureate degrees."[5] The federal government provided financial incentives and support for the development of programs for higher education of police officers.

One of the provisions of the 1994 federal crime control bill was to put more police on the streets. The money Congress provided for the Community Oriented Policing Services (COPS) program established by the 1994 statute was used in some jurisdictions for enhanced training and education of police. The 1994 statute provided funds for the development in six states (Maryland, North Carolina, Oregon, Nevada, Arkansas, and South Carolina) of programs that were modeled after the military's Reserve Officers Training Corps (ROTC). For college graduates who agreed to serve four years in policing, the program reimbursed up to $30,000 in educational costs.

A frequently cited study supporting education for police is the 1989 publication based on the research by the Police Executive Research Forum (PERF). The authors concluded that, overall, college-educated officers were more responsible and made better decisions than their less-educated counterparts. As such, officers with some college education were not only more effective in performing their jobs but also more efficient in that costs associated with lost personnel time were lower.[6]

The authors of an analysis of higher education and policing concluded the following:

> We find that higher education has two important roles to play. One is to carry education beyond the classroom in ways that encourage broad reform. The other is to help make improvements in police training and education in ways that, at least will produce higher levels of civility, and might even encourage a more humanistic police professionalism.[7]

Those who do not favor requiring a college education for police cite several reasons: First, raising educational requirements might discriminate against minority applicants. Second, there is concern that the applicant pool may be too small. Third, some police unions are opposed to higher educational requirements.[8] Finally, many of the criminal justice programs that have provided police education have come under attack. Critics argue that there is too much emphasis on technical skills at the expense of a broad educational background.[9]

Beyond the issue of how much education is required for becoming a police officer is continuing education of those who are officers. It is particularly important to focus programs on pertinent issues, such as race relations. *Racial profiling* has been a serious issue in many police departments, as we will see later in the text. One example of attempts to avoid racial profiling is a program in the New York Police Department, in conjunction with the City Council of New York and the City University of New York. The program, entitled the NYPD Police Studies Program, features critical race theory (CRT) pedagogy, provides free tuition and books, and focuses on police management and ethnic studies. The aim is to increase critical understanding of racism with a goal of changing racist thinking. Social scientists testing the effects of the program found some support for changed thinking in a positive direction, with greater changes registered among white than among black and Hispanic officers. The researchers concluded that the NYPD Police Studies Program "has produced a working example of educating officers in an undergraduate setting that gives them scholarly and critical thinking tools to deal with problems of race and racism." They suggested, however, that such courses alone are not sufficient and that organizational changes within police departments and patrol policies may be necessary before black and Latino residents have a more positive attitude toward the police.[10]

Training

In its 1967 report, the Task Force on Police of the President's Commission emphasized the importance of adequate police training, noting that the problem was particularly acute in small police departments. **Supplement 4.2** summarizes some of the Commission's findings.

Basic police training includes many areas of expertise, ranging from firing weapons to understanding the ordinances and laws that govern a particular jurisdiction. Much of the training is standard and cannot be detailed here, but it is important to go beyond the traditional, standard training. For example, a five-year study of drug-related deaths of suspects in police custody concluded

Spotlight 4.1

Equipment and Technology in Policing: A Survey

In 2015, the Bureau of Justice Statistics published the results of its 2013 survey of local police departments and their use of equipment and technology. Following are the highlights of that publication.

- The percentage of local police departments that authorized their officers to use conducted energy weapons such as Tasers increased from 60 percent in 2007 to 81 percent in 2013.
- The percentage of local police departments that required officers to wear protective armor at all times increased from 65 percent in 2007 to 71 percent in 2013.
- From 2007 to 2013, the percentage of local police departments using in-car video cameras increased from 61 percent to 68 percent.
- About a third (32 percent) of local police departments used body-worn cameras in 2013.
- About one in six local police departments used automated vehicle license plate readers in 2013, including a majority of those serving a population of 25,000 or more.
- More than 90 percent of local police departments serving 25,000 or more residents provided patrol officers with in-field computerized access to vehicle records, driving records, and outstanding warrants.
- Among local police departments serving 10,000 or more residents, more than 90 percent had their own website and more than 80 percent used social media.
- About 60 percent of local police departments provided crime statistics to citizens electronically, including more than 90 percent of those serving 25,000 or more residents.

Source: Brian A. Reaves, Bureau of Justice Statistics, "Local Police Departments, 2013: Equipment and Technology" (July 2015), https://www.bjs.gov, accessed August 29, 2018.

that approximately one-third of those deaths could have been prevented had police been adequately trained for significant intervention.[11]

One area in which police need special training is patrolling in and around schools. With the recent incidents of violence on school grounds and inside school buildings, security has become increasingly important. Many jurisdictions now train special officers who are assigned to work in the public schools.

Another relatively new area of focus for policing has occurred as a result of the terrorist acts of 9/11. Police are now trained in such areas as the following:

- Response to weapons of mass destruction
- Understanding the nature of terrorism
- Relevant federal, state, and local agencies
- Interagency information sharing
- Intelligence gathering
- Role of anti-terrorist task forces
- Related technology/equipment
- Post-incident stabilization of community
- Intelligence analysis[12]

The importance of adequate police training was emphasized in a 1989 U.S. Supreme Court decision, *City of Canton, Ohio v. Harris*, in which the Court held that inadequate police training may result in civil liability for the municipality under which the police department operates. The Supreme Court placed limitations, stating that liability may exist "only where the failure to train amounts to deliberate indifference to the rights of persons with whom the police come into contact."[13] The case is excerpted in **Supplement 4.3**.

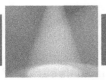

In recent years, law enforcement officers have adopted and increased their usage of improved equipment and technology, including conducted energy weapons (CEWs) (Tasers and stun guns). These changes, which reflect significant changes in law enforcement, are highlighted in Spotlight 4.1.

Some academic experts on policing are emphasizing that police training must go beyond its main focus today, which is law-related, and "focus on the scientific principles or evidence that might support practice." This would include training officers how to "understand, interpret, deploy, and develop evidence-based practice" in which police would be able to utilize sound, statistically scientific research as it applies to the problems they face.[14]

Finally, there is some recent research evidence on police training that suggests officers who were randomly assigned to training, as compared to those who were not, "were as engaged in the community . . . but they were less likely to resolve incidents with an arrest or to be involved in incidents where force was used." The investigators found this result to be most likely when officers were working in low risk areas.[15]

POLICE DISCRETION

Chapter 1 included a discussion of discretion and noted that wide discretion exists in criminal justice systems. That discretion is extreme but critical in policing. Police have wide discretion in determining whether to begin the formal processing through criminal justice systems. When they see a person who appears to be violating the law, police may refuse to acknowledge that action. Or they may investigate the situation and decide that they do not have sufficient reason to think that a crime has been committed. They might also decide that a crime has been committed but not by that suspect, or that the suspect may have committed the crime but for some reason should not be arrested.

How the officer exercises discretion may be influenced by several factors. Consider this hypothetical scenario: A police officer, while out on patrol at midnight on a Friday night, observed a car weaving down the highway, going five miles over the speed limit. The officer turned on the police car siren and lights and directed the driver to stop. After checking the operator's driver's license, the officer inquired where the person was going and why she was speeding. The driver replied that she did not realize she was speeding but that she was in a hurry to get home because a contact lens was causing pain. Something apparently had flown into her eye and blurred her vision temporarily. She considered it unsafe for a woman alone to stop by the side of a highway late at night, and she was attempting to get to her home only a mile away.

When asked where she had been, the driver replied that she was an A student in a criminal justice program and had been at a friend's house, studying, since the library closed at 11 P.M. When asked whether she had been drinking, the driver replied that she had consumed one beer. The driver answered all questions politely and nondefensively.

What would you do if you were the police officer? Would you ticket the driver for speeding? Would you believe her response about the contact lens? Would you believe what she told you about drinking only one beer? Would it make any difference in your decision if you had stopped her at 3 A.M. rather than at midnight? You could give the driver a verbal warning and let her go. You could give her a speeding ticket. If you had sufficient reason to think that she had been drinking to the point that she was legally impaired, you could ask her to get out of the car and perform some simple tests. Or you might arrest her and take her to the police station to begin official processing through the criminal justice system.

Now, think about the results of your decision. If the driver is telling the truth and you decide to arrest her, what have you accomplished by your action? Is it not possible that the negative effect of the arrest and subsequent experiences she has in the criminal justice system will outweigh any benefit that society would get from this arrest? On the other hand, if she has been drinking excessively, is it not possible that an arrest might have avoided an accident and would cause the driver to think before she gets into a car again after drinking? Or will it have no effect on her behavior? What about the behavior of her friends and other persons, who will certainly hear about your actions?

Perhaps by now you have decided what action you would take. Let's add more facts to the scenario. Suppose that, when you begin to talk to the driver, she curses you and tells you to mind your own business. Would this affect your decision to write a speeding ticket or give her roadside tests for intoxication?

Police must make decisions such as these daily. Selective enforcement of laws is necessary because our systems cannot process all cases of law violations, even if we choose to do so. Police discretion is important because police are the primary persons responsible for the initial entry of a suspect into criminal justice systems. The necessity to exercise discretion, often without adequate guidelines, puts tremendous pressure on police. That pressure is significantly enhanced when the officer decides that violent force is required by the situation.

In recent years, attention has been given to the need to prepare police for the appropriate use of discretion. The need for guidelines is recognized, although there is no agreement on what those guidelines should be or which agency should formulate them. Legislatures enact statutes for general guidance and delegate to police departments, as administrative agencies, the power to develop more specific rules. Courts have the responsibility for interpreting the guidelines, statutes, and policies in terms of state and federal constitutions.

Numerous studies of police discretion and the factors involved in police decision making have been published. The vast research was summarized and analyzed in an article by a researcher who articulated four categories of variables researched: organization variables, neighborhood variables, situational variables, and officer characteristics. *Organization variables* included the way in which the department is organized, the rotation shifts, the size of the department, the nature of its specialty units, and the degree of its professionalism. *Neighborhood variables* included the racial and socioeconomic composition of the population and the crime rate. *Situational variables* included the race, gender, and socioeconomic characteristics of the suspects and of the alleged victims, along with their demeanor and attitudes. The characteristics of the encounter, such as the seriousness of the offense, may also be a factor. *Officer characteristics* included the officer's race, gender, attitudes, extent and type of experience, and education. The researcher concluded that all four of these variables may be influential in police decision making and that further research is needed.[16]

The key, however, is that although police may use many reasons for making decisions, they may *not* use *extralegal* rather than legal factors to decide whether to stop, arrest, or take other actions.

POLICE FUNCTIONS

Although in the popular image police may spend most of their time apprehending and arresting criminals, these functions constitute a very small, albeit significant, part of the daily lives of police officers. Police also perform a variety of functions not directly related to law enforcement. These functions have been categorized as *order maintenance* and *community service*, which we will discuss prior to our analysis of law enforcement.

There appears to be agreement that law enforcement, order maintenance, and community service are the three basic areas of police functions, but there is no agreement on whether they *should* be. Nor is there agreement on how police time and resources should be allocated among the three areas. It is clear, however, that the areas are not discrete; there is considerable overlap. Attention to an order maintenance problem or provision of a particular service may prevent a situation from escalating into criminal behavior. Engaging in order maintenance functions and services may alert the police to criminal law violations. Finally, police are expected to prevent crime, and that may occur while they are performing any of their three main functions.

Before we analyze police functions in more detail, it is important to emphasize that all police functions may involve an enormous amount of paperwork, which consumes considerable police time, a fact rarely mentioned in discussions on policing. Policing recruits may have no concept of the incredible detail that will be required in filing reports. Other professions also require significant time spent in paperwork, but with policing, this work is particularly important because any errors may result in the reduction of charges, dropping of cases, or excluding evidence from trial. The defendant may be acquitted, or civil actions may be brought against the police. Reports must be filed immediately to preserve accuracy, and police rarely have access to sufficient staff assistance in writing and filing their reports.

Order Maintenance

Police are charged with maintaining order. James Q. Wilson, a noted authority on the subject, defined *order* as the absence of disorder, by which he meant behavior that tends to disrupt the peace and tranquility of the public or that involves serious face-to-face conflict between two or more persons. Wilson believed that the key to order maintenance is the management of conflict situations to bring about consensual resolution. In his view, order maintenance is the primary police function, and it is important because police encounter more problems in this area than in community service or law enforcement (with the exception of traffic violations). Wilson considered order maintenance more important than law enforcement for several reasons.[17]

First, many police departments receive more calls for help in order maintenance than in law enforcement. Some of these complaints result in arrests, but most do not. Police may be called to quiet down noisy neighbors or to intervene in disputes between friends and associates who cannot solve their differences and who appear to be on the brink of fighting. Public drunks wandering around the city alarm some people, who call the police to handle the situation. Some of these activities violate local ordinances, but many of the situations involve activities that are not criminal, although they may be obnoxious to those who call the police.

Order maintenance is an important police function for a second reason. Maintaining order may subject the police and others to physical danger. A large protest group may turn into a riot. Some domestic disputes lead to violence between the participants or against the police, and many domestic problems occur late at night, when other resources and personnel are not available to the complainant.

Washington, D.C., U.S.A., March 24, 2018. Thousands of students and supporters gather along Pennsylvania Avenue to rally against and protest school gun violence.

A third reason listed by Wilson as underscoring the importance of order maintenance is that, in this area, police exercise

> substantial discretion over matters of the greatest importance (public and private morality, honor and dishonor, life and death) in a situation that is, by definition, one of conflict and in an environment that is apprehensive and perhaps hostile.[18]

George L. Kelling analyzed order maintenance in the context of earlier policing reforms. He found that, as professionalism in policing was emphasized, the evaluation of individual police and of police departments focused on tangibles, such as arrests and quick response times of police to citizen calls. Police departments did not recognize or reward police behavior that did not lead to arrests. Police concentrated on crime prevention, arrests, and apprehension of criminals, thus emphasizing law enforcement over order maintenance or provision of services. This approach, said Kelling, decreased police corruption and improved the internal management of policing, but it resulted in less emphasis on order maintenance.[19]

Kelling argued that the focus on law enforcement had not lowered crime rates significantly but that a decreased involvement of police in order maintenance had negative effects. His position was that increased police attention to order maintenance improves relationships between the police and the community, which results in greater cooperation of citizens with the police. Citizen fear of crime is reduced, community support of the police is improved, police feel less isolated from the community, and crime detection and prevention increase.[20] Kelling, along with Wilson, advocated a significant enlargement in the time allocated to order maintenance in policing. Neither believed this approach would endanger law enforcement.[21]

The Kelling and Wilson position was challenged by Carl B. Klockars, who argued that American police maintain "an extraordinarily strong crime-fighting mandate," seen by them and by others as the primary police mission. To reduce that emphasis by increasing resources for order maintenance is undesirable. It would not reduce crime significantly because the police do not have control over most factors that produce crime. The financial cost would be much greater and would be at the sacrifice of a reduction in the number of calls for service to which police could respond quickly.

Klockars suggested that one solution might be to use foot patrols in high-density areas, particularly business areas. The increased costs might be financed partially by voluntary, tax deductible contributions by businesspeople, who stand to gain the most from the increased presence of police in the area. The problem with that suggestion, warned Klockars, was that one study of a foot patrol experiment in Newark disclosed that commercial residents perceived "a deterioration in their neighborhoods: more activity on the street, more crime-related problems, reduced safety, more victimization, poorer police service, and greater use of protective devices." Klockars was not arguing against order maintenance but only against an extended and more systematic and costly approach, which would require significant changes in the administrative structure of police departments.[22]

Two types of situations illustrate the importance of police involvement in order maintenance. The first concerns police monitoring and intervention, when necessary, of college and university sporting or campus events. Many of these events are "traditional," and if police know in advance what is expected to happen, they can be in a position to prevent riots and injuries. Police must understand what can be expected. For example, only a few students become disorderly; thus, to avoid escalating the situation, police should learn to distinguish between those students who are only observers and those who are preparing to become involved in violence. To avoid so-called party riots, police might require students to obtain permits when they plan to host a large gathering. This enables police to know when such a gathering is planned and to set conditions, such as limits on how many may attend, minimum standards regarding the event, and limits regarding alcohol consumption. "These restrictions can lessen the likelihood of a disturbance, as well as hold the hosts responsible for any negative outcomes."[23]

A second area in which police might maintain order is in assisting offenders with their reentry into society. A study by the Urban Institute's Justice Policy Center referred to police as the "eyes and ears on the street." According to this report, "the primary mission of law enforcement is to maintain peace and order and provide for a safe environment." When offenders leave incarceration and return to the community, residents are, realistically, fearful that additional crimes may be committed. Making contact with these offenders is part of policing, so it is natural that police should be involved in offenders' reentry into society.[24]

Still another issue in maintaining order in communities relates to the role of minorities both as occupants of the community and as police officers. In recent years, order maintenance policing has been criticized as racially discriminatory and procedurally unjust.[25] This has led to bitter controversies and confrontations between minorities and police, and on December 18, 2014, President Barack Obama issued an executive order appointing the President's Task Force on 21st Century Policing. Spotlight 4.2 contains comments from the conclusion of that 11-member commission.

Community Service

In addition to law enforcement and order maintenance, police perform a variety of other services for the community. Wilson maintained that community services (such as getting cats out of trees) are expected of police as a result of historical accident and convenience, that there is no good reason for police to perform these services, and that the services should "be priced and sold on the market."[26]

Removal of unnecessary community service does not mean that the police should not continue to be involved in community services either directly or indirectly related to crime prevention or order maintenance. For example, many police departments provide the equipment and officers to visit community groups and individual homes to assist residents in marking their possessions so that stolen items may be identified more quickly and easily. Officers give talks on crime prevention, emphasizing to residents what they can do to diminish the possibility that they will become crime victims. Educating women on rape prevention is a frequent topic of these sessions. Visiting with schoolchildren to educate them in crime prevention is another type of police community service.

One way to solve police time commitment problems is to train and assign special officers for community service. Community service officers generally have less training, less education, and lower salaries than other officers. The community service program, however, provides career opportunities for qualified young people who cannot or do not wish to fulfill all of the training required of police officers.

LAW ENFORCEMENT

The third major area of police functions is law enforcement. Police are empowered to detect and prevent crime, even if doing so means using force, although there are limitations on the force that may be used. The ability of police to handle crime is limited, however, and they are dependent on citizens for assistance, which may not always be forthcoming.

The law enforcement function of policing cannot be understood adequately except in the context of the legal requirements that police must observe while performing this aspect of their jobs. The legal right to use coercive force to intervene in the daily lives of people is a tremendous police power, and it cannot be unrestricted.

Chapter 1 discussed the constitutional concepts of due process and equal protection. This chapter considers the application of those constitutional rights to the police functions of stopping and questioning a suspect; arresting and conducting searches of a suspect's home, vehicle, or person; and the practices of custodial interrogation and initial investigation. The discussion begins with a brief look at traffic control, an area of law enforcement in which many police officers engage and one that may lead to the detection of serious crimes.

Traffic Control and the Enforcement of Traffic Laws

Traffic control is an important aspect of law enforcement. Police enforce state and local ordinances governing the operation of motor vehicles. This function includes enforcing requirements that vehicles be licensed and inspected, as well as ticketing motorists who commit moving violations. Normally, violations of this type

Spotlight 4.2

Highlights of President Barack Obama's Task Force on 21st Century Policing

The Task Force on 21st Century Policing, appointed by President Barack Obama in December 2014, presented its final report in May 2015. The 11-member commission was charged with researching and reaching conclusions regarding the best policies and practices for reducing crime while building public trust in policing. The lengthy report was built around six main topic areas, which it referred to as "pillars." Those pillars are enumerated below. The commission also recommended that the president create a National Crime and Justice Task Force to "examine all areas of criminal justice" and that the administration should support a study of poverty, education, and health and safety.[1]

Pillar One: Building Trust and Legitimacy

There is evidence that people are more likely to comply with laws when they believe those laws are just and are administered fairly. Specifically, "[l]aw enforcement culture should embrace a guardian—rather than a warrior—mindset to build trust and legitimacy both within agencies and with the public. Toward that end, law enforcement agencies should adopt procedural justice as the guiding principle for internal and external policies and practices to guide their interactions with rank and file officers and with the citizens they serve." The commission emphasized the need for diversity in race, gender, language, life experience, and cultural backgrounds in law enforcement agencies.

Pillar Two: Policy and Oversight

All police policies and especially those concerning the use of force, handling of mass demonstrations, relationships with races, investigations of officer-involved use of force should be carefully developed in collaboration with members of the community and specifically articulated to them. The policies should be reviewed and updated as needed. Federal agencies should provide technical training as needed.

Pillar Three: Technology and Social Media

Technology and social media should be used to assist in police practices, but their use should be clearly delineated and articulated as well as updated when necessary. National standards should be established and model policies developed.

Pillar Four: Community Policing and Crime Reduction

The community should be involved in the management of public safety, and police should work with community individuals to establish team approaches for solving problems. "Communities should support a culture and practice of policing that reflects the values of protection and promotion of the dignity of all."

Pillar Five: Training and Education

Training and education are important for effective policing, and the perspectives of members of the community should be utilized in these processes, which should reflect important changes such as those involving "terrorism, evolving technologies, rising immigration, changing laws, new cultural mores, and a growing mental health crisis." Federal agencies should assist in making this possible.

Pillar Six: Officer Wellness and Safety

Wellness and safety of law enforcement officers is important to them and to the public, and should specifically include proper shift lengths and accurate collection and assessment of data on officer deaths and "near misses." This pillar includes such policies as requirements that officers wear seat belts and proper bullet proof vests, etc.

The Commission also made recommendations for the implementations of the above, all of which are discussed in more detail in the lengthy report.

Source: Executive Summary, *Final Report of the President's Task Force on 21st Century Policing* (May 2015), pp. 1-2, http://www.theiacp.org/TaskForceReport, accessed August 31, 2018.

involve a simple procedure in which the police officer signs a statement noting the violation and gives a copy to the driver, explaining that the ticket, if unchallenged, may be handled by mail or in person at the police station. Court appearances are not required unless the motorist challenges the ticket, and most do not. The officer may decide not to issue a ticket; a verbal or written warning may be given instead.

Police play a critical role in traffic control, a job they may perform on foot, on motorcycle, or on horseback as well as by automobile.

The enforcement of statutes and ordinances designed to regulate the flow of traffic and to create safe conditions for drivers and pedestrians is also an important police function. Driving with excessive speed on any street or highway, speeding in school zones or failing to stop for school buses, and driving under the influence of alcohol or other drugs are dangerous activities. Furthermore, the apprehension of people who violate traffic ordinances may lead to disorder and violence during arrest. Thus, it is important that trained police officers be in charge of such apprehensions, which may lead police to evidence of criminal activity, such as stolen automobiles, violations of substance abuse laws, burglaries, and other crimes, as well as encountering escaped felons and wanted persons.

Some aspects of police discretion concerning moving violations have, however, been questioned. One example is the stopping of drivers who are not wearing seat belts in jurisdictions in which a statute requires drivers and passengers to wear them. A controversial case involving this issue occurred in Texas, which permitted police to stop and arrest drivers who were not buckled up (a misdemeanor in that state), in contrast to some jurisdictions that permit a stop and arrest for failure to wear a seat belt *only* if the driver has committed a moving violation. The case of *Atwater v. City of Lago Vista* is discussed in **Supplement 4.4**.

The Investigatory Stop

Traffic control obviously involves an investigatory stop. The problems often arise when police make a **pretextual stop** (a stop allegedly for a minor traffic offense but actually conducted as a pretense to look for a more serious offense, such as the possession of illegal drugs). The key case on this issue, *Whren v. United States*, was decided in 1996. The U.S. Supreme Court held that an officer who is suspicious of the behavior of the occupants of a motor vehicle but does not have grounds for stopping them may do so when a traffic violation occurs. That stop may then be used to pursue the other suspicions of illegal acts.[27] The facts of the case are noted in **Supplement 4.5**.

The U.S. Supreme Court has also held that during a routine traffic stop police may order all passengers (as well as the driver) to exit the vehicle without any reason to suspect them of wrongdoing.[28] But when police make a questionable stop of a vehicle, all persons in that vehicle have the same right as the driver to challenge the stop.[29]

Another issue arises when, in stopping motorists, police take actions that are not based on individualized suspicion. According to the U.S. Supreme Court, when this allegedly occurs, the officer's *purpose* in making the stop should be considered in deciding whether the police action was legitimate. The Court distinguished between stopping all motorists to detect illegal drugs, which it held was not permitted, and making suspicionless stops of drivers for alcohol violations, which is permitted. Two cases are briefly discussed in **Supplement 4.6**.

Profiling

A critical issue in the investigatory stop as well as in other criminal justice issues is racial profiling. In the area of traffic and other stops, police have been accused of engaging in pretextual stops based on racial profiling, in which persons are stopped for traffic violations by police who have stereotyped them as more serious law violators because of their race or ethnicity. Such traffic stops of African Americans are referred to by some as *driving while black*.[30] They are, of course, unconstitutional. Race as a reason for stopping a driver is permitted only if it is relevant to a description of a crime suspect for whom the police are looking. When racial profiling is alleged, the U.S. Department of Justice (DOJ) may investigate and, if sufficient evidence is found to support the allegations, implement orders or enter into consent decrees. An illustrative case from 1998 in New Jersey is discussed in **Supplement 4.7**, along with other issues concerning racial profiling. **Supplement 4.8** contains highlights of a study of police behavior during stops, and **Supplement 4.9** contains a brief discussion and excerpts from a key U.S. Supreme Court decision concerning stopping a black jogger: *Kolender et al. v. Lawson.*

Social scientists have conducted extensive research on racial profiling, as illustrated by the December 2017 (34, 7) issue of *Justice Quarterly*, published by the Academy of Criminal Justice Sciences. The entire volume is devoted to policing and minority communities.

More recent research and investigations by federal agencies and others have provided evidence of racial profiling in areas other than stops. In particular, the U.S. Department of Justice (DOJ) issued a report in August 2016 of its findings on policing in Baltimore. According to that report:

> Racially disparate impact is present at every stage of BPD's enforcement actions, from the initial decision to stop individuals . . . to searchers, arrests, and uses of force. . . . These racial disparities, along with evidence suggesting intentional discrimination, erode the community trust that is critical to policing.[31]

The Baltimore Police Department signed a 227-page oversight agreement with the DOJ in January 2017, just two years after Freddie Gray, a 25-year-old black suspect, died in police custody, leading to allegations of racial discrimination and charges against six officers, none of whom were convicted. In April 2017, a federal judge accepted the consent agreement.[32] The City of Baltimore settled a civil suit with Gray's family for $6.4 million.

In another recent investigation, in January 2017, the DOJ issued a scathing report concerning the Chicago Police Department. The DOJ concluded that "excessive force was rampant, rarely challenged, and chiefly aimed at African-Americans and Latinos."[33]

There is some evidence that might be described as reverse racial profiling in that in areas occupied primarily by racial minorities, police are more likely to search white suspects than black suspects. This could be due to police deciding that whites should not be in that area; thus, they must be doing something wrong. This practice could be referred to as "out-of-place" policing.[34] In addition, some researchers have reported findings that despite "clear evidence of implicit bias against Black suspects," police are more likely to use force against whites than against blacks in that officers were slower to shoot black compared to white suspects, but that study was based on laboratory findings.[35] Nevertheless, "[w]e need to move beyond the post-Ferguson atmosphere where all use of force against a racial/ethnic minority person is considered biased and unreasonable until proven otherwise."[36]

Clearly, not all researchers agree on the existence of racial profiling,[37] but that may not be as important as the *perceptions* of minorities regarding police that may influence their reactions to police and the feelings that they and others have of discrimination against minorities, especially blacks. Considerable research shows that the cumulative negative experiences of young black men with police influence their perceptions of the police.[38]

Regardless of the reality of racial profiling and action by the police, people's perceptions are important, and it is not unreasonable to think that when people witness a police shooting in person, through the mass media, or on social media, they may conclude that the shooting was unjustified. Thus, the development of movements such as "Black Lives Matter" should not be a surprise.

Research by criminologists suggests that police can do something about perceptions of racial profiling. Police can offer legitimate reasons for stops. "Several studies have shown that citizens, and blacks especially, are much more likely to cooperate with officers when they are given a reason for the stop, and that people put a premium on officers being polite, listening to citizens, and explaining their actions." It is also possible that if officers are required to explain to motorists why they were stopped, police officers might be less likely to engage in racial profiling.[39]

The U.S. Supreme Court looked at the issue of giving police too much discretion in stops, even those involving nontraffic situations. **Supplement 4.9** discusses *Kolender et al. v. Lawson*, which illustrates police abuse of the discretion to stop and question a suspect. For several reasons, this case is very important despite the fact that it was decided in 1983. First, it is still good law. Second, it was decided by the U.S. Supreme Court. Third, it stands against the recent decisions, discussed earlier, in which the Supreme Court has refused to restrict police in stopping and searching, especially in the area of traffic control. Finally, it is argued by some that the stops in *Lawson* represented a case of racial bias, which is not permitted.

The *Lawson* case makes it clear that police may not use a vague statute for purposes of stopping, questioning, and otherwise harassing individuals. But the case also makes it clear that police may stop and question individuals. How can police tell when they can go beyond initial questioning and make an arrest, or, as the next section discusses, frisk?

Finally, gender profiling is also prohibited although there is some evidence that police are more likely to stop men than women.[40]

Stop and Frisk

The police may be notified or they may observe a situation that gives them a reasonable basis for stopping a pedestrian or a driver. At this initial stop, police have wide discretion provided they do not use extralegal reasons, such as race or ethnicity, for making that stop. They can decide not to make the stop. They can stop but not arrest the suspect. They can release the suspect with a verbal or written warning. The police must make important judgment calls at the stage of stopping and questioning suspects, for it would be an inefficient use of police time and a violation of suspects' constitutional rights for police to stop persons when there is no probable cause to believe they are violating the law.

Some discretion must be allowed the police officer who, based on experience, perceives that a crime might have been committed and that the suspect may be armed, thus constituting a threat to the life or health of the officer or others. It is permissible for the police to conduct pat down searches, or **frisk** the suspect in some cases, as illustrated by the following example, a key case in constitutional law.

In *Terry v. Ohio*, Detective Martin McFadden of the Cleveland, Ohio, police department noticed two men standing on a street corner in front of several stores. The men made many trips up and down the street, peering into store windows. They talked to a third man, whom they followed up the street after his departure. McFadden, who had 39 years of experience as a police officer, suspected that the men were casing the stores for a robbery. He approached the men, identified himself as a police officer, and asked their names. The men mumbled responses, at which point the detective spun one of the men, Terry, around and patted his breast pocket. Officer McFadden removed the pistol that he felt and then frisked the second man, on whom he also found a pistol. The third man was frisked but did not have a weapon.[41]

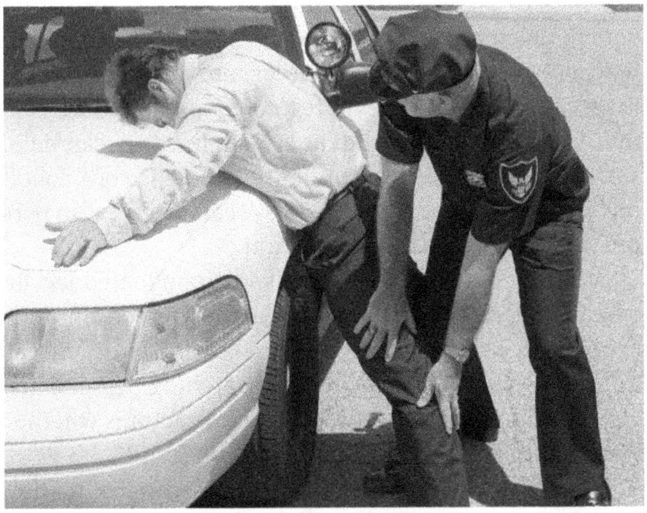

Wide discretion is permitted law enforcement officers in their initial encounter with suspects. Officers may pat down the suspects for weapons, but, in most cases, a warrant is required for a more thorough search.

In *Terry*, the U.S. Supreme Court emphasized that even brief detention of a person without probable cause for an arrest is a seizure of that person. These stops constitute a serious intrusion that can lead to strong resentment. But police officers are injured and killed in the line of duty. They cannot be expected to take unreasonable risks; thus, they may conduct a search that is limited in time and scope.

In *Terry*, the U.S. Supreme Court looked at the totality of the circumstances, holding that if, during the pat down search, the police feel an object that might be a weapon, they may continue the search until they are satisfied that it is not a weapon. The Supreme Court did not, however, answer the question of whether they could seize a **contraband** item that is not a weapon. In 1993, the Supreme Court decided that issue. In *Minnesota v. Dickerson*, the Court held that if during a *Terry* search and before an officer has concluded that the suspect is not armed, the officer feels an item "whose contour or mass makes its identity immediately apparent," that item may be seized without a warrant. The discovery of the contraband would not constitute any greater invasion of privacy than had occurred during the permissible weapons search and thus is acceptable. The Supreme Court referred to this as the *plain feel* doctrine. But officers may not go beyond the permissible scope of the weapons search to examine the item suspected of being contraband but not a weapon.[42]

The totality of the circumstances rule articulated by the U.S. Supreme Court in the *Terry* case was emphasized again in 2002 when the Court, in *United States v. Arvizu*, upheld a border patrol agent's search. The case is discussed in **Supplement 4.10**.[43]

Law enforcement officers might also have reason to stop a motorist if the driver takes flight, as illustrated by the unanimous opinion of the U.S. Supreme Court in *Illinois v. Wardlow*,[44] discussed briefly in **Supplement 4.11**. A more recent case interprets the *Terry* holding concerning pat downs based on less than probable cause even more extensively. In *Arizona v. Johnson*, Lemon Montrea Johnson was a passenger (and one of three men) in a car stopped by three officers who were members of a gang task force. The car was stopped after the officers ran a check and found that the vehicle's registration had been suspended as the result of an insurance violation. After the vehicle was stopped, each officer dealt with one of the three passengers. The officer talking to Johnson noted that he was dressed in clothing similar to that worn by members of the Crips gang. The officer also noted that Johnson had a police radio scanner, which she interpreted as unusual as these scanners are often associated with involvement in criminal activity. Upon questioning,

Johnson said he was from Eloy, Arizona, which the officer knew was the location of a Crips gang. The officer asked Johnson to exit the vehicle for further questioning, at which point she was suspicious that he had a gun. She then patted him down, felt a gun, and handcuffed him. The U.S. Supreme Court upheld the pat down search based on *Terry*, stating that two conditions must occur before such searches do not constitute an unreasonable search and seizure. First, the initial stop must be lawful, and second, to conduct a frisk, the officer must have reason to believe that the suspect is armed and dangerous. The Supreme Court's decision was unanimous.[45]

Arrest, Search, and Seizure

The process of stopping and questioning suspects may lead to a **search and seizure** or **arrest**, both of which are crucial steps in criminal justice proceedings. A clear understanding of these processes requires a brief introduction to the Fourth Amendment of the U.S. Constitution. That amendment prohibits *unreasonable* searches and seizures (see Appendix A). This provision of the U.S. Constitution is pertinent to our discussion because, under some circumstances, stopping and arresting a person may constitute a seizure of the person and therefore must follow proper procedures or be ruled unreasonable by the courts.

Warrants and Probable Cause

With some exceptions, arrests and searches may not be made until the police secure a **warrant**. A 1948 decision emphasized the purpose of the **search warrant**, but the principle also applies to arrests. According to the U.S. Supreme Court:

> The point of the Fourth Amendment, which often is not grasped by zealous officers, is not that it denies law enforcement the support of the usual inferences which reasonable men draw from evidence. Its protection consists in requiring that those inferences be drawn by a neutral and detached magistrate instead of being judged by the officer engaged in the often competitive enterprise of ferreting out crime.... When the right of privacy must reasonably yield to the right of search is, as a rule, to be decided by a judicial officer, not by a policeman or government enforcement agent.[46]

The U.S. Supreme Court emphasized the importance of search warrants in two recent cases involving searching cell phones and cell phone records. Those cases were discussed and excerpted in **Supplements 1.4** and **1.5** and should be reviewed here.

The Fourth Amendment requires that a warrant shall not be issued except upon a finding of **probable cause**. Facts sufficient to lead a reasonable person to conclude that a crime has been committed by an identifiable person or that a particular kind of contraband may be found at a specified location may be secured in various ways, such as from an **informant**, who may even have a criminal history known to the police. The U.S. Supreme Court has established rules that must be followed when police secure information from known informants. There must be underlying circumstances that would lead a reasonable person to conclude that the informant is reliable and credible in what he or she is saying, and there must be underlying circumstances that provide a basis for the conclusions drawn by the informant. If the informant is a police officer, credibility might not be questioned, although it is necessary to show why that person has reason to have such information. When the informant is a known or suspected criminal, as is frequently the case, establishing credibility is more difficult. Two cases, *Illinois v. Gates*[47] and *Florida v. J.L.*,[48] illustrate fact patterns that were or were not sufficient to establish probable cause. They are discussed in **Supplement 4.12**.

Some searches and seizures are permissible without a warrant, probable cause, or consent. One exception to the warrant requirement is a search that occurs when an officer makes a lawful arrest. The U.S. Supreme Court has emphasized, however, that the right to search the person without a search warrant or the suspect's consent—even when the arrest is proper—is a limited privilege.

After an arrest, some warrantless searches, such as searches of possessions (inventory searches) or of the person when the suspect is booked into jail, are proper. Routine searches at the border are also permitted. Inspections and searches of regulated industries are permitted, too, as are searches at certain fixed checkpoints, such as checks for drivers under the influence of alcohol. As Spotlight 4.3 notes, warrantless searches are also permissible under exigent circumstances.

Warrantless searches may also be conducted legally when a person consents to the search. This consent may be given prior to arrest, at the time of arrest, or later at the police station. It may involve searching possessions, vehicles, homes, or persons. The critical factor is whether the consent is made knowingly and voluntarily.

An arrest without a warrant is a serious matter, and the U.S. Supreme Court has placed restrictions on this procedure. Persons arrested without a warrant are entitled to a prompt judicial determination of whether

Spotlight 4.3

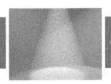

Exigent Circumstances and Warrantless Searches

Police are permitted to conduct warrantless searches in limited cases, including those with exigent circumstances. In a 1994 California case, the court refused to suppress evidence seized in a warrantless search of a home by police, who were responding to an anonymous call concerning domestic violence. Police were greeted at the door by a woman who said she was alone and safe. But police saw a man in the house, and the woman appeared to have been hit recently. The woman told police she had just fallen down the stairs.

Police entered the home and seized the illegal drugs that were in plain view. The California court held that the officers entered the home under exigent circumstances. They knew that the woman had lied about being alone, and they had reason to suspect she had been hit recently, perhaps by the man they saw in the home. For her protection, they had a right to enter. While they were in the home legally, police were justified in seizing illegal drugs that were in plain view.[1]

---

1. *People (California) v. Higgins*, 26 Cal. App. 4th 247 (4th Dist. 1994), *review denied*, 1994 Cal. LEXIS 5620 (Cal. Oct. 13, 1994).

probable cause existed. The Court has interpreted *prompt* to mean 48 hours under most circumstances. If a weekend is involved and the judicial hearing for a determination of probable cause will not be held within 48 hours, the state has the burden of showing that the delay beyond that period was reasonable.[49]

One general issue regarding search and seizure that should be noted before we go into specific areas for searches is that of the anticipatory search. In 2006, the U.S. Supreme Court upheld the constitutionality of an **anticipatory search warrant**, referring to a warrant that is issued for a search at a particular place at a particular time in the future. The case of *United States v. Grubbs* involved a defendant, Jeffrey Grubbs, who purchased from a website a videotape containing child pornography. The website was operated by an undercover postal inspector. On the basis of these facts and an affidavit that the videotape would be delivered to Grubbs' home at a controlled time and that the warrant would not be executed until the package had been delivered and taken into the home, federal agents secured a search warrant. That warrant contained two attachments describing what the authorities expected to find, along with the location of the home. The attachments but not the affidavit were included in the body of the warrant. The package was delivered to Grubbs' home, where his wife signed for it and took it into the house. A few minutes later, when Grubbs left the home, he was detained by federal agents, who then entered the home and began the search. Grubbs was given the search warrant, which contained the attachments but not the affidavit. Grubbs admitted that he had the tape. At trial, he filed a motion to suppress the videotape because the search warrant did not contain the affidavit stating the triggering events and was thus defective. His motion was denied. Grubbs then entered a guilty plea but reserved his right to appeal.[50]

Grubbs argued that anticipatory search warrants are not constitutional because they violate the requirement that warrants must be issued only upon probable cause. So, if the police execute the warrant before the stated triggering event has occurred, they do not have reason to believe the items in question are at the searched place; thus, they have no probable cause. The Court rejected this position and stated in part: "Because the probable cause requirement looks to whether evidence will be found when the search is conducted, all warrants are, in a sense, 'anticipatory.'"[51]

Home Searches

The U.S. Supreme Court has said that the "physical entry of the home is the chief evil against which the wording of the Fourth Amendment is directed."[52] The Supreme Court recognizes a difference between searches and seizures within a home or an office and the search of a person's property in other places.

An example of an unreasonable entry into and search inside of a home occurred in *Mapp v. Ohio*. Police had received information that a person wanted for questioning in a bombing was hiding out in a two-family dwelling. Mapp and her daughter by a previous marriage lived on the top floor of the home. When police arrived at the home and knocked on the door, Mapp called her attorney and then denied entrance to the officers without a warrant. The police advised their headquarters of that response and put the house under surveillance. About three hours later, with more officers on the scene, police attempted entry again. When Mapp did not come to the door quickly, the officers forced their way into the house. Mapp's attorney arrived, but the police would not let him enter the house or see Mapp.[53]

Mapp demanded to see a search warrant. The officers produced a paper they claimed to be a search warrant. Mapp grabbed that paper (which was not a warrant) and tucked it into her bosom. The officers retrieved the paper and handcuffed Mapp for being belligerent. Mapp complained that the officers were hurting her. The officers took the complaining and handcuffed suspect to her bedroom, where they conducted a search. They searched other rooms as well and found obscene materials in a basement trunk.

The seized evidence was used against Mapp at trial, and she was convicted of "knowingly having had in her possession and under her control certain lewd and lascivious books, pictures, and photographs." The U.S. Supreme Court ruled that the evidence seized in Mapp's home could not be used against her in a state trial. The Court referred to the seizure as a "flagrant abuse" of the "constitutional . . . right to privacy free from unreasonable state intrusion."[54]

Even if police have a right to search a home, there is an issue of the permissible *scope* of that search. Several factors must be considered. In *Chimel v. California*, police officers searched a house thoroughly after they entered with an arrest warrant but without a search warrant. The U.S. Supreme Court reversed the defendant's conviction and limited the areas that may be searched for weapons, if necessary, to protect the life of the officer and others. The suspect may also be searched to the extent necessary to prevent the destruction of evidence. The officer may search the area "within the immediate control" of the arrestee, such as a gun lying on a table near the suspect.[55]

In 1971, the U.S. Supreme Court held that police may seize evidence without a warrant while they are within the home to execute a lawful arrest, provided that the evidence is in plain view.[56] In 1987, the Court held that probable cause is required to invoke the **plain view doctrine**.[57]

In 1990, the U.S. Supreme Court held that an officer who is executing an arrest warrant within a private dwelling may search rooms other than the one in which the arrest is made. The Court called this a *protective sweep* search, but there are limitations. Although the search does not require probable cause or even reasonable suspicion, it is permitted only for the purpose of locating another person who might pose danger. Thus, the officers may "look in closets and other spaces immediately adjoining the place of arrest from which an attack could be immediately launched." To go further, the officers must have "*articulable* facts which, taken together with the rational inferences from those facts, would warrant a reasonably prudent officer in believing that the area to be swept harbors an individual posing a danger to those on the arrest scene." The Supreme Court emphasized that this warrantless search is permissible only for the protection of those present and cannot extend to a full search of the premises, "but [it] may extend only to a cursory inspection of those spaces where a person may be found." The protective sweep must be brief; it may last "no longer than is necessary to dispel the reasonable suspicion of danger and in any event no longer than it takes to complete the arrest and depart the premises."[58]

The U.S. Supreme Court has elaborated on the scope of the lawful search of a home's **curtilage**. The Court has held that a barn 60 yards from a house and outside the area surrounding the house enclosed by a fence is not part of the curtilage. The Court stated that

> curtilage questions should be resolved with particular reference to four factors: the proximity of the area claimed to be curtilage to the home, whether the area is included within an enclosure surrounding the home, the nature of the uses to which the area is put, and the steps taken by the resident to protect the area from observation by people passing by.[59]

The U.S. Supreme Court has ruled that the Fourth Amendment does not prohibit warrantless searches and seizures of garbage that is left outside a home's curtilage. The Court reasoned that, because the garbage is readily accessible to the public, its owner has no reasonable expectation of privacy.[60]

The U.S. Supreme Court has held that police may prevent a person outside his or her home from entering that home while police secure a search warrant, as illustrated by the Court's decision in *Illinois v. McArthur*,[61] which is discussed in **Supplement 4.13**. And in some cases, police may search a home when one occupant objects but the other consents, as illustrated by the cases of *Fernandez v. California*, decided in 2014, and *Georgia v. Randolph*, decided in 2006. These cases are discussed in **Supplement 4.14**.

Another issue concerning searches of the home is the long-standing principle of "knock and announce," meaning that police who arrive at a dwelling to search with or without a warrant must knock and announce their presence prior to entering. In 1995, the U.S. Supreme Court elevated that principle to a constitutional dimension. The rule may be relaxed under exigent circumstances, such as if there is reason to believe the evidence sought will be destroyed or if the suspects are armed and dangerous. The Court left it to lower courts to devise rules under which the knock-and-announce rule could be waived.[62]

In 1997, in *Richards v. Wisconsin*, the U.S. Supreme Court struck down a blanket exception to the knock-and-announce rule. *Richards* involved a felony drug investigation. The lower court had held that police are never required to knock and announce before entering if they have a search warrant for a felony drug investigation, the assumption being that they already have reasonable cause to believe that exigent circumstances exist in such cases. The Supreme Court upheld the no-knock in this case because the justices considered the officers' decision not to knock and announce reasonable under the circumstances of that case. But the Court rejected the blanket rule permitting no-knock in all cases involving alleged felony drug violations. The Court held that a case-by-case analysis was required.[63]

Another case concerning home searches is one in which the U.S. Supreme Court considered the time that police must wait for forcible entry after announcing their presence and intent. In *United States v. Banks*, police arrived at an apartment to execute a search warrant for drugs. They knocked and yelled, "Police search warrant." When the resident, LaShawn L. Banks, did not answer the door within 15 to 20 seconds (he was in the shower), the police entered forcibly and found crack cocaine, three guns, and $6,000 in cash. During the oral arguments before the Supreme Court, attorneys and the justices discussed the issue of whether one should be permitted to complete a shower. The justices were not at all interested in that issue and upheld the search, although they did not answer the question of how long police should wait after knocking before entering forcibly.[64]

Another issue with regard to the search of a home without a warrant is discussed in **Supplement 4.14**, which illustrates how a recent case (2014) can limit a previous one (2006).

A final area of concern that has been considered recently is the use of drug-sniffing dogs for home searches, with the U.S. Supreme Court deciding *Florida v. Jardines* in 2013. In this case, police conducted a warrantless sniff test of the front door/porch of a home using a drug detection dog. Multiple police vehicles and law enforcement personnel arrived at the suspect's home, along with an experienced dog handler and his dog, and engaged in a vigorous search of the front porch, with the sniff test taking place in full view of anyone who happened to be in the area. According to the majority, "such a public spectacle . . . will invariably entail a degree of public opprobrium, humiliation and embarrassment for the resident . . . and will be viewed as official accusation of crime." If the police can conduct this type of search without any evidence of a crime, they can do it to anyone at any time. This, the Court ruled, is not permitted by the Fourth Amendment of the U.S. Constitution as this type of "open-ended policy invites overbearing and harassing conduct."[65]

Vehicle Searches

Some of the rules concerning warrantless vehicle searches were discussed earlier in connection with traffic violation stops, but the U.S. Supreme Court has decided a number of cases that go beyond that scenario.

In *Carroll v. United States*, the U.S. Supreme Court held that, when police stop an automobile and have probable cause to believe it contains contraband, it is not unreasonable for the officers to search that vehicle. However, the Court did not deal with the scope of that permissible search. In *Chambers v. Maroney*, the Supreme Court held that a search warrant is not necessary "where there is probable cause to search an automobile stopped on the highway; the car is moveable; the occupants are alerted; and the car's contents may never be found again if a warrant must be obtained." Each case must be judged on its facts, for the U.S. Supreme Court has made it clear that not all warrantless car searches are lawful.[66]

In 1991, the U.S. Supreme Court clarified some of the procedural problems in *Carroll*, *Maroney*, and other cases, holding that "the police may search an automobile and the containers within it where they have probable cause to believe contraband or evidence is contained."[67]

In 1981, in *Robbins v. California*, the U.S. Supreme Court held that, when police stopped the driver of a car for proceeding erratically, smelled marijuana smoke as the door was opened, searched the car, and found two packages wrapped in opaque plastic, they went beyond the scope of a legitimate search without a warrant when they opened the packages.[68] One year later, in *United States v. Ross*, the Supreme Court reconsidered its position by examining the extent to which police officers who have stopped an automobile legitimately and who have probable cause to believe that contraband is concealed somewhere within it, may conduct a probing search of compartments and containers within the vehicle if its contents are not in plain view. "We hold that they may conduct a search of the vehicle that is as thorough as a magistrate could authorize in a warrant 'particularly describing the place to be searched.'" The U.S. Supreme Court emphasized that such searches must be based on probable cause.[69]

In 1985, the U.S. Supreme Court held that a warrantless search of packages held for three days after seizure by customs officials was not unreasonable. Customs officials had been observing what appeared to be a drug-smuggling operation. They saw several packages being removed from two small airplanes, which had landed at a remote section of the airport. The packages were loaded onto two pickup trucks. The customs officers approached the trucks, smelled marijuana, and saw packages that were wrapped in plastic bags and sealed with tape. Some of the individuals were arrested, and the packages were seized and placed in a Drug Enforcement Agency (DEA) warehouse. Three days later, without a search warrant, officers opened the packages and found marijuana. In ruling that the search was proper even without a warrant, the U.S. Supreme Court held that the warrantless search of a vehicle need not occur contemporaneously with the lawful seizure of the items. The Court emphasized, however, that officers may not hold vehicles and their contents indefinitely before they complete a search.[70]

As noted earlier, in some cases, police may conduct warrantless vehicle searches. This may be done to protect them from danger, to protect the owner's property while the officers have custody of the vehicle, and to protect officers against claims that items were stolen from the vehicle while it was in police custody.[71] Furthermore, the U.S. Supreme Court held that, when a driver who was stopped for an illegal turn consented to a search of his car, police could legally examine the contents of a closed container within that car.[72]

In 2009, the U.S. Supreme Court retracted its position regarding a warrantless vehicle search incident to an arrest. *Arizona v. Gant* involved a defendant who was arrested for driving with a suspended license. The arresting officers handcuffed the suspect, placed him in a rear seat of their vehicle, and then searched his car, finding cocaine in the pocket of a jacket that was located on the back seat of that vehicle. The defendant's motion to suppress that evidence was denied by the trial court and the defendant was convicted of illegal possession of a narcotic for sale and possession of drug paraphernalia. The U.S. Supreme Court ruled that this search incident to an arrest was unconstitutional. The Court articulated two reasons for its decision. First, all three suspects were handcuffed and secured in separate police vehicles. The five police officers outnumbered the three suspects. Thus, the officers could not reasonably have believed that the suspect could get to his car to destroy evidence. Second, the officers had no reason to believe that the car contained any evidence pertaining to the reason for which the suspect was arrested as normally a car would not contain such evidence. In this ruling, the Court did not specifically overrule its 1981 decision permitting vehicle searches incident to an arrest but, rather, limited its scope, stating that the previous case had been read too broadly.[73]

The search of vehicles may also include buses. In 1991, the U.S. Supreme Court held that when police board long-distance buses and, without reasonable suspicion that anyone on those buses is smuggling drugs, ask passengers for permission to search their luggage for narcotics, they are not violating those passengers' constitutional rights per se.[74] In 2002, the U.S. Supreme Court ruled that, when police board a bus to check for drugs or for other purposes, they are not required to tell passengers that they have a right to refuse to cooperate. Reasonable people understand that they are free to leave the bus or to answer questions; thus, when the police board the bus, that action does not constitute a seizure. Three justices dissented. Among them, Justice David Souter wrote that the "officers took control of the entire passenger compartment" and that "no reasonable passenger could have believed" that he or she was free to refuse to cooperate.[75]

In 1999, the U.S. Supreme Court held that an officer who has probable cause to conduct a warrantless search of an automobile may search all containers that might hold the object of the search. This includes containers that belong to a passenger. The cases of *Wyoming v. Houghton*[76] and *Maryland v. Pringle*[77] are discussed in **Supplement 4.15**.

It is also necessary to consider the issue of whether police violate a suspect's constitutional rights when they use a drug-detecting dog to sniff a vehicle after they signal the driver to pull over in a routine traffic stop. In *Illinois v. Caballes*, police stopped Roy Caballes because he was driving 71 miles per hour in a 65-mile-per-hour zone on Interstate 80. Upon request, Caballes provided police with his driver's license, vehicle registration, and proof of insurance. Caballes was asked to join the police officer in his squad car; when he did, a warning ticket for speeding was issued. Caballes refused to grant the officer's request to search his car. The officer asked Caballes if he had ever been arrested, and he replied in the negative. But the police dispatcher informed the officer that Caballes had been arrested twice on suspicion of distributing marijuana. While the officer was writing the ticket, another officer arrived with a dog trained to sniff for drugs. The dog smelled drugs; Caballes's car was searched; marijuana was found; and Caballes was arrested for drug trafficking. The U.S. Supreme Court agreed to review the case to determine whether the Fourth Amendment (see Appendix A) prohibition against unreasonable searches and seizures requires police to have a reasonable suspicion before they use drug-sniffing dogs during a legitimate traffic stop. The Supreme Court held that a well-trained narcotics-detection dog used, as in the *Caballes* case, to sniff only the outside of the vehicle during a legitimate traffic stop, is permitted by the Fourth Amendment.[78]

In 2013, the U.S. Supreme Court unanimously upheld a dog search of a car. The issue in *Florida v. Harris* was whether, during a traffic stop, the "alert" of a dog trained in drug sniffing constitutes probable cause for the search of the vehicle. The search in this case did not locate any of the specific drugs the dog, Aldo, was trained to find, but it did result in the seizure of other drugs. In a second occurrence in which the same officer pulled over the defendant, Aldo did not alert. The trial court denied the defendant's motion to suppress the evidence obtained after Aldo's alert. The Florida Supreme Court reversed, stating that "the fact that the dog has been trained and certified is simply not enough to establish probable cause." That court wanted evidence of the dog's performance history. The U.S. Supreme Court disagreed and upheld the search, stating, in part:

> If a bona fide organization has certified a dog after testing his reliability in a controlled setting, a court can presume (subject to any conflicting evidence offered) that the dog's alert provides probable cause to search.[79]

A recent and controversial type of vehicle search involves placing a Global Positioning System (GPS) on a vehicle and using it to track the driver's movements. The U.S. Supreme Court decided *United States v. Jones*, in which officers used several techniques for investigation and secured evidence that they submitted to a judge who granted their request for a search warrant to attach a GPS device on a suspect's wife's car. The judge granted the request, and the GPS device was installed on the underneath portion of the car, from which it monitored the suspect's movements for 28 days. During that time, officers changed the battery on the GPS while the car was in a parking lot. The government's failure to comply with the terms of the warrant, however, turned the situation into a warrantless search case. Eventually, the government obtained enough evidence to secure an indictment of Jones and others for allegedly conspiring to distribute cocaine. The Supreme Court held that the situation constituted a search in that the "government physically occupied private property for the purpose of obtaining information." The Court did not decide whether the search was reasonable because that issue was not raised in the lower courts and thus could not be raised on appeal.[80]

In May of 2018, the U.S. Supreme Court decided two cases involving motor vehicles. One involved a rental car and the other a motorcycle. Those cases are summarized in Spotlight 4.4.

Person Searches

The search of a suspect's body cavities is the most controversial search and seizure issue. Some body cavity searches are permitted, but there are limitations on the type, time, place, and method of search. The classic case involving body searches was decided in 1949, when three deputy sheriffs of Los Angeles County, relying on some information that a man named Rochin was selling narcotics, went to Rochin's home and entered through an open door. The officers forced open the door of the second-floor bedroom, where they found Rochin, partially clothed, sitting on the bed where his wife was lying. The officers saw two capsules beside the bed and asked, "Whose stuff is this?" Rochin grabbed the capsules and swallowed them. The officers, applying force, tried to remove the capsules and, when they were unsuccessful, handcuffed Rochin and took him to the hospital. They ordered his stomach pumped, and the drugs were used as evidence in the subsequent trial, at which Rochin was convicted. In *Rochin v. California*, the U.S. Supreme Court stated the search by officers was unconstitutional as it constituted "conduct that shocks the conscience ... [and involved] methods too close to the rack and the screw."[81]

Some body cavity searches are permitted. For example, safety and security within jails and prisons are sufficient reasons for strip-searching inmates.[82] Body cavity searches may also be conducted at the borders into the country whenever customs officials have reason to believe a person is smuggling contraband by carrying the contraband, usually illegal drugs, therein. This crime is referred to as *alimentary canal smuggling*. Probable cause is not required for the search of body cavities in these cases; customs officials need only have a reasonable suspicion that a traveler is committing the crime of alimentary canal smuggling to conduct the search. The U.S. Supreme Court has stated that the right to privacy

Spotlight 4.4

The Supreme Court Analyzes Searches of Motor Vehicles

Near the end of its 2017-2018 term, the U.S. Supreme Court decided two cases involving searching of motor vehicles. The first, *Byrd v. United States*,[1] involved an issue of privacy when renting a car. It is no doubt rather common knowledge that when one rents a car, that car may not be operated legally by anyone whose name is not on the rental agreement, and the rental contracts so state. In this case, the woman who rented the car but did not include the names of other drivers, turned the keys over to her boyfriend, Terrence Byrd, who was the sole occupant of the car when he was arrested during a traffic stop. When the police checked the rental agreement and found that Byrd was not listed on it, they informed him that they did not need his permission to search the car, including the trunk. The police found 49 bricks of heroin and body armor. Byrd entered a conditional guilty plea while reserving his right to appeal on the search issue. The U.S. Supreme Court agreed to decide "whether an unauthorized driver has a reasonable expectation of privacy in a rental car." The lower federal courts had conflicting decisions on the issue.

The Court held that the "mere fact that a driver in lawful possession or control of a rental car is not listed on the rental agreement will not defeat his or her otherwise reasonable expectation of privacy." The Court remanded the case to determine the following arguments made by the government in the case:

> that one who intentionally uses a third party to procure a rental car by a fraudulent scheme for the purpose of committing a crime is no better situated than a car thief; and that probable cause justified the search in any event.

That last point was based on the fact that when the police asked Byrd if he had anything illegal in the car, he said he had a "blunt," which he offered to retrieve. The police refused to permit him to do that, assumed he was referring to marijuana, and said that gave them probable cause to search even without Byrd's permission.

The second case, *Collins v. Virginia*,[2] involved a home and a motor vehicle. Justice Sonia Sotomayor, who delivered the opinion of the Court, framed this issue and stated the holding as "whether the automobile exception to the Fourth Amendment permits a police officer, uninvited and without a warrant, to enter the curtilage of a home in order to search a vehicle parked therein. It does not."

The police officer in *Collins* observed the driver of an orange and black motorcycle with an extended frame commit a traffic offense, but he was unable to stop the vehicle and apprehend the driver. A few weeks later another officer in the same department observed the driver of a black and orange motorcycle speeding, but he, too, was unable to apprehend the driver. The two officers exchanged their notes on the incidents and came to the conclusion that it was the same motorcycle. During their investigation, the officers learned that the vehicle was likely stolen and in the possession of Ryan Collins. They checked his Facebook profile, which contained a picture of an orange and black motorcycle parked in the driveway of a house. They tracked down the address, went to the property, and parked in front. They later discovered that Collins's girlfriend lived in the house and that he stayed there a few nights each week, which would give Collins an expectation of privacy for his vehicle parked on the premises.

While parked in front of the house, the officer saw a white tarp covering a motorcycle with an extended frame. He walked on to the property, removed the tarp, took a picture of the vehicle, recorded its vehicle numbers, and ran a check of the license plate numbers; the vehicle was stolen. He returned to his car, waited for Collins to arrive, walked to the front door of the house, knocked, and Collins came out. Collins agreed to talk to the officer, admitted that was his motorcycle and that he bought it without a title. The officer then arrested Collins, who was indicted and convicted of receiving stolen property.

The U.S. Supreme Court held that the motorcycle was parked in the curtilage of the home. "The question before the Court is whether the automobile exception justifies the invasion of the curtilage. The answer is no. . . . The reason is that the scope of the automobile exception extends no further than the automobile itself." The Court "left for resolution on remand whether Officer Rhodes' warrantless intrusion on the curtilage of Collins' house may have been reasonable on a different basis, such as the exigent circumstances exception to the warrant requirement."

1. *Byrd v. United States*, 138 S. Ct. 1518 (2018).
2. *Collins v. Virginia*, 138 S. Ct. 1663 (2018).

is diminished at the border. The suspect's rights are important, but the government has an interest in preventing drug smuggling. The test used by the Court for border searches is whether, after considering all of the facts involved, customs officials reasonably suspect that the traveler is smuggling contraband in his or her alimentary canal.[83]

One of the most controversial strip search cases that the U.S. Supreme Court has analyzed in recent years was that of a middle school student, Savana Redding, age 13, who was targeted by school officials after another student, found in possession of a prescription level dose of ibuprofen pain relievers, reported that the pills were given to her by Redding. Redding, an honors student with no record of disciplinary problems, was subjected to what she called "the most humiliating experience in her life," and no drugs were found on her person. The case of *Safford v. Redding* is included although it involves a strip search by school officials rather than by police, and the search was not as extensive as those described above. The case is important to criminal justice discussions because it illustrates the importance of the Fourth Amendment prohibition against *unreasonable* search and seizure. Even in a school setting, where officials have heightened legitimate control over students, the Fourth Amendment protections cannot be ignored. Additional facts of the case are contained, along with the Court's reasoning, in the case excerpt in **Supplement 4.16.**[84]

Finally, the issue of whether police may take blood samples of drivers without their consent when the officers suspect those persons have a blood alcohol level beyond the legal limit is an issue. As Spotlight 4.3 indicates, police may conduct warrantless searches under some exigent circumstances, and courts have held that drunk driving may constitute one of those circumstances.[85] But more recently, the U.S. Supreme Court held that may not always be the case; rather, the legality of a warrantless search in such instances must be determined on a case-by-case basis, with the police considering the totality of the circumstances.[86] In deciding three cases combined into one, in 2016 in *Birchfield v. North Dakota*, the U.S. Supreme Court held that breath tests but not blood tests may be administered without a warrant during a search incident to a lawful arrest, and a state may not impose criminal penalties on suspected drunk drivers who refuse the blood test. Despite historical "implied consent" laws, in which drivers are held to consent to tests for drunkenness or risk, for example, losing their driver's licenses, the Court held that a criminal penalty was going too far. "There must be a limit to the consequences to which motorists may be deemed to have consented by virtue of a decision to drive on public roads. . . . [W]e conclude that motorists cannot be deemed to have consented to submit to a blood test on pain of committing a criminal offense."[87]

In January 2019, the U.S. Supreme Court agreed to hear an appeal from a Wisconsin case, *State v. Mitchell*, in which the defendant was convinced of operating a motor vehicle while intoxicated. His blood was drawn without a warrant while he was unconscious. On appeal, the defendant claimed that the warrantless blood draw violated his Fourth Amendment right to be free of an unreasonable search and seizure. The Wisconsin Supreme Court held that the blood draw was reasonable under the state statute concerning implied consent when operating a motor vehicle. Under the totality of circumstances, the court reasoned, there was probable cause to believe that the defendant was driving while intoxicated and was thus *civilly* liable under the state law permitting warrantless blood draws from unconscious drunk driving suspects, but it is updated in **Supplement 4.16.1**.[88]

Interrogation

Another important law enforcement function of policing is interrogation. Police must be able to question suspects, but that need to question must be balanced with the Fifth Amendment provision that no person "shall be compelled in any criminal case to be a witness against himself" (see Appendix A). For much of our history, it was assumed that most decisions regarding police interrogation and the admission of evidence obtained by those interrogations were governed by state, not federal, law. Jurisdictions recognized various police practices, and coercion of confessions was not uncommon. In 1964, the U.S. Supreme Court declared that "today the admissibility of a confession in a state criminal prosecution is tested by the same standard applied in federal prosecutions since 1897," which meant that the Fifth Amendment's prohibition against self-incrimination was applicable to the states.[89]

Of the many cases on interrogation, this discussion will focus on the key precedent cases and the most recently decided ones. The critical case, *Miranda v. Arizona*, decided by a 5-to-4 decision in 1966, set off a flurry of reaction from liberals and conservatives but established the constitutional rights of the accused concerning interrogation. The Supreme Court engaged in a lengthy examination of police manuals, which included information on how to use psychological coercion to elicit a suspect's confession. It examined the facts of the *Miranda* case. Ernesto Miranda was arrested, taken into custody, and identified by a complaining witness. He was held and interrogated for two hours by police, who admitted that they did not tell him he had a right to have an attorney present. The police obtained from Miranda a written confession, which stated that his confession was voluntary, he had made it with full knowledge that it could be used against him, and he fully understood his legal rights. That confession was admitted into evidence at the trial, and Miranda was convicted.

The Arizona Supreme Court upheld the conviction, emphasizing that Miranda did not ask for an attorney. The U.S. Supreme Court reversed the conviction in a lengthy decision discussing the dangers of establishing psychological environments in which the accused, even if innocent, would confess. To protect suspects from impermissible psychological interrogation, the Court handed down the ***Miranda* warning**, which contains the following rights of a suspect:

- The right to remain silent
- The right to notice that anything said by the suspect can and will be used against him or her at trial
- The right to the presence of an attorney, who will be
- Appointed (that is, paid for by the government) if the suspect is indigent[90]

A suspect may waive the right to an attorney, but that waiver must be made voluntarily, knowingly, and intelligently. If a suspect indicates a willingness to talk but subsequently wishes to remain silent, police should not continue their interrogation.

The U.S. Supreme Court has decided numerous cases interpreting *Miranda.* A few of those are discussed in **Supplement 4.17**.

It is important to understand that *Miranda* applies only to a *custodial* interrogation. Police are free to ask questions in noncustodial circumstances without giving the required warning. But frequently the issue is what constitutes a custodial situation. In a 2003 Texas case, the U.S. Supreme Court refused to uphold a decision in which police went to the home of Robert Kaupp, 17, who was awakened at 3 A.M. and told, "[W]e need to go and talk." Kaupp was convicted of a 1999 murder and sentenced to 55 years in prison. The U.S. Supreme Court rejected the lower court's decision that Kaupp was not under arrest, as he was free to refuse to cooperate with the officers. Thus, his answers to police questions were admissible in court. The Supreme Court stated that a

> group of police officers rousing an adolescent out of bed in the middle of the night with the words "we need to go and talk" presents no option but "to go." ... It cannot seriously be suggested that when the detectives began to question Kaupp, a reasonable person in his situation would have thought he was sitting in the interview room as a matter of choice, free to change his mind and go home to bed.

The Court vacated the lower appellate court's decision, sent the case back for reconsideration, and instructed the court that Kaupp's confession should be excluded "unless ... the state can point to testimony undisclosed on the record before us, and weighty enough to carry the state's burden despite the clear force of the evidence shown here."[91]

In 2009, the U.S. Supreme Court decided a key case involving the right of police to question suspects without their counsel present. *Montejo v. Louisiana* involved a petitioner, Jesse Montejo, who was arrested in connection with a robbery and murder. Police suspected Montejo of being an associate of their prime suspect in this crime. Montejo waived his *Miranda* rights to an attorney and was interrogated by law enforcement officers through the afternoon, evening, and morning following his arrest. During these interrogations, Montejo often changed his story, at first claiming that he only drove the suspect to the victim's home and then stating that he killed the victim in the course of a burglary. Police videotaped these interrogations. At the hearing, required by state law to occur within 72 hours, the court automatically appointed counsel for Montejo, who was again read his *Miranda* rights. However, before Montejo consulted with counsel, he agreed to accompany officers to the area where he said he disposed of the weapon used in the crime. Also, during that time Montejo used paper and pen (provided to him by the officers) to write a letter of apology to the victim's widow. Montejo sought unsuccessfully to have that letter excluded as evidence in his trial. He was convicted of murder and sentenced to death.[92]

On appeal to the U.S. Supreme Court, Montejo argued that the letter should have been suppressed under the rule of a prior case, *Michigan v. Jackson*,[93] decided in 1986. That case required police to refrain from questioning a suspect once he or she invoked a right to counsel at a preliminary or similar hearing. In *Montejo*, the U.S. Supreme Court overruled *Jackson* specifically, stating that it was untenable and unworkable, emphasizing that Montejo had not *asked* for counsel; he stood mute at his hearing while counsel was appointed, and it was not reasonable to assume that this automatic appointment of counsel, in effect, revoked Montejo's previous waiver of his right to counsel. The Court did, however, remand the case for further proceedings, noting that Montejo might have other avenues under which he could ask the trial court to exclude the letter in question. The four dissenters in *Montejo* argued that the majority misinterpreted *Jackson* and that the police interrogation of Montejo "clearly violated" his Sixth Amendment right to counsel as there was no evidence that Montejo clearly, knowingly, and unequivocally waived his right to counsel before agreeing to be interrogated by police after his court hearing.[94]

In 2010, in *Maryland v. Shatzer*, the Supreme Court considered the issue of when the presumption of non-waiver ends. While Michael Shatzer Sr. was in prison he was approached by police, who wanted to question him about a crime other than the one for which he was incarcerated. They gave him the *Miranda* warning, and he said he did not want to talk; so they left and closed the case. Two years later another detective arrived at the prison to talk and gave Shatzer the *Miranda* warning after which Shatzer signed a waiver of his rights. As the detective questioned him, Shatzer made incriminating statements, which were admitted at his trial, and he was convicted. The key was whether Shatzer was *in the custody* of law enforcement officers. According to the U.S. Supreme Court, once Shatzer was returned to the general population after that first encounter, he was no longer in the custody of police but, rather, of prison officials. Thus, when the police came a second time to question him, they were required to give him the *Miranda* warning. However, Shatzer was not entitled to a presumption that his waiver of his *Miranda* rights prior to the second questioning was involuntary. Consequently, the police did not have the heavy burden of proof required to prove a *Miranda* waiver after a suspect asks for an attorney. The *Miranda* waiver was properly admitted at the trial.[95]

Also in 2010, in *Florida v. Powell*, the U.S. Supreme Court considered the meaning of the requirement that a suspect must be "clearly informed" of the right to remain silent and to have an attorney present if one chooses to answer questions. In *Powell*, the police told the suspect, "You have the right to talk to a lawyer before answering any of our questions" and you "have the right to use any of these rights at any time you want during this interview." On appeal, the suspect stated he did not understand those words to mean that he could have an attorney with him throughout police questioning. The Court held that although the *Miranda* warning could have been stated more clearly, the words used by the Tampa, Florida, police were acceptable under the *Miranda* requirements.[96]

A third 2010 case, *Berghuis v. Thompkins*, held that if a suspect wishes to invoke *Miranda* rights, he or she must clearly state that. The rights cannot be invoked by remaining silent. In this case, the police handed the suspect, Van Chester Thompkins, a card with five statements they used to inform a suspect of the *Miranda* warning. Thompkins was asked to read the fifth statement, which he did, but he refused to comply when police requested that he sign the statement. He did not ask for an attorney; nor did he state that he wanted to remain silent. He was questioned for about three hours during which time he said very little except that the chair in which he was sitting was uncomfortable and that no, he did not want a peppermint candy. He then answered "yes" to these questions: "Do you believe in God?" "Do you pray to God" and finally, "Do you pray to God to forgive you for shooting that boy down?" The Court ruled that Thompkins waived his right to remain silent and to have an attorney because he did not state that he wanted to exercise those rights. Writing for the four dissenters, the newest justice, Sonia Sotomayor, stated, in part:

> Today's decision turns *Miranda* upside down. Criminal suspects must now unambiguously invoke their right to remain silent, which, counterintuitively, requires them to speak. At the same time, suspects will be legally presumed to have waived their rights even if they have given no clear expression of their intent to do so. Those results . . . are inconsistent with the fair-trial principles on which . . . [our] precedents are grounded.[97]

In 2011, the U.S. Supreme Court held that police cannot interrogate juveniles without giving them the *Miranda* warning if those juveniles are considered to be "in custody." In *J.D.B. v. North Carolina*, the police escorted a 13-year-old from his classroom to a closed-door conference room in the school and asked him questions without first telling him his constitutional rights. The juvenile first denied and then admitted his involvement in the crime, and he was adjudicated delinquent.[98]

In 2013, the U.S. Supreme Court decided *Salinas v. Texas*, which involved police questioning of a suspect who was not "in custody." Police asked Genovevo Salinas to accompany them to the police station to answer questions in order to clear himself of any involvement in a murder case that they were investigating. Salinas agreed to go and answered questions until police asked him whether a ballistics test would show that the shell casings recovered from the murder scene matched his shotgun. Salinas did not answer that question, and his refusal was used against him at trial as evidence of guilt. He was convicted and appealed. Against a strong dissent of four justices, the Court held that the petitioner's claim that his right not to incriminate himself was violated failed because he did not expressly invoke his privilege against answering the officer's question.[99]

In 2014, several federal agencies, including the FBI, reversed a long-standing policy of not recording interrogations of persons in the custody of law enforcement authorities, a practice then followed in only a few jurisdictions. It was thought that numerous other jurisdictions would follow with a similar policy. U.S. Attorney General Eric Holder stated that the new policy, that reversed one that had been followed for over 100 years, would ensure an "objective account of key investigations and interactions with people who are held in federal custody." The president of the National Association of Criminal Defense Lawyers stated the following:

> Recording interrogations protects the accused against police misconduct, protects law enforcement against false allegations, and protects public safety by ensuring a verbatim record of the interrogation process and any statements.[100]

Experts on videotaping emphasize, however, that videos must be interpreted and can even be misleading as "camera angles, close-ups, lenses and dozens of other techniques shape our perception of what we see without our being aware of it."[101]

Investigation

Crime scene investigation has become a popular topic in the United States, capturing the attention of millions on television shows such as *CSI: Crime Scene Investigation*, *CSI: Miami*, and *CSI: New York*. Investigation in the real world of policing may not always be as exciting as in the TV shows, but it is a critical function of policing. The success or failure of the prosecution of a suspect for a particular crime often depends on the investigative abilities of the police before, during, or after the suspect's arrest. Evidence may be destroyed quickly or never found. Without physical evidence, it may be impossible to link the alleged criminal activity to the suspect.

In large police departments, criminal investigations may be the responsibility of specialists, and police officers may not be closely involved in the process. In many cases, however, the police officer who makes the arrest is a critical element in the investigative process. In some police departments, the patrol officer's investigative function is limited. Most of this work, at least in serious cases, is conducted by specialized officers in the criminal investigation unit of the department. These investigators conduct various activities, ranging from the maintenance of field activity records to total crime scene management, including such other activities as collecting body fluids, photographing crime scenes, following up on investigations, sketching crime scenes, obtaining search/arrest warrants, conducting interviews/interrogations, and attending autopsies.

Police use many investigative techniques. Fingerprinting is one of the most effective methods. This technique has been available in the United States since it was first used around 1900 by London's Scotland Yard. The use of computers to assist with fingerprint identification and other methods of investigation has been helpful to police in many ways.

Another investigative technique is the use of deoxyribonucleic acid, or DNA, "which carries the genetic information that determines individual characteristics such as eye color and body size." Some argue that DNA is close to 100 percent accurate, compared with traditional blood and semen tests, which are only 90 to 95 percent accurate. Advocates call this process *DNA genetic fingerprinting*.[102]

DNA results have been used to free inmates who were convicted and have served years in prison. The results have been used to win acquittals for defendants as well as to convict others. There are some issues, however. Some courts have admitted certain methods of DNA testing while excluding others or have instructed trial courts to examine the testing methods more carefully. Lawyers may also challenge the methods of collecting and analyzing DNA evidence as well as the circumstances under which DNA is collected.

In 2013, the U.S. Supreme Court decided a controversial case in which the Court upheld the practice of a DNA test without a warrant in cases involving a cheek swab by law enforcement investigators who had probable cause to believe a suspect had committed a serious crime. The case provides the focus of the criminal justice systems dilemma for this chapter.

Criminal Justice Systems Dilemma 4.1

Is a DNA Test without a Warrant Legal?

In June 2013, U.S. Supreme Court justices issued a rather surprising set of opinions in that three liberal justices, Ruth Bader Ginsberg, Elena Kagan, and Sonia Sotomayor, joined the dissent written by conservative Justice Antonin Scalia in *Maryland v. King*.[1] The case involved a suspect who, in 2003, broke into a Maryland woman's home and raped her at gunpoint. The suspect, Alonzo King, concealed his face during the crime. In 2009, King was arrested on other charges, and as part of the booking procedure for serious offenses, a DNA sample was taken from the inside of his cheeks. An analysis of that sample revealed a match between King's DNA and a DNA sample collected in a 2003 rape investigation. The evidence was presented to a grand jury, which indicted King. Law enforcement officers secured a search warrant; took another DNA sample, which matched that found in the 2003 case; used that evidence at trial; and King was convicted of the 2003 rape. He appealed, arguing that the investigative search violated his Fourth Amendment rights and thus the Maryland statute that permits authorities to collect DNA samples from "an individual who is charged with . . . a crime of violence or an attempt to commit a crime of violence; or . . . burglary or an attempt to commit burglary" is unconstitutional.[2]

The ability of authorities to link King with the 2003 rape resulted from a national DNA data base supervised by the FBI, and authorized by Congress, and involving all 50 states and numerous federal agencies. According to the Supreme Court, the Combined DNA Index System (CODIS) standardizes the points of comparisons of DNA samples. The Court noted that this cheek swab is less intrusive than the permitted collection (without a warrant in some cases) of fingerprints and blood samples and that the Fourth Amendment prohibits only *unreasonable* searches and seizures, which are interpreted in light of the state's need for the questioned intrusion.

The U.S. Supreme Court upheld the Maryland practice and stated as follows:

> In light of the context of a valid arrest supported by probable cause respondent's expectations of privacy were not offended by the minor intrusion of a brief swab of his cheeks. By contrast, that same context of arrest gives rise to significant state interests in identifying respondent not only so that the proper name can be attached to his charges but also so that the criminal justice system can make informed decisions concerning pretrial custody. Upon these considerations the Court concludes that DNA identification of arrestees is a reasonable search that can be considered part of a routine booking procedure. When officers make an arrest supported by probable cause to hold for a serious offense and they bring the suspect to the station to be detained in custody, taking and analyzing a cheek swab of the arrestee's DNA is, like fingerprinting and photographing, a legitimate police booking procedure that is reasonable under the Fourth Amendment.

The dissent strongly disagreed, stating, in part:

> The Fourth Amendment forbids searching a person for evidence of a crime when there is no basis for believing the person is guilty of the crime or is in possession of incriminating evidence. That prohibition is categorical and without exception; it lies at the very heart of the Fourth Amendment. Whenever this Court has allowed a suspicionless search, it has insisted upon a justifying motive apart from the investigation of crime.
>
> It is obvious that no such noninvestigative motive exists in this case. The Court's assertion that DNA is being taken, not to solve crimes, but to *identify* those in the State's custody, taxes the credulity of the credulous. And the Court's comparison of Maryland's DNA searches to other techniques, such as fingerprinting, can seem apt only to those who know no more than today's opinion has chosen to tell them about how those DNA searches actually work.

At the end of his opinion, Justice Scalia highlights what this text refers to as criminal justice system dilemmas, in this case, using techniques that make investigating more effective versus constitutional rights.

> Today's judgment will, to be sure, have the beneficial effect of solving more crimes; then again, so would the taking of DNA samples from anyone who flies on an airplane (surely the Transportation Security Administration needs to know the "identity" of the flying public), applies for a driver's license, or attends a public school. Perhaps the construction of such a genetic panopticon is wise. But I doubt that the proud men who wrote the charter of our liberties would have been so eager to open their mouths for royal inspection.
>
> I therefore dissent, and hope that today's incursion upon the Fourth Amendment . . . will some day be repudiated.

1. *Maryland v. King*, 569 U.S. 435 (2013), cases and citations omitted.
2. See Md. Pub. Safety Code Ann., Section 2-504(a)(3)(i) (2018).

Summary

This chapter is the second of three on policing, and it began with a discussion of preparing for policing, which looked at the issues surrounding the recruitment, selection, education, and training of police.

Police exercise wide discretion in criminal justice systems, and the chapter devoted a section to the explanation and analysis of why discretion is necessary and how it might be abused. Discretion cannot be abolished; thus, controlling it is a necessity.

The primary focus of this chapter was on the functions that police must perform in an increasingly complex society. Those functions are numerous, but they are categorized as law enforcement, order maintenance, and community service. The latter two were discussed briefly before greater attention was given to law enforcement.

The controversy over the importance of order maintenance was noted within the context of the contributions of several experts on policing. Order maintenance may be a crucial function of policing, as the absence of order may lead to law violations, even serious criminal acts, such as the violent crimes of aggravated assault and murder. Likewise, the community service function of policing may prevent or reduce actions that might lead to law violations. Furthermore, many of the activities police are called upon to perform occur after hours, when other organizations have closed for the day.

The discussion of law enforcement began with a brief overview of the constitutional limitations on policing, for it is clear that police could make more arrests and conduct more thorough investigations if they were not required to observe defendants' constitutional rights. U.S. criminal justice systems place great emphasis on the right of individuals to be free from unreasonable governmental intrusion. This does not mean that police cannot arrest, search and seize, interrogate, and investigate, but only that these functions must be performed within the limits of state and federal statutes, constitutions, and court decisions. Those limits are being challenged in many cases.

The Fourth Amendment's prohibition against unreasonable search and seizure, the Fifth Amendment's provision that a person may not be forced to incriminate himself or herself, and the Sixth Amendment right to counsel are the key constitutional bases of what police may and may not do in law enforcement. The investigatory stop, brief detention, arrest, and searching and seizing are important police activities regulated by constitutional requirements, court interpretations of those requirements, and departmental policies.

A look at a few key cases on the law of stop, arrest, and search and seizure should make it obvious that it is impossible to state what *the law* is in these areas. The facts of a particular case must be analyzed carefully in light of previous court decisions, statutes, and constitutional provisions. Reasonable minds may differ as to the conclusion in any given case. It is important to analyze case law carefully, looking at the rule of a case as well as the reasons for that rule.

In some situations, police are permitted to stop, arrest, and search and seize without a warrant, although the U.S. Supreme Court prefers warrants. Again, it is impossible for police to know in every case whether they face exceptions to the warrant requirement. Frequently, law enforcement is ambiguous, leaving considerable discretion to the individual officer, who may be second-guessed by the courts. Despite the need to analyze individual cases in terms of their unique facts, some general principles of constitutional law govern the law enforcement function of policing. Those were discussed in this chapter, with attention paid to some of the major U.S. Supreme Court cases governing each aspect of law enforcement, from the initial stop to the searching and seizing of homes, automobiles, and persons.

Interrogation is another important law enforcement function. The U.S. Supreme Court has decided many cases in this area. The *Miranda* warning must be given in cases in which a person might be deprived of his or her liberty, but it is not always clear when interrogation has begun and the warning must be given. Suspects may waive the right to counsel, but that waiver must be made knowingly and intelligently, and law enforcement officers may not initiate interrogations once that waiver has been made. Failure to comply with *Miranda* requirements may result in the exclusion of evidence from the trial, an issue discussed in Chapter 5. In an effort to reduce problems with interrogations, the FBI and other federal agencies adopted a new policy in 2014 requiring videotaping of all interrogations of suspects in custody.

Investigation was the final police function discussed in this chapter. Traditionally, police have spent considerable time investigating crimes at the scene of their occurrence without significant effectiveness. Recently, investigative techniques have been improved by the use of forensic science, especially DNA, which is now widely accepted by courts, although its reliability can be challenged in terms of how and under what circumstances it can be collected.

Policing has changed in many ways in recent years. This chapter touches on only a few areas in which changes have been attempted. Chapter 5 focuses on the primary problems and issues of policing.

Key Terms

anticipatory search warrant 85
arrest 84
contraband 83
curtilage 86
frisk 83
informant 84
Miranda warning 92
plain view doctrine 86
pretextual stop 81
probable cause 84
racial profiling 72
search and seizure 84
search warrant 84
warrant 84

Study Questions

1. If you were in charge of recruiting persons into policing, what characteristics would you emphasize? What emphasis would you place on higher education and why? What type of training would you require and why? How would you assess the ethical and moral standards of recruits? What standards would you require for policing, and what efforts would you suggest for maintaining those standards within police forces?
2. What types of training would prepare police for such terrorist acts as those of 9/11?
3. Discuss the importance of discretion in policing.
4. What is meant by *order maintenance* in policing?
5. What should be the role of police with regard to service functions within the communities they serve?
6. What functions do police have in traffic control and the enforcement of traffic laws and ordinances? Discuss the recent U.S. Supreme Court cases in this area.
7. Under what circumstances may police stop, question, and arrest a suspect? When may police frisk?
8. Explain racial profiling and its implications.
9. Why are warrants usually required for arrest and search?

10. Under what circumstances may police search without a warrant? Arrest without a warrant?

11. What is the meaning of *probable cause*, and how may it be established?

12. When may police search a home? How much of the home may be searched? Explain the plain view doctrine, and define *curtilage*.

13. After knocking and announcing, how long must police wait before entering a home forcibly to execute a search warrant?

14. May police use drug-sniffing dogs at the scene of a normal traffic stop? At a home? Discuss both.

15. Explain the *plain view* doctrine.

16. Under what circumstances may a vehicle be searched?

17. Under what circumstances may body searches be conducted? Should special provisions exist for searching young persons?

18. What is the *Miranda* warning? Why is it important? Discuss the limitations, if any, placed on this right recently by the U.S. Supreme Court interpretations.

19. Should all law enforcement interrogations be videotaped? Will this process ensure accuracy?

20. What is DNA testing and how is it used?

Notes

1. See Arthur Niederhoffer, *Behind the Shield: The Police in Urban Society* (Garden City, NY: Anchor Books, 1969), pp. 109-160.
2. "Ex-Cop Serpico Testifies on NYPD," *Miami Herald* (September 24, 1997), p. 8.
3. "One Force Shrinking, One Booming," *Dallas Morning News* (December 8, 2017), p. 1B.
4. Brian A. Reaves, Bureau of Justice Statistics, "State and Local Law Enforcement Training Academies, 2013" (July 2016), https://www.bjs.gov, accessed August 29, 2018.
5. The President's Commission on Law Enforcement and Administration of Justice, *The Challenge of Crime in a Free Society* (Washington, D.C.: U.S. Government Printing Office, 1967), p. 109.
6. David L. Carter et al., *The State of Police Education: Policy Direction for the 21st Century* (Washington, D.C.: Police Executive Research Forum, 1989), p. 15.
7. Agnes L. Baro and David Burlingame, "Law Enforcement and Higher Education: Is There an Impasse?," *Journal of Criminal Justice Education* 10 (Spring 1999): 57-74; quotation is on p. 70.
8. See Patrick Murphy, foreword to Carter et al., *The State of Police Education: Policy Direction for the 21st Century*, pp. iii-iv.
9. For an analysis of higher education and policing, see Baro and Burlingame, "Law Enforcement and Higher Education."
10. Avram Bornstein et al., "Critical Race Theory Meets the NYPD: An Assessment of Anti-Racist Pedagogy for Police in New York City," *Journal of Criminal Justice Education* 23(2) (June 2012): 174-204; quotation is on p. 202.
11. "Training Could Prevent Many Police Cell Fatalities," *Birmingham Post* (June 11, 2003), p. 6.
12. Brian A. Reaves, Bureau of Justice Statistics, *State and Local Law Enforcement Training Academies, 2006* (February 2009, revised April 14, 2009), p. 1, http://www.bjs.gov/content/pub/pdf/slleta06.pdf, accessed January 10, 2015.
13. *City of Canton, Ohio v. Harris*, 489 U.S. 378 (1989).
14. Peter W. Neyround, "More Police, Less Prison, Less Crime? From Peel to Popper: The Case for More Scientific Policing," *Criminology & Public Policy* 10(1) (February 2011): 77-83; quotation is on p. 80. See also Steven N. Durlauf and Daniel S. Nagin, "Imprisonment and Crime: Can Both Be Reduced?," in the same journal, pp. 13-54.
15. Emily Owens et al., "Can You Build a Better Cop? Experimental Evidence on Supervision, Training, and Policing in the Community," *Criminology & Public Policy* 17(1) (February 2018), pp. 41-87; quotation is on pp. 41-42. See also Lorraine Mazerolle and William Terrill, "Making Every Police-Citizen Interaction Count: The Challenges of Building a Better Cop," in the same journal, pp. 89-96.
16. Laure Weber Brooks, "Police Discretionary Behavior: A Study of Style," in *Critical Issues in Policing: Contemporary Readings*, 7th ed., Roger G. Dunham and Geoffrey P. Alpert (Long Grove, IL: Waveland Press, 2015), pp. 122-142.
17. James Q. Wilson, *Varieties of Police Behavior: The Management of Law and Order in Eight Communities* (Cambridge, MA: Harvard University Press, 1968), pp. 16, 17, 21.
18. Ibid., p. 21.
19. George L. Kelling, "Order Maintenance, the Quality of Urban Life, and Police: A Line of Argument," in *Police Leadership in America: Crisis and Opportunity*, ed. William A. Geller (Chicago: American Bar Foundation, 1985), p. 297.
20. Ibid., p. 308.
21. See James Q. Wilson and George L. Kelling, "Police and Neighborhood Safety: Broken Windows," *Atlantic Monthly* 249 (March 1982): 29-38.
22. Carl B. Klockars, "Order Maintenance, the Quality of Urban Life, and Police: A Different Line of Argument," in *Police Leadership*, ed. Geller, p. 316, quoting *The Newark Foot Patrol Experiment* (Washington, D.C.: Police Foundation, 1981), p. 88.
23. *Student Party Riots*, available from the COPS Office Response Center, cited and quoted in "Police Urged to Review Policies to Prevent Student Party Riots," *Criminal Justice Newsletter* (April 17, 2006), p. 5.

24. Nancy G. LaVigne et al., Urban Institute Justice Policy Center, *Police Reentry and Community Policing: Strategies for Enhancing Public Safety* (April 3, 2006), http://www.urban.org/publications/411061.html, accessed January 10, 2015.
25. See the discussion in Jacinta M. Gau and Eugene A. Paoline III, "Officer Race, Role Orientations, and Cynicism Toward Citizens," *Justice Quarterly Review* 34(7) (December 2017): 1246-1271.
26. Wilson, *Varieties of Police Behavior*, p. 5.
27. *Whren v. United States*, 517 U.S. 806 (1996).
28. *Maryland v. Wilson*, 519 U.S. 408 (1997).
29. *Brendlin v. California*, 551 U.S. 249 (2007).
30. See Patricia Warren et al., "Driving While Black: Bias Processes and Racial Disparity in Police Stops," *Criminology* 44(20) (August 2006): 709-737.
31. "Justice Report Cites Discriminatory and Unconstitutional Policing in Baltimore," *American Bar Association Journal*, http://www.abajournal.com, accessed August 11, 2016.
32. "Judge Upholds Police Pact," *Dallas Morning News* (April 8, 2017), p. 7.
33. "Excessive Force Is Rife in Chicago, U.S. Review Finds," *New York Times* (January 14, 2017), p. 15.
34. See Jeff Rojek et al., "Policing Race: The Racial Stratification of Searches in Police Traffic Stops," *Criminology* 50(4) (November 2012): 993-1024; and Cynthia Lum, "The Influence of Places on Police Decision Pathways: From Call for Service to Arrest," *Justice Quarterly* 28(4) (August 2011): 631-663.
35. See Lorie A. Fridell, "Racial Aspects of Police Shootings: Reducing Both Bias and Counter Bias," *Criminology & Public Policy* 15(2) (May 2016): 481-487.
36. Lois James et al., "The Reverse Racism Effect: Are Cops More Hesitant to Shoot Black than White Suspects?," *Criminology & Public Policy* 15(2) (May 2016): 457-479; quotations are on pp. 457, 476.
37. See Ronald L. Akers et al., *Criminological Theories: Introduction, Evaluation, & Application*, 7th ed. (New York: Oxford University Press, 2017), pp. 223-224.
38. For a review of the literature, see Rod K. Brunson, "'Police Don't Like Black People': African American Young Men's Accumulated Police Experiences," *Criminology & Public Policy* 6(1) (February 2007): 71-102.
39. Ronald Weitzer and Steven A. Tuch, "Perceptions of Racial Profiling: Race, Class, and Personal Experience," *Criminology* 40(2) (May 2002): 435-456; quotation is on p. 452.
40. Michael R. Smith et al., "Differential Suspicion: Theory Specification and Gender Effects in the Traffic Stop Context," *Justice Quarterly* 23(2) (June 2006): 271-295; quotation is on p. 271.
41. *Terry v. Ohio*, 392 U.S. 1 (1968).
42. *Minnesota v. Dickerson*, 508 U.S. 366 (1993).
43. *United States v. Arvizu*, 534 U.S. 266 (2002).
44. *Illinois v. Wardlow*, 528 U.S. 119 (2000).
45. *Arizona v. Johnson*, 555 U.S. 323 (2009).
46. *Johnson v. United States*, 333 U.S. 10, 13-14 (1948).
47. *Illinois v. Gates*, 462 U.S. 213 (1983).
48. *Florida v. J.L.*, 529 U.S. 266 (2000).
49. *County of Riverside v. McLaughlin*, 500 U.S. 44 (1991).
50. *United States v. Grubbs*, 547 U.S. 90 (2006).
51. Ibid. The second issue the U.S. Supreme Court faced in *Grubbs* was whether the anticipatory warrant was defective because it did not contain the affidavit with the triggering information. The Court held that it was not defective because the Fourth Amendment (see Appendix A) "does not require that the triggering condition for an anticipatory search warrant be set forth in the warrant itself."
52. *United States v. U.S. District Court*, 407 U.S. 297 (1972).
53. *Mapp v. Ohio*, 367 U.S. 643 (1961).
54. *Mapp v. Ohio*, 367 U.S. 643 (1961).
55. *Chimel v. California*, 395 U.S. 752 (1969).
56. *Coolidge v. New Hampshire*, 403 U.S. 443 (1971).
57. *Arizona v. Hicks*, 480 U.S. 321 (1987).
58. *Maryland v. Buie*, 494 U.S. 325 (1990).
59. *United States v. Dunn*, 480 U.S. 294 (1987).
60. *California v. Greenwood*, 486 U.S. 35 (1988).
61. *Illinois v. McArthur*, 531 U.S. 326 (2001).
62. *Wilson v. Arkansas*, 514 U.S. 927 (1995).
63. *Richards v. Wisconsin*, 520 U.S. 385 (1997).
64. *United States v. Banks*, 282 F.3d 699 (9th Cir. 2002), *rev'd*, 540 U.S. 31 (2003), and *rev'd, remanded*, 355 F.3d 1188 (9th Cir. 2004).
65. *Florida v. Jardines*, 569 U.S. 1 (2013).
66. *Carroll v. United States*, 267 U.S. 132 (1925); *Chambers v. Maroney*, 399 U.S. 42 (1970). See also *Florida v. Myers*, 466 U.S. 380 (1984) (*per curiam*), upholding the warrantless search by police of a car that was impounded and had been subjected to a previous legitimate inventory search.
67. *California v. Acevedo*, 500 U.S. 565 (1991).
68. *Robbins v. California*, 453 U.S. 420 (1981).
69. *United States v. Ross*, 456 U.S. 798 (1982).
70. *United States v. Johns*, 469 U.S. 478 (1985).
71. See *Colorado v. Bertine*, 479 U.S. 367 (1987); *Florida v. Wells*, 495 U.S. 1 (1990).
72. *Florida v. Jimeno*, 500 U.S. 248 (1991).
73. *Arizona v. Gant*, 556 U.S. 332 (2009). The previous case to which the Court referred is *New York v. Belton*, 453 U.S. 454 (1981).
74. *Florida v. Bostick*, 501 U.S. 421 (1991).
75. *United States v. Drayton*, 536 U.S. 194 (2002).
76. *Wyoming v. Houghton*, 526 U.S. 295 (1999).
77. *Maryland v. Pringle*, 540 U.S. 366 (1999).
78. *Illinois v. Caballes*, 545 U.S. 405 (2005).
79. *Florida v. Harris*, 568 U.S. 237 (2013).
80. *United States v. Jones*, 565 U.S. 400 (2012).
81. *Rochin v. California*, 342 U.S. 165 (1952).
82. See, for example, *Bell v. Wolfish*, 441 U.S. 520 (1979).
83. See, for example, *United States v. Montoya de Hernandez*, 473 U.S. 531 (1985).
84. *Safford United School District #1 v. Redding*, 557 U.S. 364 (2009).
85. See, for example, *Schmerber v. California*, 384 U.S. 757 (1966).
86. See *Missouri v. McNeely*, 569 U.S. 141 (2013).
87. *Birchfield v. North Dakota*, 136 S. Ct. 2160 (2016).
88. *State v. Mitchell*, 2018 WI 84 (2018), *vacated by, remanded by, Mitchell v. Wisconsin*, 2019 U.S. LEXIS 4400 (U.S. June 27, 2019).
89 *Malloy v. Hogan*, 378 U.S. 1 (1964).
90. *Miranda v. Arizona*, 384 U.S. 436, 478-479 (1966).
91. *Kaupp v. Texas*, 538 U.S. 626 (2003).
92. *Montejo v. Louisiana*, 556 U.S. 778 (2009).
93. *Michigan v. Jackson*, 475 U.S. 625 (1986).
94. *Montejo v. Louisiana*, 556 U.S. 778 (2009), Justice Stevens, dissenting.

95. *Maryland v. Shatzer,* 559 U.S. 98 (2010).
96. *Florida v. Powell,* 559 U.S. 50 (2010).
97. *Berghuis v. Thompkins,* 560 U.S. 360 (2010).
98. *J.D.B. v. North Carolina,* 564 U.S. 261 (2011).
99. *Salinas v. Texas,* 570 U.S. 178 (2013).
100. "FBI, in Historic Policy Change, to Record Interrogations," http://www.reuters.com/article/2014/05/22/us-usa-justice-record-idUSBREA4LOW320140522, accessed July 15, 2014.
101. "Can a Jury Believe What It Sees?," *New York Times* (July 14, 2014), p. 17.
102. Debra Cassens Moss, "DNA—the New Fingerprints," *American Bar Association Journal* 74 (May 1, 1988): 66.

5

Problems and Issues in Policing

Chapter Outline

Learning Objectives

After reading this chapter, you should be able to do the following:

- Explain the meaning of dilemmas in policing
- Summarize the external political pressures of policing
- Explain time allocation pressures in policing
- Discuss the meaning and importance of evidence-based policing
- Define *proactive* and *reactive* policing and discuss each in the context of domestic violence
- Explain what is meant by policing *hot spots*
- What should be the role of policing in mental health cases
- Discuss the nature and extent of police misconduct
- Explain the proper use of deadly force in the context of fleeing felons and vehicle pursuits
- Discuss the nature and implications of police brutality
- Discuss violence against police
- Explain how police activities may be controlled by police departments
- Discuss the role of the U.S. Department of Justice in regulating policing
- Explain and evaluate the exclusionary rule
- Discuss the control of policing by community relations and through civil actions
- Explain the legal actions that residents may take if they are mistreated by police officers
- Discuss the impact that affirmative action programs might have on policing in the future

Policing is a job that arouses controversy. Police are permitted to use deadly force, and in some circumstances, they would be negligent (or even charged with a crime) if they do not do so. Police are expected to stop and question persons who appear to have violated laws, but they may be criticized for doing so. Police are expected to obey all laws, but not all police meet that expectation. Police are expected to be well trained and have enough education to use reasonable judgment and discretion, but they may be stressed and bored if they are too highly educated or trained. They are expected to be alert on the job, but the dull aspects of many patrol assignments may make it difficult to remain enthused and alert at all times. In short, policing is challenging and stressful, and those who enter this profession must face the reality that the public does not always agree with their decisions and may protest even to the point of violence, as demonstrated in recent years.

In considering the problems in policing, we must realize that no problem is pervasive. This chapter discusses issues that arise in policing but does not suggest that all police—or even most police—encounter the problems and fail to resolve them successfully. Policing, like all jobs, involves some persons who are corrupt, incompetent, or in some other way unprofessional; however, most law enforcement officers probably work very hard to serve the public. They do an excellent job, and many of them find their work both challenging and rewarding.

Policing presents officers and administrators with some serious dilemmas. Conflicts arise over allocation of officers' time; investigations may compromise officers' integrity or lead the public to question officers' investigative techniques. Processing domestic violence calls, confronting the drug scene, and dealing with the reality that some suspects or victims may have communicable diseases are situations that, among others, create serious problems for police.

Role conflicts, the threat of danger, methods of evaluating job performance, job satisfaction, and other issues create stressful situations that lead to professional and personal problems for police. The dangers of terrorism, especially since the 9/11 terrorist attacks, concern all of us, but police have the responsibility to rescue, investigate, and prevent terrorist attacks.

Some police react in the same way many people react to stress: They confront the issues and deal with them successfully. They may become involved in a police subculture (discussed in the supplement) in which they feel comfortable and accepted while off duty. Others may become involved in corruption or overzealous law enforcement, or they may succumb to the use of illegal drugs or even drug trafficking. A few turn to brutality against crime suspects. The line between appropriate and excessive use of deadly force is not easy to draw, but court decisions give some guidelines. When those guidelines are violated, civil (and, in some cases, criminal) liability attaches. The control of policing is not easy but is attempted through police department regulations, federal regulations, courts, and community relationships.

The final section of this chapter focuses on affirmative action policies. The efforts of police departments to recruit minority and female applicants have increased the representation of these groups. Court cases have chipped away at affirmative action, but the U.S. Supreme Court has upheld some affirmative action policies.

DILEMMAS IN POLICING

In any work environment, it is necessary to make adjustments to conflicting demands and pressures, but conflicts may be greater in policing than in most jobs or professions. We expect the police to solve and prevent crimes. We want them to respond cheerfully, quickly, and efficiently to a host of public needs. At the same time, police are expected to be polite, even when being attacked verbally or physically, and to be effective in securing evidence of crimes without violating suspects' constitutional rights. They must use violence when necessary but not when unnecessary, and the line between those two is not always clearly established. Police should report the ethical and legal violations of their colleagues, but frequently, internal pressures push against such reporting. All of the dilemmas police face are enhanced by external political pressures.

External Political Pressures

Police are accountable to local, state, and federal agencies. Legal restrictions may be placed on police at any of these levels. Police departments must compete with other public agencies for funding, and to be competitive, they must show that, although they are using their existing resources efficiently and prudently, local, state, and federal problems have grown beyond their ability to cope successfully without additional resources.

The wide discretion police have in law enforcement may create political problems. Police are charged with enforcing law violations; however, if they arrest a popular and high-profile individual, they may find that strict enforcement is not expected or even tolerated. Political pressure to control the poor and minorities may lead to allegations that policing is for the purpose of protecting the majority's status quo, with little regard for the rights of all people. A police administrator might find it impossible to be responsive to the needs of all of his or her constituents because of political influences that could lead to job loss. Political pressures from local, state, and federal levels permeate policing and cannot be ignored. The fact that these external pressures may conflict with internal pressures makes the situation even more difficult and stressful for police.

The internal values of a police department may be at odds with those of the external constituency. To make the situation even more complicated, both the external and internal values and pressures may not be suitable for the current challenges of policing. One issue that creates conflict within and outside of the police department is how police should allocate their time.

Allocation of Police Time

There is little agreement on how police should allocate their time among law enforcement, order maintenance, and community service, the three major functions of policing (see Chapter 4). Studies of why people call police departments illustrate this time pressure. Earlier and often cited studies are the focus of **Supplement 5.1**.

More recently, the Bureau of Justice Statistics (BJS) published its findings on policing, noting that in 2011, approximately one in eight U.S. residents who were age 16 or older contacted the police. Of those, 86 percent reported that the police were helpful; 93 percent reported that the police acted properly; and 85 percent were satisfied with the police response. Approximately nine in ten persons said they were "just as likely or more likely to contact the police again for a similar problem."

Studies of the allocation of police time and the reasons residents call police have important implications for police recruitment, as well as for understanding the role conflicts of those already in policing. If people are attracted to policing because they think most of an officer's time is spent in exciting chases of dangerous criminals and they have no concept of the many dull periods of waiting for action, they might be unhappy as police officers. If they have no concept of the service functions of policing and are not trained to perform those functions, life on the beat might come as an unpleasant surprise.

An additional problem is that police officers may encounter supervisors who do not give equal credit to successful performance of the three police functions. Catching dangerous criminals might result in a faster promotion than performing order maintenance or community service functions successfully. Police officers may experience a similar response from their colleagues and from the community.

Chapter 3 discussed the use of COMPSTAT, or computer comparative statistics. This system was alleged to have been responsible for crime reduction in New York City during the tenures of police commissioner William J. Bratton. COMPSTAT and other similar programs help direct the unassigned time of police in order to make them more efficient in time management. One expert described COMPSTAT as a management process used by police departments to process, map, and analyze crime data, which is then sent to operational managers, who have the power and responsibility to discuss the information with their subunits. They are held accountable for appropriate problem-solving responses. Both the Ford Foundation and the John F. Kennedy School of Government at Harvard University gave high marks to the system.[1]

One expert on policing and racism argued that the use of COMPSTAT prevents crime because it enables police to dispatch officers to areas in which crime happens. She maintained that blacks are supportive of the system, with 68 percent of those in a survey approving of the way in which the New York City police commissioner did his job. This expert argued against the existence of racial profiling, insisting that the higher incidences of stops of blacks compared to whites was an indication of where crime has occurred. Her evaluation of COMPSTAT was as follows: "No public policy change of the last quarter-century has done as much for the city's poor and minority neighborhoods as COMPSTAT policing."[2]

Not everyone agrees, and some researchers argue that COMPSTAT is not a wise use of police time and that it discriminates against minorities, as indicated in Criminal Justice Systems Dilemma 5.1. Furthermore, COMPSTAT is not a quick fix to lower crime rates. It requires major changes in organizational structure and thinking, and we do not yet know whether its use will have long-term success in reducing crime.[3]

Evidence-Based Practice

In 1998, a policing expert, Lawrence W. Sherman, published his research on evidence-based policing, defining it as follows:

> Evidence-based policing is the use of the best available research on the outcomes of police work to implement guidelines and evaluate agencies, units, and officers. Put more simply, evidence-based policing uses research to guide practice and evaluate practitioners. It uses the best evidence to shape the best practice.[4]

Criminal Justice Systems Dilemma 5.1

Allocation of Police Time and Crime Reduction

One of the criminal justice systems dilemmas faced in policing is how to allocate the time of officers on the streets in an effort to prevent crime and to do so without discriminating against minorities. Chapter 3 discussed the *broken windows* concept of policing, referring to New York City's efforts to reduce crime by reducing so-called *incivilities* that represent disorganization and crime.

> Physical incivilities often include such things as broken windows and vacant lots, while social incivilities include loitering, loud parties, drug sales and prostitution. Within contemporary theories highlighting the importance of incivilities, social and physical incivilities are unique characteristics of neighborhoods causally linked to a number of important outcomes including crime.[1]

Politicians and police administrators argued that the decrease in New York's crime rate was due to the reduction of incivilities by the method referred to as COMPSTAT. The emphasis was on cleaning up the streets by arresting minor offenders whose presence may suggest that the police are not in control. Administrators took pride in and gave police credit for the fact that New York City became a cleaner city and a safer place to live as the police took back the streets. Not all criminologists agree, however, and some who studied the crime rates of the 1990s insisted that more careful and scientific evaluations are necessary before the conclusions of the politicians and the police can be accepted.[2]

It was also suggested that minorities suffered as a result of the use of COMPSTAT in New York City. An example was the increased arrests for smoking marijuana in public view (MPV). Researchers who studied these arrests concluded that African Americans and Hispanics were disproportionately represented, and there was "no good evidence that it contributed to combating serious crime in the city. If anything, it had the reverse effect." It was a very expensive experiment, and thus, concluded the researchers, "an extremely poor trade-off of scarce law enforcement resources."[3]

---

1. Todd Armstrong and Charles Katz, "Further Evidence on the Discriminant Validity of Perceptual Incivilities Measures," *Justice Quarterly* 27(2) (April 2010): 280-304; quotation is on p. 281.
2. See, for example, Richard Rosenfeld et al., "Did Ceasefire, Compstat, and Exile Reduce Homicide?," *Criminology & Public Policy* 4(3) (August 2005): 419-450; James J. Willis et al., "Compstat and Bureaucracy: A Case Study of Challenges and Opportunities for Change," *Justice Quarterly* 21(3) (September 2004): 463-496.
3. Bernard E. Harcourt and Jens Ludwig, "Reefer Madness: Broken Windows Policing and Misdemeanor Marijuana Arrests in New York City, 1989-2000," *Criminology & Public Policy* 6(1) (February 2007) 165-181; quotation is on p. 176. See also the special edition of *Justice Quarterly* 31(1) (February 2014).

Source: Matthew Durose and Lynn Langton, Bureau of Justice Statistics, Special Report, "Requests for Police Assistance, 2011" (September 2013), p. 2, https://www.bjs.gov/content/pub/pdf/rpa11.pdf, accessed September 6, 2018.

The focus on evidence-based policing accompanies the emphasis placed by criminologists on obtaining facts through scientific studies and applying those facts to develop guidelines and public policies. Criminologists recognized the need to go beyond their historical approach of developing theories and studying criminal law and make efforts to apply their research to the development of public policies. The American Society of Criminology focused on evidence-based research as a foundation for public policy when in 2001 it began publishing a new journal: *Criminology & Public Policy*.

For decades, social scientists have published significant research, some of which involves the field of policing; however, Sherman emphasized that the evidence-based approach focuses not only on discovery but on researching ways to improve policing goals. The approach can tell us which policies/practices, measured by scientific evidence, produce the desired result (also measured by scientific research methods). Thus, decisions need not be made in the traditional way, based on customs, opinions, and subjective impressions but, rather, based on scientific facts. Experimental research alone is not sufficient. The results must be put into practice and scientifically measured, and policy adjustments made as a result.

Evidence-based research in policing has "gathered considerable momentum in recent years," despite the fact

Professions 5.1

New Professions for Criminal Justice Students

The text discusses the original article of Lawrence W. Sherman on the subject of evidence-based policing. Sherman stated that "[o]ne way to describe people who try to apply research is the role of 'evidence cop.'"[1] Evidence-based research opens up this and numerous other job opportunities both in the public and in the private sector.

In 2013, Tara Tripp and Sutham Cobkit published their study of "unexpected pathways" consisting of criminal justice career opportunities in the private sector. They surveyed job announcements of private businesses that have hired or might hire persons with degrees in criminal justice. They concluded that criminal justice programs should involve new courses and new certificates to prepare students for these opportunities in the private sector. Jobs include positions in fraud investigation (for example, in insurance companies), research on a variety of topics, intelligence gathering, private security, assistance with victims, legal assistance, and positions with defense contractors and consulting firms. The positions require a range of background, education, and experience, and vary in salaries and benefits.

Tripp and Cobkit concluded as follows:

> Focusing solely on the criminal justice system for potential job opportunities ignores a plethora of professions in the private sector available to criminal justice students....
>
> Numerous career pathways outside of the criminal and juvenile justice systems exist for students obtaining a criminal justice degree, and this concept should be communicated.[2]

1. Lawrence W. Sherman, *Evidence-Based Policing* (Washington, D.C.: Police Foundation, 1998), pp. 3-4, http://www.policefoundation.org, accessed July 13, 2014.
2. Tara Tripp and Sutham Cobkit, "Unexpected Pathways: Criminal Justice Career Options in the Private Sector," *Journal of Criminal Justice Education* 24(4) (December 2013): 478-494; quotations are on pp. 491 and 493.

---

that it has yet to focus on all of the aspects of policing.[5] The president of the Police Foundation (and a former police chief) argued in favor, stating that evidence-based policing is "an approach to controlling crime and disorder that promises to be more effective and less expensive than the traditional response-driven models, which cities can no longer afford."[6]

In addition to the information that evidence-based research might provide to improve policing, the approach results in the development of new career opportunities in the private as well as the public sectors, as summarized in Professions 5.1.

Proactive versus Reactive Policing: Domestic Violence

In his initial development of the importance of evidence-based research, as well as in his subsequent research, Sherman focused on applying the approach to the specific police practices with regard to domestic violence. Chapter 3 noted the difference between proactive and reactive policing. In the real world of practice, police do not spend most of their time engaging in the stereotype held by many: catching dangerous criminals. In fact, many police officers spend very little time in actual crime detection. Most police work is *reactive*, not *proactive*; that is, police are dependent on the assistance of victims, witnesses, and other citizens to report crimes.

There have been some changes in recent years. Chapter 3 examined problem-oriented and community-oriented policing, whereby police identify and try to eliminate problems that may be creating a criminal situation. Police have become proactive in other areas, too, such as identifying and arresting domestic violence offenders.

In recent years, more attention has been paid to *domestic violence*, which involves spouses abusing each other, parents abusing children, and children abusing each other or their parents. Some studies include courtship violence, also referred to as *intimate partner violence (IPV)*, which includes violence toward a former spouse, girlfriend, or boyfriend, as Chapter 2 briefly noted.

In earlier times, violence among intimates, and especially within the family, was considered a domestic problem, not a crime, and if police intervened at all, they did so mainly as mediators, not as law enforcement officers. Arrests were rare. In recent years, legislation and police and prosecutor policies have changed this approach. The federal Violence Against Women Act (VAWA) of 1994 (subsequently amended), along with agency policies to implement the statute, are significant. Included are provisions for programs that train police to handle domestic violence cases, for developing policies providing sanctions for officers who refuse to arrest in such cases, for developing guidelines for when to arrest in domestic violence cases, and so on.[7] After the passage of the VAWA, many states enacted statutes giving police discretion to arrest in misdemeanor cases they had not witnessed. Police departments began training officers in how to handle domestic violence, and some jurisdictions instituted a policy of mandatory arrests in domestic violence cases. But the evidence on the impact of police arrests in domestic violence cases is contradictory.

Under a mandatory arrest policy, the police officer must arrest the alleged perpetrator of domestic violence if there is sufficient evidence that violence has occurred. This approach has resulted in more arrests in domestic violence cases in which police act on their own, without waiting for victims to insist on pressing charges.

Some of the earlier evaluations of higher arrest rates in domestic violence cases show that this approach—as compared to a nonarrest policy—is more successful in preventing further domestic violence.[8] Other studies suggest that mandatory arrest policies do not have a deterrent effect.[9]

Still other studies report that the first time an offender is apprehended by police after a domestic violence call is the most potent one and that arrest is most effective at that time. Arrest also is more effective if followed by court-mandated treatment. Subsequent monitorings of these offenders reveal that the more educated the offender, the more likely it is that he or she will not repeat domestic violence offenses.[10]

It may also be important to look at the types of violence and the degree of seriousness of alleged domestic violence. Thus, domestic violence should be examined not in isolation but, rather, in the general context of violence. Police decisions regarding arrests may be affected by the relationship between the suspect and the victim.[11]

Even in jurisdictions in which mandatory arrest policies are in effect, police encounter alleged victims who refuse to cooperate. Many spouses do not want their partners arrested; if police insist and make the arrest, the complaining partner may become hostile, belligerent, and even violent. Thus, what appears to be a positive change in policing may result in greater role conflicts for police officers and in violence against them. Mandatory arrests may also increase the number of cases beyond a reasonable level for some prosecution offices.[12]

Other variables that should be considered in analyzing domestic violence and policing are those involving reasons why alleged victims do or do not report violence. Researchers have found several reasons for the lack of reporting: privacy concerns, fear of reprisal, and the desire to protect their assailants. But research also suggests that domestic violence victims are *more* likely to report violence than are other victims because they see the violence as more serious when it occurs in the home.[13]

Another issue regarding arrest policies in IPV cases is whether negative consequences may result from mandatory arrests. There is some evidence that in mandatory arrest cases, racial minorities are more likely to be arrested than whites. Females are more likely than males to be arrested and placed in detention.[14] Victims may be in a better position than police to determine what is best for them, and arresting the alleged offender may not be in the victims' best interests with regard to child care, financial support, or other issues. Victims are more likely to be arrested along with perpetrators; retaliation after the alleged perpetrator is arrested may be a threat.[15] Spotlight 5.1 contains the highlights of a BJS analysis of police response to domestic violence.

There is evidence that in the case of alleged abuse against the elderly, more abuse is likely following intervention as contrasted with an effort to educate the alleged abuser.[16] There is also evidence that police intervention in IPV and other domestic violence cases is dangerous to police. Physical assaults on police officers are greater in these instances than during any other category of calls.[17]

One final area of domestic violence and policing that is gaining more attention is police violence against their own intimate partners. The National Center for Women and Policing reports that at least 40 percent of police families experience some type of IPV, compared to about 10 percent of non-police families. IPV is serious in any situation but more so among police families because the officer has a gun, knows the location of the area's shelters for domestic violence abuse victims, and knows how to manipulate the system. It is also more likely that victims of domestic violence at the hands of police officers will be more frightened about calling the police department for help.[18]

Finally, in early September 2018, President Donald J. Trump signed a bill to encourage lawyers to devote time to pro bono representation of domestic violence victims, the Pro bono Work to Empower and Represent Act

Spotlight 5.1

Police Response to Domestic Violence, 2006-2015: Highlights

For nonfatal domestic violence victimizations occurring during the ten-year aggregate period from 2006-2015:

- **More than half (56%) of all victimizations were reported to police.**
- **Police responded to nearly two-thirds (64%) of reported victimizations in ten minutes or less.**
- **Reasons victims did not report a victimization to police included personal privacy (32%), protecting the offender (21%), the crime was minor (20%), and fear of reprisal (19%).**
- **Female victimizations (24%) were four times as likely as male victimizations (6%) to go unreported due to fear of reprisal.**
- **Overall, the offender was arrested or charges were filed in 39% of victimizations reported to police.**
- **In 23% of reported victimizations, police arrested an offender during their initial response.**
- **The victim or other household member signed a criminal complaint against the offender in about half (48%) of victimizations reported to police.**
- **The offender was arrested or charges were filed in 89% of the victimizations reported to police where a victim was seriously injured and signed a criminal complaint.**
- **About nine in ten local police departments serving 250,000 or more residents operated a full-time domestic violence unit.**

***Source:* Brian A. Reaves, Bureau of Justice Statistics, Special Report, "Police Response to Domestic Violence, 2006-2015" (May 2017), https://www.bjs.gov/content/pub/pdf/prdv0615.pdf, accessed September 7, 2018.**

of 2018, known as the POWER Act.[19] Some of the major provisions of that bill are reprinted in **Supplement 5.2**.

Hot Spots

One other recent approach in policing that gets a lot of attention is the focus of police efforts on those usually small places where crime most often occurs, referred to as *hot spots*. In accepting an award from and addressing the American Society of Criminology in 2017, David Weisburd addressed the concept and reviewed the literature on what he refers to as *place-based prevention* of crime, which, he maintains, challenged the traditional approach to placing crime prevention attention over large areas. Studies reveal that crime is not concentrated in "bad" neighborhoods or communities but spread throughout cities, and thus, police and communities should focus on these hot spots or, what Weisburd calls, the "law of crime concentration at places."[20]

The assumption of place-based prevention is that if police focus more attention on the hot spot areas of crime, they will reduce crime. This seems logical, but the focus may not be perceived in the same way by all, and scholars suggest that we need more research on how the community perceives additional police attention to hot spots. Furthermore, we need information on whether the extra cost of policing hot spots results in an overall reduction in cost of policing as well as of crime. In one recent study, researchers found "small but noteworthy crime reductions" in their analysis of policing hot spots.[21] Finally, as Weisburd emphasized, criminologists need to refine theoretical developments concerning the effect of place-based prevention on crime prevention.[22]

In another study, the importance of evidence-based research is noted in a discussion of whether policing hot spots in New York City was the cause of the significant reduction of crime in recent years. Police claimed that the decrease was due to policing, especially their focus on eliminating "broken windows," discussed earlier. And it seems logical that that might be the case. But the police did not have a significant research evaluation program in place; there is no way to know whether their strategies worked. Herein lies a dilemma. Research is expensive, and at a time when police department budgets are reduced, as has been the case in many departments in recent years, it is not likely they will allocate significant funds to research.[23]

Policing and Mental Health Issues

The National Alliance on Mental Illness recently reported that on any given day one in five U.S. adults experience some form of mental illness, and one in 25 experience serious mental illness. Approximately 20 percent of jail and prison inmates exhibit mental illness, and that figure is 70 percent among juveniles who are incarcerated.[24]

The crisis in mental health in the United States today is a critical issue for policing, and in many of the most recent criminal incidents, such as mass shootings, mental health issues are raised. A focus on mental health issues has also involved situations concerning returning veterans and how police interact with them.[25] In its May 2015 issue of *Criminology & Public Policy*, the American Society of Criminology included a series of articles on "Police Encounters with People with Mental Illness."

How to deal with those problems in a society that clearly has inadequate facilities and personnel for taking care of the mentally ill is a serious issue for police, and many are not trained in issues regarding mental illness. The problems are exacerbated by a lack of research evidence on mental illness and how it impacts policing as well as our lack of knowledge on the degree to which mentally ill people may be expected to be dangerous. Social scientists have made some suggestions regarding how police should react to mentally ill persons,[26] and some police departments have developed successful models for reacting to mentally ill persons. The Los Angeles Police Department, for example, developed a program of partnering police officers with mental health clinicians in an effort to reduce frivolous 911 calls from mentally challenged persons. The department employs nurses, doctors, and social workers to work alongside police. As one mental health expert noted, "[d]iverting nonviolent offenders to mental health services is ultimately better for their recovery and saves taxpayers money."[27] This does not, however, solve the need for law enforcement to recognize and respond to dangerous mentally challenged persons.[28]

There are also legal issues regarding police reactions to mentally challenged persons, as illustrated by the excerpt from *City & County of San Francisco v. Sheehan*, in **Supplement 5.3**.

Dilemmas in policing lead to various reactions by police. One is the increase in stress,[29] which is noted in **Supplement 5.4**. Another is that police retreat into a **subculture**, discussed in **Supplement 5.5**, which may include a code of silence.[30]

POLICE MISCONDUCT

Police officers have many opportunities to engage in improper behavior, such as *corruption*, defined as follows:

> A public official is corrupt if he accepts money or money's worth for doing something that he is under a duty to do anyway, that he is under a duty not to do, or to exercise a legitimate discretion for improper reasons.[31]

The possibility for corruption varies, with the greater opportunities available in larger cities, but corruption can be found in all types of police departments.

James Q. Wilson analyzed police corruption according to the type of organization in a police department. He defined three types of law enforcement styles and found those styles to be related to the degree of police corruption.[32] According to Wilson, most police corruption is found in departments characterized by the *watchman style*, in which police are expected to maintain order, not regulate conduct. Low salaries and the expectation that police will have other jobs increase the probabilities that police will be involved in corruption.

Corruption is found to a lesser degree in departments characterized by the *legalistic style*, with its emphasis on providing formal police training, recruiting from the middle class, offering greater promotional opportunities, and viewing law as a means to an end, rather than an end in itself. Formal sanctions are used more frequently than informal ones, with police giving less attention to community service and order maintenance than to law enforcement.

Corruption is not a serious problem in the third type of style, the *service style*. In this management style, law enforcement and order maintenance are combined, with an emphasis on good relationships between the police and the community. Police command is decentralized, with police on patrol working out of specialized units. Higher education and promotional opportunities are emphasized, and police are expected to lead exemplary private lives.

Lawrence W. Sherman analyzed police corruption according to types. The first, the *rotten apples*, refers to a department characterized by a few police officers who accept bribes and engage in other forms of corruption. Generally, those people are uniformed patrol officers, but they are loners who will accept bribes for overlooking traffic violations, licensing ordinances, or crimes. Some officers work in groups, termed *rotten pockets*, accepting bribes for nonenforcement of the law. Many members of the vice squad are found in this type.[33]

The second type of corruption, according to Sherman, is *pervasive organized corruption*, describing the highly organized hierarchical organization of the political processes of the community, which goes beyond the police force. Some police departments are characterized by widespread but unorganized corruption, labeled as *pervasive unorganized corruption*.[34]

Two important commissions devoted to the study of police corruption, the Knapp Commission and the Mollen Commission, concerning corruption in the New York Police Department, are discussed in **Supplement 5.6**. Corruption in the Los Angeles Police Department is discussed in **Supplement 5.7**.

There are many sources of potential corruption, but in today's policing world, the existence of illegal drugs is clearly one source. The nation's declared war on drugs presents criminal justice systems and police with one of their most frustrating problems. The escalation of drug trafficking has resulted in violence, damaged and ruined lives, enormous expense, and a crushing blow to all elements of criminal justice systems. Many jails and prisons are overcrowded, primarily because of drug offenders, many of whom are creating a new underworld within prisons, with some prison correctional officers being corrupted as a result. Civil cases are backed up for years to enable courts to process the drug cases.[35]

Police face the difficulty of confronting the massive drug problem without sufficient resources, whereas drug offenders have resources to tempt officers who earn relatively low salaries in highly stressful jobs. Police patrol officers are at high risk of corruption by drug dealers because of the arrest power, but drugs also lead to corruption at other levels of law enforcement. Police have been known to extort money or property from drug dealers in exchange for not arresting them, to steal the drugs they seize from suspects, to accept bribes for tampering with evidence or committing perjury, to sell information about forthcoming drug raids, and so on (see again Spotlight 5.1).

A specific example of great proportion occurred in Tulia, Texas, population 5,000, where 46 defendants, 39 of whom were African American, were convicted of drug offenses and sentenced to a total of 750 years in prison. These defendants were convicted primarily on the basis of the undercover work and testimonies of Tom Coleman, who lied about the evidence. Coleman was convicted of perjury and sentenced to ten years' probation but could not be charged with the more serious offense of aggravated perjury because the **statute of limitations** had expired. The defendants were incarcerated, but after the case was exposed nationally on *60 Minutes*, the Texas governor pardoned 35 of them. A documentary further publicized the big drug bust and its problems.[36]

In addition to the misconduct of police that can be attributed to drugs are the allegations surrounding violence. The next section discusses violence by the police and violence against the police.

VIOLENCE AND THE POLICE

Historically, police have been viewed as agents who are necessary for establishing law and order, often by applying justice on the spot. Although violence between police and citizens had been reported earlier, the violence and unrest that occurred in the 1960s led to demands for larger and better-trained police forces. During that decade, predominantly white police and minority residents clashed in hot, crowded cities. Many student protesters also found themselves in conflict with the police, and the police experienced disillusionment with a system that they did not believe protected their interests. They, too, became more active. Police unions were established; these were viewed by some as a representation of police hostility.

In short, the 1960s brought open violence between police and residents, and the 1970s brought more cases of police violence and corruption. Meanwhile, crime rates began to rise, and people demanded greater police protection. Demands for a more professionalized police force were heard, along with allegations of police misconduct through the unreasonable use of force.

Police are entitled to use force. The issue lies with how much force and under what circumstances. The perception of some is that police use excessive force and that they do it frequently. One scholar conducted a thorough review of the literature and summarized what we know about police use of force into three categories:

- What we know with substantial confidence
- What we know with modest confidence
- What we do not know

In the first category, we know with substantial confidence that police do not use force often; that the force they use most frequently involves shoving, grabbing, or pushing, rather than more serious force; and that force by police usually occurs when they are effecting an arrest and the

Spotlight 5.2

Police and Blacks; Some Reactions to Conflict

Quotes from the respective web pages of Black Life Matters and United and Police Officers' Lives Matter are presented here to pinpoint the two organizations. Police Officers' Lives Matter was established in 2016 to assist the families of fallen police officers, and some officers also participate in a Facebook web page:

Police Officers' Lives Matter

The photograph of police officers on this page has this statement: "May God Protect Our Protectors During this Scary Time."

The following statement also appears: "This page was created to stand up for the police who sadly at times are forced to kill or be killed. We support & love our LEOs."[1]

Black Life Matters

"Black Life Matters believes that all life matters.

That being said, there are specific matters that categorically face the African American community. Issues that can only be addressed if we, the African American people, work together to solve them.

We have a unique history in our country and that history plays a part in the condition of our people today. Our mission is to bring forth the plans and solutions that take us from the dream to the physical manifestation of our excellent and complete potential.

We are a diverse people. Our strengths and weaknesses differ, but one thing is strikingly clear: we are united. Through collaboration, we aim to strengthen our people, our families and our community . . . one transformation at a time.

We've heard it said that when confronted with someone else's dilemma, it matters not what happens to you if you get involved, rather then [sic] what happens to them if you do not.

Accountability begins with us. We are not victims. We are victors.

Our mission is to see that victory through for every man, woman and child in the African American community."[2]

1. Police Officers' Lives Matter, https://www.facebook.com/pg/Policeofficerslivesmatter/about/?ref=page_internal, accessed September 10, 2018.
2. Black Life Matters. United, http://www.blacklifematters.org/our-mission, accessed September 10, 2018.

---

suspect is resisting. With modest confidence, we know that the use of force by police tends not to be related to gender, age, and ethnicity; that the use of force typically occurs when the suspects are mentally ill or are under the influence of alcohol or other drugs; and that the use of force is committed by a small percentage of police but they represent a disproportionate number of incidents.[37]

For some of these conclusions, more research is needed. Clearly, research is needed in the final category: what we do *not* know about police use of force. We do not know the incidence of the use of force. We do not know the influence of the following on police use of force: training, discipline, the use of technology, police department policies, or department organization. And finally, we do not know very much about the situations and the transactions that evoke police use of force, other than that police tend to respond to interpersonal disturbances and violent crime. Situations such as a fleeing person are also likely to evoke their response.[38]

Police use of force does not always involve excessive force; nor is the force always deadly, but it is the use of deadly force that, understandably, evokes the most intense response, particularly when that force is perceived as unreasonable, as has been the case in many police shootings of black persons in recent years. Blacks have responded by organizing Black Life Matters; Police have their Police Officers' Lives Matter. The mission statement of each is featured in Spotlight 5.2.

Although any police interaction with others can be controversial, it is the use of deadly force that is the focus of many complaints about policing.

Police Use of Deadly Force

Police use of **deadly force** has been defined as "such force as under normal circumstances poses a high risk of death or serious injury to its human target, regardless of whether or not death, serious injury, or any harm actually result."[39] Police officers may use deadly force under some circumstances, and even if that force results in injury or death, the officers will have immunity from prosecution. In a 2018 case, the U.S. Supreme Court ruled in favor of such immunity in a case in which an officer shot and wounded a woman who refused to obey at least two police orders to drop a knife as she approached another woman in her driveway. Justice Sonia Sotomayor dissented in the case, stating that the Court was permitting police to "shoot first and think later." **Supplement 5.8**, which excerpts her dissent in *Kisela v. Hughes*, contains the major facts and summarizes the law regarding qualified immunity when police use force, along with Justice Sotomayor's reaction to the Court's per curiam (not authored by a named person) opinion.[40]

If law enforcement officers use deadly force improperly, they may be prosecuted and they (and the police department and the city) may be liable to the injured person(s) (or, in the event of death, to the family of the deceased) in a civil suit.

Excessive use of force may occur while police are apprehending suspects either on foot or in vehicles, or it may occur when suspects are already apprehended. We will consider first the use of force in attempts to apprehend suspects.

Fleeing Felon Rule

In the past, shooting any fleeing felon was permitted. Because all felonies were punishable by death, it was assumed that any felon would resist arrest by all possible means. The **fleeing felon rule** developed during a time when apprehending criminals was more difficult than it is today. Police did not have weapons that could be used for shooting at a long distance; nor did they have communication techniques that enabled them to quickly notify other jurisdictions that a suspect had escaped arrest. Therefore, if fleeing felons were not apprehended immediately, they could escape and begin a new life in another community without fear of detection by the police.

As more powerful and efficient weapons were developed, it became easier for police to apprehend escaping felons, and many did so by the use of deadly force, even though the fleeing felons were not dangerous. Such actions were not necessary to protect the officer and others; nor were they necessary to apprehend felons. Despite these developments, however, most jurisdictions adopted the common law rule that permitted police officers to use deadly force in apprehending fleeing felons. This practice was condemned by many commentators and scholars, but it was considered legal until 1985, when the U.S. Supreme Court ruled that Tennessee's fleeing felon statute was unconstitutional under the facts of the case.

Tennessee v. Garner involved an unarmed youth who was killed by a police officer as he fled from an unoccupied house. The officer could see that the fleeing felon was a young male and apparently unarmed. But the officer argued that he knew that, if the youth got over the fence, he could escape, so he fired at him. The Tennessee statute allowed an officer to shoot a suspect if it appeared to be necessary to prevent the escape of a felon.[41]

In *Garner*, the U.S. Supreme Court emphasized that, to be lawful, police use of deadly force must be reasonable. Deadly force is reasonable under the following circumstances:

- To prevent an escape when the suspect has threatened the officer with a weapon
- When there is a threat of death or serious physical injury to the officer or others
- If there is probable cause to believe that the person has committed a crime involving the infliction or threatened infliction of serious physical harm and, where practical, some warning has been given by the officer

A statute that permits an officer to shoot a fleeing felon may be constitutional in some instances; however, when used against a young, slight, and unarmed youth who was suspected of burglary, deadly force was unreasonable and therefore unlawful.

Vehicle Pursuits

A second area in which police may be involved in deadly force is in vehicle pursuits. High-speed chases may end in injury or death to the suspect, the police pursuer, or innocent bystanders. It is argued that police vehicle pursuits are not worth the results in property damage, human injuries, and deaths. Some courts have held police departments liable for the consequences of such pursuits. Consequently, police departments restrict the types of cases in which vehicle pursuits are permitted or forbid them entirely.

The LAPD provides an example of policy changes, which took effect in May 2003. Los Angeles had more police pursuits than any other city, and almost 60 percent of those were the result of traffic violations or other minor infractions. Under the new policy, police may engage in vehicle pursuits only in serious cases and with a helicopter tracking them. Later the department began working with ONSTAR to use a global positioning system (GPS) to enable officers to push a switch and stop the speeding vehicle of a fleeing suspect.[42]

The U.S. Supreme Court has held that a high-speed vehicle pursuit that results in death is not a constitutional violation of the suspect's rights unless the officer in pursuit had a "purpose to cause harm unrelated to the legitimate object of arrest." The Court upheld a high-speed police chase of two boys on a motorcycle that refused to stop when the officer commanded them to do so. The officer was driving up to 100 m.p.h. in a residential area, which was a violation of the department's written policy. During the 75-second chase, the motorcycle overturned and the deputy's vehicle hit the driver, killing him. In *Sacramento County, California v. Lewis*, the Supreme Court held that the motorcyclist's constitutional rights were not violated because there was no evidence that the officer intended to harm him.[43]

Supplement 5.9 discusses subsequent vehicle chases that were or were not considered acceptable; attention is given here to a more recent case, *Mullenix v. Luna*, decided in 2015, in which the U.S. Supreme Court held a police officer's action reasonable when he fired at a speeding car in the dark from an overpass and killed the driver. The officer's supervisor had told him to wait and see whether the spikes the police had put on the road were sufficient to stop the car, but the officer fired without the supervisor's permission.

The Court noted that the driver was reportedly an intoxicated fugitive who had already threatened to fire at police and who would no doubt encounter another officer on the road if he continued driving. He had already led police on a 25-mile high-speed chase.

Justice Sotomayor dissented in this case as she did in 2018, when the Court upheld qualified immunity for an officer in another case (see again **Supplement 5.8**), and she used some of the same language, accusing the Court of adopting a "shoot now, think later" policy for police. According to Sotomayor, the officer should have waited to see whether the spike strip stopped the speeding car before he shot. "He [fired six rounds in the dark] less than a second before the car hit spike strips deployed to stop it. . . . Because it was clearly established under the Fourth Amendment that an officer in Mullenix's position should not have fired the shot, I respectfully dissent."[44]

Police Brutality

In a classic and frequently cited article on police brutality published in 1968, sociologist Albert J. Reiss Jr. began his discussion with a 1903 quotation by a former New York City police commissioner:

> For three years, there has been through the courts and the streets a dreary procession of citizens with broken heads and bruised bodies against few of whom was violence needed to [e]ffect an arrest. Many of them had done nothing to deserve an arrest. In a majority of such cases, no complaint was made. If the victim complains, his charge is generally dismissed. The police are practically above the law.[45]

Police brutality may cause serious injury or even death, and police use of deadly force is at the root of most of the controversy surrounding questionable police behavior. Significant media attention was given to several incidents of police brutality in the past. Some examples are as follows:

- In 1991 in Los Angeles, an eyewitness taped police beating Rodney King, an African-American suspect, who suffered multiple skull fractures, a broken ankle, a crushed cheekbone, internal injuries, and numerous bruises. All four officers were charged and tried in a *state* court; all but one of the charges resulted in acquittals; and the judge declared a mistrial on the remaining charge. Riots, constituting one of the most deadly disturbances to date, followed. The officers were tried for civil rights violations in a *federal* court; two were acquitted; two were convicted and served prison time.[46]
- Between 1999 and 2008, several police officers in New York City were tried for brutality against arrestees. Some were convicted. For example, Officer Justin A. Volpe entered a guilty plea to beating and sodomizing Abner Louima, a Haitian immigrant. Volpe is serving a 30-year prison sentence. Some officers were acquitted of brutality. In 2008, a judge acquitted three NYPD officers of various charges in the shooting death of Sean Bell, a 23-year-old black man, early in the morning of the day Bell was to be married.[47]
- In 2014, violent protests occurred after grand juries declined to return indictments against a white police officer who shot and killed an unarmed black teen in Ferguson, Missouri, and a black adult's life ended after police in New York City placed him in a choke hold.
- In August 2018, a white female police officer, returning to her apartment building at night, entered the wrong

apartment and shot and killed the black occupant. She was arrested and charged with manslaughter.

Numerous other examples are available, and the hostility between residents, especially minorities, and police, has been manifested in demonstrations throughout the country. Earlier discussions have looked at racism and the development of organizations such as Black Life Matters. During some of these demonstrations, there have been incidents of violence against the police.

Violence Against the Police

In July 2016, as Dallas, Texas, police officers monitored a peaceful rally in the heart of the city, where hundreds gathered to protest two recent police shootings and to show support for the families of the victims. The rally turned deadly, however, as described by the *Dallas Morning News* the following morning: "AMBUSH: 11 Officers Shot; 4 Dead: Sniper's Fire During Downtown Protest." Actually, 12 were shot; 5 officers died (one was a member of the Dallas Area Rapid Transit).[48]

A 23-year-old New Jersey police officer, Melvin Santiago, who had finished the police academy only seven months earlier, was shot to death in 2014 while responding to a report of an armed robbery. The location was not far from a gas station where Santiago had been robbed as a teen, at which time he vowed to become a police officer so he could make the area safer for his younger brother and cousins. Reportedly, 27-year-old Lawrence Campbell entered a store; asked the security guard where to find greeting cards; walked in that direction after the guard answered him; left the store; told someone to watch the news as he would become famous; reentered the store carrying a knife; overpowered the guard and took his firearm; and, after the officers arrived, shot Santiago in the head three times as he exited the squad car. Campbell apparently intended to kill two other officers as he fired three times at another squad car. Police shot and killed him; no other officers were injured. The suspect apparently had no intention of committing an armed robbery but rather, appeared to be planning to kill a police officer. An unconfirmed report suggested that the killing might have been retaliation for a police shooting.[49]

Also in 2014, officers Wenjian Liu and Rafael Ramos were ambushed in their squad car in New York City, apparently unaware that seconds earlier an all-points-bulletin had been issued concerning the alleged shooter, Ismaaiyl Brinsley. Police alleged that Brinsley "fired several rounds into the officers' heads and upper bodies" after he shot his former girlfriend in Maryland and proceeded to New York City to kill police officers. Brinsley, who had a lengthy criminal record, had posted information online and made comments such as "Watch what I'm going to do" and "[T]hey killed two; we kill two," apparently referring to the police killings of Eric Garner and Michael Brown for which no indictments were returned. Brinsley, 28, shot and killed himself a few minutes after the police were killed without ever having a chance to draw their weapons.

Policing is dangerous, and police are a close group, even with officers they do not know. It is common for large numbers of police to come from all over the country to attend the funeral of a colleague killed in the line of duty.

Although such incidents are not common, law enforcement officers are at a higher risk of workplace violence than are other types of employees. In 2017, 46 law enforcement officers (35 white, 9 black/African American, and 2 American Indian/Alaska Native; 43 men and 3 women) were killed feloniously; 60,211 officers were assaulted and of those 30.4 percent sustained injuries. Of the assaulted, the largest percentage (30.4 percent) were responding to disturbance calls, such as domestic disputes and bar fights.[50]

Police also encounter hostility that may result in verbal abuse. It is debatable which comes first and which causes which, but there are indications that both verbal and physical violence against police officers are accompanied by violence by police officers.[51]

Violence against the police has serious repercussions. Officers who survive may have physical injuries or psychological problems that preclude further work in law enforcement. In addition to financial problems, police who are subject to violence may develop feelings of hostility and fear, experience difficulty making decisions, feel alone in social situations, suffer from emotional problems, and develop sleep disorders.

THE CONTROL OF POLICING

Although only a minority of police officers may engage in misconduct, any misconduct is serious and should be subject to discipline. Policies and programs should be developed to avoid as much misconduct as possible. Police misconduct may be controlled from within or outside the department.

Regulation by Police Departments

Regulation of police conduct is not easy, given the number of persons involved, the extent of the potentially compromising situations, and the limitations on funding for recruitment and training; however, the efficient operation of any department requires the internal disciplining of employees. In the case of police departments, it is important that the public's image of internal operations also be positive.

Police departments should update their policies as needed given changing situations. Policies must be clearly articulated and enforced actively and fairly. If officers believe that they will not be reprimanded for violating departmental policies, those policies may be ineffective in curbing police abuse of discretion. Once a violation of policy is alleged, reaction should be swift and fair, with the accused being afforded an opportunity to be heard and to respond. Police departments should take measures to identify violence-prone officers in an attempt to avert problems.

A study funded by the federal office of Community Oriented Policing Services (COPS) and conducted by the Police Executive Research Forum (PERF) reported that approximately one-fourth of the larger law enforcement agencies have an *early warning system*, which is designed to detect officers who might abuse their power. According to PERF, there is evidence that these systems are successful in reducing problem behaviors. The early warning systems analyze citizen complaints, officer firings, high-speed chases, reports of the use of force, and other criteria to identify officers who are potential problems. Generally, the first reaction will be for the officer's immediate supervisor to talk with him or her and document what the officer is told and the response. This information should be reviewed by a higher-ranking commander. Some departments involve the higher-ranking person directly; some require the identified officers to attend special training classes. Officers who are identified early as potential problems may never become problems. Another advantage of early intervention is to alert supervisors to their roles in identifying and preventing problem behavior. The researchers emphasized that, for early intervention programs to be successful, they must involve accountability of supervisors and higher-up commanders. Examples of potential identifiers are frequent traffic stops of women or minorities.[52]

Local police departments can also help control policing by establishing clearly written policies to assist officers in their decision making.

Federal Regulations

Another method for regulating local and state police is for federal agencies, especially the U.S. Department of Justice (DOJ) to be involved. Federal monitors may be appointed to oversee required changes in a department after findings of corruption and other problems following federal investigations, which may be accompanied by federal court orders.

For example, in April 2014, the DOJ reported that its investigation of the Albuquerque Police Department revealed a "pattern or practice of systemic deficiencies that have pervaded" the department for "many years." The police suffered from "inadequate oversight, inadequate investigation of incidents of force, inadequate training of officers to ensure they understand what is permissible or not." The result was that the officers frequently violated the Fourth Amendment (see Appendix A) rights of citizens and engaged in excessive force with them. The DOJ called for 44 changes, including the deadly force policies.[53]

In July 2014, a federal investigation of three years concluded that the Newark, New Jersey police had engaged in a pattern of bias against minorities, especially with regard to stop-and-frisks. The investigation called for a number of reforms, including the appointment of a federal monitor to oversee police activities.[54]

In August 2016, the Department of Justice (DOJ) reported that the Baltimore Police Department had engaged in discriminatory and unconstitutional policing. Specifically: "Racially disparate impact is present at every stage of BPD's enforcement actions, from the initial decision to stop individuals on Baltimore streets to searches, arrests, and uses of force.... These racial disparities, along with the evidence suggesting intentional discrimination, erode the community trust that is critical to effective policing." According to the report, police disproportionately pulled over African Americans in traffic stops and made pat downs without grounds to believe the suspect was a threat. In addition, the police in that jurisdiction used "overly aggressive tactics that unnecessarily escalate encounters, increase tensions, and lead to unnecessary force."[55]

Regulation by Courts

If police departments do not control themselves adequately, courts may intervene. In addition to monitoring, courts have two major ways of controlling policing: excluding evidence and providing a forum for civil lawsuits against police officers and their departments.

If police seize evidence illegally or secure confessions improperly, the evidence may be excluded from trial. This procedure is the result of the U.S. Supreme Court's **exclusionary rule**. In 1914, the Supreme Court held that the Fourth Amendment (which prohibits unreasonable searches and seizures; see Appendix A) would have no meaning unless courts prohibited the use of illegally seized evidence. Consequently, when the police conducted an illegal search, the evidence they seized could not be used in *federal* cases. In 1961, the Court held that the exclusionary rule also applies to the states.[56]

The exclusionary rule is controversial, mainly because it applies after the fact. When illegally seized evidence is excluded from a trial, we know who the suspect is and may believe that guilt is obvious. Thus, for instance, when a judge rules that a gun allegedly used in a murder cannot be admitted at the suspect's trial because the evidence was obtained illegally by the police, and the suspect goes free because there is not enough legal evidence for a conviction, there may be strong public reaction of disbelief and outrage.

The exclusionary rule serves a symbolic purpose. According to one scholar, it is "a symbol of our system of criminal procedure. It is lauded as a crowning achievement of a free society."[57] If police violate individual rights to obtain evidence to convict alleged criminals, the government, in a sense, is supporting crime. When this occurs, the government becomes a lawbreaker, and in the words of a noted jurist, "it breeds contempt for law; it invites... anarchy."[58]

The second reason for the exclusionary rule is a practical one: It is assumed that the rule prevents police from engaging in illegal searches and seizures. According to the U.S. Supreme Court, the exclusionary rule "compels respect for the constitutional guarantee in the only effectively available way—by removing the incentive to disregard it."[59] It is difficult to know whether that statement is true because most illegal searches conducted to harass or punish take place in secret and may not be reported. Research on the issue is inconclusive. There is evidence, however, that the rule has led some police departments to increase the quantity and quality of police training, thus educating officers in what they may and may not do regarding search and seizure.[60]

In recent years, the exclusionary rule has come under severe attack, with calls for its abolition or modification. Most of the arguments are the reverse of the arguments in favor of the rule. First is the argument of the symbolism of abolition, based on the view that, when people see guilty persons going free as a result of a technicality, they lose respect for law and order, and criminal justice systems are weakened. The public's perception of letting guilty people go free is crucial.

Second, the abolitionists contend that the exclusionary rule should be eliminated because it results in the release of guilty people. The rule "is attacked as one of the chief technical loopholes through which walk the guilty on their way out of the courthouse to continue their depredations."[61] It makes no difference how many: One is too many, argue the abolitionists.

Third, the possibility of having evidence excluded from trial because it was not properly seized leads defendants to file numerous motions to suppress evidence, which consumes a lot of time and contributes to court congestion. In criminal cases, objections to search and seizure are the issues raised most frequently.

The U.S. Supreme Court has recognized some exceptions to the exclusionary rule. Under the **good faith exception**, illegally obtained evidence is not excluded from trial if it can be shown that police secured the evidence in good faith; that is, they had a reasonable belief that they were acting in accordance with the law. In *Massachusetts v. Sheppard*, the Supreme Court held that when police conduct a search in good faith, even if the technical search warrant is defective, the seized evidence should not be excluded from the trial.[62]

In 1995, the Supreme Court ruled that an arrest based on incorrect information as the result of a clerical error could stand because, when analyzed objectively, there was no evidence that the arresting officer was not acting reasonably.[63]

The U.S. Supreme Court has interpreted the U.S. Constitution to permit the use of evidence seized by officers who had a warrant to search one apartment but searched the wrong apartment and found illegal drugs. In *Maryland v. Garrison*, the Court reasoned that, because the search was in good faith, and because excluding its use in such cases would not deter police, who thought they were searching an apartment included in the warrant, nothing positive would be gained by applying the exclusionary rule in this fact pattern.[64]

The U.S. Supreme Court has held that a defendant's federal constitutional rights are not violated when police officers lose or destroy evidence that might have been used to establish the defendant's innocence, provided the officers' actions were made in good faith. The case of *Arizona v. Youngblood* involved Larry Youngblood, who had been convicted of the kidnapping, molestation, and sexual assault of a 10-year-old boy. The police failed to refrigerate the victim's semen-stained clothing or to make tests capable of showing whether the semen had come from Youngblood. The results of such tests might have shown that Youngblood was not the offender. Chief Justice William H. Rehnquist, writing for the majority, argued that the omission could "at worst be described as negligent."[65]

In response to the U.S. Supreme Court's adoption of the good faith exception to the exclusionary rule, some state courts have held that it does not apply under their state constitutions; therefore, all illegally seized evidence must be excluded at trial, regardless of the motivation of the officer who seized the evidence. These lower court decisions are permitted because they result in enlarging, not reducing defendants' rights.

The U.S. Supreme Court has also recognized a second major exception to the exclusionary rule: the **inevitable discovery rule**. Illegally seized evidence will be admitted at trial if it can be shown that, eventually, the evidence would have been discovered by legal methods. Writing for the Court in *Nix v. Williams*, Chief Justice Warren E. Burger said, "Exclusion of physical evidence that would inevitably have been discovered adds nothing to either the integrity or fairness of a criminal trial."[66]

In a 1990 case, the U.S. Supreme Court further demonstrated its relaxing of the exclusionary rule. In 1980, the Court had held that the Fourth Amendment prohibits police from entering a suspect's home without a warrant and without the suspect's consent to effect a felony arrest. The Court stated that its reason for this rule was to protect the physical integrity of the home. In 1990, the Court ruled that even a violation of this earlier case does not invalidate a statement made by the accused *after* the warrantless entry of the home if the accused makes a statement to police *outside* the home. It is not necessary to exclude the statement, despite the illegal entry into the home. The prohibition against the warrantless entry of the home is to protect the home's physical integrity, "not to grant criminal suspects protection for statements made outside their premises, where the police have probable cause to make an arrest."[67]

In 1991, a sharply divided U.S. Supreme Court permitted the use of coerced confessions in some circumstances. In 1967, the Supreme Court had articulated the *harmful error rule*, which holds that, if a confession is coerced, it must be excluded at trial. But in *Arizona v. Fulminante*, the Court held that the Constitution does not require the automatic exclusion of the coerced confession. Rather, a coerced confession is to be considered like any other trial error; it is to be analyzed under the circumstances, and the trial court is to make a decision regarding whether it is a harmful error beyond a reasonable doubt. If so, it must be excluded; if not, it is a *harmless error*, and the evidence may be used against the suspect.[68]

A 2009 U.S. Supreme Court case provided another example of an exception to the exclusionary rule. That case, *Herring v. United States*, is excerpted in **Supplement 5.10**. In effect, this case changes the exclusionary rule so that it now takes into account the mental state of the police when errors are made in securing evidence. In *Herring*, the Court held that the error was negligent but not reckless or deliberate. The case was decided by a 5-to-4 vote.[69]

In 2011, the U.S. Supreme Court held that when police "conduct a search in compliance with binding precedent that is later overruled," the secured evidence may be admitted in court. To exclude it would not have a deterrent effect on police and would "come at a high cost to both the truth and the public safety."[70]

In 2016, the U.S. Supreme Court decided another case, *Utah v. Strieff*,[71] involving the exclusionary rule. Portions of the Court's opinion and that of one dissent are presented in **Supplement 5.11**.

In addition to the exclusionary rule, courts assist in the regulation of police actions through civil cases. The use of civil lawsuits to bring actions against police (or other authorities) that violate citizens' civil rights is thought to be an effective deterrent for such illegal actions. Even if these lawsuits do not deter other violations, civil actions permit abuse victims (or their survivors) to recover monetary damages for their physical injuries (or death) and for emotional, psychological, and economic damages.

Civil actions are brought under federal statutes and are commonly called *1983 actions*, after the section of the U.S. Code in which the provision for such actions is codified.[72] Section 1983 actions may be brought by persons who are injured as a result of police negligence as well as for police mistreatment or "deliberate indifference" resulting in injury to persons or damage to their property. Civil actions against police represent a growing body of civil law and increasing expenses for the municipalities that are legally responsible for those actions. These civil lawsuits, however, are not easily won by plaintiffs.

Community Relations

Another method of controlling police activities is through community involvement and improved police-community relationships. It is vital that relationships between police and the community be improved. Police are not able to apprehend most criminals without the support of citizens. The U.S. Commission on Civil Rights emphasized that the men and women who are authorized to make arrests depend to a great extent on the cooperation of the public. "Perhaps the most valuable asset these officers can possess is credibility with the communities they serve."[73]

The importance of these contacts is emphasized by studies showing that citizens who have positive images of the police are more likely to report crimes than are those who have negative images. Those most likely to have negative images of the police are members of the lower socioeconomic class, African Americans, and other nonwhites—persons who feel a general alienation from the political process and those who perceive an increase in crime in their neighborhoods.

As noted in Chapter 3, community-oriented policing is in vogue today. Earlier studies disclosed some positive results, such as crime reduction[74] and crime prevention. Police educate the community about methods to prevent crime. Community organization activities in which police and the community work together to identify community problems are helpful. Herman Goldstein, who has written extensively about numerous criminal justice issues, concluded that full development of the overall concept of community policing, including a "concern with the substance of policing as well as its form," could "provide the integrated strategy for improving the quality of policing."[75]

We have already mentioned that violence by the police may evoke violence against the police. Earlier commissions underscored police violence as a catalyst for urban rioting in the 1960s.[76] But they also noted the impact of race in explaining violence by and against the police. Efforts to increase diversity in policing deserve analysis.

AFFIRMATIVE ACTION RECRUITMENT AND HIRING

Diversity in police departments is increasingly being recognized as one way to improve the services police offer to the community, as well as to improve the community's perception of police.

The need to recruit women and racial minorities was emphasized by the U.S. Commission on Civil Rights, which concluded the following:

> Serious underutilization of minorities and women in local law enforcement agencies continues to hamper the ability of police departments to function effectively in and earn the respect of predominantly minority neighborhoods, thereby increasing the probability of tension and violence.

In light of that finding, the commission recommended that "[p]olice department officials should develop and implement affirmative action plans so that ultimately the force reflects the composition of the community it serves."[77]

Recruitment of women and minority officers has had some help from the courts, with both groups having filed successful affirmative action cases under federal statutes. Women have successfully argued that they were discriminated against in hiring, on-the-job assignments, and promotions. After a decade of decisions on affirmative action policies concerning minorities and women, in 1987 the U.S. Supreme Court held that it is permissible for employers to consider gender and race in hiring.[78]

Several affirmative action cases that might be applicable to hiring in policing have been decided by the U.S. Supreme Court since the 1987 decision. They are noted in **Supplement 5.12**.

Summary

This chapter focused on problems and issues connected with policing in a complex society. Political pressures from within the department, along with pressures from the community and other outside forces, create problems. Problems may be related to the role conflicts of policing. Most officers receive more training in law enforcement than in order maintenance and performance of community services. Many of them view policing primarily as law enforcement; superiors may evaluate them by their work in that area. However, studies show that officers spend less time in law enforcement than in other police functions. Nor are the lines always clear regarding law enforcement. For example, today most departments view domestic violence as a law enforcement issue, not a social problem, yet not all police administrators, officers, or the public agree. But domestic violence among police has also become an issue.

Police encounter numerous stressors on their jobs. Some are due to the nature of the job and varying citizen expectations, and many people do not hesitate to complain if all police functions are not performed quickly, efficiently, and adequately. The real problem may lie in our unrealistic expectations of police. In theory, we want them to enforce all laws; however, in reality, we will not tolerate full enforcement—police will not and cannot do that, anyway. We expect the police to prevent crime, but that is not always possible either. We think that they should be authoritarian in enforcement situations yet maintain a supportive and friendly approach in others. We authorize them to handle all kinds of emergencies, yet we do not provide them with the resources or authority for these functions. No matter what police do, they encounter conflicts, and we cannot separate policing and its context from the rest of our society.

Stress may become a major issue for police. Officers encounter many situations that may cause concern. The chapter discussed some of them, including external political pressures and how to allocate their time among their many responsibilities. Evidence-based practice is important. Proactive versus reactive policing, especially in domestic violence cases, often leads to danger for the officers and others. Some police even become involved in intimate partner violence in their own households. Deciding where to focus their efforts in the community may be controversial, and policing in an environment in which mental illness is an issue can be a serious problem.

Police misconduct is another problem and has been studied extensively. Reports vary as to the pervasiveness and nature of misconduct, but it is clear that at least some police are involved in drug transactions and other illegal acts. Departmental efforts to eradicate this illegal behavior are not always successful.

Police use of deadly force has become a critical issue in many departments. Police are permitted to use some force, but the *abuse* of that responsibility is a focus of concern. Court decisions have required changes in the use of deadly force, and some police departments have responded with a greater emphasis on proper training in the use of deadly force. In addition, some have established more detailed departmental policies on the use of vehicular pursuits. Despite these changes, some police use excessive force, leading to allegations of police brutality.

Violence and brutality by police came into national focus in the widely publicized beating of Rodney King, an African American, by white police officers. Violence against police and police violence against residents lead to serious repercussions, as illustrated by the deadly and destructive Los Angeles riots after the state acquittals of the officers tried in the King case. Recent allegations of police violence have refocused attention on this serious policing problem. Violence against police is also an important concern in today's world.

Efforts to control improper policing have come from department regulations, court decisions, civil actions against police, and the improvement of community-police relations. The most controversial of these efforts has been the U.S. Supreme Court's exclusionary rule, whereby evidence obtained by police in violation of a suspect's constitutional rights may be excluded from that individual's trial. The Court has created some exceptions to the exclusionary rule, such as good faith and inevitable discovery and retracted the rule in other ways. Civil actions against police may serve as a deterrent to improper police behavior, and an increasing number of these suits are being filed under the federal code.

Further problems and issues in policing surround affirmative action programs aimed at employing more women and racial and ethnic minorities. These groups argue that the police cannot understand their problems and gain the support of their members unless the groups are represented adequately among police officers and administrators. Others argue that recruitment efforts have lowered standards or that court decisions upholding affirmative action programs for increasing the number of women and racial minorities on a police force are unfair and create internal problems for police. The U.S. Supreme Court's upholding of some affirmative action policies in 2003 gave a green light to universities and businesses—including law enforcement agencies—to attempt to achieve greater diversity in admissions and hiring. These cases were covered in the Supplement.

Despite problems in policing, many officers are satisfied with their profession. Problems exist in any profession, and perhaps it is good that we are never free of the opportunities for improvement that problems present. Policing is not for everyone, but for those who enjoy a challenging, exciting job in which there is opportunity for service as well as hard work, policing is a viable choice.

Joseph Wambaugh, a former police officer and an author of best-selling novels, in assessing his life in both professions, said he did not miss the tedium and bureaucracy of policing, but he did miss the loyalty and camaraderie of his former police colleagues. "I find a lot of disloyalty in show business. In police work, it's totally different.... For the period of time that you're working together [in policing] you are absolutely loyal to each other." Wambaugh concluded, "Being a cop was a good life."[79]

Key Terms

deadly force 111
exclusionary rule 115
fleeing felon rule 111
good faith exception 115
inevitable discovery rule 116
statute of limitations 109
subculture 108

Study Questions

1. What external political situations might affect policing?
2. How should police spend most of their time? Why?
3. What is meant by evidence-based policing?
4. Distinguish *proactive* and *reactive* policing and discuss changes in the former.
5. What is the relationship between domestic violence and policing?
6. Discuss the extent and result of police corruption, with particular reference to the influence of drugs.
7. What is the *fleeing felon rule*? Contrast its historical meaning with the U.S. Supreme Court's ruling currently in effect.
8. Analyze the reasons for and concern with police vehicle pursuits.
9. Discuss police brutality in the context of recent examples.
10. What is the relationship, if any, between violence against the police and violence by the police?
11. Distinguish between police department regulations and civil lawsuits as methods of controlling policing.
12. State the purpose of the *exclusionary rule* and analyze whether that purpose is being met. What exceptions has the U.S. Supreme Court recognized?
13. Discuss civil liability that may result from inadequate training of police.
14. What role should courts play in affirmative action efforts in hiring police?

Notes

1. William F. Walsh, "COMPSTAT: An Analysis of an Emerging Police Managerial Paradigm," in *Critical Issues in Policing: Contemporary Readings*, 6th ed., ed. Roger G. Dunham and Geoffrey P. Alpert (Long Grove, IL: Waveland Press, 2010), pp. 197-211; quotation is on p. 197.
2. Heather MacDonald, fellow at the Manhattan Institute, "Fighting Crime Where the Criminals Are," *New York Times* (June 26, 2010), p. 17.
3. Walsh, "COMPSTAT," p. 209.
4. Lawrence W. Sherman, *Evidence-Based Policing* (Washington D.C.: Police Foundation, 1998), pp. 3-4, http://www.policefoundation.org, accessed July 13, 2014.
5. Jack R. Greene, "New Directions in Policing: Balancing Prediction and Meaning in Police Research," *Justice Quarterly* 31(2) (April 2014): 193-228; quotation is on p. 193.
6. Quoted in David Weisburd et al., "Could Innovations in Policing Have Contributed to the New York City Crime Drop Even in a Period of Declining Police Strength?: The Case of Stop, Question and Frisk as a Hot Spots Policing Strategy," *Justice Quarterly* 31(1) (February 2014): 129-153; quotation is on p. 148. For a discussion of the research supporting evidence-based policing, see Cynthia Lum and Christopher S. Koper, "Evidence-Based Policing," in *Critical Issues in Policing: Contemporary Readings*, 7th ed., ed. Roger G. Dunham and Geoffrey P. Alpert (Long Grove, IL: Waveland Press, 2015), pp. 264-269.
7. Violence Against Women Act of 1994, USCS, Title 42, Chapter 136, Section 1381 (2019). The rule is published in the *Federal Register*, Volume 61, Section 40727-34 (August 6, 1996).
8. See, for example, Lawrence W. Sherman and Richard A. Berk, *The Minneapolis Domestic Violence Experiment* (Washington, D.C.: Police Foundation, 1984), p. 1.
9. See, for example, Franklyn W. Dunford et al., "The Role of Arrest in Domestic Assault: The Omaha Police Experiment," *Criminology* 28(2) (May 1990): 183-206.
10. Maryann Syers and Jeffrey L. Edleson, "The Combined Effects of Coordinated Criminal Justice Intervention in Woman Abuse," *Journal of Interpersonal Violence* 7 (December 1992): 490-502.
11. Richard B. Felson and Jeff Ackerman, "Arrest for Domestic and Other Assaults," *Criminology* 39(3) (August 2001): 655-676; quotation is on p. 672.
12. See, for example, Robert C. Davis et al., "Increasing the Proportion of Domestic Violence Arrests That Are Prosecuted: A Natural Experiment in Milwaukee," *Criminology & Public Policy* 2(2) (March 2003): 263-282.
13. Richard B. Felson et al., "Reasons for Reporting and Not Reporting Domestic Violence to the Police," *Criminology* 40(3) (August 2002): 617-648.
14. Meda Chesney-Lind, "Criminalizing Victimization: The Unintended Consequences of Pro-Arrest Policies for Girls and Women," *Criminology & Public Policy* 2(1) (November 2002): 89-90.
15. Drew Humphries, "No Easy Answers: Public Policy, Criminal Justice, and Domestic Violence," *Criminology & Public Policy* 2(1) (November 2002): 91-95.
16. *Results from an Elder Abuse Prevention Experiment in New York City* (Rockville, MD: National Criminal Justice Reference Service), referred to in "Study Suggests Intervention Increases Chance of Elder Abuse," *Criminal Justice Newsletter* 31(24) (January 11, 2002): 6.
17. "Domestic Disturbances: Deadly, Dangerous Calls," National Law Enforcement Officers Memorial Fund, http://www.nleomf.org/officers/stories/domestic-disturbances.html, accessed July 13, 2014.
18. "Police Family Violence Fact Sheet," National Center for Women and Policing, http://www.womenandpolicing.org/violenceFS.asp, accessed July 13, 2014.
19. The Pro bono Work to Empower and Represent Act of 2018, or the Power Act, S. 717 (2018).
20. David Weisburd, "Hot Spots and Place-Based Prevention," *Criminology & Public Policy* 17(1) (February 2018): 5-27; references are on p. 7.
21. Anthony A. Braga et al., "The Effects of Hot Spots Policing on Crime: An Updated Systematic Review and Meta-Analysis," *Justice Quarterly* 31(4) (August 2014): 633-663.
22. Weisburd, "Hot Spots of Crime and Place-Based Prevention." See this article for an excellent overview of this approach.
23. Weisburd et al., "Could Innovations in Policing Have Contributed to the New York City Crime Drop?"
24. National Alliance on Mental Illness, "Mental Health by the Numbers," https://www.nami.org, accessed July 10, 2017.
25. See Fred E. Markowitz and Amy C. Watson, "Police Response to Domestic Violence: Situations Involving Veterans Exhibiting Signs of Mental Illness," *Criminology* 53(2) (May 2015): 231-252.
26. See, for example, the discussion by Wesley G. Jennings and Edward J. Hudak, "Police Response to Persons with Mental Illness," in *Critical Issues in Policing*, 7th ed., ed. Dunham and Alpert, pp. 435-451, with particular reference to their list of "dos and don'ts" on p. 447.
27. "In Los Angeles, A National Model for How to Police the Mentally Ill," *The Christian Science Monitor* (June 15, 2015), n.p.
28. See Geoffrey P. Alpert, "Police Use of Force and the Suspect with Mental Illness," *Criminology & Public Policy* 14(2) (May 2015): 277-283. For a brief discussion of policing and mental illness, see Chapter 5, "First Responders and Street Encounters," in Anne F. Segal et al., *Mental Health and Criminal Justice* (New York: Wolters Kluwer, 2019), pp. 141-171.
29. For a discussion on the issue of whether stress differs between male and female officers, see Ni He, Jihong Zhao, and Carol A. Archbold, "Gender and Police Stress: The Convergent and Divergent Impact of Work Environment, Work-Family Conflict, and Stress Coping Mechanisms of Female and Male Police Officers," *Critical Issues in Policing*, 7th ed., ed. Dunham and Alpert, pp. 362-384.
30. For a discussion, see Geoffrey P. Alpert et al., "Solidarity and the Code of Silence," in *Critical Issues in Policing*, 7th ed., ed. Dunham and Alpert, pp. 106-121.
31. Lawrence W. Sherman, ed., *Police Corruption: A Sociological Perspective* (Garden City, NY: Doubleday, 1974), p. 6.
32. James Q. Wilson, *Varieties of Police Behavior: The Management of Law and Order in Eight Communities* (Cambridge, Mass.: Harvard University Press, 1968), Chapters 5-7, pp. 140-226.

33. Sherman, ed., *Police Corruption*, pp. 7-8.
34. Ibid., pp. 1-39.
35. For details on these and other issues concerning drug abuse and drug trafficking, see Sue Titus Reid, *Criminal Law*, 9th ed. (New York: Oxford University Press, 2013), pp. 315-347, especially "The Impact of Drugs on Criminal Justice Systems," pp. 327-328; and Reid, *Crime and Criminology*, 14th ed. (Wolters Kluwer Law & Business, 2015), pp. 319-346.
36. "Perry Shouldn't Delay in Pardoning Tulia 35," *Austin America-Statesman* (July 31, 2003), Editorial, p. 14; *60 Minutes* (July 4, 2004); "Story of a Drug Bust Gone Wrong," *Houston Chronicle* (February 9, 2009), p. 6.
37. Kenneth Adams, "What We Know About Police Use of Force," in *Use of Force by Police: Overview of Local and National Data*, National Institute of Justice Research Report (Washington, D.C.: U.S. Department of Justice, 1999), reprinted in *Critical Issues in Policing*, 6th ed., ed. Dunham and Alpert, pp. 532-547.
38. Ibid., pp. 543-546.
39. Catherine H. Milton et al., *Police Use of Deadly Force* (Washington, D.C.: Police Foundation, 1977), p. 41.
40. *Kisela v. Hughes*, 138 S. Ct. 1148 (2018), Justice Sotomayor, dissenting.
41. *Tennessee v. Garner*, 471 U.S. 1 (1985).
42. "New Pursuit Rules Held a Week: Police Intend to Work Out Kinks Before Changing Policy," *Daily News of Los Angeles* (May 3, 2003), p. 3N; "New Technology to End High-Speed Police Chases," CBS News Transcripts: *The Early Show* (October 9, 2007), 7 A.M.
43. *Sacramento County, California v. Lewis*, 523 U.S. 833 (1998).
44. *Mullenix v. Luna*, 136 S. Ct. 305 (2015), Justice Sotomayor, dissenting.
45. Albert J. Reiss Jr., "Police Brutality," *Transaction Magazine* 5 (1968), reprinted in *Police Behavior: A Sociological Perspective*, ed. Richard J. Lundman (New York: Oxford University Press, 1980), pp. 274-275.
46. "One Fourth of L.A. Riot Deaths Found Unrelated to Violence," *St. Petersburg Times* (Florida) (June 2, 1992), p. 4. The case is *United States v. Koon*, 34 F.3d 1416 (9th Cir. 1994), *aff'd in part, rev'd in part, remanded*, 518 U.S. 81 (1996).
47. "Three Are Guilty of Cover-Up Plot in Louima Attack," *New York Times* (March 7, 2000), p. 1; "Sean Bell's Family and Friends Outraged by Verdict," *New York Times* (April 26, 2008), p. 9B.
48. *Dallas Morning News* (July 8, 2016), p. 1.
49. "Jersey City Officer Is Shot to Death by a Gunman at a Walgreens," *New York Times* (July 14, 2014), p. 12.
50. Federal Bureau of Investigation, *Uniform Crime Reports 2017* (2018), https://www.fbi.gov/, accessed September 11, 2018. For a series of recent articles on police officers' deaths, see *Criminology & Public Policy* 18 (1) (February 2019): 7-46.
51. Milton et al., *Police Use of Deadly Force*, p. 3.
52. *Early Warning Systems: Responding to the Problem Police Officer* (Rockville, MD, 2001), as cited in "Police Creating Warning Systems for Potential Problem Officers," *Criminal Justice Newsletter* 31(17) (September 19, 2001): 4.
53. "Justice Dept. Accuses Albuquerque Police of Excessive Force," *New York Times* (April 11, 2014), p. 11.
54. "Inquiry of Newark Police Cites a Pattern of Bias," *New York Times* (July 23, 2014), p. 23.
55. "Justice Report Cites Discriminatory and Unconstitutional Policing in Baltimore," *American Bar Association Journal* (August 10, 2016), http://www.abajournal.com, accessed September 12, 2018.
56. *Weeks v. United States*, 232 U.S. 383 (1914); *Mapp v. Ohio*, 367 U.S. 643 (1961).
57. Lawrence Crocker, "Can the Exclusionary Rule Be Saved?," *Journal of Criminal Law & Criminology* 84 (Summer 1993): 310-351; quotation is on pp. 310-311.
58. *Olmstead v. United States*, 277 U.S. 438, 485 (1928), Justice Brandeis, dissenting.
59. *Elkins v. United States*, 364 U.S. 206, 217 (1960).
60. See Stephen H. Sachs, "The Exclusionary Rule: A Prosecutor's Defense," *Criminal Justice Ethics* 1 (Summer/Fall 1982).
61. Crocker, "Can the Exclusionary Rule Be Saved?," p. 311.
62. *Massachusetts v. Sheppard*, 468 U.S. 981 (1984). See also *United States v. Leon*, 468 U.S. 897 (1984) (decided the same day).
63. *Arizona v. Evans*, 514 U.S. 1 (1995).
64. *Maryland v. Garrison*, 480 U.S. 79 (1987).
65. *Arizona v. Youngblood*, 488 U.S. 51 (1988).
66. *Nix v. Williams*, 467 U.S. 431 (1984).
67. *New York v. Harris*, 495 U.S. 14 (1990), referring to the previous case, *Payton v. New York*, 445 U.S. 573 (1980).
68. *Arizona v. Fulminante*, 499 U.S. 279 (1991).
69. *Herring v. United States*, 555 U.S. 135 (2009).
70. *Davis v. United States*, 131 S. Ct. 2419 (2011).
71. *Utah v. Strieff*, 136 S. Ct. 2056 (2016).
72. USCS, Chapter 42, Section 1983 (2019).
73. U.S. Commission on Civil Rights, *Who Is Guarding the Guardians?*, p. 2.
74. See Jerome H. Skolnick and David H. Bayley, *The New Blue Line: Police Innovation in Six American Cities* (New York: Free Press, 1986); Albert J. Reiss Jr., *Policing in a City's Central District: The Oakland Story* (Washington, D.C.: National Institute of Justice, 1985).
75. Herman Goldstein, "Toward Community-Oriented Policing: Potential, Basic Requirements, and Threshold Questions," *Crime & Delinquency* 33 (January 1987): 28.
76. U.S. Commission on Civil Rights, *Who Is Guarding the Guardians?*, p. vi.
77. Ibid., p. 2.
78. See *Johnson v. Transportation Agency*, 480 U.S. 616 (1987).
79. Quoted in Claudia Dreifus, "A Conversation with Joseph Wambaugh," *Police Magazine* (May 1980), pp. 37-38.

Part III

Processing a Criminal Case: Criminal Court Systems

The processing of a criminal case involves a complex series of stages that center on adult criminal courts. The chapters in Part III examine the pretrial, trial, and appellate procedures of adult criminal court systems. Chapter 6 explores the structure of courts, how they are administered, what role judges and justices play in court systems, and what might be done about the current crisis in courts created by the increase in cases.

Attorneys play important roles in criminal cases. Prosecutors and defense attorneys are portrayed in the media as fighting their battles in the drama of criminal courtrooms. Their roles are far more complex than the media portray. Chapter 7 looks at the differences between the prosecution and the defense and analyzes their respective roles in criminal justice systems. Particular attention is given to prosecutorial discretion. Chapter 7 also covers pretrial procedures, including the frequently used and highly controversial process of plea bargaining.

Chapter 8 focuses on the trial of a criminal case, examining each step of the trial and explaining the roles of defense, prosecution, and judges. But perhaps the most controversial process in criminal justice systems is the sentencing of persons who are found guilty, especially those sentenced to death. Chapter 8 examines recent trends in sentencing, along with the sentencing process and an analysis of issues raised by sentencing. The chapter closes with a discussion of appeals.

6

Criminal Court Systems

Chapter Outline

Learning Objectives

After reading this chapter, you should be able to do the following:

- Discuss the judicial branch of government, define basic legal terminology regarding courts, and distinguish between trial and appellate courts
- Diagram the levels of state and federal court systems, and explain what happens at each level
- Discuss the history and purpose of the U.S. Supreme Court, and explain and evaluate its functions and operations
- Describe the role of judges in criminal trials
- Explain and evaluate the sentencing role of trial judges
- Contrast the role of an appellate judge with that of a trial judge
- List and explain two methods for selecting judges
- Explain briefly the training, retention, and control of judges
- Describe court congestion and suggest remedies

Courts, which are located within the judicial branch of government, are central agencies in American criminal law systems. The actions that occur within courts affect all other aspects of criminal justice systems, but courts are under more severe attacks than ever before. A former American Bar Association president expressed his concern regarding the "alarming increase in rhetorical and physical attacks on the judiciary" and concluded that we need to teach our citizens the reasons our country established an independent judiciary. He concluded his brief remarks with these words:

> Those who would tear down our courts, for short-term political or other gain threaten the very fabric of our republic. It is our responsibility to ensure that judges are able to decide cases fairly and without fear of retribution, and that the judiciary receives the resources and respect it must have to do its job. If we do not protect our courts, our courts cannot protect us.[1]

The U.S. Constitution gives Congress the power to create courts inferior to the U.S. Supreme Court. Congress determines the type of cases that will be handled by those courts, determines how many judges there will be and where they will work, confirms (or refuses to confirm) presidential appointments, and determines the courts' budgets.

This chapter provides an overview of courts, with many of the particular functions that occur within them discussed in later chapters. The chapter begins with an examination of the judicial branch of government and explains some legal concepts that must be understood for an adequate explanation of courts. It then discusses and distinguishes trial from appellate courts before examining court structures and pointing out the distinctions between federal and state court systems. It discusses the levels of state and federal courts and pays particular attention to the highest court in the United States, the U.S. Supreme Court. The next major section of the chapter examines the judge's role. The final section focuses on court congestion and discusses solutions to this major problem.

THE JUDICIAL BRANCH OF GOVERNMENT

The framers of the U.S. Constitution established three branches of government at the national level—legislative, executive, and judicial—and provided for the establishment of one supreme court. They envisioned a separation of the powers of these three branches, although there is some overlap. Federal **judges** and U.S. Supreme Court justices are appointed by the president, representing the executive branch, and confirmed by the Senate, representing the legislative branch. Because courts have limited enforcement powers, they rely on the executive branch for enforcement of their decisions. The court systems must depend on the legislative branch of government for financial appropriations.

In U.S. criminal justice systems, a separate judicial branch is viewed as necessary for assuring that the constitutional and statutory rights of citizens are not controlled by political pressures. In practice, however, political pressures may enter into the selection of judges, as well as into the organization and administration of courts and the judicial decision-making process.

Definitions of Legal Terms

For an understanding of criminal court systems, it is necessary to explain some legal terms and concepts. *Jurisdiction* refers to a court's power to hear and decide a case. This power is given by the constitution or statute that created that court. A court's jurisdiction may be limited to a certain age group (e.g., juvenile courts, with jurisdiction over juvenile delinquency, child custody, and adoption proceedings) or to a particular type of law (e.g., criminal, civil, bankruptcy) or specialized areas (e.g., drug courts, mental health courts, domestic courts). Some courts have jurisdiction only over minor offenses, or *misdemeanors.* Others hear only the more serious kinds of offenses, called *felonies.* Some courts hear only civil cases, others only criminal cases. This text is concerned primarily with courts that have jurisdiction over criminal law, although at appellate levels, most courts hear both criminal and civil cases.

It is necessary to distinguish types of jurisdiction. *Original jurisdiction* refers to the jurisdiction of the court that may hear a case first—that is, the court that may try the facts. When more than one court may hear a case, those courts have *concurrent jurisdiction.* When only one court may hear a case, that court has *exclusive jurisdiction. Appellate jurisdiction* refers to the jurisdiction of the court that may hear the case on appeal. **Supplement 6.1** contains an example of a jurisdictional question in a highly controversial case.

Another limitation on courts is that they hear only actual cases and controversies. Courts do not decide hypothetical issues, and normally they do not give advisory opinions. Only when a dispute involves a legal right between two or more parties will a court hear the case. If the controversy ends before the completion of the trial or the appeal, usually the court will not decide the case, as the issue is **moot**, meaning that it is no longer a real case because no legal issue between the parties remains to be resolved. Thus, if a defendant has appealed the exclusion of evidence at trial but the case is decided on a plea bargain, there is no reason for the appellate court to hear the appeal on the evidence issue. That issue is moot once the defendant and the prosecution have agreed to a plea that has been accepted by the trial court judge.

Because law needs stability, courts follow the rule of ***stare decisis*** ("to abide by, or adhere to, decided cases"), whereby previous decisions become precedents for current and future decisions. But law is flexible, and courts may overrule (specifically or by implication) their previous decisions, although this does not occur frequently.

It is important to distinguish between the rule of the court and the **dicta** of the judges or justices. *Dicta* refers to judicial comments on issues that are not part of the court's ruling. These comments, even if they represent the opinion of a majority of the court, must be recognized as dicta and not confused with the holding or rule of law of the court. For this reason, it is necessary to read cases carefully.

Most appellate court judges and justices issue written opinions that are recorded in official reports. Decisions of the U.S. Supreme Court are officially recorded in the *United States Reports*, usually referred to as the *U.S. Reports*, but this official printing may take several years. Prior to that publication, U.S. Supreme Court opinions are published in the *Supreme Court Reporter* (S. Ct.), the *U.S. Law Week* (USLW), or a legal computer service, such as Lexis-Nexis, which also provides access to important information, such as the prior decisions in those cases, as well as any subsequent court action. Today, U.S. Supreme Court cases are also available on the Internet, as are many lower court decisions.

Decisions of the U.S. Supreme Court are binding on all lower federal courts. They are also binding on state courts when applicable—that is, where *federal* statutory or constitutional rights are involved.

Trial and Appellate Courts

Trial and appellate courts both exist at the state and federal levels. Both are involved in interpreting laws, but generally, trial courts try the *facts* of the case, and appellate courts are concerned only with *law*. There are some exceptions.

Trial courts are the major fact finders in a case. The trial jury (or judge if the case is not tried before a jury) decides the basic questions of fact. In a criminal trial, for example, the trial jury decides whether the accused committed the crime for which he or she is being tried, whether a defense (such as insanity) was proved, and so on. In making these findings, the jury considers evidence presented by both the defense and the prosecution. Because the trial judge and jury hear and see the witnesses, they are in a better position than the appellate court to decide whether those witnesses are credible. Thus, it is argued, the appellate court should be confined to issues of law (e.g., whether specific evidence should have been excluded) and not be permitted to reverse a trial court's decision regarding ultimate fact issues, such as guilt or innocence.

After the judge or jury has made a decision at the trial level, the defendant, if found guilty, may **appeal** that decision. At the appellate level, the **appellant** (the defendant at trial) alleges error in the trial court proceeding (e.g., admission of an illegal confession or exclusion of minorities from the jury) and asks for a ruling on the issue, arguing that he or she was prejudiced by the error. The **appellee**, the prosecution at trial, argues either that errors did not exist or that the errors did not prejudice the appellant.

The U.S. Supreme Court, the highest court in the U.S. court system, hears and issues opinions from its historic building in Washington, D.C. Passes are available for persons who wish to attend the oral arguments before this Court.

Appellate cases are heard by judges or justices rather than juries. The appellate court looks at the trial court record, considers written briefs submitted by attorneys who use them to establish and support their legal arguments, and may hear oral arguments from counsel for the defense and the prosecution regarding alleged errors of law during the trial. The appellate court makes a ruling on those issues. The court may hold that no errors were committed at the trial level, in which case the appellate court *affirms* the lower court's decision. It may hold that there were errors but that the errors did not prejudice the defendant, and thus the conviction (or sentence if that is the issue) stands. The court may hold that there were errors and that one or more of those errors prejudiced the defendant, which means that the defendant may not have received a fair trial. In that case, the appellate court may reverse the case and send it back for another trial with instructions concerning the errors. This process is referred to as *reversed and remanded.* The court may also reverse the case *with prejudice,* meaning that no further trials are permitted on those charges.

In essence, appellate courts are assessing the work of trial courts. This system allows appellate courts to exercise some administrative control over trial courts, thus achieving more uniformity among courts than would otherwise exist. Trial court judges and juries exercise considerable power in criminal justice systems, however, as most cases are not appealed. In cases that are appealed and retried, the trial court frequently reaches the same decision on retrial or resentencing.[2]

In addition to the power to hear and decide cases appealed on facts of law in criminal trials, appellate courts have **judicial review** over acts of the legislative and executive branches of government if those acts infringe on freedoms and liberties guaranteed by the state statutes and state constitutions (in state cases) and by the U.S. Constitution or federal laws (in federal cases). This power of judicial review represents the great authority of courts. The U.S. Supreme Court also has the power to declare acts of the president or of Congress unconstitutional. The power of judicial review by courts was established in 1803 by the U.S. Supreme Court.[3]

The highest court of each state determines the constitutionality of that state's statutes in relation to its constitution. The U.S. Supreme Court is the final decision maker in the process of judicial review of federal statutes and U.S. constitutional issues.

Figure 6.1

U.S. Dual Court Systems

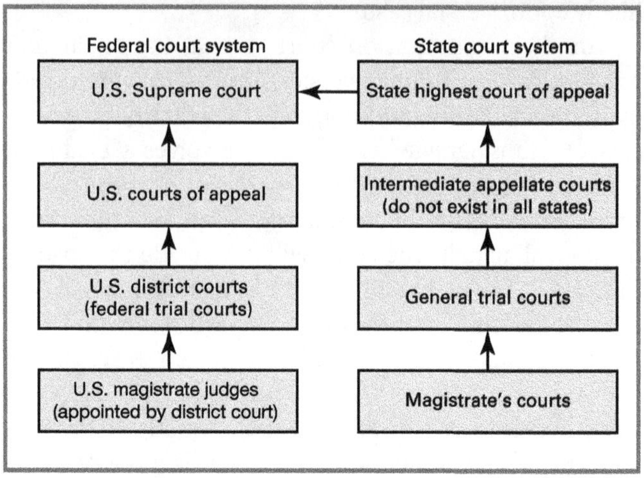

Note: Arrows indicate general avenues of appeal: there may be some exceptions. State court systems are explained in more detail in Table 6.1.

THE DUAL COURT SYSTEM

The United States has a dual court system consisting of state and federal courts, as diagrammed in Figure 6.1. State crimes are prosecuted in state courts, and federal crimes are prosecuted in federal courts. State crimes are defined by state statutes, federal crimes by Congress. Some acts violate both federal and state statutes, in which case the defendant may be tried in a state or a federal court or both.

Lower federal and state courts constitute separate systems. Cases may not be appealed from a state court to a federal court, except to the U.S. Supreme Court, and then only when a *federal* statutory or constitutional right is at issue. Federal and state courts may hear only cases over which they have jurisdiction. Many of the cases brought in federal courts by state inmates are appropriate to those courts because the inmates are alleging that federal rights have been violated.

A closer look at the structure and organization of state and federal court systems facilitates understanding of the subsequent material in this chapter, as well as the analysis of pretrial and trial processes in subsequent chapters. Because most criminal cases are tried in state and local courts, this discussion begins with the state court systems.

State Courts

Considerable variation exists in the organization of state court systems. Diversity also exists *within* state systems, leading to problems that have prompted some states to move toward a unified court system. Despite the variety in systems, however, it is possible to make some general observations that provide an overview of state court systems. This discussion focuses on courts that process criminal cases (although some may also process civil cases). The main aspects of the structure, function, and jurisdiction of state courts are summarized in Table 6.1.

Courts of Limited Jurisdiction

In discussions about courts, frequent references are made to *lower* courts. These are the courts of limited jurisdiction, so called because their jurisdiction is usually limited to minor civil cases and criminal misdemeanors. Jurisdiction over criminal cases may be limited to certain kinds of misdemeanors, such as those that carry a jail or short prison term or some other, less serious, sanction.

A court's jurisdiction may also be limited to certain activities. The judge or magistrate who presides over courts of limited jurisdiction, for example, may conduct some pretrial procedures, such as issuing warrants for searches or arrests, deciding bail, appointing counsel for indigent defendants, or presiding over the initial appearance or preliminary hearing.

Lower courts, which are called by various names, as noted in Table 6.1, should not be considered insignificant because of their limited jurisdiction. Certainly, the power of limited court judges to grant or deny bail or some other method of pretrial release is tremendous.

Table 6.1

Structure and Jurisdiction of State Court Systems

Court	Structure	Jurisdiction
Highest state appellate court (usually called the supreme court)	Consists of five, seven, or nine justices, who may be appointed or elected; cases decided by this court may not be appealed to the U.S. Supreme Court unless they involve a federal question, and then there is no right of appeal except in limited cases.	If there is no intermediate appellate court, defendants convicted in a general trial court have a right of appeal to this court; if there is an intermediate appellate court, this court has discretion to limit appeals with few exceptions, such as in capital cases.
Intermediate appellate court (also called court of appeals; exists in approximately half of the states)	May have one court that hears appeals from all general trial courts or may have more than one court, each with appellate jurisdiction over a particular area of the state; usually has a panel of three judges.	Defendants convicted in general trial courts have a right of appeal to this level.
General trial courts (also called superior courts, circuit courts, district courts, court of common pleas)	Usually, state is divided into juridical districts, with one general trial court in each district, often one per county; courts may be divided by function, such as civil, criminal, probate, domestic.	Jurisdiction to try cases usually begins where jurisdiction of lower court ends, so this court tries more serious cases; may have appellate jurisdiction over cases decided in lower courts.
Courts of limited jurisdiction (also called magistrate's courts, police courts, justice of the peace courts, municipal courts)	Differ from state to state: some states divide the state into districts, with each district having the same type of lower court; in other states, courts are located in political subdivisions, such as cities or townships, in which case the structure may differ from court to court; may not be a court of record, in which case the system will permit trial *de novo* in general trial court; particularly in rural areas, magistrates may not be lawyers and may work only part-time.	May be limited to specific proceedings, such as initial appearance, preliminary hearing, issuing of search and arrest warrants, setting of bail, appointing of counsel for indigent defendants; jurisdiction of cases is limited to certain types, usually the lesser criminal and civil cases; some jurisdictions may hear all misdemeanors; others are limited to misdemeanors with minor penalties.

Professions 6.1

Careers in Criminal Court Systems

A wide variety of positions exist in criminal court systems. Not all require a law degree. The most common positions are noted here.

Lawyers perform various functions in court systems. *Prosecutors* represent the government and prosecute cases; *defense attorneys* represent those who are accused of violating the law. Lawyers must receive a law degree (usually a three-year program) and pass the state bar. Although some states are reciprocal and permit attorneys from other states to be admitted to practice through a petitions process, many require that a bar exam be taken in that state. Some permit attorneys from other states to become members of the bar by taking only part of the exam, provided they have passed the bar of another state and have engaged in some years of practice.

Most *judges* are lawyers. Some of them have practiced law; others have not. Judges may or may not have received special training for their new roles, although it is becoming more common to provide judicial training for attorneys who become judges.

Paralegals may perform some legal functions in criminal court systems, but they are not recognized as lawyers and generally must be supervised by attorneys. They have some legal training, but it is not as extensive as that required for a law degree. *Legal assistants* and *law clerks* may assist attorneys, but they, too, must be supervised. Although the position of *law clerk* usually does not pay well, that is not the case with legal assistant and paralegal positions, which, in some jurisdictions, are relatively high-paying.

The *court clerk*, normally a position that does not require formal legal training, is the court officer charged by statute or court rules with the responsibility of maintaining all court records. The court clerk files the pleadings and motions and records any decisions made by the court. These are very important functions because judgments are not enforceable if they have not been filed properly. The court clerk is assisted by a staff, which in large jurisdictions may include a deputy for each of the court's divisions (e.g., traffic, probate, civil, and criminal). Various personnel may be employed to handle the paperwork of the court.

The *bailiff*, perhaps best known for pronouncing, "Hear ye, hear ye, this court of the Honorable Judge . . . is in session; all rise" before the judge's entry into the courtroom, has a variety of functions. The bailiff is charged with keeping order in the courtroom and may eject or otherwise discipline people who do not observe proper courtroom behavior. In small courts, the bailiff may also be the person who screens all persons who wish to enter the courtroom. He or she may transport defendants to and from the court, pass papers and exhibits to and from attorneys and the judge, run errands for the judge, escort the jury from place to place and protect them from outside influence, and guard the jury room when jurors are deliberating. In some courts, a deputy sheriff performs the bailiff's functions. In federal courts, a deputy marshal may serve as bailiff. In state courts, the bailiff's position may carry a different title, such as *court service officer*.

In courts of record, a verbatim account of all proceedings is kept by a *court reporter*. The proceedings are not transcribed unless one or both of the parties request it, in which case there is a fee. If a criminal defendant is indigent, the state pays for the transcript when it is required for an appeal. Court reporters also record proceedings outside of court when attorneys are securing evidence for trial by questioning witnesses. Court reporters must have extensive training, and generally, the pay is very good. Many court reporters have their own businesses; others are employed by the courts.

The *minute clerk* is an employee of the court who records an outline of what happens during the proceedings but does not maintain a verbatim account. The minute clerk might record the charges against the defendant, summarize the process of selecting the jury, note the time spent in that process, list the names of the jurors and alternates, summarize the presented evidence, and record the court's decision.

Larger court systems employ other professionals. *Counselors* or *social workers* may be available, along with *psychologists*, *statisticians*, *probation officers*, and *clerical personnel*. And in today's modern courtrooms, a variety of positions might be available to handle electronic devices and programs.

General Trial Courts

General trial courts are called by various names, as noted in Table 6.1. Usually, these courts have a wider geographical base than lower courts. In large areas, the general trial court may be divided by functions, such as traffic cases, domestic cases, civil cases (excluding domestic and traffic cases), probate, estates and wills, and criminal cases. Smaller jurisdictions may have fewer divisions. A civil and a criminal division is one frequently used model.

In most systems, the jurisdiction of general trial courts begins where the jurisdiction of the lower courts ends and includes the more serious cases. If the lower court is not a court of record, meaning that the court does not make provision for a transcript of the proceedings, a case appealed from the lower court to the general trial court may be tried ***de novo***, which means a new trial. In that instance, the evidence will be presented again.

Both of the court levels discussed thus far are at the trial level. The personnel and their functions in trial courts may vary among jurisdictions, but most are fairly common and are noted in Professions 6.1. Some of these positions are also characteristic of appellate courts.

Appellate Courts

Unsuccessful defendants at the trial level may have grounds for appeal. Some states have an intermediate appellate court, usually called a *court of appeals*. In those states, only one court may hear all appeals, or courts in various districts may hear appeals from their respective geographical areas. If the state does not have an intermediate appellate court, cases may be appealed directly from the general trial courts to the highest court, which in most states is called the *state supreme court*. Justices of this court are either elected or appointed. In states having intermediate appellate courts, except in a few types of cases, the highest appellate court has the power to limit the cases it hears and decides. This court has the final decision on cases that involve legal issues pertaining to the constitution or statutes of the state in which the case is brought. If the case involves any federal issues, the defendant may appeal to the U.S. Supreme Court, although that Court accepts only a limited number of the cases for which review is requested.

Texas and Oklahoma have two final appellate courts: a final court of appeals for criminal cases and a second one for civil case appeals. Cases may not be appealed from one of these courts to the other.

Lower Federal Courts

The basic trial courts in the federal system are the *U.S. district courts*. These courts hear cases in which individuals have been accused of violating federal criminal laws. They try civil cases that meet specified criteria. Each state has at least one federal district court, and some states have several. In the federal district courts, cases are prosecuted by U.S. attorneys and presided over by federal trial judges. These are appointed positions.

Cases appealed from federal district courts go to the appropriate intermediate federal appellate courts, called the *circuit courts of appeal*. Decisions of the federal appellate courts are not binding on state courts unless they involve federally created procedural rights that have been held to apply to the states or federally protected constitutional rights, such as the right to counsel. The decision of one federal appellate court is not binding on another one. If federal circuit courts decide similar cases differently, the resulting conflict may be resolved only by the U.S. Supreme Court, the final appellate court in the federal system.

The U.S. Supreme Court

The U.S. Supreme Court is the only specific court established by the federal Constitution, which designates a few cases in which the Court has original jurisdiction. The Court has appellate jurisdiction under such exceptions and regulations as determined by Congress. This Court also has the power to review state court decisions whenever those decisions involve *federal* rights. The basic function of the U.S. Supreme Court is to interpret federal laws and the federal Constitution. **Supplement 6.2** contains pertinent information concerning what one might expect to see and hear during a Supreme Court session, along with some of the career opportunities (such as law clerk) available in that venue.

Nine justices (one chief justice and eight associate justices) comprise the U.S. Supreme Court. The Court began its 2017-2018 term with six men and three women. Upon the death of Chief Justice William H. Rehnquist in 2005, Judge John G. Roberts Jr. was nominated and confirmed as the chief justice, who presides over the Court. Associate Justice Sandra Day O'Connor, the first woman to serve on the Court, retired in 2005 and was replaced by Samuel A. Alito Jr. Justice David Hackett Souter retired in June 2009 and was replaced by Sonia Sotomayor, the first Latina on the Court (see **Supplement 6.3**). In June

2010, Associate Justice John Paul Stevens retired and was replaced by Elena Kagan, the third woman currently on the Court and the fourth to serve.

Associate Justice Antonin Scalia died unexpectedly in 2016. President Barack Obama nominated Chief Judge Merrick B. Garland of the District of Columbia Court of Appeals, but the Republican-led Senate refused to conduct the required hearings and vote on his confirmation. Shortly after he was sworn in, Republican President Donald J. Trump nominated federal judge Neil M. Gorsuch, who was confirmed and took his place on the Court in the spring of 2017. In 2018, Associate Justice Anthony M. Kennedy retired. President Trump nominated Judge Brett Kavanaugh of the District of Columbia Court of Appeals. Shortly before the scheduled vote on his confirmation in September 2018, information surfaced that a California psychology professor, Dr. Christine Blasey Ford, alleged that Judge Kavanaugh sexually assaulted her at a party when both were in high school. The vote on Judge Kavanaugh was postponed and a public hearing for both parties to testify was set for September 24, 2017, but Dr. Ford refused to testify unless an FBI investigation was conducted, a request denied by the Senate Judiciary Committee. The contentious hearing was held a few days later; other woman accused the judge of sexual harassment but were not permitted to testify at that hearing. The judge was confirmed and subsequently sworn in to serve on the U.S. Supreme Court.

The other associate justices on the Court during the 2018-2019 term were Ruth Bader Ginsburg, Stephen G. Breyer, and Clarence Thomas, the second African American to serve on the Court.

A case gets before the U.S. Supreme Court if the Court grants a **writ of *certiorari*** on an appealed case. A *writ* is an order from a court authorizing or ordering that an action be taken. *Certiorari* literally means "to be informed of." When the Supreme Court grants a writ of *certiorari*, in effect it is agreeing to hear a case appealed by an appellant from a lower court and is ordering that court to produce the necessary documents for that appeal. If the Court denies *certiorari*, it is refusing to review the case, which means that the decision of the lower court stands. Four of the justices must vote in favor of a writ of *certiorari* in order for it to be granted. If the Court hears a case, five justices must vote to decide in favor of the appealed decision for it to stand. If an even number of justices is sitting and there is a tie vote, the lower court's decision on the appealed case stands.

In an average term, the Court hears only a small fraction of the cases filed. One of the reasons for limiting the number of cases is the time required for oral arguments as well as for the deliberations and opinion writing of the justices. The second reason the U.S. Supreme Court hears only a percentage of the cases filed was emphasized by a former chief justice of the Court: "To remain effective, the Supreme Court must continue to decide only those cases which present questions whose resolution will have immediate importance far beyond the particular facts and parties involved."[4]

In recent years, the U.S. Supreme Court has decreased the number of cases it decides. For example, in the 1990s, the Court handled about 150 cases per year. In its 2000-2001 term, the Court decided 85 cases, but it decided only 73 during its 2012-2013 term and 67 during its 2013-2014 term. During its 2017-2018 term, the Court decided 63 cases.[5]

The U.S. Supreme Court may hear cases when lower court decisions on the issues in question have differed. The Court's decision becomes the final resolution of the issue, unless or until it is overruled by a subsequent U.S. Supreme Court decision, by a constitutional amendment, or by congressional legislation. To illustrate, in a case involving federal sentencing guidelines, 116 U.S. district court judges had ruled in favor of the guidelines, while 158 had ruled against them by the time the U.S. Supreme Court settled the issue, upholding the guidelines in *Mistretta v. United States* in 1989.[6]

Cases that are accepted for review by the U.S. Supreme Court must be filed within a specified time before oral arguments. The attorneys who argue before the Court are under strict guidelines and considerable pressure. They must be well prepared and are subject to being interrupted at any time by a justice's question. Attorneys are expected to argue their cases without reading from the prepared briefs. Each is limited to 30 minutes (sometimes an hour) for oral arguments.

Most U.S. Supreme Court decisions are announced in written opinions, which may represent majority (or plurality) opinions. A **concurring opinion** may be written by a justice who voted with the Court but disagreed with one or more of its reasons, who agreed with the decision but for reasons other than those in the Court's opinion, or who agreed with the Court's reasons but wishes to emphasize or clarify one or more points. Opinions concurring in part, dissenting in part, and dissenting entirely may also be written.

U.S. Supreme Court decisions are handed down on opinion days, usually three Mondays of each month of the term, although at times the Court also issues opinions on other days. The announced decisions are public and available on the Internet. Judicial opinions, especially those of U.S. Supreme Court justices, are a very important part of U.S. legal systems. These opinions are read carefully by lawyers, who use the reasoning and conclusions of law in arguing future cases.

JUDGES IN CRIMINAL COURT SYSTEMS

Historically, judges have been held in high esteem by the U.S. public. In recent years, however, the position of judge has come under intense scrutiny and criticism. In their decisions on pretrial releases, judges have been accused of releasing dangerous persons who prey on the public, commit more crimes, and terrorize citizens. In their sentencing decisions, judges have been accused of coddling criminals. Judges are easy scapegoats, and some critics take the opportunity to accuse them of causing most of the critical problems in the handling of criminals. Although some of the criticism is justified, much of it is not. Recently, the politics of judging has come under scrutiny.

In 2018, U.S. Supreme Court Chief Justice John G. Roberts Jr. fired back at President Donald J. Trump after the president referred to a judge appointed by former president Barack Obama as an "Obama judge" after the judge ruled against the president in an asylum immigration case. According to the chief justice:

> We do not have Obama judges or Trump judges, Bush judges or Clinton judges. . . . What we have is an extraordinary group of dedicated judges doing their level best to do equal right to those appearing before them. That independent judiciary is something we should all be thankful for.[7]

Judges begin their participation in criminal justice systems long before the trial. They determine when there is probable cause to issue a search or an arrest warrant. After arrest, a suspect must be taken before a neutral magistrate or judge, who will determine whether there is probable cause to hold the alleged offender. Judges determine whether the accused is released on bail or some other pretrial procedure, or is detained in jail awaiting trial.

Judges hear and rule on motions made by attorneys before, during, and after a trial. They approve plea bargains made between the prosecution and the defense. In most cases, trial judges determine the sentences of convicted offenders. Judges (or justices, at the appellate level) determine whether errors were made at the trial or lower appellate levels and whether cases should be reversed or affirmed.

Trial Judges

At a trial, judges are referees. Theoretically, they are neither for nor against a particular position or issue but, rather, are committed to the fair implementation of the rules of evidence and law. They are charged with the responsibility of ensuring that all parties before the court, including attorneys, follow the rules.

In the role of referee, the judge has immense power. If the defense makes a motion to have evidence suppressed on the grounds that it was allegedly obtained illegally, the judge's decision whether to grant that motion might be the deciding factor in the outcome of the case. Without the evidence, the prosecution might not be able to prove its case. Likewise, the judge's decision to admit evidence offered by the defendant, such as the testimony of a psychiatrist regarding the defendant's mental state, may be the deciding factor in the ability of the defense to convince the jury of its position.

The importance of trial judges is underscored by the fact that most of their decisions are not appealed. Many decisions that are appealed are not reversed, and even if the defense wins on appeal, considerable time is lost—time that might have been spent by the accused in jail. Furthermore, it is important to *prevent* problems at trial whenever possible and that responsibility frequently lies with the trial judge.

Another important responsibility of the trial judge is to rule on whether **expert witness** testimony may be admitted. Many issues in criminal cases are beyond the common knowledge of jurors, so it is necessary to introduce expert testimony, which involves knowledge beyond that of a typical juror. In addition to deciding whether the area of expertise is fitting, the judge must determine whether the offered expert is qualified to testify about that evidence and whether the proposed evidence is acceptable. Generally, judges make these decisions after hearing oral arguments from the defense and the prosecution, and some judges require written motions and briefs from attorneys prior to those arguments.

Another responsibility of the trial judge is to decide whether there is sufficient evidence to send a case to the jury for a decision or whether the case should be dismissed for lack of evidence. Even if the judge sends the case to the jury and the jury finds the defendant guilty, the trial judge may reverse that decision if he or she believes the evidence is not sufficient to determine guilt beyond

Criminal Justice Systems Dilemma 6.1

Judicial Power in Question: The *Au Pair* Case

In U.S. criminal justice systems, trial judges are responsible for deciding motions concerning the introduction of evidence. They are also responsible for instructing the jury concerning the law that applies to the case they must decide. If the evidence that has been presented is not sufficient to support the charges, the judge should not send the case to the jury. Judges are reluctant to do this, but on occasion, they reverse a jury decision that is based on insufficient evidence. A case that received international media attention is illustrative.

Louise Woodward, age 19, was convicted of second-degree murder in the death of Matthew Eappen, 8 months old. Woodward was a British *au pair* hired by Matthew's parents to take care of the baby and his older brother. The prosecution argued that Woodward had shaken the baby and knocked his head against a wall or the tub. The defense claimed that Matthew died of a skull injury he had incurred several weeks prior to his death.

The defense asked the judge to instruct the jury on murder charges only, taking the gamble that, if the jury had to choose between murder and acquittal, it would choose acquittal. After deliberating for 27 hours, the jury found Woodward guilty of second-degree murder and she faced life in prison.

At a subsequent hearing, the trial judge listened to arguments from both the defense and the prosecution, took a few days to contemplate, and then announced his decision: Louise Woodward's conviction for second-degree murder was not supported by the evidence. "Having considered the matter carefully, I am firmly convinced that the interests of justice . . . mandate my reducing the verdict to manslaughter. I do this in accordance with my discretion and my duty."[1]

The judge ruled that, had the jury been instructed on manslaughter, it might have chosen that option, which he believed was one rational conclusion based on the evidence. He did not believe the evidence supported a murder conviction. At a subsequent hearing, the judge sentenced Woodward to the time she had already served and set her free.

1. "Excerpts from the Judge's Decision Reducing Conviction of Au Pair," *New York Times* (November 11, 1997), p. 16.

a reasonable doubt. This power is given to judges so they can serve as a check on jurors who might be influenced by passion or prejudice despite the evidence in the case.

The role of the trial judge in deciding whether to accept a jury verdict is illustrated by the trial and conviction of Louise Woodward, an *au pair* (a person hired to take care of a home or children—or both—and often from a foreign country, usually living with the family and perhaps even exchanging services for room and board), discussed in Criminal Justice Systems Dilemma 6.1. Additional details about the Louise Woodward case are presented in **Supplement 6.4**.

After hearing the evidence in a case, a trial judge may direct the jury to return a verdict of **acquittal**. This may occur before the judge hears all of the evidence, as well as after a jury verdict of guilty. Once the verdict of acquittal has been entered, the defendant may not be retried on the same charge; to do so would violate the defendant's constitutional right not to be tried twice for the same offense.

Another role of the judge is to instruct the jury regarding the law in the case it must decide. In addition, the judge must monitor all activities of the trial, ensuring that the defendant's constitutional and statutory rights are protected, that all rules and regulations are followed, and that all participants and spectators (including the media) behave appropriately during all judicial proceedings and under any other conditions set by the judge (such as a gag order in talking to the media). Spotlight 6.1 presents an example of a judge disciplining those in his courtroom for not behaving properly. A judge may go too far in that process, however, as illustrated by the Oklahoma judge who retired "after he was accused of using his contempt powers to jail people for infractions such as leaving sunflower seeds in his courtroom and talking in court."[8]

Spotlight 6.1

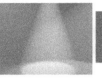

Judicial Control of Improper Courtroom Behavior

Failure to behave properly in a judicial proceeding can result in a citation for contempt of court, a fine, and even incarceration. In the highly publicized 2011 Florida trial of Casey Anthony for the murder of her toddler, Caylee, Judge Belvin Perry made several threats to cite the defense and the prosecution for contempt. But Matthew Bartlett, a spectator, got more than a threat. He was assessed a $400 fine and $223 in court costs and sentenced to six days in jail for flipping his middle finger at the prosecutor during court proceedings. Bartlett's appeal was denied, and the 28-year-old served the jail term.[1]

A loud yawn and an "offensive" sound landed 33-year-old Clifton Williams in jail after Judge Daniel Rozak found him in contempt of court in his Illinois courtroom. Williams was attending court to support his cousin, who was sentenced on a drug felony charge. The cousin was placed on two years' probation, while Williams was given a six-month jail term, although after three weeks of confinement, he was brought, in shackles, back to court where the judge released him.[2]

A committee of federal judges ordered attorney Vincent Schmelz, who claimed he did not see the sign forbidding photographs and recordings inside the courtroom, to pay $5,000 to the Chicago Bar Foundation for tweeting photos during a trial. He was also required to attend a course on ethics in social media and "donate at least 50 hours to the pro se desk at the federal courthouse in Chicago."[3]

1. "Judge Keeps Spectator in Jail: Contempt Order Appealed," *Orlando Sentinel* (Florida) (July 2, 2011), p. 9B.
2. "No Babies, No Yawning, No Bears," *Chicago Tribune* (August 16, 2009), p. 3C.
3. "BigLaw Partner Is Ordered to Donate $5,000 for Tweeting Photos During Federal Trial," *American Bar Association Journal* (December 15, 2015), http://www.abajournal.com, accessed December 16, 2015.

The role of the trial judge at sentencing is one of the most important of all judicial functions. Despite the importance of sentencing, until recently little attention was paid to preparing judges for this role. Nor was there any emphasis on the importance of thorough presentence reports by probation or other officers of the court to assist judges in making the decision. Likewise, little attention was given to appellate review of judicial sentencing.

Concern with the extensive power of judges over sentencing, along with other sentencing issues, has led to sentence reform, which is discussed in Chapter 8. The purpose of most of the reform efforts has been to reduce judicial sentencing discretion, thought to cause sentence disparity. Some of the alleged disparity results from a consideration of legally acceptable factors, such as the defendant's prior record and the nature of the current charge(s). However, some of the differences may be the result of unacceptable factors, such as the gender, age, race, sexual orientation, disability, or ethnicity of a defendant, as well as the personalities, backgrounds, and prejudices of the sentencing judges. Before concluding that judicial sentencing differences are unfair, unreasonable, or unconstitutional, it is important to consider all the variables involved in the decision-making process. Spotlight 6.2 discusses an unusual case but one that demonstrates how much power judges may have at sentencing.

The sentencing decision is a difficult one. As one judge concluded, "I am sure that I speak for my many colleagues when I state that the imposition of a criminal sentence is the most delicate, difficult, distasteful task for the trial judge."[9] Sentencing issues are discussed in greater detail in Chapter 8. In all of these and other activities at trial, not only the decision but also the demeanor and attitude of the judge, are important. The judge's behavior may influence the attitudes and decisions of jurors, witnesses, and victims at the trial, as well as the general public's image of criminal justice systems. In addition, the judge influences the flow of cases through the criminal courts. Poor management of a caseload contributes to court congestion and risks impairing the rights of defendants to a speedy trial. High-profile televised cases in particular challenge the judicial demeanor. **Supplement 6.5** briefly details the outstanding career of a high-profile trial judge.

Spotlight 6.2

A Sentence Enhanced: Sometimes It Does Not Pay to Brag

New York defense attorney Lynne Stewart was sentenced to 28 months in prison. She indicated that she would do it all over again and announced to the press that she could do 28 months "standing on my head." When the appellate court ruled that the sentence was too short and sent the case back to the trial court for resentencing, the trial judge imposed 120 months in prison. The sentencing judge praised the earlier legal work of the defendant but said her comments to the press showed "a lack of remorse." Although we will probably never know why the judge imposed a sentence as long as 120 months, it is suspected that his perception of the "lack of remorse" was the reason.[1]

Stewart, a New York attorney who represented Sheik Omar Abdel-Rahman, the "blind cleric," was indicted in 2002. Prosecutors accused her of aiding her client "in continuing to direct the terrorist activities of the Islamic Group from his prison cell in the United States." Stewart's client was sentenced to life in prison after his conviction in 1995 for plotting to blow up the World Trade Center and other New York City buildings. Prosecutors portrayed Stewart as the mastermind behind two other defendants (one of whom was her Arabic translator) in a conspiracy to evade prison regulations concerning the contact that her client could maintain with the world outside the prison and in lying to the government when they said they would abide by those regulations. Stewart maintained that she did not go beyond what an attorney can do to represent her client and that what happened to her "could happen to anyone, at any time, any place and anywhere for lawyers who represent clients charged with heinous crimes."[2]

Stewart's attorney said:

> My client denies that she committed crimes. She denies that she did anything wrong. . . . I think [the prosecution of Stewart is] an attempt to send a message to the legal community. "If you represent people who we, the Justice Department, determine to be social pariahs, whether we call them terrorists or predators, there's going to be a price to pay."[3]

Stewart was convicted in 2005, but her original sentencing was postponed until 2006 to enable her to get treatment for breast cancer. She appealed her conviction and the government appealed the sentence. She was out on bail until a decision on those appeals was made in November 2009, at which time her conviction was upheld and the lower court was instructed to revoke her bail and order her to report for prison. The trial court was also instructed to reconsider her sentence. The U.S. Supreme Court refused to review that decision. Stewart was resentenced by the trial court, at which time she was 70 years old and still in poor health. She made an effort to soften her earlier statement about being able to do 28 months standing on her head by saying that being incarcerated in a prison was much worse than she had imagined.[4]

In late December 2013, Stewart was granted a compassionate release from prison based on her doctors' assessment that she had less than 18 months to live. She was released in early January 2014. During the next two years, she gave political speeches and solicited funds. She died in 2017.

---

1. "Sentence Is Sharply Increased for Lawyer Convicted of Aiding Terror," *New York Times* (July 16, 2010), p. 22.
2. "Indicted Lawyer: It Could Happen to You: Terrorists' Attorney Paints a Chilling Picture," *New Jersey Lawyer* (October 7, 2002): 4.
3. "DOJ Says Four Lawyers Broke Anti-Terror Rules," *Fulton County Daily Reporter* (April 18, 2002), n.p.
4. "Sentence Is Sharply Increased." The case is *United States v. Lynne Stewart et al.*, 590 F.3d 93 (2d Cir. 2009), *cert. denied, Sattar v. United States*, 559 U.S. 1031 (2010).

Appellate Judges

Decisions of trial judges may be upheld or reversed on appeal. In most cases, however, appellate courts defer to trial courts on issues in which trial judges have an advantage because of their direct observation of the events that occurred at trial. In some cases, however, an appellate court may instruct the trial judge to give further analysis to a decision he or she made. Only a fraction of cases are reversed on appeal; those cases are important not only to the individual defendants but also to the justice system as precedents for future cases.

Appellate judges and justices are often faced with interpreting the laws and constitutions of their jurisdictions in ways that will have an effect on more than the parties before the court. In that respect, their decisions have a much broader impact than the decisions of trial courts. Usually, their decisions—in contrast to those of trial courts—are accompanied by written opinions, thus placing an even greater responsibility on judges to articulate why they decided a specific issue in a particular way.

Judicial Selection, Training, and Retention

The first issue in deciding how to select, train, and retain judges is to decide what qualities are desired. Historically, judges have been white, male, Protestant, and conservative. Only recently have more women and minorities joined the judiciary, along with liberals and persons of varying faiths.

Judges should be impartial and fair. They should be able to approach a case with an objective and open mind concerning the facts. If for any reason a judge cannot be objective in a case (or could not be perceived to be impartial given his or her association with the case or any parties before the court), he or she should withdraw from that case, a process known as **recusal**. Objectivity enables the judge to be fair, and to insist that attorneys abide by the laws and procedures of the judiciary, the jurisdiction, and the state and federal (where applicable) constitutions. Judges should be well educated in substantive and procedural law, the rules of evidence, and the Constitution. They should be able to think and write clearly. Their opinions are important to attorneys and other judges, who use them to analyze how future cases might be argued and decided. Judges should have high moral and ethical standards, enabling them to withstand political and economic pressures that might influence decisions. They should be in good physical, mental, and emotional health. They should be good managers because they have considerable power over court systems. They should be able to assume power sensibly, without abuse, and to exercise leadership in social reform where necessary and desirable.

Finding persons with the desired judicial qualifications is not always easy. Several methods have been used for selecting judges in the United States. During the colonial period, judges were appointed by the king, but after the American Revolution, this practice ceased. In a majority of the colonies, judges were appointed by the legislators. In some colonies, the appointment was made by the governor, with or without the required approval of his council.

As the colonies became states, they gradually began to select judges by popular election, but that method came under criticism, with frequent allegations that undue political influence led to the selection of incompetent and corrupt judges. Today most states use the election process for some of their judges. Another method of selecting judges, the merit plan, is traced to Albert M. Kales, one of the founders of the American Judicature Society. The plan was first adopted by Missouri in 1940. It is referred to as the *Missouri plan* or, less commonly, the *Kales plan* or *commission plan*.

Merit selection plans vary extensively from state to state, but most plans include a nonpartisan commission, which solicits, investigates, and screens candidates when judicial openings occur. The commission sends a select number of names (usually three to five) to the executive branch, where an appointment is made. The new judge may serve a probationary period (usually a year) and may be required to run unopposed on a general election retention ballot. Voters are polled with a yes or no vote to determine whether this judge should be retained in office. A judge who receives a majority of votes (which is usually the case) will be retained. A merit selection plan does not assure that politics will not enter into the selection process, but arguably, the prescreening by a nonpartisan commission places only qualified candidates in a position for election. Criticisms remain, however, and politics plays an important role.

In an effort to avoid public pressure on judicial decision making, federal judges, along with U.S. Supreme Court justices, are appointed. Technically, they are appointed by the president of the United States and confirmed by the Senate, but frequently, the attorney general or the deputy attorney general recommends individuals, and the president accepts those recommendations. Members of the U.S. House of Representatives and the U.S. Senate are also influential in nominating candidates for judicial positions. Federal judges and justices hold their appointments for life. They may be removed only for bad behavior, but that process is very difficult and is not often undertaken, even when there are reasons to do so.

Most U.S. jurisdictions do not have required formal training for judges, but we are making progress in providing training programs for newly appointed or elected judges. States generally provide some training, and many are offering continuing education courses for judges already on the bench.

Recruiting the right kind of attorneys and giving them proper training in the judiciary is important, but retention of the best judges is becoming a serious problem. In the past, a judicial appointment, especially to the federal bench, was the ultimate goal of many lawyers. But the increasing number of resignations of federal judges has led some to refer to the revolving door of the federal judiciary, with some of the best candidates refusing nominations or accepting them, staying a few years, and then leaving. For those who do stay, morale may be affected as they realize the substantial pay cut they take by leaving private practice to accept an appointment to the bench.

According to the Administrative Office of the U.S. Courts, the "real pay" for federal judges has declined significantly in recent years, and many other federal employees now earn more than federal district judges. Many of the federal judges who have left the bench in recent years have stated that they did so for financial reasons. In 2018, federal judges' salaries were as follows:

District judge	\$208,100
Circuit judge	\$220,600
Associate justices	\$255,300
Chief justice	\$267,000[10]

State judicial salaries vary significantly from state to state. Although, generally, salaries are higher in the federal system, the late Judge Irving R. Kaufman wrote an open letter to President Ronald Reagan in 1981, declaring, "[W]e receive for our services little more than those fresh-faced lads a few years out of Harvard at the larger New York firms."[11] Salaries of federal judges have increased since Judge Kaufman made that statement, and federal judges now get cost-of-living raises, but the salaries have not kept pace with the increases in other professions, leaving Chief Justice John Roberts Jr. of the U.S. Supreme Court to make these statements:

> Inadequate compensation directly threatens the vitality of life tenure, and if tenure in office is made uncertain, the strength and independence judges need to uphold the rule of law—even when it is unpopular to do so—will be seriously eroded.
>
> If judicial appointment ceases to be the capstone of a distinguished career and instead becomes a stepping stone to a lucrative position in private practice, the Framers' goal of a truly independent judiciary will be placed in serious jeopardy.[12]

Stress is another problem that judges face. Judges handle issues that are very important and highly controversial but must be decided. As Judge Kaufman said, "Much tension accompanies the job of deciding the questions that all the rest of the social matrix has found too hard to answer."[13]

In addition to the stresses faced by any professional person, judges face several stressors not common to other professions. It may be a lonely transition from the practice of law to a judicial position about which lawyers may know very little except as outside observers. Usually at the peak of their legal careers when they become judges, they must give up many of their positions and even their friendships. Additional stresses on judges come from the judicial code of conduct that places limitations on their financial and social lives. For example, contacts that might compromise a judge's decisions must be avoided; close associations with attorneys who might appear before them must be restricted; and they are limited in terms of when and with whom they may discuss cases. **Supplement 6.6** reproduces the code of conduct for federal U.S. judges.

Violence is another area of stress for judges and justices. Violence has invaded courtrooms, as illustrated by the shootings in Atlanta, Georgia, in March 2005, when Brian Nichols entered the Fulton County courtroom of Superior Court Judge Rowland W. Barnes and shot and killed the judge and his court reporter, Julie Ann Brandau. Nichols, 33, and a defendant in a criminal trial presided over by Judge Barnes, overpowered his guard, Cynthia Hall, who was critically injured, took her weapon, and went to the judge's chambers, where he overpowered another deputy, handcuffing him and stealing his gun. After killing Barnes and Brandau, Nichols went to the parking garage, attacked and pistol-whipped a reporter, and stole his car. Outside the courthouse, a third murder victim, Sergeant Hoyt Teasley, was shot in the abdomen and killed. Other acts of violence were also attributed to Nichols after he left the courthouse area. Nichols was convicted but the jury could not agree on the death penalty; he was sentenced to life in prison.

Most courthouses provide security checks on all persons who wish to enter, and in high-profile cases, it is now customary to have extra courthouse security, such as metal detectors and additional security personnel. Security has been increased in recent years for federal judges, who are protected by the U.S. Marshals Service. Penalties for those who threaten or harm federal judges have been increased as well, but it is impossible to remove all potential violence against judges. The same is true for state judges.

Diversity and Judging

Diversity is important in all phases of criminal justice systems. In 2008, the House of Delegates of the American Bar Association (ABA) adopted four goals in its commitment to diversity. The following is the description of one of those goals:

GOAL III: ELIMINATE BIAS AND ENHANCE DIVERSITY

Objectives:

1. Promote full and equal participation in the Association, our profession, and the justice system by all persons.

2. Eliminate bias in the legal profession and the Justice System.[14]

In 2013, the ABA published a report regarding the association's work on Goal III. Among other comments were these:

> Increasing diversity and inclusion in a practice area and . . . a profession, are lofty, but achievable goals. The process toward a fully diverse and inclusive profession will evolve slowly and will most likely be fraught with ups and downs, progress and setbacks. However, those entities that commit for the long haul will recap the ultimate reward.[15]

In April 2010, the ABA published the results of an extensive analysis of diversity in legal systems. **Supplement 6.7** presents information from that study, "Diversity in the Legal Profession: The Next Steps."[16]

The judiciary is a key area in which diversity in criminal justice systems is important. In recent years, the numbers of women and racial and ethnic minorities have increased in the judiciary but not in proportion to their numbers in the population. Women, for example, have made up around one-half of the law student population for the past 25 years, but they hold only one-third of federal judiciary positions, and a smaller percentage of federal judges are women of color.[17]

The American Constitution Society published a study in which it referred to the "gavel gap," meaning that judges in the United States are not representative of the populations they serve. Women, who represent approximately 50 percent of the population, occupy about 30 percent of state judicial positions. Racial and ethnic minorities, representing 40 percent of the population, occupy only 20 percent of state judicial positions. Most people in the United States who come into contact with courts do so in state, not federal courts.[18] Finally, in 2017, the Associated Press (AP) reported that President Trump's nominees to the federal bench were less diverse than those of any other president for the previous three decades. The AP reported that Trump's nominees were 91 percent white and 81 percent male.[19]

Judge Sonia Sotomayor was nominated by President Barack Obama in May 2009 and became the first Latina justice and the third woman to serve on the U.S. Supreme Court. Justice Sotomayor, an outspoken member of the Court, began her legal career as a prosecutor and later served as a corporate litigator, a trial judge, a circuit judge, and a law professor. She shared her interesting life story from her birth in the Bronx, New York, to her confirmation as a justice on the highest court in her autobiography, My Beloved World.

Judicial Control

Like all other professions, the judiciary is characterized by some members who engage in questionable behavior in their professional and personal lives. Their shortcomings may affect their abilities to function effectively as judges. Excessive drinking may be tolerated in some circles, but excessive drinking by a judge, particularly one convicted of driving while intoxicated, is unacceptable. And although the private sexual behavior of most adults may be considered their business as long as it is private, consensual, and does not involve minors, the public consider it their business when judges engage in any sexual behavior that comes to public attention. Sexual harassment by anyone is unacceptable, but sexual

Spotlight 6.3

A Personal Relationship Between a Judge and a Prosecutor: Private Business?

Behavior that might be accepted in some jurisdictions (e.g., legal behavior) may not be considered acceptable for a judge and other court personnel. Consider the case of a judge who engages in an extramarital affair with a prosecutor who tries a death penalty case before that judge.

In 1990, a Texas jury found Charles Dean Hood guilty of murdering and robbing a couple. He was sentenced to death. Subsequently, it was discovered that the prosecutor, district attorney Thomas S. O'Connell Jr., and the district judge, Verla Sue Holland, had engaged in a "romantic" relationship for years although it was not clear when that relationship began and when it ended. At the time of the trial, rumors had circulated, but the information was not disclosed during the trial. On the day of Hood's scheduled execution, his attorneys asked the Court of Criminal Appeals (the highest court in the criminal division in Texas) for a stay of execution based on an affidavit signed by another district attorney and stating that it was "common knowledge" that the judge and the prosecutor had been involved in a "romantic relationship." The court rejected the motion on the grounds that the attorney filing the affidavit did not have first-hand knowledge of the alleged affair. The execution was not carried out that night for technical reasons (the state could not do so in the time remaining on the death warrant).

The execution was rescheduled, followed by several appeals on procedural issues. Eventually Hood was granted a new sentencing hearing, but to avoid that, he entered a guilty plea and was sentenced to life in prison.[1]

1. The case is *Ex parte Hood*, 2009 Tex. Crim. App. Unpub LEXIS 561 (Tex. Crim. App. September 16, 2009), *cert. denied*, *Hood v. Texas*, 559 U.S. 1072 (2010).

---

harassment by a judge is even more shocking. Even if the sexual behavior does not rise to the level of harassment, if engaged in by a judge, it is cause for concern, as illustrated by the case discussed in Spotlight 6.3.

How do we control improper judicial behavior? It is not easy to unseat judges, even after they have been convicted of a crime. Usually, they are asked to resign, but if they do not, it may take months or even years to go through appropriate channels to unseat them. Elected judges may be unseated by a recall vote, as illustrated in the case of Judge Aaron Persky in Santa Clara County, California. Judge Persky was recalled by voters who were upset by his sentencing of Brock Turner, a Stanford University swimmer, who was accused of sexually assaulting an unconscious woman. Brock testified that he thought the sex was consensual. Brock served three months in jail. Judge Persky had refused to resign, stating that judicial independence was at stake. "The problem with this recall is, it will pressure judges to follow the rule of public opinion as opposed to the rule of law." In this case, the California Commission on Judicial Performance had refused to remove the judge despite numerous requests to do so. The commission found that there was no "clear and convincing evidence of bias, abuse of authority or other misconduct."[20]

When judges are appointed, a removal is more difficult. At the federal level, where judges serve for life and may be removed only by impeachment and conviction by Congress, legislation provides some avenues for disciplining judges. The Judicial Councils Reform and Judicial Conduct and Disability Act of 1980 provides several sanctions: certify disability, request the judge to retire, strip the judge of his or her caseload "on a temporary basis," and censure or reprimand privately or publicly.[21]

Another method for controlling judicial misconduct and compensating those who are victimized by judges is to permit federal civil rights charges to be brought against judges. In 1997, the U.S. Supreme Court considered a case appealed from a lower federal court, which had held that the federal civil rights statute involved in a Tennessee case did not provide notice that it covered simple or sexual assault crimes. The Supreme Court held that the statute need not specify the *specific* conduct covered and sent the case back for the lower court to reconsider the issue in light of the Supreme Court's holding that the rule is "whether the statute, either standing alone or as construed [interpreted], made it reasonably clear at the relevant time that the defendant's conduct was criminal." The case, *United States v. Lanier*,[22] is discussed in **Supplement 6.8**.

CRISIS IN THE COURTS

Numerous problems exist in our criminal courts, some of which are mentioned in this chapter. But by far the most serious problem is the pressure placed on courts, on defendants, and on society by the increased number of cases tried and appealed. This increase has led to a crisis in our courts, which continues despite additional judges in both state and federal court systems, although many judicial positions, especially in the federal system, remain unfilled.

The greatest number of criminal offenses in federal criminal courts involve drug offenses, leading to recommendations that most drug cases be tried in state courts. In addition to drug cases, the federal court caseload has grown because of the increased number of crimes that have been made *federal* offenses by statute. Over a decade ago, Chief Justice William H. Rehnquist warned against this trend of "one new federal statute after another," but his warnings have not been heeded.[23]

Shifting federal cases to state courts might ease the problem in federal courts, but state courts also face case backlogs and budget problems. In recent years, most—if not all—states faced budget shortfalls. In many states, cutbacks were made in criminal justice systems, with courts facing cuts in personnel, including judges, court-appointed attorneys, and prosecutors. Some courts cut back on services. In New Hampshire, one court began closing at 1 P.M. daily because of the cutback in staff, while a local jail increased the use of bail to save money on medical expenses of the accused who would otherwise be held in jail awaiting their trials.[24]

Among other problems, court congestion results in delayed trials. It is argued that justice delayed is justice denied. That concept is based on the belief that, when a trial is delayed for a significant time, there is a greater chance for error. Witnesses may die or forget. Crowded court dockets have created pressures that encourage plea bargaining and mass handling of some cases. Delayed trials may deny defendants their constitutional right to a speedy trial.

For the accused who are not released before trial, court congestion may result in a long jail term in overcrowded facilities. Because their court-appointed attorneys are so busy with other cases, defendants may not see them during that period. The accused are left with many questions, no answers, and a long wait. Those who are incarcerated before trial face more obstacles in preparation for trial.

Obvious injustices are created by overcrowded courts that must decide cases presented by overworked prosecutors and defense attorneys. The image of inefficiency and injustice that the crowded court dockets and delayed trials project colors the public's perception of criminal justice systems.

In addition to the delays caused by overcrowded court dockets, court delays are also caused by the use of a **continuance**, or postponement. The purpose of granting continuances is to ensure a fair hearing. The defense or the prosecution may need more time to prepare; additional evidence might have come to light and need evaluating; additional witnesses may need to be located.

Another reason for congestion in criminal courts is that courts must handle some cases that perhaps should be processed in some other way. Criminal law is used in an effort to control behaviors such as some types of alcohol and other drug abuse, consenting sexual behavior between adults in private, prostitution, and gambling. This is not to suggest that we should be unconcerned with these activities but only to question the reasonableness of using the criminal law to attempt to regulate them. Removal of some or all of these actions from the criminal court system would reduce the number of cases in those courts.

Many suggestions have been made for solving court congestion. The first is to reduce the number of offenses covered by criminal law. Building new court facilities and expanding the number of judges, prosecutors, defense attorneys, and support staff are other possible solutions. Better management of court proceedings and court dockets may also be helpful. Court personnel need to update their equipment and make use of improved technology. Some courts are using computers to speed up the paperwork. Other courts have been reorganized for greater efficiency.

Other suggestions are to use lay judges, volunteers who would handle misdemeanor cases (e.g., disorderly conduct, petit larceny, prostitution, and criminal mischief), as a method of relieving pressures in the regular court system. Volunteers may be used as prosecutors in some cases, while special courts (e.g., drug courts, mental health courts, and domestic violence courts), some of which are discussed in Chapter 11, are becoming more common.

Another suggestion is the use of alternatives to courts, based on the assumption that, in many cases, courts could and should be avoided. Although most of the alternatives, such as arbitration and mediation, apply primarily to civil cases, some are also used in criminal cases. The expanded use of plea bargaining, whereby defense and prosecution reach an agreement out of court, is an example.

The costs of these proposals must be evaluated. Expanding courts and increasing the number of judges involves the direct cost of the expansions along with support staff and an increase in the number of prosecutors, defense attorneys, courtrooms, other facilities, and police and correctional personnel and facilities.

Finally, some criminal justice systems have instituted special courts to handle cases that perhaps are best handled through treatment rather than punishment through incarceration. Examples of special courts are domestic violence courts, drug courts, truancy courts, veterans' courts, and mental health courts.

Summary

An understanding of the nature and structure of criminal court systems is necessary for a study of the activities taking place within those systems. Terminology is also important. If a court does not have jurisdiction, it cannot hear and decide a case. Cases must be brought before the proper court, and this is determined by the seriousness of the offense, the type of offense, or both. Some courts hear criminal cases, others hear civil, and some hear both. Some hear petty offenses or misdemeanors, whereas others have jurisdiction over felony cases.

Trial courts must base their decisions on facts, which may or may not establish whether the defendant committed the alleged criminal act or acts. Usually, appellate courts are concerned only with questions of law. They ask, "During the trial, did the trial court commit any serious errors in law, such as the admission of evidence that should have been excluded, and if so, was that error prejudicial to the defendant's right to a fair trial?" If a serious error occurred, the case is reversed and sent back for retrial, resentencing, or both. The appellate court might find less serious errors in law and not reverse the case.

Criminal cases may be appealed, but not necessarily to the highest court. Cases in the state system may not be appealed to the lower federal appellate courts. If a federal constitutional right is involved in a state case, the U.S. Supreme Court may hear that case. Cases decided in state courts must be followed in the states in which they are decided but are not binding on other states' courts.

Decisions at one level or jurisdiction may be used by other courts as reasons for their decisions if the judges choose to do so. Decisions of the U.S. Supreme Court are binding on all lower federal courts and on state courts when a federal right is involved. However, because the Supreme Court hears only a few of the cases it is asked to hear, many issues remain unsettled because federal courts in different jurisdictions decide similar cases differently.

The primary figure in court efficiency and administration is the judge. Despite the importance of judges in U.S. court systems, some who become judges are not trained in judicial decision making or trial and appellate procedures. Some have had limited experience as trial lawyers, yet they are given vast powers in criminal justice systems. Most perform admirably; some need to be disciplined or removed; but the system is not very well equipped for those processes. Diversity is important; gender, age, disability, racial and ethnic issues were noted.

Today, courts are criticized for being in a state of crisis as a result of the large backlog of cases, criminal and civil, at both the trial and appellate levels. Some steps must be taken to reduce this backlog. Lawyers and judges have a responsibility to solve this problem, but the role of the public is also important although difficult to accomplish during dire economic circumstances.

Significant changes cannot be made in court systems without public support, especially financial support. Changes are needed in all areas of criminal justice systems. Significant changes in the courts also affect other criminal justice areas. If we create more courts, so that we can try, convict, and sentence more people to prison, yet do not build adequate facilities to accommodate that increase, we push the problems from one area of the system to another. Courts must be analyzed and altered in the total social context in which they operate.

Key Terms

acquittal 135
appeal 127
appellant 127
appellee 127
concurring opinion 132
continuance 141
de novo 131
dicta 127
expert witness 133
judge 126
judicial review 128
moot 127
recusal 137
stare decisis 127
writ of *certiorari* 132

Study Questions

1. Distinguish the judicial branch from other branches of government.
2. What is meant by *jurisdiction*? How does it apply to the dual court system?
3. What is the difference between trial and appellate courts?
4. What is the relationship between state and federal courts?
5. What are the levels of courts in each of the two main court systems, state and federal?
6. What is the purpose of the U.S. Supreme Court, and how does a case get before the Court? What happens to a case that is appealed to but not accepted by the Court?
7. What are the main roles of judges in trial courts? In appellate courts?
8. How are judges and justices selected? What are the advantages and disadvantages of each method?
9. Should an effort be made to recruit more female and minority judges? Why or why not? What methods do you suggest if you think more should be recruited?
10. What actions do you think should be sufficient to disqualify a person for a state judgeship? A federal judgeship? Appointment to the U.S. Supreme Court?
11. To what extent, if any, should public opinion be permitted to influence judicial appointments or judicial retention?
12. How would you suggest that the current caseload crisis in trial and appellate courts be resolved?

Notes

1. "Lawyers Have a Lot to Teach," *American Bar Association Journal* 91 (October 2005): 6.
2. See, for example, the resentencing ordered by the appellate court in the case of the officers who assaulted Rodney King: *United States v. Koon*, 34 F.3d 1416 (9th Cir. 1994), *aff'd in part, rev'd in part, remanded*, 518 U.S. 81 (1996), *on remand, remanded by United States v. Koon*, 91 F.3d 1313 (9th Cir. 1996).
3. *Marbury v. Madison*, 5 U.S. 137 (1803).
4. Chief Justice Fred M. Vinson, quoted in Ronald L. Carlson, *Criminal Justice Procedure*, 2d ed. (Cincinnati, OH: Anderson, 1978), p. 243.
5. "Justices Opt for Fewer Cases, and Professors and Lawyers Ponder Why," *New York Times* (September 29, 2009), p. 20; "Chemerinsky: What We Learned About SCOTUS This Term," *American Bar Association Journal* (July 2, 2013), http://www.abajournal, accessed January 12, 2015; Erwin Chemerinsky, "Chemerinsky: Conservatives' Victories in Key Cases Are a Harbinger of What Is to Come," *American Bar Association Journal* (July 2, 2018), http://www.abajournal.com, accessed July 2, 2018.
6. *Mistretta v. United States*, 488 U.S. 361 (1989).
7. Debra Cassens Weiss, "Chief Justice Roberts Defends Judicial Independence After Trump's 'Obama Judge' Criticism," *American Bar Association Journal* (November 21, 2018), http://www.abajournal, accessed November 28, 2018.
8. "Judge Resigns After He Is Accused of Using Contempt Powers to Jail More than 200 People," *American Bar Association Journal* (August 23, 2018), http://www.abajournal.com, accessed August 23, 2018.
9. *United States v. Wiley*, 184 F. Supp. 679 (N.D. Ill. 1960).
10. Federal Judicial Center, https://www.fjc.gov, accessed September 19, 2018.
11. Irving R. Kaufman, "An Open Letter to President Reagan on Judge Picking," *American Bar Association Journal* 67 (April 1981): 444.
12. Administrative Offices of U.S. Courts, "Federal Judicial Pay Increase: Fact Sheet," http://www.uscourts.gov, accessed March 7, 2011.
13. Quoted in "By and Large We Succeed," *Time* (May 5, 1980), p. 70.
14. American Bar Association, "Defending Liberty, Pursuing Justice" (May 1, 2011), p. 1 (The other goals are to serve the ABA members, improve the profession, and advance the rule of law), http://www.americanbar.org, accessed July 16, 2014.
15. Commission on Racial and Ethnic Diversity in the Profession, American Bar Association, "2013 Goal III Report/Executive Summary," p. 3, http://www.americanbar.org, accessed July 16, 2014.
16. American Bar Association press release, "ABA Presidential Commission Report Calls for More Nuanced Diversity" (February 4, 2010). The full report, *Diversity in the Legal Profession: The Next Steps: Report and Recommendations*, was published in April 2010, available at http://www.americanbar.org, accessed July 16, 2014.
17. National Women's Law Center, "The Vacancy Crisis in the Federal Judiciary: What's at Stake for Women" (September 10, 2014), http://www.nwlc.org, accessed April 25, 2015.
18. Lorelei Laird, "Study Finds a 'Gavel Gap' Between Diversity of Judges and That of the Populations They Serve," *American Bar Association Journal* (June 23, 2016), http://www.abajournal.com, accessed June 24, 2016.
19. Lorelei Laird, "Trump's Judicial Nominees Are the Least Diverse in Almost 3 Decades," *American Bar Association Journal* (November 16, 2017), http://www.abajournal.com, accessed November 18, 2017.
20. Debra Cassens Weiss, "Judge Criticized for Stanford Swimmer's Sexual Assault Sentence Is Ousted in Recall Vote," *American Bar Association Journal* (June 6, 2018), http://www.abajournal.com, accessed July 7, 2018.
21. Judicial Councils Reform and Judicial Conduct and Disability Act of 1980, Public Law 96-458, incorporated into Complaints of Judicial Misconduct or Disability, USCS Ct. App. Fed. Cir. R 51 (1994). The statute is USCS, Title 28, Section 351 (2019).
22. *United States v. Lanier*, 520 U.S. 259 (1997).
23. "Troubling Review: Rehnquist Sees Rough Times Ahead of Federal and State Courts," *American Bar Association Journal* 90 (January 1994): 94.
24. "Backlog Forces Court to Close Early Each Day," *Conway Daily Sun* (New Hampshire) (July 23, 2010), p. 3; "Court Loosens Bail to Save on Medical Expenses," *Conway Daily Sun* (June 24, 2010), p. 11.

7

Prosecution, Defense, and Pretrial Procedures

Chapter Outline

Learning Objectives

After reading this chapter, you should be able to do the following:

- Discuss briefly the historical background of the legal profession
- Explain the organization and structure of prosecutorial systems
- Recognize the importance and problems of prosecutorial discretion regarding whether to prosecute
- Evaluate ways to control prosecutorial discretion and especially prosecutorial misconduct
- Explain the role of the defense attorney
- Explain and analyze the right to be represented by defense counsel
- Discuss the reasons for private defense counsel in contrast to public defense counsel
- Explain the meaning of effective assistance of counsel and the right to refuse counsel
- List and explain the major steps in the criminal justice pretrial process
- Explain the importance of bail to defendants and to society
- List and explain the ways in which a defendant may be released pending trial
- Explain the process of entering a plea in a criminal case
- Discuss the arguments for and against plea bargaining
- Analyze the importance of the right to counsel at plea bargaining

The adversary philosophy that characterizes U.S. criminal justice systems applies not only to the trial and appeal of a criminal case but also to the processes that occur prior to a trial. This chapter examines those critical pretrial procedures, but first it is necessary to examine the role that lawyers play. Underlying the adversary philosophy is the belief that the best way to obtain the facts of a criminal case is for each side to have an advocate, or attorney, to present evidence and cross-examine the witnesses and examine the evidence and arguments presented by the opposing side.

Attorneys are important at various stages in criminal justice systems. This chapter examines the primary functions of each side and then focuses on the pretrial procedures in which attorneys engage, along with the judge and other participants in criminal cases. The chapter begins with a general overview of lawyers and the legal profession.

LAWYERS AND THE LEGAL PROFESSION

Law and lawyers play a critical role in the administration of justice in any society, although that role has changed over the years, as **Supplement 7.1** indicates in its brief history of lawyers and the legal profession.

The terrorist acts of 9/11 caused some U.S. lawyers to renew their commitment to their chosen profession, as they were encouraged to do so in a letter sent by the president of the American Bar Association (ABA) to all of the association's members one year after the events. Excerpts from that letter are contained in Professions 7.1.

Like most other professions, the legal profession suffered significant cutbacks during the economic downturns after 9/11 and, to some extent, these cutbacks have continued to the present. Many law firms decreased their number of employees, including staff as well as attorneys, even at the highest levels, while others reduced the hiring of new attorneys. In 2018, the ABA offered buyouts to longtime staff members as it engaged in a comprehensive staff restructuring.[1] But that same year, the ABA announced that in 2017, some of the largest law firms were increasing their hiring of recent graduates as well as raising the entry level salaries. The average salary for newly hired lawyers in 2017, for example, increased $5,000 from that of 2016. Law firms with over 500 attorneys were offering starting salaries of $180,000.[2]

The year 2018 also saw encouraging signs in law school admissions. Despite the previous decline in the number of law schools, law faculty, and law school enrollments, and the increasing cost of attending law school, the ABA announced that law school applications for the fall classes of 2018 had increased by 8 percent.[3]

Despite these signs, a 2016 report of law graduates in seven law schools reported that only 38 percent said they had a "good job" (and most of those lawyers graduated in the 1960s), and only 20 percent strongly agreed that going to law school was worth the cost of that education. The researchers acknowledged that the study did not represent all law graduates,[4] but there were other signs of dissatisfaction among lawyers. In 2018, the ABA called on law firms to develop programs for the well-being of their attorneys after the ABA released a survey showing that mental health issues and problem drinking were higher among lawyers than indicated by previous studies. Nearly 21 percent of respondents reported drinking problems, 28 percent reported depression, 19 percent reported anxiety, and 23 percent reported stress.[5] The problems with substance abuse and mental health issues were more likely to occur with younger than older lawyers.[6]

Law school classes, such as this one, train students to enter the legal profession, but with increasing costs for a legal education, law schools have initiated alternatives, such as eliminating the third year or one semester of that year from classes and permitting students to spend time in internships. Some states are now permitting students to take the bar prior to the completion of six semesters of classes. The job market for new lawyers has improved in some locations.

In 2018, a study reported that lawyers "outranked other professionals on a 'loneliness scale,'" which included "61 percent of lawyers, compared to 57 percent of engineers, 55 percent of research scientists, 51 percent of workers in food preparation and serving, and 45 percent of workers in education and library services."[7] However, an earlier study noted that lawyers who work more than 60 hours a week appear happier with their

Professions 7.1

An Open Letter to American Lawyers

Reprinted here is part of an open letter written to members of the American Bar Association (ABA) via e-mail on September 10, 2002 by the ABA president, Alfred P. Carlton Jr.

"The seasons have now cycled since that moment when we saw a blue September sky turn the darkest of gray. One year ago, forces from outside our imagination attacked innocent and earnest people for no other reason than they were workaday participants in the wondrous journey that is America.... [Carlton discussed many of the values that are important to Americans and to the world before he continued.]

Such an allegiance to these ideals is not just rhetorical. It is written into, and facilitated by, our laws. It is our law, above all else, that binds us all to a common moral code. Our law protects us from tyranny, rewards our creativity, punishes our corruptness. Our law facilitates that which is the greatest moral concept our species has ever had the temerity to develop—the concept of justice. As lawyers, you and I see justice every day. Fair hearing, due process, presumption of innocence, are the foundations on which everything else rests. It is you and I, the American lawyer, whose calling it is to ensure that justice is done.

Most of us become lawyers because of a desire to be involved in the operation of the social construct. As officers of the court, we seek to ensure that our vast universe of human endeavor moves with the grace of justice. We are sworn to pursue this calling with our common oath to 'uphold, defend and protect the Constitution and the laws of the United States of America.'

I hope all lawyers have felt, as I have, a renewed passion for our chosen profession in these new times. No matter how far removed your daily work seems from the founding principles of this nation we know that it is not. Justice exists every day, each a fair hearing, each served by due process. The law is, and always will be, our collective shelter from the storm."

Source: E-mail to author and all other members of the American Bar Association, September 13, 2002.

---

career choice than those who worked fewer than 60 hours weekly, although they were less likely to state that the legal profession permitted them "a life outside work."[8] One final comment on the legal profession is that it has recently faced significant changes and will continue to do so. Global and technological changes mandate adjustments and new skills, including languages. Today's lawyers must understand data and how to manipulate it. They must have technological skills and update them. They must adjust to the changing business nature of law firms as they compete with legal websites and apps that offer everything from wills and trusts to contracts and business solutions.[9]

"The legal profession is experiencing an era of turbulence and transformation" leading some to fear that "the headlong rush to remake the profession will cause a shift from the practice of law to the business of law, with the profession losing its moral and cultural footing along the way."

The discussion of the roles lawyers play in the prosecution and defense of criminal cases begins with the prosecution.

PROSECUTION

The **prosecution** of a criminal case is the process by which formal charges are brought against a **defendant** accused of committing a crime. Formal prosecutions are a modern phenomenon, and **Supplement 7.2** contains a brief history of the development of the process and the types of prosecution systems. All states have local and state prosecution systems. Local jurisdictions may have ordinances applicable only to them, with local prosecutors responsible for prosecuting violations of those ordinances. Serious offenses are designated by state statutes, although generally, they are prosecuted in local courts by local prosecutors. In a few states, minor offenses may be prosecuted by the police chief (or his or her designate within the police department), even if that individual is not an attorney.

The Organization and Structure of Prosecution Systems

Most local and state prosecutors are elected officials, although the elected prosecutor may appoint other attorneys to serve as deputy (or assistant) prosecutors within the office. Election means that prosecutors may be subject to the pressures of local and state politics, but it is argued that the election of this important official makes the prosecutor more accountable to the people. Many young attorneys view the office of the prosecutor as a good place to gain experience in a legal career. It is excellent preparation for other types of law practice and provides young lawyers with valuable contacts in the legal profession.

Federal prosecutors, or United States attorneys (provided for by the Judiciary Act of 1789), are appointed by the president (who often accepts the recommendations of the members of the U.S. Senate and the U.S. House of Representatives from the area in which the U.S. attorneys will work) and approved by the Senate. These officials and their assistant U.S. attorneys, along with other lawyers in the U.S. Department of Justice (DOJ), have jurisdiction for prosecuting alleged violations of federal statutes. The DOJ is headed by the attorney general, an attorney who is appointed by the president and confirmed by the Senate.

U.S. attorneys are responsible to the attorney general (to whom they report through the deputy attorney general) and are generally free to develop their own priorities within the guidelines provided by the DOJ. This freedom may result in greater job satisfaction for the attorneys who occupy these positions and provide the needed flexibility for federal prosecutions to be concentrated on the types of crime characteristic of specific areas. However, it may also result in different types of law enforcement throughout the federal system, which in turn may lead to charges of unjust practices.

Although most crimes are prosecuted at the state level, federal prosecutors handle a significant number and variety of criminal offenses. Finally, some prosecution systems employ a **community prosecution** system, which is similar in form to community policing. More details on this approach are contained in **Supplement 7.3**.

The prosecutor is the key figure in prosecution, as it is he or she who has the discretion to bring (or decline) charges, to determine the nature and extent of those charges, and who has the burden of proving the charges beyond a reasonable doubt.

The Prosecutor's Role

According to the American Bar Association's criminal justice standards, the duty of the **prosecuting attorney** is to "seek justice, not merely to convict."[10] In a criminal case, the prosecutor is responsible for assessing the allegations and the evidence and deciding whether to bring charges against persons accused of committing crimes. If charges are brought, the prosecutor must turn over certain evidence to the defense, decide whether to plea bargain a case, recommend to the judge that the charges be dropped if additional evidence suggests that is the just approach, or if the case goes to trial, develop and present the evidence against the accused. Prosecutors also participate in the sentencing phase of a criminal case. Most of these functions are discussed in this chapter; the importance of this section is to assess the role of discretion in prosecutorial decisions whether to charge or to proceed with a case.

The importance of a fair and just prosecution was emphasized in a 1935 U.S. Supreme Court case. It refers to a U.S. attorney, but the same general principles and rules apply to local and state prosecutors.

> The United States attorney is the representative not of an ordinary party to a controversy, but of a sovereignty whose obligation to govern impartially is as compelling as its obligation to govern at all; and whose interest, therefore, in a criminal prosecution is not that it shall win a case, but that justice shall be done. As such, he is in a peculiar and very definite sense the servant of the law, the twofold aim of which is that guilt shall not escape or innocence suffer. He may prosecute with earnestness and vigor—indeed, he should do so. But, while he may strike hard blows, he is not at liberty to strike foul ones. It is as much his duty to refrain from improper methods calculated to produce a wrongful conviction as it is to use every legitimate means to bring about a just one.[11]

These comments were made by a court in 1935, but they must ring in the hearts and minds of numerous defendants today who are serving (or have served) prison terms for crimes they did not commit, all because prosecutors withheld exculpatory evidence that would have exonerated them. Criminal Justice Systems Dilemma 7.1 discusses the issue of wrongful convictions and recognizes one person who was a victim of a prosecutor's wrongful acts.

Criminal Justice Systems Dilemma 7.1

Wrongful Convictions and Prosecutorial Involvement: Texas Reacts

Michael Morton walked out of prison on October 4, 2011, after serving 25 years for a murder he did not commit. Morton's case is particularly unusual in that it resulted in a state statute and charges against the prosecutor who brought Morton's case and succeeded in convicting him. The 2013 Texas Legislature enacted the Michael Morton Act,[2] which pertains to discovery in a criminal case. The new law requires that defendants have access to information that might lead to acquittals. Morton was not in the legislature for the final moments of this victory: He was in court in another town, witnessing the conviction of the man who killed Morton's wife, the murder for which Morton was convicted. Mark Alan Norwood entered a guilty plea in March 2013, admitting that he murdered Morton's wife, beating her to death in her bedroom one morning in 1986 after Morton left for work.

The evidence that the prosecution did not give to the defense prior to Morton's trial was that neighbors had seen a suspicious van in the area prior to the murder of Morton's wife and that their 3-year-old son had said that "a monster" hurt his mother. Morton was not even told that their son witnessed the murder. The man who prosecuted Morton, Ken Anderson, who later became a judge, was investigated for wrongfully withholding evidence that could have exonerated Morton. Anderson, who said he was sickened by the wrongful conviction, denied any wrongdoing but agreed to a plea deal in which he was sentenced to nine days in jail and surrendered his law license.

1. The Innocence Project, "DNA Exoneree Case Profiles," http://www.innocenceproject.org/know/, accessed July 18, 2014.
2. The Michael Morton Act is codified as 2013 Tex. SB 1611 (2013).

In late December 2014, Rickey Dale Wyatt was exonerated of a rape for which he served 31 years in prison, making him Texas's longest-serving exoneree. Officials said that, in the original trial, both police and prosecutors withheld evidence that would have assisted in Wyatt's defense. Although Wyatt was released from prison three years earlier, he was not declared innocent until December 2014. The state district judge held, "The state finds the defendant is actually innocent." In 2015, Wyatt was awarded state compensation in the amount of $2,480,000 and a monthly annuity of $15,075.[12]

Prosecutorial Discretion

The prosecutor in most jurisdictions has extensive discretion in deciding whether to bring formal charges against the accused. Statutes vary but generally provide that the prosecutor or assistant prosecutors shall appear at all trials and shall prosecute all actions for crimes committed in their jurisdictions. These statutes have been interpreted to mean that prosecutions must be brought by prosecutors or their assistants and not that prosecutors must file charges in *all* crimes brought to their attention. Consequently, prosecutors have the discretion to refuse to prosecute. This discretion is virtually unchecked, as noted by a New Jersey appellate court:

> A decision to prosecute or not to prosecute is to be accorded judicial deference in the absence of a showing of arbitrariness, gross abuse of discretion or bad faith. . . . It is fundamental that the mental processes of public officials by means of which governmental action is determined are generally beyond the scope of judicial review.[13]

In the real world, however, the prosecutor may bring a weak case and ruin lives before that fact is discovered. Consider the prosecutorial allegations against three white Duke University lacrosse players for allegedly raping a young black woman who was hired as a dancer for one of the fraternity parties. The case is summarized in **Supplement 7.4**.

What influences prosecutors in their decisions whether to prosecute? It is, of course, possible that extralegal factors (e.g., race, ethnicity, disability, gender, or sexual orientation) or, as noted in the Duke University case, political gain, influence prosecutorial decisions. The accused in the Duke lacrosse case retained excellent defense attorneys, who were able to pick the case apart, but not everyone has that opportunity. And despite the availability of legal recourse, it is difficult to win a case of false prosecution. Some of the legal issues regarding false prosecution are noted in **Supplement 7.5**.

Legitimate, practical reasons may lead to a refusal to prosecute, especially in cases that involve a lot of time, resources, and expense. Other reasons are as follows:

- There may not be enough physical evidence to support a conviction.
- Evidence may be tainted because of the manner in which it was collected or the evidence in some other way violates defendants' rights.
- Witnesses may be unsure of the alleged facts to which they must testify, unwilling to testify, or not convincing enough to cause prosecutors to conclude that their testimony will be meaningful and effective.
- Prosecutors may secure a guilty plea to one or more charges in exchange for declining prosecution on other charges.
- Prosecutors may agree not to charge (or to drop charges) if the accused enters a treatment program.
- It may not be in the interests of justice to prosecute a particular case.

These and other reasons for declining to prosecute may also apply to a prosecutor's decision to request a dismissal after a case has been filed.

Once the prosecutor decides to prosecute, he or she must decide the appropriate charge(s) to bring. Many criminal statutes overlap. Some offenses, such as first- or second-degree murder, are defined by degrees of seriousness. There may be evidence that the suspect has committed more than one crime. The prosecutor must decide which charges to make in each case, and there is no requirement that the suspect be charged with all possible crimes. In jurisdictions in which separate charges may not be prosecuted in the same trial, or for other reasons, prosecutors may decide to bring charges only on the more serious allegations.

Once the prosecutor has decided on specific charges, formal charges must be made. The law specifies where and how those charges are to be filed with the court. The prosecutor prepares an **information**, a document that names a specific person and the specific charge(s) against that individual. Formal charges may also begin by means of an **indictment** by a **grand jury**. In some cases, the law *requires* a formal grand jury indictment, but even then, the prosecutor may have considerable influence over the grand jury's decision. Although the grand jury is viewed as a safeguard against unfounded criminal charges—thus serving as a check on the prosecutor—most grand juries follow prosecutors' recommendations, especially in urban jurisdictions faced with a large number of alleged criminal violations, many of which may be serious crimes. In smaller jurisdictions, especially in rural areas, grand juries may have more time to consider cases and be less influenced by prosecutors.

When charging decisions are made, most prosecutors have scant evidence about the defendant or the alleged crime. Charging decisions may be based on intuition, personal beliefs about the usefulness of punishment, the relation of the crime to the possible penalty, and even personal bias or prejudice. Most prosecutors must make charging decisions without adequate guidelines or established goals. Where goals and guidelines exist, they differ from one jurisdiction to another. However, some general goals of prosecution are commonly accepted.

One goal of charging decisions is crime reduction. Prosecutors attempt to control crime by prosecuting and, therefore, incapacitating offenders and presumably deterring potential criminals. Charging practices may be affected by decisions to concentrate on cases involving repeat offenders and the use of habitual criminal statutes with enhanced penalties. Thus, defendants who are convicted of multiple specified crimes may be given longer prison terms than they could receive for each crime individually or for all of them cumulatively. In addition, crime control efforts may focus on high-rate, dangerous offenders.

Another goal of charging decisions is the efficient use of resources in the prosecutor's office. Funds and staff limit the number of cases that can be processed. The cost of prosecuting some cases may be too great, and charging decisions must emphasize early case disposition in offices that cannot afford many trials.

Still another goal may be the rehabilitation of the defendant. The prosecutor may set the level of charge for a defendant with the goal of diverting that person into an alternative treatment program, such as job training or alcohol or other drug rehabilitation, rather than incarceration in prison.

Judicial Review and Prosecutorial Misconduct

One way to control prosecutorial discretion is by the exercise of judicial review. Defendants who think they have been treated unfairly might appeal their convictions on the basis of prosecutorial misconduct. This is possible but difficult, as noted in the discussion in the *Armstrong* case in **Supplement 7.5**, mentioned earlier.

The landmark case using the equality principle to overturn a prosecutor's decision is over a century old. In 1886, the U.S. Supreme Court held that, if the prosecutor uses a law that is fair and impartial as written and applies it with "an evil eye and an unequal hand," so that

Spotlight 7.1

Prosecutorial Misconduct

All attorneys who serve the courts should be held to a high standard of conduct. This includes how they act and what they say, both in and out of court. Defense and prosecution attorneys may be placed under a complete or restricted gag order by the judge. If they violate the order and discuss the case, for example, with the media, they may be sanctioned. Attorneys may also be sanctioned for making improper comments during court proceedings. When their statements or actions are challenged by the opposing side, courts analyze the questioned statements in the context in which they were made and consider whether the effect of the words was to deny the defendant a fair trial.

Consider the case of *Darden v. Wainwright*. Among other questionable comments, the prosecutor stated that the defendant

> shouldn't be out of his cell unless he has a leash on him and a prison guard at the other end of that leash. I wish [Mr. Turman] had had a shotgun in his hand when he walked in the back door and blown [sic] his [Darden's] face off. I wish I could see him sitting here with no face, blown away by a shotgun.[1]

The crime involved in *Darden* was a particularly heinous one. Darden was attempting an armed robbery of Mrs. Turman in a furniture store in 1973. When Mrs. Turman's husband unexpectedly came in the back door, Darden shot him. As Mr. Turman was dying, Darden attempted to force Mrs. Turman into a sexual act. A young neighbor entered the store and tried to help Mr. Turman but was shot three times by Darden, who fled after the assault. In his rush to escape, Darden had an automobile accident. A witness to that accident testified that Darden was zipping his pants and buckling his belt. Officers traced the car and, with this evidence, charged Darden with the crimes against the Turmans.

During the trial, in addition to the comment quoted above, the prosecutor said repeatedly that he wished Darden had used the gun to kill himself. The U.S. Supreme Court held that, although the prosecutor's comments were improper, they were not sufficient to deny Darden a fair trial. Four justices dissented. In 1988, Darden was executed in Florida by electric chair.

1. *Darden v. Wainwright*, 477 U.S. 168 (1986).

---

the prosecutor creates discrimination, the defendant has been denied equal protection of the laws, and the decision may be overturned.[14]

In short, appealing a prosecutor's decision is difficult and rarely successful—unless the prosecutor has engaged in misconduct or a criminal act.

Prosecutors may engage in various types of misconduct, most of which will go unchallenged because of wide prosecutorial discretion and the lack of judicial review of their decisions. There are, however, some acts for which courts and bar associations hold prosecutors responsible.

Overcharging is one type of prosecutorial misconduct for which judicial review may be a remedy. Prosecutors abuse their discretion when they file charges that are not reasonable in light of the evidence available at the time those charges are filed. Overcharging may be done on purpose to coerce the defendant to plead guilty to a lesser charge.

Allegations of overcharging are difficult to prove. Prosecutors may legally charge a suspect with any crime for which there is sufficient evidence to connect that person. If the prosecutor decides not to file the most serious charge(s) that could be filed, and if the defendant refuses to plead guilty to the lesser charge(s), the prosecutor may file the more serious charge(s). This is not an abuse of discretion.

Prosecutorial misconduct can involve withholding evidence that would be favorable to the defense. A landmark 1963 U.S. Supreme Court case, *Brady v. Maryland*, held that prosecutors who suppress evidence favorable to defendants and material to the issue of guilt or innocence are violating the due process rights of those defendants.[15] In a December 2013 decision, the dissent in a Ninth Circuit case declared, "There is an epidemic of Brady violations abroad in the land. Only judges can put a stop to it."[16]

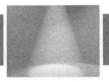

Prosecutorial misconduct can occur in or out of court by the manner in which the prosecutor talks or acts. Spotlight 7.1 summarizes one case. There is a fine line, however, between prosecutorial misconduct and questionable judgment. Among the types of prosecutorial misconduct are the failure of prosecutors to disclose evidence in their possession that might be of assistance to the defense; the mishandling of evidence or use of false evidence; purposely misleading the jury on the meaning of the evidence or presenting evidence known to be inflammatory; referring to the defendant or the defense attorneys in a hostile manner; discriminating on the basis of race, gender, sexual orientation, ethnicity, or any other recognized extralegal reason; filing charges without credible evidence that the alleged acts occurred, and so on.

Some prosecutors go beyond misconduct and engage in criminal acts by committing the same type of crimes they prosecute. An example is the case of Richard J. Roach, who was elected district attorney for five counties in the Texas Panhandle. Roach was so enthusiastic about prosecuting drug offenders that he would bound into his office in the morning, exclaiming, "Let's go." Roach, who had previously spent time in a drug treatment center, had resumed his illegal habit. In February 2005, FBI agents entered a courtroom and arrested Roach for suspicion of violating drug and weapons offenses. Roach plea bargained quickly, pleading guilty to possessing a firearm while using illegal drugs, and resigned his position. The remaining charges against him were dropped.[17]

DEFENSE

One of the most effective ways to control prosecutorial misconduct is to provide adequate defense counsel for those accused of crimes. This section focuses on the role of the attorney as defense counsel in U.S. criminal justice systems, giving particular attention to the right to counsel.

The Defense Attorney's Role

The **defense attorney** is charged with the responsibility of protecting a defendant's constitutional rights at all stages of the legal proceedings, which begin before trial.

The defense of a criminal case is extremely important in the adversary system. The primary job of a defense attorney is to protect the defendant's legal rights and thereby preserve the adversary system. It is not the function of the defense attorney to judge the guilt or innocence of the defendant; that is a factual question to be decided by the jury (or the judge if the case is not tried to a jury). The defense attorney gathers and presents evidence and witnesses that support the defense and examines the evidence and witnesses introduced by the prosecutor.

This basic defense function is critical. The adversary system requires that, for a person to be convicted of a criminal offense, all of the elements of that offense must be proved by the prosecutor and the question of guilt decided by a jury or judge. The evidence must be strong enough to determine the defendant's guilt beyond a reasonable doubt, a much tougher burden than that required in a civil case.

The first encounter that a defense attorney usually has with a client is at the jail. Normally, after arrest and booking, a suspect is permitted one phone call. That call is usually to a lawyer or to a friend, requesting that the friend call a lawyer. If the suspect cannot afford an attorney, the judge appoints counsel at the first court appearance. Typically, defendants who can afford to retain counsel are visited by their attorneys before that court appearance.

The defense attorney's first responsibility is to interview the client and obtain as many facts as possible. The attorney must gain the confidence of the client so that the defendant is willing to disclose all facts. The attorney should explain that this information is confidential between the attorney and the defendant. The defense attorney may begin an investigation by interviewing witnesses or friends, going to the scene of the alleged crime, and securing physical evidence. The attorney will also talk to the prosecutor to determine what information the police and prosecution have secured against the defendant.

The initial interview with the defendant is a very important one. Defendants may be confused about the law. They may have little or no understanding of their constitutional rights. They may not understand the importance of certain facts to their defense. The attorney must be able to elicit the needed information while maintaining a sense of perspective and understanding.

As soon as the defense attorney has enough information, he or she should advise the defendant concerning the strategy that could be used in the case. It might be reasonable for the defendant to plead guilty rather than go to trial. Negotiating pleas before trial is a frequent and very important procedure. The defense attorney should explain to the defendant the pros and cons of pleading guilty, but the attorney must be careful about encouraging a guilty plea when there is evidence that the defendant is legally not guilty. Even in those cases, a particular defendant, because of his or her prior record or the nature of the alleged offense, might be advised to plead guilty to a lesser offense rather than risk conviction on a more serious charge. All of these issues involve trial strategy, which includes knowing what to expect from the prosecutor as well as trying to predict what the judge and jury will do should the case go to trial.

In some cases, defense attorneys talk to their clients' families and inform them of what to expect during the initial stages of the criminal justice processes. Families and friends might be valuable sources of information for the attorney in preparing a defense, as well as in sentencing recommendations if the defendant is found guilty. Getting the facts from defendants and their families and friends is a difficult task in many cases. It is emotionally draining as well, and some defense attorneys are not trained for this process. Defense attorneys devise strategies to elicit information from clients. Some use sworn police statements to shock the defendant into being honest. Others appear nonjudgmental and use hypothetical questions to allow clients to save face. Some attorneys admit that they browbeat their clients by being tyrannical. Others try to be friendly, but they may resent the time required to discover the facts.

The defense attorney must keep track of the scheduled procedures for the remainder of the time the case is in the criminal justice system. Defense attorneys may request a delay in the proceedings by asking for a continuance because they have not had sufficient time to prepare for hearings. At other times, the requested delays are unreasonable and should be denied by the trial judge.

Even while obtaining facts and additional forms of evidence from defendants and others, most defense attorneys begin preparing the case for trial, should that occur. Trial strategy is important, and an unprepared attorney does a disservice to the defendant. If the case results in a trial and the defendant is convicted, the defense attorney must be prepared to present evidence at sentencing. He or she must also prepare for an appeal if the case warrants one, although some defendants, for their appeals, retain lawyers who specialize in the appellate process.

Defense and the Right to Counsel

The most important aspect of the defense of a criminal case is that the accused has a **right to counsel**. The drafters of the U.S. Constitution recognized that in a criminal trial the state's powers are immense compared with those of the defendant. The Sixth Amendment to the U.S. Constitution states that "in all criminal prosecutions, the accused shall enjoy the right . . . to have the Assistance of Counsel for his defense" (see Appendix A). Many scholars consider the right to counsel to be the most important of all the defendant's constitutional rights. If a defendant cannot afford counsel, the government will provide an attorney for him or her. This provision has been the subject of considerable litigation, some of which is summarized in **Supplement 7.6**, which includes the important cases of *Powell v. Alabama* and *Gideon v. Wainwright* and their progeny.[18]

The right to counsel involves a right to refuse counsel, but a **waiver** of the right to counsel must be made voluntarily and knowingly. Judges know that the trial process is complicated, and they guard against the possibility that defendants will create an unfair disadvantage by appearing ***pro se***. Judges question defendants carefully about their knowledge of criminal law and procedure and their understanding of the advantages of having counsel present. But if the defendant insists, he or she must be given the right to proceed to trial without counsel, although most judges require standby counsel to be present with the defendant to explain the basic rules, formalities, and etiquette in the courtroom. Some defendants refuse all such advice and proceed on their own, although they must observe court rules.

The right to counsel also involves the right to retain the counsel of one's choice within reason. Refusal of that right may be reversed, as illustrated by the discussion in **Supplement 7.7**.

One final and extremely important issue concerning the right to counsel is that defendants have the right to *effective* assistance of counsel, although the nature and meaning of that phrase is not clear. This aspect of the right to counsel is not mandated by the U.S. Constitution, but it has been held to be implied by that document. The right to counsel would have little or no meaning without effective counsel. The U.S. Supreme Court used the concept of "effective and substantial aid" in *Powell v. Alabama* (mentioned earlier and discussed in **Supplement 7.6**).

The Supreme Court has also considered the meaning of effective assistance of counsel in several subsequent cases. In 1945, the District of Columbia Court of Appeals articulated the standard that representation would not be considered ineffective unless counsel's actions reduced the trial to a "farce or mockery of justice." Other lower courts adopted this standard; some courts developed higher standards, such as "reasonably effective assistance."[19]

In 1984, the U.S. Supreme Court adopted the "reasonably effective assistance" standard then used by all the lower federal courts and stated that no further definition was needed than the establishing of a two-pronged test, explained in *Strickland v. Washington* as follows:

> First, the defendant must show that counsel's performance was deficient. This requires showing that counsel made errors so serious that counsel was not functioning as the "counsel" guaranteed the defendant by the Sixth Amendment. Second, the defendant must show that the deficient performance prejudiced the defense. This requires showing that counsel's errors were so serious as to deprive the defendant of a fair trial.[20]

Although a court may conclude that counsel was ineffective based on a single error, *Strickland* requires the court to consider the *totality of circumstances* of the case, and there is a strong presumption that counsel provided effective assistance. The problem comes in deciding which facts are sufficient to constitute ineffectiveness. **Supplement 7.8** considers some examples. This discussion focuses on two recent cases decided by the U.S. Supreme Court: *McCoy v. Louisiana*, decided in 2018, and *Garza v. Idaho*, decided in 2019.

The first case involved Robert McCoy, who was charged with first-degree murder in the deaths of his estranged wife's mother, stepfather, and son. McCoy pleaded not guilty and insisted to his attorney that he was out of town when those murders were committed. He insisted that his attorney not admit his guilt. Yet the court permitted McCoy's attorney to tell the jury during the guilt phase of the trial that there was "no way reasonably possible" that, after hearing the prosecution's evidence, they could reach "any other conclusion" than that McCoy committed those murders. According to Justice Ruth Bader Ginsburg, who delivered the opinion of the Court, which granted McCoy a new trial,

> We hold that a defendant has the right to insist that counsel refrain from admitting guilt, even when counsel's experienced-based view is that confessing guilt offers the defendant the best chance to avoid the death penalty. . . . With individual liberty—and, in capital cases, life—at stake, it is the defendant's prerogative, not counsel's, to decide on the objective of his defense: to admit guilt in the hope of gaining mercy at the sentencing stage, or to maintain his innocence, leaving it to the State to prove his guilt beyond a reasonable doubt.[21]

In the second recent case, *Garza v. Idaho*, decided by a 6-3 vote in February 2019, the U.S. Supreme Court ruled that even though the defendant had signed appeal waivers in his plea agreement, he was entitled to a presumption that he was prejudiced when his attorney declined to file an appeal despite being told to do so by his client on several occasions after his sentencing. According to the majority opinion, "When counsel's deficient performance forfeits an appeal that a defendant otherwise would have taken, the defendant gets a new opportunity to appeal." Justice Clarence Thomas wrote a dissent in which he implied that the *Gideon* decision was wrongly decided and that the Supreme Court was going too far in its interpretation of the Sixth Amendment. According to Thomas, the "Sixth Amendment appears to have understood at the time of ratification as a rejection of the English common-law rule that prohibited counsel, not as a guarantee of government-funded counsel. . . . The right to counsel is not an assurance of an error-free trial or even a reliable result. It ensures fairness in a single respect: permitting the accused to employ the services of an attorney." Clarence Thomas was joined in his dissent by justices Samuel Alito and Neil M. Gorsuch, although Alito did not join with the statements concerning the suggested overreach of the *Gideon* case.

In 2018, the U.S. Supreme Court refused to review a case in which the lower federal appellate court had declined to hold that a defendant received ineffective assistance of counsel when his lawyer failed to present at trial, or in the postconviction appeal, evidence that the defendant suffered from a major neurocognitive disorder. Excerpts of the dissent from the Court's decision are presented in Spotlight 7.2.

Defense Systems for Indigents

Providing court-appointed counsel for indigent defendants represents a critical part of U.S. criminal justice systems. In recent years, funding of indigent defense programs has been threatened or cut back, while demand has increased. There are many examples of indigent defense programs that are improperly staffed, overcrowded, and lack adequate resources. Defense counselors' caseloads are too high, salaries are too low to attract many of the brightest law graduates, and capital case appeals have increased and are complicated, with an insufficient number of well-trained attorneys to handle them.

In 2003, during the 40th anniversary year of the *Gideon* case, the American Bar Association (ABA) held hearings on the status of the right to counsel in the United States. Witnesses from across the country testified concerning the issues, leading the ABA to entitle its report Gideon*'s Broken Promise: America's Continuing Quest for Equal Justice*. The nine main findings of that report are reproduced in Spotlight 7.3.

Many jurisdictions have not provided sufficient funds for defense systems. An interesting reaction to that situation occurred in Missouri in 2016, when the state's top **public defender** wrote a letter to the governor, who blocked a budget increase for the system, ordering the governor, a licensed lawyer, to serve as counsel in the case of an indigent defendant. This letter was written pursuant to the state's law giving the public defender the authority to "delegate the legal representation of any person to any member of the state bar of Missouri."[22]

Spotlight 7.2

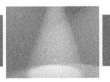

Justice Sotomayor Dissents on the Issue of Effective Assistance of Counsel

As noted in the text, the U.S. Supreme Court refused to review a case involving the issue of whether defense attorneys provided effective assistance of counsel when they failed to discover what might have been mitigating circumstances in the sentencing of a defendant charged with a capital crime.

Justice Sonia Sotomayor wrote a dissent to that decision. Excerpts from her opinion in *Wessinger v. Vannoy* are presented here.[1]

> Wessinger suffers from a major neurocognitive disorder that compromises his decision-making abilities. As a child, he experienced a stroke in his left frontal lobe that affected how the left and right sides of his brain communicate. He also suffered from childhood seizures, and he has a hole in the area of his brain associated with executive functioning that resulted from some form of cerebrovascular illness. The jury never considered this evidence at sentencing, or other mitigation about Wessinger's family history of poverty, alcoholism, and domestic violence....
>
> This Court repeatedly has held that the failure to perform mitigation investigation constitutes deficient performance....
>
> The Court's denial of certiorari here belies the "bedrock principle in our justice system" that a defendant has a right to effective assistance of trial counsel, and undermines the protections this Court has recognized are necessary to protect that right. Indeed, the investigation of mitigation evidence and its presentation at sentencing are crucial to maintaining the integrity of capital proceedings. The layers of ineffective assistance of counsel that Wessinger received constitute precisely the type of error that warrants relief under this Court's precedent. Yet, Wessinger will remain on death row without a jury ever considering the significant mitigation evidence that is not apparent. Because that outcome is contrary to precedent and deeply unjust and unfair, I dissent from the denial of certiorari.

1. *Wessinger v. Vannoy*, 864 F.3d 387 (5th Cir. 2017), *cert. denied*, 138 S. Ct. 952 (2018), cases and citations omitted, Justice Sotomayer dissenting.

Also in 2016, the lack of sufficient attorneys in the Louisiana public defender offices to service the state adequately led to the appointment of city attorneys to represent criminal defendants. Many of these attorneys had no experience in practicing criminal law and were not given sufficient time to learn about and prepare for individual cases. One report stated, "Anyone with a law license, a professional address in the [Caddo] parish, and a pulse" might be appointed to represent an indigent defendant. One insurance attorney, who proclaimed his lack of experience, declared, "I wouldn't want me representing me."[23]

Louisiana's experience is not atypical, as noted by the ABA in a 2017 article, "The *Gideon* Revolution: Starved of Money for Too Long, Public Defender Offices Are Suing and Starting to Win." The author referred to the lack of funding in the New Orleans office and noted that successful lawsuits were being filed by public defender offices, with five settled or reaching successful results in the previous five years and at least six lawsuits regarding inadequate funding filed against states in 2016.[24]

The ABA adopted the following ten principles for a public defense delivery system:

- "The public defense function, including the selection, funding, and payment of defense counsel, is independent.
- Where the caseload is sufficiently high, the public defense delivery system consists of both a defender office and the active participation of the private bar.
- Clients are screened for eligibility, and defense counsel is assigned and notified of appointment, as soon as feasible after clients' arrest, detention, or request for counsel.
- Defense counsel is provided sufficient time and a confidential space within which to meet with the client.
- Defense counsel's workload is controlled to permit the rendering of quality representation.

Spotlight 7.3

Gideon's Broken Promise: America's Continuing Quest for Equal Justice

The nine findings of the American Bar Association's hearings on the status of defense systems in the United States are as follows:

- "Forty years after *Gideon v. Wainwright*, indigent defense in the United States remains in a state of crisis, resulting in a system that lacks fundamental fairness and places poor persons at constant risk of wrongful conviction.
- Funding for indigent defense services is shamefully inadequate.
- Lawyers who provide representation in indigent defense systems sometimes violate their professional duties by failing to furnish competent representation.
- Lawyers are not provided in numerous proceedings in which a right to counsel exists in accordance with the Constitution and/or state laws. Too often, prosecutors seek to obtain waivers of counsel and guilty pleas from unrepresented accused persons, while judges accept and sometimes even encourage waivers of counsel that are not knowing, voluntary, intelligent, and on the record.

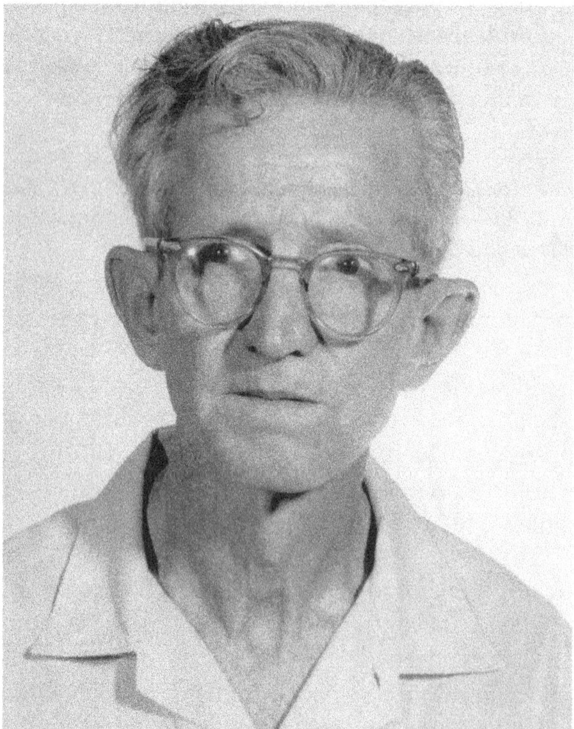

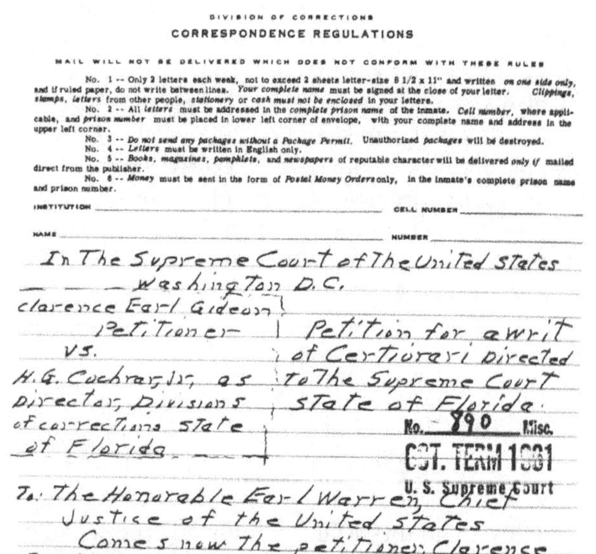

DIVISION OF CORRECTIONS
CORRESPONDENCE REGULATIONS

MAIL WILL NOT BE DELIVERED WHICH DOES NOT CONFORM WITH THESE RULES

No. 1 -- Only 2 letters each week, not to exceed 2 sheets letter-size 8 1/2 x 11" and written *on one side only*, and if ruled paper, do not write between lines. *Your complete name* must be signed at the close of your letter. *Clippings, stamps, letters* from other people, *stationery* or *cash must not be enclosed* in your letters.

No. 2 -- All *letters* must be addressed in the *complete prison name* of the inmate. *Cell number*, where applicable, and *prison number* must be placed in lower left corner of envelope, with your complete name and address in the upper left corner.

No. 3 -- *Do not send any packages without a Package Permit.* Unauthorized *packages* will be destroyed.

No. 4 -- *Letters* must be written in English only.

No. 5 -- *Books, magazines, pamphlets*, and *newspapers* of reputable character will be delivered *only if* mailed direct from the publisher.

No. 6 -- *Money* must be sent in the form of *Postal Money Orders* only, in the inmate's complete prison name and prison number.

INSTITUTION ______ CELL NUMBER ______

NAME ______ NUMBER ______

In The Supreme Court of The United States
Washington D.C.

clarence Earl Gideon, Petitioner vs. H.G. Cochran, Jr, as Director, Divisions of corrections State of Florida | Petition for a writ of Certiorari Directed to The Supreme Court State of Florida.

No. 890 Misc.
OCT. TERM 1961
U. S. Supreme Court

To: The Honorable Earl Warren, Chief Justice of the United States

Comes now The petitioner, Clarence Earl Gideon, a citizen of The United states of America, in proper person, and appearing as his own counsel. Who petitions this Honorable Court for a Writ of Certiorari directed to The Supreme Court of The State of Florida. To review The order and Judgement of The court below denying The petitioner a writ of Habeus Corpus.

Petitioner submits That The Supreme Court of The United States has The authority and jurisdiction to review The final Judgement of The Supreme Court of The State of Florida The highest court of The State Under sec. 344(B) Title 28 U.S.C.A. and Because The "Due process clause" of The

Clarence Earl Gideon's plea for appointed counsel when he was accused of breaking and entering was denied by Florida judges, who claimed that such appointment was provided only in capital cases. Gideon defended himself, was convicted, and appealed to the U.S. Supreme Court, which reversed his case. His petition requesting the Court to hear and decide his case is shown, in part, at right.

- **Judges and elected officials often exercise undue influence over indigent defense attorneys, threatening the professional independence of the defense function.**
- **Indigent defense systems frequently lack basic oversight and accountability, impairing the provision of uniform, quality services.**
- **Efforts to reform indigent defense systems have been most successful when they involve multifaceted approaches and representatives from a broad spectrum of interests.**
- **The organized bar too often has failed to provide the requisite leadership in the indigent defense area.**
- **Model approaches to providing quality indigent defense services exist in this country, but these models often are not adequately funded and cannot be replicated elsewhere absent sufficient financial support."**

Source: *Gideon's Broken Promise: America's Continuing Quest for Equal Justice*, **A Report on the American Bar Association's Hearings on the Right to Counsel in Criminal Proceedings (December 2004), p. v, available at http://www.americanbar.org, accessed January 12, 2015.**

- Defense counsel's ability, training, and experience match the complexity of the case.
- The same attorney continuously represents the client until completion of the case.
- There is parity between defense counsel and the prosecution with respect to resources and defense counsel is included as an equal partner in the justice system.
- Defense counsel is provided with and required to attend continuing legal education.
- Defense counsel is supervised and systematically reviewed for quality and efficiency according to nationally and locally adopted standards."[25]

In 2017, the ABA published an article entitled "The Gideon Revolution," in which the author discussed the increasing number of lawsuits focusing on the lack of adequate defense resources. Several public defender offices had initiated lawsuits over this issue, and some were winning. According to this source, "[a]t least five lawsuits have reached successful decisions or settlements over the past five years. . . . More are coming."[26] In 2017, the ABA released a report of its finding that in Louisiana, the public defender system was understaffed by about 1,400 lawyers and thus might deny defendants adequate assistance of counsel.[27] The previous year, the chief district defender for Orleans Parish in Louisiana wrote an article discussing the situation and concluded, "It is little wonder that Louisiana has the nation's highest rates of incarceration *and* exoneration for wrongful conviction."[28]

There are some recent indications of improvement. For example, the governor of New York announced in 2017 that the *state* would begin providing some funding for indigent defendants. This action was in response to the 2014 settlement reached in the case of *Hurrell-Harring v. New York*,[29] a lawsuit regarding indigent defense brought by the New York Civil Liberties Union. The case is excerpted and the settlement discussed in **Supplement 7.9**.

Three models are used for organizing the provision of defense counsel for indigent defendants in states and localities: public defender systems (which employ **public defenders**), **assigned counsel** systems, and **contract systems**. These systems are discussed in **Supplement 7.10**.

PRETRIAL PROCEDURES

The prosecution and the defense begin playing their respective roles and interacting with each other during a series of important pretrial procedures, the focus of the rest of this chapter. This section explores the important stages of the processes and procedures that occur prior to criminal trials. These stages are not discrete. They do not always happen one after the other; some stages overlap. Nor are the functions of the police, prosecutors, defense attorneys, and judges limited to particular stages. Citizens—as victims, witnesses, or members of a jury—also function at different stages.

Spotlight 7.4

Steps in the Criminal Justice Process Before Trial

1. Report of a crime
2. Investigation prior to arrest
3. Arrest
4. Booking
5. Post-arrest investigation
6. Prosecutor's decision to charge suspect with a crime
7. Initial appearance
8. Preliminary hearing
9. Grand jury review
10. Arraignment
11. Pretrial motions
12. Pretrial conferences

Steps in the Criminal Justice Process

Figure 1.1 in Chapter 1 diagrammed the steps in the criminal justice process. The specific stages occurring before trial are enumerated in Spotlight 7.4 for easy reference.

The stages in the criminal justice process are important for two reasons. First, most people who are arrested are not tried in a criminal court (see again Figure 1.2). After the initial investigation, there may not be sufficient evidence for an arrest. There may be sufficient evidence, but the police may be unable to locate the suspect, or for some other reason, the police may not arrest. Those who are arrested may not be prosecuted, for any number of the reasons previously discussed. If the prosecutor files charges, they may be dropped by the prosecutor (which may require judicial approval) or dismissed by the judge. This action may occur during any of the court sessions before or after the trial begins.

The procedures listed in Spotlight 7.4 begin with the report of an alleged crime, which may be followed by a formal arrest and **booking**. In the second step, the alleged crime must be investigated. Early investigation of a reported crime is very important—later, evidence may be lost or destroyed, or witnesses may disappear. Thus, police prefer to question potential witnesses at or near the scene of a crime as soon as possible. Police use various methods to investigate an alleged crime. Defense attorneys may use the same methods or even retain private investigators to search for evidence that would assist in the defense of the case. They check for physical evidence by analyzing the victim's clothing and looking for hair, blood, or other evidence that might associate the accused with the reported crime. They look for a weapon or weapons that might have been used in the offense. They question all parties who might know something about the alleged crime or the suspect, looking for information such as motive as well as any evidence linking a specific individual with the crime.

Securing physical evidence that a crime has occurred may involve searching the suspect's automobile, home, or office. It may also involve securing physical evidence from the accused. For example, police may obtain body fluids or hair samples from the suspect. Police cannot compel suspects to testify against themselves; that would be a violation of the Fifth Amendment (see Appendix A). However, samples of hair, fiber, blood, saliva, and other body fluids may be secured from suspects without violating their due process rights.

The results of tests on evidence may lead the prosecution to decide not to file charges or to drop charges already filed. In earlier stages, the police may decide not to arrest after conducting a preliminary investigation. For example, a person suspected of driving under the influence may be given a field test for alcohol and perform so well that the officer decides not to pursue the matter.

These initial investigations at the time of a suspected crime or shortly after a crime has been reported may be followed by more intensive investigations by the police or prosecution. Investigations may continue throughout the case and for a very long time before a case is settled—even before an arrest.

Examinations may be required of alleged violent crime victims to secure physical evidence of the crimes they report. Psychological examinations of victims may be given to obtain evidence that might be useful to the prosecution. A psychological or psychiatric examination of a defendant may be ordered at some point before trial in order to determine whether he or she is mentally competent to stand trial.

During investigations, both sides look for testimonial as well as for physical evidence. Both sides may use the services of an expert witness to testify regarding a crucial element of the case. An *expert witness* is an individual who has specialized knowledge in a recognized area, such as medicine. Both the prosecution and the defense also look for eye witnesses to the crime. One frequently used method of obtaining eyewitness identification of a suspect is to conduct a **lineup**, which involves several people. The witness (who may also be the alleged victim) is asked to look at all of the people in the lineup and decide whether he or she can identify the person(s) who allegedly committed the crime. Lineups are permissible, provided they are conducted properly.

It is improper in most instances to ask a witness to identify the suspect in a **showup** involving only that suspect. This kind of identification procedure has been condemned by courts but is allowed under limited circumstances. Pictures may be shown to witnesses for identification of suspects, although restrictions are placed on this procedure. It must be shown that the witnesses had a good opportunity to see the suspect. The pictures must be viewed soon after the alleged crime while the memory of the witnesses is clear. Multiple witnesses may not view the pictures in the company of each other. The police may not make suggestive comments regarding the pictures and the suspect. Usually, it is not permissible to offer the witness only one photograph, that of the accused.

If the investigation convinces the prosecutor that sufficient evidence is available to lead a reasonable person to think that a particular suspect committed a crime, and if the prosecutor decides to file formal charges against the suspect, in most cases, that suspect must be taken before a magistrate for an **initial appearance**. The initial appearance is for the purpose of having the court determine whether there is probable cause to charge the suspect with the criminal allegations.

A suspect who has been retained in custody must be taken before the magistrate without unreasonable delay. The time involved in processing the suspect at the police station usually means that the initial appearance cannot take place until the following day. If the suspect is booked on a weekend, the initial appearance cannot take place until the following Monday, unless special provisions have been made. In some metropolitan areas, because of the high volume of weekend arrests, magistrates' courts hold special sessions on weekends to permit initial appearances earlier than usual and thus decrease the amount of time suspects must spend in jail prior to the hearing.

Most initial appearances are brief. Magistrates verify the names and addresses of the defendants and inform them of the formal charges against them and of their constitutional rights. Although the procedures differ among jurisdictions, at this stage in many areas, the process of appointing counsel for accused indigents is started. Most defendants who have retained counsel have their attorneys with them at their initial appearances.

If the defendant is charged with a minor offense, such as a misdemeanor, he or she may enter a plea at the initial appearance. Many defendants enter guilty pleas at this stage. Defendants who do not plead guilty are informed of the next steps in the proceedings. Defendants charged with felonies may not enter a plea at the initial appearance. In some felony cases, the defendant is not required to appear in court at this stage, although defense counsel will do so. For defendants who have been detained in custody to this point, magistrates make determinations whether to release them pending trial. If the police have released defendants after booking, then at the initial appearance magistrates review the terms of those releases and decide whether they were properly made under the circumstances.

In some jurisdictions, the initial appearance is followed by a **preliminary hearing**, at least in cases involving felonies. Normally, the preliminary hearing occurs between one and two weeks after the initial appearance. During the interval between these two stages, some or all charges may be dropped as prosecutors discover that there is insufficient evidence to proceed. If the charges are not dropped, a preliminary hearing is held to determine whether there is probable cause to continue with those charges. A preliminary hearing is not required in all jurisdictions. If it is not required, prosecutors may take the case directly to a grand jury where that is required. If a grand jury is not required, prosecutors may proceed on their own.

At the preliminary hearing, the prosecution and the defense must present sufficient evidence to enable the magistrate to decide the issue of probable cause. Normally, the preliminary hearing is open because of the First Amendment right (see Appendix A) of the press to cover and of the public to know about such hearings. The hearing may be closed if a defendant shows that he or she cannot get a fair hearing without closure. Defendants may waive the preliminary hearing, and many choose to do so, but the waiver must be a knowing and intelligent one.

In the United States, an official criminal charge begins in one of two ways. First, the prosecutor may initiate the proceedings by returning an *information*. That may be done in cases not requiring action by the grand jury or when the grand jury review is waived. Second, the case may begin with a grand jury *indictment*, which some states require in felony cases, although the states differ in the crimes for which an indictment is required. The indictment is the official document stating the name of the accused, the charge, and the essential facts supporting that charge. Some states limit the requirement to serious felonies. In federal courts, grand jury indictments are required for the prosecution of capital or otherwise infamous crimes, with the exceptions noted in the Fifth Amendment (see Appendix A).

The grand jury is composed of private citizens, usually 23 persons, although some states have reduced that number. Originally, a majority vote was required for a decision, but today, some states, particularly those with grand juries smaller than 23, require more than a majority vote. The grand jury review differs from the initial appearance and the preliminary hearing in that, in this review, only the prosecutor presents evidence. The defendant does not have a right to present evidence or to be present. The grand jury is not bound by all the evidence rules that are required at a trial, and its deliberations are secret.

The basic function of the grand jury is to hear the prosecutor's evidence and to decide whether there is probable cause to return an indictment. An indictment returned by a grand jury is called a **true bill**. In returning that indictment, the grand jury is not bound by the magistrate's decision at the preliminary hearing. Generally, a grand jury indictment is not required in misdemeanor or petty offense cases. Those are begun officially when the prosecutor returns an information.

Once it is in session, the grand jury may initiate investigations. This may be done, for example, when there are allegations of widespread corruption in public agencies. The grand jury may also be used to investigate organized crime. When the grand jury begins an official prosecution in this manner—that is, by action on its own knowledge without the indictment presented by the prosecutor—it returns a **presentment**, which is an official document, an accusation asking for the prosecutor to prepare an indictment.

In theory, the grand jury serves as a check on prosecutorial discretion. The U.S. Supreme Court recognized this important function when it said that the grand jury serves the significant function of standing between the accuser and the accused, whether the latter is an individual, a minority group, or another entity, to determine whether a charge is founded on reason or is dictated by an intimidating power or by malice and personal ill will.[30]

Usually, however, the grand jury is considered to be an arm of the prosecution. In most cases presented by prosecutors to grand juries, the indictment is returned as a true bill. Of course, some procedures must be observed by the grand jury, and the body of case law in this area is extensive and at times conflicting. Like the selection of trial juries (discussed in Chapter 8), the selection of the grand jury may not involve systematic exclusion because of race or ethnicity, gender, or other extralegal categories.

After the indictment or information is officially filed with the court, an **arraignment** is scheduled. At that hearing, judges or magistrates read the indictments or informations to the defendants, inform them of their constitutional rights, and ask for pleas to the charges. If a defendant pleads not guilty, a trial date is set. If a defendant pleads guilty, a date is set for formal sentencing, unless that takes place at the arraignment, as is often the case with less serious offenses.

In some jurisdictions, a defendant is permitted to plead ***nolo contendere***, which literally means "I will not contest it." That plea in a criminal case has the legal effect of a guilty plea. The difference is that the *nolo* plea may not be used against a defendant in a civil case. Thus, if the defendant pleads *nolo* to felony charges of driving while intoxicated and leaving the scene of an accident, that plea may not be used in a civil case filed by a victim who suffered injuries or property damage in the accident.

Throughout the pretrial proceedings both sides may file motions. A **motion** is a document submitted to the court, asking for a rule or an order. Some motions are inappropriate before trial; a motion for a new trial is an example. Other motions may be made before the trial begins. The defense may make a motion to suppress evidence on the allegation that the evidence was secured in violation of the defendant's rights. Defendants may make motions to dismiss the case because of insufficient evidence. There could be other reasons, such as a defense attack on the technical sufficiency of the charging document, a question on the composition of the grand jury, or a claim of prosecutorial misconduct.

It is common for the defense to file a motion requiring the prosecutor to produce evidence, a process called **discovery**. Discovery procedures are defined by court rules and procedural statutes, but the nature of discovery rules varies from permitting extensive discovery to allowing rather limited discovery. Discovery is a two-way street. The prosecution and the defense are entitled to certain advance notice (or copies) of information that the other side plans to use at trial. Lists of witnesses, prior statements obtained from those witnesses, and the nature of physical evidence are the kinds of information that the prosecution and defense might obtain. Prosecutors and defense attorneys may be sanctioned for violating discovery rules or for not observing them in a timely manner.

Under some circumstances, both the prosecution and the defense may obtain oral statements from witnesses outside of court and before trial. These statements are called **depositions**. They are taken under oath, are recorded verbatim (usually by a court reporter), and may be used in court. They are permitted when there is a court order or procedural rules that allow depositions. Attorneys for both sides are present. Witnesses or other parties may also be given **interrogatories**, a series of questions that are to be answered truthfully, with the respondents signing notarized statements of oath that, to the best of their knowledge, their answers are correct.

Discovery is very important in criminal as well as in civil cases. The deposition is one of the best tools for gathering information (although it is not permitted, or may be limited, in criminal cases). Although we are accustomed to movies and television shows in which surprise witnesses appear unexpectedly in court and change the nature of the case, or known witnesses blurt out an incriminating fact to the surprise of everyone, this does not normally occur in actual cases.

Another motion the defense might file is for a change of **venue**, which is the place of trial. If the case has received considerable media attention, the defense may succeed with the argument that the defendant could not get a fair trial in that jurisdiction, and therefore, a change of venue should be granted. Changing the venue of a trial is usually controversial, and extended hearings may be held in court over this issue.

The prosecutor might file motions, too, including a motion to drop the case or change the charges. In some jurisdictions, once formal charges have been filed, prosecutors may not drop or change those charges without the court's permission. Frequently, the prosecutor files a motion to drop or lower charges as a result of a plea arrangement made with the defense.

In addition to motions that the prosecution and defense might wish to make individually, or other issues they want to discuss with the judge, there are times when both sides want to meet with the judge to ask for more time to secure evidence, to prepare pretrial motions, to negotiate a plea, or to handle any other pretrial matters. In some instances, these arrangements are made between the prosecution and the defense and do not require the judge's presence or approval. In other cases, the judge might keep a tight hold on the management of the case and not permit any changes (such as an extension of the discovery period) without judicial approval.

Pretrial conferences can also be referred to as *status conferences*. They may be informal, with the prosecution and the defense discussing the status of the case and enumerating the issues on which they agree so that no court time is wasted on arguing issues that are not in dispute. The judge may ask each attorney to estimate the time he or she expects to take to present the case. The answer is important for time management in courts, and the defense and prosecution might be limited by their predictions during these conferences; thus, the estimates should be made only after close scrutiny of the evidence each attorney thinks should be presented.

Both the prosecution and the defense use the pretrial period to prepare for trial. Preparation includes further investigation and testing of physical evidence; attempts to locate witnesses; interviewing witnesses; obtaining depositions of expert and other witnesses; and reviewing all evidence pertinent to the case. Attorneys spend time with their own witnesses, ensuring that they know what information they will be asked to present at the trial and preparing them for the questions that opposing counsel might ask.

Attorneys keep records of their expenses for trial preparation, which include costs of their own time (even if they are public defenders paid by the case and not by the hour or prosecutors on salary, most keep an hourly record of their activities); out-of-pocket expenses for investigations, depositions, interrogatories; fees for expert witnesses; and so on. Most attorneys who require set retainers in advance for specific types of criminal cases in all probability still keep an annotated record of the time they spend on each case.

Lists of witnesses who will be called for trial must be prepared, and the proper papers for notifying those witnesses must be filed. If the witnesses do not want to appear, the attorney may request a court order to subpoena them. A **subpoena** is an order to appear in court at a particular time and place and to give testimony on a specified subject or issue. As a precautionary measure, subpoenas might be issued to all potential witnesses to make it more difficult for them to change their minds and refuse to appear in court or at a deposition to testify. Witnesses may also be ordered to produce documents or papers that are important to the trial.

Pretrial conferences are very important to attorneys as they assess and prepare their cases. For example, the prosecutor may decide that the defense position is strong enough that a guilty verdict is unlikely. The attorneys may offer and accept (or reject) plea bargains for a plea to the charge(s) or to lesser charges. Many issues may be discussed during these pretrial conferences.

Release or Detention: Bail or Jail?

Once a person has been charged with a crime and arrested, the decision whether to release or detain that individual pending trial is an important one. According to the U.S. Supreme Court, for the defendant, it is a time "when consultation, thoroughgoing investigation and preparation ... [are] vitally important."[31] During this period, the defendant retains an attorney or is assigned counsel. The defense counsel and the prosecutor negotiate and consider possible plea arrangements. Witnesses are interviewed, and other attempts are made by both sides to secure evidence for the trial. Uncovering additional evidence may change the nature of the case and may even result in dropping or reducing charges before trial.

For society, the issue of whether the defendant is released or detained before trial is critical. Public outcries, accusing courts of coddling criminals, are common when persons charged with serious crimes are released, especially when those releasees commit additional crimes.

The procedures by which the **bail** decision to release a defendant is made vary among jurisdictions, but a hearing is required, and the defendant is entitled to the benefit of counsel at that hearing. In the federal system, the hearing must take place within 24 hours of arrest. Some jurisdictions have ordinances or statutes specifying what types of offenses are bailable, while others have specifications concerning what the magistrate may consider in making the release decision. In many cases, however, the magistrate has wide discretion and there is virtually no check on this.

The magistrate also has wide latitude in setting the amount of bail. In the federal system, the factors most closely related to the level of bail, in order of importance, are the seriousness of the current charge, the district in which the bail hearing occurs, and the offender's criminal record.[32]

Defendants may petition the court to reduce the amount of bail or to grant bail if it has been denied. Some judges grant these motions, particularly when the defense has had more time to gather evidence that favors the defendant's pretrial release.

The Eighth Amendment to the U.S. Constitution prohibits requiring excessive bail (see Appendix A). This provision has been interpreted to mean that, when bail is set, its amount may not be excessive, but there has been no clear definition of what that means. In 1951, in *Stack v. Boyle*, the U.S. Supreme Court considered this issue and held that bail set at a "figure higher than an amount reasonably calculated to fulfill this purpose [assuring the presence of the defendant at trial] is 'excessive' under the Eighth Amendment."[33]

In 1970, with the passage of the District of Columbia Court Reform and Criminal Procedure Act, **preventive detention** was recognized as a legitimate purpose of bail. The statute permits judges to deny bail to defendants charged with dangerous crimes if the government has clear evidence that the safety of others would be endangered if the accused were released. In addition, bail can be denied in cases involving persons who have been convicted of violent crimes while on probation or parole. The statute was upheld by the District of Columbia Court of Appeals in 1981, and the U.S. Supreme Court refused to review, thus leaving that court's decision standing.[34]

Other jurisdictions followed the District of Columbia in passing statutes or changing their constitutions to permit the denial of bail for preventive detention. In 1984, in *Schall v. Martin*, the U.S. Supreme Court upheld the preventive detention of juveniles.[35]

The most controversial changes in bail, however, occurred in the Bail Reform Act of 1984, a federal statute that permits judges to deny bail if they have sufficient reason to think a defendant poses a dangerous threat to the community. The defendant is entitled to a prompt hearing on that issue, but if the hearing is not prompt, the government is not required to release a defendant who otherwise meets the criteria for detention. If there is sufficient evidence to charge the defendant with drug or certain other serious offenses, there is a presumption of dangerousness. This means that bail may be denied unless the defendant can prove to the court that he or she is not dangerous. This burden is a difficult one to sustain.[36]

In 1987, the U.S. Supreme Court decided a case challenging the Bail Reform Act's provision for the preventive detention of dangerous persons. *United States v. Salerno* involved the detention of defendants charged with numerous acts associated with organized crime. At the **pretrial detention** hearing the government presented evidence that both defendants were in high positions of power in organized crime families. The government contended that the only way to protect the community was to detain these persons pending trial, and the Supreme Court agreed that under the facts of the case, preventive detention was permissible.[37]

There is evidence that, like some other phases of criminal justice systems, the bail system suggests discrimination against minorities as compared to whites. Consider the following conclusions by one criminologist:

- "Black and Hispanic defendants are more likely than white defendants to be denied bail.
- Hispanic defendants are less likely to receive a non-financial release option (e.g., ROR [release on own recognizance]) than either white or black defendants.
- The amount of bail required for release is higher for Hispanic defendants than white defendants; there is no black-white difference in bail amount.
- Hispanic and black defendants are more likely than white defendants to be held on bail because of an inability to post bail. Indeed, the inability to 'make bail' accounts for the majority of black and Hispanic defendants' overall greater likelihood of pretrial detention."[38]

Many defendants are indigent and cannot post bail; thus, a bail **bond** system developed. The bail system is discussed briefly in **Supplement 7.11**, which also presents a table of the methods of pretrial release in state courts. Recent changes in bail systems, however, have eased the bail burdens on indigent defendants, although some of these changes are controversial. A few jurisdictions making significant bail changes are noted.

In Harris County (Houston, Texas), federal judge Lee H. Rosenthal of the Southern District of Texas ruled in 2017 that the jurisdiction's cash bail system discriminated against indigent defendants and was thus unconstitutional under the Texas and the federal constitutions. The case was appealed to the Fifth Circuit Court of Appeals, which made some changes in the judge's orders and sent the case back for additional consideration. The county will no longer be permitted to establish bail based on a schedule rather than a consideration of the defendant's ability to pay. The county is now required to release defendants on their personal bond (which requires no money) if the county's criminal judges "have found, based on a new risk assessment tool," that those individuals "should presumptively be released on personal bonds." The ruling involves such crimes as drunken driving, petty theft, or passing bad checks, as long as the accused "do[es] not have any formal holds for outstanding warrants, federal immigration detainers, upcoming hearings to determine their mental health, or any family violence restraining orders."[39]

In January 2018, in New York, Judge Maria Rosa of Dutchess County ruled that it is unconstitutional to set bail without considering the ability of the defendant to pay, but in April 2019, the U.S. Supreme Court refused to hear a case appealed from Georgia that raised the issue of bail that does not consider a defendant's ability to pay. *Walker v. City of Calhoun, Ga.* involved a pedestrian who was arrested for being under the influence of alcohol in violation of a state statute. The statute provided only for a fine upon conviction, but the defendant was in jail because he was held pending a bail hearing and could not pay the standard $160 cash bond required for persons charged under the statute. The American Bar Association had filed a "friend of the court" brief urging the Supreme Court to hear the case and reverse the lower appellate court's upholding of the city's practice of utilizing a fixed-bail policy to hold a defendant prior to a bail hearing without any consideration of a person's ability to pay. According to the ABA, jailing defendants "solely because they cannot afford to purchase their freedom" violates their equal protection rights under the Fourteenth Amendment (see Appendix A).[40]

In August 2018, California governor Jerry Brown signed the first-in-the-nation statute to end cash bail. According to Brown, the California Money Bail Reform Act will treat rich and poor defendants alike. Bail decisions for all will be determined on the basis of their risk of flight and danger to society.[41]

California governor Jerry Brown, during a ceremony on August 28, 2018, hands to one of its co-authors a copy of the bill that makes that state the first in the nation to eliminate bail for suspects awaiting trial.

The Guilty Plea

The guilty plea is very important in U.S. criminal justice systems because approximately 90 percent of defendants plead guilty. Although many guilty pleas are entered after plea negotiations begin, defendants may choose to plead guilty without any negotiations between the prosecution and the defense, and they may do so throughout the process until the judge (or jury) reaches a verdict.

Why would a defendant plead guilty rather than go to trial? Some defendants are guilty and see no reason to go to trial, thinking that they have no chance of an acquittal or a conviction on a lesser offense. They may not want to engage in any kind of plea bargaining because, as in a trial, that might take more time than they are willing to devote to the process. Some defendants want a quick decision. This may be true particularly if they have been denied bail and must wait in jail until a plea deal is reached or a trial is completed. Still other defendants may not want to experience the public exposure of the evidence the prosecution will present at trial.

In cases involving minor offenses, most defendants are placed on probation. That means they are not required to serve time in jail or prison. They might prefer to plead guilty and get on with their lives. Pleading guilty will save attorney fees for defendants who do not qualify for publicly supported counsel. Defendants who can go back to work can continue to support their families and reduce the stress placed on everyone by an indecisive situation or by incarceration.

Defendants who plead guilty may be familiar with the court process and the reputation of the prosecutor in that jurisdiction. If the prosecutor has a reputation for recommending stricter sentences for defendants who insist on trials, compared with those who plead guilty, defendants may choose to plead guilty. If juries in that jurisdiction have a reputation for being tough on defendants, that information might lead defendants to plead guilty.

Defense attorneys may encourage their clients to plead guilty. In some cases, this is the best advice that attorneys can give defendants and should not be viewed as a dereliction of the defense attorney's duty to the client. If defendants have little chance of an acquittal, they are entitled to know that. In addition, most attorneys will explain what may be expected financially and otherwise if the case goes to trial. In other cases, it may be bad advice to counsel defendants to enter a guilty plea. In all cases, however, the final decision about whether or not to plead guilty should be made by the defendant.

In deciding whether to plead guilty, the defendant may consider carefully the implications of studies showing that defendants who plead guilty are less likely to be sentenced to prison than defendants who go to trial and are convicted. Many who plead guilty receive shorter sentences than those who go to trial. The difference, however, may be associated with the nature of the offense or other factors that are not in themselves related to whether guilt is determined by a guilty plea or by a trial.

Jurisdictions vary in the processes by which defendants plead guilty, but generally, the plea is entered in open court and recorded on a form signed by defendants and their attorneys. By signing this form, defendants swear that they are of sound mind, that they are not under the influence of alcohol or other drugs, that they understand fully that they are waiving the rights associated with a trial, and that nothing has been promised in return for their signatures on the form. The form contains the sentence recommended by the prosecutor. The judge is not required to follow that recommendation but usually does.

After the form is completed, the defendant, the defense attorney, and the prosecutor appear before the magistrate or judge for formal entering of the plea. At that time, the judge questions the defendant. Before the plea is accepted, the judge must be convinced that the defendant entered into the plea agreement knowingly, intelligently, and voluntarily. The U.S. Supreme Court has made it clear that, because a defendant who pleads guilty gives up several constitutional rights, including the right to a trial by an impartial jury, a guilty plea requires "an intentional relinquishment or abandonment of a known right or privilege" and must be declared void if it is not a knowing and intelligent plea.[42]

If the judge decides that the plea is a knowing and intelligent one, he or she may accept that plea, in which case a formal record is made with the court. Generally, the form specifies how long the defendant has for an appeal on a sentence imposed by the court. Defendants who change their minds and wish to withdraw their guilty pleas may petition the court to do so. If that request is made prior to sentencing, the judge may grant it; usually motions to withdraw a guilty plea after sentencing are not granted. There is no absolute right to withdraw a guilty plea at any time.

Plea Bargaining

One of the most controversial practices in U.S. criminal justice systems is **plea bargaining**, the process in which the prosecution and the defense attempt to negotiate a plea. The negotiation may involve reducing charges, dropping charges, or recommending a sentence. Plea bargaining became a part of U.S. criminal justice systems after the Civil War but was not practiced widely until the 1990s. Little attention was paid to the process until crime commissions began their studies in the 1920s.

Plea bargaining may occur during any stage of the criminal process, but most defense attorneys begin negotiations as soon as possible. The longer a defendant has been in the system, the less likely prosecutors are to plea bargain because of the time and effort already spent on the case. Prosecutors may want to initiate plea bargaining early to dispose of a heavy caseload. Or, they might stall on the process, thinking that defendants will be more cooperative the longer they have to wait, especially if they are being detained in jail.

Plea bargaining may be initiated by either the prosecution or the defense. Prosecutors may refuse to discuss any kind of bargain and insist on a trial. Likewise, defendants may refuse to bargain and insist on a trial, but defendants who enter a guilty plea cannot withdraw it merely because they chose the wrong strategy. It is possible for the parties to negotiate a final plea after the trial has begun, as illustrated by the discussion of the Unabomber case in Spotlight 7.5, which presents examples of other highly controversial plea bargains.

Generally, judges may not participate in plea negotiations in federal cases, although some state and local jurisdictions permit this practice. When judges participate in plea bargaining, they may suggest directly or indirectly the sentence that might be imposed in the case, encourage defense attorneys and prosecutors to reach a settlement, nudge defendants to accept the plea negotiation decision, or intervene actively in the negotiations.

Some jurisdictions permit victims to be a part of the plea negotiations if they choose to do so. Some victims do not want to participate; others may be too vindictive or too lenient. At a minimum, however, victims should be kept informed of the proceedings at all stages in the pretrial procedures. Whether they should participate actively in plea negotiations is controversial. Some argue that it would give defendants a chance to begin the rehabilitation process by being confronted by the victim, and it would give victims an opportunity to see the defendant as a whole person. Others take the position that the participation of victims would be disruptive to the system and would have a negative impact on victims.

It was not until the 1970s that the U.S. Supreme Court recognized plea bargaining as appropriate and even essential in criminal justice systems. In the federal system, 97 percent of defendants enter guilty pleas; in state systems 94 percent do so.[43] In 1971, the Court approved plea bargaining as a means of managing overloaded criminal dockets, referring to the process as "an essential component" of the criminal process, which "properly administered . . . is to be encouraged."[44] Over 90 percent of defendants do enter a guilty plea although not all those pleas involve plea bargaining. **Supplement 7.12** gives a brief discussion of the history of plea bargaining in the U.S. federal criminal justice system, summarizing the significant case of *Bordenkircher v. Hayes*, decided in 1978.[45]

In 2012, the U.S. Supreme Court held that once a plea bargain is reached, the defense and prosecution submit formal papers to the judge, who must accept or reject the agreement. The judge is not required to abide by any promises made by the prosecution. Thus, after plea negotiations, it is possible for the defendant to enter a guilty plea with the understanding that a particular sentence will be imposed but subsequently be faced with a different, even harsher sentence.

There is no legal right to a plea bargain. According to the U.S. Supreme Court, the states and Congress may abolish plea bargaining; however, where it does exist, it is not improper to offer leniency "and other substantial benefits" to defendants in exchange for a guilty plea.[46] In 1984, the U.S. Supreme Court upheld a prosecutor's withdrawal of an offer that had been accepted by a defendant. After he had accepted the prosecutor's offer, the defendant was told that the offer was a mistake and was being withdrawn. He appealed; the federal appellate court agreed with the defendant that the withdrawal was not permissible. The Supreme Court disagreed, reversed the lower federal court, and stated that an agreement to a plea bargain is an "executory agreement that does not involve the constitutional rights of the accused until it is embodied in the formal pleas." In upholding the prosecutor's withdrawal of the plea, the Court said, "The Due Process Clause is not a code of ethics for prosecutors" but, rather, is concerned "with the manner in which persons are deprived of their liberty."[47]

Although there is no right to plea bargaining, when it exists, defendants are clearly entitled to effective assistance of counsel. In two cases decided in 2012, the U.S. Supreme Court held that plea bargaining is a critical stage in the criminal justice process; thus, defendants are entitled to counsel, and that means effective assistance. In *Missouri v. Frye*,[48] the defendant's lawyer did not tell him about the prosecutor's plea offers, which involved only 90 days in jail. The defendant was convicted and sentenced to three years in prison. In *Lefler v. Cooper*, the defendant was told of a plea offer with a recommended sentence of 51 to 85 months in prison for multiple charges including assault with intent to commit murder. He made that decision after his attorney told him that the prosecutor would be unable to prove intent to commit murder because the victim was shot below the waist. The defendant, who was convicted of all charges, was sentenced to prison for 185 to 370 months. The Court had decided in 2010 in *Padilla v. Kentucky* that an attorney's failure to inform his client of the immigration consequences if he entered a guilty plea constituted ineffective assistance of counsel.[49]

In 2017, in a case involving a defendant who had spent most of his life in the United States as a lawful permanent resident but who did not become a citizen, the

Spotlight 7.5

High-Profile Plea Bargain Cases

Plea bargaining in high-profile cases is controversial, especially when those cases involve murder, as some of the following cases illustrate.

In April 2017, Dylann Roof entered guilty pleas in a South Carolina court to nine counts of murder, three counts of attempted murder, and one weapons charge to avoid the death penalty under that state's laws. In June 2015, Roof had entered a historically black church in Charleston, sitting with parishioners in a Bible study prior to drawing his weapons during a prayer and shooting repeatedly, killing nine and wounding others. He was sentenced to nine consecutive life sentences and three consecutive 30-year sentences. He was already under a federal death sentence on charges of hate crime and obstruction of the practice of religion.

In November 2003, the prosecution in King County (Seattle) offered a plea deal to Gary L. Ridgway, who was accused in the murders of 48 young women in the Green River area of Seattle. Many of the victims were prostitutes or runaways and had been sexually assaulted and strangled. This case, which baffled police for 20 years, was unusual in that plea bargains normally are not offered in cases involving multiple murders, but the prosecution's position was that the plea deal was the only way to bring closure to all of the victims' families. Ridgway, showing no emotion, entered a guilty plea to all 48 counts, making him the deadliest serial killer in U.S. history. A statement made previously by Ridgway was read in court:

> I killed the 48 women. . . . In most cases, when I murdered these women I did not know their names. Most of the time I killed them the first time I met them, and I did not have a good memory for their faces. I killed so many women, I have a hard time keeping them straight.

When asked in court whether that statement was true, the defendant said, "Yes, it is." The statement continued as follows:

> I placed most of the bodies in groups which I called clusters. I did this because I wanted to keep track of all the women I killed. I liked to drive by the clusters around the county and think about the women I placed there.[1]

Ridgway had been charged with only seven of the Green River killings and was scheduled to go on trial in 2004; the prosecution was asking for the death penalty. By entering guilty pleas Ridgway spared his own life. He was sentenced to one prison life term for each murder.

In April 2005, Eric Rudolph pleaded guilty to multiple terrorist acts in the 1990s. Rudolph's bombings during the 1996 Summer Olympics in Atlanta; at an Atlanta office building (an abortion clinic inside that building was thought to be the target); at an Atlanta bar frequented by gays and lesbians in 1997; and at an abortion clinic in Birmingham, Alabama, in 1998, resulted in the deaths of two persons, including a police officer, and injuries to over 100 others. Rudolph was a fugitive and listed on the FBI's Ten Most Wanted Fugitives list, but he eluded law enforcement officials until his capture in 2003 near Murphy, North Carolina, while he was scavenging for food. Rudolph was to be tried first in Alabama, where prosecutors were seeking the death penalty. After jury selection began, the prosecution announced that they had struck a plea bargain with Rudolph. He would plead guilty to all of the bombings in return for a life sentence. In an 11-page statement released by his attorneys, Rudolph made no apologies, but lashed out at what he called a morally corrupt government that permits abortions and makes accommodations for gays and lesbians. Some victims were angry that Rudolph did not get the death penalty; others were relieved that there would not be a trial and that they had some explanation for his terrorist acts.

In the case of Ted Kaczynski (known as the Unabomber because he sent bombs through the mail to university professors and airlines, among other targets), a few weeks before the scheduled date of the trial, the defense offered to plead guilty in exchange for a sentence of life without parole. The U.S. Department of Justice recommended that the plea be rejected, and it was. This decision was questioned by some who pointed out the irony that, after the defendant's alleged attempt at suicide, "having insisted on the death penalty, the government is now engaged in the bizarre exercise of trying to prevent Mr. Kaczynski from killing himself so that it can continue to spend enormous amounts of money and court time trying to execute him." The *New York Times* editorialist concluded that pressing a capital trial in this case "will only prolong this costly legal farce." The amount of evidence suggesting that the defendant was mentally ill probably would have been sufficient to trigger a successful appeal if he had been convicted.[2]

A plea was accepted in this case, and the defendant was sentenced to life without parole. Kaczynski, who was representing himself at the time of the plea, subsequently claimed that his plea was involuntary. He appealed his conviction, but it was upheld by the federal appellate court, and the U.S. Supreme Court refused to hear the case, thus permitting the conviction to stand.[3]

Plea bargains can be highly controversial, as illustrated by the 2018 sentencing of Jacob Walter Anderson, a former fraternity president at Baylor University in Texas. Anderson was accused of "violently and repeatedly" raping a student who was devastated when Anderson was permitted to plead no contest to a lesser charge of felony restraint. According to the plea accepted by the trial judge, Anderson was not required to serve jail or prison time or register as a sex offender. He was required to serve "three years of deferred adjudication probation, pay a $400 fine, and undergo counseling." As of December 11, 2018, 96,000 people had signed petitions opposing the plea bargain that led to this sentencing. The prosecutor said she agreed to the plea deal because she could not prove guilt beyond a reasonable doubt under the evidence she had in the case. Anderson was expelled from Baylor but was scheduled to graduate from the University of Texas at Dallas. The fraternity was suspended.[4]

1. "In Deal for Life, Man Admits Killing 48 Women," *New York Times* (November 6, 2003), p. 1.
2. "The Unabomber Travesty," *New York Times* (January 10, 1998), p. 24.
3. *United States v. Kaczynski*, 239 F.3d 1108 (9th Cir. 2001), *cert. denied*, 535 U.S. 933 (2002).
4. Debra Cassens Weiss, "Former Frat President Accused of Rape Pleads Guilty to Lesser Charge in Deal without Jail Time," *American Bar Association Journal*, (December 11, 2018), http://www.abajournal.com, accessed December 12, 2018.

U.S. Supreme Court agreed that his attorney did not offer effective assistance of counsel when he told his client that he would not be deported if he accepted a plea deal. The defendant had no viable defense to his drug conviction and would thus have probably been convicted had he gone to trial. One could argue that in that circumstance he could not show that he was prejudiced by pleading guilty. In *Lee v. United States*, the Court stated:

> We cannot agree that it would be irrational for a defendant in Lee's position to reject the plea offer in favor of trial. But for his attorney's incompetence, Lee would have known that accepting the plea agreement would *certainly* lead to deportation. Going to trial? *Almost* certainly.... Not everyone in Lee's position would make the choice to reject the plea. But we cannot say it would be irrational to do so.
>
> Lee's claim that he would not have accepted a plea had he known it would lead to deportation is backed by substantial and uncontroverted evidence. Accordingly we conclude Lee has demonstrated a "reasonable probability that, but for [his] counsel's errors, he would not have pleaded guilty and would have insisted on going to trial."[50]

Summary

This chapter discussed the attorneys who prosecute and defend in criminal cases, and then provided an overview of the pretrial procedures in which they engage. The chapter began with a historical overview of the legal profession before turning to the prosecution of a criminal case. In its analysis of the prosecution, the chapter looked briefly at the historical emergence of public prosecution, contrasting that approach with the method of private prosecution that was its predecessor in the United States and that still exists in some other countries.

U.S. public prosecution systems are varied. Although most prosecutors are elected officials, their functions and the structures of their offices differ, depending on the size of the jurisdiction and the complexities of local needs. State systems of prosecution, like those at the federal level, may be large. They differ from local systems in some respects. State and federal prosecutors may issue opinions on the constitutionality of their respective state and federal statutes. In addition, they are charged with the prosecution of state and federal crimes, and like local prosecutors, they must make important decisions on which cases to prosecute and which charges to bring in each case.

This authority to determine whom to prosecute and which charges to bring when there are several options gives prosecutors tremendous power. Generally, a decision not to prosecute ends the case. Once the initial decision to prosecute has been made, prosecutors may drop charges. Charges may be dropped for a lack of evidence or for political or personal reasons. This power is virtually unchecked. Even when the prosecutorial decision to drop charges occurs after the defendant has made a court appearance and the judge must approve the prosecutor's decision, the prosecutor has immense power in the final determination. Frequently, judges defer to prosecutors, who may insist that they are overworked, that their resources are limited, and that there is not enough evidence to continue the prosecution.

Such extensive power may lead to abuse. Prosecutors may abuse their discretion in many ways. They may charge defendants with crimes for which they have little or no evidence in order to coerce them to plead guilty to crimes for which they have sufficient evidence. This avoids trials and reduces prosecutors' caseloads while providing them with "victories."

The next focus of the chapter was on the defense of a criminal case. The discussion began with an overview of the defense attorney's role, followed by a discussion of the right to counsel. The evolution and current status of the right to appointed counsel for indigent defendants was explored, culminating with the critical *Gideon* decision in 1963, in which the U.S. Supreme Court held that the right to appointed counsel for indigents is not limited to capital cases but applies to other felonies as well. The Supplement noted that the right to appointed counsel for indigents was later extended to less serious offenses.

The right to appointed counsel does not exist at all pretrial and posttrial stages, although it does exist at critical stages. The right to counsel also involves a right to refuse counsel. Defendants may serve as their own attorneys, provided their waivers of counsel have been made knowingly and intelligently. They may retain private counsel if they prefer and can afford to do so.

The right to counsel implies a right to effective counsel, which the U.S. Supreme Court defined in *Strickland* v. *Washington* as involving a two-pronged test. The defendant must show that counsel was deficient and that the deficiency resulted in prejudice to the defendant, who as a result did not get a fair trial. This standard is very difficult to prove, but the courts must consider the totality of the circumstances in making their decisions concerning whether a defendant had effective assistance of counsel.

The interaction of the defense attorney and the prosecutor is important during criminal proceedings. The pretrial procedures that are the focus of their interaction were the subject of the chapter's final section. These procedures include some of the most critical issues and most difficult procedures in criminal justice systems. All of the pretrial court hearings are crucial, for at any stage, failure to find probable cause must result in the defendant's release. If any rights of the accused are violated during arrest, interrogation, investigation, or search and seizure, the evidence secured as a result of those violations may be excluded from the trial. Without the illegally seized evidence, many cases must be dismissed for lack of probable cause. The initial appearance, the preliminary hearing, the grand jury review, and the arraignment are concerned with the issue of determining whether there is sufficient evidence to continue the case.

The roles of the prosecution and the defense in these stages are critical. Prosecutorial discretion to drop the charges after the police have arrested a suspect may negate police crime control efforts. However, that discretionary power may serve as a check on overzealous police officers. Even after formal charges are filed with the court, through either a prosecutorial information or a grand jury indictment, the prosecutor has considerable influence in getting those charges dismissed. This dismissal may be done for good reasons, such as lack of evidence, or for bad reasons, such as discrimination or political pressure. Prosecutors have great power at the stage of grand jury review because grand juries usually return a true bill on indictments submitted by the prosecution.

The role of defense attorneys is to protect defendants' rights at all pretrial stages and to plan the defense strategy should the case go to trial. The role of judges is important as well. They preside over all formal court hearings and have the power to grant or deny motions, to grant or deny bail in most cases, and to accept or reject guilty pleas. To a great extent, judges control the timing of all the stages, as they set dates for the court hearings and for the trial. If a guilty plea has been accepted, judges usually have the power to impose sentencing at that time.

Two critical procedures discussed in this chapter raise controversial issues in our criminal justice systems: the decision whether to release or to detain defendants pending trial and the practice of plea bargaining. The decision whether to release a defendant on bail or to allow another alternative requires the judge to predict whether that person would appear for trial if released prior to trial. With recent legislation in some jurisdictions permitting pretrial detention for preventive purposes, some judges have the power to detain if they think the defendant is a danger to society. These are not easy decisions in a world in which predicting human behavior is inaccurate, yet the decision to detain imposes great burdens on defendants, who are inconvenienced and may lose their jobs, endure the indignities and embarrassments of a jail term, and in some cases, suffer physical attacks by other inmates. For those who are acquitted of the crimes for which they are charged, pretrial detention is an incredible injustice. For society, pretrial release may mean more crime; however, pretrial detention creates the need for more facilities, thus increasing the cost of criminal justice systems.

Some defendants enter guilty pleas and thus avoid a trial, while others may plead guilty after the trial begins and the evidence is mounting against them. Some enter guilty pleas as part of a plea bargain concerning other charges or sentencing or both.

Plea bargaining is a procedure that raises many issues. The practice is necessary as long as we have high crime rates and insufficient facilities and personnel to try all cases. The practice allows the flexibility necessary if the system is to respond with any degree of concern for the circumstances of individual cases. But that flexibility may lead to abuse of discretion, resulting in bitter defendants, some of whom have reasonable justification for believing that the system has treated them unfairly. Thus, the right to effective assistance of counsel is important at this stage. Plea bargaining may entice defendants to plead guilty to crimes they did not commit rather than risk their constitutional right to trial. Such a choice might, and usually does, result in conviction.

Many of the subjects discussed in this chapter are also important to Chapter 8, "Trial, Sentencing, and Appeal." Attorneys and judges are the major professionals in trials, as well as during pretrial procedures. Plea bargaining may continue. Many of the motions made at pretrial may be made during the trial. The issue of whether a detained defendant should be released from jail may be reconsidered; likewise, the decision to release a defendant pending trial may be revoked when changes in the circumstances warrant that decision. Both prosecution and defense may continue the investigation to secure more evidence to present at trial, particularly during a long trial. The stages in criminal justice systems are not separable. Some procedures and issues, however, are peculiar to the criminal trial, the focus of Chapter 8, which also discusses the stages of sentence and appeal.

Key Terms

arraignment 160
assigned counsel 157
bail 162
bond 163
booking 158
community prosecution 148
contract system 157
defendant 147
defense attorney 152
deposition 161
discovery 160
grand jury 150
indictment 150
information 150
initial appearance 159
interrogatories 161
lineup 159
motion 160
nolo contendere 160
plea bargaining 164
preliminary hearing 159
presentment 160
pretrial detention 162
preventive detention 162
pro se 153
prosecuting attorney 148
prosecution 147
public defender 157
right to counsel 153
showup 159
subpoena 161
true bill 160
venue 161
waiver 153

Study Questions

1. How have lawyers been viewed by the public in recent years?
2. Why did a system of public prosecution develop, and what is the difference between public and private prosecution? Which system do you think is better?
3. What is the main function of a prosecutor? Why is the prosecutor allowed so much discretion in fulfilling that role? What are the problems with allowing such discretion?
4. How can prosecutorial discretion be kept within reasonable limits? Evaluate one example of prosecutorial misconduct discussed in the chapter.
5. What is meant by the *right to counsel*? Describe briefly what that right means today, compared with its historical meaning in the United States.
6. What is the importance of the *Gideon* case?
7. Do you think a defendant should have the right to refuse counsel? Explain your answer.
8. What does the U.S. Supreme Court mean by *effective assistance of counsel*? If you had the opportunity to define that term for the Court, what would you include?
9. How would you suggest improving the availability and quality of legal defense counsel?
10. Would you prefer to be a defense attorney or a prosecuting attorney? Why?
11. Define each of the major steps in the criminal justice process before trial.
12. Describe the main purposes of the *initial appearance*, *preliminary hearing*, and *arraignment*.
13. What is a *grand jury indictment*? How does that process differ from a prosecutor's information?
14. Distinguish between *depositions* and *interrogatories*.
15. What is the *bail bond system*, and why is it controversial today?
16. What should be the goals and purposes of detention prior to trial?
17. Describe the process of pleading guilty before trial. Does it make any difference whether the plea is a negotiated one?
18. Do you think plea bargaining should be abolished? Why? If it is, what might be the result?
19. Evaluate some of the recent high-profile cases involving plea bargaining.
20. What is the status of the right to counsel at plea bargaining?

Notes

1. Lee Rawles, "ABA Offers Buyouts to Longtime Staff in Advance of Its Planned Reorganization," *American Bar Association Journal* (February 15, 2018), http://www.abajournal.com, accessed February 17, 2018.
2. Debra Cassens Weiss, "Median Salaries for New Law Grads Jump to $70K as BigLaw Boosts Hiring of Newbie Lawyers," *American Bar Association Journal* (August 2, 2018), http://www.abajournal.com, accessed August 2, 2018.
3. Stephanie Francis Ward, "While Number of Lawyer Jobs Have Been Decreasing, Law School Applications Are Up 8%," *American Bar Association Journal* (July 31, 2018), http://www.abajournal.com, accessed August 3, 2018.
4. Debra Cassens Weiss, "Was Law School Worth It? Only 20% of Recent Grads Strongly Agree, Pilot Study Says," *American Bar Association Journal* (March 24, 2016), http://www.abajournal.com, accessed March 25, 2016.
5. "ABA Calls on Firms to Pledge to Tackle Lawyer Mental-Health and Substance-Use Issues," *American Bar Association Journal* (September 10, 2018), http://www.abajournal.com, accessed September 11, 2018.
6. James Podgers, "Younger Lawyers Are Most at Risk for Substance Abuce and Mental Health Problems, A New Study Reports," *American Bar Association Journal* (February 7, 2016), http://www.abajournal.com, accessed February 8, 2016.
7. Debra Cassens Weiss, "Lawyers Rank Highest on 'Loneliness Scale,' Study Finds," *American Bar Association Journal* (April 3, 2018), http://www.abajournal.com, accessed April 6, 2018. See also Jeena Cho, "Lawyer Loneliness: Facing and Fighting the

'No. 1 Public Health Issue,'" *American Bar Association Journal* (July 2018), p. 28.
8. Debra Cassens Weiss, "Lawyers Who Work the Most Appear Least Likely to Regret Their Career Choice, Indiana Study Finds," *American Bar Association Journal* (November 24, 2015), http://www.abajournal.com, accessed November 25, 2015.
9. Sarah Kellogg, "The Uncertain Future: Turbulence and Change in the Legal Profession," *American Bar Association Journal* 30(8) (April 2016), p. 19.
10. *ABA Standards for Criminal Justice: The Prosecution Function*, Standard 3-1.2, approved by the ABA House of Delegates, February 1992.
11. *Berger v. United States*, 295 U.S. 78 (1935).
12. "Judge Exonerates Man in '80 Rape," *Dallas Morning News* (December 25, 2014), 1B; Innocence Project, https://www.innocenceproject.org, accessed September 28, 2018.
13. *State v. Mitchell*, 395 A.2d 1257 (Sup. Ct. App. Div. N.J. 1978).
14. *Yick Wo v. Hopkins*, 118 U.S. 356 (1886). In *Yick Wo*, a public board that was authorized to issue laundry licenses denied licenses to Chinese applicants and granted licenses to most white applicants.
15. *Brady v. Maryland*, 373 U.S. 83 (1963).
16. *United States v. Olsen*, 737 F.3d 625 (9th Cir. 2013), Judge Kozinski, dissenting.
17. "A Zealous Prosecutor of Drug Criminals Becomes One Himself," *New York Times* (February 15, 2005), p. 14; "I Inject, Your Honor," *Texas Monthly* (April 2005), n.p.; "Drug Plague upon the Panhandle; Former District Attorney Just Another Casualty in Region Where Methamphetamine Pervades," *Austin (Texas) American-Statesman* (March 6, 2005), p. 1.
18. *Powell v. Alabama*, 287 U.S. 45 (1932); *Gideon v. Wainwright*, 372 U.S. 335 (1963).
19. *Diggs v. Welch*, 148 F.2d 667 (D.C. Cir. 1945); *cert. denied*, 325 U.S. 889 (1945).
20. *Strickland v. Washington*, 466 U.S. 668 (1984).
21. *McCoy v. Louisiana*, 138 S. Ct. 1500 (2018); *Garza v. Idaho*, 139 S. Ct. 738 (2019).
22. "Governor Who Blocked Public-Defender Budget Increases Is Ordered to Represent Indigent Defendant," *American Bar Association Journal* (August 4, 2016), http://www.abajournal.com, accessed August 5, 2016.
23. "Louisiana's PD System Is So Underfunded that Tax Lawyers and Even a Prosecutor Handle Defense Work," *American Bar Association Journal* (September 8, 2016), http://www.abajournal.com, accessed September 9, 2016; "Louisiana Courts Are So Strapped for Public Defenders, Civil Attorneys Are Used for Criminal Cases," *American Bar Association Journal* (September 16, 2016), http//www.abajournal.com, accessed September 19, 2016.
24. Lorelei Laird, "The *Gideon* Revolution: Starved of Money for Too Long, Public Defender Offices Are Suing—and Starting to Win," *American Bar Association Journal* 103(1) (January 2017): 44-51.
25. American Bar Association, "ABA Ten Principles of a Public Defense Delivery System" (February 2002), p. 1, http://www.americanbar.org, accessed December 28, 2013.
26. Laird, "The *Gideon* Revolution," p. 46, 103(1) 46.
27. Debra Cassens Weiss, "Louisiana's Public Defender System Is Understaffed by About 1,400 Lawyers, ABA Study Finds," *American Bar Association Journal* (February 2017), http://www.abajournal.com, accessed October 4, 2018.
28. Derwyn Bunton, "No Lawyers to Spare for Poor in New Orleans," *New York Times*, Op-Ed (February 19, 2016), p. 27.
29. Lorelei Laird, "For the First Time, New York Will Provide Some State Funding for Indigent Defense," *American Bar Association Journal* (April 14, 2017), http://www.abajournal.com, accessed October 4, 2018, *Hurrell-Harring v. New York*, 930 N.E. 2d 217 (N.Y. 2010).
30. *Wood v. Georgia*, 370 U.S. 375, 390 (1962).
31. *Powell v. Alabama*, 287 U.S. 45, 57 (1932).
32. See USCS, Title 18, Section 3142(c)(1) (2019).
33. *Stack v. Boyle*, 342 U.S. 1 (1951).
34. *United States v. Edwards*, 430 A.2d 1321 (D.C. Ct. App. 1981), *cert. denied*, 455 U.S. 1022 (1982).
35. *Schall v. Martin*, 467 U.S. 253 (1984).
36. The Bail Reform Act is codified at USCS, Chapter 18, Sections 3141 et seq. (2019).
37. *United States v. Salerno*, 481 U.S. 739 (1987).
38. Stephen Demuth, "Racial and Ethnic Differences in Pretrial Release Decisions and Outcomes: A Comparison of Hispanic, Black, and White Felony Arrestees," *Criminology* 41(3) (August 2003): 873-908; quotation is on p. 899.
39. Cameron Langford, "Federal Judge Orders Texas County to Release Poor Defendants Without Bail," https://www.courthousenews.com, accessed July 4, 2018. The Fifth Circuit case is *Odonnell et al. v. Harris County, Texas*, No. 17-20333 (February 14, 2018).
40. Debra Cassens Weiss, "New York Judge Rules It's Unconstitutional to Set Bail Without Regard to Ability to Pay," *American Bar Association Journal* (February 8, 2018), http://www.abajournal.com, accessed February 10, 2018. The Georgia case is, *Walker v. City of Calhoun, Ga.*, 901 F.3d 1245, *cert. denied*, 2019 U.S. LEXIS 2446 (U.S. Apr. 1, 2019). The Georgia statute is codified at Ga. Code Ann., Section 40-6-95 (2019). See also Weiss, "ABA Urges Supreme Court to Review Constitutionality of Fixed-Bail System," *American Bar Association Journal* (January 29, 2019), http://www.abajournal.com, accessed January 30, 2019.
41. "California Is the First State to Scrap Cash Bail," *New York Times* (August 28, 2018), https://advance.lexis.com/, accessed October 4, 2018. See Cal. SB 10 (2018).
42. *Johnson v. Zerbst*, 304 U.S. 458 (1938).
43. See the U.S. Supreme Court decisions on plea bargaining decided in 2012: *Missouri v. Frye*, 566 U.S. 134 (2012); *Lafler v. Cooper*, 566 U.S. 156 (2012). For a brief discussion of plea bargaining in the federal system, see *United States of America v. Charles York Walker, Jr.*, U.S. Dist. Ct. for the Southern District of West Virginia, Charleston Division, Criminal Action No. 2:17-cr-00010 (June 26, 2017).
44. *Santobello v. New York*, 404 U.S. 257, 260-261 (1971).
45. *Bordenkircher v. Hayes*, 434 U.S. 357 (1978).
46. *Corbitt v. New Jersey*, 439 U.S. 212 (1978).
47. *Mabry v. Johnson*, 467 U.S. 504 (1984).
48. *Missouri v. Frye*, 566 U.S. 134 (2012).
49. *Lafler v. Cooper*, 566 U.S. 156 (2012); *Padilla v. Kentucky*, 559 U.S. 356 (2010). See also *Hill v. Lockhart*, 474 U.S. 51 (1983).
50. *Lee v. United States*, 2017 U.S. LEXIS 4045 (2017).

8

Trial, Sentencing, and Appeal

Chapter Outline

Learning Objectives

After reading this chapter, you should be able to do the following:

- State an overview of defendants' constitutional rights
- Explain a defendant's right to a speedy, public trial by an impartial jury
- Discuss the variables of gender, race (and ethnicity), age, disability, and sexual orientation in jury selection
- List and explain the stages in the trial and appeal of a criminal case in the United States
- Explain how evidence is presented in a criminal trial, and discuss the various types of evidence and objections to evidence
- Distinguish the prosecution's case from that of the defense
- Discuss the role of the jury in deciding a criminal case
- Explain and analyze the concept and process of sentencing and sentencing strategies
- Discuss the sentencing hearing and decision
- List and define the major types of sentences
- Describe the use of sentencing guidelines by states and the federal government
- Explain the difference between indeterminate and determinate sentencing and evaluate each
- Assess the current status of capital punishment in the United States
- Explore the meaning, causes, and consequences of sentence disparity
- Discuss the meaning and impact of three-strikes and truth-in-sentencing legislation
- Consider the impact of a treatment approach to sentencing
- Summarize the provisions of the First Step Act of 2018
- Describe appeals and writs
- Explain and analyze the issue of wrongful convictions

Chapter 7 noted that most cases do not go to trial. For the cases that do proceed to trial, especially in the criminal area, it is important to know the rules and constitutional principles that govern the processes involved. This chapter begins with a discussion of some of defendants' constitutional rights at trial and explains the major processes that occur during criminal trials.

Sentencing, which often occurs even in cases that are not tried, is a critical part of criminal justice systems and is discussed at some length in this chapter. The chapter explains the concept and process of sentencing, the death penalty, and selected sentencing issue. These issues include sentence disparity and the punitive approaches of three-strikes legislation, truth in sentencing, and treatment and sentencing, along with recent changes in those and other sentencing policies and statutes. The First Step Act, enacted in 2018, is highlighted.

The chapter overviews the procedures through which convictions and sentences are challenged, by discussing appeals and writs. It concludes with an analysis of wrongful convictions.

CONSTITUTIONAL ISSUES AT TRIAL

This analysis of constitutional issues at trial is not meant to be exclusive. It must be understood in the context of the discussions in earlier chapters, but it focuses on the constitutional issues and rights that pertain primarily to trials in U.S. adult criminal courts. First is the right to a speedy **trial**, which is embodied in the Sixth Amendment (see Appendix A) to the U.S. Constitution. The U.S. Supreme Court has held that this right "is as fundamental as any of the rights secured by the Sixth Amendment."[1]

In 1974, Congress passed the Speedy Trial Act. It is possible for the defendant to be tried so quickly that there would not be adequate time for preparing a defense. Thus, the Speedy Trial Act provides that, without the consent of the defendant, "the trial shall not commence less than thirty days from the date on which the defendant first appears through counsel or expressly waives counsel and elects to proceed pro se [on his or her own]."[2]

Some delays are permissible under the Speedy Trial Act. Several are listed in the act, including the obvious ones, such as those delays caused by examinations to determine whether the defendant is competent to stand trial and delays caused by deferred prosecution when that is agreed upon by the prosecutor, the defendant, and the court. The act permits delays due to continuances requested by the defense or the prosecution when they are granted to serve the ends of justice. Most state constitutions and statutes also cover the right to a speedy trial. **Supplement 8.1** presents the provision for a speedy trial in Vermont, along with an excerpt from the U.S. Supreme Court's interpretation of the Vermont law.

To avoid what might appear ambiguous with regard to how long one must wait for a speedy trial, some jurisdictions specify the period by statutory or procedural rules.

A second important Sixth Amendment provision is that it guarantees the right to a *public* trial, but that does not mean that the defendant may be tried by the media. Media publicity in criminal cases raises a delicate problem: the conflict between the First Amendment (see Appendix A) free speech right of the press and the public's right to know and the defendant's right to a trial by an impartial jury not biased by media reports. If it can be shown that the defendant cannot get a fair trial because of media publicity in the jurisdiction in which the case is to be tried, the trial should be moved to another jurisdiction.

The U.S. Supreme Court has had several occasions to consider the conflict between the defendant's right to a fair trial and the First Amendment rights of the press. In a 1966 case, the Court overturned the conviction of Dr. Sam Sheppard, who had served ten years in prison after his conviction for murdering his wife. In overturning Sheppard's conviction, the Supreme Court stated in part:

> Murder and mystery, society, sex and suspense were combined in this case in such a manner as to intrigue and captivate the public fancy to a degree perhaps unparalleled in recent annals. Throughout the preindictment investigation, the subsequent legal skirmishes and the nine-week trial, circulation-conscious editors catered to the insatiable interest of the American public in the bizarre.... In this atmosphere of a "Roman holiday" for the news media, Sam Sheppard stood trial for his life.[3]

At his retrial Sheppard was acquitted.

In subsequent cases, the U.S. Supreme Court has continued to wrestle with the rights of defendants versus those of the press and the public. The Court has held that, under some circumstances, the former must give way to the latter. For example, in *Globe Newspaper Co. v. Superior Court*, the Court invalidated a Massachusetts statute that had been interpreted to require the exclusion of the press from *all* trials when sexual offense victims under the age of 18 were testifying. The Court held that each case must be examined in terms of its own facts, such as "the minor victim's age, psychological maturity and understanding, the nature of the crime, the desires of the victim, and the interests of parents and relatives."[4]

In some highly publicized cases, it has been argued that the defendant cannot get a fair public trial in *any* jurisdiction. Timothy McVeigh, who was tried on capital charges and convicted for the murders resulting from the bombing of the federal building in Oklahoma City, Oklahoma, on April 19, 1995, argued unsuccessfully that he could not get a fair trial. In addition to immense publicity about the bombing and its victims, the media carried articles stating that McVeigh had confessed to his attorneys. After two of these articles were published, McVeigh's attorneys asked the court to dismiss the charges against their client—or, in the alternative, to grant a long continuance. The district court denied the motions, and the federal appellate court affirmed. The venue of the trial was moved from Oklahoma to Denver, Colorado; an action, the appellate court claimed, that significantly lessened the chance of prejudice in jury selection. Members of the jury pool were subjected to numerous questions in an attempt to secure jurors who could analyze the evidence objectively, and the appellate court refused to reverse McVeigh's conviction.[5] McVeigh was convicted and sentenced to death. He was executed in June 2001.

In state cases, the venue of a trial may be moved from the place of the crime, but it must remain in that state. If publicity throughout the state is an issue, the judge may grant a long continuance before the case is tried.

The Sixth Amendment also guarantees the defendant in a criminal case the right to a trial by a **jury**. Technically, the jury that sits in a trial is called the **petit jury**. The word *petit* means minor, small, or inconsequential, but in this context, it is used to distinguish the trial jury from the larger grand jury, rather than to carry the connotation of inconsequential.

The importance of the right to a jury trial, along with a brief history of its evolution, was emphasized by the U.S. Supreme Court in 1968 in *Duncan v. Louisiana*. This case involved a defendant who was charged with simple battery, a misdemeanor punishable by a maximum of two years' imprisonment and a $300 fine. A Louisiana trial court denied Gary Duncan's request for a jury trial. At that time, the Louisiana constitution granted jury trials only in cases in which convicted defendants could be sentenced to imprisonment at hard labor or to capital punishment. Duncan was convicted, sentenced to 60 days in the parish prison, and fined $150. The Louisiana Supreme Court denied his request for an appeal. Duncan appealed to the U.S. Supreme Court, alleging that he had been denied his constitutional right to a jury trial. That Court agreed, but emphasized that the right to a jury trial does not extend to petty crimes.[6] The right to a jury trial may be waived, provided it is done knowingly, intelligently, voluntarily, and in writing, and it is accepted by the trial court judge.

The U.S. Constitution does not specify how many jurors must be present for the defendant's right to a jury trial to be legal. Although 12 is the usual number of petit jurors, the U.S. Supreme Court has upheld the use of smaller juries in some cases. But there must be at least six jurors, and a jury that small must be unanimous. A unanimous vote is required in all federal jury trials. **Supplement 8.2** discuses whether that requirement should be applied to the states.

The Sixth Amendment provides for the right to trial by an *impartial* jury, which includes the right to a jury not prejudiced unduly by media publicity. If the media publicity cannot be nullified by a change in venue, the judge may order not only a continuance but sequestration of the jury. However, a long sequestration might work against the defense (or the prosecution, if the sequestration is perceived as prolonging the trial unnecessarily). Sequestration is also disruptive to the lives of the jurors, their families and friends, and their employers.

The constitutional right to a trial by a jury has been interpreted to mean a jury of the defendant's peers, which means the jury must be selected from a pool of persons who are representative of the community. Potential jurors may not be excluded from the jury on the basis of specific characteristics, such as race and ethnicity, disability, gender, and religion. It is the *systematic* exclusion of particular groups of persons from the jury pool or jury selection that constitutes a constitutional issue, illustrated primarily by the U.S. Supreme Court's rulings regarding the exclusion of African Americans from juries. In 1880, the Supreme Court held that a statute permitting only white men to serve on juries was unconstitutional. In 1965, the Court held that it was permissible to exclude individual African Americans by using a **peremptory challenge** (a challenge that does not require the attorney to state a reason), but the Court left open the issue of systematic exclusion of African Americans.[7]

Other decisions were made in the intervening years, but the key decision did not come until 1986 in *Batson v. Kentucky*, in which the defendant proved that he was a member of a cognizable racial group whose members were excluded from the jury under circumstances that raised an inference that they were excluded because of race. Portions of *Batson* are included in **Supplement 8.3**.

In *Batson*, the U.S. Supreme Court articulated a three-pronged test to use when analyzing an allegation that the peremptory challenge was used to eliminate a potential juror because of race:

- A defendant must show a *prima facie* (on its face) case that a peremptory challenge was based on race.
- If the defendant makes that showing, the prosecution must give a race-neutral explanation for why the juror in question was challenged.
- The trial court judge must consider the evidence submitted for the preceding two reasons and determine whether the defendant has shown purposeful discrimination based on race.[8]

Since *Batson*, lower courts and the U.S. Supreme Court have dealt with variations in fact patterns in which *Batson* might apply, including holding that a criminal defendant is not required to be of the same race as the excluded juror to object to race-based exclusions because excluded jurors have a constitutional right not to be excluded from juries based on their race; holding that *Batson* applies equally to the removal of white as well as African-American potential jurors and to the defense, as well as to the prosecution; holding that a defendant may challenge a prosecutor's race-based exclusion of a potential juror regardless of whether the defendant and the excluded juror are of the same race; and holding that *Batson* applies to civil as well as to criminal cases. **Supplement 8.4** discusses racial bias in jury selection in a Texas case.

In 2005, the U.S. Supreme Court held that, to state a *prima facie* case under *Batson*, a criminal defendant is *not* required to prove that "peremptory challenges . . . were more likely than not based on race." That standard is too strict. In 2019, in *Flowers v. Kentucky*, a death penalty case involving a *Batson* issue, the Supreme Court reversed a conviction on the basis of prosecutorial discrimination on the basis of race in jury selection.[9]

Gender is another important category in jury selection. Women have a right to serve on juries, and defendants have a right to have women serve as jurors. In 1994, the U.S. Supreme Court's decision in *Batson* was extended to include gender. *J.E.B. v. Alabama ex rel. T.B.* was a civil rather than a criminal case, but it is likely that the holding will apply to criminal cases as well. In this case, Alabama sued J.E.B. to establish paternity and award child support to T.B. (the real names are omitted to protect the child), who alleged that J.E.B. was the father of her minor child. During jury selection, the state used most of its peremptory challenges to remove men from the jury pool, whereas the defense used most of its peremptory challenges to remove women from the pool. An all-female jury was empaneled. The U.S. Supreme Court held that the prosecution's use of peremptory challenges to exclude men from the jury was unconstitutional because it did not show "an exceedingly persuasive justification" for doing so. One of the dissenting opinions noted that for every man the prosecution excluded, the defense excluded a woman; thus, men were not singled out for discriminatory treatment.[10]

The U.S. Supreme Court has not decided a case regarding the issue of sexual orientation in jury selection, but in 2014, a panel of the Ninth Circuit Court of Appeals did so in *SmithKline Beecham v. Abbott Laboratories*,[11] which is summarized in **Supplement 8.5**.

The right to a jury of peers does not include the right of young adults to be tried by a jury composed of other young adults. The absence of young adults on the jury does not necessarily mean that the young defendant's right to be tried by a jury of peers was violated. The defendant must show that the underrepresented group has characteristics that can be defined easily and that the group has common attitudes, experiences, or ideas in addition to a community of interest.[12]

Disability is another issue that must be considered in jury selection. With the emphasis on the rights of physically challenged persons, exemplified by the passage of and the numerous cases being brought under the Americans with Disabilities Act (ADA), consideration must be given to extending the right to serve on juries to those whose physical or mental challenges might have precluded such service in the past.

Finally, those who serve on juries must conduct themselves properly both inside and outside the courtroom. The same is true for defendants, who have a right to be involved in the trial but must behave properly. The classic case of a defendant who failed to observe this rule, *Illinois v. Allen*, is discussed in **Supplement 8.6**.

THE TRIAL PROCESS

In this section, the stages of a criminal trial are discussed in the order in which they generally occur. Spotlight 8.1

Spotlight 8.1

Stages in the Trial and Appeal of a U.S. Criminal Case

1. Opening of the court session
2. Jury selection
3. Opening statement by the prosecutor
4. Opening statement by the defense attorney
5. Presentation of evidence by the prosecutor
6. Cross-examination by the defense
7. Redirect examination by the prosecutor
8. Cross-examination by the defense
9. Presentation of the defense's case by the defense attorney
10. Cross-examination by the prosecutor
11. Redirect by the defense
12. Cross-examination by the prosecutor
13. Rebuttal proof by the prosecutor
14. Closing statement by the prosecutor
15. Closing statement by the defense
16. Rebuttal statement by the prosecutor
17. Submittal of the case to the jury
18. The verdict
19. Postverdict motions
20. Sentencing
21. Appeals and writs

lists those stages, and the discussion follows the order in that list. These stages are not always distinct, however, and some of the procedures may occur at various stages. For example, motions might be made throughout the trial. An obvious motion is one to dismiss the charges or to declare a **mistrial**, which is made by defense counsel after the prosecutor or a prosecution witness has said something improper. A defense motion for change of venue (change of location for trial) might be made before and during the trial as increased media attention to the trial leads the defense to argue that it is impossible for the defendant to have a fair trial in that area.

Opening of the Court Session

When it is time for the trial court session to begin, the bailiff arrives and calls the court to order with such words as "Hear ye, hear ye, the court of the Honorable Judge Decider is in session—all rise." At that point, everyone in the courtroom should rise. The judge, usually dressed in a robe, enters the courtroom and sits, after which everyone else may sit. The judge announces the case, for example, "The State of California versus Jordan Jones, Case No. 45629-16." The judge asks whether the prosecution is ready; if so, the judge asks whether the defense is ready. If both sides are ready, the case begins with jury selection, assuming that the court has no additional business regarding the case, such as pretrial motions, that needs to be heard prior to the beginning of the trial.

After the jury has been selected and sworn in, the judge reads the indictment or information and informs the court that the defendant has entered a plea of not guilty (or not guilty by reason of insanity, if that is applicable in the case), and the trial begins with opening statements. Variances may occur in these procedures; for example, the jury may be selected and sent home (or sequestered), while attorneys argue various motions before the judge.

Jury Selection

Jurisdictions differ in their procedures for selecting persons to form the pool from which jurors will be selected. Those selected are notified by means of a **summons**. After arriving at the designated place, potential jurors may sit all day and not be picked for a jury. If that happens, they may be instructed to return for jury selection the following day. This procedure may go on for days, but many judges try to avoid this inconvenience to potential jurors.

Usually, the members of the jury pool are seated in the courtroom before the judge enters for jury selection. After the formal opening of the court session, the judge instructs the jury pool about procedures. The minute clerk begins by selecting names from a jury wheel, drawing names out of a fishbowl, or using some other similar procedure. As each name is drawn, the minute clerk reads and spells the name. The first selected person sits in the first seat in the jury box and so on until the jury box is filled or contains the number the judge wishes to process at one time.

Questioning of the potential jurors follows, a process called ***voir dire***, which means "to speak the truth." The defense attorney and the prosecuting attorney *voir dire* the jury pool; that is, they question each potential juror and decide whether or not they will approve the selection of that person. Judges may also question potential jurors. In the federal system, judges may refuse to permit attorneys to question prospective jurors. Normally, in the federal system, jury selection takes only a few hours; in some states, the process may take weeks or even months.

After they are questioned, potential jurors may be excused from jury duty in two ways. First, if they are excused for *cause*, they are presumed to be biased in the case. Bias may be presumed on the basis of the potential jurors' answers to the questionnaire or to questions in court, association with or knowledge of the defendant or some other person involved in the trial, personal financial interest in the case, or a background that might prejudice them. For example, a person whose spouse has been murdered might be presumed to be prejudiced against a defendant on trial for murder. Attorneys are entitled to an unlimited number of challenges for cause. The judge may also exclude potential jurors for cause.

The second way a potential juror may be excused is by *peremptory challenge*, which means that the attorneys may excuse without cause. No reason need be given; that is the purpose of the challenge. But the peremptory challenge may not be used for extralegal reasons, such as to exclude minorities from the jury. Jurisdictions vary in the number of peremptory challenges permitted.

Some attorneys retain consultants to assist them in the questioning and selection of jurors. Through empirical studies, social scientists provide information on characteristics that are related to opinions and therefore may influence the decision of a juror. In a particular case, a retained jury consultant may conduct a survey to determine factors that might influence a juror in that town on that case.

Opening Statements

After the jury is selected, attorneys may make opening statements. The prosecutor makes the first opening statement. This is the prosecution's chance to outline what he or she intends to prove during the trial. The opening statement is very important; it should be planned carefully and delivered convincingly.

The opening statement should be brief but long enough to present an adequate statement of the facts the prosecution expects to prove. It should be interesting but not overly dramatic. The prosecutor must not overstep his or her boundaries and raise the ire of the judge, the defense, or the jury. Inflammatory and prejudicial statements are not permitted.

The defense is entitled to follow the prosecution with an opening statement, and many defense attorneys do so. The same principles apply to the defense as to the prosecution. The opening statement should raise the jury's interest to listen further but should not be too long or too dramatic. A defense attorney has the option of waiving the opening statement until the prosecution has presented its evidence. Some do so in order to hear that evidence before revealing the defense. Prosecutors, knowing that this might occur, may make comments in their opening statements that would lead the jury to expect the defense to make a statement or to be suspicious if the defense does not do so. Like the prosecution, the defense attorney should not include within the opening statement any information that is misleading.

Presentation of the Evidence

Before looking at the types of evidence that the prosecution and the defense may present, it is necessary to understand some general rules of evidence and to look at the categories of evidence that apply to both the prosecution and the defense. The rules of evidence in criminal cases must be established through statute or other proper rule making procedures, and they may be interpreted through case law. They are complex, and they differ from one jurisdiction to another; however, a few general rules are important to a basic understanding of a criminal trial.

Any evidence presented must be *relevant*, *competent*, and *material* to the case. The meaning of those words has been litigated often, and over time, changes have been made concerning admissible evidence. For example, in rape cases, historically the defense was permitted to ask the complainant about her prior sexual experiences, to imply that the alleged rape was a voluntary sexual act, not one of force. If she had engaged in sexual relationships with other men, particularly if it could be inferred that she had been promiscuous, a rape conviction was unlikely. Most U.S. jurisdictions have changed that rule. Some permit such questions only if the evidence is relevant to motive or conduct during the alleged crime or if the evidence shows that the alleged victim had sex with someone other than the accused during the time period at issue. Other jurisdictions do not permit any questions about the victim's sexual experiences other than with the defendant and may limit that evidence to the case on trial. This change in what is defined as material evidence may not only affect the outcome of the case but also may make it much more likely that victims will report rapes and agree to testify at trial.

Attempts by the prosecution or the defense to introduce evidence or to ask questions thought by the opposing side to be incompetent, irrelevant, or immaterial may be followed by an objection by opposing counsel. If the judge sustains the objection, the evidence is not admitted. If the objection involves a question posed to the witness, the judge tells the witness not to answer the question. If the question has already been answered, the judge instructs the jury to disregard the answer, unless the information is so prejudicial that the judge declares a mistrial, which means the case cannot continue with that jury. A new jury must be selected or the charges dropped.

An important evidence rule is that of *discovery*, which refers to the process during which one side obtains the information that will be presented in court by the other side. Although in a criminal case, the defense is not required to produce all of its evidence through discovery, the prosecution is required to present evidence that might exonerate the defendant. The purpose of discovery is to prevent surprises in the trial and to enable each side to prepare adequately for its cross-examination of the evidence introduced by opposing counsel. If discovery procedures are violated, the judge may impose fines or a more severe sanction, such as excluding the evidence in question or even citing the attorney for **contempt of court**. A contempt citation might result in a fine or even a jail sentence. In extreme situations, the judge might grant a new trial.

Several types of evidence may be presented at trial. **Demonstrative evidence** is real to the senses, in contrast to evidence presented by the verbal testimony of sworn witnesses (including the alleged witness). Examples of demonstrative evidence are the weapon alleged to have been used in the crime, blood samples, hair samples, and clothing. The integrity of demonstrative evidence may be, and often is, challenged.

Some evidence may be competent, relevant, and material to the case but be excluded because it was secured in violation of the defendant's rights or because it is considered to be too prejudicial or inflammatory. Deciding which evidence to admit and which to exclude is the judge's responsibility. He or she may be overruled on appeal, but many of the decisions made at the trial (or pretrial) stages stand, and often, they are crucial to the outcome of the case.

A second type of evidence that may be introduced at trial is that of witnesses, which is referred to as *testimonial evidence*. Witnesses may be called by the prosecution or by the defense, and they are sworn in before they are permitted to testify. If they do not tell the truth, they may be prosecuted for perjury. There are several types of witnesses.

The testimony of a *victim-witness* is a preferred type of testimonial evidence. In many cases, prosecutors drop charges if victims will not agree to testify against the accused. *Eyewitnesses* who are not the victims of the alleged crime are also prime candidates for being called to testify in criminal cases, although some psychologists question the use of eyewitnesses, citing evidence that some jurors place too much weight on their testimonies and that they are not always accurate in their memories or perceptions.

The defense or the prosecution may also call *expert witnesses*. Expert witnesses testify regarding subjects on which they have expertise beyond that of the average person. To illustrate, ballistics experts may be called to testify about the specifics of when and where a gun was fired and what kind of gun was used. Medical experts might testify regarding the cause of death in a murder case or the cause of injury in a case of assault and battery. Psychologists and psychiatrists might testify concerning the mental or emotional state of the defendant or other topics relevant to the trial. Before expert evidence is admitted, the judge must rule that the science about which the expert will testify is advanced sufficiently to qualify for presentation to the jury. The judge must also rule on whether a particular person is qualified to testify on the subject in question. The attorney who presents the expert offers evidence to qualify that person. Opposing counsel may challenge the expert's credentials, but in most cases, they are accepted, although after the expert finishes testifying opposing counsel will try to discredit the content of the testimony during cross-examination. Both the prosecution and the defense might present experts from the same field. If the experts disagree, it is the jury's responsibility to determine credibility. A particular expert may be allowed to testify to some but not all issues about which the attorney wishes to question him or her.

Generally, witnesses must testify to facts—not opinion—although in some instances, opinions are allowed by expert witnesses. Witnesses are not permitted to testify to the ultimate question of fact in a criminal case: the guilt or innocence of the defendant. One way for counsel to get around the requirement of factual testimony is to ask hypothetical questions concerning facts similar to those in the case on trial. The expert witness may be permitted to answer the hypothetical questions.

In most instances, experts and other witnesses are permitted to testify only to what they know, not to what they have heard from others, which constitutes **hearsay evidence**. Hearsay evidence is not admissible because there is no opportunity to cross-examine the source of the information. However, there are a number of exceptions to the hearsay evidence rule, such as a *dying declaration*. Since it might be presumed that one who is dying has no reason to lie, courts may permit a witness to testify (either in a deposition or at trial) to information that otherwise would be considered hearsay.

One further distinction important to the presentation of evidence is the difference between *direct* and *circumstantial* evidence. A witness who testifies that he or she saw the defendant using the alleged weapon is providing **direct evidence**. Much evidence, however, is not direct; rather, it is *inferred* from a fact or series of facts and is called **circumstantial evidence**.

After the prosecution presents its witnesses, in a process called **direct examination**, the defense attorney may question those witnesses through **cross-examination**. The defense may reserve the right to cross-examine a witness later in the trial. After the defense cross-examines a prosecution witness, the prosecutor may follow with additional questions, in a process called *redirect examination*. If that occurs, the defense may cross-examine the witness again. The same process occurs in reverse after the defense has presented its witnesses.

The Prosecution's Case

The prosecutor is the first to present evidence. Its case may include the presentation of demonstrative evidence as well as the testimony of the alleged victim(s), other witnesses, and experts. Usually, police officers involved in the arrest or the investigation of the case are called to testify. The prosecutor's case may consume days, weeks, even months in some trials and may involve very complicated evidence.

After the defense has rested its case, the prosecutor has the option of presenting additional proof to rebut the case presented by the defense. Not all prosecutors choose to exercise this option to present what is called *rebuttal* evidence. When the option is exercised, the prosecution may call or recall police officers or others to testify regarding facts that have been in dispute among witnesses at the trial.

The Defense Attorney's Case

After the prosecution has presented its case and all cross-examinations and redirect examinations have occurred, the prosecution rests and the defense presents its case. At this point, some special issues arise.

The defendant has a right not to testify (see Appendix A, the Fifth Amendment). The reason is that even innocent persons might appear guilty if they take the stand. If the defendant does not testify, neither the prosecution nor the judge may make unfavorable comments about that fact.

Some defendants choose to testify. In that case, they are sworn in, and they may be prosecuted for perjury if they testify falsely. They may be cross-examined by the prosecutor. Rules vary, but generally, the rules applied to other witnesses also apply to the defendant. In most jurisdictions, this means that the cross-examination may encompass only those subjects covered on direct or redirect examination. Where that is the case, the defense attorney has the ability to limit the subject matter about which the prosecution may ask questions to the subjects the defense attorney includes in direct examination. Some jurisdictions, however, permit the prosecution to go beyond those subjects once the defendant takes the stand.

The defense may call *character witnesses*, who testify about the defendant's good character; if that occurs, the prosecution may call witnesses to testify to the defendant's bad character. The prosecution may not begin this line of evidence. Character witnesses, like all other witnesses, may be subjected to stringent cross-examination. This is difficult for many people, and therefore, it is important that attorneys who plan to call character or other kinds of witnesses spend time with those witnesses, preparing them for trial.

Another important element of the defendant's case is the presentation of defenses. Commission of a criminal act, even with the required criminal intent, is not sufficient for a guilty verdict if the defense proves a legally acceptable reason that the law should not be applied to this defendant. Many defenses might be raised. Infancy, intoxication, duress, involuntary action, entrapment, public duty, legal impossibility, self defense or defense of others, action under authority of law (e.g., a justifiable killing by a police officer), and insanity are some examples.

Jurisdictions differ regarding which of these defenses are acceptable and under what conditions. Differences exist in the type of proof required for the defense to be successful.[13]

Closing Statements

After all of the evidence has been presented, attorneys may offer closing statements. The closing statement is given first by the prosecution, then by the defense; this may be followed with a rebuttal by the prosecutor. In the closing statement, as in the entire trial, the prosecutor must be careful not to go too far. If he or she does so, the judge must determine whether the statements are so prejudicial or erroneous that they might have undue influence on the jury's determination of guilt. If so, they are considered **prejudicial errors**, and the judge orders a mistrial. If not, they are considered *harmless errors*. Prejudicial errors and harmless errors may be committed by the defense or the prosecution and may refer to actions or comments made at various stages in the criminal process or to evidence presented (or not presented). **Supplement 8.7** discusses a U.S. Supreme Court decision concerning an example of a case returned to a lower court to consider whether the errors were harmless.

The defense offers a closing statement after that of the prosecutor, unless the defense chooses to waive this step. The defense should also be careful not to go beyond the evidence or be too emotional, but as a practical matter, defense attorneys' closing statements are rarely the subject of appeal. This is because the prosecution may not appeal an acquittal; if the defendant is convicted and the defense appeals, that appeal will be concerned only with alleged errors made by the prosecution or rulings made by the judge.

Submittal of the Case to the Jury

After all of the preceding steps have been completed, most cases are submitted to a jury, although some cases are tried without a jury. The judge may not direct the jury to return a guilty verdict. However, in many jurisdictions, trial judges, on their own or by granting a motion from the defense, may order a **directed verdict**, a direction to the jury to return a verdict of not guilty.

Why would a trial judge have that power? If the evidence is so weak that it is unreasonable to conclude beyond a reasonable doubt that the defendant is guilty, it would be a travesty of justice to send the case to the jury, let the jury return a guilty verdict, and then make the defendant wait for an appeal to get justice.

Before the case is given to the jury for deliberation, the judge has the responsibility of *charging* the jury, which means instructing jurors on matters of law relating to the case they must decide. In many jurisdictions, patterned jury instructions are given for the most commonly raised issues. The judge accepts suggested instructions from the prosecution and the defense and usually schedules a conference with them on these. The judge determines the final instructions (which may be subject to appeal) and presents them orally to the jury. The charge of the judge is very important, for it can be influential, perhaps determinative, in the jury's decision.

The jury charge should be as clear and simple as possible without distorting the meaning of the law. The law as applied to many cases is complicated and difficult to understand, especially for people who are not legally trained, yet it is the jury's responsibility to apply that law to the evidence it has heard. It is the duty of the trial judge to explain the law in terms that the jury can understand. If the judge's charge is too complicated or is an inaccurate interpretation of the law in the case, the defense may appeal. In some instances, the case is reversed and necessitates a new trial.

The judge's charge must explain to the jury the law that applies to the case, and it must clarify what the jury may do. For example, if the defendant has been charged with first-degree murder but the law permits the jury to return a guilty verdict for second-degree murder, that must be explained, along with the elements that must be proved for conviction of each of those charges. The judge should explain the meaning of evidence and distinguish among the types of evidence. If conflict exists in the testimonial evidence, the jurors need to understand that they are the final determiner regarding the credibility of the testimony. This is true particularly when expert opinions conflict. Jurors may expect conflict between the testimony of a victim and that of a defendant but be very confused when two physicians give contradictory statements. Experts do differ; the jury is to decide whom to believe. Jurors may also ignore the testimony of any or all experts.

The judge may instruct the jury to disregard certain evidence that has been admitted but that for some reason should not be considered. In the federal and in some state systems, the judge is permitted to summarize and comment on the evidence when the charge is given to the jury. This is an immense responsibility, for the judge's obligation to be a neutral party continues throughout the trial unless the right to a jury trial is waived and the judge determines the ultimate fact of guilt or innocence.

The judge might cover many areas of law in the instructions. The details of each charge depend on the nature of the case being tried. Two issues deserve further attention in this section: (1) the presumption of innocence, and (2) the burden and standard of proof.

In U.S. criminal justice systems, the defendant is presumed innocent. The **presumption of innocence** is an important principle. It means that the prosecution has the responsibility of proving every element required for conviction and that the defendant cannot be required to prove innocence. The defendant's attorney may choose not to present any evidence during the trial and still win an acquittal for the defendant if the government does not prove its case.

Some judges instruct the jury regarding the presumption of innocence, although the U.S. Supreme Court has held that it is not constitutionally required that an instruction be given. According to the Supreme Court, all circumstances must be examined to determine whether the defendant had a fair trial without an instruction on the presumption. If so, the case will not be reversed for failure to give the instruction.

The presumption of innocence is essential in protecting those who are falsely accused. Innocent people are convicted in some cases, and these convictions may be devastating to their personal and professional lives. The criminal justice system is impaired when the rights of innocent persons are violated, particularly when a violation leads to a conviction (or in some cases, execution).

The standard of proof in a criminal case is **beyond a reasonable doubt**. That burden is a heavy one; it means that, when jurors look at all the evidence, they are convinced, satisfied to a moral certainty, that guilt has been established by the facts. Some judges refuse to define *beyond a reasonable doubt* on the assumption that not much more can be said. We all understand those words, and any attempt to define them further might be confusing or misleading.

After the charge is read to the jury, the bailiff takes the jurors to the jury room to deliberate. These deliberations must be conducted in secret. It is the bailiff's responsibility to ensure that no one talks to the jurors; nor are the jurors permitted to seek advice. If they need further instruction, they may send the bailiff to ask the judge, who may or may not give that instruction, depending on the nature of the request. Any communication between the jury and the judge is conducted in the presence of the attorneys for both the prosecution and the defense.

If the jurors are sequestered, the bailiff (or another court person, such as a deputy sheriff) escorts them not only in and out of the courtroom but also to all meals and to the hotel rooms where they are staying. Access to television and newspapers is not permitted unless special arrangements are made to avoid any possibility that jurors are exposed to media accounts of the trial. For example, jurors might be offered newspapers only after the articles about the trial have been removed.

Normally, when the jurors deliberate, they have access to the demonstrative evidence that has been introduced during the trial. If they have been permitted to take notes during the trial, they may have their notes for the deliberation. Generally, the trial judge has the discretion to decide whether jurors may take notes.

In some trials, jurors deliberate for hours and do not reach verdicts. They report to the judge, who may tell them to go back and try again. The number of times a judge may send the jury back and how long they must deliberate is a matter of jurisdictional rules and judicial discretion, but the judge may not require jurors to deliberate for an unreasonable period of time. The definition of *reasonable* depends on the complexity of the trial. If the jury cannot reach a verdict, it is deadlocked, also called a *hung jury*, and the judge should declare a mistrial.

Mistrials may also be declared under other circumstances, such as the serious illness or death of the judge or one of the attorneys or jurors (in the case of the latter, alternate jurors may be assigned, but the jury deliberations must then start over and include that person). Mistrials may be declared during the trial as a result of a prejudicial error made by one of the parties involved in the trial. Other reasons include prejudicial media publicity that comes to the attention of the jury and efforts of someone to bribe some or all of the jurors.

If the jury is not deadlocked and returns a verdict, the verdict may be not guilty. In that case, the judge may order a verdict of acquittal, and the case is ended. The judge may not reverse a not guilty verdict. The judge may, but rarely does, reverse a guilty verdict. This may happen if the judge believes the evidence was not sufficient to support the guilty verdict. In addition, the judge may find the defendant guilty of a lesser charge than the one on which the jury based its verdict.

After the verdict and before sentencing, the attorneys may file postverdict motions. If the jury returns a guilty verdict, the defense may file a motion for a judgment of acquittal. That motion may also be made before the case goes to the jury and probably is more appropriately done at that time. The motion is based on the argument that the evidence is not sufficient to support a guilty verdict. The court may be more likely to grant that motion before the jury has returned a verdict, particularly in a close case.

The more common motion made by the defense after a guilty verdict is a motion for a new trial. This motion may be made on several specific grounds or on general grounds; that is, a new trial is in the interest of justice. Court rules or statutes may enumerate the specific grounds on which this motion may be based.

SENTENCING

After a guilty verdict, the court imposes a **sentence**, which may or may not involve a jury recommendation to the judge. In some jurisdictions, the jury determines the sentence. In others, the jury is permitted to make a sentencing recommendation, but the judge is not required to follow it, although there are exceptions, such as in capital cases. The jury must determine all issues of fact, as noted below.

Frequently, the sentencing process takes place at a later hearing to allow time for presentence reports. The court may hold an extensive sentencing hearing, or the judge may impose a sentence without a hearing, depending on the rules of the jurisdiction and, in some cases, the preferences of the judge. Sentencing is an important stage, and in recent years it has come under intense scrutiny by the public and the media, as well as by the courts.

The Concept and Process of Sentencing

A *sentence* is a term of punishment imposed by a court on a convicted offender. Sentencing is one of the most controversial topics in criminal justice systems. It can be one of the simplest or one of the most complex processes. Sentencing involves numerous people, ranging from the legislators who formulate sentencing laws to the probation officers who compile the presentence reports judges use in making sentence decisions.

An understanding of sentencing is complicated because sentencing differs significantly from state to state, from court to court within a state, from county to county, and even from time to time within any of these jurisdictions. Sentencing policies in the federal system differ from those in the states. Attitudes toward what is and is not appropriate in sentencing also differ.

Sentencing Strategies

Four main strategies are used for sentencing: indeterminate, presumptive, mandatory, and determinate sentences. Most states use a combination of these.

An **indeterminate sentence** involves legislative specifications of sentence ranges that permit judges to exercise discretion in determining actual sentences. In its purest form, the indeterminate sentence would be from one day to life, but usually, it involves legislative specification of a maximum and minimum term for each offense. For example, if the legislative sentence for armed robbery is not more than 25 or less than 10 years, judges have discretion to set the sentence at any point in between.

Another sentencing strategy is the **presumptive sentence**. In presumptive sentencing, the normal sentence is specified for each offense, but judges are permitted to deviate from that norm. Some jurisdictions require that any deviation from a presumptive sentence be accompanied by written reasons for the deviation. Furthermore, the law may specify which conditions and circumstances may be considered for deviating from the presumptive sentence.

A **mandatory sentence** is one that must be imposed upon conviction. Mandatory sentences are specified by state legislatures (or by Congress for the federal system) and usually involve a prison term. The mandatory approach leaves the judge no discretion in sentencing.

In recent years, a popular approach in many jurisdictions (including federal) has been the statutory requirement of imposing mandatory minimum sentences. Generally, these sentences are long, and, in recent years, they have become highly controversial, as noted in **Supplement 8.8**. Recent changes in the practice are discussed later in this chapter.

Another type of sentencing strategy is the **determinate sentence**, which requires a specific sentence for a particular crime, although the trial judge may have the option of suspending that sentence or imposing probation (or some other sanction, such as work service) rather than a jail or prison term. However, once the judicial sentence is imposed, the parole board does not have the discretion to reduce the sentence by offering early parole. The determinate sentencing scheme may involve a provision for mandatory parole after a specified portion of the determinate sentence has been served. It may include a provision for sentence reduction based on **good-time credits** the inmate earned.

Determinate sentences may include a provision for raising or lowering the sentence if there are **mitigating circumstances** or **aggravating circumstances**. For example, the determinate sentence for rape might be 15 years; however, if a weapon is used to threaten the victim, there may be a provision for increasing the penalty. Likewise, if there are circumstances that reduce the moral culpability of the offender, the sentence might be reduced. An example is extreme passion in a homicide, as when the accused finds his or her spouse in bed with another and, in a fit of anger, kills that person.

For less serious offenses, particularly when the case is not tried before a jury, the judge may pronounce sentence immediately upon finding the defendant guilty or upon accepting a guilty plea. Sentencing may also be immediate when the judge has no option but to assess the statutory penalty. Sentencing may be set for a future date but may not involve any special investigations, with the judge taking recommendations from the defense and the prosecution. However, the trend is toward having a separate sentencing hearing. After the trial verdict, the judge sets a formal date for sentencing, leaving sufficient time to consider appropriate presentence investigations. It is common in capital cases to have a separate hearing on the issue of whether the defendant will be sentenced to death, life, or a term of years, depending on the legislative options in that jurisdiction.

The **presentence investigation (PSI)** may include information based on interviews with the defendant, family, friends, employers, or others who might have facts pertinent to a sentencing decision. Medical, psychiatric, or other reports from experts may be included. Information on prior offenses, work records, school records, associates, pastime activities, attitudes, willingness to cooperate, and problems with alcohol or other drugs might be included as well.

If the PSI is conducted thoroughly, it is a time-consuming job. In some jurisdictions, the reports are prepared by the Department of Corrections (DOC). Most of these departments have diagnostic facilities and may be better equipped to conduct the investigations than probation officers, who conduct the PSI in some jurisdictions.

After the sentencing hearing comes the sentencing decision. Judges decide most sentences (unless the legislature has removed all judicial discretion), but in some cases (usually in serious offenses, such as first-degree murder), juries have sentencing power. The judge is not required to follow the jury's recommendation in all jurisdictions, although U.S. Supreme Court decisions place some restrictions on judges. Many of those decisions relate to sentencing in capital cases; they are complex, extensive, and beyond the scope of this text, but **Supplement 8.9** summarizes some of the major cases.

In addition to constitutional requirements, a sentencing decision is regulated by procedural rules. In jurisdictions in which the jury has sentencing power, the judge instructs the jury concerning the law and its application to sentencing. Many factors might be considered in the sentencing decision. Those factors may be designated by statute. Some states have formalized and restricted the factors that may be considered. Many require that evidence of aggravating or mitigating circumstances be presented. Some jurisdictions use sentencing formulas, which indicate the weight to be given to specific factors, such as the nature of the crime.

If the defendant has been convicted of more than one offense, the judge usually has the authority to determine whether the sentences are to be imposed concurrently or consecutively. With a **concurrent sentence**, the defendant satisfies the terms of all sentences at the same time. For example, if the defendant is sentenced to 20 years for each of three counts of armed robbery, the total number of years served will be 20 if the sentences are concurrent. With a **consecutive sentence**, the defendant will have to serve 60 years (unless the term is reduced by parole or good-time credits or is commuted or pardoned). Most multiple sentences are imposed concurrently. The U.S. Supreme Court has held that states may permit judges rather than juries to determine whether sentences must be served consecutively or concurrently.[14]

After the sentence is determined, the judge reads the sentence to the defendant, and the sentence is recorded in court records. If the sentence involves incarceration, the defendant generally is taken into custody immediately (or returned to custody if he or she had not been released before trial). The judge may allow the defendant some time to prepare for incarceration, but that rarely occurs and generally applies only in the cases of government officials or other people who might, in the eyes of the judge, need time to get their affairs in order and who would not be a danger to society or flee the jurisdiction.

In any of the sentencing strategies, the power to determine sentence length may be altered by other factors. Power may be given to the governor to commute a sentence of life to a specified term of years or to commute a death sentence to a life sentence. The governor may also have the power to **pardon** an offender. In the case of a federal crime, the pardoning power resides with the president of the United States. Such pardons are often controversial, as illustrated by negative reactions to those issued by Jerry Brown on December 24, 2018 before he left the governorship of California. Brown granted pardons to 143 and issued 131 commutations, including some to those who faced deportation.

Victims' Participation in Sentencing

In some jurisdictions, crime victims are permitted to express their concerns and opinions on issues such as sentencing. The role of victims in sentencing was limited by the U.S. Supreme Court in *Booth v. Maryland*, a 1987 decision in which the Court held that the defendant's constitutional rights are violated when Victim Impact

Statements (VIS) contain information such as the severe emotional impact of the crime on the family, the personal characteristics of the victim, and the family members' opinions and characterizations of the crime and the offender. When the issue arose in the sentencing phase of a capital case, the Court emphasized its concern that, in such serious cases, decisions should be based on reason, not on emotion. Thus, the jury should not hear this type of information, which "can serve no other purpose than to inflame the jury and divert it from deciding the case on the relevant evidence concerning the crime and the defendant."[15]

In 1991, the U.S. Supreme Court reversed itself on the ruling in *Booth* and another case. In *Payne v. Tennessee*, the Court ruled that a VIS may be used at capital sentencing hearings.

> A state may legitimately conclude that evidence about the victim and about the impact of the murder on the victim's family is relevant to the jury's decision as to whether or not the death penalty should be imposed.[16]

In 1995, the Washington Supreme Court upheld that state's provision for admitting victim impact evidence during the sentencing phase of a capital trial. The U.S. Supreme Court refused to hear an appeal, thus permitting the lower court decision to stand.[17]

Capital Punishment

A form of punishment that was used extensively in the past is **capital punishment**. Over the years, capital punishment has been in and out of favor, with abolition movements beginning in the 1700s, gaining momentum in the late 1800s, and leading to actual abolition of the death penalty in many states during the twentieth century, only to have it reinstated in some jurisdictions. But in 2018, for the fourth year in a row, death sentences and executions were low in number, with the Death Penalty Information Center's December report stating that support for the death penalty is eroding; Washington becoming the twentieth state to abolish the death penalty, and a Gallup poll finding that only 49 percent of Americans believe the death penalty is applied fairly, "the lowest level in the 18 years that Gallup has asked that question."[18]

Other changes regarding capital punishment that have occurred recently have been noted in the media, such as the 2019 announcement that newly elected California governor Gavin Newsome issued a moratorium on the death penalty in his state. That decision means that the 737 people on California's death row received a stay of execution.

Supplement 8.10 presents a brief history of recent developments in the execution of adults (the issue of executing juveniles is discussed in Chapter 12), covering such as the constitutionality of execution methods, the constitutionality of delays, and the execution of persons who are mentally challenged.

One of the current issues regarding capital punishment concerns the difficulty states are having obtaining the drugs they use for lethal injections. One problem is that those in charge of manufacturing the drugs are concerned about being associated with executions and thus wish to remain anonymous. In July 2014, a panel of the Ninth Circuit Court of Appeals, in a divided vote (2-1) became the first federal court to rule that a defendant has a legal right to know the source of the drugs to be used in a forthcoming execution. The State of Arizona appealed to the full court for a rehearing. The panel's ruling was issued just four days before the plaintiff was scheduled for execution. A federal public defender successfully led the challenge for Joseph Wood in his claim that the state's refusal to name the source of the drugs violated his First Amendment right to have access to public proceedings. According to the two members of the panel, the state's secrecy "ignores the ongoing and intensifying debate over lethal injection . . . and the importance of providing specific and detailed information about how safely and reliably the death penalty is administered." The entire Ninth Circuit upheld the stay; the U.S. Supreme Court overturned the stay.[19] Wood was executed on July 23, 2014.

The number of executions from 1976 through May 31, 2019, is graphed by year in Figure 8.1, with the race of those executed presented in Figure 8.2, and the race of death penalty case victims graphed in Figure 8.3.

Another point about capital punishment is critical: the number of death row inmates who have been exonerated because new evidence pointed to the fact that they did not commit the crimes for which they were given the death sentence. Death row exonerations by state are graphed in Figure 8.4.

The large number of exonerations of death row inmates raises the issue of the qualifications of attorneys who represent them. Generally, those attorneys should have additional training, referred to in legal circles as *death penalty qualified*. But in 2016, in *Elmore v. Holbrook*, the U.S. Supreme Court refused to hear a case involving the issue of a defense attorney who had never tried a death penalty case and whether that constituted ineffective assistance of counsel given the evidence the attorney did not introduce. Justice Sotomayor

Figure 8.1

Number of Executions Since 1976: 1499

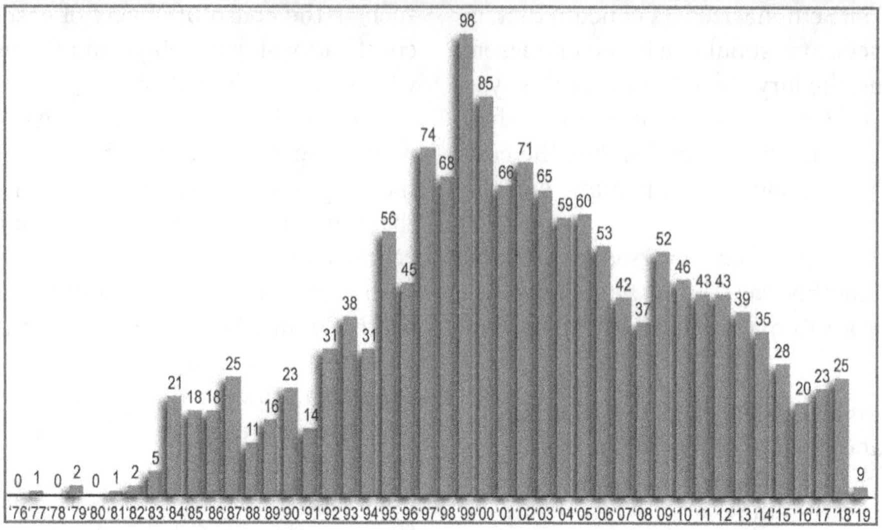

Source: Death Penalty Information Center, "Facts About the Death Penalty" (updated May 31, 2019), https://files.deathpenaltyinfo.org/legacy/documents/FactSheet.pdf, accessed June 15, 2019.

Figure 8.2

Race of Defendants Executed

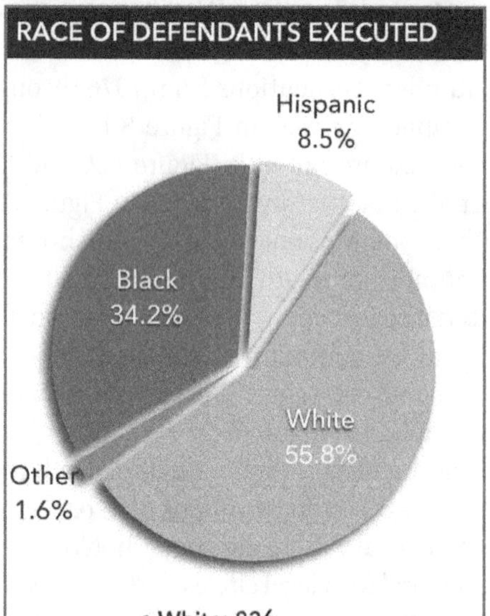

Source: Death Penalty Information Center, "Facts About the Death Penalty" (updated May 31, 2019), https://files.deathpenaltyinfo.org/legacy/documents/FactSheet.pdf, accessed June 15, 2019.

Figure 8.3

Race of Victims in Death Penalty Cases

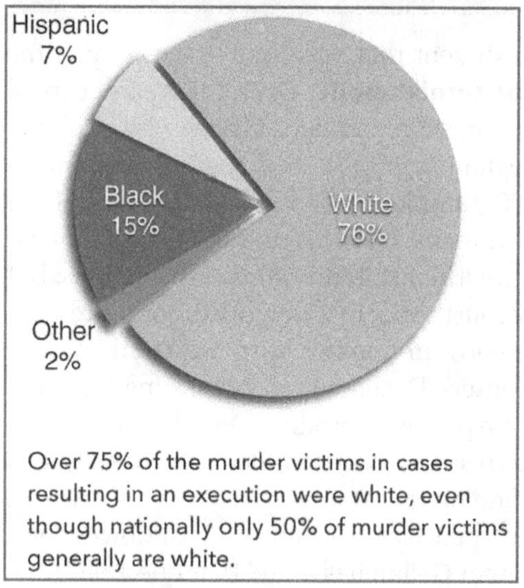

Source: Death Penalty Information Center, "Facts About the Death Penalty" (updated May 31, 2019), https://files.deathpenaltyinfo.org/legacy/documents/FactSheet.pdf, accessed June 15, 2019.

Figure 8.4

Capital Punishment and Innocence

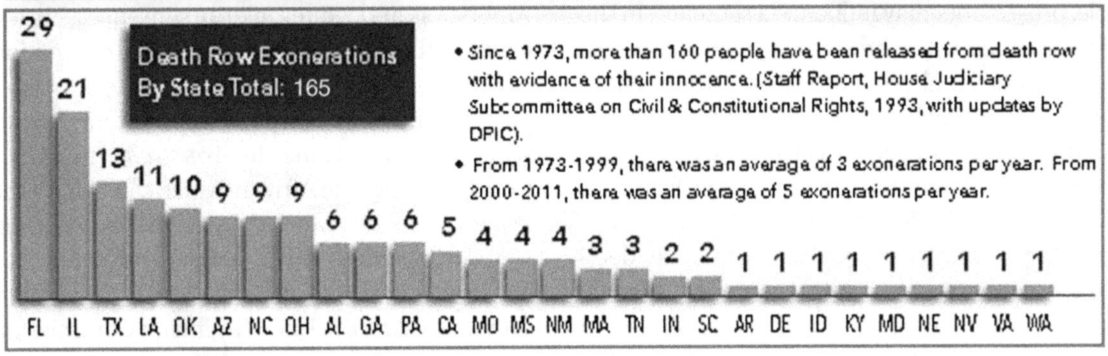

Death Row Exonerations
By State Total: 165
• Since 1973, more than 160 people have been released from death row with evidence of their innocence. (Staff Report, House Judiciary Subcommittee on Civil & Constitutional Rights, 1993, with updates by DPIC).
• From 1973-1999, there was an average of 3 exonerations per year. From 2000-2011, there was an average of 5 exonerations per year.
29 21 13 11 10 9 9 9 6 6 6 5 4 4 4 3 3 2 2 1 1 1 1 1 1 1 1 1
FL IL TX LA OK AZ NC OH AL GA PA CA MO MS NM MA TN IN SC AR DE ID KY MD NE NV VA WA

Source: Death Penalty Information Center, "Facts About the Death Penalty" (updated May 31, 2019), https://files.deathpenaltyinfo.org/legacy/documents/FactSheet.pdf, accessed June 15, 2019.

dissented, joined by Justice Ginsburg, and declared that the evidence introduced in the penalty phase of the case fell well below the bare minimum guaranteed by the Constitution.... Had the jury known that Elmore—who had never before been convicted of a crime of violence and felt searing remorse for the heinous act he committed—might be brain damaged, it might have sentenced him to life rather than death.[20]

Finally, the issue of the mental capability of a person sentenced to death continues to be at issue. **Supplement 8.9** mentions the case of *Atkins v. Virginia*,[21] in which the U.S. Supreme Court held that it is unconstitutional to execute a mentally retarded (but not necessarily mentally ill) person. The Court has visited this issue in other cases since, including *Moore v. Texas*,[22] decided in 2017, in which the Court remanded Moore's case after noting that the Texas court crafted "a constitutional holding based solely on what it deems to be medical consensus about intellectual disability [the term the Court recently adopted after dropping the earlier term it used: mentally retarded]. The Court emphasized that the medical profession should determine that consensus and courts should determine "the content of the Eighth Amendment." The Texas Court of Criminal Appeals, on remand, again found that Moore was not intellectually disabled. The U.S. Supreme Court again heard an appeal and on February 19, 2019, held that Moore had shown that "he is a person with intellectual disability." Chief Justice John R. Roberts, Jr. in a brief concurring opinion, stated that it was still difficult to know how to apply the *Atkins* holding, but it was clear that the Texas Court of Criminal Appeals had not applied *Atkins* properly in Moore's case. Justice Samuel Alito wrote a dissenting opinion, in which he was joined by Justices Clarence Thomas and Neil M. Gorsuch. The result is that the criteria for determining whether defendants should not be executed due to mental challenges remains unclear.[23]

In terms of data concerning mental disability and the death penalty, a late 2018 report noted that "11 of the 25 people executed in 2018 had significant evidence of mental illness; at least nine had evidence of intellectual disability or brain damage."[24]

Sentencing Issues: A Sample

There are many issues in sentencing. This section considers four: (1) sentence disparity; (2) three-strikes legislation; (3) truth-in-sentencing legislation; and (4) treatment practices.

Sentence Disparity

Although there is concern about alleged **sentence disparity**, its meaning is not clear. Some use the term to refer to any differences that they think are unfair or inappropriate. Thus, the differences between legislatively determined sentences in two jurisdictions might be viewed as disparate. Others limit the definition of the term to the differences in sentences imposed by judges in similar cases. Some include any differences; others look to the circumstances surrounding the crime before determining whether sentences are disparate.

Sentence disparity may stem from legislative, judicial, or administrative decisions. Sentence length may vary from jurisdiction to jurisdiction because legislatures establish different terms for the same crime. Legislatures may differ with regard to whether a defendant with multiple sentences serves them concurrently or consecutively. Legislative sentences may be disparate if within a system there are sentences that are considered unfair. Sentence disparity may also result from decisions made by others. For example, prosecutors may influence a sentence. In the plea bargaining process, the prosecutor may offer a deal that involves a lesser penalty for one offense if the offender pleads guilty to another or to several other offenses. Sentencing disparity may occur because juries have considerable discretion in their power to determine facts that will impact sentences, as noted in previous discussions.

Administrative discretion may also result in decisions that are perceived as creating sentence disparity. For example, although parole has been abolished in some states, where it does exist, parole authorities have great latitude in deciding actual time served. Even when the legislature specifies by statute the percentage of a term that must be served before an offender is eligible for parole, the parole board has the power to determine when, if ever, that person will be released before the end of the actual sentence (parole is discussed in Chapter 11).

Most of the allegations of sentence disparity have involved the variables of race, ethnicity, and gender. Earlier studies examining these variables in sentencing did not agree on whether discrimination existed and, if it did, to what extent and why. Modern scholars do not agree either, and the debate continues. A few studies are illustrative. First, we look at race and ethnicity and sentencing.

Some criminologists argue that criminal justice systems are racist in sentencing. Two criminologists, in their explanation of radical criminology (an approach to the study of crime and criminals that suggests a connection between economic reality and social phenomena, such as racism), referred to numerous studies that support this position.

> These studies show that minorities, particularly blacks, are discriminated against in the sentencing process. Blacks receive longer sentences than whites for the same crime, and blacks who victimize whites receive longer sentences than blacks who victimize blacks. Recent research . . . on rape indicates that this bias remains in force today.[25]

In an earlier publication, a noted law professor reported his analysis of jail and prison data and concluded that racial disparities in sentencing had "steadily gotten worse since 1980." The professor alleged that drug arrests are easier to make in inner-city minority areas than in predominately middle- and upper-class areas. Increased penalties have been aimed primarily at the illegal use of crack cocaine, used by minorities more frequently than powder cocaine, a similar drug purchased primarily by whites.[26]

In *United States v. Armstrong*, African-American defendants challenged the differences between African Americans and whites in drug sentences. The defendants claimed that they were denied equal protection because of the higher sentences (approximately 100 to 1) for the illegal distribution or possession of crack, as compared with powder cocaine. In *Armstrong*, the U.S. Supreme Court held that the African-American defendants had not shown racial discrimination despite presenting evidence that 88.3 percent of all federal prosecutions for crack cocaine violations were against African Americans.[27] In previous years, the U.S. Sentencing Commission had recommended changing the 100-to-1 ratio; some changes were made, and finally, in 2010, a new statute changed the ratio. The Fair Sentencing Act of 2010 is discussed in Spotlight 8.2.

A 2013 publication, reporting on an analysis of 50 of the studies of race and sentencing published in refereed journals since the late 1990s, along with updated data on race and sentencing, led the researcher to conclude that "there are good reasons to be skeptical of the conclusions drawn from many of the existing studies." That is not to suggest that racial disparity in sentencing does not exist but, rather, that research has not identified the *why* and other aspects of that diversity.[28]

Racial stereotypes may also play a role in sentencing. In 2017, the U.S. Supreme Court considered this issue in a capital sentencing case. *Buck v. Davis* involved a black defendant in Texas who alleged that his public defender did not provide him with adequate assistance of counsel when he called an alleged expert to testify. One prerequisite for assessing the death penalty in Texas is that the convicted murderer is likely to be violent in the future. The expert (a psychologist) testified that Duane Buck probably would not be violent in the future but that he was statistically more likely to commit future violent acts because he is black. According to the appellate attorney for Mr. Buck:

> This evidence encouraged the sentencing jury to make its critical future dangerousness decision which was a prerequisite for a death sentence and the central disputed issue at sentencing based not on the individual facts and circumstances of Mr. Buck's crime or his life history but instead based on a false and pernicious group-based stereotype.[29]

This case was about effective assistance of counsel, and the Court discussed the requirements for that charge

Spotlight 8.2

The Fair Sentencing Act of 2010

For years scholars, sentencing organizations such as The Sentencing Project, and many other agencies and organizations, including the U.S. Sentencing Commission (which establishes sentencing guidelines for federal crimes), as well as President Barack Obama, urged Congress to reduce the ratio of penalties for crack and powder cocaine. The argument was that the 100-to-1 ratio discriminated against minorities, who are more often arrested and convicted for possessing crack cocaine, while whites are more often arrested for possessing powder cocaine.

On July 28, 2010, Congress enacted The Fair Sentencing Act of 2010, S. 1789, which was signed by President Barack Obama on August 3, 2010. The act became effective on November 1, 2010. The major changes of this act involve penalties for convictions for possession of crack compared to powder cocaine. The 100-to-1 ratio (50 grams of crack and 5 kilograms of powder cocaine both trigger a 10-year prison sentence) was changed to an 18-to-1 ratio. The statute eliminates the five-year mandatory minimum prison sentence for simple possession of crack cocaine. It increases penalties for drug offenses that involve vulnerable victims, violence, and other aggravating factors. It requires that data be kept on the effectiveness of drug courts that are federally funded.[1]

The statute does not state whether it is retroactive. Normally, statutes are not applied retroactively unless Congress indicates that is its wish. The U.S. Supreme Court held that Congress did so intend and stated its reasons in *Dorsey v. United States*, decided in 2012.[2]

In 2013, the U.S. Sentencing Commission published data on the implementation of the Fair Sentencing Act. The sentences of over 7,300 federal inmates were shortened as a result of the law. The average reduction was 29 months. According to the news media, that represented a total of 16,000 years at a cost of approximately half a billion dollars. In 2015, the Sentencing Commission issued another statement after its analysis of the results of the FSA, stating in conclusion:

> [T]he FSA reduced the disparity between crack and powder cocaine sentences, reduced the federal prison population, and appears to have resulted in fewer federal prosecutions for crack cocaine. All this occurred while crack cocaine use continued to decline.[3]

The Sentencing Commission and President Obama requested that the 18-to-1 reduction be changed to 1 to 1. That did not occur.

1. The Fair Sentencing Act of 2010, 124 Stat. 2372 (2014).
2. *Dorsey v. United States*, 567 U.S. 260 (2012).
3. The full reports are available from The U.S. Sentencing Commission's *Preliminary Crack Retroactivity Data Report: Fair Sentencing Act*, http://www.ussc.gov, accessed August 9, 2013; *Report to the Congress: Impact of the Fair Sentencing Act of 2010* (August 2015), https://www.ussc.gov, accessed October 11, 2018.

---

and then concluded that "[i]t would be patently unconstitutional for a state to argue that a defendant is liable to be a future danger because of his race. No competent defense attorney would introduce such evidence about his client.... Buck has demonstrated prejudice."

In terms of data, black males are more likely to be incarcerated than white males, and in 12 states more than one-half of male inmates are black. In 11 states, "at least 1 in 20 adult black males is in prison."[30]

One final case: In October 2018, the Washington Supreme Court held that the state's death penalty statute was unconstitutional because, in its application, it discriminated against defendants based on race. The court unanimously held that all death penalty sentences should be converted to life in prison due to the unconstitutionality of the statute, which served no penological goal due to its unequal application. Brief excerpts are included in Spotlight 8.3.

It has also been alleged that sentence disparity is related to an offender's gender. Some researchers say that women are treated differentially at every stage in U.S. criminal justice systems and that this treatment is sexist; that is, women are discriminated against *because* of their gender.

Spotlight 8.3

Washington State Abolishes the Death Penalty

On October 11, 2018, the State of Washington became the twentieth state to outlaw capital punishment, ruling that the state's statute was unconstitutional under the state's constitution because its imposition of the provision constituted racial bias. The court's ruling was unanimous.[1] Here are a few of the court's statements in the case.

STATE v. GREGORY
2018 Wash. LEXIS 696 (October 11, 2018), cases and citations omitted

Washington's death penalty laws have been declared unconstitutional not once, not twice, but three times. And today, we do so again. None of these prior decisions held that the death penalty is per se unconstitutional. Nor do we. The death penalty is invalid because it is imposed in an arbitrary and racially biased manner....

The most important consideration is whether the evidence shows that race has a meaningful impact on imposition of the death penalty. We make this determination by way of legal analysis, not pure science....

Given the evidence before this court and our judicial notice of implicit and overt racial bias against black defendants in this state, we are confident that the association between race and the death penalty is *not* attributed to random chance....

The arbitrary and race based imposition of the death penalty cannot withstand the "evolving standards of decency that mark the progress of a maturing society." ... When the death penalty is imposed in an arbitrary and racially biased manner, society's standards of decency are even more offended....

Given our conclusion that the death penalty is imposed in an arbitrary and racially biased manner, it logically follows that the death penalty fails to serve penological goals.

1. Debra Cassens Weiss, "Washington Supreme Court Strikes Down State Death Penalty as Racially Biased," *American Bar Association Journal* (October 11, 2018), http://www.abajournal.com, accessed October 12, 2018.

Others conclude that the system is more lenient toward women than toward men at every level and that, in particular, women receive lighter sentences than men for the same offenses. That, too, must be analyzed in terms of the legal factors courts may consider in sentencing, such as prior convictions and the seriousness of the current offense. It is argued that, when these factors are analyzed, there is little or no evidence of gender bias in sentencing.

In one of his earlier articles on gender and sentencing, Darrell J. Steffensmeier reviewed the empirical evidence comparing the sentencing of men and women and concluded that, although preferential treatment of women exists, it is of small magnitude.[31]

In a later study, Steffensmeier and his colleagues analyzed gender and imprisonment decisions during a two-year period in Pennsylvania. They found support for earlier research, concluding that, in general, women received more lenient sentences than men. However, unlike some of their predecessors, these scholars concluded that the differences were due to "the type or seriousness of the crime committed and the defendant's prior record, not the defendant's gender (or, for that matter, age, race, or other background/contextual variables)."[32]

The latest official sentencing data show that in 2017, more men than women were incarcerated, with women constituting only approximately 7 percent of the total U.S. prison population. The imprisonment rate for black females was almost double that of white females. Women were more frequently than men sentenced for drug and property offenses.[33]

What can be done to control sentence disparity? Most allegations of sentence disparity are aimed at judges, and many of the recent changes in sentencing laws have been enacted to control or remove judicial sentencing discretion. One of the main methods is to enact sentencing guidelines, which are viewed as a way to control discretion without abolishing it, while correcting the extreme disparity that can result from individualized sentencing.

Basically, guidelines work as follows: A judge has an offender to sentence. Without guidelines, the judge may consider the offender's background, the nature of the offense, and other variables. When guidelines are available, presumably the relevance of these and other variables has been researched. Thus, the judge has a benchmark of an appropriate penalty in such circumstances. However, the judge may decide that it is reasonable in a given case to deviate from the guidelines; in that situation, reasons should be given.

Sentencing guidelines may be based on an empirical analysis of what *has* been done in the jurisdiction, not a philosophy of what *ought* to be done. Sentencing guidelines may be based on what it is thought *should* be done. This may occur in a variety of ways. The guidelines may be recommended by a committee and accepted and thus mandated by the legislature, or they may be adopted by judges to apply to their jurisdictions.

Sentencing guidelines have been challenged at both the federal and state levels. The federal judiciary reacted sternly to a law enacted on April 30, 2003 as a part of the PROTECT (Prosecutorial Remedies and Other Tools to End the Exploitation of Children Today) Act of 2003. Among other provisions, the PROTECT Act limits the cases in which a federal judge may issue a lighter sentence than the federal sentencing guidelines, gives Congress (without the permission of the sentencing judge) access to certain documents from the case, and requires the reporting of lighter sentences. The act also requires that, when a federal court of appeals reviews a sentencing decision of a federal district court, it must do so *de novo*, which means anew, as if the hearing had not been held before. A number of federal judges protested the new law and called for its repeal, with some retiring rather than enforce the law. In September 2003, the Judicial Conference of the United States, which is headed by the U.S. Supreme Court chief justice (at that time, William H. Rehnquist) and includes the 27 federal judges who make policy for the federal judiciary, called for a repeal of the law.[34]

In January 2004, Chief Justice Rehnquist focused his annual state of the judiciary address on the PROTECT Act. The chief justice stated that the law "could appear to be an unwarranted and ill-considered effort to intimidate individual judges in the performance of their judicial duties." The chief justice continued by declaring, "It seems that the traditional interchange between the Congress and the judiciary broke down" when the law was passed without any formal input from the judiciary. The chair of the House Judiciary Committee said there was no breakdown in communication. Congress knew the judiciary would oppose the bill, but it was necessary because federal judges were using downward departures in applying the federal sentencing guidelines.[35] But significant changes have been made in the impact of the federal sentencing guidelines as a result of recent decisions by the U.S. Supreme Court holding that the guidelines are advisory, not compulsory. Some portions of the PROTECT Act were upheld in 2008.[36]

The proposal to reduce or remove judicial sentencing discretion was manifested primarily in the adoption of determinate sentencing, which began in the 1970s. One of the most rigid of the new determinate sentencing statutes was that of California, the state that pioneered the indeterminate sentence and that used it most extensively.[37] The California statute removed the rehabilitation philosophy and substituted punishment as the reason for incarceration. It specified that sentences were not to be disparate and that defendants charged with similar offenses should receive similar sentences. The judge may decide on the basis of aggravating or mitigating circumstances to raise or lower the presumed sentence, but written reasons must be given for deviating from it. However, in January 2007, in *Cunningham v. California*, the U.S. Supreme Court held that this sentencing provision is unconstitutional because it violates a defendant's right to a jury trial under the Sixth Amendment (see Appendix A).[38]

Three Strikes Legislation

The emphasis on reducing sentence disparity has been manifested most clearly in the national focus on the habitual offender, summarized in the 1994 political slogan **three strikes and you're out**. The phrase figured prominently at the state and national level after 12-year-old Polly Klaas was kidnapped from her home in 1993 while her parents and her friends (who were attending her slumber party) were sleeping. Polly was sexually assaulted and murdered. Richard Allen Davis, who had two prior kidnap convictions, was convicted and sentenced to death for the crimes against Polly. California led in the enactment of three-strikes legislation and was quickly followed by most states and the federal government. But California's legislation was one of the toughest. It provided for a mandatory sentence for all persons convicted of a third felony, and that third strike could be any felony. The first two felonies, however, must be serious or violent ones. California also provided harsher penalties for two strikes.

In 2004, California voters failed to pass Proposition 66, which would have required that the third strike for the three-strikes legislation must be a serious felony. The state's prison populations skyrocketed, and by 2012, the state's voters demanded a change. They voted to require that the third strike must be a violent or serious felony to trigger a life sentence. But, in 2003, the U.S. Supreme Court decided two three-strikes cases, including *Ewing v. California*,[39] and upheld the legislation in question. These cases are critical ones in sentencing and, despite changes in state statutes in recent years, they remain good law. Thus, a brief excerpt from the decision upholding California's stricter version of three strikes is included in **Supplement 8.11**.

In November 2014, California voters passed Proposition 47, known as the Safe Neighborhoods and Schools Act, which took effect on November 5, 2014. Among other provisions, this statute permits persons convicted of certain drug and theft felonies, which were reclassified as misdemeanors with shorter sentences, to apply for resentencing "unless the court, in its discretion, determines that resentencing the petitioner would pose an unreasonable risk of danger to public safety." The act mandates that "non-serious, nonviolent crimes" are to be reclassified as misdemeanors rather than felonies unless the offender had previous convictions for murder, rape, certain other sex offenses, or specified gun crimes. The law requires a thorough review of each applicant for resentencing prior to any resentencing.[40]

Truth in Sentencing

Another current trend in sentencing is **truth in sentencing**. These laws require that inmates serve a specified percentage of their sentences before they are released from prison. Most states have such laws, which are encouraged by federal government grants. The Violent Offender Incarceration and Truth in Sentencing Incentive Grants Act of 1995 offers states some grants for prison construction and operation but provides that those states must require violent offenders to serve 85 percent of their sentences.[41]

Some states require that murderers (or other specified types of offenders) must serve all of their time before they are released. For example, an Illinois statute provides that "a prisoner who is serving a term of imprisonment for first degree murder shall receive no good conduct credit and shall serve the entire sentence imposed by the court." The statute then specifies that inmates serving sentences for certain crimes (such as aggravated kidnapping and attempted first-degree murder) may receive only 4.5 days of good conduct credit (toward early release) per month. Those serving time for crimes that are not enumerated may receive one day of good conduct credit for each day they serve.[42]

Treatment and Sentencing

The final sentencing issue this chapter addresses is that of treatment. After years of "locking them up and throwing away the key," some jurisdictions are beginning to review that approach and back away. The recent changes have come about because of the increased costs of incarceration at a time when government budgets are being cut significantly. There has also been some concern that the punitive approach, at least in some cases, such as drug offenses, is less effective than a treatment approach.

By 2003, with most states facing severe budget cuts, many state legislatures had begun changing sentencing policies to reduce the number of inmates on the states' payrolls. According to one professional organization, "[w]ith the third straight year of budget shortfalls looming and most of the easy cuts already enacted, services once considered untouchable were falling prey to legislators desperate for additional savings."[43]

The U. S. economic situation has improved, but closer scrutiny is still given to the extremely high criminal justice expenditures. In an effort to reduce prison populations and thus costs, states and the federal government are looking at alternatives to incarcerating large numbers of people for long periods of time. The recent major attempts at the federal level consist of the Smarter Sentencing Act of 2015, which would significantly reduce mandatory minimum sentences for some nonviolent drug offenses, provide for early release of thousands of inmates who were sentenced under the disproportionate sentencing law regarding cocaine, and give judges more discretion to sentence below mandatory minimums in some cases. The Recidivism Reduction and Public Safety Act would permit early release of some inmates who earned credits by participating in drug treatment, education, and job training programs. These proposed statutes did not pass, however, and despite calls for sentencing reform to reduce the mass incarceration that has characterized the United States, significant progress has not occurred although some jurisdictions have reduced sentences for minor drug offenses. Both former president Barack Obama and current president Donald J. Trump recognized the need for sentencing reform and other changes to combat the drug crisis, and both issued executive orders, but most would agree that the orders had little effect. President Obama's 2015 National Drug Control Strategy is reprinted in **Supplement 8.12**. President Trump's executive order issued in 2017 is presented in **Supplement 8.13**.

Early indications were that the Department of Justice under the Trump administration would pursue a strict policy of following the current federal sentencing guidelines. The directive issued to that effect on May 10, 2017, by the Office of the U.S. Attorney General is reproduced in **Supplement 8.14**. It is not clear what effect the firing in 2018 of Jeff Sessions, the attorney general at that time, would have on sentencing. However, a bipartisan bill passed Congress and was signed by the president in late 2018. That law is the focus of the next section.

Recent Sentencing Reforms

For several years, numerous politicians, social scientists, and others have called for criminal justice reforms, especially sentencing reforms. Finally, in December 2018, both houses of the U.S. Congress passed, and President Donald J. Trump signed, the First Step Act of 2018, a bipartisan criminal justice reform bill enacted for the purpose of reducing recidivism after inmates are released from prison and to alter harsh sentencing policies. According to the *New York Times*, this bill represents "the most substantial changes in a generation to the tough-on-crime prison and sentencing laws that ballooned the federal prison population." The Senate vote was 87-12; the House vote was 358-36.[44]

Some of the provisions of this new statute, which pertains only to federal penal facilities, are as follows:

1. Shorten the three-strikes sentencing policies in particular.
2. Shorten other federal sentencing policies.
3. Permit the judicial bypass of some mandatory sentencing policies by making inmates eligible to qualify for "safety valves."
4. Reduce the sentencing disparity between convictions for possession of crack and powder cocaine by making the Fair Sentencing Act of 2010 retroactive.
5. Establish a risk and needs assessment system to be applied to all inmates.
6. Prohibit use of restraints on inmates during pregnancy and postpartum recovery.
7. Placement of inmates close to families.
8. Expand inmate employment through Federal Prison Industries.
9. Utilize home confinement for low-risk inmates.
10. Provide programs that permit some inmates to become eligible for time credits toward early release while prohibiting some inmates from such programs.
11. Conduct ongoing research on evidence-based programs that enhance the reduction of recidivism and other issues.
12. To the extent possible, assess the risk for recidivism for each inmate and reassess that risk periodically and reassign inmates where appropriate based on that reassessment.
13. Determine when inmates are ready for transfer to prerelease custody.
14. Allow phone and visitation privileges for inmates who are participating in evidence-based recidivism programs.
15. No longer "stack" sentences for first offenders who are convicted for possession of a firearm during commission of another federal crime.
16. Shorten mandatory minimum sentences from 20 to 15 years for serious violent crimes and drug crimes offenses.
17. Provide credits for early release for inmates who participate in vocational training, educational courses, or faith-based programs.
18. Eliminate sentences of life without parole and solitary confinement for juvenile offenders.
19. Provide for compassionate release of elderly and terminally ill inmates.
20. Support the Second Chance Act, which makes programs available to assist inmates to transition successfully back into the community upon release from custody.[45]

APPEALS AND WRITS

Defendants who have been convicted may have grounds for appealing their convictions or sentences. But appeals are limited to *issues of law*, not fact. Thus, a defendant cannot appeal a guilty verdict per se but, rather, must have a legal issue, such as a violation of state or federal constitutional rights. For example, an appealable issue might be that evidence was excluded or included in violation of existing laws or procedures.

A successful appeal does not necessarily mean that the case is over and the defendant is released from the criminal justice system. Generally, a successful appeal means that the case is sent back (remanded) to the lower court for another trial or resentencing. In most of the retrials, the defendant is again convicted. A successful appeal on a sentence—for example, the death penalty—may result in another death sentence. The difference is that, in the retrial (or resentencing), the state must not commit the errors made in the previous trial (or sentencing). On appeal, a defendant may be successful on some issues but not on others. Appendix B explains how to read an appellate court citation and defines such terms as *reversed, affirmed,* and *remanded.*

In addition to appeals, defendants may petition for a **writ**, which is a court order. A writ gives permission to do whatever was requested or orders someone to do something specific. A common writ filed by offenders is a writ of *habeas corpus*, which means "you have the body." Originally, a writ of *habeas corpus* was an order from the court to someone, such as a sheriff or a jailer, to have the person in court at a specified time and to state the legal theory under which the person was being held. Today, it is more extensive, and its use is governed by statutes, which differ from jurisdiction to jurisdiction. Often, it is used by inmates who are questioning the legality of their confinement. The writ does not question the issue of guilt or innocence but asserts that some due process rights of offenders are being violated or have been violated.

Under some circumstances, sentences may be appealed. Occasionally, a sentence is reversed, and the case is sent back for resentencing. In practice, this rarely occurs; most appellate courts show great deference to the sentences that trial judges impose. As long as the sentence is within the statutory provisions and the sentencing judge has not abused his or her discretion or shown undue prejudice, it is difficult for defendants to challenge a judicial sentence successfully. In rare cases, courts may declare a legislatively determined sentence to be in violation of the defendant's rights.

Not all inmates can afford to file appeals, however, and various programs are available to assist some of them. The Innocence Project is one of them. According to its website:

> The Innocence Project, founded in 1992 by Peter Neufeld and Barry Scheck at Cardozo School of Law, exonerates the wrongly convicted through DNA testing and reforms the criminal justice system to prevent future injustice.[46]

WRONGFUL CONVICTIONS

When criminal justice systems fail, wrongful convictions may occur. Throughout the first eight chapters of this text, we have seen examples of failures within criminal justice systems: victims do not report crimes; reporting agencies misreport their data; police arrest the wrong persons; prosecutors charge without sufficient evidence or violate discovery rules; prosecutors may not charge in cases in which the public thinks they should; defense attorneys are not adequately prepared to represent their clients; courts are overcrowded and cannot handle the caseloads, and so on. On occasion, any of these failures can lead to wrongful convictions: An innocent person is charged, convicted, and sentenced to prison. Some serve years before the mistakes are brought to light; some are never exonerated. The ultimate wrongful conviction is the execution of an innocent person. According to the Death Penalty Information Center, since 1973, 165 death row inmates were freed from death row as of May 31, 2019. For those inmates, the average number of years from sentencing to exoneration was 11.3. To qualify for inclusion on the Death Penalty Information Center's "Innocence List," defendants must have been convicted, sentenced to death and subsequently either:

- "Been **acquitted** of all charges related to the crime that placed them on death row, or
- Had all charges related to the crime that placed them on death row **dismissed** by the prosecution, or
- Been granted a complete **pardon** based on evidence of innocence."[47]

Exonerations have occurred for crimes with sentences other than the death penalty and for crimes other than murder. On July 29, 2010, Michael Anthony Green, 45, was released on bail after serving 27 years in prison, the longest in Texas history to that date, for a rape he did not commit (see again Chapter 7 and, in particular Criminal Justice Systems Dilemma 7.1 for more information on exonerations). Green was sentenced to a prison term of 75 years. He was the second Houston inmate to be exonerated and released from prison within a week. A DNA test of the jeans stored in a warehouse and worn by the victim the night of the rape excluded Green. Furthermore, four men were identified as being involved in the crime, with three of them alleged to have sexually assaulted the victim, but none could be charged because the statute of limitations had expired. Three were convicted of other charges and served time in prison; two are still in prison. Allen Wayne Porter was also released in July 2010 after he, too, was exonerated of the rape for which he was wrongfully convicted. He served 19 years.[48]

Several other recent Texas exonerations illustrate the seriousness of wrongful convictions. In 2011, Michael Morton was released from prison after serving 25 years

Michael Morton was freed from death row and released from prison after serving 25 years for the murder of his wife. He was in court when the person responsible for the murder was convicted. Morton's exoneration led to the passage of the Michael Morton Act, a Texas statute that provides additional safeguards for defendants, including the right to access of information obtained by the prosecution and relevant to the defense. Morton's prosecutor (who later became a judge), Ken Anderson, withheld information. Anderson served a brief jail term and forfeited his law license as the result of a plea arrangement in the case against him.

for his wife's murder. In Morton's case, prosecutor Ken Anderson withheld evidence that would have exonerated Morton. Anderson, who later became a judge, denied wrongdoing but accepted a plea deal in which he was required to surrender his law license; he spent nine days in jail. Morton's case and his own work led to the passage of the Michael Morton Act in 2013, an act requiring that defendants be given information that might lead to their acquittals. Morton was unable to attend that legislative session. He was in a courtroom in another city witnessing the conviction of Mark Alan Norwood, who admitted that he beat Morton's wife to death.[49]

Another recent Texas case that is unusual is that of Anthony Graves, who was released from prison after serving 18 years on death row for his wrongful convictions for murdering a family of six. This exoneree gave a portion of the $1.4 million compensation from the State of Texas to endow a scholarship in the name of the attorney who worked so diligently to free him: the Nicole B. Casarez Endowed Scholarship at the University of Texas College of Law. Casarez graduated from that law school.[50]

In 2009, the U.S. Supreme Court agreed to review an Iowa case that raised the issue of whether prosecutors have immunity for their pretrial actions with regard to a case that results in a exoneration. The Court heard oral arguments in *McGhee v. Pottawattamie County* but subsequently dismissed the case after the parties settled.[51] Criminal Justice System Dilemma 8.1 discusses the civil liability issue in wrongful conviction cases.

McGhee v. Pottawattamie County involved one of two African-American men who, as teens, were tried by an all-white jury and convicted for a 1977 murder of a retired police department captain who at the time was serving as a security guard. Both defendants were sentenced to life without parole. Terry J. Harrington was released in 2003 after the state supreme court vacated his conviction; shortly thereafter Curtis W. McGhee Jr. was released. Two years later both men filed civil claims against the prosecutors and the police, leading to several years of motions before various courts and an ultimate settlement. The defendants in this civil case settled with the plaintiffs in January 2010 for approximately $12 million.[52]

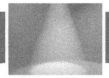

Wrongful Convictions: A Court Reacts

Considerable attention has been given to wrongful convictions now that DNA and other types of evidence are available to confirm or exclude the involvement of specific persons in specific cases. In some cases, honest mistakes are made. As the excerpt below indicates, that is not always the explanation for wrongful convictions. But whatever the reason, criminal justice systems face a serious dilemma: How do you respond to the wrongfully convicted (and usually lengthily incarcerated) person, and, in cases of willful manipulation of evidence, how do you respond to the persons who withheld evidence, tampered with evidence, or committed perjury during the proceedings? This excerpt from one case reveals explicit framing of suspects through conspiracy, intentional misconduct, and subornation of perjury (procuring another to commit perjury—false statements made willingly and knowingly under oath in a judicial proceeding). In this case, a federal court ruled that the former police detective and the retired FBI agent involved were not immune to a civil lawsuit by the plaintiffs. The two plaintiffs were released from prison; the other two involved in the wrongful convictions had subsequently died.

LIMONE v. UNITED STATES

497 F. Supp. 2d 143 (D. Mass. 2007), *aff'd*, 579 F.3d 79 (1st Cir. 2009) cases and citations omitted

The conclusions that the plaintiffs have asked me to draw—that government agents suborned perjury, framed four innocent men, conspired to keep them in jail for three decades—are so shocking that I felt obliged to analyze this complex record with special care in order that the public, and especially the parties, could be fully confident of my conclusions.

I have concluded that the plaintiffs' accusations that the United States government violated the law are proved....

Now is the time to say and say without equivocation: This "cost" to the liberty of four men, to our system of justice is not remotely acceptable. No man's liberty is dispensable. No human being may be traded for another. Our system cherishes each individual. We have fought wars over this principle. We are still fighting those wars.

Sadly, when law enforcement perverts its mission, the criminal justice system does not easily self-correct. We understand that our system makes mistakes; we have appeals to address them. But this case goes beyond mistakes, beyond the unavoidable errors of a fallible system. This case is about intentional misconduct, subornation of perjury, conspiracy, the framing of innocent men. While judges are scrutinized—our decisions made in public and appealed—law enforcement decisions like these rarely see the light of day. The public necessarily relies on the integrity and professionalism of its officials.

It took nearly thirty years to uncover this injustice. It took the extraordinary efforts of a judge, a lawyer, even a reporter, to finally bring out the facts. Proof of innocence in this democracy should not depend upon efforts as gargantuan as these....

[The court discussed the civil actions involved in the case.]

The government's position is, in a word, absurd. The law they cite does not apply to the extraordinary facts of this case. The issue here is not discretion but abuse, not independent charging decisions but the framing of four innocent men, not the failure to produce exculpatory evidence but procuring convictions by misrepresentation, not letting perjured testimony proceed uncorrected but facilitating it....

In the end I conclude that the defendant is liable to these men and their families. As to damages, plaintiffs' loss of liberty, and, in effect, a lifetime of experiences, is obviously not compensable. To the extent that damages can approach this task, my total award is One Hundred One Million, Seven Hundred Fifty Thousand, And 00/100 ($101,750,000.00) Dollars.

Summary

This chapter focused on the criminal processes during the stages of trial, sentencing, and appeal. The procedures and issues surrounding these aspects of U.S. criminal justice systems are extensive and complicated and are governed by numerous statutes and court decisions. It is not possible to state "the law" in many of these areas because often the judges of state courts and lower federal courts differ in their analyses of how statutes and constitutions apply to the facts before them.

Even when the U.S. Supreme Court agrees to hear and decide some of the controversies, often we do not know how these decisions will be applied in similar cases. Some of the Court's decisions are close, with many decided by a 5-to-4 vote. Thus, a change of one member of the Court may alter the direction of what has been called the revolution in criminal procedure of the past several decades.

It is possible, however, to state generally what happens in the trial of a criminal case and how the constitutional guarantees apply to any or all of the stages of a trial. This chapter began with a brief overview of those constitutional rights and gave closer attention to the rights that are more specific to the trial and appellate stages. The right to a speedy trial, the right to a public trial by an impartial jury, and the right to the confrontation and cross-examination of witnesses, along with defendants' right to remain silent and not be forced to testify against themselves, are crucial to understanding the implementation of the various stages of the trial. Although states have considerable freedom in establishing the procedures by which they will conduct criminal trials, they may not violate federal (or state) constitutional provisions.

The importance of constitutional rights that apply to the trial is underscored by the fact that, when those rights are violated, with only a few exceptions, the demonstrative or testimonial evidence secured as a result of those violations should be excluded from the trial. In some cases, it is not possible to prove guilt beyond a reasonable doubt without this tainted evidence; thus, the case must be dismissed.

This use of the exclusionary rule has led to considerable controversy concerning U.S. criminal justice systems. Its implications are extensive. Police may become discouraged and refuse to arrest in certain situations, thinking the case will not result in a conviction. Society may become critical of a system that appears to let the guilty go free. Potential criminals may decide to commit crimes, thinking they will not be convicted even if arrested. But those protections are to ensure that, when people are convicted of crimes, their convictions occur only after proper procedures have been followed and constitutional safeguards have been observed.

In this chapter, each stage of the criminal trial was explained and discussed, beginning with the opening of the court session in which charges against the defendant are read, through jury selection, the presentation of evidence, the final arguments, and the verdict. In all of these stages, the defense, the prosecution, and the judge are primary figures in assuring that proper procedures are followed. But following proper procedures does not end the matter. It is important to consider and reconsider the issues involved in U.S. criminal justice systems.

Some of those important issues were raised in this chapter. The right of the public to know and of the media to tell may conflict with the right of the defendant to be tried fairly and impartially. Which right should give way? The right of the defendant to a trial by jury creates enormous expenses and consumes considerable time of all participants in the criminal trial. At what point, if ever, should that right give way to cost?

The criminal trial has an enormous effect on the rest of the criminal justice system. Long criminal trials increase the backlog in civil and criminal courts and result in a greater likelihood that defendants are denied their right to a speedy trial and that society must spend more money to keep the system operating. Mistrials increase the amount of time and money devoted to trials. Failure to convict in numerous cases might lead the public to question the effectiveness of the system. Conviction of the innocent undermines the entire system, but acquittal of those whom most believe guilty has led to rioting. Repeated appeals lead many to question whether there is any finality in the law.

Throughout this discussion of the procedures and issues of the trial, however, it should be remembered that the vast majority of defendants do not go to trial. Therefore, it is important not to let the issues of the trial overshadow the need to give attention to the pretrial stages of criminal justice systems. In addition, it is important to understand and analyze what happens after defendants plead guilty or are found guilty at trial. Sentencing is a critical stage of the system and was the focus of the next major section of the chapter.

The sentencing process, ranging from the sentencing hearing to the formal stage of imposing the sentence on the convicted defendant, involves numerous issues and problems. The discussion began with an overview of the various sentencing strategies and includes the issues of whether victims should participate in this phase of criminal justice systems. Particular attention was given to the most severe sentence, that of capital punishment. The sentencing hearing was noted, along with some of the processes and issues involved in the decision-making process of sentencing.

The various types of sentences, ranging from probation to the most severe—capital punishment—were noted, followed by a discussion of the current issues and trends in sentencing. The concern with alleged sentence disparity led to a return to determinate sentences, many of which are longer than they were previously. The current concepts of three strikes and you're out and truth in sentencing embody this return to longer and more determinate sentences. More recently, however, some jurisdictions have turned to treatment rather than punishment in an attempt to balance budgets and reduce crime. Perhaps the most important of recent developments in criminal justice reforms was the enactment of the First Step Act of 2018, which was passed by Congress and signed by President Trump in December 2018. As of this writing, it is impossible to know what impact this law will have on criminal justice reforms as it will require financial backing for implementation.

The next section of the chapter focused on appeals and writs, both means by which individuals may challenge the legality of their incarceration, their sentences, or even their convictions. Finally, the chapter closed with a brief look at what happens when the system fails: wrongful convictions.

This chapter concluded our study of what happens in adult criminal court systems. As we have seen, most people accused of crimes do not go through the entire system. But for the small percentage who do, and for a society that needs and deserves protection for property as well as from violent offenders, confinement and incarceration have become the solutions. Whether they are adequate solutions is the underlying issue in the next section of the text, which includes three chapters.

Key Terms

aggravating circumstances 183
beyond a reasonable doubt 182
capital punishment 185
circumstantial evidence 180
concurrent sentence 184
consecutive sentence 184
contempt of court 179
cross-examination 180
demonstrative evidence 179
determinate sentence 183
directed verdict 181
direct evidence 180
direct examination 180
good-time credits 183
hearsay evidence 180
indeterminate sentence 183
jury 175
mandatory sentence 183
mistrial 177
mitigating circumstances 183
pardon 184
peremptory challenge 175
petit jury 175
prejudicial errors 181
presentence investigation (PSI) 184
presumption of innocence 182
presumptive sentence 183
sentence 183
sentence disparity 187
summons 177
three strikes and you're out 191
trial 174
truth in sentencing 192
voir dire 178
writ 194

Study Questions

1. Explain the importance of constitutional rights in a criminal trial.
2. What is the purpose of the Speedy Trial Act of 1974? What kinds of delays does it permit?
3. Why is the right to a public trial important to defendants? What are the legal problems and issues with public trials as far as the media are concerned?
4. Why is the jury system considered important in the United States? Should it be abolished? Why or why not? Do you think a fair and impartial jury can be selected in high-publicity trials?
5. What are the requirements for jury size and the selection of names for the jury pool? What is meant by an *impartial jury*? A *jury of peers*?
6. What is the role of the judge in controlling the conduct of defendants at trial?
7. Should people who are chosen for the jury pool be permitted to be excused from jury duty at their own request, or should all persons called be required to serve? Which, if any, requests should be honored? Which reasons should not be considered?
8. What is the significance of *Batson v. Kentucky*? Does the case apply to gender? Does it apply to any other issues?
9. How do opening statements differ from closing statements? Are both required for the prosecution and the defense?
10. Define *demonstrative evidence*. How does it differ from witness testimony as evidence?
11. What is the *hearsay rule*?
12. What is the difference between direct and circumstantial evidence?
13. What is meant by *direct examination*, *cross-examination*, and *redirect examination*?
14. Contrast the prosecution's case with that of the defense.
15. Describe the role of the judge in presenting the case to the jury.
16. Describe and evaluate the role of the jury in a criminal trial.
17. Discuss the importance of sentencing, and explain sentencing strategies.
18. Is a sentencing hearing necessary? Is it required? What occurs in a sentencing hearing? What is the value of a presentence investigation? Should the presentence investigation be available to the prosecution and the defense, as well as the judge? Why or why not?
19. What are the legal issues concerning the role of victims in the sentencing process? What is your opinion regarding the role victims should be permitted to play?
20. Should capital punishment be abolished? Why or why not?
21. What is meant by *sentence disparity*? Discuss the issues of gender and racial discrimination in sentencing.
22. What are sentencing guidelines?
23. What is the difference between *determinate* and *indeterminate sentences*?
24. What do you think will be the effect of three-strikes legislation? Evaluate the U.S. Supreme Court's recent decision on this concept. Explain the meaning of and the reason for California's Proposition 47. What is the effect of truth in sentencing?
25. Should we treat rather than punish? Discuss.
26. Explain the meaning of *appeals* and *writs*.
27. What is a wrongful conviction and what measures should be taken when it occurs?

Notes

1. *Klopfer v. North Carolina*, 386 U.S. 213 (1967).
2. USCS, Title 18, Sections 3161-3174 (2019).
3. *Sheppard v. Maxwell*, 384 U.S. 333, 356 (1966), quoting 135 N.E.2d 340, 342 (1956).
4. *Globe Newspaper Co. v. Superior Court*, 457 U.S. 596 (1982).
5. *United States v. McVeigh*, 955 F. Supp. 1281 (1997).
6. *Duncan v. Louisiana*, 391 U.S. 145 (1968).
7. *Swain v. Alabama*, 380 U.S. 202 (1965).
8. *Batson v. Kentucky*, 476 U.S. 79 (1986).
9. See *Johnson v. California*, 545 U.S. 162 (2005) and *Flowers v. Mississippi*, 240 So.3d 1082 (Miss. 2017), *reversed and remanded*, Docket No. 17-9562, 588 U.S. ____ (June 21, 2019).
10. *J.E.B. v. Alabama ex rel. T.B.*, 511 U.S. 127 (1994).
11. *SmithKline Beecham v. Abbott Laboratories*, 740 F.3d 471 (9th Cir. 2014), *rehearing en banc denied*, 759 F.3d 990 (9th Cir. June 24, 2014).
12. See *Barber v. Ponte*, 772 F.2d 982 (1st Cir. 1985) (*en banc*), *cert. denied*, 475 U.S. 1050 (1988).
13. For a discussion of defenses, see Sue Titus Reid, *Criminal Law*, 9th ed. (New York: Oxford University Press, 2013), Chapter 4, pp. 85-127; and Reid, *Criminal Law: The Essentials*, 3d ed. (New York: Oxford University Press, 2017), pp. 65-97.
14. *Oregon v. Ice*, 555 U.S. 160 (2009).
15. *Booth v. Maryland*, 482 U.S. 496 (1987), *overruled in part by Payne v. Tennessee*, 501 U.S. 808 (1991).
16. *Payne v. Tennessee*, 501 U.S. 808 (1991). The other case that was overruled is *South Carolina v. Gathers*, 490 U.S. 805 (1989).
17. *State v. Gentry*, 888 P.2d 1105 (Wash. 1995), *cert. denied*, 516 U.S. 843 (1995).
18. Cited in Lorelei Laird, "Death Sentences, Executions Stay Low for Fourth Straight Year, Report Says," *American Bar Association Journal* (December 17, 2018), http://www.abajournal.com, accessed December 17, 2018.
19. *Wood v. Ryan*, 2014 U.S. App. LEXIS 13867 (9th Cir. 2014), *cert. denied, stay denied, Ryan v. Wood*, 573 U.S. 976.
20. *Elmore v. Holbrook*, 137 S. Ct. 3 (2016).
21. *Atkins v. Virginia*, 536 U.S. 304 (2002).
22. *Moore v. Texas*, 137 S. Ct. 1039 (2017).
23. *Moore v. Texas*, 139 S. Ct. 666 (2019).
24. Laird, "Death Sentences."
25. Michael J. Lynch and W. Byron Groves, *A Primer in Radical Criminology*, 2d ed. (New York: Harper and Heston, 1989), pp. 106-107, citations omitted.
26. Michael Tonry, "Racial Politics, Racial Disparities, and the War on Crime," *Crime & Delinquency* 40 (October 1994): 483-488; see p. 475.
27. *United States v. Armstrong*, 517 U.S. 456 (1996).
28. Eric P. Baumer, "Reassessing and Redirecting Research on Race and Sentencing," *Justice Quarterly* 30(2) (April 2013): 231-281; quotation is on p. 233.
29. Transcript of the oral argument of Christina A. Swarns, Esq., on behalf of the Petitioner, case of *Buck v. Davis*, 137 S. Ct. 759 (2017).
30. Ashley Nellis, The Sentencing Project, "The Color of Justice: Racial and Ethnic Disparity in State Prisons" (June 14, 2016), http://www.sentencingproject.org, accessed October 10, 2018.
31. Darrell J. Steffensmeier, "Assessing the Impact of the Women's Movement on Sex-Based Differences in the Handling of Adult Criminal Defendants," *Crime & Delinquency* 26 (July 1980): 344357.
32. Darrell Steffensmeier et al., "Gender and Imprisonment Decisions," *Criminology* 31 (August 1993): 411-446; quotation is on p. 435.
33. Jennifer Bronson and E. Ann Carson, Bureau of Justice Statistics, "Prisoners in 2017" (April 2019), pp. 3, 15, https://www.bjs.gov, accessed April 28, 2019.
34. "In Angry Outbursts, New York's U.S. Judges Protest New Sentencing Procedures," *New York Times* (December 8, 2003), p. 25; "Judges Seek Repeal of Law on Sentencing," *New York Times* (September 24, 2003), p. 17. The PROTECT Act is codified as Public Law 108-21 (2009).
35. "Chief Justice Attacks a Law as Infringing on Judges," *New York Times* (January 1, 2004), p. 10.
36. *United States v. Williams*, 553 U.S. 285 (2008).
37. Cal. Penal Code, Section 1170 et seq. (2018).
38. *Cunningham v. California*, 549 U.S. 270 (2007).
39. *Ewing v. California*, 538 U.S. 11 (2003), footnotes and case citations omitted. See also *Lockyer v. Andrade*, 538 U.S. 63 (2003). The statute in question is Cal. Penal Code, Section 667(b) (2018).
40. Proposition 47's resentencing provision is codified at Cal. Penal Code, Section 1170.18 (2018).
41. Violent Offender Incarceration and Truth in Sentencing Incentive Grants, USCS, Title 34, Section 12104 (2019).
42. Ill. Comp. Stat., Chapter 730, Article 6, Section 5/3-6-3 (2018).
43. "Budget Deficits Forcing Changes in Sentencing, Lawmakers Say," *Criminal Justice Newsletter* (October 1, 2003), p. 8, referring to the report *Dollars and Sentences: Legislators' Views on Prisons, Punishment, and Budget Crisis*, available from the Vera Institute of Justice, 233 Broadway, 12th Floor, New York, N.Y. 10279, (212) 334-1300.
44. Debra Cassens Weiss and Jason Tashea, "Congress Passes Bipartisan Criminal Justice Reform Bill: ABA Applauds 'First Step,'" *American Bar Association Journal* (December 20, 2018), http://www.abajournal.com, accessed December 21, 2018.
45. First Step Act of 2018, Public Law 391 (2018).
46. The Innocence Project, "About Us," https://www.innocenceproject.org, accessed June 15, 2019.
47. "The Innocence List," Death Penalty Information Center, https://www.deathpenaltyinfo.org/innocence-list-those-freed-death-row, accessed June 15, 2019. Emphasis in the original.
48. "27 Years Wrongly Behind Bars to End: Houston Man Jailed Longer Than Any Exonerated Texan for a Rape He Didn't Commit," *Houston Chronicle* (July 29, 2010), p. 1.
49. Michael Morton Act, 2013 Tex. SB 1611 (2014).
50. "Exonerated Man Creating UT Law Scholarship," *Dallas Morning News* (October 25, 2013), p. 3; "Prosecutor of Ex-Death Row Inmate Could Be Disbarred," *Dallas Morning News* (July 8, 2014), p. 3.
51. *McGhee v. Pottawattamie County*, 547 F.3d 922 (8th Cir. 2008), U.S. Supreme Court *cert. dismissed by Pottawattamie County v. McGhee*, 130 S. Ct. 1047 (2010).
52. "King & Spalding Marks Start of Its 129th Year with Successful Settlement of Pro Bono Civil Rights Case," *Marketwire* (January 20, 2010), n.p.

Part IV

Confinement and Corrections

After defendants are convicted and sentenced, society is faced with the issue of what to do with them. Historically, convicted offenders were treated informally by means of various psychological and physical punishments. Physical, or corporal, punishments became severe, however, and for humanitarian and other reasons, reformers decided corporal punishment should be replaced with confinement.

Confinement facilities—formerly used primarily for detaining the accused temporarily while they awaited trial or the convicted while they awaited corporal or other forms of punishment—were viewed as places for punishment and reformation. Although many reformers saw confinement facilities as a replacement for corporal punishment, others saw them as an environment in which offenders would be reformed through work, would have time for reflection, and in some cases, would be subjected to corporal punishment.

The history of the emergence of prisons and jails as places of punishment is a fascinating study, but it is laced with controversy, idealism, and unfulfilled promises. Part IV traces that development from its beginning through modern times. Chapter 9 focuses on the history and structure of confinement, pointing out the differences between state and federal systems, the different levels of security that characterize confinement, and the emergence of prisons as places for punishment. The nature of private corrections is discussed, along with the problems of prison and jail overcrowding. This chapter provides the background needed for an analysis of some of the issues surrounding modern correctional practices.

Chapter 10 examines the administration and inmate life of today's prisons, looking particularly at the ways in which the internal structure of the prison may be used to control inmates. That control is not always successful, however, as illustrated by the discussions of prison violence and the lawsuits filed as a result of alleged violations of inmates' constitutional rights. Part IV closes with a chapter on community corrections, probation, and parole.

Confinement and Corrections

[illegible]

9

The History and Structure of Confinement

Chapter Outline

Learning Objectives

After reading this chapter, you should be able to do the following:

- Explain the reasons for the emergence of institutions for confining offenders
- Explain the significance of the Walnut Street Jail
- Distinguish the Pennsylvania system from the Auburn system, and evaluate the contributions of each
- Recall the contributions of Europeans to the emergence and development of prisons
- Explain the relevance of the Elmira Reformatory
- Summarize the development of modern U.S. prison systems
- Distinguish among jails, prisons, and community corrections
- List and describe the purposes of prison security levels
- Analyze the differences between prisons for men and women
- Describe state and federal prison systems, and evaluate the differences between them
- Discuss the distinguishing features of jails, and analyze the role of the federal government in local jails
- Discuss the implications of the growth in jail and prison populations, with particular attention to the effects of overcrowding
- Analyze the role of privatization in correctional facilities

In the distant past, lengthy confinement of offenders would have been impractical in a less-populated world, where formal police protection did not exist and conditions were so unstable that populations moved from one place to another in search of food and shelter. Under those conditions, the punishment of persons who violated society's norms usually was carried out by quick methods, such as **corporal punishment**, or, in extreme cases, capital punishment. Generally, confinement was for very short periods while defendants awaited these punishments or trial.

Places of confinement for suspects or convicted defendants should reflect the purposes for which they are intended. If confinement is for holding a person only briefly, little attention need be paid to the confinement facility except to keep it secure. The architecture, conditions, and administration should reflect the security goal. If humanitarian concerns are not important, the conditions of confinement are relatively unimportant. Likewise, if the reason for confinement is to remove offenders from society and punish them for their criminal acts, then programming, treatment personnel, and prison conditions are unimportant. Prison is a place of custody and punishment; confinement is the punishment. The rationale is that offenders are getting what they deserve as a result of their criminal acts.

If the purpose of confinement is to rehabilitate offenders, more attention should be given to confinement conditions, which are important because they are related to inmates' rehabilitation. Even the location of confinement facilities is important; facilities should be close enough to inmates' homes to enable family members to visit. Treatment programs, educational and work opportunities, fairness in discipline, and many other activities behind prison walls are relevant. Administration and management must reflect a treatment-rehabilitation orientation while also maintaining security within the institution.

This chapter looks at the historical development of the confinement of defendants prior to trial or for the incarceration of convicted and sentenced offenders. Throughout the discussion, the purposes of confinement—retribution, incapacitation, deterrence, and rehabilitation—should be kept in mind. The focus on one or more of these purposes is not necessarily chronological in the history of prisons, but the purpose is tied to the type of prison that emerges.

The chapter explores the history of the emergence of jails and prisons, overviews modern prisons, explains the differences among the various types of prisons, distinguishes prisons for men and for women, contrasts the federal and state prison systems, analyzes jails as places of short-term detention, and looks at the significant issue of jail and prison populations and suggests solutions for reducing them where necessary. The focus is on adult facilities; juvenile facilities are discussed in Chapter 12.

THE EMERGENCE OF PRISONS FOR PUNISHMENT

The transfer from the use of secure penal facilities primarily for *punishment* occurred in the eighteenth century. In 1704, Pope Clement XI erected the papal prison of San Michele in Rome. In 1773, the prison in Ghent, Belgium, was established by Hippolyte Vilain XIII. In 1776, England was faced with a rising crime rate, the elimination of the need for galley slaves, and decreasing opportunities for the **transportation** of criminals to its colonies. England legalized the use of hulks, usually broken-down war vessels, for the housing of **offenders**, and by 1828, at least 4,000 of them were confined in hulks. The ships were unsanitary, poorly ventilated, and vermin-infested. Contagious diseases killed many inmates, and punishments were brutal. There was little work for inmates, and idleness was demoralizing. Moral degeneration set in because of the "promiscuous association of prisoners of all ages and degrees of criminality."[1] This system of penal confinement in England lasted until the middle of the nineteenth century.

The spirit of **humanitarianism** that arose during the Enlightenment was among the reasons for the substitution of imprisonment for transportation and corporal and capital punishment. People began to realize the horrors inherent in the sordid treatment of incarcerated offenders. The French prison built in Paris in the fourteenth century, the Bastille, became a symbol of such treatment, as well as of tyrannical prison administration. French philosophers, shocked by what they called *judicial murders*, sought changes in criminal justice systems.[2]

Another important philosophical development in France during the French Revolution was the emphasis on rationalism. This approach was important in the history of prisons because of its influence on social and political philosophy. Philosophers believed that social progress and the greatest happiness for the greatest number would only occur through revolutionary social reform, which could be brought about only by applying reason.

These reform ideas flourished in the United States because many French people lived here during the French Revolution and many influential Americans had been to France. In fact, the Constitutional Convention was influenced significantly by the political philosophy of French philosophers.

There are other important reasons for the rise of the prison system in the United States. The increasing emphasis on personal liberty meant that the deprivation of liberty could be seen as punishment. In addition, after the Industrial Revolution, there was an increasing need for labor, which inmates could supply. It has been argued, too, that prisons were developed by those in power for the purpose of suppressing persons who were not in power.

Although these general conditions are important in explaining the rise of prisons, attention must also be given to one individual who was highly influential in the process: John Howard (1726-1790), known as the great European prison reformer. Howard, an Englishman, was credited with the beginning of the **penitentiary** system. He traveled throughout Europe and brought to the world's attention the sordid conditions under which inmates were confined. Howard's classic work, *State of Prisons*, published in 1777, was influential in prison reform in Europe and in the United States. Among his other ideas, Howard suggested that inmates should be housed individually, in sanitary facilities, and provided clean clothing; that women, men, and children should be segregated from each other; and that jailers should be trained and well paid.[3]

The history of correctional institutions can be traced back to Roman, French, and English systems. An early English gaol (jail) is featured in **Supplement 9.1**. The unique contribution of the United States was the substitution of imprisonment for corporal punishment, an innovation of the Quakers of West Jersey and Pennsylvania in the eighteenth century. They combined the prison and the **workhouse** to achieve a system of confinement at hard labor.

In 1787, Pennsylvania enacted a statute reducing the number of capital crimes, substituting imprisonment for many felonies, and abolishing most corporal punishments. A 1794 statute abolished capital punishment except for first degree murder and substituted fines and imprisonment for corporal punishment in the case of all other crimes. The Pennsylvania criminal code reform set the stage for similar developments in other states. The main feature of early Pennsylvania reform was the Walnut Street Jail.

The Walnut Street Jail

In 1787 in Pennsylvania, Benjamin Rush, Benjamin Franklin, and others met to discuss punishment. Rush proposed a new system for the treatment of offenders. This system included **classification**, individualized treatment, and prison labor to provide jobs for inmates and to make prisons self-supporting. A 1790 statute codified the principle of solitary confinement and established the Walnut Street Jail, in which individual cells were provided for serious felons. Inmates were separated by gender and by whether they had been sentenced after being convicted of a crime or were being detained awaiting a trial or punishment. This law was the beginning of the modern prison system in the United States, and the Walnut Street Jail is often cited as the first U.S. prison.

The Walnut Street Jail, established by a 1790 Pennsylvania statute, is often referred to as the first U.S. prison. Among other characteristics, the facility featured classification of inmates by gender, work opportunities that kept the inmates busy and made the institution self-supporting, and solitary confinement.

Some scholars have argued that the Walnut Street Jail was not the first American prison. According to one, Connecticut's Newgate Prison was the "first true colonial prison for the long-term punishment of serious offenders."[4] That prison was used for the incarceration and punishment of offenders who committed robbery, burglary, forgery, counterfeiting, and horse thievery. Unlike the Walnut Street Jail, Newgate was much more like the English houses of corrections and other early penal facilities, with an emphasis on punishment rather than rehabilitation.[5]

Offenders in the Walnut Street Jail worked an eight- to ten-hour day and received religious instruction. They labored in their cells and were paid for their efforts. Guards were not permitted to use weapons, and corporal punishment was forbidden. Inmates were allowed to talk only in the common rooms at night before retiring. With some variations, this plan was followed in other states. By 1800, problems with the system had become obvious. Crowded facilities made work within individual cells impossible; there was not enough productive work for the large number of inmates, and vice flourished. Ultimately, the Walnut Street Jail failed as a result of politics, inadequate finances, lack of personnel, and overcrowding, but not before it had gained recognition throughout the world.

The Walnut Street Jail and other early prisons faced serious problems. Despite the thick walls and high security, **inmates** escaped. To combat that problem, some **wardens** required inmates to wear uniforms; in some prisons, the color of the uniform reflected whether the convict was a first-, second-, or third-time offender. Discipline was a major issue; some wardens reinstituted corporal punishment; others used solitary confinement for punishment.

Funding was a challenge in these early prisons, and facilities were needed for exercise. To alleviate these problems, work programs (such as gardening) were begun, but they were not effective. Inmates were neither reliable nor efficient, and administrators were not skilled in managing prison labor. The result was that most prisons operated at a loss. In 1820, the viability of the entire prison system was in doubt, and even its most dedicated supporters conceded a nearly total failure. Institutionalization had failed to pay its own way and had encouraged and educated the criminal even more extensively to a life of crime.[6]

In response to these problems, two types of prison systems developed: the Pennsylvania, or separate, system, based on solitary confinement; and the New York, or Auburn, system, known as the **silent system**. These two systems were the subject of intense debate. Tourists flocked to see the prisons; foreign nations sent delegates to examine the two systems. By the 1830s, the two American penitentiary systems were famous throughout the world.

The Pennsylvania System

With the demise of the Walnut Street Jail, solitary confinement with hard labor appeared to be a failure. Consideration was given to a return to corporal punishment. But in 1817, the Philadelphia Society for the Alleviation of the Miseries of Prisons began a reform movement, which led to a law providing for the establishment of the separate system of confining inmates in solitary cells without labor.

The first separate system prison was opened in Pittsburgh in 1826 and subsequently was known as the Western Penitentiary. The problems resulting from inmate idleness in this prison led to legislative changes to permit work in solitary confinement. The design of the Western Penitentiary became the basic architectural model for the Pennsylvania system.

The Eastern Penitentiary—or Cherry Hill as it was called because of its location in a cherry orchard—was established in 1829. It was the first large-scale attempt to implement the philosophy of solitary confinement at all times, with work provided for inmates in their cells. The law that authorized construction of this prison specified that, although the commissioners could make some alterations and improvements in the plan used for the Western Penitentiary, the principle of solitary confinement must be incorporated.

John Haviland, the architect of Cherry Hill, was faced with the problem of creating a structure that would permit solitary confinement but would not injure inmates' health or permit their escape. His solution was seven wings, each connected to a central hub by covered passageways. Each inmate had a single inside cell with an outside exercise yard. Inmates were blindfolded when taken to the prison and were not permitted to see other inmates. They were not assembled even for religious worship. The chaplain spoke from the rotunda, with inmates remaining in their cells.

Before Cherry Hill was completed, it became the focus of discussion among prison reformers around the world. Although it was the architectural model for most of the new prisons in Europe, South America, and later Asia, the design was unpopular in the United States. Despite that fact, John Haviland's contributions to American prison architecture should not be minimized, as one criminologist stated:

> Compared with the penitentiaries of their day, Haviland's prisons were overwhelmingly superior, both technically and stylistically. . . . Haviland's great service to penology would seem to be in establishing high standards of construction, standards which were to have an influence on almost all of the prison construction of the 19th century.[7]

Haviland should also be remembered for the fact that his prison architecture embodied a treatment philosophy.

The Auburn System

The prison system that became the architectural model for the United States was the Auburn system. In 1796, New York enacted a statute that provided for the building of two prisons. Newgate in New York City was first occupied in 1797. That prison soon became so crowded that, to make room for new inmates, as many inmates had to be released as were admitted.

The second prison, Auburn, built in 1816, was similar to Newgate, with workshop groups during the day and several inmates to a cell at night. Discipline was a problem, however, so a new system, which became known as the *Auburn system*, developed. The Auburn system featured congregate work during the day, with an enforced silent system. Inmates were housed in individual cells at night. The architecture created a fortress-like appearance, with a series of tiers set in a hollow frame, a much more economical system than that of Cherry Hill.

The early New York prison at Auburn was characterized by a silent system, in contrast to the Pennsylvania system, which featured solitary confinement. The Auburn system also featured a strict system of inmate discipline.

The silent system was strictly enforced at Auburn. The inmates ate face to back. They stood with arms folded and eyes down, so that they could not communicate with their hands. They walked in lockstep with a downward gaze. Strict regulation of letters and visits with outsiders and few or no newspapers further isolated the inmates. Inmates were brought together for religious services, but each sat in a booth-like pew, which prevented their seeing anyone other than the speaker.

Strict discipline was maintained at Auburn. The warden, Captain Elam Lynds, thought that the spirit of a person must be broken before reformation could occur. He was credited with the Auburn punishment philosophy. It is said that he changed discipline rules without legislative authority, instituted the silent system, fed inmates in their cells, and required lockstep in marching. A committee from the legislature visited the prison, approved of the way it was being run, and persuaded the legislature to legalize the new system.

In 1821, a system of classification was instituted. It placed dangerous offenders in solitary confinement, which led to mental illness and inmates pleading for work. Some committed suicide. A commission established to study prisons recommended abolishing solitary confinement and putting all inmates to work.

The Auburn system emphasized the congregate but silent system; the Pennsylvania system emphasized solitary confinement. Both featured the importance of a disciplined routine and isolation from bad influences. Both reflected the belief that, because inmates were not inherently bad but, rather, the product of defective social organization, they could be reformed under proper circumstances. Scholars, practitioners, and politicians debated the advantages and disadvantages of these two systems, but few questioned the premise on which both rested: Incarceration is the best way to handle criminals.[8]

The architecture of the two systems resulted in cost differentials. The Auburn system was more economical to build, although the Pennsylvania system was less expensive to administer. It was argued that the Auburn system was more conducive to productive inmate labor and less likely to cause mental illness. The silent system continued into the twentieth century, not for the original purpose of preventing inmates from negatively influencing each other, but because it was easier to run an institution if the inmates were not allowed to speak to each other.

Finally, the Pennsylvania and Auburn systems were important in that both were based on treatment philosophies, with architecture designed to accommodate those philosophies.

The Emergence of the Reformatory Model

The disagreement over the Pennsylvania and Auburn systems led to an emphasis on reformation, along with a prison system characterized by indeterminate sentences, parole, work training, and education. This reformation was heavily influenced by the work of Captain Alexander Maconochie, a Scotsman, and Sir Walter Crofton, an Irishman, whose contributions to prison reform are summarized in **Supplement 9.2**.

American reformers visited the Irish prison system in the 1860s and returned with enthusiasm for its reformation philosophy. On October 12, 1870, penologist Enoch C. Wines led a meeting in Cincinnati, Ohio, to settle the dispute between the Pennsylvania and Auburn systems. This meeting led to the organization of the American Correctional Association, then called the *National Prison Association*. The group drafted 37 principles calling for such changes as indeterminate sentences, cultivation of inmates' self-respect, inmate classification, and advancement of the philosophy of reformation rather than punishment.

The Elmira Reformatory, established in 1876, emerged from this meeting. It became the model for a **reformatory**, which was designed for young offenders. The architecture was similar to that of the Auburn system, but greater emphasis was placed on educational and vocational training. Indeterminate sentences with maximum terms, opportunities for parole, and the classification of inmates according to conduct and achievement were the greatest advances of this new institution.

Elmira was established at the same time that other reforms, such as the juvenile court, probation, parole, and indeterminate sentences, were emerging. It was predicted that Elmira would dominate U.S. prison systems.[9]

The significant contribution of the Elmira reformatory system was its emphasis on rehabilitation through education, which led to greater prison discipline, indeterminate sentences, and parole. The system declined eventually, mainly as a result of the lack of trained personnel to conduct the educational programs and to carry on the classification system adequately. Some scholars argue that the Elmira system was never intended to be a real reform but rather, was developed for the purpose of controlling the lower classes, women, and minorities. The system, it was said, promised benevolent reform but delivered only repression.[10]

An increase in the prison population in the late 1800s resulted in severe overcrowding. Eventually, new prisons were built, including Attica (New York) in 1931, and Stateville (Illinois) in 1925. Most of the prisons of this period followed the Auburn architectural plan and were characterized by increasing costs per inmate, Sunday services, a chaplain on duty most of the time, and insufficient educational and vocational training programs. The training programs were based on the needs of institutions, not the interests or needs of inmates. Insufficient funds were available to hire and retain adequate personnel.

These early institutions provided work for some inmates, and the prison products were sold on the open market. This industrial period of prison history irritated those in private industries, who complained that competition from prisons was unfair because of the low wages paid to inmates. In 1929, the Hawes-Cooper Act was passed, followed in 1935 by the Ashurst-Summers Act to restrict the sale of prison goods:

> These [federal statutes] in turn were followed by state laws designed to do the same. With the passage of these laws, the Industrial Prison was eliminated. In 1935 for the great majority of prisoners the penitentiary system had again reverted to its original status: punishment and custody.[11]

MODERN PRISONS: AN OVERVIEW

When they emerged, U.S. prisons were viewed as a substitute for corporal punishment, but corporal punishment continued. Supposedly, prisons were places in which inmates could be reformed.[12] However, the early reform approach was eventually abandoned in favor of a custody philosophy. According to David I. Rothman, this occurred for several reasons. The change was not inherent in prison designs. Some disappointment was inevitable because of the great expectations the founders had for the success of the prison movement. Change also came about as a result of the resources drained from prisons during the Civil War. Additionally, the rehabilitation goal promoted but also disguised the shift from reformation to custody. Too often, prison administrators assumed that incarceration was reformation, and no one recognized that reformation programs were lacking. The administrators relaxed their reform efforts, and abuses of power arose within the prisons.[13]

The nature of inmates' offenses was also related to the change from a reformation to a custodial emphasis. The silent, segregated systems were not designed for hardened offenders serving long-term or life sentences. The founders who envisaged reformation of the offender had not contemplated what to do with the hardened adult offender or the juvenile already committed to a life of crime. When the situation arose, **custody** seemed the best answer. The public accepted that approach because of the need for safety and security.[14] As cities became larger and their populations became more heterogeneous, including an influx of immigrants as well as distinct social classes, traditional methods of social control became ineffective. When those persons entered prison, an emphasis on custody seemed appropriate.

By the late 1800s, it had become clear that reformation was no longer a major punishment goal. Later studies reported corruption between correctional officers and inmates, cruel punishment of inmates, overcrowded prisons with financial problems, and severe criticism of both the Pennsylvania and Auburn systems. As hardened offenders were held for long periods of time, prisons turned into holding operations, where wardens were content if they could prevent riots and escapes.

Some reformers began to express dissatisfaction with incarceration per se, criticizing long sentences as counterproductive and large expenditures on prisons as foolish and unnecessary. Probation and parole were advocated but slow to be adopted. Most reformers and the public seemed content to incarcerate for the sake of security.

Why did the public stand for the decline of the original prison philosophy? David Rothman suggested that part of the explanation was that usually it is easier to capture public interest "with predictions of success than with the descriptions of corruption." Some may have believed that incarceration was synonymous with rehabilitation. But, said Rothman, the reasons went deeper. Many persons saw the prison as performing an important social function, for they noted that the majority of inmates were from the lower social class and many were immigrants. Few upper-class or upper-middle-class persons were incarcerated.

In recent years, reformation and rehabilitation were dealt a severe blow by researchers claiming that empirical evidence showed that rehabilitation had failed. Some evidence of the rehabilitative ideal remained, but it was no longer the dominant reason for punishment. It was replaced by an emphasis on deterrence and retribution. In those jurisdictions in which reformation or rehabilitation was emphasized, the focus was usually on diversion from prison rather than on prison programs designed to reform. As we shall see, however, just within the past decade or so, a reemphasis on rehabilitation and treatment has emerged.

Many aspects of modern U.S. prisons are examined in this chapter and in Chapter 10, and they demonstrate that some modern prisons are characterized by disruption, violence, monotonous daily routine, lack of work opportunities, and unconstitutional living conditions. Some jails and prisons are under federal court orders to improve inmates' living conditions and to reduce inmate populations or be closed. Are these modern prisons an improvement over the earlier ones? Some may say the question is not relevant; offenders should be punished, which is just what the system is doing.

CONFINEMENT INSTITUTIONS

Offenders are confined in various types of institutions. These institutions are classified most commonly as jails, prisons, and community-based correctional facilities.

Although the terms **jail** and **prison** are used interchangeably and the two types of institutions have common characteristics, they can be distinguished by their purposes. Jails and detention centers confine persons awaiting trial. They are also used for the short-term detention of persons in need of care when no other facilities are available immediately. For example, a public drunk might be detained until sober or until arrangements are made for admittance to a treatment facility. Occasionally, jails are used to detain witnesses to a crime if it is thought that otherwise they might not be available for trial. Finally, jails are used to incarcerate convicted offenders who are sentenced to short terms, usually less than one year.

Prisons are used for the incarceration of offenders who have been convicted of serious offenses, usually felonies, and who have been sentenced to lengthy terms (usually over one year), or to capital punishment.

Another type of facility that is used for confinement is a **community-based correction facility**, which houses offenders but permits them to leave during part of the day to work, attend school, or engage in treatment programs. Offenders may also be confined in special-purpose facilities, such as treatment centers for abusers of alcohol or other drugs, for sex offenders, or for the mentally challenged.

Prison Security Levels

Prison security levels may be divided into three main categories: maximum, medium, and minimum custody. The federal government and most states have all three types. The architecture and degree of security of the levels differ from one jurisdiction to another.

Many of the maximum-security prisons currently in use were built before 1925, when most inmates were housed in maximum-security prisons, although for many of them, that security level was excessive. Unfortunately, this also occurs in some jurisdictions today. Maintenance of these old maximum-security facilities is difficult and costly; many of the complaints about prison conditions are related to the problems of maintaining these old facilities. An example is that of California's San Quentin Prison, featured in **Supplement 9.3**.

Maximum-, medium-, and minimum-security prisons differ in the emphasis on treatment and related programs and in the freedom permitted inmates. In maximum-security prisons, inmates are detained in their cells for longer periods of time and are given less freedom of movement within the cell blocks than are those in the other security levels.

Another type of prison is the **open prison**. Open prisons make use of the natural environment for security. An example was Alcatraz Island, located in San Francisco Bay. Called "the Rock" because the island is mainly rock, Alcatraz has been used for numerous purposes, including a military prison and a maximum-security federal prison. Officially, it became a federal prison on January 1, 1934, and its purpose was to incarcerate the most dangerous federal offenders. A former U.S. attorney general described Alcatraz as a prison that would make no pretense at rehabilitation. Rather, it was a place for "the ultimate punishment society could inflict upon men short of killing them; the point of no return for multiple losers." Alcatraz was described by one writer as "the great garbage can of San Francisco Bay, into which every federal prison dumped its most rotten apples."[15]

Alcatraz Island (in the background) was the venue for a military prison and then a federal maximum-security prison that housed the "worst of the worst" inmates and made no pretense at a rehabilitation philosophy. The secure facility was expensive to operate, however, and was closed as a federal prison in 1963. In 1991, the facility was opened as a museum and quickly became the top tourist attraction in the San Francisco area.

Alcatraz incarcerated some of the most notorious federal offenders, men such as George "Machine Gun" Kelly (who arrived at Alcatraz in 1934), a college-educated man from a prosperous family, convicted of bootlegging, and Robert F. Stroud (who was transferred from another federal prison in 1942), a young pimp who killed a customer after he had attacked one of Stroud's prostitutes. Stroud became known as the "Birdman of Alcatraz" because of his knowledge of bird diseases. Men such as Kelly and Stroud were sent to Alcatraz because it was considered the most secure U.S. prison at the time. It was assumed that no one could survive in the icy waters and current long enough to swim from the prison to San Francisco. There are no records of successful escapes, although on June 11, 1962, three inmates escaped, and their bodies were never found.

The cost of keeping an offender at Alcatraz was three times as high as it was at any other federal prison, and costly capital improvements were needed. On March 21, 1963, the prison was closed as a federal penitentiary. Inmates were transferred to other federal prisons. After a period of occupation by Native Americans between 1969 and 1971, Alcatraz became a tourist attraction, the most frequently visited one in the San Francisco area. In recent years, Alcatraz has been renovated, and in 1991, a museum filled with "Alcatrivia" was opened on the island. Numerous books have been written about the prison and the island, some by former inmates and others by prison staff or their families.[16]

Alcatraz illustrated some of the problems with open prisons. They may be more secure, but they are costly and inconvenient. Land is scarce, and finding appropriate places for prison colonies is difficult. It is unlikely, therefore, that the open prison system will be used extensively in the future. The former federal penitentiary on McNeil Island (off the coast of Washington State) became a state prison, but in 2011, that was closed as such although the state continues to house sex offenders there in the state's Special Commitment Center.

In recent years, special prisons for high security needs have been built. These secure facilities are referred to as *maxi-maxi prisons* or *supermaximum-security (supermax) prisons*. The author of a federal correctional report urged a conservative approach toward classifying inmates for supermax prisons and implored states not to use them to confine mentally challenged inmates, those who need protective custody from other inmates, or those who are merely a nuisance. Supermax prisons are expensive to build and to operate, but they are popular with politicians. It is argued that the presence of these institutions—and thus the threat of being incarcerated in them—serves as a deterrent to inmates who might otherwise become disruptive within less secure facilities.[17]

A federal supermax prison was opened in 1994 in Florence, Colorado. It was a state-of-the-art prison designed and built specifically for predator inmates—that is, those who have demonstrated that they cannot live in other prisons without causing trouble for inmates as well as staff and administration. The facility, located at the foot of the Rockies, was built for 400 inmates. The inmates live

Spotlight 9.1

Supermax Prisons: A Look at the Federal System

The federal supermax prison in Florence, Colorado, is the most secure in the federal system, having surpassed Marion, Illinois, which held that position for many years. One of its occupants is Eric Rudolph, who in April 2005 pleaded guilty to multiple terrorist acts in the 1990s, including the bombings at the 1996 Summer Olympics in Atlanta. Another inmate at the Colorado supermax prison is Richard Reid, the shoe bomber terrorist who attempted to blow up a flight from Paris, France, to Miami, Florida, in 2002.

The Colorado supermax prison also houses other terrorists, such as Theodore "Ted" Kaczynski, the Unabomber (who used the mails to kill three people and injure 22 over a period of 17 years, serving four life sentences plus 30 years); Ramzi Abmed Yousef (convicted of masterminding the 1993 bombing of the World Trade Center, which killed six and injured more than 1,000 people, serving a life sentence); and Khalfan Khamis Mohamed, also serving life, who, along with three others, was convicted of bombing the U.S. embassies in Kenya and Tanzania in 1998, killing 224 people.

The inmates at the Florence prison spend most of their days and nights in their cells in isolation. As one behavioral therapist said, Florence is the only U.S. prison "specifically designed to keep every occupant in near-total solitary confinement. . . . The worst behaved men could serve an entire sentence—decades—in isolation." The isolation is brutal but, said the therapist, so are the inmates. "This is it. The end of the line."[1] Some of the inmates are under court orders that severely restrict their communications with the outside world—for example, Yousef is not permitted to communicate by mail, telephone, or visits without court permission. Inmates are constantly monitored by surveillance cameras. The prison cost $150 million to build and is expensive to operate.[2]

The model of a supermax prison emerged in the 1970s and 1980s after inmates murdered numerous correctional officials. Various security measures were taken, including locking down an entire prison population. Soon, the idea of building special facilities for the "worst of the worst" emerged, with the philosophy of almost total lockdown for these inmates.

Supporters claim that the supermax prisons have resulted in fewer inmate and staff deaths; critics warn that locking inmates down in almost total isolation for years may have serious repercussions. Furthermore, there is evidence that in some states the guidelines for supermax eligibility are ignored, resulting in the incarceration of some inmates who do not need or deserve such intense security and isolation. As one news article concluded, "the available numbers suggest that casual overuse of these facilities is common. For in tough-on-crime America, imposing grim conditions on prisoners is all too often seen as a good in itself, regardless of the long-term costs."[3]

1. Quoted in "Monsters Doomed to Rot in a Hellish Dungeon," *New York Post* (October 19, 2001), p. 6.
2. Ibid.
3. Sasha Abramsky, "Return of the Madhouse: Supermax Prisons Are Becoming the High-Tech Equivalent of the Nineteenth-Century Snake Pit," *The American Prospect* (February 11, 2002), p. 26.

in a "super-controlled environment that enforces a hard-edged solitude to contain the risk of social mixing and violence. Even the cell windows deny them all views of the outside except the sky above."[18] A British newspaper described this prison as looking "more like a chemical weapons installation than anything else" because of the obvious security measures, including 14-foot-high razor wire bundles and a "triangular ring of mirrored-glass towers guarding the new tomblike highest security prison," which "can be seen from six miles across the prairie wastelands of Colorado's Rockies."[19] Spotlight 9.1 presents more information on this secure federal prison.

Scholars who have conducted empirical research on supermax prisons have raised serious questions. After a three-year study of Florida's supermax housing of inmates, researchers concluded that such confinement may actually increase the number of violent crimes committed by those inmates if they are released. The researchers concluded that there was no evidence of a "substantial specific deterrent effect of supermax incarceration."[20]

In a case involving the Ohio supermax prison (OSP), the U.S. Supreme Court held that conditions were so severe that inmates have a right to due process before they are assigned to such institutions. In that particular case, however, the unanimous Court found that the state had given the inmate adequate due process. A brief excerpt from *Wilkinson v. Austin* is presented in **Supplement 9.4**.

Although the U.S. Supreme Court did not detail all of the elements of due process that it considered to be required before a decision is made to assign an inmate to a maximum-security prison, the Court did emphasize that one of the most important of the acceptable policies of the OSP is the requirement that the inmate who is being considered for assignment to the OSP be given the reasons and a chance to refute them. The Court also spoke with favor about the requirement that three decision makers—the warden, the classification committee, and the Bureau of Classification—must agree to the proposed assignment, and the assignment can be negated by any one of those three.

Women's Prisons

Until the late nineteenth century, women, men, and children occupied the same dungeons, almshouses, and jails. The institutions were plagued with physical and sexual abuses. Prison reform led to segregated areas for women within the existing institutions. There were few female inmates, and that fact was used to justify not providing separate facilities. Some women's sections did not have a female matron. Vocational training and educational programs were not considered important.

In 1873, the first separate U.S. prison for women, the Indiana Women's Prison, was opened. Its emphases were rehabilitation, obedience, and religious education. Other institutions followed: in 1877 in Framingham, Massachusetts; a reformatory for women in 1891 in New York; the Westfield Farm (also in New York) in 1901; and in 1913 an institution in Clinton, New Jersey.

In contrast to penal institutions for adult men, most institutions for women are more aesthetic and less secure. Most female inmates are not considered high security risks and are not as violent as male inmates. There are some exceptions, but on the whole, the institutions are built and maintained to reflect the assumption that the occupants are not great risks to themselves or to others. Usually, female inmates are permitted more freedom and greater privacy than incarcerated men and may even be allowed to wear their own clothes rather than prison-issued uniforms.

Historically, female inmates have had fewer educational, vocational, and treatment programs than their counterparts in all-male penal institutions. The movement toward inmates' rights that began in the 1970s led to a recognition of these discrepancies, as discussed in Chapter 10 (and its supplement), along with a discussion of the special needs of female inmates, such as pregnancy and childbirth and the resulting issues of caring for those infants.

Having a parent in prison creates problems for any child, but the problems may be more severe when the mother is incarcerated. This is because most children whose mothers go to prison are not cared for by their fathers (the reverse is more likely when fathers go to prison). Some children of female inmates do live with other relatives, but the children of female inmates are five times more likely than those of male inmates to be placed in foster homes or be put up for adoption. Only about one-third of female inmates have even talked by phone with their children since incarceration; the children of approximately one-half of female inmates have never visited their mothers in prison. Some are not permitted to do so; many just live too far away to be able to make the trip. Yet, approximately two-thirds of all female inmates have at least one child under age 5.[21]

Some of the problems faced by children of inmates (especially those whose mothers are in prison) are noted in Criminal Justice Systems Dilemma 9.1. The number of minor children with at least one parent in prison has increased significantly in recent years, and minorities have been most severely impacted.[22]

To accommodate female inmates and their children, most prison systems would need to engage in expensive renovations. Some have done so, while others are providing special arrangements and programs within existing facilities by, for example, providing help with mothering skills. Another approach is illustrated by the Bedford Hills Correctional Facility, New York's maximum-security prison for women, which has for years provided summer

Criminal Justice Systems Dilemma 9.1

Female Inmates and Their Children

According to The Sentencing Project, the rate of incarceration for women in the United States is increasing at almost twice that of men, and two-thirds of female inmates have at least one minor child.[1]

In the following excerpt, The Sentencing Project highlights the impact that incarceration has on inmates' children, especially those of minority inmates.

"Mass incarceration has had significant and long-lasting impacts on American society, and particularly on communities of color. There is now a growing awareness that parents who go to prison do not suffer the consequences alone; the children of incarcerated parents often lose contact with their parent and visits are sometimes rare. Children of incarcerated parents are more likely to drop out of school, engage in delinquency, and subsequently be incarcerated themselves.

In 2007 there were 1.7 million children in America with a parent in prison, more than 70% of whom were children of color. Children of incarcerated parents live in a variety of circumstances. Some were previously in homes of two-parent families, where the non-incarcerated parent can assume primary responsibility for the children. Many children, especially in cases of women's incarceration, were in single-parent homes and are then cared for by a grandparent or other relative, if not in foster care. And in some cases, due to substance abuse and other factors, incarcerated parents had either not lived with their children or not provided a secure environment for them. Following release from prison both parents and children face challenges in reuniting their families. Parents have to cope with the difficulty of finding employment and stable housing while also reestablishing a relationship with their children.

The increasing incarceration of women means that more mothers are being incarcerated than ever before. There is some evidence that maternal incarceration can be more damaging to a child than paternal incarceration, which results in more children now suffering negative consequences. The number of incarcerated mothers has more than doubled (122%) from 29,500 in 1991 to 65,600 in 2007. The effect of parents' incarceration on children is related to a number of factors, including whether the child was living with the parent, whether the family unit was a one-parent or two-parent household, whether the parent was the sole earner, the age of the child, and the surrounding support network. While the effects can differ among children, the consequences of incarceration of a parent on a child are long-lasting and need to be considered when analyzing the ramifications of an expanding prison population."[2]

1. The Sentencing Project, "Children Are Affected by Incarceration," http://www.sentencingproject.org, accessed July 27, 2014.
2. The Sentencing Project, *Incarcerated Parents and Their Children: Trends 1991-2007* (February 2009), pp. 1-2, http://www.sentencing-project.org, accessed July 27, 2014.

camps for inmates' children. In Kentucky, two private charities take newborns and other babies to visit with the inmate mothers. Once a quarter, the mothers who qualify are permitted to spend a whole day with their children. Several states provide live-in nurseries for the infants of female inmates. Washington State provides special facilities for children from birth to age 3 to stay with their inmate mothers, while mothers of newborns may keep their infants with them in two-person cells.[23] Other examples of the ways in which prisons have made accommodations for inmate parents to interact with their children are summarized in **Supplement 9.5**.

FEDERAL AND STATE PRISONS

Most U.S. prisons are state institutions, but the federal government also has a large prison system.

The Federal System

The chapter's earlier discussion of the emergence of U.S. prisons referred to state-supported prisons. The federal government, which did not have prisons until the 1900s, contracted with states to incarcerate federal inmates. One of the first acts of Congress was to pass a statute encouraging states to permit the incarceration of federal inmates, at the federal government's expense, in state prisons. Most federal inmates with less than a year to serve or those awaiting trial were kept in local jails.[24]

In 1870, Congress established the Department of Justice (DOJ), which had a general agent in charge of the federal inmates in local jails and state prisons. Later, that position was called the *superintendent of prisons*. The superintendent was in charge of the care and custody of federal inmates and reported to an assistant attorney general in the DOJ.

Overcrowding in state prisons after the Civil War made some state officials reluctant to house federal offenders; other states accepted only federal offenders from within their borders. Transporting federal offenders to other states was expensive. In 1891, Congress authorized the purchase of land for three federal prisons.

The first federal prison was taken over from the War Department at Fort Leavenworth, Kansas. The facility had been used to house military offenders. It was found to be inadequate for the federal prison system, and Congress authorized the building of a prison on the Fort Leavenworth military reservation. Federal offenders housed at Fort Leavenworth built the prison. On February 1, 1906, inmates were moved to the new prison, and Fort Leavenworth was returned to the War Department. Final work on Leavenworth was not completed until 1928. Leavenworth was followed by the construction of federal prisons—all for men—in Atlanta, Georgia, and McNeil Island, Washington (which, as noted earlier, subsequently became a state facility). These prisons followed the architecture and philosophy of the Auburn system.

Prison overcrowding, poor conditions, and inconsistent administration of prisons, which were run primarily by local wardens, led to the need for more organization in the federal system. On May 14, 1930, President Herbert Hoover signed the law that created the federal Bureau of Prisons (BOP). Today, that bureau is a complex system, consisting of a main office in Washington, D.C., headed by an acting director, Hugh J. Hurwitz. The BOP operates regional offices, staff training centers, community corrections offices, and correctional institutions. Approximately 35,470 employees supervised the inmate population of 180,501 as of April 30, 2019. The BOP has a prison industries division as well as a research arm, the National Institute of Corrections (NIC). The bureau has an extensive legal department and divisions overseeing programming, medical services, and administration. Eighty-three percent of the federal institutions are operated by the BOP; 11 percent are privately managed; 6 percent are managed by entities other than the BOP or private companies.[25]

Overcrowding is a serious problem in some U.S. jails and prisons. Such arrangements as pictured above magnify the problems inherent in close confinement, exacerbating the spread of disease and violence.

Three figures portray the federal inmate population as of April 30, 2019, with Figure 9.1 containing data on gender, Figure 9.2 graphing the race of federal inmates, and Figure 9.3 noting that the largest percentage of federal inmates are incarcerated for convictions of drug offenses. Professions 9.1 contains information on job opportunities in the federal prison system. The federal system also has provisions for volunteers, as noted on the bureau's web page.

Staffing in the federal prison system has been a problem in recent years. President Donald J. Trump implemented a hiring freeze after he took office, and although that freeze in the overall federal system was lifted in April 2017, it lasted longer in the federal prison system. Approximately 5,000 unfilled jobs, including approximately 1,500 correctional officers, were eliminated. The result was that in 2018, some prisons were assigning teachers, nurses, secretaries, clerks, and other support staff to serve as correctional officers, and this was done with limited training for that position. There was concern that despite previous reductions in federal prison populations, the numbers would rise as a result of the "get tough" policies of Jeff Sessions,

Figure 9.1

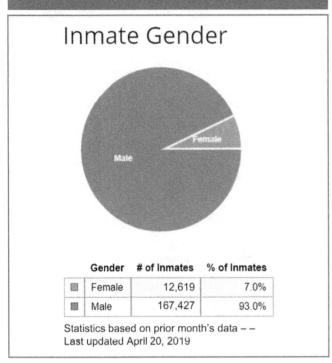

Gender Characteristics of the Federal Inmate Population as of April 20, 2019

Inmate Gender

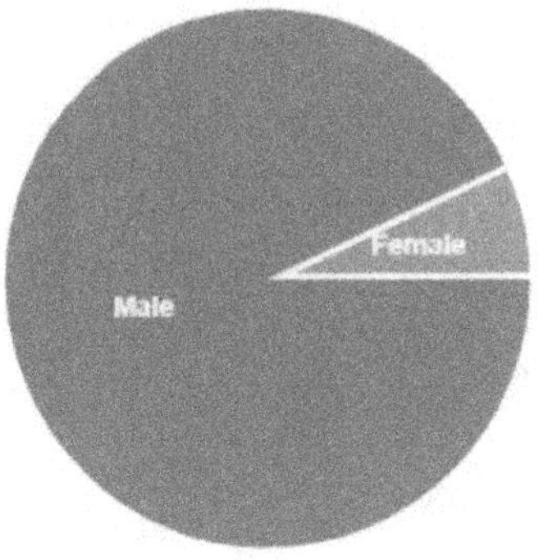

	Gender	# of Inmates	% of Inmates
■	Female	12,619	7.0%
■	Male	167,427	93.0%

Statistics based on prior month's data – –
Last updated April 20, 2019

Source: Bureau of Prisons, https://www.bop.gov/about/statistics/statistics/_inmate_gender.jsp, accessed April 30, 2019.

Figure 9.2

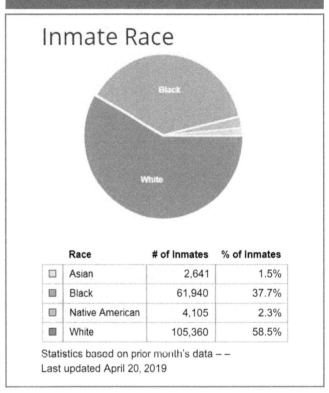

Race of the Federal Inmate Population as of April 20, 2019

Inmate Race

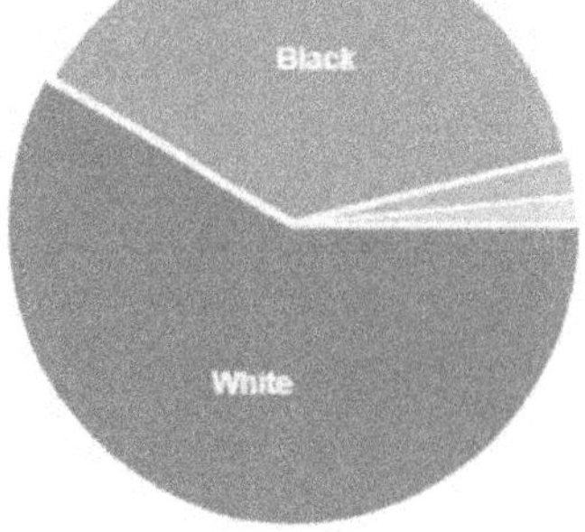

	Race	# of Inmates	% of Inmates
□	Asian	2,641	1.5%
■	Black	61,940	37.7%
■	Native American	4,105	2.3%
■	White	105,360	58.5%

Statistics based on prior month's data – –
Last updated April 20, 2019

Source: Bureau of Prisons, https://www.bop.gov/about/statistics/statistics/_inmate_race.jsp, accessed April 30, 2019.

the attorney general, and the transfer in 2018 of approximately 1,600 immigration detainees to federal prisons by April 2019, however, the BOP's website was headlined, "The Bureau of Prisons Is Hiring."[26]

State Systems

All states have correctional systems; most are centralized and headed by a director, who reports to the governor. The director is responsible for overseeing all correctional facilities. Most states have all levels of security for male offenders, in addition to separate institutions for juveniles and women and treatment centers in the communities. Not all levels of security are available for women because of the small number of female inmates.

States may contract with other states for the incarceration of some inmates. After a riot, it is not uncommon for inmates to be transferred to another state until the riot-damaged facilities are remodeled, repaired, or replaced. Such transfers may also be made to remove the riot's leaders. Some states contract with other states to house inmates whose lives are in danger in their own states. Such arrangements may also be made between a state and the federal system, or when a state's facilities are inadequate to house all of its inmates.

State prison systems differ considerably from each other in size and complexity, as well as in prison conditions and facilities, administrative problems, and the cost of maintaining inmates. Some state prison systems are under financial constraints, with some facing federal court orders to reduce their populations and make significant other changes.

LOCAL SYSTEMS: THE JAIL

Jails are local facilities that are used to confine persons awaiting trial; individuals for whom there are no

Figure 9.3

Offense Convictions of the Federal Inmate Population as of April 20, 2019

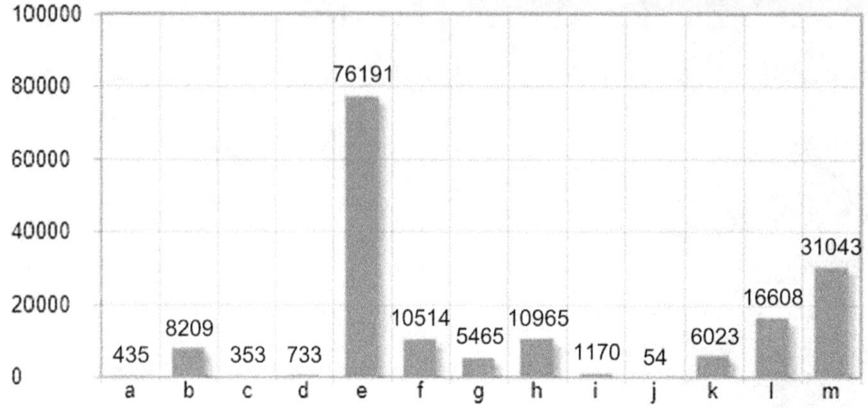

Chart Label	Offense	# of Inmates	% of Inmates
a	Banking and Insurance, Counterfeit, Embezzlement	435	0.3%
b	Burglary, Larceny, Property Offenses	8209	4.9%
c	Continuing Criminal Enterprise	353	0.2%
d	Courts or Corrections	733	0.4%
e	Drug Offenses	76,191	45.4%
f	Extortion, Fraud, Bribery	10,514	6.3%
g	Homicide, Aggravated Assault, and Kidnapping Offenses	5,465	3.3%
h	Immigration	10,965	6.5%
i	Miscellaneous	1,170	0.7%
j	National Security	54	0.0%
k	Robbery	6,023	3.6%
l	Sex Offenses	16,608	9.9%
m	Weapons, Explosives, Arson	31,043	18.5%

Offenses

Statistics based on prior month's data -- Last updated April 20, 2019

Source: Bureau of Prisons, https://www.bop.govabout/statistics/statistics_inmate_offenses.jsp, accessed April 30, 2019.

alternative facilities immediately available (such as suspects arrested for driving while intoxicated who do not have a responsible driving adult to whom they may be released); and inmates serving short sentences, usually less than a year. Most jails are operated by counties.

Jails may be the most important facilities in criminal justice systems because they affect more people than do any other criminal justice facilities. The "jail is [not only] a major intake center . . . for the entire criminal justice system, but also a place of first or last resort for a host

Professions 9.1

Federal Bureau of Prisons: Career Opportunities

The following information was posted on the website of the Federal Bureau of Prisons (BOP) on October 15, 2018, beginning with the heading, "Do Your Career Justice."

"We are a family and career-oriented agency, offering a broad range of exciting career opportunities in a work environment that promotes integrity, diversity, and professional development. And with over 35,000 highly motivated individuals, we are one of the most unique agencies in the United States Department of Justice where each employee's day-to-day performance makes a difference."

The site then discusses opportunities, openings, and life at the BOP. Some of the specific jobs are as follows:

Accountant
Attorney
Chaplain
Clinical Nurse
Clinical Psychologist
Computer Specialist
Correctional Officer
Dentist
Drug Treatment Specialist
Educational Specialist
Electrician
Engineering Technician
Health Technician
Human Resource Specialist
Medical Records Technician
Nurse (psychiatric)
Nurse Practitioner
Painter
Pharmacist
Physical Therapist
Plumber
Physician Assistant
Recreation Specialist
Registered Nurse
Sheet Metal Mechanic
Supervisor Correctional Officers
Teacher
Utility Systems Repairer
Vocational Technical Instructor

Source: Federal Bureau of Prisons, https://www.bop.gov/, accessed April 30, 2019.

of disguised health, welfare, and social problem cases."[27] **Supplement 9.6** lists other functions of local jails.

Jails may be traced far back into history, when they made their debut "in the form of murky dungeons, abysmal pits, unscaleable precipices, strong poles or trees, and suspended cages in which hapless prisoners were kept."[28] The primary purpose of those jails, also called *gaols* (see again Spotlight 9.1), was to detain people awaiting trial, transportation, the death penalty, or corporal punishment. The old jails were not escape-proof, and frequently, the person in charge received additional fees for shackling inmates. Inmates were not separated according to classification, physical conditions were terrible, food was inadequate, and no treatment or rehabilitation programs existed.

These early detention centers were followed in the fifteenth and sixteenth centuries in Europe by facilities characterized by work and punishment, called *workhouses*, or *houses of correction*. After the breakup of the feudal system, all of Western Europe experienced a significant increase in pauperism and public begging. To combat this problem, a workhouse called the Bridewell was established in London in 1557. The dominant philosophy at the Bridewell was a belief that, if people had to work at hard and unpleasant tasks, they would abandon their wantonness and begging.

The sordid conditions of jails and workhouses in Europe were brought to the attention of the world by John Howard, the prison reformer mentioned earlier in this chapter. In 1773, after his tour of European institutions, Howard proclaimed that more inmates died of jail fever than of execution.[29]

The first jails in the American colonies were places of confinement used primarily to hold suspects awaiting trial, persons who could not pay their debts, and convicted offenders waiting to be transferred to prisons. Jails were rarely used for punishment. Most of the offenses for which people may be sentenced to jail or prison today were handled in other ways then: by corporal punishment, capital punishment, fines, or publicly humiliating activities, such as sitting in the stocks or pillory, where people could jeer at the offenders. In the stocks, the victim's ankles were chained to holes in a wooden frame. The pillory was a device of varying shapes and sizes, to which the offender was secured in several ways, one of which was to be nailed to boards. The pillory was driven through town so that people could throw rotten eggs or vegetables at the offenders.

In the 1600s, Pennsylvania Quakers suggested that such punishments be replaced with what they considered to be a more humane form of treatment, the use of jails *as* punishment. U.S. jails came to be used not only for the detention of those awaiting trial but also as confinement for those serving short-term sentences.

The sordid conditions of American jails continued over the years. In 1923, Joseph F. Fishman, a federal prison inspector, investigator, and consultant, wrote a book, *Crucible of Crime*, in which he described U.S. jails. He based his descriptions and evaluations on visits to 1,500 jails. He said that some of the convicted would ask for a year in prison in preference to six months in jail because of the inhumane jail conditions.

According to Fishman, most jails were characterized by a lack of space; inadequate amenities, such as meals, bathing facilities, and hospitals; and no separate facilities for juveniles. Although Fishman said jail conditions were terrible nationwide, the facilities were worse in the South. Fishman's conclusions might be summarized by his definition of a U.S. jail as

> an unbelievably filthy institution. . . . Usually swarming with bedbugs, roaches, lice, and other vermin; has an odor of disinfectant and filth which is appalling; supports in complete idleness thousands of ablebodied men and women, and generally affords ample time and opportunity to assure inmates a complete course in every kind of viciousness and crime. A melting pot in which the worst elements of the raw material in the criminal world are brought forth, blended and turned out in absolute perfection.[30]

Today, the typical U.S. jail is small, at least 30 years old, and in need of renovation. It is located in a small town, usually the county seat of a predominantly rural county. These small, rural jails constitute the majority of jails but house a minority of the total U.S. jail populations. Some are used infrequently, and many are not crowded, in contrast to jails in urban areas. The typical jail is locally financed and administered.

Today's jails are not necessarily an improvement over those described above by Fishman. In March 2019, the sheriff, undersheriff, five deputies, and most of the staff of an Oklahoma jail resigned over what they considered to be dangerous jail conditions. Citing the existence of mold throughout the jail, unsafe electrical conditions such as exposed wires in showers and other places in the facility, improper plumbing resulting in the presence of methane gas throughout the jail, the lack of a mandated alarm system, and other dangerous conditions, the sheriff proclaimed that the job was not worth going to jail. Sheriff Terry Barnett of Nowata County had been threatened with a contempt citation by a judge because she refused to reopen the jail after she closed it when four of the employees had been taken to the emergency room because of a carbon monoxide leak. The interim sheriff who was sworn in after the resignations, said she would not reopen the jail until it was declared safe.[31]

Some states have assumed partial control of their jails and have established statewide minimum standards. Professional organizations have also become involved with jail standards. In the 1980s, the American Correctional Association sponsored the Commission on Accreditation for Corrections. That commission develops jail standards and certifies jails that meet those standards, but supervision or evaluation by states or professional organizations may not be sufficient to raise jail standards to an acceptable level. Federal courts have become involved, and their actions are discussed in Chapter 10 (and its supplement) in conjunction with court orders concerning jail and prison conditions.

The influence of the federal government on jails is also seen in other areas, such as federal technical assistance, financial assistance, and the imposing of standards. In addition, the federal government has provided states and local governments with assistance to build new correctional facilities and to remodel existing ones.

CORRECTIONAL POPULATIONS

Figure 9.4 diagrams the total population of correctional institutions in the United States from 2006 through 2016, representing a 0.9 percent decrease during 2016 and indicating that in 2016 approximately 1 out of every 38 persons in the United States was under probation, prison, parole, or jail supervision. These figures represent the ninth consecutive year of a decrease in these overall populations.[32] We look more closely at jail and prison

Figure 9.4

Total Population Under the Supervision of U.S. Adult Correctional Systems, 2006-2016

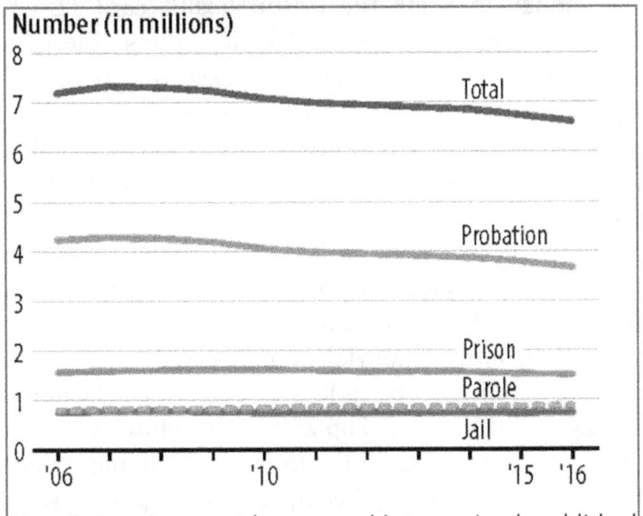

Note: Estimates may not be comparable to previously published BJS reports because of updated information or rounding. See *Methodology* for details.

Source: Bureau of Justice Statistics, Annual Probation Survey, Annual Parole Survey, Annual Survey of Jails, and National Prisoner Statistics program, 2006–2016.

Source: Danielle Kaeble and Mary Cowhig, Bureau of Justice Statistics, "Correctional Populations in the United States, 2016" (April 2018), p. 1, https://www.bjs.gov, accessed April 30, 2019.

Figure 9.5

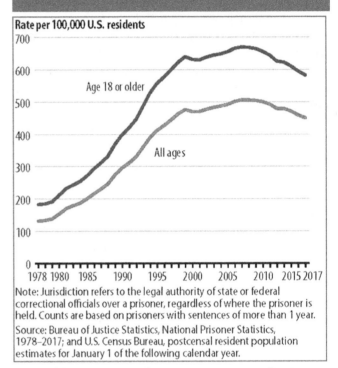

Imprisonment Rate of Sentenced Prisoners Under the Jurisdiction of State or Federal Correctional Authorities, per 100,000 U.S. Residents, 1978-2017

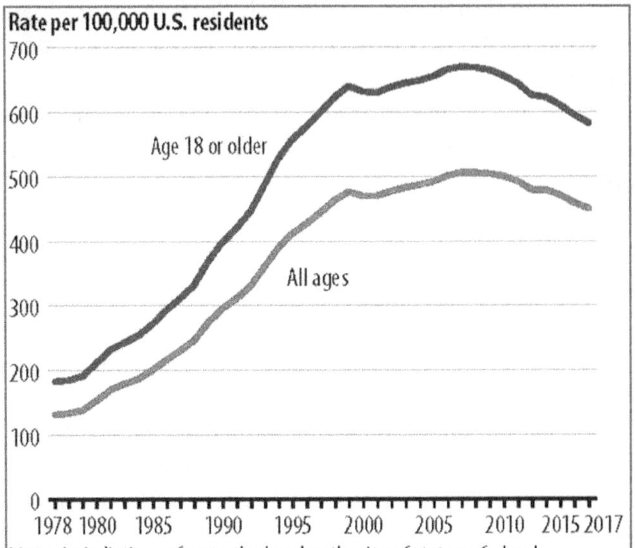

Note: Jurisdiction refers to the legal authority of state or federal correctional officials over a prisoner, regardless of where the prisoner is held. Counts are based on prisoners with sentences of more than 1 year.

Source: Bureau of Justice Statistics, National Prisoner Statistics, 1978–2017; and U.S. Census Bureau, postcensal resident population estimates for January 1 of the following calendar year.

Source: Jennifer Bronson and E. Ann Carson, Bureau of Justice Statistics, "Prisoners in 2017" (April 2019), p. 1, https://www.bjs.gov, accessed April 30, 2019.

populations here and at probation, parole, and community corrections in Chapter 11.

Since 2000, jail populations peaked at 785,500 at midyear 2008 and were relatively stable through 2017, when the population at midyear was 745,200, down from over 780,000 at the same time in 2016. The incarceration rate in 2017 was 229 per 100,000 persons over age 18, with males constituting 85 percent of jail inmates, but between 2000 and 2017, the percentage of female jail inmates increased from 11 percent to 20 percent of the total. Almost one-half of jail populations in 2017 were white. One-third were black. The percentage of inmates who were black decreased from 41 percent in 2000 to 39 percent in 2017. Approximately 65 percent of jail inmates in 2017 were not convicted but were incarcerated awaiting trial or some other legal action.[33]

Prison populations increased significantly from 1978, peaking in 2009, but the imprisonment rate began to decline in recent years, as graphed in Figure 9.5. In 2017, the number of inmates in state and federal prisons was 1.2 percent lower than in 2016. One-third of the decrease occurred in federal prisons. Over one-half (55 percent) of prison inmates in state prisons in 2017 were incarcerated for violent offenses, while half of federal inmates were incarcerated for drug offenses. In 2017, women constituted 7 percent of the prison population, which was a slight decrease (470 inmates) over 2016. In federal prisons, 47 percent of inmates were sentenced for drug offenses. In state prisons, 25 percent of female inmates, compared to 14 percent of male inmates, were serving time for drug offenses. Twelve percent of inmates in state and federal prisons were 55 or older.[34]

But despite the overall declining prison populations in recent years, there remains a concern with overcrowding and with prison conditions. The situation is fluid and differs among jurisdictions. For example, between 2011 and 2017, Texas closed eight prisons due to reduced budgets, declining populations, and falling crime rates, but the head of Oklahoma's Department of Corrections warned that the state's prisons were crumbling; guards were overworked and underpaid, and there was concern that the prison populations would increase as longer sentences were imposed. In 2018, Oklahoma had the second highest incarceration rate in the nation, second only to that of Louisiana.[35]

Many individual jails and prisons were already operating beyond their rated capacity. In 2016, the federal system and 14 states "met or exceeded the maximum measure of their prison facilities' capacity."[36] This situation has resulted in lawsuits, leading to federal court monitoring of jails and prisons as a result of the recognized harmful effects of overcrowding.

Overcrowding and Its Effects

Social scientists and federal judges have noted the negative impact of jail and prison overcrowding on inmates. In a Texas prison case, which was in the federal courts for almost two decades, an appellate court concluded during the initial stages that inmates were "routinely subjected to brutality, extortion, and rape. . . . The overcrowding . . . exercises a malignant effect on all aspects of inmate life." The court noted that inmates were in the presence of other persons almost constantly, sleeping with the knowledge that they might be attacked by cell mates. "There is little respite from these conditions, for . . . inmates have wholly inadequate opportunities to escape the overcrowding in their living quarters."[37]

The overcrowding in the California prison system is also illustrative. In 2005, approximately 10,000 inmates were housed in what officials called *ugly beds*, beds that were located in areas that were not designed for housing, such as recreation rooms and hallways. A nonpartisan legislative committee reported that between 1997 and 2003, when the California prison system experienced significant growth, the rate of inmate altercations rose 18 percent. A corrections consultant stated it this way: "The problem with overcrowding is that you lose flexibility in how you house inmates." The overcrowding in California prisons was thwarting the governor's promise to overhaul the state's prison system and restore it to its position as a leader in corrections.[38]

Between 1980 and 2008, California prison populations increased sevenfold. New prisons were built but they were soon operating beyond their approved capacity. The prison system threatened to bankrupt the state, accounting for approximately 10 percent of state expenses, with costs increasing by about 50 percent since 2000.[39]

A federal panel of three judges issued a temporary order in early 2009 that California must reduce its prison population by 37,000 to 55,000, while the federal monitor of the state's health care system demanded the money to bring the prison health care system into compliance with federal court orders. The governor, Arnold Schwarzenegger, refused that request.[40] Escalating prison costs led Schwarzenegger to suggest early release of prison inmates, changes in sentencing practices, or the removal over the next three years of 23,000 state inmates to local jails that were already overcrowded.[41]

In 2011, California passed the Public Safety Realignment (PSR) Act in an effort to reduce prison populations by moving nonviolent, nonserious, and nonsex offenders from prisons to jails and treatment facilities. In August 2013, the U.S. Supreme Court refused to stay a lower court order that the California prison inmate population be reduced as required by law, which gave the state two years to reduce the populations to 137.5 percent of the prisons' design capacity. In October 2013, federal judges gave the state an additional month, extending the deadline into late February 2014, at which time federal judges extended the deadline two more years. California was given until February 2016 to make severe reductions in its prison populations, but the state had interim deadlines that it was required to meet prior to that time. A federal monitor was in place to check on the state's progress toward those deadlines.[42] In March 2015, the state submitted to a three-judge federal panel an exhibit showing that it had met the reduction orders. In 2016, the voters of the state passed Proposition 57, the Public Safety and Rehabilitation Act of 2016, an effort to reduce the number of people incarcerated and emphasize rehabilitation as well as to enhance public safety. A summary of the requirements of Proposition 57 are included in **Supplement 9.7**, which contains the October 15, 2018 report to the Three-Judge Court. The state is required to submit a report every October, and this one confirms that the state has met the requirements of the panel concerning the reduction of California's prison populations and other issues.

California has also made other changes in procedures and policies to affect its prison populations. In 2014, California voters approved Proposition 47,[43] the Reduced Penalties for Some Crimes Initiative. This measure "reduces certain drug possession felonies to misdemeanors. It also requires misdemeanor sentencing for petty theft, receiving stolen property and forging/writing bad checks when the amount involved is $950 or less." Proposition 47 does not provide automatic resentencing but does permit an inmate currently serving a sentence for any of the affected crimes to petition to be resentenced.[44] Approximately 10,000 inmates were eligible for resentencing after a thorough risk assessment to ensure the state did not release inmates who might harm the public. It created a Safe Neighborhoods and Schools Fund to receive appropriations of the savings the state made compared to expenses prior to the implementation of Proposition 47, an estimated $150 million to $250 million per year. Twenty-five percent of that fund would be distributed to the Department of Education, 10 percent to the Victim Compensation and Government Claims Board, and 65 percent to the Board of State and Community Correction.

The changes in California's statutes and propositions affected jails as well as prisons. For example, between 2011 and 2012, the state's jail populations increased by 7,600 inmates. One of the reasons for that increase was a change in the state statute made in 2011, referred to as the Post-release Community Supervision Realignment (AB 109, after the name of the Assembly Bill authorizing the change). This law moved many lower felonies out of the state prison category for punishment. Those offenses are now punished by jail terms. This largest change in California's sentencing policies in about 30 years also provides that most parolees cannot be returned to prison for technical violations and that post-release community supervision is required for most inmates who are released from state prisons.[45]

The harmful effects of prison overcrowding, along with other issues, have led to numerous lawsuits, some of which are noted in Chapter 10 and its supplement, along with a more detailed discussion of medical issues in correctional facilities.

Prison and Jail Expansion

Some jurisdictions have responded to overcrowding by building new facilities, an extremely costly measure. Others have remodeled existing facilities, resulting in a corrections business that is one of the fastest-growing industries in the United States. Construction costs are not the only expenses to be considered in the expansion of facilities or the building of new ones. Operational costs of jails and prisons are high, and they continue to increase, outstripping the ability of many jurisdictions to cover them. A dramatic example in June 2010 was the inability of Los Angeles County to open a new $74 million state-of-the-art jail because it did not have the money to hire sufficient correctional officers.[46]

Construction time is also a factor. Because some jurisdictions are under federal court orders to reduce their prison and jail populations, they need available space quickly. As a result, some have sought faster construction plans and methods, which may result in construction problems. Others have turned to private correctional facilities.

PRIVATE CORRECTIONAL FACILITIES

One solution to prison problems has been to hire private firms to build and operate prisons or to provide special services, such as medical care or food. Privatization of correctional facilities, thought by many to be a modern movement, was actually used in the 1800s, in many cases for the same reasons as today, such as prison overcrowding.

The private sector is involved in corrections in three main areas: (1) prison work programs, (2) the financing of construction, and (3) the management of facilities. A state or the federal government might contract for one, two, or all three of these functions. In some cases, the private agencies actually buy the correctional facilities.

Many states and the federal government have used some private contractors for the management and operation of correctional institutions. The latest BJS data show that at the end of 2017, 27 states and the federal system housed 8 percent of their inmates in private correctional facilities. Between 2016 and 2017, the number held in federal prisons decreased by 19 percent, and in August 2016, the DOJ announced that the federal system would phase out the use of private prisons after a report revealed safety and security issues in them.[47] Shortly after he took office, however, President Donald J. Trump issued an executive order reversing that position, and indications are that the Trump administration may increase the use of private prison facilities. In particular, President Trump ordered the detention of more immigrants, most of whom were men held in private minimum-security prisons.[48]

In April 2013, Corrections Corporation of America (CCA) celebrated its thirtieth anniversary of providing private services to government correctional facilities. The CCA was the first and is the largest provider of correctional services to federal and state governments in the United States. In 2015, CCA had over 15,000 employees in over 60 facilities with a total of approximately 85,000 beds and over 600 inmate programs.[49]

Although we do not know whether private prisons can exist successfully with traditional government programs, some believe there are definite advantages. The private sector can concentrate on special offenders. This includes women, juveniles, illegal aliens, and inmates who are at risk in the general prison population, such as child molesters, former law enforcement officials, and prison informants.

The private sector may also provide an invaluable service simply by showing jail and prison officials that efficient and flexible management is possible in corrections. The private sector may be more likely to be characterized by competitive business principles, creative use of staff, adaptation of existing buildings and programs to meet changing needs, and experimentation with new ideas. Private involvement in corrections may encourage correctional administrators to modernize management styles, staff relations, and inmate care.

The private sector's involvement in corrections, however, raises many questions. First is the issue of whether private companies can deliver what they promise, such as high-tech prisons that are not crowded, are more carefully managed, and offer more vocational, educational, and other rehabilitative programs.

Another issue is whether private corrections facilities are effective. A study by Florida scholars concerning private prisons in that state concluded that there was no evidence that inmates released from private prisons (including those for adult males, adult females, and juveniles) were less likely to become recidivists once they were released. The authors did, however, acknowledge that there is limited empirical information on this subject and that studies should be conducted in other states as well.[50]

In reacting to the Florida study, a scholar at the National Institute of Justice stated:

> The original promise was that prison privatization would increase service quality. The premise was that the free market would introduce efficiency previously unknown.... The resulting performance suggests that neither promise nor premise was correct. The research results are clear.[51]

Another scholar pointed out that there were methodological problems with both the Florida study and the earlier ones by other scholars that suggested that private prison releasees were less likely to recidivate than those released from public facilities, and that these problems resulted in limitations on their conclusions.[52]

There are also allegations that privatization of correctional facilities may be dangerous. Specifically, it is argued that private security firms cut security short to save money. One labor economist stated that "the daily pressures that these [private] companies face to satisfy Wall Street [cause] them to pay employees low wages, and to under-staff facilities, under-train employees and hire unqualified staff." The labor economist concluded that, if the government thinks airport security is so critical that it requires government rather than private regulation, it does not make sense to contract out the security of our prisons. A noted criminal justice policy analyst also believes that government prisons are better managed than private ones and that "inmate assaults on other inmates and guards, drug use and escapes occur at higher rates in private prisons."[53]

The next chapter will note safety and other concerns in U.S. jails and prisons, but some point specifically to private facilities as the worst offenders. In the extreme, for example, in 2012 a federal judge concluded that the Walnut Grove Correctional Facility, a privately operated prison in Mississippi, was run by gangs and corrupt correctional officers. The prison "paints a picture of such horror as should be unrealized anywhere in the civilized world." In 2016, the state announced that for budgetary reasons, it would close the prison, which was operating under a federal consent decree due to violations of inmates' constitutional rights.[54]

There are other issues concerning private prisons. Politically, it is argued that corrections is a government function that should never be delegated. To do so increases problems, leading to lobbying for programs that might not be in the best interests of the public or of corrections. The profit motive reduces the incentive to decrease the number of incarcerated people. The profit incentive encourages larger and larger private prisons. To make a profit, those facilities must be occupied. When the incentive for full prisons is combined with the public's call for longer and harsher sentences, the result may be more inmates serving more time.

Finally, it is argued that politics and financial support are issues. For example, private corporations have spent money lobbying Congress concerning appropriations bills in general and bills concerning private prisons in particular. Furthermore, it was reported that two private prison corporations each donated $250,000 to the Trump inaugural activities and that one made donations to Trump-affiliated organizations.[55]

Summary

This chapter set the stage for the next two chapters, which discuss life in prison and community corrections. It is important to understand the history of jails and prisons in order to evaluate what is happening today. The chapter began with the European background of incarceration, emphasizing the reform efforts of John Howard. Howard was influential in America, but the Quakers led the movement toward incarceration, intended as a milder sanction to replace the death penalty and the inhuman methods of corporal punishment that prevailed in U.S. criminal justice systems.

Two systems that emerged in the United States—the Pennsylvania system, with its emphasis on solitary confinement, and the Auburn system, with its emphasis on the silent system—competed for recognition in the United States and in Europe. The influence of the systems is still seen today; many of our maximum-security prisons, built in the late 1800s and early 1900s, reflect an architecture typical of the Auburn system. In Europe, many prisons built on the architectural model of the Pennsylvania system remain in use.

The system of reformatories that emerged in the United States was focused on the Elmira Reformatory, established in 1876, but this institution did not survive long as a place of reformation, although it did set the stage for the movement toward rehabilitation and established the reformatory model that became characteristic of institutions for juveniles.

It is impossible to talk about a prison system in the United States because states have their own unique systems, the jail systems of local communities differ widely, and the federal government has a separate system. The federal system has traditionally been considered the most efficient and effective, but it is also the fastest growing. State prisons have been the sites of most of the riots and overcrowded conditions that are discussed in subsequent chapters. But many local jails also face problems of overcrowding and inadequate facilities, leading to the establishment of jail standards by the federal government, the American Correctional Association, and some states. Overcrowding has also led to inmate lawsuits, some resulting in federal court orders to reduce prison and jail populations or make changes in prison conditions.

Many of the problems of incarceration are related to overcrowding. There are two basic ways to solve this problem. First, we can build more facilities. The costs, however, are overwhelming. Perhaps even more important, if we build them, we fill them, and the problem of a lack of prison space remains. The second solution is to reduce prison populations. This has been done in some states by enacting statutes that permit governors to declare an emergency and authorize early release of some inmates when prison populations reach 95 percent (or some other figure) of legal capacity. Problems occur, however, when the releasees commit new crimes.

The cost of building new facilities to handle the overcrowding of jails and prisons, coming at a time when many government budgets were being cut, led to the involvement of the private sector in the financing and management of jails and prisons. This is a controversial innovation, as the chapter discussion demonstrated, and it can be expected to grow.

Inadequate conditions, overcrowding, and management problems in jails and prisons increase the problems of living behind the walls, as we will see in Chapter 10.

Key Terms

classification 205
community-based correction facility 209
corporal punishment 204
custody 208
humanitarianism 204
inmates 206
jail 209
offenders 204
open prison
penitentiary 205
prison 209
reformatory 208
silent system 206
transportation 204
wardens 206
workhouse 205

Study Questions

1. Explain why prisons emerged in Europe, and relate your discussion to the contributions of John Howard.
2. What characterized the emergence of prisons in the United States, and how did the Walnut Street Jail contribute to this development?
3. Compare and contrast the Pennsylvania and the Auburn systems.
4. What is a reformatory? Why were reformatories developed? Explain the importance of European reformers to this development. How did European reform programs influence the emergence of the Elmira Reformatory?
5. How do jails differ from prisons and from community-based correction facilities?
6. What is the difference between prisons centered on a philosophy of custody and those that focus on rehabilitation?
7. Distinguish among the levels of prison security. What is meant by a *supermax* or a *maxi-maxi* prison? Evaluate.
8. Explore the general and unique features of prisons for women, and compare them with the features of those for men. Discuss the issues with regard to inmate children and suggest ways to solve those problems.
9. Distinguish between the state and federal prison systems, and analyze population growth in each.
10. How does the present-day purpose of jails compare with their historical purpose? What are the problems of administering jails? What role, if any, should the federal government play in the administration of local jails?
11. What are the effects of prison and jail overcrowding?
12. Discuss recent efforts in California to handle prison overcrowding.
13. What is the place of the private sector in jails, prisons, and in other security areas?

Notes

1. Harry Elmer Barnes, *The Story of Punishment* (Boston: Stratford, 1930), pp. 117, 122. The introductory material on the history of prisons is based on this source unless otherwise noted.
2. Stephen Schaefer, *Theories in Criminology* (New York: Random House, 1969), pp. 104-105.
3. John Howard, *State of Prisons*, 2d ed. (Warrington, England: Patterson Smith, 1792).
4. Alexis M. Durham III, "Social Control and Imprisonment During the American Revolution: Newgate of Connecticut," *Justice Quarterly* 7 (June 1990): 293.
5. Alexis M. Durham III, "Newgate of Connecticut: Origins and Early Days of an Early American Prison," *Justice Quarterly* 6 (March 1989): 89-116.
6. David J. Rothman, *The Discovery of the Asylum: Social Order and Disorder in the New Republic* (Boston: Little, Brown, 1971), pp. 92-93.
7. Norman B. Johnston, "John Haviland," in *Pioneers in Criminology*, ed. Herman Mannheim (Montclair, NJ: Patterson Smith, 1960), p. 122.
8. Rothman, *The Discovery of the Asylum*, p. 83.

9. Orlando G. Lewis, *The Development of American Prisons and Prison Customs* (1922; reprint, Montclair, NJ: Patterson Smith, 1967), p. 7.
10. See Alexander W. Pisciotta, *Benevolent Repression* (New York: New York University Press, 1994).
11. Howard Gill, "State Prisons in America 1787-1937," in *Penology*, ed. George C. Killinger and Paul F. Cromwell (St. Paul, MN: West, 1973), p. 53.
12. See Michael Foucault, *Discipline and Punish: The Birth of the Prison*, trans. Alan Sheridan (New York: Pantheon, 1977).
13. Rothman, *The Discovery of the Asylum*, pp. 238-253. This source was used for the following paragraphs as well.
14. Ibid., pp. 243-253.
15. Francis J. Clauss, *Alcatraz: Island of Many Mistakes* (Menlo Park, CA: Briarcliff, 1981), p. 35. The brief history of Alcatraz comes from this source.
16. See, for example, Jolene Babyak, *Eyewitness on Alcatraz: Life on THE ROCK as Told by the Guards, Families & Prisoners* (Berkeley, CA: Ariel Vamp Press, 1988, revised 1996); Darwin E. Coon (former inmate), *Alcatraz: The True End of the Line* (Sacramento, CA: New Desmas Press, 2002); Pierre Odier, *Alcatraz: The Rock: A History of Alcatraz: The Fort/The Prison* (Eagle Rock, CA: L'Image Odier, 1982).
17. National Institute of Corrections, *Supermax Prisons: Overview and General Considerations*, summarized in "Supermax Prisons Established in Most States, Study Finds," *Criminal Justice Newsletter* 29 (December 15, 1999): 4-5.
18. "A Futuristic Prison Awaits the Hard-Core 400," *New York Times* (October 17, 1994), p. 1.
19. "There Are Jails ...," *The Daily Telegraph* (August 10, 1996), p. 22.
20. Daniel P. Mears and William D. Bales, "Supermax Incarceration and Recidivism," *Criminology* 47(4) (November 2009): 1131-1166; quotation is on p. 1154.
21. The Sentencing Project, "Women in the Criminal Justice System" (May 2007), http://www.sentencingproject.org/, accessed July 27, 2014.
22. Ibid. See also Lauren E. Glaze and Laura M. Maruschak, Bureau of Justice Statistics, *Parents in Prison and Their Minor Children* (August 2008, last revised March 30, 2010), p. 1, http://bjs.ojp.usdoj.gov/content/pub/pdf/pptmc.pdf, accessed March 26, 2011.
23. "Having Summer Camp Behind a Prison's Fence," *New York Times* (August 22, 2007), p. 19; "Family Ties in Prison," *Courier-Journal* (Louisville, KY) (July 11, 2009), p. 1.
24. This history of the federal prison system comes from a publication by Gregory L. Hershberger, *The Development of the Federal Prison System* (Washington, D.C.: U.S. Department of Justice/Federal Prison System, 1979). See also the Federal Bureau of Prisons, http://www.bop.gov/, accessed January 12, 2015.
25. Federal Bureau of Prisons, https://www.bop.gov, accessed April 30, 2019.
26. Debra Cassens Weiss, "As Position Cuts Hit Federal Prisons, Teachers and Nurses Are Tapped to Act as Guards," *American Bar Association Journal* (June 19, 2018), http://www.abajournal.com, accessed June 19, 2018. Also see the Federal Bureau of Prisons' website at https://www.bop.gov, accessed April 30, 2019.
27. Hans Mattick, "The Contemporary Jails of the United States: An Unknown and Neglected Area of Justice," in *Handbook of Criminology*, ed. Daniel Glaser (Skokie, IL: Rand McNally, 1974), p. 781.
28. Edith Elisabeth Flynn, "Jails and Criminal Justice," in *Prisoners in America*, ed. Lloyd E. Ohlin (Englewood Cliffs, NJ: Prentice Hall, 1973), p. 49.
29. Jerome Hall, *Theft, Law and Society* (Boston: Little, Brown, 1935), p. 108.
30. Joseph F. Fishman, *Crucible of Crime: The Shocking Story of the American Jail* (New York: Cosmopolis Press, 1923), pp. 13-14.
31. Debra Cassens Weiss, "Citing Unsafe Jail Conditions and Judge's Order, Sheriff Resigns along with Her Deputies," *American Bar Association Journal* (March 21, 2019), http://www.abajournal.com, accessed April 30, 2019.
32. Dielle Kaeble and Mary Cowhig, Bureau of Justice Statistics, *Correctional Populations in the United States, 2016* (April 2018), p. 1, https://www.bjs.gov/, accessed April 30, 2019.
33. Zhen Zeng, Bureau of Justice Statistics, *Jail Inmates in 2017* (April 2019), p. 1, https://www.bjs.gov/, accessed April 30, 2019.
34. Jennifer Bronson and E. Ann Carson, Bureau of Justice Statistics, "Prisoners in 2017" (April 2019), pp. 1, 13, 14, https://www.bjs.gov/, accessed April 20, 2019.
35. "Prisons Close as Crime Falls," *Dallas Morning News* (July 10, 2017), p. l; "Oklahoma Prison Chief Warns of Crisis," *Dallas Morning News* (January 17, 2018), p. 4.
36. Ibid., p. 14.
37. *Ruiz v. Estelle*, 503 F. Supp. 1265 (S.D. Tex. 1980), *aff'd in part, vacated in part, modified, in part, appeal dismissed in part*, 679 F.2d 1115 (5th Cir. 1983), *cert. denied*, 460 U.S. 1042 (1982). Numerous other proceedings in this lawsuit have occurred over the years.
38. "Crowding at Prisons Has State in a Jam," *Los Angeles Times* (March 13, 2005), Metro Desk, Part A, p. 1.
39. "The California Prison Disaster," *New York Times*, final edition (October 25, 2008), p. 22.
40. *Coleman v. Schwarzenegger*, 2009 U.S. Dist. LEXIS 67943 (E.D. Cal. 2009), *stay denied, Schwarzenegger v. Coleman*, 557 U.S. 963 (2009).
41. "Bid to Shift State Inmates to County Jails Denounced," *Los Angeles Times* (home edition) (May 23, 2009), p. 8A; "Guards Fire Rounds During Fatal Prison Riot," *Los Angeles Times* (home edition) (March 20, 2009), p. 17A; "Forcing Their Hands: Budget Crisis Pushes Governor and Lawmakers on Prison Reform," *San Diego Union-Tribune* (May 17, 2009), p. 2F.
42. *Brown et al. v. Plata and Coleman et al.*, 134 S. Ct. 1 (August 2, 2013), *motion denied by, motion granted by Coleman v. Brown*, 2013 U.S. Dist. LEXIS 115403 (E.D. Cal. August 9, 2013), *stay denied, Coleman v. Brown*, 2013 U.S. Dist. LEXIS 127407 (E.D. Cal. 2103); "California: Short Delay Granted for Inmate Cuts," *New York Times* (October 22, 2013), p. 13; "Court Gives California More Time on Prisons," *New York Times* (late edition—final) (February 11, 2014), p. 12.
43. For a discussion of California's Proposition 47, see the following articles, both in *Criminology & Public Policy* 17(3) (August 2018): Gerald G. Gaes, "Reducing the Rate of U.S. Incarceration One State at a Time: California and the Impact of Proposition 47," pp. 689-493; and Bradley J. Barton and Charis E. Kubrin, "Can We Downsize Our Prisons and Jails Without Compromising Public Safety?: Findings from California's Prop 47," pp. 693-716.
44. Proposition 47, California Department of Corrections and Rehabilitation, http://www.cdcr.ca.gov, accessed November 24, 2016.
45. See Cal. AB 109 and Cal. Penal Code 1170 (2018).

46. "$74M Jail Has It All Except Inmates, *Los Angeles Times* (June 24, 2010), p. 12.
47. Bronson and Carson, "Prisoners in 2017," p. 14.
48. Lorelei Laird, "Prison Pays: Trump Administration Reverses Federal Plans to Phase Out Use of Private Facilities," *American Bar Association Journal* (September 2017): 16-17.
49. Corrections Corporation of America (CCA), www.cca.com/careers, accessed May 2, 2015.
50. William D. Bales et al., "Recidivism of Public and Private State Prison Inmates in Florida," *Criminology & Public Policy* 4(1) (February 2005): 57-82.
51. Gerald G. Gaes, "Prison Privatization in Florida: Promise, Premise, and Performance," *Criminology & Public Policy* 4(1) (February 2005): 83-88.
52. Charles W. Thomas, "Recidivism of Public and Private State Prison Inmates in Florida: Issues and Unanswered Questions," *Criminology & Public Policy* 4(1) (February 2005): 89-100.
53. "Experts Argue Against Prison Privatization," *Federal Human Resources Week* 9(3) (April 29, 2002): n.p.
54. "Privately Run Mississippi Prison, Ruled a Scene of Horror and Correction, Closes," *New York Times* (September 16, 2016), p. 12.
55. Laird, "Prison Pays," p. 17.

10
Life in Prison

Chapter Outline

Learning Objectives

After reading this chapter, you should be able to do the following:

- Relate the historical to the more recent position of federal courts on the issue of inmates' rights
- State the general criteria the U.S. Supreme Court uses to determine whether inmates' rights, such as to be free of cruel and unusual punishment, have been violated
- Trace the evolution of prison management styles, and compare them with today's needs
- Explain the functions of correctional officers, exploring ways in which they controlled inmates historically and how that has changed recently
- Discuss gender and other issues concerning correctional administrators
- Identify some of the issues that new inmates face, and give a brief overview of inmate prison life
- Explain the inmate subculture, discuss its origin, and explore how it affects the adjustment of male and female inmates
- Analyze the social control role of the inmate system
- Discuss the influence of prison gangs in men's prisons
- Analyze the needs of female inmates and of those requiring special care and programs and discuss how those needs are or are not accommodated
- Comment on the problems of children whose parents are incarcerated
- Analyze the use of solitary confinement of inmates
- Explain the Prison Rape Elimination Act of 2003

- **Contrast same-gender sexual behavior of female and male inmates**
- **Comment on the problems of the elderly, and physically and mentally challenged inmates, and discuss the latest developments in caring for these inmates**
- **Discuss the nature and availability of prison programs**
- **Analyze the impact of prison violence**

From the inmates' point of view, imprisonment is a series of status degradation ceremonies intended to destroy their identities and to assign them new identities of a lower order.[1] The way offenders are treated when they enter prison exemplifies society's rejection; they are stripped of most of their personal belongings, given a number, searched, examined, inspected, weighed, and documented. To the inmates, these acts represent deprivation of their personal identities. The actions may be conducted in a degrading way that emphasizes their diminished status. They face the correctional officers, who have contacts and families in the outside world but who are there to ensure that the inmates conform to institutional rules.

Gresham M. Sykes referred to the psychological and social problems that result from the worst punishment, deprivation of liberty, as the "pains of imprisonment." In his classic study of male inmates in a maximum-security prison, Sykes discussed the moral rejection by the community, which is a constant threat to the inmate's self-concept; the deprivation of goods and services in a society that emphasizes material possessions; the deprivation of heterosexual relationships and the resulting threat to the inmate's masculinity; and the deprivation of security in a population in which inmates face threats to their safety, their health, and even their lives.[2]

In their attempts to adjust to the pains of imprisonment, inmates devise ways of manipulating the prison environment. Sometimes, this manipulation creates serious control problems for the correctional officers, staff, and administrators charged with the ultimate responsibility of maintaining safety and order within the prison and keeping inmates from escaping. This is not an easy task, and the problems are becoming more serious. But at the same time, federal courts have interpreted various constitutional amendments as providing standards for the treatment of inmates, along with reasonable accommodations while they are incarcerated.

This chapter examines life in prison for inmates, as well as for the prison administrators and correctional officers charged with the responsibility of maintaining prisons. The chapter begins with an overview of life in prison and then looks at some of the major legal issues associated with incarceration. The traditional approach to inmates' rights is contrasted with the modern approach as we analyze substantive and procedural issues raised by the U.S. Constitution and the modern cases interpreting that document. The roles of the primary persons charged with administering prisons—administrators and correctional officers—are explored historically and in light of recent developments.

The chapter then focuses on how inmates adapt to prison life, their daily routines, and the process of prisonization. A general discussion of inmate subcultures is followed by a look at the inmate social system as a method of social control, followed by a discussion on prison gangs. The special needs of female inmates are noted, along with the issues concerning the children of inmates. A section on prison issues begins with solitary confinement and then explores visitation policies. Male and female inmates are contrasted in how they engage in sexual behavior. Among other critical issues associated with prison life are the growing concerns with inmates who are elderly, or physically or mentally challenged. Prison programs are highlighted before the chapter closes with a discussion of prison violence, a growing concern in many institutions.

THE INCARCERATION OF OFFENDERS

Prison overcrowding has already been discussed, noting a decrease in inmate populations, but the United States, with the highest incarceration rate in the world—25 percent of the world's inmates and only 5 percent of the world's population—continues to experience overcrowding in many institutions. Calls for ending this mass incarceration have garnered attention, with a Yale University professor, James Forman Jr., receiving a Pulitzer Prize for his book on mass incarceration: *Locking Up Our Own: Crime and Punishment in Black America.* The book's title emphasizes one of the main characteristics of U.S. inmates: They are persons of color. At least 1 in 20 adult black males in 11 states are incarcerated. Overall in the United States, blacks, compared to whites, are incarcerated at a rate of 5 to 1, with a rate of 10 to 1 in Iowa, Minnesota, New Jersey, Vermont, and Wisconsin. Maryland's prison population is 72 percent black, while in 11 other states blacks constitute over 50 percent of the inmate populations.

The previous chapter discussed the late 2018 efforts of Congress and the president to reduce prison populations through various approaches, but it is too early to know what impact these measures might have. Despite their impact, some issues, such as processing offenders into the system, remain.

After offenders have been sentenced, official papers are prepared to turn them over to the custody of the state's department of corrections (or the Federal Bureau of Prisons in the federal system). They may be transported to prison immediately or retained in jail for a short period. In some states, they are sent to a diagnostic center for a physical examination, psychological testing, and orientation, and they are assigned to a particular institution after an evaluation of the test results. In other states, the placement decision may be made according to the seriousness of the offense, the age and gender of the offender, and whether the offender has a prior record (and if so, the extent and nature of that record). In the case of female offenders, there may be no choice; the state may have only one institution, which must accommodate all security levels, unless the state contracts with another state (or the federal system) to house some of its inmates.

If the state has a central diagnostic unit, inmates must be transported from that unit to their individual assignments for incarceration. Upon arrival at the assigned institution, usually they are isolated from the general population for several days or even a week or longer. During that period, they are told the rules or given a rule book to read. They undergo physical exams, and in most institutions, all incoming inmates are strip searched for drugs and weapons. They may be required to take a bath with a disinfectant soap and shampoo. Urine samples are collected to determine whether they are on drugs, and laxatives may be given to determine whether they are smuggling drugs.

The inmates' clothing may be taken and special prison clothing issued. In lower-security institutions, especially in some women's prisons, inmates may be permitted to wear their own clothing, although there may be restrictions concerning the type of clothing. The rules differ from state to state and even within states, depending on the institution's security level and other factors. When inmates are not allowed to keep personal clothing, they may be required to pay to have the clothing shipped home or may find upon release that their clothes were donated to charity. When the inmate is released, many prisons issue only one new set of clothes.

A correctional officer at the Deuel Vocational Institute in Tracy, California, escorts recently arrived inmates through the institution. These inmates have already received their prison-issued clothing, the recognizable orange jumpsuits, and probably have already gone through the initial orientation process and are ready for their assigned housing arrangements.

During the orientation period, inmates are required to complete numerous forms concerning their backgrounds, medical histories, and potential visitors. They may be asked whether they fear any persons in the prison; some inmates may need to be placed in protective custody for protection from the general population. Other inmates and correctional officials may test the inmate during the orientation period; seasoned inmates suggest that it is wise to be respectful to the officers and to be careful about making friends among other inmates. Generally, inmates are not permitted to have visitors during this orientation period. Phone calls are prohibited or limited. Thus, it is a lonely, frustrating, and stressful time. Inmates may be interviewed for job assignments or educational programs in an effort to determine placement within the institution.

Inmates are permitted to buy personal items from the **commissary**, but times for purchases and frequency of purchases are limited. Inmates cannot keep money in most institutions; it is placed in a trust fund against which they may draw for purchases. Money that may be received from the outside is limited. Any or all of the rules in effect during the orientation period may also apply to the inmate's life in the general population.

Eventually, inmates are relocated in the facility to which they are assigned, and normal prison life begins. Before we look at the details of adaptation to prison life, it is important to discuss the legal implications of incarceration.

LEGAL IMPLICATIONS OF INCARCERATION

The recognition of inmates' legal rights has a short history. The earlier judicial position on inmates' rights was expressed in an 1872 case, in which a state court declared bluntly that by committing a crime the convicted felon forfeits his or her liberty and "all his personal rights except those which the law in its humanity accords to him. He is for the time being the slave of the state."[3]

From 1872 until the 1960s, the federal courts generally observed a **hands-off doctrine** toward inmates and prisons, reasoning that prison administration is a part of the executive, not the judicial, branch of government. In 1974, however, the U.S. Supreme Court held that, although an incarcerated person loses some rights because of institutional needs, "a prisoner is not wholly stripped of constitutional protections when he is imprisoned for crime. There is no iron curtain drawn between the Constitution and the prisons of this country."[4]

Even before the 1974 decision, lower federal courts had begun looking into inmates' claims that they were being denied basic constitutional rights. By the 1980s, inmates had filed numerous lawsuits, and federal courts had scrutinized prison conditions, particularly regarding overcrowding. Entire prison systems were placed under federal court orders to reduce populations and to make other changes in prison conditions. By the 1990s, jail and prison overcrowding had resulted in an explosion of federal lawsuits concerning incarceration conditions. Recently, however, many jurisdictions have been taking steps to remove their prison systems from federal court oversight, and some have succeeded in doing so.

What was responsible for the increasing recognition of inmates' rights in federal courts? Among other issues, the **civil rights** activism of the 1960s included the treatment of inmates, and during that period, federal courts began to look at what was happening inside prisons. Many of the earlier cases involved allegations of physical brutality, as well as questionable living conditions. For example, in 1970, a federal district court that heard evidence on the prison conditions in Arkansas concluded that inmates were living under degrading and disgusting conditions, and found the prison system unconstitutional. The need for judicial intervention into the administration of prisons was stated emphatically by the federal court: "If Arkansas is going to operate a Penitentiary System, it is going to have to be a system that is countenanced by the Constitution of the United States."[5]

The dilemma that courts face regarding the hands-off policy is illustrated by the following excerpt from a federal court opinion:

> In the great majority of cases, it would be sheer folly for society to deny prison officials the discretion to act in accordance with their professional judgment. At the same time, it would be an abrogation of our responsibility as judges to assume (or, more precisely, to reassume) a "hands off" posture, requiring categorical acquiescence in such judgments. Where an inmate alleges that precious constitutional rights are being abridged, the judiciary has the power, and indeed the duty, to intervene in the internal affairs of a prison. Balancing the wisdom of judicial deference against the need for courts to involve themselves in preserving precious liberties is a task of inordinate difficulty. But face it we must if we are to discharge our arduous and delicate duty as protectors and defenders of the Constitution.[6]

Since the 1970s, federal courts have heard numerous cases on prison conditions. Federal intervention has also been extended to jails. Some prison officials have been ordered to close facilities until conditions are corrected; others have been ordered to change specific conditions. Some officials who have defied these orders have been held in contempt of court. Federal judges require that some jails and prisons be monitored to ensure that progress is made toward specified changes. Judges continue to defer to prison authorities concerning day-to-day prison operations, but they intervene when federal constitutional rights are violated. It is important to look at those issues more closely and consider how actions are brought by inmates who seek legal remedies to alleged unconstitutional conditions.

Historically, prison officials spoke of the difference between *rights* and *privileges.* Rights require constitutional protection; privileges are there by the grace of prison officials and may be withdrawn at their discretion. In 1971, the U.S. Supreme Court rejected the position that "constitutional rights turn upon whether a governmental benefit is characterized as a 'right' or a 'privilege.'"[7]

It is clear, however, that a hierarchy of rights is recognized. Some rights are considered more important than others and therefore require more extensive due process before they may be infringed upon. For example, an inmate's right to be released from illegal confinement is more important than the right to canteen privileges. Some of the other rights high in the hierarchy are the right to protection against willful injury, access to courts, freedom of religion, freedom of communication, and freedom from cruel and unusual punishment. Inmates who succeed in their lawsuits against prison officials may be entitled to civil damages, as noted in **Supplement 10.1**.

The recognition of inmates' rights and of the hierarchy of rights does not mean that the government (or prison officials acting as government agents) may not restrict those rights. Rights may be restricted if prison officials can show that the restriction is necessary for security or for other recognized penological purposes, such as discipline and order.

Another important issue concerns the tests used for determining whether an inmate's constitutional rights have been violated. One right is illustrative—the Eighth Amendment's ban against cruel and unusual punishment (see Appendix A). Generally, the U.S. Supreme Court's tests regarding this ban are stated broadly and thus are open to interpretation. In 1976, in examining allegations of cruel and unusual punishment with regard to prison conditions, the Court held that an inmate may bring a successful action against prison officials who deny him or her adequate medical care for a serious medical problem only if it can be shown that the officials acted with *deliberate indifference* to the inmate's needs. In *Estelle v. Gamble*, the Court stated that allegations of "inadvertent failure to provide adequate medical care" or of a "negligent . . . diagnos[is]" do not establish the requisite state of mind for a violation of the cruel and unusual punishment clause.[8]

In subsequent years, the U.S. Supreme Court has interpreted the cruel and unusual punishment prohibition further. Some of the cases are summarized in **Supplement 10.2**, along with cases involving violations of the First Amendment (see Appendix A).

Other constitutional rights are also involved in litigation; some are noted in subsequent discussions.

PRISON ADMINISTRATION

State prison systems have a director, who reports to the governor or a corrections board. In the federal system, the director of the U.S. Bureau of Prisons (BOP) reports to the U.S. attorney general's office in the U.S. Department of Justice (DOJ).

Wardens or Superintendents

Prison directors hire and fire wardens or superintendents of the institutions within their respective jurisdictions and manage the correctional agency's central staff. Preparing and managing a budget is one of the director's most important functions, along with supervision over those who manage the prisons. The day-to-day administration of adult prisons is the responsibility of the warden or superintendent of each institution.

In early prisons, wardens had great power. Although some exercised control as a result of strong personalities, most controlled their institutions with the authority that came from their positions. The strict chain of command from the warden down to the inmates was emphasized by the military atmosphere of most institutions: the wearing of uniforms, the use of job titles, lockstep marching, and total deference to the warden and his staff. Strict discipline, and in some cases corporal punishment, were part of that traditional, authoritarian management style. The earlier prison wardens also exercised authoritarian management styles in their interactions with the staff. The wardens had total authority to hire and fire the staff, and they could command undivided loyalty, which in staff selection could be a more important factor than competence. The warden also controlled the institution's resources. Most wardens lived on the grounds of the institutions, and the warden's household budget was included in that of the prison. The authoritarian style dominated prison management until the middle of the twentieth century.[9]

During the 1970s, significant changes took place in many American prisons. First, there were demographic changes. Harsh drug laws led to the incarceration of more young people with drug problems. The percentage of the prison population that was poor, minority, and urban increased. Attempts to suppress gang activity resulted in the incarceration of greater numbers of gang members, many of whom maintained close ties to their colleagues outside prison. Increased politicization within prisons occurred as the younger, more radical prison populations viewed incarceration as a political process. The inmates looked with disdain on the traditional rewards the officers might offer in exchange for their cooperation.

A second factor that precipitated change during the 1970s was the warden's decreased power. Many inmates and **correctional officers** (COs) were unwilling to accept the authoritarian governance style, and their rejection of that style has been supported by federal court orders. Court decisions that require changes in prison physical conditions as well as provisions for due process in some correctional proceedings reduced the traditional power of prison administrators and COs.

There are numerous obstacles to significant changes in prison management. First, the values of each group within the prison may clash. Second, the conflict between the goals of custody and rehabilitation remains. Third, there are insufficient facts on which to base decisions. Part of this results from limited research, a lack of evaluation of treatment programs, and insufficient knowledge of the applicability of new management techniques to prison settings. With a lack of knowledge of treatment and management, the prison administrator may fall back on rule books and manuals, which are likely to produce a more rigid and authoritarian type of organization.

Finally, some prisons continue to be faced with financial problems, which have reduced expenditures for management training programs and resulted in difficulties in recruiting trained persons at competitive salaries. Budget cuts have reduced the degree to which prison managers can provide the resources that are needed for many prison programs, as well as to hire sufficient staff and COs.

Some signs of progress are evident in the area of corrections management. First, more institutions are implementing research techniques to measure the success of programs and evaluation strategies for personnel. Therefore, an increasing amount of information is available to correctional managers. Second, professional organizations are developing standards for criminal justice administration, including correctional administration. These standards reflect a general concern with effective management. More important, the standards being developed by correctional managers in the field may be more responsive to problems and more acceptable to administrators.

The third, and the most important, reform in prison administration is the increased attention to professionalism. More attention has been given to attracting highly educated people to the correctional field. Management has sought to improve correctional training and to introduce new management techniques. An issue arises, however, when professionalism is viewed as the *solution* to organizational problems, which may result in a better image of the organization without sufficient attention to underlying problems.

Some research suggests, for example, that more highly educated correctional officers do not have more positive and humane attitudes toward inmates than do less educated officers. Furthermore, the more highly educated officer may be more frustrated in the job. Thus, the appearance of professionalism may be only that, unless adequate prior and on-the-job training programs are implemented to prepare correctional officers for the difficulties they will face. Important organizational changes must also be made.

Correctional Officers

The goals of the correctional institution and the management style of the warden or superintendent are very important in determining the institution's success or failure. However, the individuals with the most extensive contact and perhaps the greatest effect on inmates are the COs, or guards. Professions 10.1 presents the qualifications for the CO position in Florida.

COs in maximum-security prisons spend almost all of their workdays behind bars in close contact with inmates. It is impossible to generalize the working conditions or the reactions of COs, but the job is often monotonous and boring. Salaries are low, fringe benefits are limited, and the stress and risk are immense. Recruiting is difficult, and the turnover among officers is high in many institutions.

Attempts are being made to assist officers in adjusting to the stress caused by violence and other problems within prisons. Stress management is becoming an important element of CO training. The American Correctional Association (ACA) provides numerous publications and correspondence courses to assist COs in dealing with the daily problems they face. Criminal justice institutes provide continuing education programs. Some prison systems are giving COs a taste of life as an inmate by sending them to prison to be treated as inmates for a short period of time, but these programs are expensive and not used widely.

The initial formal training of COs is also critical. Usually, training is conducted at a central place within the prison system, and the nature of the training varies from one system to another. Of necessity, it covers institutional security; however, in addition, COs must learn how to protect themselves from inmates who attack them physically and how to react when inmates curse at, spit at, or urinate on them. Recruits are taught the rules and regulations that govern inmate behavior in prisons, and they must learn the rules and constitutional provisions that govern the behavior of COs in relation to inmates.

The fact is, however, that the primary function of COs is to maintain internal security and discipline. In the past, when corporal punishment was allowed, COs controlled inmates by physical force and, if necessary,

Professions 10.1

Professional Opportunities in Corrections

Numerous opportunities are available for persons who desire to enter the area of corrections within criminal justice systems. The website of any system will give the specifics for jurisdiction. Florida is one of the largest correctional systems and is featured here. A state statute and an administrative code section list the following as the minimum qualifications for a correctional officer career.

"**1.** Be at least 19 years of age.
2. Be a citizen of the United States notwithstanding any laws of the State to the contrary.
3. Be a high school graduate or its 'equivalent' as the term may be determined by the Criminal Justice Standards and Training Commission.
4. Not have been convicted of any felony or of a misdemeanor involving perjury or a false statement, nor have received a dishonorable discharge from any of the Armed Forces of the United States. Any person who, after July 1, 1981, pleads guilty or nolo contendere or is found guilty of a felony or of a misdemeanor involving perjury or a false statement shall not be eligible for employment or appointment as an officer, notwithstanding suspension of sentence or withholding of adjudication.
5. Have his/her processed fingerprints on file with the employing agency.
6. Have passed a medical examination by a licensed physician based on specifications established by the Commission.
7. Have a good moral character as determined by a background investigation under procedures established by the Commission.
8. Have completed the basic recruit training course for Correctional Officers and be eligible for, or possess a current employment certificate of compliance for Correctional Officers issued by the Criminal Justice Standards and Training Commission.
9. Have a valid driver's license."

***Source:* Florida Department of Corrections, "Correctional Officer Careers," http://fldocjobs.com/paths/co/qualifications.html, accessed August 1, 2014.**

brutality. Although courts have held that excessive force is not permitted constitutionally, recent evidence confirms that some COs have brutalized inmates. For example, in July 2014, New York City agreed to one of the largest settlements in such cases in its history: $2.75 million in civil damages for the death of Ronald Spear, who died in 2012 of blunt force trauma to his head, which caused fatal injuries while he was incarcerated at Rikers Island and suffering from serious kidney problems. During that same month, the city began investigating 129 allegations of inmate injuries at Rikers Island during 11 months in 2013. In December 2014, Terrence Pendergrass, a Rikers Island correctional officer, was convicted in the death of 25-year-old Jason Echevarria, an inmate in that facility, who was in need of but did not receive medical care. The deceased inmate cried out in pain after he swallowed a toxic detergent; the CO did not give him medical care but left him to suffer and die alone in his cell. At sentencing, the judge stated that Pendergrass showed little compassion or remorse: "A man died here, a 25-year-old man, because of your indifference and your callousness." The judge sentenced Pendergrass, who had requested a sentence of 21 to 27 months, to five years in prison and a $5,000 fine. Pendergrass had faced up to ten years in prison.[10]

The 2014 problems at Rikers Island led to the resignation of three top staff officials, while the city's newly elected mayor, Bill de Blasio, declared that one of his top priorities was to change the culture at Rikers Island. The mayor referred to the agency that oversees Rikers Island, the New York State Department of Corrections and Community Supervisors, as the "city's most troubled agency," and admitted that for years, some inmates who left Rikers Island were "more broken than when they came in." Among other changes at the facility, the mayor said he would triple the number of surveillance cameras (at a cost of $15.1 million) as many of the acts of brutality by COs against inmates occurred in areas that were not under camera surveillance. The city had already allocated $32 million for the expansion of programs to aid mentally challenged inmates, who made up 40 percent of the jail population. The jail administrator had already replaced 90 percent of the jail's senior leaders, which included 12 of the 14 wardens, but critics claimed all those changes were not positive, as illustrated by the fact that three of them (mentioned above) had already stepped down.[11] **Supplement 10.3** provides more information on the problems at Rikers Island.

Other than the use of force, COs in the past used manipulation of the inmates' **social system** to control them. COs permitted selected inmates to have positions of authority and control over other inmates. In recent years, however, federal courts have prohibited the practice of elevating inmates to positions of power over other inmates. In some cases, the changes resulting from the removal of inmate power over other inmates have occurred quickly without the addition of more COs to fill the power void. In other cases, inmates have gained control of institutions for temporary periods, leading to devastating riots.

In some institutions, COs' use of inmates to help control other inmates led to corruption, including officers' acceptance of bribes from inmates. Some COs have taken *contraband* (forbidden items, such as alcohol, other drugs, weapons, cell phones, and pornography) into prisons for this purpose. More recently, some institutions have permitted COs to use force (e.g., pepper spray or stun devices) to reduce or eliminate prison violence. An example is the *stun belt*, which is attached to the officer's waist. From a distance as far away as 300 feet, the device can be activated to send an eight-second, 50,000-volt electric stun. Some judges permit the use of the device for the purpose of keeping defendants or inmates in order; others do not approve its use.

One suggestion for improving the control COs have over inmates is increased professionalism and more intensive and appropriate training of officers, along with increased educational requirements. In many jurisdictions, a high school diploma is sufficient for the entry-level officer, although it would be difficult today for someone without college experience to advance to an administrative position. Good physical health is also required, for the duties of a CO may involve strenuous physical work, particularly during a riot or other prison disturbance. Mental and emotional health are also important, although many jurisdictions provide inadequate testing and training in this area.

Despite the problems, along with high turnover, corruption and brutality, difficulties in recruiting, and stress, some correctional officers see themselves as correctional agents (not just as officers primarily responsible for maintaining security and order), with a belief that the system can have positive effects on inmates.

One final emphasis of note is that many penal institutions have made efforts to increase the presence of female and minority COs. Minorities represent a significant portion of inmate populations, and female inmates, though smaller in number, have unique problems in the correctional setting, and it can be argued that those problems are best understood by female COs. In addition, female COs argue that, to gain parity with male COs, they must be able to work in prisons that incarcerate male inmates. **Supplement 10.4** discusses these issues in more detail.

ADAPTATION TO PRISON LIFE

Adapting to prison is difficult for both male and female inmates, and much of the information in this section applies to both genders. However, the initial studies of inmate prison life were conducted solely on male inmates. With the increasing number of women and their special needs, in recent years female inmates have also become a focus of research. We begin by looking at the traditional approaches; the next major section focuses primarily on female inmates.

Daily Routine and Prisonization

Life in prison is monotonous and routine. In maximum-security prisons, inmates are regulated for most of each day, beginning with the time for rising in the morning. Meal schedules may be unusual; for example, in some prisons, inmates eat breakfast at 3 or 4 A.M. and then go back to bed for naps before beginning the regular workday. This is done because of the long time period required to feed a large population in a secure facility. Dinner may be served as early as 3 P.M. Some inmates are fed in their cells. During lockdown, when there has been internal trouble among inmates and particularly after riots, inmates may be confined to their cells most of the day, with all meals served there.

Most prisons do not have sufficient jobs for all inmates to work an eight-hour day, so many inmates must find ways to fill their time. In some prisons, depending on the security needs of the institution, along with inmates' classification status, inmates are permitted to move about rather freely within certain areas of the complex.

Recreational facilities may be available in the prison's common areas. Ping-pong and board games are examples. Some prisons have gyms; others have weight rooms or a provision for outdoor recreation, such as baseball or basketball, but hours of use are limited. Some books are available for inmates to take to their cells or rooms. In large prisons, particularly maximum-security institutions, inmates are limited to a specified number of showers per week (e.g., three) and are marched to and from and are supervised during their showers. Privacy is nonexistent in most prisons. During the hours of the regular workweek, inmates may be assigned to jobs or be permitted to attend educational or vocational classes. Others may have no organized activities.

After dinner, inmates may be permitted to socialize informally in the common areas. The institution may provide activities such as movies, Alcoholics Anonymous meetings, drug-abuse seminars, or other self-help programs. Some institutions make television available; some permit inmates to have a television and radio in their cells, provided the equipment is purchased from the commissary to avoid the problem of contraband being brought into the institution by this means. However, as prisons have become crowded and more expensive in a society that has become more punitive, some prison systems have eliminated television and other amenities for inmates.

Part of the inmate's day may be spent writing letters to friends and family, although there may be limits on the number of letters that may be sent and received. Gifts from the outside are limited or excluded. Inmates may spend time taking care of their personal or prison-issued clothing and working at institutional assignments.

In minimum-security institutions, some inmates may be permitted to leave the institution from time to time for various purposes. For the most part, however, inmates are confined day and night for the duration of their sentences. During confinement, particularly in maximum-security prisons for men, inmates may be subjected to violence by other inmates; some are raped (discussed later in this chapter). Prison life is bleak for most inmates.

How do inmates adapt to this restrictive environment? In earlier prisons, they were not allowed to interact with other inmates. With the end of the segregated and silent systems discussed in Chapter 9 came the opportunity for inmates to interact. One result of this interaction has been the opportunity for inmates to form a prison subculture, or community. The new inmate encounters this subculture through the process of socialization or **prisonization**.

In 1940, Donald Clemmer reported his study of the male prison community in the Illinois maximum-security prison at Menard. Many of the more recent studies of prisons have been conducted as tests of Clemmer's theories, the most important of which was his concept of prisonization. Clemmer defined *prisonization* as "the taking on, in greater or lesser degree, of the folkways, mores, customs, and general culture of the penitentiary." The process begins as the newcomer learns his or her status as an inmate.[12]

The degree to which prisonization is effective on a specific inmate depends on several factors: (1) the inmate's susceptibility and personality; (2) the inmate's relationships outside the prison; (3) the inmate's membership in a primary group in prison; (4) the inmate's placement in the prison, such as which cell and cell mate; and (5) the degree to which the inmate accepts the dogmas and codes of the prison culture. Clemmer contended that the most important of these factors is the primary group in prison.

Clemmer saw prisonization as the process by which new inmates become familiar with and internalize prison **norms** and values. He argued that, once inmates become prisonized, they are, for the most part, immune to the influences of conventional value systems. Other scholars have tested Clemmer's conclusions. Some of the findings are noted in **Supplement 10.5**.

The Inmate Subculture and Social Control

In earlier studies, scholars analyzed the emergence and development of the inmate subculture and created two models for explaining the phenomenon: deprivation and importation. In the **deprivation model**, the inmate's pattern of behavior is an adaptation to the deprivations of his or her environment. The inmate social system is functional for inmates; it enables them to minimize the pains of imprisonment through cooperation. For example, inmate cooperation in the exchange of favors not only removes the opportunity for some to exploit others but also enables inmates to accept material deprivation more easily. Their social system redefines the meaning of material possessions. Inmates come to believe that material possessions, so highly valued on the outside, result from connections instead of hard work and skill. This realization enables inmates to insulate their self-concepts from failures in work and skill. In addition, those goods and services that are available may be distributed and shared if the inmates have a cooperative social system. Because of the pains of imprisonment and their degradation, inmates repudiate the norms of the staff, administration, and society and join forces with each other, developing a social system that enables them to preserve their otherwise threatened self-esteem. By rejecting their rejecters, they avoid having to reject themselves.[13]

The more traditional approach to an understanding of the inmate subculture, according to John Irwin and Donald R. Cressey, is that inmates take patterns of behavior with them to prison. This constitutes the **importation model**. Irwin and Cressey argued that social scientists have overemphasized inside influences as explanations for the prison inmate culture. In reality, the prison subculture is a combination of several types of subcultures that inmates import from past experiences and use within prison to adjust to the deprivations of prison life.[14] **Supplement 10.6** provides summaries of additional research on the deprivation and importation models.

The inmate social system may create problems for correctional officers and other prison personnel, for inmates upon release, and for society. The inmate social system serves as a social control agency within the prison, wielding a powerful influence over inmates because it is the only reference group available. It is powerful because inmates need status. In addition, they may be more susceptible than usual to peergroup pressure and more prone to look to the peer group than to authority figures for social support. This form of social control is functional to the prison when it maintains order within the institution. To understand it, we must look more carefully at the control problems that penal institutions face.

Within the prison, two powerful groups seek to control one another: the COs, whose primary responsibilities are custody and security, and the inmates, who are interested in escaping as much as possible from the pains of imprisonment. Richard A. Cloward studied the power struggle between these two groups. Cloward noted that in most institutions inmates reject the legitimacy of those who seek to control them. A serious social control problem may result. In many ways, the job of the custodian in prison is an impossible one. He or she is expected to maintain control and security within the institution but may not use the traditional method of doing this—force. The new, more liberal philosophy of recognizing due process and other inmates' rights has increased problems of social control for correctional officers.[15]

Under the authoritarian regime of prison administration and management, inmate cooperation was necessary to maintain peace within institutions. The few COs could not have kept a disorganized body of inmates under control. Inmates ran the institutions, and the COs cooperated. For example, COs permitted the inmate leaders to take the supplies they needed. When a "surprise" search was conducted, the COs told the inmate leaders in advance. The leaders spread the word as a form of patronage. The COs were aiding certain inmates in maintaining their positions of prestige within the inmate system; in return, inmate leaders maintained order. The system was a fairly stable one, with little disorder.

Federal court orders to abolish inmate power positions changed the traditional system of inmate-officer interaction and altered the role of the inmate social system in social control. The results are illustrated by the Texas prison system, which has been plagued with administrative attempts to maintain order. After a disturbance in 1985, during which eight inmates were killed in eight days, Texas prison officials announced that they were declaring war on the prison system. They locked down 17,000 inmates in 13 prisons. Sociologists studying the Texas prison system had reported earlier that the elevation of inmates to positions of power had kept racial tension in check, and little violence existed.[16]

Prison Gangs

When inmates were removed from positions of power over other inmates in the Texas prison system, a power vacuum occurred. This vacuum was filled by gangs, beginning with one in 1983 (the Texas Syndicate, 56 members) and increasing to eight gangs with a total of 1,400 members less than two years later. Violence increased, with gang warfare occurring between the Texas Syndicate and the Mexican Mafia, two of the largest prison gangs. In an earlier analysis of the organizational structure of these two gangs, one scholar described them as similar. Among other characteristics, each followed a code of rules, called the *constitution*. The penalty for violating any of those rules was death.[17]

Gangs exist in many, if not all, prisons and may be very influential in prison social control, with actions ranging from rape to murder. Effective control of gang influence demands knowledge of the gang members and their activities. Gangs are difficult to control, but the collection of data on gang crime and the analysis of gang activities and memberships have increased in recent years. Some of the studies include prison settings; others do not. Some focus on gangs and drugs, but regardless of the focus, the research leaves many questions unanswered. It is clear, however, that gangs have a significant, negative impact on prison life. Inmates cite gang formation as one of the reasons for the increased turmoil within prisons. The presence of gangs, along with administrative policies concerning them, adds to the increasingly unpredictable world in which inmates live.

The best way to control prison gangs may be to become familiar with their expected activities, so intelligence gathering is critical. In California, where prison gangs are a constant threat, "intelligence gathering is the method and the cornerstone of all efforts to curb, suppress and prevent gang activity that is both criminal and disruptive to public safety and the safety and security of penal institutions."[18] Some progress has been made in the prosecution of prison gangs. Federal prosecutors successfully prosecuted the Aryan Brotherhood prison gang, which, they claimed, was one of the most violent and controlling gangs in the country. This gang emerged in the 1960s at the California prison in San Quentin. The gang was accused of using terror, including murder, to control inmates nationwide. Guilty verdicts were returned against the defendants, who included the gang's top leaders: Barry "The Baron" Mills and Tyler "The Hulk" Bingham. The defendants were eligible for the death penalty under California law, but they were sentenced to life in prison.[19] **Supplement 10.7** excerpts a case involving California's prison gangs.

FEMALE INMATES

Characteristics of the female offender may help explain the nature of her adaptation to prison life and the differences between her methods of adapting and those of the typical male offender. Women constitute only a small percentage of prison populations, but their numbers have increased more rapidly than those of male inmates in recent years. Female jail inmates have also increased more rapidly in recent years than have male inmates and, in 2017, constituted 15.2 percent of jail populations.[20]

Women are more likely than men to be serving time for drug and property offenses. It is argued that women are the "silent victims" of the war on drugs, as their increasing numbers in prison have occurred in conjunction with mandatory minimum sentences for drug offenses. "[W]omen now represent the fastest growing prison population nationwide for drug offenses."[21] Female inmates are more likely than male inmates to have children in their homes when they are incarcerated, and they are more likely to be married and unemployed at the time of their incarceration.

Like men, women often develop an inmate subculture while in confinement. In her earlier and classic study of the Federal Reformatory for Women, Rose Giallombardo considered the issue of whether the female inmate subculture is an adaptation to the pains of imprisonment or is imported from outside experiences. Giallombardo concluded that the female prison inmate culture, or social system, cannot be explained solely as a response to prison deprivations, although those may precipitate its development. She illustrated her point primarily by looking at gender roles within correctional institutions for women and girls. Those gender roles reflected the roles women play in society. Her point was that attitudes and values, as well as roles and statuses, are imported into the prison system. Prison deprivations provide the structure in which these roles are performed.[22]

The evidence seems to suggest that, although roles within the inmate systems of men and women differ, they reflect the differences in the attitudes, values, and roles that have distinguished men and women traditionally. For example, in his study of a men's prison, Sykes suggested that loss of security was the greatest problem the male inmate faced. For the female inmate, however, it appears that the loss of liberty and autonomy is the major deprivation. Women miss the freedom to come and go and resent the restrictions on their communications with family and friends. In the institutions, everything is planned for them. Furthermore, female inmates may be frustrated because they have no control over events that occur in the outside world: Their children may be neglected, a loved one may become sick or die, and husbands or boyfriends may be unfaithful.

For some female inmates, prison life is a deprivation of the goods and services to which they are accustomed. As soon as they enter the institution, female inmates, like male inmates, are stripped of most of their worldly possessions, a kind of symbolic death. They must endure supervised baths and bodily examinations for drugs and contraband. They may have to give up their personal clothing and wear prison uniforms, although in some institutions, female inmates are permitted to wear their own clothes. Generally, personal items such as jewelry, pictures, cosmetics, and other beauty products are banned or limited. Furthermore, many female inmates have "significant histories of physical and sexual abuse, high rates of HIV infection, and substance abuse."[23]

Many female inmates leave minor children when they become incarcerated. Chapter 9 looked briefly at the dilemmas presented to criminal justice systems as a result of inmates who are parents, focusing in particular on the need to accommodate inmate mothers. A publication by the Bureau of Justice Statistics (BJS) presents data on parents in prison and their minor children. Some of the details are reproduced in Spotlight 10.1.

Spotlight 10.1

Parents in Prison and Their Minor Children

Some of the conclusions concerning incarcerated parents and their minor children as reported by the Bureau of Justice Statistics are as follows:

- "Parents of minor children held in the nation's prisons increased by 79% between 1991 and midyear 2007. . . .
- The number of children under age 18 with a mother in prison more than doubled since 1991. . . .
- More than 4 in 10 fathers in state or federal prisons were black; almost 5 in 10 mothers were white. . . .
- The majority of prisoners reported having a minor child, a quarter of which were age 4 or younger. . . .
- More than a third of minor children will reach age 18 while their parent is incarcerated. . . .
- Drug and public-order offenders in state and federal prisons were more likely than violent offenders to have children . . . .
- Inmates in state and federal prisons with a criminal history were more likely to be parents of minor children than those with no criminal history. . . .
- More than 4 in 10 mothers in state prison who had minor children were living in single-parent households in the month before arrest. . . .
- Fathers living with their minor child relied heavily on someone to provide daily care. . . .
- Fathers most commonly reported the child's mother as current caregiver of their children, while mothers most commonly reported the child's grandparents. . . .
- More than three-quarters of state prison inmates who were parents of minor children reported that they had some contact with their children since admission. . . .
- Mothers in state prison (58%) were more likely than fathers (49%) to report having a family member who had also been incarcerated. . . .
- Mothers in state prison [were] more likely than fathers to report homelessness, past physical or sexual abuse, and medical and mental health problems. . . .
- Mothers in prison had served less time at time of interview and expected to be released in a shorter amount of time than fathers."

Source: Lauren E. Glaze and Laura M. Maruschak, Bureau of Justice Statistics, *Parents in Prison and Their Minor Children* (August 2008, last revised March 30, 2010), https://bjs.gov/content/pub/pdf/pptmc.pdf, accessed October 23, 2018.

Most female inmates who have children were living with them when they were incarcerated. Care for their children is a primary concern of many inmate mothers, and separation from them is one of the greatest pains of their incarceration. An inmate mother must face her inability to care for her children, along with the loss of self-esteem that may come with incarceration. She must cope with the readjustment she and her children face when she is released from prison. She must deal with the lack of visitation opportunities for children and the difficulty of telling her children what is happening. Some may face lawsuits over the legal custody of their children. All of these factors may affect the ways in which incarcerated mothers adapt to prison life.

Children suffer when one or both parents are incarcerated. Young children may have separation anxiety, which appears to be magnified when it is the mother who is incarcerated. The reason may be that when women are incarcerated their children usually live with grandparents (53 percent of the cases) or other relatives, or even in foster homes (almost 10 percent), rather than with their fathers. But when men are incarcerated, the children of 90 percent of them live with their mothers. Women are incarcerated in institutions that are, on the average, 160 miles from their homes, compared to only 100 miles for men.[24]

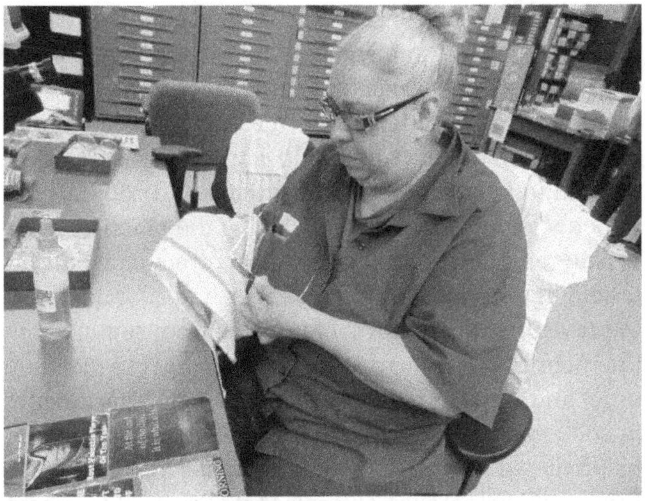

Jill, an inmate at the state women's prison in Cambridge Springs, Pennsylvania, works on a pair of eyeglasses May 31, 2018. She hoped to be out of prison in January and planned to seek a job as an optician.

Female inmates also have unique medical needs that present challenges when they are incarcerated. All inmates are legally entitled to basic health care needs, but the issue of whether special medical care for women should be available in prisons, along with legal issues surrounding the differences in programs that are available to male as compared to female inmates, has led to numerous court cases, some of which are discussed in **Supplement 10.8**.

There are still overall problems in the ways in which prison systems care for the medical and other needs of female inmates. There are concerns with mental health care, education, employment, and other programs. An intensive study of female inmates from the District of Columbia published in 2016 made numerous recommendations for changes in the processing and treatment of these inmates, including permitting new mothers to spend at least six months with their babies. Only nine states had nursery programs (or plans to create them) for newborns whose mothers were in prison, citing research showing that such programs increase bonding between mothers and their newborns and decrease the number of repeat offenses for released mothers. In addition, the report recommended increased programs for drug treatment and mental health issues as well as more educational and job training programs.[25]

PRISON ISSUES

This section focuses on only a few of the many issues regarding prison life, including solitary confinement; visitation policies; inmate sexual behavior; elderly, or physically or mentally challenged inmates; prison programs; and prison violence.

Solitary Confinement

The practice of confining inmates for long periods of time without contact with other persons is a long-standing method of punishment in jails and prisons, but currently, the practice of solitary confinement is being challenged as a violation of constitutional rights. In June 2014, Governor John Hickenlooper of Colorado signed a statute making that state the second state (New York was the first) to impose restrictions on the practice, especially as it relates to mentally challenged inmates. This step was a reaction to the 2013 murder of the state's prison chief, Tom Clements, who was killed by Evan Ebel after his release from prison. Ebel spent most of his eight-year prison stay in solitary confinement. He was released into society from solitary confinement, murdered a pizza delivery person to get his uniform, and went to Clements's house in that uniform, apparently to entice him to open the door to his assassin. Ebel was later murdered in Texas during a shootout with police who stopped him for a traffic violation.[26]

Rick Raemisch, executive director of the Colorado Department of Corrections, who succeeded the murdered director, spent 20 hours in a solitary confinement cell in that state's prison system. Raemisch took this action to understand what the experience is like, but of course, his short stay was not comparable to that of inmates who spend years in solitary. Of his experience, the director said:

> Whatever solitary confinement did to that former inmate and murderer, [referring to Ebel] it was not for the better.
>
> When I finally left my cell at 3 P.M., I felt even more urgency for reform. If we can't eliminate solitary confinement, at least we can strive to greatly reduce its use. Knowing that 97 percent of inmates are ultimately returned to their communities, doing anything less would be both counterproductive and inhumane.[27]

The length of stays in solitary confinement varies from state to state and within prisons, but one inmate released from prison in 2013 had been in solitary confinement for 41 years. He died a few days after he was released from prison. Herman Wallace had always maintained his innocence; a federal judge had ruled that he was entitled to a new trial; he was quickly indicted again but did not live for the retrial. His attorneys, commenting on their client's endurance of a situation few of us could even imagine, "did it with grace, dignity, and empathy to the end." One of the last phrases from Wallace to his lawyers was, "I am free. I am free."[28]

Wallace and Albert Woodfox were convicted in 1974 of killing a corrections officer. They (and another inmate) were each placed in solitary confinement cells (6 feet by 9 feet) for up to 23 hours a day in the Louisiana State Penitentiary in Angola. They became known as the Angola 3 and were the subjects of a 2011 report by Amnesty International and featured in a documentary film, *In the Land of the Free.*[29]

An attorney who has litigated prison law issues reported that 44 states permit solitary confinement in prisons. He cited a 2005 report indicating that over 80,000 inmates at that time were being held in solitary confinement. Some described the condition as "being trapped in a coffin." Inmates had no books or other diversions, and lights were often kept on 24 hours. The attorney pointed out that the United States is a nation of laws based on a constitution. He asked, "Do we really find this kind of treatment of prisoners acceptable?"[30]

In 2015, President Barack Obama became the first sitting U.S. president to visit a federal prison. During his visit to the medium-security prison in El Reno Federal Correctional Institution (near Oklahoma City), the president called for ending solitary confinement for months and years. In 2017, a spokesperson for the Texas Department of Criminal Justice announced, "While reviewing solitary confinement as a policy and practice we determined that as a department we can effectively operate without it." The system continued to use administrative segregation, which is nonpunitive and imposed for security or protective reasons, but its use had "plummeted over the past decade."[31]

Supplement 10.9 focuses on two cases involving solitary confinement in which the U.S. Supreme Court refused to grant a review in 2018. However, Justice Sonia Sotomayor, who agreed with the Court's decision, wrote her comments on the seriousness of the practice, expressing her "deeply troubling concern" about the practice. Ironically, one of the defendants in these cases was the director of corrections mentioned above, Rick Raemisch.

Finally, the negative effects of solitary confinement were among the issues raised in recent years in California. Judge Claudia Wilkin of the U.S. Federal District Court in Oakland, California, granted the class action status petition from inmates in Pelican Bay Prison who had spent over a decade in solitary confinement. The inmates alleged that such treatment constitutes cruel and unusual punishment and thus is a violation of their Eighth Amendment rights (see Appendix A). The granting of class action status meant that a decision in the forthcoming lawsuit would impact more than just the plaintiffs who brought the lawsuit and could be the impetus for court decisions negating the practice. Judge Wilkin refused to permit California correctional officials to join in the suit. They claimed they had a legal interest in preventing the removal of inmates from solitary confinement in that such treatment is necessary to maintain order and security within the prison. Most of the inmates in solitary were alleged to be gang members who could be predicted to be violent. In addition to the Pelican Bay Prison, officials at the California State Prison at Corcoran placed alleged gang members in solitary confinement.

In February 2015, Judge Wilkin ruled from the bench that inmates who had been transferred out of Pelican Bay to other prisons but who were detained in solitary confinement while in the Pelican Bay Prison could be included as plaintiffs in the lawsuit. The judge issued her written opinion in March 2015. The California lawsuit contended that the practice in the Pelican Bay Prison was extreme and "renders California an outlier in this country and in the civilized world." The case of *Ashker v. Governor of California* resulted in a settlement, which is summarized in **Supplement 10.10**.

Visitation Policies

Even inmates who are not in solitary confinement have needs for visitation. As noted previously, some provision for parental/child interaction is important for inmates with children. But it is also important for inmates to have visits from other family members and friends. Some inmates do not have anyone to visit them; others have families who cannot visit because of cost and distance between their homes and the confinement facilities. But for inmates who have family and friends who wish to visit, prisons establish strict rules. Some of these rules are necessary for security reasons; others are questionable.

In 2003, in *Overton v. Bazzetta,* the U.S. Supreme Court approved the Michigan corrections policies that limited the number of visitors inmates could receive. Michigan authorities argued that as their prison populations grew, resulting in increased numbers of visitors, their problems with discipline (e.g., the use of alcohol and other drugs and maintaining order) also increased. It was necessary, they argued, to limit visits, especially from children, who require additional supervision.[32]

Under the Michigan policy in question in the *Overton v. Bazzetta* case, most inmates could receive visits only from persons on their approved lists (excluding clergy and attorneys). Each inmate could list an unlimited number of members of his or her immediate family plus ten other individuals (with some restrictions). Children under 18 could not be listed unless they were the inmates' children, stepchildren, grandchildren, or siblings. Children of inmates whose parental rights had been terminated could not visit. Furthermore, "[a] child authorized to visit must be accompanied by an adult who is an immediate family member of the child or of the inmate or who is the legal guardian of the child." The Michigan policies also provided that inmates who were cited for multiple substance abuse violations not have any visitors except clergy and attorneys.[33]

The U.S. Supreme Court reviewed its precedent cases concerning inmate rights, especially the right of association, and concluded that the Michigan policies did not violate them. In particular, the Court noted, "freedom of association is among the rights least compatible with incarceration. . . . Some curtailment of that freedom must be expected in the prison context." The Court concluded that the prison authorities had presented rational reasons for the visitation rules and the goal of security, and that was all they were required to do. With regard to the curtailing of visits for inmates with multiple substance abuse violations, the Court emphasized that this restriction was subject to removal in two years. The restriction, however, "serves the legitimate goal of deterring the use of drugs and alcohol within the prisons. Drug smuggling and drug use in prison are intractable problems."[34]

In the early 1900s, the Mississippi prison at Parchman began a program of conjugal visiting in which some inmates were permitted brief but private visits from spouses. In 2014, that program was ended amid concerns that the result might be pregnancies and the spread of HIV. The cost was also a factor.[35]

Currently, some prisons and jails permit video visitations, and some institutions use the offering of these visits to justify denying in-person visits. The justification is that some inmate families live too far away to visit in person, and the institution's cost for monitoring personal visits is high. Video visits also eliminate the possibility that visitors can introduce contraband into the jail or prison. The negative aspects are that the cost of video visits is high (50 cents per minute in 15-minute increments in an Arkansas prison in 2018) and such visits remove the personal aspect of visitations, which are especially important with family members.[36]

Inmate Sexual Behavior

Inmates face sexual harassment and abuse from other inmates, which is reported more frequently by male than by female inmates. The issue of same-gender sex and especially rape has been a topic of research in male prisons for years.

Isolation from the opposite gender implies abstinence from the satisfaction of heterosexual relationships at a time when the sex drive is strong. Earlier studies reported that between 30 and 40 percent of male inmates had some same-gender experiences while in prison. These estimates were discussed at a conference on prison homosexuality in the early 1970s. Peter C. Buffum wrote a synthesis of the five working papers presented at that conference. Buffum contended that the belief that we can eliminate same-gender sex in prisons by establishing other outlets for sexual drives is a myth.[37] Others have not agreed, however, and the subject deserves further attention.

In prison, same-gender sexual behavior among male inmates seldom involves a close relationship. In some cases, a man who is vulnerable to sexual attacks enters into a sexual relationship with another man, who agrees to protect him from abuse by other inmates. Earlier studies found that sexual acts between male inmates seemed to be a response to their sexual needs coupled with their socialization. Men are taught to be aggressive, and playing the male role (the wolf) in a sexual act with another man might enable the inmate to retain this self-concept. Furthermore, male inmates may see a prison sexual relationship as little more than a search for a casual, mechanical act of physical release.[38]

Some researchers have found prostitution to be the most frequent type of same-gender sexual behavior among male inmates. Usually, the behavior is not the result of violence; however, when violence occurs, it often has racial implications.[39] It is a power play, which may be compared to the rape of a woman by a man. It represents the need to dominate, control, and conquer.

Daniel Lockwood, who reported on his study of male inmates in New York prisons, interviewed men designated as targets of sexual propositions or sexual abuse, as well as those who were identified as sexual aggressors. He found that many verbal threats of sexual aggression did not result in actual aggression.[40]

Perhaps most inmate same-gender rape victims do not report the acts, primarily because of the fear of reprisal from other inmates. Some fear for their lives if they cooperate with officials in trying to solve violent acts.

These fears may or may not be unreasonable. For those who do report being raped and file lawsuits, the standard for review was articulated by the U.S. Supreme Court in 1994 in *Farmer v. Brennan*. In this case, an inmate who considered herself a woman, but whom prison officials classified as a man, alleged that she was raped in her cell in a high-security federal prison in Terre Haute, Indiana, where she was incarcerated for credit card fraud. In deciding Farmer's case, the U.S. Supreme Court focused on the meaning of *deliberate indifference*, defining the term for the first time. The concept is similar to criminal negligence and calls for subjective rather than objective knowledge. "The officials must both be aware of facts from which the inference could be drawn that a substantial risk of serious harm exists, and he must also draw the inference." The case was sent back to determine more facts.[41]

In contrast to the same-gender sexual behavior of many male inmates, same-gender sexual behavior among female inmates may develop out of mutual interest to alleviate the depersonalization of the prison and to gain status.[42] For a female inmate, a lesbian relationship may take the place of the primary group relationship for some male inmates. Talk of loyalty, sharing, trust, and friendship among female inmates may refer to the same-gender relationship, not to primary groups per se. Lesbian relationships represent an attempt to simulate the family found outside the prison and are not primarily for sexual gratification. One study reported that same-gender relationships were the most important relationships among female inmates.[43]

For female inmates, pseudo families may compensate for the lack of a close family environment on the outside. They permit the exercise of dominant and submissive roles, which the women learned outside of prison. Within these pseudo families is an opportunity for sexual behavior, but sexual behavior does not appear to be the primary reason that female inmates form family relationships.[44]

Another characteristic of the sexual behavior of female inmates distinguishes their behavior from that of male inmates' sexual involvement. Whereas in most cases male sexual behavior, especially rape, is manifested in actual physical sexual contact (oral or anal sex), for female inmates, sexual relationships may involve only a strong emotional relationship, with some bodily contact that would be acceptable outside prison (e.g., embracing upon seeing one another). However, some women may hold hands or engage in more serious forms of sexual contact that attempts to simulate heterosexual intercourse.[45]

Another issue regarding sexual behavior, especially in women's prisons, is contact (including rape) between inmates and COs. Allegations that male COs have sexually abused female inmates have been substantiated in several studies. The General Accounting Office (GAO) conducted a study of the correctional facilities in the District of Columbia, along with the three largest systems: California, Texas, and the federal system, which house more than one-third of all female inmates in the United States. The study found that some of the allegations were substantiated but noted that the actual number of incidents is not known because "many female inmates may be reluctant or unwilling to report staff sexual misconduct, and jurisdictions lack systematic data collection and analysis of reported allegations." Sexual misconduct includes "consensual" sexual activities. Inmates are not legally permitted to consent to sex with staff. Most of the reported incidents of sexual activity involved "verbal harassment, improper visual surveillance, improper touching, and/or consensual sex," with allegations of rape and related forms of sexual violence noted only rarely.[46]

More recent studies, however, have shown that more than half of the sexual assaults committed against female inmates are perpetrated by other female inmates, not male staffers. Two researchers from the University of South Dakota studied sexual abuse in three midwestern medium- and maximum-security prisons that house women. The researchers studied sexual activity by coercion as well as by force. They found greater coercion (about double) in the larger prison, which was more racially diverse and housed women who had committed more serious crimes. In that institution, approximately 25 percent of the interviewed women said they had been sexually coerced while in prison, over 33 percent of them by one assailant and 40 percent by two or three persons together. Less than one-third of these victims reported the attacks to prison officials.[47]

Female inmates are not the only targets of sexual abuse by prison officials. Male inmates are abused by female correctional officers, as noted in Spotlight 10.2.

Legislation is one way to reduce or eradicate sexual assaults against both female and male inmates. An example is the federal Prison Rape Elimination Act (PREA) of 2003, which pertains not only to sexual assaults but also to other prison issues, such as AIDS, mental illness, general violence, and psychological problems.[48] Portions of the law are presented in **Supplement 10.11**.

The PREA requires annual hearings to collect evidence on prison rapes to enable improved conditions for preventing such violence. It requires an annual report by

Spotlight 10.2

Sexual Abuse of Male Inmates by Prison Officials

Two female former correctional officers at the supermax federal prison in Florence, Colorado, Kellee S. Kissinger, 34, and Christine Achenbach, 42, were accused of engaging in oral sex or sexual intercourse with male inmates. Achenbach, who held the fourth highest position at the prison, executive assistant to the warden, was convicted in December 2002. In May 2003, she was sentenced to five years' probation and four months' home detention, and fined $3,000. The sentencing judge, commenting that she had no option but to require the defendant to register as a sex offender, stated, "Even though I personally would not want to see this kind of conviction treated as a sex-offender conviction, I must apply the law as it is written, not as I wish it were written." Of the inmates, the judge said, "I don't think they felt victimized at all.... They probably enjoyed it." Kissinger, who accepted a plea bargain that Achenbach refused, was sentenced to four years' probation and a $2,400 fine. She was given the option of serving 100 hours of community service in lieu of the fine.[1]

In February 2014, a female former correctional officer at the federal Metropolitan Detention Center located in Brooklyn, New York, was sentenced to one year and one day in prison for having sex with an inmate sentenced to death row in his second sentencing (his first death sentence was reversed by an appellate court). Nancy Gonzalez gave birth to a son, Justus, by the inmate, Ronell Wilson. The sentencing judge assessed a prison sentence to Gonzalez because she found her to be manipulative despite the fact that she is severely emotionally dysfunctional and "broken" and had "the most horrendous upbringing of anyone that I've ever seen being sentenced." According to the judge, Wilson used Gonzalez "with her full knowledge and cooperation to create a tinder box" in the facility. He used his relationship with her to intimidate other inmates and thus created security risks.[2]

1. "Official Gets Probation for Inmate Sex," *Denver Post* (May 16, 2003), p. 4B.
2. "Year in Jail for Ex-Guard Who Had Child with an Inmate," *New York Times* (February 20, 2014), p. 14.

June 30 of each year. The highlights of the latest available report are presented in Spotlight 10.3.

Inmates Who Are Elderly, or Physically or Mentally Challenged

Another characteristic of changing prison life is the increase in the number of inmates who are elderly, or physically or mentally challenged. Physically and mentally challenged persons have been incarcerated for years, but recently, some courts have held that the Americans with Disabilities Act (ADA) and its predecessor, the 1973 federal Rehabilitation Act, apply to inmates in some circumstances. The Ninth Circuit Court of Appeals has held that in its administration of programs, prison officials may not discriminate against inmates with disabilities who are "otherwise qualified" (a requirement of the ADA statute).[49] It has been held, however, that the statutes do not apply to inmate employment.[50] The U.S. Supreme Court refused to review either of these cases.

In 2014, an inmate in Oregon filed a federal lawsuit under the ADA, claiming that as a deaf person, he is entitled to a qualified sign language interpreter. David D. VanValkenburg, 48, alleged that he was excluded from full participation in many prison activities, such as intake interviews, because of the prison's failure to provide him with an interpreter. In 2016, the plaintiff was awarded $400,000 in noneconomic damages. In 2017, he was awarded $683,873.13 in attorney fees, $18,155.19 in costs, and $3,924.79 in litigation expenses.[51]

Another special group of inmates are those who are elderly. The aging of the prison population presents new challenges, as noted in Criminal Justice Systems Dilemma 10.1.

Spotlight 10.3

Highlights of the Prison Rape Elimination Act Data

On June 29, 2018, the Bureau of Justice Statistics published the following highlights of data collected during 2017 and 2018 under this act.

- "Correctional administrators reported 24,661 allegations of sexual victimization in 2015, nearly triple the number recorded in 2011. . . .
- Substantiated allegations rose from 902 in 2011 to 1,473 in 2015 (up 63%). (Substantiated allegations are those in which an investigation determined an event occurred, based on a preponderance of the evidence.)
- In 2014, unfounded allegations (8,372) exceeded unsubstantiated allegations (7,783) for the first time in SSV data collection. Prior to 2014, more allegations were unsubstantiated than were unfounded. (Unfounded allegations are those in which an investigation determined that an event did not occur.)
- Among the 24,661 allegations of sexual victimization in 2015, a total of 1,473 were substantiated, 10,142 were unfounded, 10,313 were unsubstantiated, and 2,733 were still under investigation.
- The sharp rise in unfounded or unsubstantiated allegations of sexual victimization coincided with the release of the National Standards to Prevent, Detect, and Respond to Prison Rape in 2012. It reflects improvements in data collection and reporting by correctional authorities, and increased reporting of allegations by inmates."

Source: Jessica Stroop, Bureau of Justice Statistics, "PREA Data Collection Activities, 2018" (June 29, 2018), https://www.bjs.gov, accessed October 25, 2018.

The special needs of mentally challenged inmates should also be addressed. The BJS reported that over one-half of all jail and prison inmates have a mental health problem. Approximately 15 percent of state prison inmates and 24 percent of jail inmates meet the criteria for a psychotic disorder. Nearly one-fourth of the mentally challenged prison and jail population have served three or more sentences for previous convictions, and approximately three-fourths meet the criteria for substance abuse or dependency. More female inmates than male inmates are mentally challenged. Mentally challenged inmates are more likely than other inmates to report being physically or sexually abused in the past.[52]

A later BJS publication noted that more white than black or Hispanic prison and jail inmates are likely to meet the threshold of serious psychological distress (SPD) in the previous 30 days, and more prison inmates (14%) and jail inmates (26%) "met the threshold for SPD in the past 30 days than the standardized general population (5%)."[53]

Concerned persons and organizations have called for investigations into the way mentally challenged inmates are treated. Many are kept in isolation 23-24 hours a day in tiny rooms with little ventilation or light, conditions that, according to mental health experts, may lead to deterioration, depression, and even suicide. After judges found that a disproportionate number of mentally ill inmates were being housed in isolation in the Wisconsin and Ohio prisons, those states agreed to be monitored. The American Civil Liberties Union (ACLU) filed suits in several jurisdictions concerning the manner in which mentally ill persons are confined in prisons, and they have had some success. To cite one example, in 2007 the ACLU settled out of court with the Indiana Department of Corrections, with an agreement to discontinue extreme sensory deprivation of mentally ill inmates. Prison officials promised "to avoid housing seriously mentally ill prisoners in long-term isolation and to provide additional mental health services for all prisoners housed in the SHU [Secured Housing Unit.]"[54]

In April 2009, the ACLU released its findings concerning what it referred to as nightmarish conditions in the nation's largest detainment facility: the Los Angeles County Jail system, which houses approximately 20,000 detainees on any given day. Inmates with mental illness

Criminal Justice Systems Dilemma 10.1

Elderly Offenders: Incarcerate or Treat in the Community?

Elderly inmates present criminal justice systems with a serious dilemma. These inmates are considerably more expensive to house and care for, and they are increasing in numbers. The Pew Charitable Trusts analyzed Bureau of Justice Statistics data and noted that the number of older inmates increased by 280 percent between 1999 and 2016. This increase occurred while the number of younger inmates was decreasing. "As a result, older inmates swelled from 3 percent of the total prison population to 11 percent."[1]

Even more expensive is the medical care needed for elderly inmates. New York estimated that it costs the state $150,809 a year to incarcerate and care for a gravely ill inmate.[2] To accommodate its elderly and sick population of inmates, the state developed a special-needs facility, possibly the first in the nation. It specializes in treating inmates with dementia-related conditions such as Alzheimer's disease. The 30-bed facility opened in 2006. Staff members are specially trained to understand the behavior of inmates with such cognitive problems. The behavior may at first appear problematic and requiring disciplinary action, but it really is simply a manifestation of the inmates' cognitive problems.[3]

After conducting a study of elderly California female inmates age 55 or older, a geriatrician at the San Francisco Veterans Administration Medical Center concluded: "Prison is not a safe place for vulnerable older people. . . . Prisons are not geared to the needs of older people." Approximately 69 percent of the elderly female inmates had difficulty in one or more of the following daily activities: standing in line, listening to orders, climbing into a top bunk, dropping to the floor rapidly when the alarm sounded, or walking to and from the dining hall. Within the previous year, 55 percent of the women had fallen; 16 percent needed assistance to perform at least one daily function. That percentage was twice the national average for nonincarcerated persons age 65 or older.[4]

Some of the difficulties the elderly face call for physical adjustments in facilities (e.g., installing grab bars on showers, tubs, and toilets), or rearrangements (e.g., assigning them to lower bunks) or housing them closer to the dining hall or other facilities that they need. Other issues, such as medical care, are not so easily solved.

A 2014 editorial referred to prisons as "Nursing Homes Behind Bars," emphasizing the increased costs of prisons to house the elderly, which it described as "the largest and fastest-growing segment of the American prison population," a segment that quadrupled between 1995 and 2010, costing approximately $16 billion per year by 2014.[5]

Compassionate release of elderly inmates is noted in the next chapter and is one way to alleviate the high cost of incarceration of those 50 and over.

---

1. Matt McKillop and Alex Boucher, Pew Charitable Trusts, "Aging Prison Populations Drive Up Costs: Older Individuals Have More Chronic Illnesses and Other Ailments That Necessitate Greater Spending" (February 20, 2018), https://www.pewtrusts.org, accessed October 25, 2018.
2. "Law Has Little Impact on Compassionate Release for Ailing Inmates," *New York Times* (January 30, 2010), p. 17.
3. "Spotlight July/August 2008—Prison Gray" (July 29, 2008), http://www.docs.state.ny.us/NewsRoom/external_news/2008-07-09_Prison_Gray.pdf, accessed June 18, 2010; "Dementia Behind Bars," Editorial, *New York Times* (March 26, 2012), p. 11.
4. "Study: U.S. Prisons Fall Short in Caring for Elderly Inmates," *Corrections Professional* 11(14) (April 7, 2006): n.p.
5. "Nursing Homes Behind Bars," *New York Times* (September 29, 2014), p. 22.

cost approximately $140 per night (over $50,000 a year) to detain, and many low-risk detainees are held for months because they do not have the money to post bond. With regard to mental illness specifically, the report concluded: "[I]dleness and massive overcrowding at the jail leads to violence, victimization, custodial abuse and ultimately psychotic breakdown even in relatively healthy people, as well as potentially irreversible psychosis in detainees with pre-existing illness."[55]

In December 2014, the Los Angeles County jail system agreed to oversight by a three-person panel appointed by a federal court and having extensive oversight authority. Extensive changes were to be made in policies and the administration of those policies. According to one of the FBI agents who reviewed the system's records, the "level of violence and brutality" was "astonishing." The agent said "he had never seen anything like it in the United States or elsewhere in the world."[56]

In 2003, a federal appeals court upheld the decision of a U.S. district judge in Portland, Oregon, who ruled that the state violated the rights of mentally challenged persons by keeping them in county jails for weeks or months before they were sent to the state hospital, where they could receive psychiatric care. According to the Ninth Circuit Court of Appeals, mentally challenged persons who are awaiting trial have a higher rate of suicide and "are often locked in their cells for 22 to 23 hours a day, which further exacerbates their mental illness." Only the state hospital is charged with their psychiatric care; thus, if they are held in jail and not transferred to that facility, they will not get the psychiatric care they need to become competent to stand trial.[57]

There have been some improvements. In August 2014, a federal judge approved California's plan to reduce its practice of placing mentally challenged inmates in solitary confinement, provide mental health treatment and suicide prevention programs, and develop other policies.[58] On June 18, 2015, the U.S. Supreme Court reversed a lower court decision denying a death row inmate's petition for an evidentiary hearing on his claim that he is mentally challenged. According to the Court, the standard is that the inmate's petition must only raise a reasonable doubt that he is challenged to be entitled to an evidentiary hearing. The Court sent *Brumfield v. Cain* back for an evidentiary hearing.[59]

Congress enacted the Mentally Ill Offender Treatment and Crime Reduction Act of 2004 to divert mentally ill persons to special mental health courts for treatment. The statute provides up to $100 million a year in grants for states and localities.[60] The stated purpose of this legislation is reprinted in **Supplement 10.12**.

One final mental health issue concerning prisons and jails is the increasing use of these facilities to house mentally challenged persons who have not even been charged with crimes. In January 2019, the American Bar Association (ABA) published an article on the issue, noting that in 2016 "the number of state and county psychiatric beds hit 37,769, down from its peak of 559,000 beds in 1995." But an estimated 10.4 million adults in the United States had a serious mental illness. The result has been a serious lack of available mental health treatment, leading the director of advocacy at Mental Health Colorado to state, "What we've done is made our jails and prisons the new mental health institutions." According to the ABA article, the efforts in the 1980s to end warehousing mentally challenged persons in large state hospitals, removing federal funds from those institutions, and establishing small community centers for treating mentally challenged persons not charged with crimes, caused the problems. "[M]ost of those centers have never materialized, forcing many people with mental illness to live without psychiatric care." As a result, some have been held in prisons and jails.[61]

In addition to mental challenges, jail and prison inmates face medical issues, with one-half reporting chronic conditions such as heart disease, asthma, arthritis, kidney, and liver problems. Twenty-one percent of prison inmates and 14 percent of jail inmates reported having health issues such as tuberculosis and sexually transmitted diseases. Most inmates were overweight, obese, or morbidly obese, with women less likely than men to be overweight but more likely to be obese or morbidly obese.[62] All of these conditions, along with less serious health issues, increase the cost of care and the potential problems of housing and controlling inmates.

Prison Programs

This section delves into the programs that might be implemented for the well-being of most, if not all, inmates regardless of their mental or physical challenges or their ages. In particular, education and work are examined.

Despite the importance of education, correctional institutions give insufficient attention to educational opportunities. It is estimated that as many as 50 to 75 percent of American adult inmates are illiterate. The BJS reported over a decade ago (and some prison programs have been cut since then) that inmates had significantly less education than the general public. Approximately 18 percent of the general public have not completed high school, compared to 40 percent of state prison inmates, 27 percent of local jail inmates, and 31 percent of probationers. In terms of college-level or postsecondary vocational classes, which are taken by approximately 48 percent of the general population, the corresponding figures for correctional populations are as follows: 11 percent of state prison inmates, 24 percent of federal inmates, 14 percent of jail inmates, and 24 percent of probationers.[63]

If inmates are to return to society as law-abiding individuals, they must have skills, many of which are gained primarily through formal education. Most prisons provide some educational opportunities; some have college courses. Jails lag far behind prisons in this and in many other program areas.

Despite the evidence of the beneficial effects of education, those who argue that prisons should be for punishment and that state or federal government money should not be used for educating inmates may be winning in some jurisdictions. For example, the 1994 revision of the federal criminal code eliminated grants that provided college courses in prisons. Furthermore, courts have not ruled that inmates have a *right* to any educational opportunities they may choose, and some courts have held that inmates do not have a right to a free college education.[64]

In recent years, several states, in cutting their overall budgets, have cut funding for prison education. However, in 2008, the Ninth Circuit Court of Appeals ruled that the Orange County Sheriff's Department must make changes in its practice of housing all physically challenged inmates in the two jails at Santa Ana, California. The jails do not have all of the educational and recreational programs that are available to inmates in other jails.

> The county may not shunt the disabled into facilities where there is no possibility of access to those programs. . . . [Physically challenged inmates cannot] by reason of such disability, be excluded from participation in or be denied the benefits of the services, programs, or activities of a public entity, or be subjected to discrimination by any such entity.

Although the court in *Pierce v. County of Orange* rejected many of the constitutional claims of the pretrial jail detainees, it held that the county violated the ADA in its lack of provision for specific physical access for the disabled and the lack of available programs, such as education, for those inmates in the Santa Ana jails.[65]

There are some college education programs available for inmates, such as the one provided by the John Jay College of Criminal Justice in New York City. Inmates who have a high school diploma (or its equivalent) and are eligible to be released in the next five years may apply to a highly competitive program through which they take courses taught at the prison and earn credits at John Jay. After their release from prison, the inmates may complete their college programs at John Jay.[66]

The Second Chance Act of 2007, which became law in 2008 and is discussed in Chapter 11, provides, among other opportunities, access to educational classes and vocational programs for inmates. The legislation is designed to reduce recidivism by preparing inmates for meaningful work upon release back in to society.[67] As noted in Chapter 9, a bipartisan law enacted by Congress and signed by the president in December 2018 also includes prison programming.

Work programs are a second area of important focus in prisons. One criminologist emphasized that "the most difficult prison to administer is the one in which prisoners languish in idleness. Absence of work leads to moral and physical degradation and corrupts institutional order."[68] Historically, work has been an important part of U.S. prisons, and some of the early prison industries were profitable. That changed, however, as state laws prohibiting the sale of prison-made goods to the general public, along with federal laws prohibiting shipping prison-made goods across state lines into states with these statutes, altered the nature of prison labor. Prisons were confined primarily to making goods for state (or federal) use.

In recent years, additional attempts have been made to introduce meaningful vocational opportunities into prisons, along with "just plain work" to keep inmates busy and provide needed services for state and federal institutions. The BOP led the way, announcing in 1994 the need to expand the Federal Prison Industries (FPI), which was created by federal statute in 1934 and now operates under the trade name UNICOR. All federal inmates are required to work, but the increase in the inmate population was outstripping available jobs. Furthermore, most of the inmates work in jobs that maintain the institution and thus may not provide them with the marketable skills they need when they are released from prison. Federal prisons are limited to producing goods for federal institutions in order to avoid competition, but some have suggested a change in that policy.[69]

In recent years, the Texas prison system has developed new work opportunities for its inmates, such as training service dogs for veterans, a practice that also occurs in other prison systems, such as in Maryland, where dogs spend the weekends in homes to experience the outside world. The president of the North American chapter of Assistance Dogs International reports that service dogs trained by inmates "graduate at a higher level" than those who receive their training outside of prisons. And not to be outdone by their competition as America's most wanted pet, cats are in prison too. Mistreated felines in Washington are placed in prisons to socialize the inmates and the cats! Two inmates, who share a cell with a cat, learn teamwork while training their cat to "have better manners."[70]

In Louisiana, inmates at the Angola prison are learning horticulture. Although many in the program are serving life and thus may never work outside in the jobs for which they are getting training (licensed landscaping and horticulture), the work and learning assist the inmates while in prison. As one commented, even with a life sentence, "you've got to find something to do—to pass the time, to help others go out and find jobs, and look forward to getting out ourselves."[71]

At California's San Quentin, inmates' jobs include writing for the prison newspaper. Noted criminologist and law professor Franklin E. Zimring, in referring to the greatest prison problem as boredom, said this prison newspaper "is an operational anti-depressant that keeps its participants structured and psychologically well organized."[72]

In Nevada, Arizona, Colorado, California, Kansas, and Wyoming, inmates help "gentle" wild horses, which means to work with the horses until they respond to the inmates' commands. In essence, the inmates and horses are helping each other.[73] In 2017 in California, male and female inmates were working to help contain wildfires at a pay rate of $2 per day plus $1 an hour for time on the fire line. The assignment was controversial, however, as three inmates died during the previous two years. The inmates' work helped save $124 million a year in taxpayer costs for fire.[74]

Inmates may be paid for their work, but pay is not required. A 1990 federal court ruling held that "compelling an inmate to work without pay is not unconstitutional."[75]

Prison Violence

Prisons are places of violence, manifested in the injuries to or murders of other inmates or prison officials, escapes, or riots that may result in serious property damage, injuries, or deaths. Earlier discussions in this chapter referred to violence by correctional officers (for example, in the New York jail at Rikers Island). **Supplement 10.13** highlights some examples of violence by inmates, with a focus on riots and escapes. Although few in number, such incidents are serious in their injuries, which in some cases result in death, as well as in their destruction of property. **Supplement 10.13** also covers other types of violence as well as unconstitutional conditions, such as those reported by the U.S. Department of Justice in its April 2, 2019 report of its findings in the Alabama men's prison.

Two of the most destructive and highly publicized U.S. prison riots occurred in 1971 in Attica, New York, and in 1980 in Santa Fe, New Mexico. The Attica riot is summarized in a 1985 opinion of a federal judge whose court heard allegations of violations of constitutional rights in that facility. The judge noted that 43 persons (32 inmates and 11 correctional employees) were killed during the riot. Prior to the riot, the prison was overcrowded, with 2,200 inmates in a facility built for 1,700. Although 54 percent of the inmates were African American and 9 percent were Puerto Rican, all officers were white. The institution had no meaningful programs for inmates. As was noted in **Supplement 10.1**, the civil suits regarding this riot continued for years.[76]

On February 2, 1980, a riot as devastating as the Attica riot occurred at the state prison in Santa Fe, New Mexico. Estimates of damage ranged from $20 million to repair to $80 million to replace the prison. At least 90 persons required hospitalization, and 33 inmates were killed. Characteristic of the violence was the torture and incredible brutality of inmates toward inmates, which led National Guardsmen to regurgitate on the scene and firefighters who had fought in Vietnam to proclaim that they had not seen such atrocities as those that were committed during this riot.[77]

Another form of prison disruption that is dangerous but occurs infrequently is escape. In June 2015, two convicted murderers cut through walls and escaped through pipes at the maximum security prison at the Clinton Correctional Facility in Dannemora, New York. A massive hunt was in place for over three weeks. One of the men was captured and returned to prison; the other was killed by authorities during the capture. Joyce E. Mitchell, a prisoner supervisor, pleaded guilty to aiding and abetting. She smuggled hacksaw blades, chisels, concrete bits, and a steel punch into the prison for the men with whom she was reportedly infatuated. Mitchell had promised to meet them after the escape and provide them with weapons and a car. She defaulted on that promise. She was sentenced to at least 28 months in prison. Two others were implicated in the escape.

One final form of violence is less obvious but very important, and that is inmate self-inflicted violence. This violence may not be reported in jails and prisons for a variety of reasons, but when self-violence leads to suicide, the acts become known and may trigger investigations by public officials and lawsuits by survivors. Suicides are more common in jails than in prisons, and little is known about the reasons for inmate death by suicide. It has been linked to overcrowded institutions, mental illness, the extended use of solitary confinement, and the psychological consequences of being victimized in jail or prison. Some inmates who are threatened with rape or other violence become depressed and desperate about their physical safety. If they submit to violence, they are branded as weak and forced to face further violent attacks from other aggressive inmates. If they seek help from the prison administration, they are branded as snitches or rats. Furthermore, the inmate social system rewards violence against weaker inmates.

What can be done to prevent jail and prison suicides? In 2001, a jail that opened in South Bend, Indiana placed a psychiatrist on duty in an attempt to prevent suicides after two recent suicides had occurred in the county jail. After two jail inmates committed suicide within a six-month period in 2002, a new cellblock was opened in 2003 at the Madison County Jail in Missouri. The facility houses male inmates who may be suicide risks because of depression or mental illness. The sheriff commented, "We want to see the inmates who walk into this jail walk out, and not be carried out."[78]

Summary

In 1984, the U.S. Supreme Court said that the continuing guarantee of substantial rights to prison inmates "is testimony to a belief that the way a society treats those who have transgressed against it is evidence of the essential character of that society."[79] This chapter explored life in prison, historically and currently. It began with a brief look at the events that might accompany an inmate's arrival at prison and proceeded to an overview of the legal issues that govern incarceration today.

The U.S. Supreme Court has made it clear that inmates forfeit some rights and that prison security needs may justify the restriction in prison of some rights normally recognized in other settings. This chapter surveyed the historical and current approaches to inmates' legal rights, beginning with a look at the traditional hands-off doctrine, in which federal courts refused to become involved in daily prison administration and maintenance. As a result of the recognized abuse of inmates and the civil rights movement, which brought the nation's attention to the problems not only of minorities in society but also to the conditions under which inmates lived, courts began to abandon the hands-off doctrine. Courts continue to defer to prison officials, but they do not tolerate violations of basic rights. The concept of cruel and unusual punishment, along with ways of determining what that means, was discussed as an example.

The chapter next focused on prison administration and its relationship to security goals. In earlier days, authoritarian prison wardens or superintendents and correctional officers maintained security by keeping inmates separated and by not permitting them to talk to each other, or by using fear and force, often involving corporal punishment. Those methods are not permitted today, and new management techniques are necessary.

Correctional officers are crucial to prison management. They have primary responsibility for maintaining internal discipline, order, and security. Their jobs are difficult and at times boring, but the position can also be challenging and rewarding. This chapter emphasized the importance of selecting and training officers carefully and of including women and minorities within their ranks. It also noted examples of brutality by prison COs.

When we think of life behind bars, however, we think mainly of inmates serving time within those facilities. This chapter noted how inmates adjust to prison life through the prisonization process. The resulting subculture was discussed in view of its origin: whether inmates develop the prison subculture as a method of adapting to the deprivations of prison or whether they import outside values to create the prison subculture.

The male inmate subculture is characterized by social roles that assist inmates in maintaining some self-esteem and positive self-concepts. Some accomplish these goals at the expense of other inmates: social control through economics, racial and gang violence, and homosexual attacks. Prison gangs play a critical role in these interactions.

Female inmates develop patterns of adaptation to prison life, too, but normally, their adaptations are less violent than those of male inmates. Their social roles mirror the roles they have played in society. Women face many of the same deprivations as male inmates, but they face the additional problems of adjusting to daily life without their children. Mothers behind bars have become a subject of research only recently, and even today, few provisions are made for female inmates to interact with their children. Women also have special medical needs, and some jurisdictions are attempting to accommodate those needs, although some are doing so only under court orders or the threat of such orders.

Special attention was given to six current prison issues, beginning with solitary confinement. The negative effects of this practice—especially with regard to mentally challenged inmates—have resulted in some changes. Inmate visitation policies were noted, and the sexual behavior of male and female inmates was contrasted and discussed with attention given to the incidences of violent sex. The implications of the federal statute, the Prison Rape Elimination Act, were noted.

The chapter gave special attention to the needs of inmates who are elderly, or physically or mentally challenged, noting legal changes for their treatment.

Adaptation to prison is made more difficult by the lack of activities, including education and work. Recent attention to the need for such programs, along with budget cuts that have reduced prison programs, was discussed.

The final section looked at the impact of prison violence, with attention given to the major prison riots of recent times. The Attica riot of 1971 and subsequent studies of that riot illustrated the devastation of riots in terms of personal injury, death, and property damage, as well as the slowness with which meaningful changes were made. The New Mexico riot illustrated the torture and brutality of which inmates are capable. The more recent riots and other violent incidents discussed in the supplement reminded us that serious prison disturbances still occur.

Eventually, most inmates are released from prison. The meaning that has for them and for society is the topic of Chapter 11.

Key Terms

civil rights 230
commissary 229
correctional officer 231
deprivation model 235
hands-off doctrine 230
importation model 236
norms 235
prisonization 235
social system 234

Study Questions

1. What is the *hands-off doctrine*, and to what extent (and why) has it been abandoned?
2. What is meant by a *hierarchy of rights*?
3. What were the characteristics of the authoritarian warden? What do you think should be the characteristics of the ideal warden or prison superintendent?
4. What events have occurred within prisons during the past three decades and forced changes in prison administration?
5. How did early correctional officers control inmates?
6. Describe some of the daily aspects of inmate prison life.
7. Define *prisonization* and *subculture*, and explain the development and importance of each in a prison setting. Would the importance be different in prisons for female as compared to male inmates?
8. Distinguish the importation and deprivation models of prisonization, and explain the social control role of inmate social systems.
9. What is the significance of prison gangs? What could be done to lessen their influence?
10. What provisions do you think should be made for incarcerated women who have children at home or for women who give birth during incarceration? What provisions should be made for incarcerated mothers and fathers to visit with their children?
11. Do female inmates have special problems other than child care, and if so, how should those problems be handled? Should inmate fathers have the same access to visitation arrangements that inmate mothers have?

12. Explain the Prison Rape Elimination Act of 2003, and discuss what impact you think the statute has on inmate behavior.

13. Distinguish the sexual behavior of male and female inmates.

14. Discuss the situations that prison officials face as the result of aging inmate populations.

15. What are the special needs of physically and mentally challenged inmates?

16. If most inmates are relatively poorly educated, why do we not make a greater effort to provide education classes in prisons?

17. Should inmates be required to work within the prisons? If there is a lack of jobs, how should that problem be solved?

18. What policies would you recommend to prison administrators if they were to ask you how to prevent prison riots? What policies might prevent jail or prison suicides?

Notes

1. See Harold Garfinkel, "Conditions of Successful Degradation Ceremonies," *American Journal of Sociology* 61 (March 1956): 420-424.
2. Gresham M. Sykes, *The Society of Captives* (Princeton, NJ: Princeton University Press, 1958), pp. 63-83.
3. *Ruffin v. Commonwealth*, 62 Va. 790, 796 (1872).
4. *Wolff v. McDonnell*, 418 U.S. 539 (1974).
5. *Holt v. Sarver*, 309 F. Supp. 362 (E.D. Ark. 1970). This case has a long history of remands and reversals leading to the U.S. Supreme Court case, *Hutto v. Finney*, 437 U.S. 678 (1978).
6. *Abdul Wali v. Coughlin*, 754 F.2d 1015 (2d Cir. 1985).
7. *Graham v. Richardson*, 313 F. Supp. 34 (D. Ariz. 1970), *aff'd*, 403 U.S. 365, 375 (1971).
8. *Estelle v. Gamble*, 429 U.S. 97, 106 (1976).
9. Norman Holt, "Prison Management in the Next Decade," *Prison Journal* 57 (Autumn/Winter 1977): 17-19. Unless otherwise noted, this discussion of prison management comes from this source.
10. "New York City Agrees to Pay $2.75 Million in Death of Rikers Island Prisoner," *New York Times* (July 21, 2014), p. 14; *"Ex-Captain at Jail Is Found Guilty in Inmate's Death," New York Times* (December 18, 2014), p. 31; "Ex-Captain Gets 5 Years in Inmate's Death," *New York Times* (June 19, 2015), p. 23.
11. "Mayor Urges 'Culture Changes' at Rikers as He Vows Jail Reforms and Plans Visit," *New York Times* (November 21, 2014), p. 22.
12. This discussion of Clemmer's concept of prisonization comes from his book, *The Prison Community* (New York: Holt, Rinehart and Winston, 1958), pp. 298-301.
13. See Sykes, *The Society of Captives*; and Gresham M. Sykes and Sheldon L. Messinger, "The Inmate Social System," in *Theoretical Studies in Social Organization of the Prison*, ed. Richard A. Cloward et al. (New York: Social Science Research Council, 1960).
14. See John Irwin and Donald R. Cressey, "Thieves, Convicts and the Inmate Culture," *Social Problems* 10 (Fall 1962): 142-155.
15. Richard A. Cloward, "Social Control in the Prison," in *Theoretical Studies*, ed. Cloward et al.
16. James W. Marquart and Ben M. Crouch, "Coopting the Kept: Using Inmates for Social Control in a Southern Prison," *Justice Quarterly* 1(4) (1984): 491-509.
17. Robert S. Fong, "The Organizational Structure of Prison Gangs," *Federal Probation* 54 (March 1990): 36-43.
18. Ibid.
19. "Trial Begins for Members of Aryan Prison Gang," *New York Times* (March 15, 2006), p. 17; "4 Leaders of Aryan Brotherhood Prison Gang Found Guilty in O.C.," *Los Angeles Times* (July 30, 2006), p. 3B.
20. Zhen Zeng, Bureau of Justice Statistics, *Jail Inmates in 2017*, (April 2019), p. 4, https://www.bjs.gov/, accessed May 3, 2019.
21. "Women Are Silent Casualties of War on Drugs," Public Access Journalism (December 24, 2006), reprinted on the website of The Sentencing Project, http://www.sentencingproject.org, accessed August 3, 2014.
22. Rose Giallombardo, *The Social World of Imprisoned Girls: A Comparative Study of Institutions for Juvenile Delinquents* (New York: John Wiley, 1974).
23. "Women in the Justice System," The Sentencing Project, http://www.sentencingproject.org/template/page.cfm?id=138, accessed August 3, 2014.
24. Justice Policy Center, *Families Left Behind: The Hidden Costs of Incarceration and Reentry*, a 12-page report, summarized in "Incarceration of Parents Causes Enormous Problems, Report Says," *Criminal Justice Newsletter* (November 17, 2003), p. 5.
25. Debra Cassens Weiss, "Imprisoned Mothers Should Be Allowed to Spend Six Months with Newborns, Report Says," *American Bar Association Journal* (March 25, 2016), http://www.abajournal.com, accessed March 25, 2016.
26. Rich Raemisch, "My Night in Solitary," *New York Times* (February 21, 2014), p. 23.
27. Ibid.
28. "Inmate Held 41 Years in Solitary Dies Just Days After Court Orders his Release from Prison," American Bar Association, http://www.abajournal, accessed February 21, 2014.
29. Obituary/Herman Wallace, "One of 'Angola 3,' in Solitary 41 Years," *Dallas Morning News* (October 6, 2013), p. 12B.
30. Martin Garbus, "Cruel Punishment Isn't That Unusual in Prisons," *New York Times* (October 5, 2014), p. 5P.
31. "Prisons Drop Punitive Solitary Confinement," *Dallas Morning News* (September 23, 2017), p. 6B.
32. *Overton v. Bazzetta*, 539 U.S. 126 (2003).
33. Mich. Admin. Code R 791.6609 (2014).

34. *Overton v. Bazzetta*, 539 U.S. 126 (2003).
35. "As Conjugal Visits Fade, a Lifeline to Inmates' Spouses Is Lost," *New York Times* (January 13, 2014), p. 8.
36. Debra Cassens Weiss, "Another Jail Eliminates In-Person Visits and Adopts 50-Cent-a-Minute Video Visitation," *American Bar Association Journal* (July 24, 2018), http://www.abajournal.com, accessed July 24, 2018.
37. Peter C. Buffum, *Homosexuality in Prisons* (U.S. Department of Justice et al., Washington, D.C.: U.S. Government Printing Office, 1972), p. 13.
38. Sykes, *The Society of Captives*, p. 97.
39. Leo Carroll, *Hacks, Blacks, and Cons: Race Relations in a Maximum Security Prison* (Lexington, MA: D.C. Heath, 1974), p. 194.
40. Daniel Lockwood, *Prison Sexual Violence* (New York: Elsevier Science Publishing, 1980), p. 21.
41. *Farmer v. Brennan*, 511 U.S. 825 (1994).
42. David A. Ward and Gene G. Kassebaum, "Women in Prison," in *Correctional Institutions*, ed. Robert M. Carter et al. (Philadelphia: J. B. Lippincott, 1972), pp. 217-219.
43. Rose Giallombardo, *Society of Women: A Study of a Woman's Prison* (New York: John Wiley, 1966).
44. John Gagnon and William Simon, "The Social Meaning of Prison Homosexuality," *Federal Probation* 32 (March 1968): 27-28.
45. David Ward and Gene Kassebaum, "Sexual Tensions in a Women's Prison," in *Crime and Justice: The Criminal in Confinement*, ed. Leon Radzinowicz and Marvin E. Wolfgang (New York: Basic Books, 1971), pp. 146-155.
46. The report, *Women in Prison: Sexual Misconduct by Correctional Staff* (June 1999), is available at http://www.gao.gov/assets/230/227683.pdf, accessed August 3, 2014.
47. "Inmates Commit Most Sexual Assaults in Women's Prisons," *Corrections Professional* 8 (January 20, 2003): n.p.
48. The Prison Rape Elimination Act, Public Law 108-79, is codified at USCS, Title 42, Sections 15601-15609 (2019).
49. *Bonner v. Lewis*, 857 F.2d 559 (9th Cir. 1988), *cert. denied*, 498 U.S. 1074 (1991).
50. See *Torcasio v. Murray*, 57 F.3d 1340 (4th Cir. 1995), *cert. denied*, 516 U.S. 1071 (1996).
51. *VanValkenburg v. Or. Dept. of Corr.*, 2014 U.S. Dist. LEXIS 153738 (D. Or. 2014).
52. Doris J. James and Lauren E. Glaze, Bureau of Justice Statistics Special Report, *Mental Health Problems of Prison and Jail Inmates* (September 2006), p. 1, https://www.bjs.gov/content/, accessed October 25, 2018.
53. Jennifer Bronson and Marcus Berzofsky, Bureau of Justice Statistics, "Indicators of Mental Health Problems Reported by Prisoners and Jail Inmates, 2011-12," (June 2017), p. 1, https://www.bjs.gov, accessed October 25, 2018.
54. See the ACLU web page, http://www.aclu.org/, accessed March 28, 2011.
55. "ACLU Releases Expert's Report on Nightmarish Conditions at Men's Central Jail in Los Angeles," *ACLU Webpage* (April 14, 2009), http://www.aclu.org/, accessed March 28, 2011.
56. "A New Day for L.A.'s Brutal Jails," *New York Times* (December 17, 2014), editorial page; "Panel to Set Terms to End Abusive Reign at Jail System," *New York Times* (December 17, 2014), p. 17.
57. "Court Orders Swifter Review of Mentally Ill Defendants," *Metropolitan News Enterprise* (Los Angeles, CA) (March 7, 2003), p. 3. The case is *Oregon Advocacy Ctr. v. Mink*, 322 F.3d 1101 (9th Cir. 2003).
58. "Federal Judge Approves California Plan to Reduce Isolation of Mentally Ill Inmates," *New York Times* (August 30, 2014), p. 10.
59. *Brumfield v. Cain*, 2015 U.S. LEXIS 4058 (U.S. June 18, 2015).
60. Mentally Ill Offender Treatment and Crime Reduction Act of 2004, Public Law 108-414 (2004).
61. Julianne Hill, "Prisons Are Housing Mental Health Patients Who've Committed No Crimes," *American Bar Association Journal* (January 2019), http://www.abajournal.com, accessed January 3, 2019.
62. Laura M. Maruschak and Marcus Berzofsky, Bureau of Justice Statistics, "Medical Problems of State and Federal Prisoners and Jail Inmates, 2011-12" (February 2015), https://www.bjs.gov, accessed October 25, 2018.
63. Caroline Wolf Harlow, Bureau of Justice Statistics, *Education and Correctional Populations* (Washington, D.C.: U.S. Department of Justice, January 2003, revised April 15, 2003), pp. 1-2, http://www.bjs.gov/content/pub/pdf/ecp.pdf, accessed August 3, 2014.
64. See *Hernandez v. Johnston*, 833 F.2d 1316 (9th Cir. 1987).
65. *Pierce v. County of Orange*, 526 F.3d 1190 (9th Cir. 2008), *cert. denied, Orange County v. Pierce*, 555 U.S. 1031 (2008). The Americans with Disability Act is codified at USCS, Title 42, Section 12101 et seq. (2019).
66. "Prison Program Turns Inmates to Intellectuals," *New York Times* (June 1, 2014), p. 24.
67. Second Chance Act of 2007, 110 Public Law 199 (2008).
68. Elmer H. Johnson, *Crime, Correction, and Society*, rev. ed. (Homewood, IL: Dorsey, 1968), p. 559.
69. "Bureau of Prisons Cites Need to Expand Prison Industries," *Criminal Justice Newsletter* 25 (May 16, 1994): 4.
70. "Raising Dogs, Spirits in Prison," *Dallas Morning News* (January 6, 2013), p. 6; "In Prison, Troubled Cats Get Another Life," *Dallas Morning News* (May 4, 2012), p. 12; "A Prison Alliance: Dog Trainers and Veterans," *New York Times* (March 23, 2014), p. 27B.
71. "Inmates Cultivating Plants and New Lives," *Dallas Morning News* (December 6, 2014), p. 3.
72. "Inmates' Newspaper Covers a World Behind San Quentin's Walls," *New York Times* (May 21, 2014), p. 14.
73. Debra Cassens Weiss, "Program Helps Inmates Learn to 'Gentle' Horses at Nevada Ranch," *American Bar Association Journal* (October 10, 2017), http://www.abajournal.com, accessed October 25, 2018.
74. Debra Cassens Weiss, "Prisoners Making a Top Hourly Pay of $1 Help Fight California Wildfires," *American Bar Association Journal* (October 13, 2017), http://www.abajournal.com, accessed October 25, 2018.
75. *Murray v. Mississippi Department of Corrections*, 911 F.2d 1167 (5th Cir. 1990), *cert. denied*, 498 U.S. 1050 (1991).
76. *Abdul Wali v. Coughlin*, 754 F.2d 1015 (2d Cir. 1985).
77. Cited in Joseph W. Rogers, "Postscripts to a Prison Riot" (paper presented at the annual meeting of the Academy of Criminal Justice Sciences, Louisville, KY, March 25, 1982).
78. "Jail Changes to Target Inmate Suicide," *South Bend Tribune* (Indiana) (May 22, 2003), p. 4D; "Jail Adds Unit for Suicidal Inmates," *St. Louis Post-Dispatch* (February 25, 2003), p. 1B.
79. *Hudson v. Palmer*, 468 U.S. 517, 523, 525 (1984).

11

Community Corrections, Probation, and Parole

Chapter Outline

Learning Objectives

After reading this chapter, you should be able to do the following:

- Explain the meaning of *community corrections*, and state the advantages of using this approach
- Explore substance abuse and its implications for criminal law
- Discuss the development and impact of drug courts and other diversionary programs
- Assess the contributions of California to the modern treatment approach toward minor, nonviolent drug offenders
- Comment on mental health issues regarding community corrections and evaluate mental health courts
- Be conversant with problems inmates face on release
- Discuss the nature and importance of the Second Chance Act of 2007
- Distinguish probation from parole, and analyze recent data on each
- Explain felony probation, and analyze recent approaches to its use
- Recognize the advantages and disadvantages of intensive probation supervision (IPS)
- Identify three organizational models of parole systems
- Explain the parole process, with particular attention to due process
- Discuss and evaluate medical parole
- Explain the legal controls on parole and probation revocation
- Analyze the future of probation and parole
- Discuss the issues surrounding probation or parole revocation
- Assess the practical and constitutional issues involved in sex offender registration laws and the civil commitment of released sex offenders

Supervision of offenders within the community is an alternative to imprisonment, although the conditions placed on offenders may be severe. This chapter focuses on community treatment of offenders, probation, and parole. It begins with an overview of community-based corrections, noting the historical development and discussing problems offenders face when they enter these programs. It looks at the decriminalization of minor drug offenses in the context of diversionary programs, such as drug courts, and the general treatment approach provided by statute in some jurisdictions today. It discusses the diversion of mentally challenged persons before examining how problems might be minimized through programs that prepare inmates for their release from prison back into the community. The importance of such programs is emphasized by a focus on the Second Chance Act.

Probation, the most frequently imposed sentence, and parole, until recently a major method of release from prison, are discussed in their historical contexts and with their modern changes. Both have been the focus of considerable attention in recent years. Frequently, crimes committed by probationers and parolees receive widespread publicity, leading to public pressure to reduce the use of probation and parole. In some jurisdictions, these pressures have been successful.

Like other changes in criminal justice systems, however, changes in the use of probation and parole must be viewed in terms of their effects on the other aspects of criminal justice systems. A significant reduction in the use of probation and parole, for example, places severe strain on correctional systems, increasing prison overcrowding and all of its consequences. In addition, it may result in the incarceration of offenders who do not need such severe restraints. But crimes committed by probationers and parolees reduce the safety and security of society. It is not possible to predict with great accuracy who will harm society while on probation or parole.

The Supplement considers some of the major federal constitutional issues that govern community corrections, probation, and parole, and the chapter focuses on sex offender registration and commitment laws, which evolved in an effort to protect communities from released sexual predators.

SUPERVISION OF OFFENDERS IN THE COMMUNITY

Discussions in earlier chapters described some methods used in the past to permit the accused or the convicted offender to remain in the community. Family members, friends, or attorneys served as sureties to guarantee the presence of the accused at trial. Later, sureties were replaced by a variety of methods for posting bond. Early reformers were successful in their efforts to have convicted persons placed on probation in the community. In the late 1880s in New York City, **halfway houses** were used to permit inmates a gradual readjustment to the community.

The major impetus for the modern movement toward supervision of the offender within the community grew out of the Federal Prisoner Rehabilitation Act of 1965 and the reports of the President's Commission on Law Enforcement and the Administration of Justice. The latter stated in a 1967 report that the new direction in corrections recognized that crime and delinquency represent community as well as individual failures. The commissioners saw the task of corrections as one of reintegrating offenders into the community, restoring family ties, assisting offenders to get an education or employment, and securing for them a place in the normal functioning of society. That requires changes in the community and in offenders. The commission reports described the traditional methods of institutionalizing offenders as fundamentally deficient. They concluded that **reintegration** was likely to be more successful if we worked with offenders in the community rather than confining them in prisons.[1]

In 1973, the National Advisory Commission on Criminal Justice Standards and Goals called for an increased emphasis on probation. This commission concluded: "The most hopeful move toward effective corrections is to continue to strengthen the trend away from confining people in institutions and toward supervising them in the community."[2]

In recent years, beginning in 2002, a movement referred to as Justice Reinvestment has focused on reducing prison populations and reintegrating offenders successfully back into the community. Spotlight 11.1 provides more information on this movement.

There are a number of possibilities for treating offenders within the community. Some jurisdictions use only a **fine**, which is a punishment in which the offender is ordered to pay a sum of money to the state in lieu of or in addition to other forms of punishment. Fines are used in combination with probation and other alternatives to confinement discussed later in this chapter. Historically, fines were used primarily in cases involving traffic violations or other nonviolent offenses. Recently, with the increasing interest in victim compensation, including compensation for violent and property crimes, some jurisdictions have begun to assess fines against offenders convicted of more serious offenses.

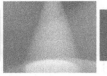

Spotlight 11.1

Ending Mass Incarceration: Charting a New Justice Reinvestment

Burgeoning jail and prison populations during the past several decades, along with their significant costs coming at a time of state and federal budget problems, led to prison overcrowding. A prominent effort to reverse the trend toward mass incarnation has come from Justice Reinvestment. In a paper entitled "Ending Mass Incarceration: Charting a New Justice Reinvestment," the authors describe the Justice Reinvestment as follows:

> "Justice Reinvestment Initiative" or "JRI" refers to the formal implementation strategy spearheaded by the Council of State Governments (CSG) and its now principal funders, Pew Charitable Trusts (PEW) and Bureau of Justice Assistance (BJA). Of the 27 states that have participated in the JRI, approximately 18 have enacted JRI legislation for the purpose of stabilizing corrections populations and budgets. JRI has played a major role in educating state legislators and public officials about the bloated and expensive correctional system, persuading them to undertake reforms not previously on the table. Considering the country's four-decade addiction to mass incarceration and harsh punishment, the general refusal to acknowledge its failures and the monumental resistance to change, JRI's most enduring contribution to date may be having created a space and a mindset among state officials to seriously entertain the possibility of lowering prison populations.[1]

The publication cited the following percentage increases in correctional populations in the United States (with a 37 percent overall population increase between 1980 and 2011):[2]

Prisons	371 percent
Probation	255 percent
Parole	287 percent
Jails	279 percent

These correctional populations are overwhelmingly poor, black, and Latino, and they come primarily from areas of the community characterized by "unemployment and poverty; homelessness; and sub-standard schools, healthcare, and other basic services." When released, most of the offenders return to those conditions, a situation that breeds resentment and hostility among the released men and women, "undermines the legitimacy of the justice system," increases the costs to society, and produces "a level of mass incarceration on a scale never before experienced."[3]

---

1. James Austin et al., *Ending Mass Incarceration: Charting a New Justice Reinvestment* (April 17, 2013), p. 1, citation omitted, http://www.sentencingproject.org, accessed January 1, 2015.
2. Ibid., p. 2.
3. Ibid., p. 3.

Another type of sentence that is growing in use is *restitution*, which requires offenders to reimburse victims financially or with services. The primary rationale for restitution is victim compensation; retribution is another. It is also argued that the state (or federal government in the case of federal offenders) should assist crime victims, and restitution provides one source of revenue at the expense of the offender. Finally, the offender might experience some rehabilitation during the restitution process.

Restitution may be combined with work assignments. The work assignments may be designed to benefit only the victim or a larger group, as in the case of **community work service** assignments. Some administrative questions are left open by the statutes providing for restitution or community work service. Some are ambiguous about the kind of work that may be assigned. Others require work programs or restitution of a nature that aids the victim but also fosters rehabilitation of the offender. Usually, community work service orders impose strict rules on the offender and, in many cases, are combined with probation, which is the most frequently used sanction for criminal activity.

Some punishments that do not involve incarceration do not fall within the definition of *corrections*. Fines and restitution are alternatives to incarceration, but they are not corrections. The important factor in community-based corrections is the relationship between those involved in the program, both clients and staff, and the community. Community-based programs involve an element of supervision aimed at assisting offenders to reintegrate into the community. In some programs, supervision may not be adequate, but it is the effort to supervise and improve that distinguishes community-based programs from fines and restitution, both of which could be combined with community-based corrections.

Community-based corrections should be distinguished from **diversion**, a process of directing the offender away from the criminal (or juvenile) systems and into other programs. Diversion usually occurs instead of, not in addition to, criminal (or juvenile) court processing. Diversion has been used primarily in the processing of juveniles, but it is also utilized for adult offenders. The substance abuser who is apprehended for petty theft might be directed to a drug and alcohol treatment program in the community and told that successful completion of that program will result in the dropping of criminal charges. That program could be a community-based treatment program. Supervised programs may be offered within prisons to prepare offenders for release. They may also be offered outside of prisons, with inmates reporting back to their prisons on a part-time basis prior to their release. Or the programs may be provided for convicted offenders who are placed on probation or released from prison on parole.

Community-based programs and supervision may be provided in residential facilities, such as community treatment centers, group homes, or foster homes. Foster homes and group homes may be used for juveniles who do not need specialized treatment programs but who have experienced difficulties living in their own homes. They may house juveniles who need specialized programs, which may be provided in nonresidential community treatment centers, schools, or other institutions. Chapter 12 covers these and other provisions for juvenile offenders.

Diversion of offenders may also occur through the use of halfway houses, which are places for offenders nearing the end of their terms to live during a period of gradual reentry into society. The offender lives in a supervised environment but may leave that facility during the day to work or to participate in vocational, treatment, educational, or other rehabilitative programs.

Residential facilities may also be used for more than halfway programs. Some are viewed as long-term housing for offenders, usually juveniles, who need intensive treatment and supervision. They may be designed for offenders with particular needs. For example, some are limited to first offenders; others are limited to repeat offenders who do not function effectively without intensive supervision. Residential facilities may include community treatment centers that provide housing and supervision for persons who have not been to prison, such as those who are on probation and need more supervision than may be provided in a nonresidential environment.

Some community treatment facilities are nonresidential. Offenders live in their own homes or with relatives or friends but go to the treatment centers for individual or group therapy and for participation in seminars and other programs designed to assist them with adjustment problems.

Diversion of Nonviolent Drug Offenders

Prison overcrowding and the expenses that entails, dissatisfaction with severe sentencing, a belief that offenses associated with substance abuse should not be criminalized, and humane concern have led some states to enact statutes providing for the diversion from incarceration of minor, nonviolent drug offenders. This is accomplished by (1) the decriminalization of minor, nonviolent drug offenses; (2) processing those offenders through special drug courts; and (3) making statutory provisions for the treatment rather than the incarceration of offenders processed through the adult criminal courts.

Chapter 1 discussed behaviors (such as private, consensual sexual behavior among adults) that some people believe should not be a focus of criminal law. Nonviolent, minor drug offenses constitute another type of behavior in which some people question the use of criminal law to regulate. Although many people would agree that criminal law is an appropriate mechanism for controlling the manufacture and sale of certain drugs, there is no general agreement with regard to its employment to control the *use* of some drugs, such as marijuana, and the nonviolent, minor offenses that may accompany such use.

Several reasons are given for including acts related to substance abuse within criminal law. First is the symbolic value of the legislation: By criminalizing the acts, society makes it clear that they are unacceptable. Second, it is assumed that criminalization has a deterrent effect; if the act is criminal, most people will decline to commit it. This reason requires more careful consideration. For example, there is no significant evidence that the threat of criminal punishment is a deterrent to public drunkenness. In fact, as far back as 1986, a California court concluded that jailing public drunks might even be counterproductive.[3]

For the criminalization of offenses associated with substance abuse to be a deterrent, it could be argued that the abuser must have the ability to control his or her actions. There is some evidence, however, that the abuse of alcohol and other drugs is a disease, not a "moral failing" over which the abuser has control. The Obama administration took that position in its 2014 National Drug Control Strategy, outlined in **Supplement 11.1**.

It is not clear which position the U.S. Supreme Court would take on this issue. In 1988, in *Traynor v. Turnage*, a case involving veterans' benefits, the U.S. Supreme Court upheld the statutory categorization of alcoholism as "willful misconduct" when the alcoholism is unrelated to mental illness, but the Court noted that it did not have to decide whether alcoholism is a disease. According to the justices, "[i]t is not our role to resolve this medical issue on which the authorities remain sharply divided."[4]

It has also been maintained that, because the use of alcohol (and other drugs) is related to criminal behavior, substance abuse should come under the jurisdiction of criminal law, and in recent years, U.S. jurisdictions moved toward more strict drug laws and more stringent enforcement of those laws, which was the major factor in the massive increase in prison population. But in the past decade changes have occurred to reduce this impact. Chapter 8 discussed some of those changes, such as the passage in December of the First Step Act of 2018, which, among other changes, reduced the sentencing disparity between convictions for possession of crack and white powder cocaine even beyond those changes made by the Fair Sentencing Act of 2010. The reader is referred back to Chapter 8 for a review of other recent changes in sentencing related to the use of illegal drugs and other crimes.

In addition, within the past decade 33 states, Washington, D.C., and the U.S. territories of Guam and Puerto Rico (as of May 2019) have enacted statutes that provide for the use of marijuana for medical reasons. In addition,

> an estimated 73 million Americans now reside in jurisdictions where anyone over the age of 21 may possess cannabis legally. Voters overwhelmingly support these policy changes. According to a 2017 Quinnipac University poll, 59 percent of Americans support full marijuana legalization and 71 percent believe that states, not the federal government, should set marijuana policy.[5]

These state changes to legalize the use of marijuana, however, present problems in that its use remains a violation, of federal law. That would be changed if Congress enacts the Ending Federal Marijuana Prohibition Act of 2019, which would remove marijuana from the federal Controlled Substances Act. That had not occurred as of this writing.[6]

The federal system and some states have placed increasing emphasis on alternative methods for processing minor drug offenders. A brief look at the 2010 National Drug Control Policy is illustrative. Described as the "inaugural drug control plan for the Obama Administration," this policy statement outlined a five-year program for combating drug abuse and its consequences. It included reducing the rate of drug use among young people; reducing the number of chronic drug users; reducing drug-induced deaths; and reducing driving while under the influence of drugs. The policy included treatment and prevention programs, including the use of drug courts, discussed below. The Obama administration implemented subsequent drug control strategies, culminating in the 2015 National Drug Control Strategy outlined in **Supplement 11.2**.

President Donald J. Trump, who succeeded President Barack Obama, has not shown signs of promoting the trend toward decriminalization of marijuana but has focused on the opioid crisis. **Supplement 11.3** contains portions of the executive order signed by President Donald J. Trump on March 29, 2017. On October 30, 2018, the White House web page stated the following under the head "The Opioid Crisis."

> More than 300,000 Americans have died from overdoses involving opioids since 2000. President Donald J. Trump has mobilized his entire Administration to address opioid abuse by directing the declaration of a nationwide Public Health Emergency.[7]

One approach to reducing the number of drug offenders in prison is the use of drug courts. Drug courts began in Miami, Florida, in 1989 and spread to all states. According to a December 2003 speech by a Massachusetts judge, in 2000 all of the chief justices and court administrators in the 50 states signed a statement supporting drug courts. The judge explained drug courts as follows:

> The typical drug court combines substance abuse treatment in the community, strict case management with direct judicial involvement, regular drug testing, and graduated incentives and sanctions based on performance in treatment. The ultimate reward is avoidance of a jail sentence or the expunging of criminal charges. The ultimate sanction is imprisonment.[8]

The judge maintained that mandatory treatment within drug courts is more effective than voluntary treatment or imprisonment "if the goal is to keep addicts from relapsing into drug habits and crime." He stated that the sentences for drug offenders were too harsh and that decriminalization, which offers treatment with little threat of punishment, "diverts scarce resources from those who can most benefit: addicted offenders. Drug courts deal with the shortcomings of both approaches, favoring treatment over jail but constructing a system that allows treatment to stick."[9]

The judge contended that in his 13 years on the bench, he had learned the following:

- "Substance abuse is a significant factor in the majority of criminal cases that enter the judicial system each year. . . .
- Almost all substance abusers and addicts need treatment to become clean and sober. The vast majority of them will not do it on their own.
- The longer someone remains in treatment, the more successful he or she generally is in maintaining sobriety and law-abiding behavior. . . .
- Coerced treatment works. Most addicts and substance abusers will not enter treatment or stay very long if treatment is voluntary. . . .
- Treatment that is not only coerced but coordinated has an even higher success rate. . . .
- Success in treatment should be rewarded. Treatment is hard work. Most addicts have zero self-esteem and no track record of accomplishment in life. Rewarding offenders is a strange concept to most judges and court officials, but it is essential in substance-abuse cases."[10]

New York's chief judge agreed. Referring to what she called a "startling fact"—that almost one-half of New York's inmates were serving sentences for drug-related offenses—she emphasized that courts cannot ignore drug offenses. Because of the serious impact of drug offenses on the state's courts, New York instituted drug courts less than a decade previously, and "their effectiveness in halting the destructive cycle of addition and criminality is indisputable." To support her conclusions, the judge referred to the study of the U.S. Department of Justice (DOJ) and the Center for Court Innovation. That report, one of the most comprehensive about state drug courts, concluded that the New York drug courts reduced **recidivism** by almost 32 percent. Over 18,000 offenders had participated in the state's drug courts, resulting in an estimated savings to the state of over $254 million in incarceration costs alone.[11] Not everyone agrees with these judges, however, and the controversy over drug treatment continues.

Drug courts may focus on particular types of offenses or problems, such as those that occur in families when parents are accused of drug violations and their children are removed from the families for their own protection. Reintegrating those children back into the family is important. Drug courts may also focus on types of offenders—for example, first- or second-time minor offenders—or they may focus on types of drug offenses, such as possession of small amounts of illegal drugs.

A variation of the drug court is the family drug court. An example is the Kentucky court designed to help mothers who are addicted to drugs (and who as a result have lost custody of their children) to come clean and recover custody.[12] Drug courts may also focus on offenders convicted of driving while intoxicated; others focus solely on rehabilitating any drug offender.

Another approach to the treatment rather than punishment of selected categories of drug offenders is illustrated by the California statute reproduced in **Supplement 11.4**. California led the way, and its legislation includes minor nonviolent first- or second-time drug possession offenders. Under the California system, once a drug offender completes the treatment program successfully, that person's conviction is removed from the records.

Another way to decrease prison populations and increase community-based corrections is to divert mentally challenged persons.

Diversion of Mentally Challenged Persons

Chapter 10 emphasized that many offenders are mentally challenged. **Supplement 10.12** (see again Chapter 10) reproduced portions of the Mentally Ill Offender Treatment and Crime Reduction Act, which advocates that the majority of mentally challenged persons who come into contact with criminal justice agencies can benefit from treatment. It is suggested that many of these offenders should be diverted to treatment programs through mental health courts, which are established specifically for handling mentally challenged offenders. Mental health courts are similar to drug courts in that they are geared toward the treatment rather than punishment of offenders.

Mental health courts were started in Broward County, Florida, in 1997; other states followed. The Center for Court Innovation (the research and development arm of the New York state court system) studied the mental health courts in Florida, California, Washington, and other states. These courts are optional for offenders. The targets for these courts—which have their own special judges and some support staff, such as clinical persons—are offenders with serious mental illnesses who face nonviolent misdemeanor charges. According to the Center for Court Innovation report, these special courts aim

> to move beyond standard case processing to address the underlying problems that bring people to court.... In the process, they seek to shift the focus of the courtroom from weighing past facts to changing the future behavior of defendants.[13]

Congress enacted a provision for federal mental health courts, providing for federal grants for up to 100 programs to establish special mental health courts that target offenders charged with nonviolent offenses or misdemeanors. The statute provides for training law enforcement and judicial personnel to identify persons who should qualify for the special programs. There is a provision for "voluntary outpatient or inpatient mental health treatment, in the least restrictive manner appropriate, as determined by the court, that carries with it the possibility of dismissal of charges or reduced sentencing upon successful completion of treatment." The statute provides for the centralized management of all charges against a defendant and "continuing supervision of treatment plan compliance for a term not to exceed the maximum allowable sentence or probation for the charged or relevant offense and, to the extent practicable, continuity of psychiatric care at the end of the supervised period."[14]

For those offenders who are incarcerated, assistance is needed for their transition back into society.

PROBLEMS OF OFFENDERS ON RELEASE

Efforts should be made to assist inmates in their transitions back into society. In that regard, in 2006, the National Institute of Corrections (NIC) announced its new program, Transition from Prison to the Community Initiative. This initiative was "intended to help states improve their transition processes, thereby increasing public safety, reducing recidivism, reducing new victimization, and making better use of resources in correctional facilities and communities." One of the key components in assisting an inmate to transition from prison to society is individual mentoring once the inmate is released. According to the NIC, 97 percent of inmates will eventually be released back into society, and many of them will not be prepared without this type of transition program.[15]

Many offenders will become **recidivists**, committing additional crimes, some of them rather quickly after release. All will face problems. Some problems will be individualized; others will be difficulties that most, if not all, releasees face. For example, releasees need street and work clothing. Although most prisons provide clothing or permit inmates to receive clothing from home for release, this practice is not adequate in many cases. The prison may provide only one set, and the inmate may not have family or friends who can supply additional clothing. Even a pre-arranged job may not be of immediate financial help, for the inmate will not get a paycheck for a week or longer.

Inmates may receive a small amount of money upon release from custody. The amount varies from state to state but may be as low as $50. With these funds, many inmates must buy bus tickets to their immediate destinations; pay for additional clothing, housing, and food; and repay debts incurred before incarceration. Some may be under court orders to pay restitution to their victims; many have families who need financial support, and some may face court-ordered child support payments.

Employment is another problem a released offender faces. Institutions may or may not provide offenders assistance in seeking employment. Inmates also must deal with social adjustments upon release. The day of release may be characterized by a sense of optimism, the belief that life will be different and more pleasant. Release from prison may be viewed as a positive life change, but inmates also experience uncertainty, loneliness, depression, and disorganization.

For many ex-offenders, release from prison means frustration and anxiety over how to act and what to say in social situations and on the job. Feelings of helplessness, insecurity, fear, indecision, and depression may result in physical problems, such as loss of appetite, chronic exhaustion, sleeping problems, or sexual difficulties. Fear of the unknown may be particularly acute for inmates who have not been able to maintain close ties with friends and families during incarceration.

Relationships with family members may create problems for ex-offenders. Spouses and children suffer as a result of the offender's incarceration; anger and hostility may greet the offender who returns home. Years of absence, with few opportunities for family members to visit their loved ones in prison, may create interpersonal problems that are beyond repair. Financial hardships caused by the offender's absence may compound the interpersonal tensions. Some may even prefer to be back in prison, as the example in Spotlight 11.2 illustrates.

Spotlight 11.2

Achieve Your Prison Dream: Rob a Bank

In 2014, Walter Unbehaun had one wish: to return to the place he called home: prison. Unbehaun, in his early 70s, had spent many years in prison for numerous crimes, including home invasion and kidnapping. In 2013, he robbed a bank, pulling a gun on the teller but saying he would not harm her. He took the money, drove to a motel, and waited for police to arrest him. During his court hearing, he told the court that he just wanted to go home. They thought he meant that he wanted bail but he was stating his desire to return to prison. No family members attended the hearing; no one posted letters of support. He was apparently all alone. His attorneys said he was bored and lonely outside prison.

When police arrested him in the parking lot at the motel, Unbehaun seemed overjoyed. His attorney said, "It is, without a doubt, one of the saddest and most disturbing cases I've dealt with." The prosecutor noted that sending the defendant to prison was not a punishment; thus, the judge faced a dilemma: A jail sentence gave the defendant what he wanted! "Did the system fail Mr. Unbehaun? Or was his inability to stay out of jail his own free will?"

The judge sentenced the defendant to three and a half years in prison.

Summarized from "Bank Robber Gets His Wish—Prison," *Dallas Morning News* (April 18, 2014), p. 12.

Financial, economic, social, and other difficulties that inmates encounter on release from prison may be eased if the community provides adequate services for ex-offenders, but preparation for release is also important. **Furlough** and **work release** programs are discussed in **Supplement 11.5**. Prerelease programs are noted in **Supplement 11.6**.

Finally, the preparation of inmates for release is not sufficient to ensure that they will make adequate adjustments when they leave prison. Families of inmates also need to be prepared for the adjustments that they must make when their loved ones are released from prison; thus, counseling should be provided for families. The importance of making adequate preparations for inmate reentry into society is illustrated by the enactment of the Second Chance Act of 2007.

FOCUS ON THE SECOND CHANCE ACT OF 2007

In April 2008, President George W. Bush signed into law the Second Chance Act, emphasizing that our country was built on the belief that everyone matters and that even ex-offenders may have "brighter days ahead." The president emphasized that we should assist former inmates to "build new lives as productive members of society." The Second Chance Act provided $330 million for programs involving reentry, substance abuse, mentoring services, housing, counseling, education, and so on. The legislation provides for grants to states as well as for federal programs both inside and outside jails and prisons. It includes provisions for drug treatment programs as alternatives to incarceration and for family-based treatment. The stated purposes of the legislation are reprinted in **Supplement 11.7**.[16]

Selected findings cited by Congress in the Second Chance Act of 2007 are presented in Spotlight 11.3. The act's provisions stress the importance of involving the offender's family in treatment programs. Offenders must be released from custody at the end of their terms, but many are released prior to serving their entire sentences or they are not incarcerated but are supervised within the community. The next section analyzes the methods involved in both approaches.

PROBATION AND PAROLE: AN OVERVIEW

Probation and parole have been the most frequently used and probably the most controversial alternatives to prison. **Probation** is a sentence that does not involve

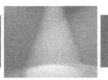

Spotlight 11.3

The Second Chance Act of 2007

Among the congressional findings stated in the Second Chance Act of 2007 (signed into law in 2008 and subsequently reauthorized) are the following:

- Each year approximately 650,000 inmates are released from state and federal incarceration and over 10 million are released from jails.
- Within three years after their release, two-thirds of these offenders will be arrested for additional offenses.
- Between 1982 and 2002, the cost of corrections alone increased from $9 billion to $59.6 billion. Additional expenditures were made for arrests and prosecutions; victims also incurred expenses.
- In the 1990s, the number of children who had a parent in custody increased from approximately 900,000 to 2 million.
- Each year approximately 100,000 juveniles are released from correctional facilities. Their chances of rehabilitation are greater if they are involved in aftercare programs. Their rates of recidivism range from 55 to 75 percent when they have been confined in secure facilities.
- Upon their release from custody, 15 to 27 percent of inmates are homeless.
- Most inmates (70 percent) "function at the lowest literacy levels." Whereas 82 percent of the general population has achieved a high school diploma or its equivalent, only 32 percent of state prison inmates have done so.
- Approximately 57 percent of federal and 70 percent of state inmates experienced regular use of alcohol or other drugs prior to the offense for which they were incarcerated, and up to 84 percent were using drugs or alcohol at the time of the offense. There is evidence that drug treatment programs are effective, but more programs are needed.

Source: Public Law 110-199, Section (b) Findings (2008).

confinement but may involve conditions imposed by the court. The term *probation* refers to the status of a person placed on probation, to the subsystem of the criminal justice system that handles this disposition of offenders, and to a process that involves the activities of the probation system: preparing reports, supervising probationers, and providing or obtaining services for probationers.

Parole is the release of persons from correctional facilities after they have served part of their sentences. It is distinguished from unconditional release, which occurs when the full sentence (or the full sentence minus time reduced for good-time credits) has been served.

Probation and parole permit convicted persons to live in the community, with conditions imposed on their behavior and, in some cases, under supervision. Both are based on the philosophy that the rehabilitation of some individuals might be hindered by imprisonment (or further imprisonment) and could be aided by supervised freedom. The processes differ in that parole is granted after a portion of the prison term has been served, whereas probation is granted in lieu of incarceration. Probation is granted by the judge. Parole is usually granted by a **parole board** appointed or elected specifically for that purpose, although in some states the board recommends and the governor makes the final decision.

Probation and parole are important elements of criminal justice systems, with probation the most widely used method of correctional supervision in the United States. Figure 11.1 graphs the number of adults under probation, parole, and total community supervision between 2000 and 2016, the latest data available. At the end of 2016, the number of adults on community supervision (approximately 1 out of every 55 adults) was at its lowest level since 1999 and had decreased by 1.1 percent from the previous year. The number on probation had declined 1.4 percent and the number on parole had increased by 0.5 percent during the previous year.[17]

Figure 11.1

Adults Under Community Supervision, Probation, and Parole on December 31, 2000-2016

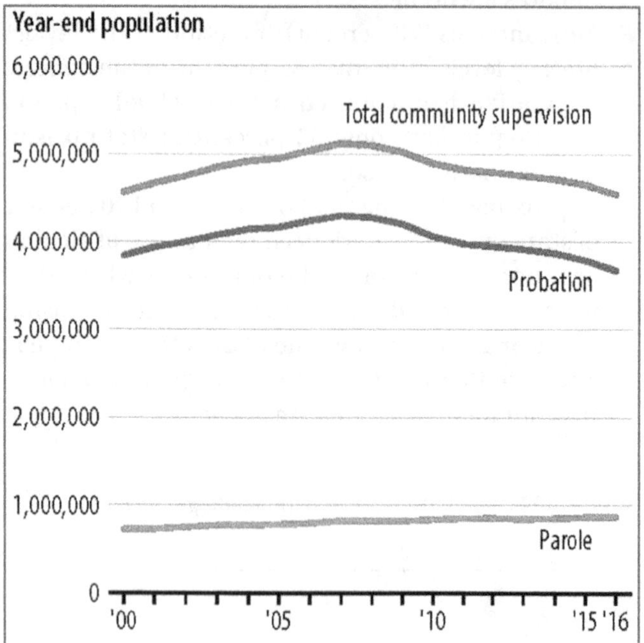

Note: Estimates are based on most recent data and may differ from previously published statistics. See *Methodology*. The total community supervision population excludes parolees on probation to avoid double counting and will not equal the sum of probation and parole populations.

Source: Bureau of Justice Statistics, Annual Probation Survey and Annual Parole Survey, 2000–2016.

Source: Danielle Kaeble, Bureau of Justice Statistics, "Probation and Parole in the United States, 2016" (April 2018), p. 1, https://www.bjs.gov/, accessed February 21, 2019.

PROBATION

In the United States, probation is traced to John Augustus, a prosperous Boston shoemaker. He asked that offenders be given their freedom within the community under his supervision, and Massachusetts responded with a statute in 1878. By 1900, six states had probation statutes; by 1915, 33 states had statutes providing for adult probation; and by 1957, all states had probation statutes. In 1925, Congress enacted a statute authorizing probation in federal courts.[18]

Probation may be administered in several ways. In some cases, it is reserved for only minor offenses; supervision may or may not be imposed. But there are several other types of probation.

The use of probation for offenders convicted of *serious* offenses is referred to as **felony probation**. Studies by the Rand Corporation disclosed that many felony probationers committed additional crimes while they were on probation. Thus, they were *recidivists*.[19] The latest data from the BJS show a very high rate (83 percent) of recidivism among all adults released from prison, with four in nine arrested during the first year.[20]

The Rand Corporation study concluded that probation in its current form was not successful, but the researchers emphasized that sending felons to overcrowded prisons would not solve the problem either. They suggested alternatives:

> The answer may be intensive surveillance programs that include intense monitoring and supervision, real constraints on movement and action, requirement of employment, mechanisms to immediately punish infractions, and added requirements of community service, education, counseling, and therapy.[21]

Other studies suggested that some felony probation programs were more successful than those Rand evaluated. After reviewing the Rand research and studies of more successful programs, one scholar recommended that more attention be given to such problems of probationers as drug abuse and employment and that the studies of felony probation be scrutinized more carefully.[22]

Probation or parole may be combined with **house arrest** (or home detention or confinement). Offenders who are confined to house arrest are placed under specific restrictions. They may live at home or in another designated facility, but they may leave only under specified conditions and go only to restricted places, such as work, church, the grocery store, and so on. In some jurisdictions, house arrest is accompanied by *electronic monitoring*, in which monitors are attached to the offender, usually at the ankle or the wrist. The devices are monitored by corrections personnel, who can determine whether the probationer leaves his or her area of confinement or violates curfew.

Although electronic monitoring is not new to criminal justice systems, the technology has become increasingly sophisticated and has been used effectively in tracking terrorists as well as criminal offenders and in searching for lost persons in, for example, heavily wooded areas.

The use of government satellites gives local and state law enforcement officials extensive coverage. For example, child abductions often result in the child being taken to another state; this could be tracked with a GPS. A spokesperson for a company that manufactures these monitoring devices described their security as second only to keeping inmates behind bars.[23]

Electronic monitoring is used extensively with abusers of alcohol and other drugs. As substance abuse violations have increased in number and have swelled prison populations, as well as court dockets, many jurisdictions have turned from incarceration to alternative treatment programs combined with electronic monitoring.

Electronic monitoring may also be used with violent offenders, including sexual predators. Sophisticated systems can track and notify authorities when released offenders are near areas they are forbidden to visit, such as any place where children can be expected to play. Some empirical evidence indicates that electronic monitoring is reasonably safe with sex offenders, although not with violent offenders in general.[24]

A concern with the use of electronic monitoring (and also house arrest), however, is that the system is too lenient. But both electronic monitoring and house arrest may be accompanied by **intensive probation supervision (IPS)** (discussed later in the chapter), fines, restitution,[25] or a combination of these. Electronic monitoring and house arrest may also be combined with brief jail or prison sentences. For example, some statutes permit sending offenders to prison for a short period of time and then placing them on probation. It is assumed that this procedure will shock offenders into appropriate behavior. This process is called *shock probation*, although technically, that term is incorrect because probation is an *alternative* to incarceration. The purpose of shock probation is to expose offenders to the shock of prison before placing them on probation and to release them before they are influenced negatively by the prison experience.

Probation may also be combined with a jail term, a procedure called *periodic sentencing*. The offender may be confined to jail during the night but be permitted to go to work or school during the day. The jail term might be served on weekends only, with the offender free to move about in the community during the week, although under some probation terms. The weekend alternative is often used for offenders who have been convicted of driving while intoxicated, particularly in jurisdictions in which jails are crowded and the offender has a steady job.

Probation Administration

In most jurisdictions, probation administration is a court function and thus located within the judicial branch of government. The trial judge makes the decision whether to grant probation and may reject a probation recommendation made by the attorneys.

Despite the role of the trial judge in making probation decisions, it is possible for various courts within a particular jurisdiction to have probation departments, resulting in an overlap of services and other administrative problems. Other jurisdictions may have a statewide probation system with branches at the city and county levels. Probation departments may be found in the executive branch, too, reporting to the governor in the case of statewide systems. Probation departments differ in size and complexity and in the extent and quality of services that they provide for clients.

One division of the probation department provides services to courts. Usually, the probation department prepares the *presentence investigation (PSI)* by interviewing clients and related parties, investigating and compiling materials relevant to each case, and developing recommendations for the sentencing body. In addition, the department provides the court with processing and reporting services for probation cases and keeps records of all persons on probation, the status of their probation, whether probation has been revoked, and other pertinent data. Probation departments also provide their clients with services such as counseling, referral to other community sources, and supervision. Some probation departments counsel substance abusers and their families.

Usually, probation departments are headed by a chief **probation officer**, who has the primary responsibility for hiring, training, and firing probation officers and for managing all sections of the probation department. The chief probation officer also has public relations functions and works with community leaders, attorneys, police officers, and court personnel.

A large probation department may have an assistant chief probation officer who reports to the chief probation officer and may be assigned such responsibilities as coordinating volunteer efforts and administering the department. A supervisor might be in charge of coordinating the efforts of those who prepare the PSI, assign cases, and handle other administrative functions.

Probation officers work directly with probationers. These officers should have training in the various aspects of probation work, including skills in interpersonal relationships. They provide counseling for probationers and engage in surveillance to determine whether their clients are violating probation conditions.

Probation officers do most of the investigative work in preparing the PSI and may be required to make a sentence recommendation to the judge. This involvement in the sentencing decision and then in supervising the probationer may present problems. Probationers may resent the position the probation officer has in relationship to the judge. Furthermore, it is questionable whether probation officers can be effective counselors while also being responsible for surveillance.

Professions 11.1

Federal Probation Services

Most people in the United States who are under the supervision of criminal justice systems are on probation. Theoretically, probationers are supervised by probation officers, who perform a variety of functions. This Professions box features the federal probation system, but many state systems are similar. Reference is made to several specialties within the federal probation system.

The Functions of Federal Probation Officers[1]

Probation officers have two basic duties: presentence investigations and the supervision of offenders. Both require written and oral skills; a broad understanding of criminal justice systems, federal probation and parole systems, the federal prison system, federal sentencing guidelines, and federal case law; and an ability to work with diverse populations.

Presentence investigations require a probation officer to prepare for the court a document that includes information on the offense in question, the offender's history and personal characteristics, sentencing options, and the application of federal sentencing guidelines. Collecting and analyzing the data may require extensive time by the officer, who must make recommendations regarding the potential risk of the offender as well as the need for restitution, treatment, or other options. Probation officers prepare these reports by interviewing the offender and other persons, reading available documents, and analyzing other evidence. Probation officers also supervise inmates. Such supervision may involve extensive visits or be limited to phone calls, depending on the officer, the offender, the offense, and available resources.

Functions of Federal Pretrial Services Officers[2]

Federal pretrial services officers have two main functions: investigation and supervision. They investigate each offender in order to recommend to the court whether the individual should be released pending trial. If the offender is released, they provide supervision for some but not all offenders. The court may determine that some offenders do not pose a threat to themselves or to society and can be predicted to show up for trial; thus, they need no supervision.

Pretrial services officers also attend court sessions concerned with pretrial services and detention. They prepare release status reports for the courts. These reports summarize the offender's compliance with prerelease orders and make recommendations for release or detention if the offender is released after sentencing and pending an appeal. Supervision may include meeting with offenders to counsel them about the details of their release, the need to attend treatment programs for the abuse of alcohol or other drugs, other treatment programs, job opportunities, and so on.

To be eligible for the position, an applicant must have a bachelor's degree in an academic subject, such as sociology, criminology, or criminal justice, psychology, or some other social science, although occasionally those with majors in other disciplines, such as business, are hired. Many individuals working as pretrial services officers have graduate degrees, and many of the federal officers have experience at the local or state level.

Functions of Substance Abuse Specialists[3]

Most probation officers must deal with offenders who have abused alcohol or other drugs, but the substance abuse specialists are senior-level officers whose job is to oversee and manage a substance abuse program. They are in charge of the budget for substance abuse, which includes the contracts for substance abuse treatment programs. They may provide in-service training for those who supervise offenders with drug problem and may or may not have their own caseloads.

---

1. Adapted from John P. Storm, "What United States Probation Officers Do," *Federal Probation* 61 (March 1997): 13-18.
2. Adapted from Thomas J. Wolf, "What United States Pretrial Services Officers Do," *Federal Probation* 61 (March 1997): 19-24.
3. Adapted from Edward M. Read, "Challenging Addiction: The Substance Abuse Specialist," *Federal Probation* 61 (March 1997): 25-26.

Average beginning salaries for probation officers are not high enough to attract applicants who have baccalaureate degrees, as the National Advisory Commission recommended. Efforts should be made to raise salaries and to improve working conditions for probation officers. Opportunities to work in the federal probation system are discussed in Professions 11.1.

One final point on the administration of probation systems is that some departments charge probationers for services. In Texas, for example, in one year adult probationers paid $237 million in court-ordered fines and probation fees and performed 8.5 million hours of unpaid community service, which otherwise would have cost the state approximately $45 million in pay to minimum-wage workers. These fees, fines, and work service accommodated approximately one-half of the probation supervision costs of the state for that year.[26]

Probation Supervision

Conditions are generally imposed on convicted persons who are released on probation. **Supplement 11.8** discusses several cases focusing on this topic. For many probationers, success in observing the various conditions is related to adequate supervision by a probation officer. The type and degree of supervision vary. In some probation departments, the probation officer counsels probationers. In other departments, a probation officer is expected to supervise only the activities of probationers, and that supervision may be limited. The model that is chosen depends on the availability of resources, the caseloads of probation officers, their professional training, probationers' needs, and many other factors. Essentially, the officer's function is to assist the probationer in making important transitions—from law-abiding citizen to convicted offender, from free citizen to one under supervision, and finally, back to free citizen.

There are various ways in which probation officers can improve their supervisory relationships with their clients. Some probation officers go beyond supervision and serve as treatment agents for their clients. Treatment of probationers may be multidimensional. Many probationers need to learn the social skills involved in successful interpersonal relationships. Most offenders have long histories of personal failures, and probation officers are crucial in helping them increase their self-confidence and acquire the social skills and habits necessary for successful interpersonal relationships.

When probation officers go beyond supervising their clients and begin a treatment process, however, some problems may occur. Officers may lack sufficient training in treatment techniques. Even if probation officers are trained, skilled, and licensed in treatment techniques, the very nature of the position may preclude successful treatment. Because of the legal nature of probation work, probation officers cannot promise the confidentiality that an effective treatment relationship needs. In reality, probation officers have a conflict of interest. The officers represent the interests of the state in taking action against violations of probation agreements or of the law; they also represent the interests of clients in treatment and supervision.

The National Institute of Corrections (NIC) has suggested that probation, parole, and community corrections staff need more training to cope with their dual roles of treatment *and* surveillance. In the past, these workers were primarily social workers who focused on their clients' rehabilitation. While performing that role only, the staff rarely had to be concerned with personal safety. Now, however, the supervisors may be in danger of physical harm as they check on their clients to determine whether they are violating the terms of their releases.[27]

Probation supervision has come under severe criticism, especially when persons on probation have committed additional crimes. In response, a panel of probation experts (including several from the American Parole and Probation Association), called the Reinventing Probation Council (RPC), suggested much stronger probation supervision, with such measures as no "free" violations—that is, any probation violation would carry sanctions. Probationers would not be told in advance that they might be subject to drug testing. Furthermore, probation supervisors should meet with probationers in the probationers' homes at all hours—not just regular probation office hours—a process the panel called *fortress probation*. The panel recommended lighter caseloads, noting the absurdity of expecting any meaningful supervision when an officer has a caseload of 500. The panel also noted that attitudes and policies of probation staff must be changed. For example, the policy of avoiding dangerous neighborhoods may increase the safety of officers, but it makes it essentially impossible to be a probation officer, as many probationers live in those areas. The RPC concluded: "We believe probation is at once the most troubled and the most promising part of America's criminal justice system." However, the members admitted that "perhaps more candidly than leading members of our profession have ever admitted, that widespread political and public dissatisfaction with community corrections has often been totally justified."[28]

The subject of probation supervision needs to be explored in more detail. In the past, researchers debated the effect of the officer's caseload size on the success or failure of probationers. That issue is not settled, and many factors are important in determining what type of caseload is most efficient. Today, the focus of probation has shifted in many jurisdictions. No longer is rehabilitation the primary purpose of probation. The function of probation is to divert from prison persons who might not need that intensive security and supervision, and through that diversion process, reduce the populations that are swelling prisons. It is argued that many offenders can succeed on probation if they are under intensive probation supervision (IPS).

IPS programs began developing in the 1960s. Two researchers who studied earlier programs suggested that three conclusions may be drawn from those analyses:

1. Intensive supervision is difficult to achieve.
2. Close contact does not guarantee greater success.
3. Intensive supervision produces an interactive effect.

The third conclusion refers to the evidence that, although IPS appears to assist some offenders, "it is entirely reasonable that intensive supervision might interfere with the functioning of some clients who would otherwise be successful."[29]

PAROLE

Parole is an administrative decision to release an offender after he or she has served some but not all of a sentence to a correctional facility. Rehabilitation, justice, prison overcrowding: These are the three main reasons for parole in the United States. Ironically, the movement to abolish parole, a movement that paralleled the one toward determinate sentencing in the late 1970s and 1980s, was propelled by the cry for justice, disillusionment with rehabilitation, and the argument that the lack of justice in the parole decision process hindered rehabilitation. Parole was called the "never-knowing system" by many inmates, who argued that it was granted for arbitrary and capricious reasons.

Parole has come under severe attack in the United States primarily as a result of violent crimes committed by parolees. For example, the 1988 killing of a police officer in New York City led to proposals to abolish parole. Anthony Mosomillo, age 36 and the father of two, was called a hero by New York City's mayor, who proclaimed the 14-year veteran "an exceptional police officer." Mosomillo was gunned down by a parolee whom he and his fellow officers were attempting to arrest for a parole violation. The offender, Jose Serrano, managed to get another officer's gun and shoot Mosomillo four times in the neck and body. Before he died, Mosomillo killed Serrano.

Serrano was on parole after serving time for a drug conviction, but he was wanted for a parole violation when he was arrested in April 1998 on a minor drug offense. At that time, he was released from custody after giving police an alias. He was ordered to return to court on May 18. Serrano had been fingerprinted, but those prints were not available when he gave police the alias.

When Serrano failed to show up for his court date, a warrant was issued for his arrest. Mosomillo and his colleagues apprehended Serrano, who was hiding under a bed. Serrano's girlfriend, who was on probation until the year 2005 for her conviction for smuggling heroin, struggled with a female officer, whose gun was knocked away. Serrano then grabbed the gun and began shooting. Mosomillo was taken to a hospital, where he died, with his wife and children, one a toddler, by his side.

The killing of Officer Mosomillo by a parolee led to calls for the abolition of New York's parole system. In August 1998, the state enacted a statute that limited access to early release for first-time violent felons. The statute requires that these felons serve 85 percent of their maximum sentences before they are covered by mandatory release. Previously, these offenders were released after they had completed two-thirds of their maximum sentences unless they had been involved in disciplinary problems while in prison. The new law was the result of lobbying by the parents of Jenna Grieshaber, who was killed in her apartment in Albany, New York, in 1997 by a parolee, and it is called "Jenna's Law," although it was Mosomillo's death that gave impetus to the law's passing. **Supplement 11.9** contains another example of reaction to the crimes of a parolee.

Such crimes by inmates granted clemency give rise to demands for parole abolition. After a decade of attempts, the federal criminal code was revised when President Ronald Reagan signed the Comprehensive Crime Control Act of 1984. That act abolished early release by parole in the federal system and, over a five-year period, phased out the U.S. Parole Commission. Under the new statute, inmates in the federal system could receive only a maximum of 15 percent good-time credits on their sentences. Under the former statute, they were eligible for parole after serving only half of their sentences.[30]

By January 1999, 15 states had abolished parole boards, although criminologists had warned that there was no significant evidence that abolishing parole reduces crime. Some of the states that abolished parole boards later reinstituted them because of prison overcrowding that resulted in a need to release some inmates before they had completed their sentences. Some politicians argued that parole boards were such failures that their abolition would have no effect on criminal justice systems. Others insisted that parole boards may actually result in some inmates serving longer terms than they would under some sentencing structures that allow for a reduction in sentences for good time and other reasons. For example, criminologist Joan Petersilia noted that Richard Allen Davis, who was convicted of kidnapping, raping, and killing Polly Klaas, was rejected for parole six times before California abolished its parole board. But the state was required by law to release Davis after he had served a specified period of time; shortly thereafter, he killed Klaas.[31]

The Organization and Process of Parole Systems

The organization of parole is complex. One reason for this is the variety of sentencing structures under which parole systems must operate. In jurisdictions where sentences are long, with little time off for good behavior, parole may involve a lengthy supervision period. In jurisdictions where sentences are short, parole may be unimportant as a form of release, and supervision is for shorter periods.

Despite the wide variety of parole programs, there are three common organizational models: institutional, independent authority, and consolidated. Under the *institutional model*, found mainly in the juvenile field, the decision to release is made by the correctional staff. The assumption is that those who work closely with offenders are in the best position to make release decisions. Arguments against this model are that institutions may make decisions in their own best interests, not in the best interests of offenders or of the community. Decisions may be based on institutional overcrowding. Staff members may be less objective in the decisions because they are closely involved with the offenders. Abuse of discretion may be more likely under this model.

As a result of those problems, many parole boards for adult correctional facilities follow the *independent authority model*, in which the parole board is established as an agency independent of the institution. This model has been critized severley. In some cases, the parole board is composed of people who know little or nothing about corrections. The board is removed from the institution and may not understand what is taking place there. Decisions may be made for inappropriate reasons, and as a result, parole boards may release those who should not be paroled and retain those who should be released.

The *consolidated model* of organization for parole boards involves consolidating correctional facilities into one common administration—usually, a department of corrections. Under the consolidated model, the parole-granting board is within the administration of the department of corrections but possesses independent powers.

Parole board members should have an understanding of all correctional programs available in the system. It is more likely that such understanding will occur under the consolidated model than under the other two models. However, the board should possess independence, so that it can act as a check on the rest of the system.

With the exception of the institutional model, most parole systems are located in the executive branch of government and are administered at the state level. Most systems have one parole board, whose members are appointed by the executive branch. In most states, that board has final authority to decide who is granted parole. In other states, the board makes recommendations to someone else, who has the final decision-making authority. That person might be the governor, as noted earlier.

Some parole board members serve full time; others serve part time. They may or may not be required to meet specific qualifications. As political appointees, parole board members may be appointed for reasons unrelated to expertise in the kind of decision making that is the board's function. The board may have the authority to revoke as well as to grant parole.

The parole system has a division responsible for parole services, which includes parole supervision. Parole services may be delegated to smaller divisions throughout the state. Generally, the parole system provides some parole services at the institutions in which inmates are incarcerated. Often, one person has the responsibility of interviewing all those eligible for parole and making written recommendations to the parole board.

Parole officers should have the same qualifications as probation officers. Increasingly, professional organizations and commissions recommend that parole and probation officers hold a bachelor's degree, and some prefer additional education as well. In-service training is also important and should be continued throughout the officer's period of work and evaluated periodically.

Finally, in some states, parole as such has been replaced with statutory provisions for early release when prison and jail populations reach a crisis stage.

Even in those cases, however, parole *supervision* remains important.

In those jurisdictions with a parole release system, the parole *process* is very important, and adequate preparation should be made for the parole hearing. The inmate's ability to convey an improved self-image and to demonstrate the ability to work with others and to stick with a job may influence the board's decision. Inmates who have maintained strong family ties may have an edge in the decision-making process. Inmates who have had successful experiences on work, education, or furlough release may also have an advantage. A good behavior record in the institution may also be viewed favorably.

Inmates should be told what to expect regarding the timing of the decision and the kinds of questions to anticipate. Demeanor and behavior are important; some inmates are put through mock decision-making situations to prepare them for the parole board hearing. It is also important to prepare the inmate for the parole board's decision; a negative decision may have a disastrous effect on an inmate who has not been adequately prepared for that result.

The determination of eligibility for parole varies, but usually there are statutory specifications, such as requiring that inmates serve a certain percentage of their sentences before they are eligible for parole. Good-time credits may reduce that period. Many jurisdictions require that inmates have job commitments before parole is granted; others grant parole on the condition that the inmate has a job by the time he or she is released on parole.

The parole candidate may appear before the entire parole board or only a committee of the board. Larger boards may split into smaller groups to process paroles faster. Usually, the parole hearing is held at the institution in which the inmate is incarcerated. However, if only a few inmates at one institution are eligible for parole, the state (or the federal government) may transport them to a central location for the parole hearing.

Many parole systems allow inmates to participate in the hearings, although that participation might be short. This gives inmates a greater sense of fairness in that they have an opportunity to express to the board members their perceptions of their chances for success.

Numerous factors may be considered in a parole decision. Those factors require information from the past, present, and future. They include statements made by the sentencing judge concerning the reasons for sentencing, as well as the inmate's future plans. They include disciplinary actions (if any) that have occurred during the inmate's incarceration. Documentation on changes in attitude and ability is also important. The crimes for which the inmate is serving time, along with any prior experiences on parole or probation, are considered, as are family relationships, the ability to get along with others, and employment records and opportunities.

The parole decision is a critical one. Historically, parole boards have had almost total discretionary power in determining parole. Parole was viewed as a privilege, not a right. Because parole was not a right, no reasons had to be given for denial. Elements of due process were not required at the time the decision was made. Courts reasoned that due process is not required at the determination of parole because parole granting is not an adversary proceeding. Parole granting is a complicated decision, and the parole board must be able to use evidence that would not be admissible in an adversary proceeding, such as a trial. The general lack of due process at the parole decision stage has resulted in bitter complaints from inmates. Perhaps the late Justice Hugo Black of the U.S. Supreme Court best summarized the view of many inmates toward the parole board:

> In the course of my reading—by no means confined to law—I have reviewed many of the world's religions. The tenets of many faiths hold the deity to be a trinity. Seemingly, the parole boards by whatever names designated in the various states have in too many instances sought to enlarge this to include themselves as members.[32]

Today parole hearings and decisions must meet some due process standards. The Fourteenth Amendment (see Appendix A) prohibits the denial of life, liberty, or property without due process of law. Claims by inmates for due process at the parole decision are based on the argument that they have a liberty interest in parole. The U.S. Supreme Court has held that, although there is no constitutional right to parole, statutes may create a protected liberty interest. When that is the case, parole may not be denied if the conditions of those statutes are met.

How do we know whether a protected liberty interest has been created and therefore due process is required? According to the U.S. Supreme Court, if a state creates a parole system and provides that if inmates meet certain conditions, they are entitled to parole, a liberty interest has been created. Under those circumstances, the state has created a presumption that inmates who meet certain requirements will be granted parole. If the statute is general, however, giving broad discretion to the parole board, no liberty interest is created.

In *Greenholtz v. Nebraska*, decided in 1979, the U.S. Supreme Court examined the Nebraska statute, which provided for two hearings before a final parole decision. At the first hearing, an informal one, the inmate is interviewed, and all relevant information in the files is considered. If the board decides the inmate is not ready for parole, parole is denied, and the inmate is given reasons. If the board finds evidence that the inmate might be ready for parole, it notifies the inmate of a formal hearing, at which time the inmate may present evidence, call witnesses, and be represented by retained counsel.

In *Greenholtz*, the Supreme Court found that a liberty interest was created by the Nebraska statute but that the procedures required by the statute met due process requirements. "The Nebraska procedure affords an opportunity to be heard and when parole is denied it informs the inmate in what respects he falls short of qualifying for parole; this affords the process that is due under these circumstances. The Constitution does not require more."[33]

In 1987, while analyzing the Montana parole statute, the U.S. Supreme Court reaffirmed its holding in *Greenholtz* that, although the existence of a parole system does not by itself give rise to an expectation of parole, states may create that expectation or presumption by the wording of their statutes. In *Board of Pardons v. Allen*, the Supreme Court held that the Montana statute, like the Nebraska statute examined in *Greenholtz*, created an expectation of parole, provided certain conditions were met. Thus, if those conditions are met, parole must be granted.[34]

In both of these cases, the U.S. Supreme Court emphasized that the language—the use of the word *shall* rather than *may*—creates the presumption that parole will be granted if certain specified conditions are met. Thus, the Supreme Court injected some procedural requirements into the parole-granting process in the states that use mandatory language in their parole statutes.

A final issue regarding parole decisions is that parole conditions are an essential element of the release process. The U.S. Supreme Court has stated:

> The essence of parole is release from prison, before the completion of sentence, on the condition that the prisoner abide by certain rules during the balance of the sentence....
>
> [T]he conditions of parole . . . prohibit, either absolutely or conditionally, behavior that is deemed dangerous to the restoration of the individual into normal society.[35]

Parole conditions vary from jurisdiction to jurisdiction and are similar to probation conditions. Many parole conditions have been challenged in court. The conditions are valid, however, if they are reasonably related to the crimes in question, if they are not against public policy, and if it is reasonably possible for the parolee to comply with them.

Medical Parole: A New Focus?

The aging prison population, along with the expense of incarcerating older inmates, especially those with medical problems, and overcrowded prisons, have led some jurisdictions to provide for medical parole for inmates who are frail, who have life-threatening diseases, or, for other reasons, are near death. Two prime examples were in the news recently.

High-profile New York attorney, Lynne F. Stewart, convicted of aiding terrorism by smuggling letters from her convicted client out of prison, petitioned for a medical release, stating that she was dying of cancer. The release was granted on December 31, 2013 after which Stewart was released from a Texas correctional facility. She died March 7, 2017, at the age of 77. On June 21, 2013, 89-year-old Anthony D. Marshall, convicted of fraud with regard to the estate of his mother, wealthy socialite Brooke Astor, was released from a New York prison. Marshall died on November 30, 2014, at the age of 90.

With regard to keeping elderly offenders in prison, consider the cost of medical care for inmates by looking at the State of California. Approximately one-fourth of California's health care bill for inmates is spent on special care inmates. One inmate, for example, cost the state $1 million the year before he died, while 1,175 inmates in California accounted for $185 million in health care in one year. In June 2010, backed by the advice of the state's federal monitor, the state senate passed a bill for medical parole to release inmates whose release "would not reasonably pose a threat to public safety." The provision does not apply to death row or to inmates serving a term of life without parole. The bill passed and was signed into law. Among other issues, the bill raises these questions:

> Does it make sense for the state to pay for two correctional officers to guard an inmate 24-hours-a-day as the inmate lies comatose or in a permanent vegetative state in a hospital bed? Does it make sense for CDCR [California Department of Corrections and Rehabilitation] to become a long-term care facility for inmates with, for example, end-stage Alzheimer's disease, whose dementia is so severe they no longer understand that they are in prison? California is paying tens of millions of

dollars every year to incarcerate these very high-cost inmates. These offenders were sent to prison to protect society and to punish them for their crimes. Because of their medical condition, however, they are no longer a threat and the ones being punished are the taxpayers.[36]

The next section discusses the revocation of parole and probation, and **Supplement 11.10** discusses other constitutional issues, such as those relating to search and seizure and the Americans with Disabilities Act.

PROBATION AND PAROLE REVOCATION

Historically, **probation revocation** and **parole revocation** occurred without due process hearings. In probation cases in which the offender had been sentenced to prison but the judge suspended the sentence and placed the offender on probation, a violation of probation conditions could, without a due process hearing, result in incarceration to serve the original sentence.

In 1967, in *Mempa v. Rhay*, the U.S. Supreme Court held that, when sentencing has been deferred and the offender placed on probation, the revocation of that probation and the determination of a sentence of incarceration require the presence of counsel. The Court reasoned that this situation, in which in reality the offender is being sentenced, invokes the requirement that "at every stage of a criminal proceeding where substantial rights of a criminal accused may be affected," counsel is required. This case and others pertinent to probation and parole revocation are noted in **Supplement 11.11**. Probation revocation that does not involve deciding a sentence, however, does not always require counsel, although there are some due process requirements.

Historically, like probation, parole revocation was conducted with little concern for due process. Lack of due process was justified on the basis that parole was a privilege—not a right—and that it involved a contract. The inmate contracted to behave in exchange for freedom from incarceration. If that contract were broken, the inmate could be returned to prison. Others argued that parole is a status of continuing custody, during which the offender is subject to prison rules and regulations; thus, revocation requires no greater due process than that required for any action against the inmate while incarcerated.

In 1972, in *Morrissey v. Brewer*, the Supreme Court looked at parole revocation in the case of two offenders, Morrissey and Booher. Morrissey's parole was revoked for these allegations:

- He had bought a car under an assumed name and operated it without permission.
- He had given false statements to police concerning his address and insurance company after a minor accident.
- He had obtained credit under an assumed name.
- He had failed to report his place of residence to his parole officer.

Booher's parole was revoked because of these allegations:

- He had violated the territorial restriction of his parole without consent.
- He had obtained a driver's license under an assumed name.
- He had operated a motor vehicle without permission.
- He had violated the employment condition of his parole by failing to keep himself in gainful employment.[37]

No hearing was held before parole was revoked in these two cases. In its discussion of the cases, the U.S. Supreme Court made several findings. According to the Court, the purpose of parole is rehabilitation. Until parole rules are violated, an individual may remain on parole, and parole should not be revoked unless those rules are violated. Parole revocation does not require all the due process rights of a criminal trial, but some due process elements must be observed. Informal parole revocation hearings are proper, and the requirements of due process for parole revocation change with particular cases.

In *Morrissey*, the U.S. Supreme Court enumerated the minimum requirements for revocation; they were reproduced earlier in **Supplement 11.11**. The Court also ruled that there should be two hearings before the final decision is made. The first is to determine whether there is probable cause to support a parole violation. At the second and more formal hearing, the final decision is made whether to revoke parole.

One year after *Morrissey*, the U.S. Supreme Court extended these minimum due process requirements to probation revocation, but in *Gagnon v. Scarpelli*, the Supreme Court also discussed whether counsel is required at probation and parole revocations. The Supreme Court had not decided that issue in *Morrissey*. In *Gagnon*, the Court held that there might be some cases in which counsel is necessary in order for the offender to have a fair hearing, but counsel is not constitutionally required in all revocation cases.[38]

Two other cases of significance to revocation hearings are summarized in **Supplement 11.11**. Taken together, *Bearden v. Georgia* and *Black v. Romano* demonstrate that there are some restrictions on probation revocation. In *Bearden*, the U.S. Supreme Court held that it is improper to revoke the probation of an indigent who has not paid a fine and restitution unless there is a finding that the indigent has not made a sufficient effort to pay. Even then, the court must look at other alternatives before revoking probation and incarcerating the offender. But in *Romano*, when the offender's probation was revoked because he was charged with leaving the scene of an automobile accident (a felony), the U.S. Supreme Court held that due process does not require that, before incarcerating the offender on the original sentence, other sentencing alternatives be considered.[39]

It is clear from these decisions, read in conjunction with those involving the decision whether to grant parole, that the U.S. Supreme Court sees a significant difference between granting parole and revoking parole. The Court stated it this way:

> The Court has fashioned a constitutional distinction between the decision to revoke parole and the decision to grant or to deny parole. Arbitrary revocation is prohibited by *Morrissey v. Brewer*... whereas arbitrary denial is permitted by *Greenholtz v. Nebraska*.[40]

The courts have also considered other issues regarding parole and probation revocation. In a 1998 decision, a divided U.S. Supreme Court held that the exclusionary rule, which bars the use at trial of illegally seized evidence, would not bar the use of the same material at a parole revocation hearing. In *Pennsylvania Board of Probation and Parole v. Scott*, Justice Clarence Thomas, writing for the majority, emphasized that "[t]he costs of allowing a parolee to avoid the consequences of his violation are compounded by the fact that parolees (particularly those who have already committed parole violations) are more likely to commit future criminal offenses than are average citizens." Thus, the U.S. Supreme Court held that a weapon found during a home search of a parolee, who was forbidden to have weapons, was admissible at his parole revocation hearing. The four dissenting justices argued unsuccessfully that, if the exclusionary rule is necessary to deter police from making unreasonable searches and seizures, it is also necessary to deter parole officers from doing so.[41]

A March 2019 judicial decision raised a critical constitutional issue concerning parole revocation, and the same legal analysis could be applied to probation revocation. The issue concerns sending parolees back to prison without due process for allegedly violating parole for technical reasons "such as crossing a state line, missing a parole appointment or losing a job because their employer found out about their criminal record." U.S. District Judge Stephen R. Bough in Kansas City, Missouri, issued a summary judgment in favor of plaintiff parolees who filed a lawsuit alleging that the Missouri Department of Corrections and its Division of Probation and Parole did not follow the guidelines established by the U.S. Supreme Court concerning the due process rights of parolees.[42] Thousands of immigrants could be released as a result of this ruling.

SEX OFFENDER REGISTRATION LAWS

Another measure taken in some jurisdictions to avoid recidivism by offenders released from prison or parole is to require registration and notice of sex offenders living in the community. Such laws were enacted after the deaths of children at the hands of sexual predators who were released from prisons. **Supplement 11.12** gives a brief history of sex registration laws; three specific laws are discussed here, beginning with the first to be enacted.

In 1994, New Jersey enacted a community notification statute, commonly called **Megan's Law**, in memory of Megan Kanka, who was sexually assaulted and murdered earlier that year. Jesse K. Timmendequas, a neighbor (living with two other sex offenders) with two sex offense convictions, was charged, convicted, and sentenced to death for Megan's murder.[43]

Megan's parents turned the tragedy into a national effort to enact legislation requiring that, when sex offenders are released from prison, notification must be given to the law enforcement officers in the areas in which the offenders plan to live. New Jersey's statute was followed by statutes in most other states and the District of Columbia as well as the federal system.[44] The statutes vary in their provisions, but many require that residents be notified of the presence of a sex offender in the neighborhood.

Megan's Law may also require that schools, community organizations, and entire neighborhoods be notified when sex offenders move into the area. Notification includes the offender's name, address, description, picture, license plate number, and place of employment, depending on the assessment assigned to the offender by the prosecutor's office. That office may be required to assess whether the released sex offender is a low, moderate, or high risk for subsequent sex crimes, a difficult task that requires considerable prosecutorial time. Not all jurisdictions have this provision, and in some jurisdictions, all sex offenders must register for life and there is no ranking of types of offender according to dangerousness.

In July 27, 2006, the U.S. Congress passed, and President George W. Bush signed, the Adam Walsh Child Protection and Safety Act.[45] This act is named for a young Florida boy, Adam Walsh, age 8, who had been kidnapped and murdered 25 years previously. Adam's head (but not the rest of his body) was found near a Florida shopping mall. It was not until late 2008 that the case was possibly solved. Police believe that Adam was abducted and murdered by Ottis Toole, a pedophile, who died in a Florida prison in 1996 for an unrelated murder. Toole confessed but subsequently retracted his confession. In 2010, his confession was challenged in a lawsuit filed by Willis Morgan, a witness, who asked the court for copies of the files of the retired police officer on whose report the conclusion regarding Toole was based. Morgan claimed that serial killer Jeffrey Dahmer was in Sears at the time Adam Walsh was abducted, and hence was a strong suspect in the case.[46] Police have stuck to their conclusion and closed the case.

President George W. Bush, joined by Senate and House members, welcomes John and Reve Walsh prior to signing H.R. 4472, the Adam Walsh Child Protection and Safety Act of 2006 at a ceremony Thursday, July 27, 2006, in the Rose Garden at the White House. The bill is named for the Walsh's six-year-old son Adam Walsh who was abducted and killed 25 years ago.

Adam's father, John Walsh, hosts the media program *America's Most Wanted*, and in that capacity has assisted law enforcement officers in apprehending persons wanted for sexually assaulting and murdering young children. Walsh was instrumental in the establishment of the National Center for Missing and Exploited Children. The Walsh Act increased the effectiveness of law enforcement attempts to apprehend sexual pedophiles by permitting officers to share information across state lines. The act also tightened and broadened sex offender registration requirements. For example, the act precludes the right to use the Internet to ensnare children for sexual purposes. Registration is required prior to, not after, release, along with registering any subsequent address changes. Sex offenders must report to offices within their jurisdictions to update their information; the frequency of reporting depends upon their sex offender level of dangerousness. The act also requires that offenders wear tracking devices; that states maintain statewide registries (in addition to local ones); and that states adopt felony penalties for offenders who do not comply with the requirements, along with many other requirements.

The Walsh Act includes the Sex Offender Registration and Notification Act (SORNA), which requires the establishment of three tiers of sex offenders, ranging from high risk to low risk.

The Walsh Act was amended in 2008, with the enactment of the Keeping the Internet Devoid of Sexual Predators (KIDS) Act, which requires sex offenders to register their e-mail and instant messenger addresses with the National Sex Offender Registry. This amendment was an effort to curtail sexual predators' use of the Internet to lure potential victims. KIDS makes it a crime for Internet users to misrepresent their ages to lure children into sexual conduct, and it requires GPS monitoring at all times for released sex offenders.[47]

Supplement 11.13 presents an excerpt from *Nichols v. United States*,[48] decided by the U.S. Supreme Court in 2016 and resolving a legal issue concerning the Adam Walsh Act's registration requirement.

Sex offender registration laws have been made stricter in many jurisdictions, with statutes patterned after the Florida law that resulted from the death of Jessica Lunsford in March 2005. The body of Jessica, age 9, was found three weeks after she was last seen in the Florida home where she lived with her father and his parents. John E. Couey, 46, a registered sex offender and neighbor, was convicted and sentenced to death for Jessica's rape and murder. Her father has fought for stricter sex offender laws as a result of these crimes against his daughter. The Jessica Lunsford Act includes numerous requirements, including longer sentences for convicted sex offenders and more stringent monitoring requirements for those offenders who are living in the community.[49]

Spotlight 11.4

Sex Offender Registration and Notification: Limited Effects in New Jersey

"Researchers for the first time have conducted an independent scientific assessment of the impact of [Megan's Law] in New Jersey. . . . They found that:

- Sex offense rates in New Jersey have been on a consistent downward trend since 1985. . . .
- Megan's Law did not reduce the number of rearrests for sex offenses, nor did it have any demonstrable effect on the time between when sex offenders were released from prison and the time they were rearrested for any new offense, such as a drug, theft, or sex offense.
- The majority of sexual offenders sentenced in New Jersey are convicted of incest and child molestation. In more than half of the cases, the victim and offender know each other. Megan's Law did not have an effect on this pattern. . . .
- Megan's Law had no demonstrable effect on the number of victims involved in sexual offenses. . . .
- Sexual offenders convicted after Megan's Law was passed received shorter sentences than those convicted before the law."

Source: Kristen M. Zgoba and Karen Bachar, U.S. Department of Justice, "Sex Offender Registration and Notification: Limited Effects in New Jersey" (April 2009), pp. 1-2, http://www.ncjrs.gov/pdffiles1/nij/225402.pdf, accessed August 8, 2014.

California's version of a **Jessica's Law** is one of the toughest and was enacted after 70 percent of that state's voters approved Proposition 83, effective November 8, 2006. The Sexual Predator Punishment and Control Act (SPPCA) eliminates good-time credits for sex offenders and increases the minimum mandatory sentence for sex offenders. The statute permits labeling some released sex offenders as violent offenders who are eligible for civil commitment on the basis of one sex offense. The offenders must wear GPS monitoring systems for life and they are not permitted to live within 2,000 feet of a school or any other place in which children can be expected to congregate. The act also includes penalties for providing date-rape drugs and pornography.[50]

Some of the limitations placed on registered sex offenders have been challenged in the courts. Some are discussed in the Supplement. **Supplement 11.14** excerpts *In re Taylor*,[51] a California case concerned with the issue of housing restrictions. In **Supplement 11.15**, in *Packingham v. North Carolina*,[52] the U.S. Supreme Court rules on the issue of whether registered sex offenders may be prohibited from using the Internet. **Supplement 11.16** considers the issue of requiring GPS monitoring of registered sex offenders as discussed in a 2016 case in the Seventh Circuit, *Belleau v. Wall*.[53]

Effectiveness Issues

A major concern with these and other sex offender registration laws is whether they are effective in reducing recidivism among sexual predators. A survey of the empirical research has led some to conclude that the results are questionable. Most children who are sexually assaulted are victimized by relatives or other persons they know; these laws do not affect those crimes. Other research suggests that we do not have enough pre- and post-evidence to conclude that crimes are deterred by sex registration laws.[54]

Spotlight 11.4 relates brief conclusions on a study of the effectiveness of New Jersey's Megan's Law as reported by the U.S. Department of Justice (DOJ). Furthermore, a lack of funding has resulted in offices in which there is no indication of which sex offenders are in the area or where they are living. These problems with recordkeeping make it easier for offenders to engage in additional sex crimes. In fact, the Department of Justice reports that over 52 percent of sex offenders in the nation are recidivists.[55]

A study conducted by the California Bureau of State Audits reported that in that state, the registered sex offender database contained "thousands of errors, inconsistencies, and out-of-date information" and that these mistakes placed the public at risk. On the one hand, the public could be misled in checking the database and finding no sexual offenders in their neighborhoods when they, in fact, do reside there. On the other hand, the public could become unreasonably alarmed by the erroneous reporting that 1,142 convicted sex offenders are in the community. In addition, the state violated the privacy of 42 juvenile sex offenders by including their names within the registry, thus making public the names of juvenile offenders. And although the failure of a sex offender to register is a crime, the state rarely knows who is avoiding the registry unless those offenders, most of whom move often, are arrested for other crimes.[56]

In January 2001, California's Sexual Offender Management Board (CASOMB), a 15-member commission established by law to advise the state's governor and the legislature, issued a report that raised critical questions about how that state's sex offender registration laws were working. Among other issues, CASOMB blasted the assumption that children will be protected if sex offenders are not permitted to live near areas in which children congregate, stating that there is "almost no correlation between sex offenders living near restricted areas and where they commit their offenses." The report concluded that money is wasted because the state cannot concentrate its limited resources on the most dangerous sex offenders because the "one-size-fits-all system of registration" does not distinguish sex offenders. CASOMB concluded that not all sex offenders should be required to register for life. The board also recommended significant improvements in law enforcement with regard to sex offender registration issues.[57]

A January 2010 report by CASOMB contained a scathing report that raised significant questions about California's statutes regarding sex offenders in the community. The report challenged the premise of Jessica's Law with regard to residence restrictions. "The hypothesis that sex offenders who live in close proximity to schools, parks and other places children congregate have an increased likelihood of sexually re-offending remains unsupported by research. . . . On the contrary, there is almost no correlation between sex offenders living near restricted areas and where they commit their offenses." The report noted that the law requires the state to send more sex offenders through mental health analysis to determine whether they should be civilly committed (discussed later). The monthly costs of that process had escalated from $161,000 prior to the passage of Jessica's Law to more than $1 million after the law was enacted. The report questioned the wisdom of GPS and noted its expense and the lack of evidence of its effectiveness. The report emphasized that California had 90,000 registered sex offenders, 68,000 of whom lived in communities; all were required to register for life. The public has no way to distinguish the dangerousness of these offenders. "In this one-size-fits-all system of registration, law enforcement cannot concentrate its scarce resources on close supervision of the more dangerous offenders or on those who are at higher risk of committing another sex crime." The board recommended the following:

- "Not all California sex offenders need to register for life in order to safeguard the public and so a risk-based system of differentiated registration requirements should be created.
- Focusing resources on registering and monitoring moderate to high-risk sex offenders makes a community safer than trying to monitor all offenders for life.
- A sex offender's risk of re-offense should be one factor in determining the length of time the person must register as a sex offender and whether to post the offender on the Internet. Other factors which should determine duration of registration and Internet posting include:
  - Whether the sex offense was violent
  - Whether the sex offense was against a child
  - Whether the offender was convicted of a new sex offense or violent offense after the first sex offense conviction
  - Whether the person was civilly committed as a sexually violent predator
- Monitoring of registered sex offenders once they are no longer under any form of formal community supervision is critical to public safety."[58]

Still another issue with regard to the many statutes regulating sex offenders who live in communities is the impact on minorities. Some researchers have found that these restrictions more negatively impact sex offenders in disadvantaged as compared with affluent neighborhoods and that convicted sex offenders are more likely to live in the disadvantaged areas.[59]

Constitutional Issues

Aside from the practical problems of whether sex offender registration laws are effective are the legal issues. Some courts have ruled that the registration statutes (or portions of them) are unconstitutional, while other courts have upheld all or a portion of challenged statutes.

In 2003, the U.S. Supreme Court upheld the sex offender registration statutes in Alaska and Connecticut.

The Alaska case raised the issue of whether the law violated the *ex post facto* clause of the U.S. Constitution, while the Connecticut case raised the due process issue. The Alaska case was challenged by two men, each having served eight years for sexually molesting their own daughters. After the Alaska Megan's Law was enacted in 1994, the men (both of whom had been released from prison in 1990) were required to register as sex offenders. They argued on appeal that since the law was not in effect when they committed their crimes, it could not be imposed on them. To do so would constitute additional punishment, which is prohibited by the *ex post facto* clause of the U.S. Constitution. The Connecticut statute was challenged by appellants who argued that the lack of a requirement to determine whether a released sex offender was dangerous before requiring registration violated due process.

The U.S. Supreme Court rejected both challenges. By a 6-to-3 vote in *Smith v. Doe*, the Court held that the Alaska statute does not violate the *ex post facto* clause. According to the majority, sex offender registration requirements do *not* constitute punishment. The *purpose* of required registration is to protect society, not to punish defendants.[60]

In *Connecticut Department of Public Safety v. Doe*, by a unanimous vote, the U.S. Supreme Court upheld the Connecticut statute, which, the Court stated, does not violate due process of law. No hearing on the issue of whether a sex offender is dangerous is necessary prior to requiring that offender to register. About one-half of the state sex offender registration laws in effect at the time of this case did not require a hearing.[61]

Another legal issue with regard to requiring sex offenders to register in the communities in which they live relates to making failure to do so a *federal* crime. The issue was raised in a 2009 decision by the Eleventh Circuit Court of Appeals, which reversed a decision by a federal judge in Tampa, Florida. The federal judge, who acknowledged the "commendable" congressional goal of protecting society from sexual predators, concluded that "a worthy cause is not enough to transform a state concern (sex offender registration) into a federal crime." The case of *United States v. Powers* involved Robert Powers, who has an IQ of 68 and reads at a second-grade level. While living in South Carolina in 1995, Powers was convicted of a sex crime and required to register as a sex offender. In 2007, he moved to Florida and did not register as a sex offender as required by SORNA. He was arrested and indicted for the federal crime of *failure to register as a sex offender*. On appeal, the court reversed the lower court's decision that SORNA was unconstitutional under the Commerce Clause of the U.S. Constitution and ordered the lower court to reinstate the indictment against Powers.[62]

In June 2010, however, the U.S. Supreme Court handed down its decision in *Carr v. United States*. This case differed from *Powers* in that the appellant in *Carr* traveled interstate prior to the effective date of SORNA. Carr was arrested, convicted, and sentenced to prison in Alabama but released on probation on July 3, 2004. He registered as a sex offender as required by Alabama law. Prior to the enactment of SORNA, Carr relocated to Indiana but did not register as required by Indiana law. He subsequently became involved in a fight, which brought him to the attention of Indiana law enforcement authorities. He was charged by federal prosecutors with violating SORNA. He challenged that charge on the grounds that it constituted an *ex post facto* (and thus illegal) application of SORNA. His challenge was rejected. He entered a guilty plea, reserving his right to appeal the legal issue, which he did. The U.S. Supreme Court did not decide the *ex post facto* issue, holding it was not necessary because the Court held that SORNA does not extend to travel prior to the effective date of the statute. Specifically, SORNA applies to a person who "is required to register under the Sex Offender Registration and Notification Act."[63]

In June 2019, the U.S. Supreme Court decided two cases concerning sex offender registration. Those cases, *United States v. Haymond* and *Gundy v. United States*, are discussed in **Supplement 11.17**.[64]

CIVIL COMMITMENT OF RELEASED SEX OFFENDERS

Because registration requirements for released sex offenders may not be effective, some states provide for the civil commitment of sex offenders after they complete their prison terms. In 1997, the U.S. Supreme Court upheld the Kansas civil commitment statute in the case of Leroy Hendricks, who was convicted in 1984 of indecent liberties with two 13-year-old boys. After serving most of his ten-year sentence, Hendricks was scheduled for release from prison, but a jury determined that he was a sexual predator, and the judge found that he had a mental abnormality. He was involuntarily confined indefinitely under the Kansas Commitment of Sexually Violent Predators Act, which defines a *sexually violent predator* as "any person who has been convicted of or charged with a sexually violent offense and who suffers from a mental abnormality or personality disorder which makes the person likely to engage in the predatory acts of sexual violence." In a 5-4 decision, the U.S. Supreme Court upheld the commitment.[65]

More recently, the U.S. Supreme Court decided a limited legal issue with regard to the civil commitment of sex offenders after they have completed their prison sentences. In May 2010, in *United States v. Comstock*, the Court considered whether Congress has the constitutional authority under Article I of the U.S. Constitution to authorize such civil commitments. At issue was the Adam Walsh Child Protection and Safety Act, mentioned earlier, which authorizes the civil commitment of federal sex offenders judged dangerous to society. The *Comstock* case did not involve state jurisdiction but focused only on the U.S. Constitution's delegation to Congress of the power to enact statutes that are "necessary and proper for carrying into execution" the other powers delegated to Congress. The U.S. Supreme Court, by a vote of 7 to 2, ruled that Congress does have that power.[66]

There are many social, practical, and constitutional issues regarding sex offenders and other types of offenders. Of significant importance is whether any civil rights should be restored when those individuals are released back into society. One big issue was emphasized in October 2018, when Frederick Clay was released after serving 38 years in prison for a crime he did not commit. Clay was permitted to vote for the first time, but he had been exonerated of the crime for which he served time. The right to vote is not usually granted to all who are released from prison. According to Clay:

> They say one voice can make a difference, and maybe my voice will make a difference through voting. I feel happy about that. I'm going to vote for all the people who never had the chance to vote and gave their live [sic] for it. I'm ready to do my part.[67]

One final consideration is whether any lenience should be given by judges when considering release conditions or even whether to sentence to prison a person who is convicted of a serious crime committed without realizing the significance of the act. **Supplement 11.18** excerpts the case of *United States v. Nesbeth*,[68] in which a New York judge refused to incarcerate a young woman, a student, who was asked by friends to bring two suitcases into the United States not realizing they contained illegal drugs.

Summary

This chapter covered some critical areas of criminal justice. Despite the public demand for stricter reactions to criminals, overcrowded jails and prisons force most jurisdictions to use some types of community corrections. Many jurisdictions retreated from rehabilitation as a purpose for punishment and corrections; that position, however, is changing, and offenders are (and will continue to be) in the community, usually with limited or no supervision. The issue is not whether we wish to have community corrections; the issue is how much attention and funding we will provide to make sure the use of community corrections does not impair the goal of security.

In recent years, there has been somewhat of a return to a rehabilitation philosophy, especially in the processing of substance abuse offenders. The chapter discussed changes in drug laws and the use of drug courts, as well as statutory provisions for the treatment, rather than punishment, of first- or second-time drug offenders. The chapter discussed the diversion and treatment of physically and mentally challenged persons.

The chapter began with an overview of community-based corrections. It considered the history of this approach to corrections, along with the cost. Financing is a problem, particularly with the cutbacks in federal and state budgets. However, the costs for community corrections are far less than the costs of incarceration, and that is true even when intensive supervision is provided for offenders residing in the community. The problems that offenders face when they live in the community were discussed, along with the need for services in assisting them to cope with these adjustments. In particular, attention was given to furlough, work release, and prerelease programs. A particular focus was the federal Second Chance Act.

Probation and parole were discussed in greater depth in this chapter than were other community corrections because they are the methods used most frequently.

Probation is the sentence imposed most often and is used today for serious as well as for minor offenders. The prognosis for success is not great, although it is thought that with intensive probation supervision the probability for success improves. Attention was given to the types of probation.

Brief attention was given to the administration of probation systems before focusing on probation supervision. The discussion on parole noted that it has been the most frequently used method of release from prison, but its use for early release has been restricted in recent years. The various methods of organizing parole systems were discussed in the chapter, along with the parole process, including eligibility for parole and the parole hearing. The due process requirements for the parole decision-making hearings were also discussed. Attempts to decrease the perceived arbitrariness of parole decisions have involved the use of parole guidelines. Due process in the revocation of probation and parole has helped remove the arbitrariness and unfairness of those important processes.

The movement away from rehabilitation has resulted in problems for community corrections. Perhaps the bitterest criticisms have been hurled at parole, resulting in action in many states to abolish or at least curtail its use. Despite the call for parole abolition, it has become obvious that some form of discretion in the release of offenders must be retained, especially if sentences are long. Consideration of medical parole for the aging prison population was noted.

No one can say which is the real problem: the failure of parole per se or the abuse of discretion by parole-granting authorities. In 1975, Maurice H. Sigler, chairman of the U.S. Board of Parole, argued that parole "has now become the scapegoat of all of corrections' ills." He suggested that the system deserves the same objective, dispassionate analysis that its critics demand of parole decisions:

> To those who say "let's abolish parole," I say that as long as we use imprisonment in this country we will have to have someone, somewhere, with the authority to release people from imprisonment. Call it parole—call it what you will. It's one of those jobs that has to be done.[69]

The abolition of parole may result only in shifting discretion to another area, such as prosecution. Prosecutors may refuse to prosecute; juries may refuse to convict in cases involving long, mandatory sentences with no chance of parole. Efforts to control discretion within the parole system may be a more reasonable approach than the total abolition of the system.

The final section of the chapter analyzed sex offender registration laws, looking in particular at Megan's Law, the Adam Walsh Child Protection and Safety Act, and Jessica's Law. The discussion noted practical problems with sex offender registration laws and included an analysis of constitutional issues. Attention was given to the civil commitment of sexual offenders after they serve their prison sentences. We can expect continued controversy over these sex offender registration laws and civil commitment as courts balance society's rights against those of ex-offenders.

The text now turns to a special area of criminal justice as Chapter 12 looks at issues regarding juvenile offenders.

Key Terms

community work service 255
diversion 256
felony probation 262
fine 254
furlough 260
halfway house 254
house arrest 262
intensive probation supervision (IPS) 263
Jessica's Law 273
Megan's Law 271
parole 261
parole board 261
parole officer 263
parole revocation 270
probation 260
probation officer 263
probation revocation 270
recidivism 258
recidivists 259
reintegration 254
work release 260

Study Questions

1. Define *community-based corrections,* and give reasons why some argue that this approach is preferred over incarceration of offenders.
2. What changes have been made in drug laws, especially those regulating the use of marijuana?
3. Evaluate the role of drug courts and other diversionary processing and treatment of nonviolent drug offenders.
4. Do we need mental health courts? Why or why not?
5. What problems do offenders face when they return to the community from incarceration? What is being done to assist them in coping with those problems?
6. Explain the meaning and importance of the Second Chance Act of 2007.
7. What is the difference between probation and parole?
8. What is meant by *intensive probation supervision*? How does it compare in effectiveness with traditional methods of supervision?
9. What effect do due process requirements have on parole granting? On parole and probation revocation?
10. What is medical parole and why is it important?
11. Explain and discuss the practical and legal implications of sex offender registration laws. Distinguish the types of laws.
12. What is meant by civil commitment of sex offenders? Should it be utilized?

Notes

1. President's Commission on Law Enforcement and Administration of Justice, *The Challenge of Crime in a Free Society* (Washington, D.C.: U.S. Government Printing Office, 1967), p. 121.
2. National Advisory Commission on Criminal Justice Standards and Goals, *A National Strategy to Reduce Crime* (Washington, D.C.: U.S. Government Printing Office, 1973), p. 121.
3. *Sundance v. Municipal Court,* 729 P.2d 80 (Cal. 1986).
4. *Traynor v. Turnage,* 485 U.S. 535 (1988), superseded by statute as stated in *Larrabee v. Derwinski,* 968 F.2d 1497 (3d Cir. 1992).
5. National Organization for the Reform of Marijuana Laws, "Federal: Bipartisan Bill to End Federal Marijuana Prohibition," NORML, https://norml.org/, accessed May 4, 2019. See this source for continuing updates on the changes in law concerning the use of marijuana for medical and recreational purposes.
6. The Controlled Substance Act is codified at 21 USCS, Section 812 (2019). The Ending Federal Marijuana Prohibition Act of 2019 is HR 1588.
7. "The Opioid Crisis," The White House, https://www.whitehouse.org, accessed October 31, 2018.
8. "Treatment with Teeth: A Judge Explains Why Drug Courts That Mandate and Supervise Treatment Are an Effective Middle Ground to Help Addicts Stay Clean and Reduce Crime," *The American Prospect* (December 2003), p. 45.
9. Ibid.
10. Ibid.
11. Quoted in "Drug Courts Reduce Recidivism by 32 Percent," *The Daily Record of Rochester* (Rochester, NY) (November 14, 2003), n.p.
12. "Drug Court Is All About Family," *The Courier-Journal* (Louisville, KY) (December 24, 2003), p. 1B.
13. "Mental Health Courts Offer Detention Alternatives," *Legal Intelligencer* 231(12) (July 19, 2004): 4.
14. The statute is codified at 34 USCS, Section 10471 (2019).
15. "NIC Aids Corrections with Inmate Transition Program," *Corrections Professional* 11(13) (March 24, 2006): n.p.
16. The quotations from President Bush are printed in "Prisoner Reentry Measure Is Signed by President Bush," *Criminal Justice Newsletter* (April 15, 2008), p. 4.
17. Danielle Kaeble, Bureau of Justice Statistics, "Probation and Parole in the United States, 2016" (April 2018), p. 1, https://www.bjs.gov/, accessed October 31, 2018.
18. See Sanford Bates, "The Establishment and Early Years of the Federal Probation System," *Federal Probation* 51 (June 1987): 4-9.
19. Joan Petersilia, "Rand's Research: A Closer Look," *Corrections Today* 47 (June 1985): 37.
20. Mariel Alper and Matthew R. Durose, Bureau of Justice Statistics, "2018 Update on Prisoner Recidivism: A 9-Year Follow-up Period (2005-2014)" (May 2018), p. 1, https://www.bjs.gov, accessed October 31, 2018.
21. *Criminal Justice Research at Rand* (Santa Monica, CA: Rand Corp., January 1985), p. 11.

22. John T. Whitehead, "The Effectiveness of Felony Probation: Results from an Eastern State," *Justice Quarterly* 8 (December 1991): 525-543.
23. "Long Arm of the Law Has Them by the Anklet," *Los Angeles Times* (June 27, 2003), Part 2, p. 2.
24. See the study by Mary A. Finn and Suzanne Muirhead-Steves, "The Effectiveness of Electronic Monitoring with Violent Male Parolees," *Justice Quarterly* 19(2) (June 2002): 293-312.
25. For a recent analysis of the relationship between restitution and recidivism, see the three articles on "Restitution Payment and Recidivism," in *Criminology & Public Policy* 17(4) (November 2018), pp. 783-825.
26. "Probationer Fees Cover Half of Supervision Costs in Texas," *Criminal Justice Newsletter* (January 2, 2003), p. 7.
27. National Institute of Corrections, *New Approaches to Staff Safety*, 2d ed., summarized in *Criminal Justice Newsletter* (May 1, 2003), pp. 7-9.
28. *"Broken Windows" Probation: The Next Step in Fighting Crime*, Manhattan Institute, http://www.manhattan-institute.org, accessed April 2, 2011.
29. Todd R. Clear and Patricia L. Hardyman, "The New Intensive Supervision Movement," *Crime & Delinquency* 36 (January 1990): 42-44. The entire journal is devoted to issues on intensive probation supervision.
30. The Sentencing Reform Act was passed as part of the Comprehensive Crime Control Act of 1984, Public Law 98-473, 98 Stat. 1837, 1976 (1984), and is codified with its subsequent amendments in 18 USCS, Section 3551 et seq. (2019) and 28 USCS, Sections 991-998 (2019).
31. "Eliminating Parole Boards Isn't a Cure-All, Experts Say," *New York Times* (January 10, 1999), p. 11.
32. Quoted in Jessica Mitford, *Kind and Usual Punishment: The Prison Business* (New York: Alfred A. Knopf, 1973), p. 216.
33. *Greenholtz v. Nebraska*, 442 U.S. 1 (1979).
34. *Board of Pardons v. Allen*, 482 U.S. 369 (1987).
35. *Morrissey v. Brewer*, 408 U.S. 471, 478 (1972).
36. See Cal. Penal Code, Section 3550 (2018).
37. *Morrissey v. Brewer*, 408 U.S. 471 (1972).
38. *Gagnon v. Scarpelli*, 411 U.S. 778 (1973).
39. *Black v. Romano*, 471 U.S. 606 (1985); and *Bearden v. Georgia*, 461 U.S. 660 (1983).
40. *Jago v. Van Curen*, 454 U.S. 14 (1981).
41. *Pennsylvania Board of Probation and Parole v. Scott*, 524 U.S. 357 (1998).
42. Dan Margolies, "Thousands of Missouri Inmates whose Paroles Were Revoked May Be Entitled May Be Entitled to Relief, Judge Rules," St. Louis Public Radio (March 1, 2019); Beth Schwartzapfel, The Marshall Project, "Parole Process Puts too Many People Back Behind Bars, Missouri Lawsuit Says," *American Bar Association Journal* (February 22, 2019), http;//www.abajournal,com, accessed February 26, 2019.
43. The statute is codified in N.J. Stat., Section 2C:7-1 et seq. (2018).
44. The federal statute is part of the Violent Crime Control and Law Enforcement Act of 1994, Public Law 103-323 (September 13, 1994), Section 20417.
45. Adam Walsh Act Child Protection and Safety Act, 18 USCS, Section 2250(a) (2019).
46. "Witness in Adam Walsh Case Seeks Report," *Orlando Sentinel* (June 4, 2010), p. 9B.
47. Keeping the Internet Devoid of Sexual Predators (KIDS) Act of 2008, Public Law 110-440, 24 USCS, Section 1690 (2019).
48. *Nichols v. United States*, 136 S. Ct. 1113 (2016).
49. Florida's Jessica Lunsford Act is codified at Fla. Stat., Section 948.06 et seq. (2018).
50. Cal. Penal Code, Section 3003.5 et seq. (2018).
51. *In re Taylor*, 343 P.3d 867 (Cal. 2015).
52. *Packingham v. North Carolina*, 137 S. Ct. 1730 (2017).
53. *Belleau v. Wall*, 811 F.3d 929 (7th Cir. 2016).
54. For a review of the research, see the document published by the U.S. Department of Justice, *Megan's Law: Assessing the Practical and Monetary Efficacy*, by Kristen Zgoba et al. (December 2008), http://www.ncjrs.gov/, accessed April 2, 2011.
55. "Nearly Half of Calif. Sex Offenders Not Tracked," *St. Petersburg Times* (Florida) (January 8, 2003), p. 5.
56. California State Auditor, *California Law Enforcement and Correctional Agencies: With Increased Efforts, They Could Improve the Accuracy and Completeness of Public Information on Sex Offenders*, http://www.bsa.ca.gov/pdfs/reports/2003-105.pdf, accessed April 2, 2011.
57. California Sex Offender Management Board (CASOMB), California Department of Mental Health, *Decrease Victimization, Increase Community Safety Recommendations Report* (January 2010), http://www.casomb.org, accessed January 2, 2015.
58. California Sex Offender Management Board (CASOMB), California Department of Mental Health, *Recommendations Report* (January 2010), p. 51, http://www.casomb.org, accessed January 2, 2015.
59. See Lorine A. Hughes and Keri B. Burchfield, "Sex Offender Residence Restrictions in Chicago: An Environmental Injustice?," *Justice Quarterly* 25(4) (December 2008): 647-673; Hughes and Colleen Kadleck, "Sex Offender Community Notification and Community Stratification," *Justice Quarterly* 25(3) (September 2008): 469-495. See also Michelle L. Meloy et al., "Making Sense Out of Nonsense: The Deconstruction of State-Level Sex Offender Residence Restrictions," *American Journal of Criminal Justice* (Fall 2008): 209-222.
60. *Smith v. Doe*, 538 U.S. 84 (2003).
61. *Connecticut Department of Public Safety v. Doe*, 538 U.S. 1 (2003).
62. *United States v. Powers*, 544 F. Supp. 2d 1331 (M.D. Fla. 2008), *vacated and remanded*, 562 F.3d 1342 (11th Cir. 2009).
63. *Carr v. United States*, 560 U.S. 438 (2010). The Court was quoting from 18 USCS, Section 2250(1) (2019).
64. United States v. Haymond, 588 U.S. ____ (2019); Gundy v. United States, 588 U.S. ____ (2019).
65. Commitment of Sexually Violent Predators, Kan. Stat. Ann., Section 59-29a02 (2012). The case is *Kansas v. Hendricks*, 521 U.S. 346 (1997).
66. *United States v. Comstock*, 560 U.S. 126 (2010).
67. E-mail to the author from the Innocence Project, October 30, 2018.
68. *United States v. Nesbeth*, 188 F. Supp. 3d 179 (E.D.N.Y. 2016).
69. Maurice H. Sigler, "Abolish Parole?," *Federal Probation* 39 (June 1975): 48.

Part V

Juvenile Justice: A Special Case

Juvenile court systems emerged as separate systems for processing juveniles who engage in criminal and delinquent activities or who are dependent or neglected. Historically, these special courts and systems were viewed as being concerned with the welfare of children who did not need the procedural safeguards characteristic of adult criminal court systems.

In recent years, that orientation has changed. Some but not all procedural safeguards recognized in adult criminal courts have been extended to juvenile court systems, leaving the two systems far less distinguishable than was originally the case. Whether these are positive or negative changes is debatable, but clearly the increased attention given to the involvement of juveniles in violent crimes has resulted in efforts to change juvenile justice systems or to process violent juveniles in adult criminal court systems.

Chapter 12 discusses the early development and recent changes that have been made in juvenile court systems, along with the development and changes that have occurred in juvenile correctional systems.

12

Juvenile Justice Systems

Chapter Outline

Learning Objectives

After reading this chapter, you should be able to do the following:

- List and explain the basic procedural and philosophical differences between juvenile courts and adult criminal courts historically and currently
- Discuss current data on delinquency
- Describe juvenile court proceedings and note the role of attorneys
- Explain and evaluate the processing of juvenile offenders in adult criminal courts
- Assess the wisdom of sentencing juveniles to life without parole, referring to the U.S. Supreme Court's decision on this topic
- Analyze the practice of confining juveniles in adult jails and prisons and discuss 2018 legislation on this issue
- Summarize recent changes in juvenile corrections
- Should juveniles be guaranteed a right to treatment? Discuss
- Discuss the wisdom of supervising juveniles within the community rather than in institutions
- Evaluate the current legal status of the capital punishment of juveniles
- Comment on the future of juvenile court systems

Criminal responsibility in adversary systems is based on the premise that accused persons have the ability to understand and control their behavior. Most people are presumed to have this ability, but among the exceptions have been persons of tender years. In the late 1800s, separate systems for juveniles emerged in the United States. In recent years, these systems have gone through significant changes. This chapter looks at some of those changes.

The chapter begins with a brief historical overview of the background of U.S. juvenile justice systems. The origin of juvenile courts is discussed, along with the dispute over the purposes of juvenile justice systems. Delinquency data are analyzed, with special consideration to race and ethnicity and gender. The chapter examines juvenile court organization and procedures, followed by an analysis of juveniles in adult criminal courts, including the role of attorneys. Significant attention is given to the coverage of issues regarding the processing of juvenile offenders through adult criminal courts, including constitutional law issues with this approach, particularly with a focus on life without parole and confining juveniles in adult facilities. Registration laws for sex offenders, discussed in Chapter 11 with reference to adults, are analyzed in the supplement as they apply to juveniles.

Numerous issues concerning juveniles in corrections are covered before the chapter turns to the analysis of supervising juvenile offenders in the community rather than incarcerating them. The recent U.S. Supreme Court case on the execution of juveniles is mentioned in the text discussion of capital punishment, with its facts and an excerpt from the case presented in the supplement. A final section of the chapter contains a brief assessment of adult criminal and juvenile justice systems.

JUVENILE JUSTICE SYSTEMS: AN OVERVIEW

Special justice systems for children rest on the belief that a **juvenile delinquent** should be treated separately from and different than adults. Juveniles need special handling and processing when they engage in delinquent or criminal acts. They are considered amenable to treatment, to change, and to rehabilitation. The law of New Hampshire is illustrative, as noted in **Supplement 12.1**.

Although the first discussion of **juvenile** problems of which we have records dates back 4,000 years to the Code of Hammurabi, the treatment of children in the United States can be traced to the philosophy of the English, who in the eleventh and twelfth centuries developed the practice of treating children differently from adults. A child under the age of 7 was considered incapable of forming the intent required for criminal prosecutions. A child between the ages of 7 and 14 years was presumed to be incapable of forming the intent, but that presumption could be refuted. A child over 14 was treated as an adult.

During this earlier period of English history, when the death penalty was provided for many crimes, children were not exempted, although few children were executed. Later in England, the *chancery courts*, or equity courts, were established for the purpose of avoiding the harshness of the strict technicalities of the English common law. Equity courts were to decide cases on the principles of justice and fairness. These courts were called chancery courts because they were under the jurisdiction of the king's chancellor. Equity courts had jurisdiction over many types of cases, including those involving children.

The English king could exercise the power of a parent over children and others, a concept called ***parens patriae***, literally meaning the "parent of the country." In time, this concept became so important that England enacted statutes permitting the legal rights of parents and other family members to be terminated in the cases of persons who needed the legal guardianship of the king.

Parens patriae was interpreted in England to mean that the sovereign had the responsibility to oversee any children in the kingdom who might be neglected or abused. The court exercised this duty only when it was thought necessary for the welfare of the child, and that rarely occurred. The protection of society and the punishment of parents were not considered to be sufficient reasons to invoke the responsibility. In the English system and in the system as adopted during the early period of American history, the *parens patriae* doctrine applied only to children who were in need of supervision or help because of the actions of their parents or guardians, not to children who were delinquent. These children were categorized as *children in need of supervision, persons in need of supervision*, or *dependent or neglected children*. The extension of juvenile court jurisdiction over delinquent children was an innovation adopted in Illinois in 1899.[1]

In the United States, juvenile court jurisdiction was extended to children considered incorrigible because they would not obey their parents or other adults. Even if they were not violating the law, these juveniles could be accused of committing a **status offense**, such as running away from home. The trend in recent years has been to remove status offenses from juvenile court jurisdiction; however, where jurisdiction remains, the status offender generally is included within the definition of juvenile delinquent. Some states have a minimum age for juvenile court jurisdiction, but as a practical matter, most courts do not decide cases involving very young children.

Prior to the emergence of the **juvenile court**, children in the United States were treated as adults. Capital punishment was permitted but seldom used; however, many children were deprived of adequate food, incarcerated with adults, or subjected to corporal punishment. Some institutions were established to separate incarcerated juveniles from adults. The New York House of Refuge, established in 1824, was the first and served as a model. These early institutions eliminated some of the evils of imprisoning children with adult criminals, although some scholars have questioned whether they provided much improvement in the treatment of juveniles.[2]

By the mid-1800s, probation for juveniles had been established in the United States, and separate **detention centers** had been built. The 1800s saw the evolution of progressive ideas in the care and treatment of dependent and neglected children. Protective societies, such as the Society for the Prevention of Cruelty to Children (developed in New York in 1875), paved the way for the first juvenile court, established in 1899 in Illinois. Other states quickly followed.

Table 12.1 lists some of the historical differences between U.S. adult criminal courts and juvenile courts. The juvenile court, with its emphasis on individualized treatment, was visualized as a social agency or clinic rather than a court of law, a vision that has encountered much criticism in recent years. The court was to be a social institution designed to protect and rehabilitate the child, rather than to determine the child's guilt or innocence. Juvenile courts were to be treatment-oriented, not punishment-oriented. The purpose of juvenile courts was to prevent children from becoming criminals by catching them in the budding stages and giving them the protection and concern that a parent would be expected to provide.

The vocabulary of juvenile and criminal courts also differed. Children would not be arrested but, rather, summoned or apprehended; they would not be indicted, but a **petition** would be filed on their behalf. If **detention** were necessary, children would be placed in special facilities separate from adults rather than in jails. They

Table 12.1

U.S. Adult Criminal and Juvenile Courts: Some Historically Important Contrasts

Adult criminal court	Juvenile court
Court of law	Social institution, agency, clinic
Constitutional court	*Parens patriae* approach — supra-constitutional rights
Purpose to punish, deter	Purpose to salvage, rehabilitate
Begins with arrest	Begins with apprehension, summons; process of intake
Indictment or presentment	Petition filed on behalf of child
Detained in jails or released on bail	Detained in detention centers or released to family or others
Public trial	Private hearing
Strict rules of evidence	Informal procedures
Right to trial by jury	No right to trial by jury
Right to counsel	No right to (or need for) counsel
Prosecuted by state	Allegations brought by state
Plea bargaining	No plea bargaining; state acting in child's best interests
Impartial judge	Judge acting as wise parent
Pleads guilty, innocent, or *nolo contendere*	Admits or denies petition
Found guilty or innocent	Adjudicated
Sentenced	Disposition of the case
Probation	Probation
Incarcerated in jail or prison	Placed in reformatory, training school, foster home, etc.
Released on parole	Released to aftercare

would not have a public trial but a private hearing, in which juries and prosecuting attorneys would rarely, if ever, be used. In most cases, they would not have an attorney.

The juvenile hearing would be informal, for the ordinary procedures of the adult criminal courtroom would be out of place. Judges would not act as impartial observers, as was their function in criminal courts. Rather, they would act as wise parents, disciplining their children with love and tenderness and deciding in an informal way what was best for those children. Juveniles would not be sentenced as the concept is used in adult criminal courts. Instead, after the hearing, there would be an **adjudication**. A **disposition** would be made only after a careful study of the juvenile's background and potential, and the decision would be made in the best interests of the child.

The juvenile court hearing differed from that of the adult criminal court in procedure as well as in philosophy. Rules of evidence required in criminal courts were not applied to juvenile courts. Adult criminal court procedural safeguards were set aside in the interest of treatment and the welfare of children. Because the state, in recognizing its duty as parent, was helping, not punishing, children, no constitutional rights were violated. The emphasis in juvenile court was not on what the child *did* but who the child *was*. Juvenile courts were to be concerned with children as individuals, and this enabled judges to save children from criminal careers through proper treatment. In contrast, the adult criminal court was concerned at trial with the narrow issue of the guilt or innocence of the accused.

Early advocates of juvenile courts believed that law and humanitarianism were not sufficient for the treatment of juveniles. They expected juvenile courts to rely heavily on the findings of the physical and social sciences. It was anticipated that these research findings would be applied scientifically in the adjudication and disposition of juveniles. The inability of the social sciences to develop sufficient research to implement this philosophy adequately, the failure of the legal profession to recognize and accept those findings that would be of assistance, and the abuse of discretion by correctional officials all contributed to the tensions that developed over the lack of procedural safeguards in juvenile courts.

The rehabilitative ideal of the founders of juvenile courts has not been realized. In actuality, many juveniles receive punishment, not treatment, and being processed through juvenile rather than adult criminal courts does not remove the stigma of *criminal*.

Not only may a juvenile suffer the worst of both the adult criminal and the juvenile court worlds, but some scholars take the position that this was the intent. Disputing the benevolent motives of the founders of the juvenile court system, these scholars have argued that juvenile courts diminish the civil liberties and privacy of juveniles, and that the child-saving movement was promoted by the middle class to support its own interests.[3]

Others have contended that the development of juvenile courts represented neither a great social reform nor an attempt to diminish juveniles' civil liberties and arbitrarily control them. Rather, it represented another example of the trend toward bureaucratization and an institutional compromise between social welfare and the law. The juvenile court "was primarily a shell of legal ritual within which states renewed and enacted their commitment to discretionary social control over children."[4]

Changes have occurred in the juvenile court philosophy and procedures; some of those are discussed in this chapter, but first, we take a brief look at delinquency data, an area of research that provides interesting job opportunities, as noted in Professions 12.1.

JUVENILE DELINQUENCY DATA

It is impossible to get accurate data on the amount of **delinquency**, since jurisdictions differ in their definitions of the term. Theoretically, *delinquency* does not refer to children processed through juvenile courts because they are in need of supervision, dependent, neglected, or abused; rather, it refers to youth who have been adjudicated by the juvenile court as having violated a statute or an ordinance or other provision (such as a curfew) that applies only to juveniles. Nevertheless, some jurisdictions include in delinquency data all categories of juveniles over which juvenile courts have jurisdiction. Generally, that jurisdiction is over youth under 18, although some states have had lower ages.

Methods of collecting delinquency data vary, too, and in most cases, juvenile records are confidential; some states require that the records be destroyed or sealed. How, then, do we know about juvenile offenses? Chapter 2 discussed the use of self-report studies, in which respondents are asked to state the types of offenses they have committed and how often they have committed them. From carefully selected samples of the population, predictions may be made on the overall extent of delinquency by the use of this method.

Professions 12.1

Careers in Juvenile Justice

Juvenile crimes, especially violent crimes, have led officials to pay greater attention to research into juvenile crime. Research provides numerous job opportunities for those who are trained in research methodology. The opportunities exist in all areas of criminal justice, but juvenile justice is one area that may appeal to young people. The desire to find out why crime happens and what to do — how to treat — may lead to intriguing days at the office.

Those who prefer the hands-on approach will also find numerous chances to become involved in juvenile justice. Jobs are available in juvenile detention and correctional facilities, juvenile probation and parole, school services, community treatment programs, court services, and many other areas. Others may be interested in teaching positions that focus on children with behavior problems, as well as on those who have already committed juvenile or criminal offenses.

Another area of service to juveniles is in victimization, as larger numbers of children, some very young, become crime victims, often at the hands of other children or juveniles.

A variety of agencies offer employment in working with juveniles. One is the Office of Juvenile Justice and Delinquency Prevention (OJJDP), a component of the Office of Justice Programs (OJP) of the U.S. Department of Justice. Visit the website of the OJP (https://www.ojp.usdoj.gov/about/jobs.htm, accessed January 15, 2019), which offers a variety of job opportunities, including student employment programs.

States also have juvenile justice offices that offer positions in research, data analysis, and other areas.

Figure 12.1

Percentage of Total Arrests for Selected Crimes, 2017, Involving Youths Under 18 Years of Age

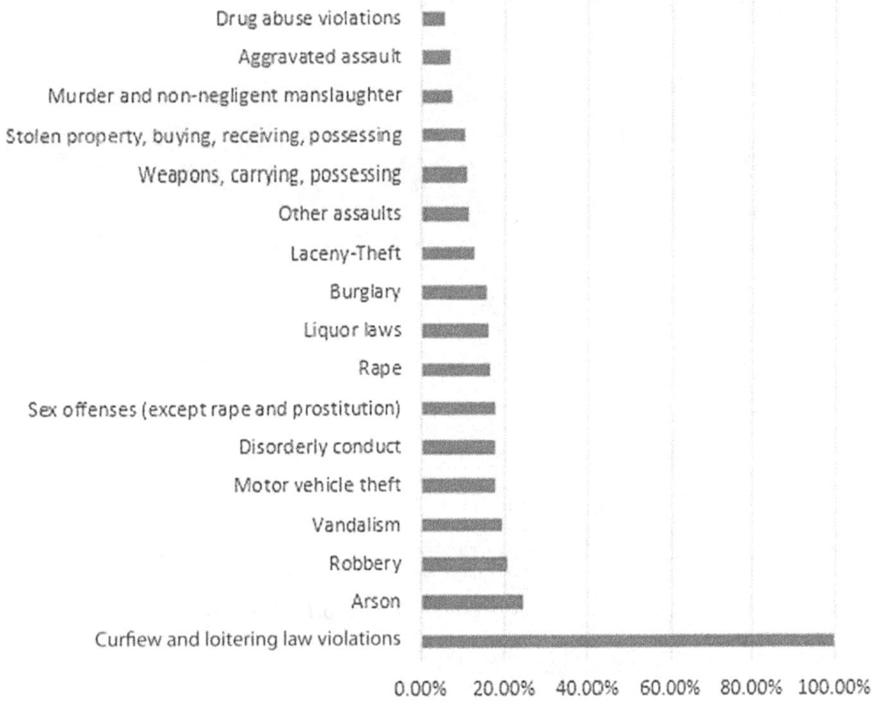

Source: Federal Bureau of Investigation, *Uniform Crime Reports, Crime in the United States, 2017* (September 2018), https://ucr.fbi.gov, accessed November 4, 2018.

Figure 12.2

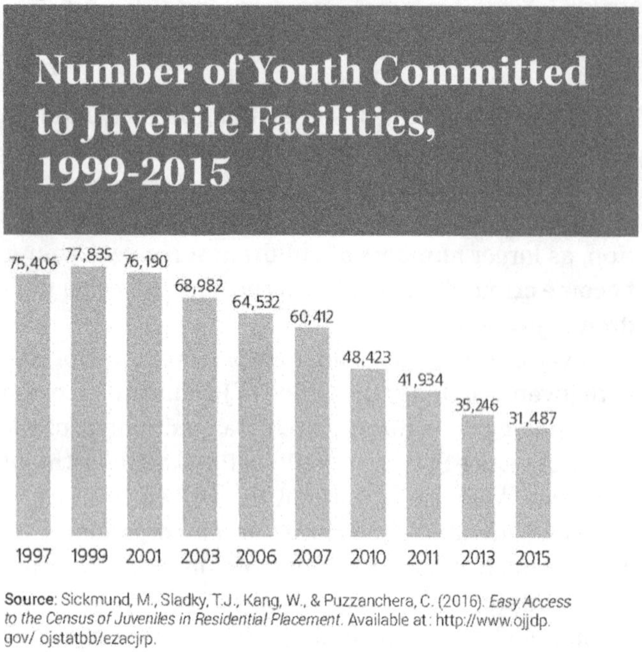

Source: The Sentencing Project, "Fact Sheet: Trends in U.S. Corrections — Youth," p. 6, https://www.sentenceproject.org, accessed November 3, 2018.

Official arrest rates recorded by age brackets and published by the FBI are another source of data. The official data reveal that in 2017, persons under age 18 accounted for 10.1 percent of arrests for serious violent crimes and 13.4 percent of all arrests for serious property crimes. Figure 12.1 graphs the percentage of total arrests in 2017 of persons under age 18 for all serious offenses and several other crimes. The figure demonstrates that, according to official data, juveniles under age 18 do *not* commit most of the violent crimes.[5]

Other significant data show that since 1999, the number of youth committed to secure juvenile facilities has declined. The data showing commitments from 1999 through 2015 are graphed in Figure 12.2. Data showing the number of youth in adult facilities are shown later. Despite those declines, the data show a disproportionate number of commitments by race and ethnicity, as graphed in Figure 12.3. And youth of color are sentenced more harshly than are white youth.[6]

Race and Ethnicity Issues

Race and ethnicity are important characteristics to consider in analyzing juvenile justice data. A study sponsored by the National Council on Crime and Delinquency (NCCD) reported that at every stage of criminal justice systems, race and ethnicity are factors.

- "African American rates of residential placement were over 4 times, Hispanic rates over 2 times, and Native American 3 times those for Whites.

Figure 12.3

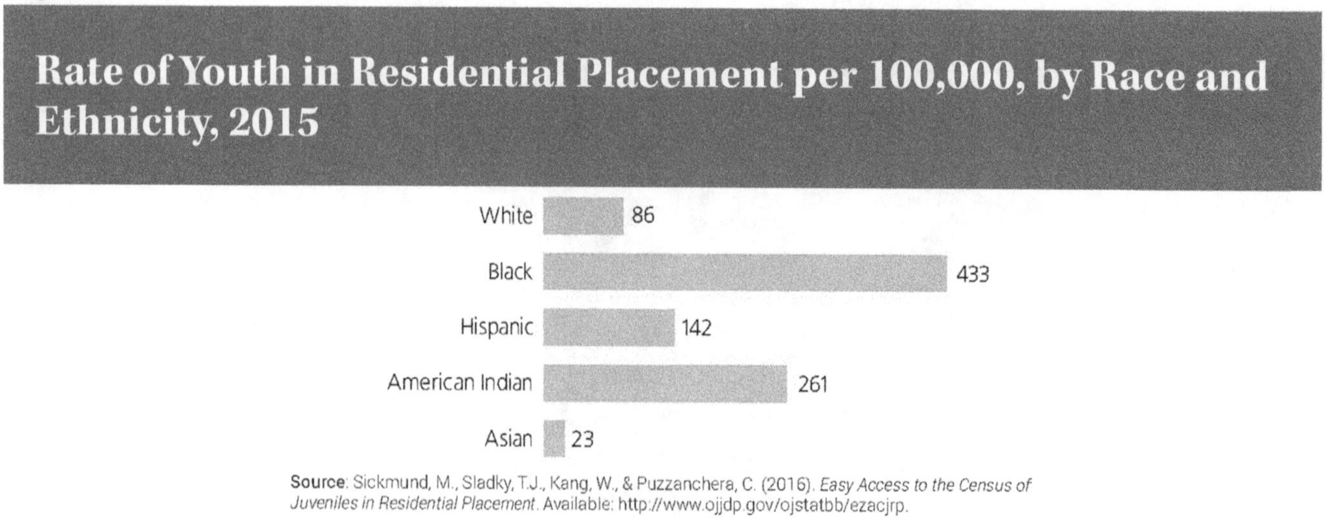

Source: The Sentencing Project, "Fact Sheet: Trends in U.S. Corrections — Youth," p. 6, https://www.sentenceproject.org, accessed February 21, 2019.

- Rates of youth admitted to adult prisons were 7 times higher for African Americans and over 2 times as high for Native Americans as for White youth.
- Disparity in the juvenile system is the worst at the deepest levels of the system."[7]

The NCCD also reported that although African-American juveniles constitute only 16 percent of the population, they represent

- "28 percent of juvenile arrests
- 30 percent of referrals to juvenile court
- 34 percent of youth formally processed by the juvenile court
- 35 percent of youth judicially waived to criminal court
- 38 percent of youth in residential placement
- 58 percent of youth admitted to state adult prisons"[8]

There are other views, such as those of two criminologists, who conducted a study supported by a grant from the Office of Juvenile Justice and Delinquency Prevention (OJJDP) and concluded that police decisions to take alleged juvenile offenders into custody were not based on race. According to this report, the data did indicate, however, that nonwhite juveniles were more likely to be taken in to custody if the complaining victims were white as compared to nonwhite.[9]

One way to reduce racial disparities is to ensure that juveniles have adequate legal representation. The American Bar Association has reported that minorities may be more affected by the problem of a lack of legal representation among youth than are nonminorities.[10]

There are some signs of successful efforts to reduce apparent racial and ethnic disparity among juveniles in our justice systems. According to the Justice Policy Institute (JPI), a national nonprofit organization, a study of the detention of juveniles in two counties demonstrated

> that jurisdictions can not only reduce the number of youth behind bars . . . but also the odds that kids of color will be detained. After more than a decade of focus and dozens of studies, we now have examples of success — not on paper, but in emerging models, whose lessons are relevant to all who aspire for a fairer justice system for juveniles.

The successful efforts included hiring more minority personnel, seeking additional alternatives to detention, and establishing written criteria for selecting those youths who should be detained.[11]

But that was 2015. In September 2018, the Marshall Project reported that under the Trump administration the department that was delegated (by Congress in 1988) the job of reducing racial disparities among youth in prison, the OJJPD, "has taken a quiet but decisive turn away from that mandate." That was being accomplished by dissolving the research arm of OJJDP, which collects the data that could lead to improving racial disparities. The new director of OJJPD said the agency, which had already received millions for the project, had not accomplished its goals and she could not continue to pour millions into it. According to Caren Harp, the states "have been spending too much time and money compiling data without real-life outcomes."[12]

Gender Issues

Another issue crucial to an analysis of differential reactions within juvenile justice systems is that of gender. The 1974 Juvenile Justice and Delinquency Prevention Act (JJDPA) encouraged states to find means other than incarceration for juveniles who had committed nonserious offenses (status offenders, most of whom were girls) and for juveniles who were dependent or neglected but who had not committed any offenses. The statute called for an end to incarcerating juveniles with adults.[13]

On its website in 2014, the National Council on Crime and Delinquency (NCCD) cited evidence that compared to boys, girls in juvenile justice systems "present with higher rates of serious mental health conditions including post traumatic stress disorder, psychiatric disorders, attempts of self harm, and suicide." The NCCD continued with the following information comparing girls and boys under correctional supervision:

- "Of all youth incarcerations, 42 percent of girls are 15 and younger, compared to 31 percent of boys 15 and younger.
- Girls are incarcerated for status offenses (18 percent) compared to boys (4 percent).
- Girls are more likely to be returned to detention for longer periods for technical violations for minor infractions such as contempt of court or violations of probation.
- Girls are more likely to be sexually victimized in juvenile facilities than are boys. Girls constitute 11 percent of the incarcerated population but were victims of 34 percent of substantial abuse cases."[14]

Some jurisdictions have made changes in the manner in which they treat girls, especially those apprehended for status offenses. In New York State, for example, where such offenders are called *persons in need of supervision (PINS)*, the legal age was extended to include 16- and 17-year-old juveniles as the result of parents who looked to governmental agencies to assist them with problem teens. This statutory change meant that the number of PINS could increase by up to 105 percent, with a resulting cost of millions of dollars. A review of the state's PINS programs revealed that many status offenders were being placed in the court systems, after which court orders were violated, and the process escalated. The new approach was to increase diversionary programs and try to avoid placing status offenders in courts. One program, entitled *Family Keys*, involves dispatching counselors to families within two hours after teen problems are reported. Initial reports were that fewer juveniles were processed through the courts, which are now considered a last resort. New York counties are also looking at alternatives to foster care for teens who defy their parents or engage in other status-type offenses without violating the law. Teens are kept within their homes but provided intensive supervision and services under a program entitled *Juvenile Release Under Supervision (JRUS)*. The Vera Institute of Justice reported that these programs resulted in cutting $1.5 million from the Albany County's $2.3 million detention budget.[15]

Federal laws prohibit placing status offenders in locked juvenile detention or correctional facilities, but implementation of the provisions of the JJDPA have been challenging. According to the Vera Institute of Justice:

> One of the best ways that the United States can begin to ensure that juvenile justice is fair, humane, and effective is to stop responding to adolescent behavior as if it were a criminal offense and to begin viewing offenders for who they are: children who committed no crime but who need a helping hand in getting back on track.[16]

It is, however, the violence by juveniles, often with juvenile victims, that raises great concern, along with the types of violent crimes that are being committed, a few of which are noted in **Supplement 12.2.** Such crimes are not typical and, fortunately, do not occur with great frequency, but it is such serious crimes that lead some to call for abolishing the juvenile court and processing all offenders in adult criminal courts. A closer look at the juvenile court is warranted.

JUVENILE COURTS

In 2018, the National Center for Juvenile Justice published its 2016 data, estimating that courts that had jurisdiction over juveniles handled an estimated 850,500 delinquent cases, of which 72 percent were male; 44 percent were white; 36 percent were black; 18 percent were Hispanic; 2 percent were American Indian, and 1 percent were Asian.[17] Juvenile courts differ somewhat from jurisdiction to jurisdiction, but the discussion in this section involves the organization and procedures that are found in most U.S. juvenile court systems. Figure 12.4 diagrams a typical organizational model and should be used as a reference for this discussion.

Juveniles may be referred to a juvenile justice system in various ways. Although most juvenile offenders are referred by law enforcement agencies, some referrals come from parents, relatives, schools, probation officers, other courts, and miscellaneous other sources. Juveniles may be counseled and released to their parents. Some may be diverted to social services or other programs. In juvenile systems, diversion historically was used to remove the juveniles from *official* juvenile or criminal proceedings before a hearing. If a decision was made not to divert the juvenile to some other agency or to his or her parents, other dispositions had to be made.

In some cases, after a referral has been made and the police have observed delinquent behavior, or an offense has been reported and juveniles are suspected, the police may begin surveillance and investigation. There is no way of knowing how many cases are handled by the police without any formal action being taken, but most juveniles are not taken into custody after apprehension by police. Police are not the only people who may take children into custody. Officials in child protective services, probation offices, family services, and youth services may do so in many jurisdictions.

Historically, there were few guidelines for taking juveniles into custody. In the *In re Gault* case, discussed in **Supplement 12.3** along with other cases involving the constitutional rights of juveniles, the U.S. Supreme Court, in its analysis of the due process rights of juveniles, did not cover such actions as police apprehension. Some lower courts have held that taking a juvenile into custody is not an arrest, and therefore, the due process requirements that must be observed in the arrest of an adult are not applicable. But most courts appear to consider the process an arrest, which should be accompanied by due process requirements.[18]

If a juvenile is taken into custody, the issues of search and seizure may arise. Most state courts have interpreted *Gault*'s fundamental fairness test to mean that the constitutional prohibition against unreasonable searches and seizures applies to juvenile proceedings. Some states have incorporated exclusionary rules into their statutes; thus, evidence seized illegally in juvenile cases may not be admitted as evidence against the offenders.

Figure 12.4

The Stages of Delinquent Case Processing in the Juvenile Justice System

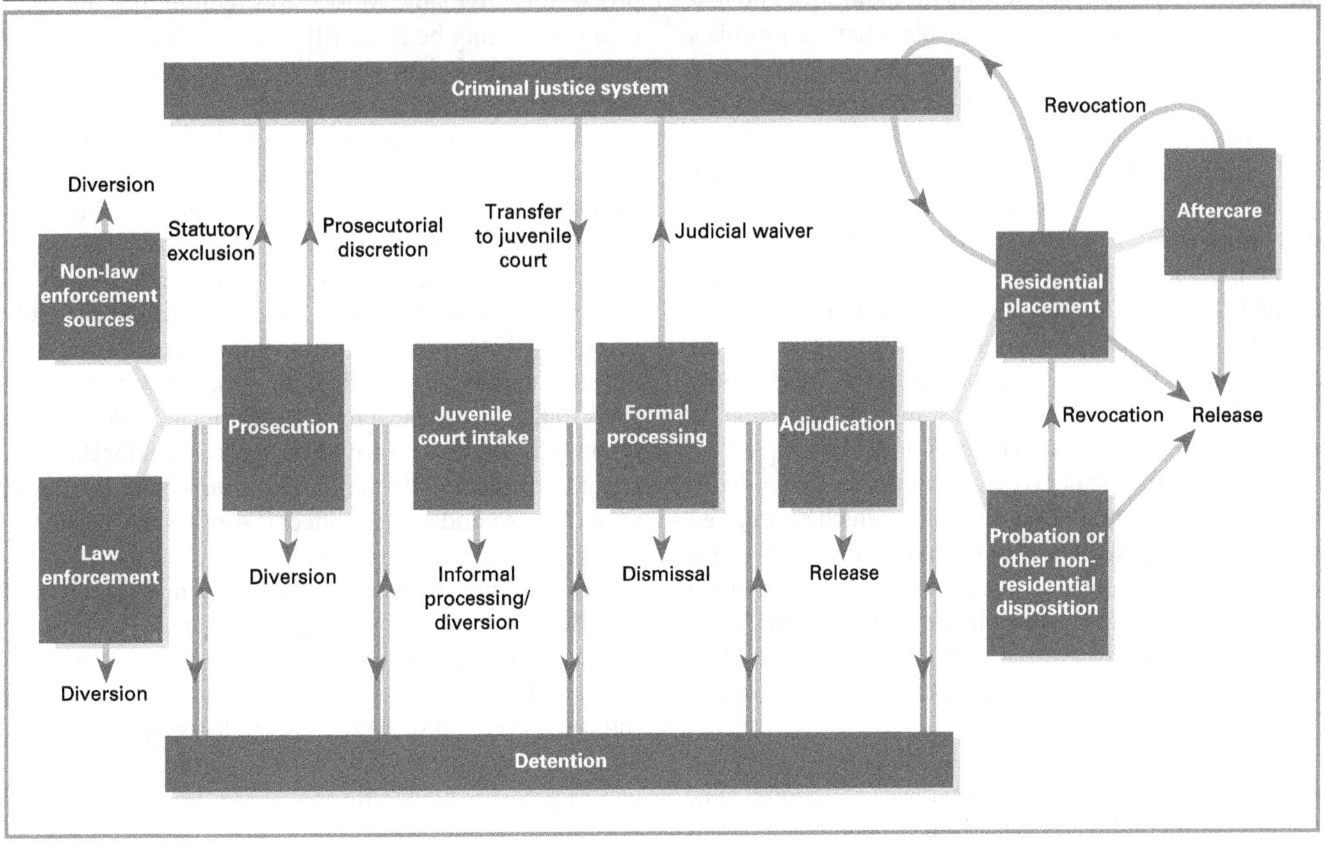

Source: Melissa Sickmund, Bureau of Justice Statistics, *Juveniles in Court* (Washington, D.C.: U.S. Office of Juvenile Justice and Delinquency Prevention, U.S. Department of Justice, June 2003), p. 3.

Whether or not a search is conducted, there may be a decision to detain the juvenile. Most often, juveniles are taken into custody without a summons or a warrant. Police must then decide what to do with the juveniles in their custody. Most are released to their parents. When that is not possible or reasonable, most jurisdictions require that juveniles be placed in juvenile detention centers. Approximately one in five apprehended juveniles is detained; of those, approximately 83 percent are in secure areas (e.g., locked within a part of a locked building that is within a locked area that is behind a secure fence) despite the fact that most (over two-thirds) of these youth are apprehended for nonviolent offenses. One-fourth of the facilities are at or beyond their rated capacity.[19]

In *Schall v. Martin* (see again **Supplement 12.3**), the U.S. Supreme Court upheld preventive detention for juveniles. After noting that juveniles have a substantial interest in liberty, the Court said, "But that interest must be qualified by the recognition that juveniles, unlike adults, are always in some form of custody." The justices reiterated their belief that courts have special powers over children, as compared with adults. "[C]hildren, by definition, are not assumed to have the capacity to take care of themselves," and therefore, they need additional protection. Preventive detention of juveniles may be appropriate to protect the juveniles themselves, not just to protect society, as in the case of preventive detention of adults, which the U.S. Supreme Court upheld in 1987.[20]

Bail is another issue with regard to juvenile detention or incarceration. Some states grant juveniles the right to release on bail; others have no bail provisions for them; and still others provide that it is not an issue because of the provision of special facilities for juvenile detention.

Consider also the question of whether juveniles should be interrogated by police. Originally, it was assumed that it would be therapeutic for children to confess; thus, juveniles had few procedural protections concerning police interrogation. Today the rule is that juvenile confessions may be used against them in court, provided those confessions are made voluntarily and reasonably. It is, however, questionable whether juveniles can meet those requirements without adequate legal representation, which, as noted in **Supplement 12.4**, they do not always have.

Certain police procedures, however, may not be applicable in juvenile cases. Most statutes covering juvenile proceedings attempt to protect juveniles from some of the harshness of adult criminal courts and therefore prohibit publication of the names and photographs of suspects and the taking of fingerprints. The use of lineups and showups, however, has been left to the courts, most of which have held that the same standards applicable to adults must also be applied in juvenile proceedings.

If a decision is made to detain a juvenile, that individual will be brought to intake screening, which is designed to remove the juveniles who should be diverted if that decision was not made earlier. A decision could be made at this stage to refer the juvenile to another agency or to his or her parents to await a hearing. A third alternative is to detain (or continue to detain) the juvenile before the hearing.

The **intake decision** is made by an intake officer, who may also be in the probation division. Theoretically, these officers conduct an investigation before making the intake decision; however, with heavy caseloads, this may not be done thoroughly, if at all. Some states have placed statutory requirements on the intake officer regarding referrals out of the system or dismissals. For example, in some jurisdictions, an intake officer may not dismiss a case without the prosecutor's written permission. In others, the case may not be dismissed or diverted if the complaining witness insists that formal action proceed beyond this stage.

If the juvenile is detained with the intent that a petition will be filed to bring formal procedures, a hearing usually is held to determine whether there is reason to continue with the case. This is true whether the juvenile is being held as an alleged dependent, neglected, or delinquent child. The hearing must be held within a reasonable period after detention begins, but it does not involve all procedural safeguards.

After the preliminary inquiry or hearing, the juvenile may be released from detention, or the case may be dismissed. If the case is not dismissed, it may proceed only with the filing of a petition, the formal document for initiating a case in the juvenile system. This petition is in contrast to a grand jury indictment or a prosecutor's presentment in adult criminal courts.

The *Gault* case requires that juveniles and their parents be given adequate notice of the charges and of the proceedings to follow. Most states require that the adjudicatory hearing be held within a specified period after the petition is filed. In some jurisdictions, if this does not occur, the case must be dismissed.

Juveniles may admit or deny guilt; most admit that they committed the acts of which they are accused. This plea must be a knowing and voluntary one, and juveniles have the right to counsel if they are involved in proceedings that could lead to confinement in an institution.

Since the *Kent* case, discussed in **Supplement 12.3**, some jurisdictions have enacted statutes to permit juveniles some discovery procedures. *Discovery* involves the right to find out the evidence the opposing side plans to use in the case. This information is necessary for the juvenile and his or her attorney to know how best to proceed with the case, and it might affect the juvenile's decision to admit or deny the allegations.

The juvenile court hearing is less formal than that of the adult criminal court, but the same general procedures occur. The prosecutor presents the evidence against the juvenile, the defense has an opportunity to cross-examine the witnesses, and some rules of evidence apply. Hearsay evidence may be presented in a juvenile hearing, in contrast to an adult criminal court trial. Evidence is presented to a judge and not to a jury unless the jurisdiction provides for a trial by jury and the juvenile has not waived that right.

At the end of the presentation of evidence, there is an adjudication of whether the juvenile did what he or she was accused of doing. Technically, the terms *guilty* and *not guilty* are not used in juvenile proceedings, although the obvious purpose is to determine whether the alleged acts were committed. To support a finding of responsibility, the evidence must be sufficient to convince the judge beyond a reasonable doubt.

In traditional language, juveniles are not sentenced; dispositions are made. Dispositions tend to be indeterminate, although the court loses jurisdiction over the child when he or she reaches the age of majority. Several types of dispositions are available. Figure 12.3, presented earlier, illustrates that the court may take one of three routes. Nominal dispositions, such as warnings and reprimands, are common. Conditional dispositions in juvenile courts are similar to those in adult criminal courts, and they may involve work assignments, restitution, fines, community service, suspended disposition, community supervision (probation), or a combination of these and other dispositions. A final method of disposition is to place juveniles in secure or nonsecure facilities.

What procedures must be followed at the disposition hearing? In *Gault*, the U.S. Supreme Court stated that it was not answering the question of which federal constitutional due process rights apply to the pre- or post-adjudicatory hearing stages of the juvenile process. Therefore, the required procedures are established by state statutes or by state court decisions, and they vary from state to state. Because many juvenile cases do not involve a dispute over the facts, the disposition hearing becomes the most significant part of the process, and the right to counsel is important. Normally, disposition of a juvenile case involves a separate hearing from that of adjudication, and it is preceded by an investigative report, or social report, on which the decision may be based.

The social report is crucial to the philosophy that juveniles are to be treated individually and that it is possible to rehabilitate them. The social report should include any information that might have a bearing on assessing the needs of the particular child. The types of evidence that may be admitted at the dispositional stage are much broader than those permitted at the adjudicatory hearing.

After the disposition, the juvenile may have grounds for an appeal. In *Gault*, the U.S. Supreme Court did not rule on the issue of whether there is a constitutional right to appeal from a juvenile court decision, but today all jurisdictions have some statutory provisions for appeals.

One important issue in all of these proceedings is the role of attorneys when they are permitted. The defense attorney's primary function in a juvenile court case is to ensure that the juvenile's constitutional rights are protected during all of the proceedings. The attorney should be familiar with all the facts of the case and be prepared to present the defense at the hearing. The lack of formality in the hearing does not mean that the defense is any less important in a juvenile than in an adult criminal court hearing.

The interaction between those who serve as prosecutors and those who serve as defense attorneys is as important in juvenile as in adult criminal court systems. The relationship between prosecutors and defense attorneys in juvenile systems is similar to the relationship they share in adult criminal court systems. They may serve as checks on the potential abuse of power, or they may cooperate to the point of violating juveniles' rights. They may serve diligently and competently, with the best interests of juveniles as their goals. But in some cases, those who take that perspective find their goals thwarted by a system that has inadequate resources and insufficient personnel.

Another interaction that occurs between prosecutors and defense attorneys in criminal court proceedings is also applicable to juvenile proceedings. Plea bargaining does occur, and it is frequently in the best interests of the juvenile and society for attorneys to negotiate a plea rather than subject the juvenile to a formal process in the juvenile court or a trial in the adult criminal court.

Before moving to the more serious practice of processing juveniles through adult criminal courts, it is important to note that in some jurisdictions, juveniles may be subjected to juvenile court jurisdiction not because they violate a law that applies to all but because they violate juvenile curfews or are truant. Those subjects are discussed in **Supplement 12.5** and **Supplement 12.6**.

JUVENILES IN ADULT CRIMINAL COURTS

Many U.S. criminal justice systems provide that, in certain cases, juveniles may be tried, sentenced, or incarcerated through adult criminal courts. Juvenile cases may be tried in adult criminal courts as the result of mandatory statutes or through **waivers** from juvenile courts. Some jurisdictions permit the prosecutor to determine whether to charge a juvenile in an adult criminal court. Other jurisdictions have a presumption that certain crimes, such as murder, should be tried in adult courts; some require that juveniles charged with murder and other serious crimes be tried in adult criminal courts. But many juvenile cases that are tried in adult criminal courts go through a process of *waiver*. A waiver, also called a *transfer* or **certification**, means that the juvenile court waives jurisdiction, the case is transferred from the juvenile court to the adult criminal court, or the juvenile court certifies that the juvenile should be tried as an adult. After hearing motions by the defense and the prosecution, a judge will determine whether the case is waived.

An estimated 250,000 youths each year are processed through adult criminal courts, and most of those are charged with nonviolent offenses.[21] The number of cases waived to adult criminal courts peaked in 1994 at 13,600 and declined during most years through 2011. In 2011, the number of juvenile cases waived to adult criminal courts (5,400) was 61 percent lower than the waivers in 1994. The main reason for the decline in waivers was the decline in violent crimes attributed to juveniles.[22]

The cases of boys are much more likely than those of girls to be waived, and cases involving minorities are more likely than those involving whites to be waived. Boys' cases involving personal injury are more likely to be waived; for girls the most likely are cases involving drug offenses.[23]

When waiver occurs, the juvenile goes through the same procedures as those required in adult criminal courts and has the same constitutional rights as adults who are tried in those courts. The procedural requirements for waiver were articulated by the U.S. Supreme Court in the *Kent* case, discussed in **Supplement 12.3**. Although that case applied only to a statute at issue in Washington, D.C., most courts have interpreted it as stating the minimum due process requirements for transfer from a juvenile court to an adult criminal court. The juvenile is entitled to a hearing on the issue of transfer, and the right to counsel attaches to that hearing. Upon request, the defense counsel must be given access to the social record that the court has compiled on the juvenile. If jurisdiction is waived from the juvenile court to the adult criminal court, the juvenile must be given a statement of the reasons for the waiver.

The issue of a right to counsel is critical. For example, many juveniles who are tried in adult courts are not legally competent. A study published by the MacArthur Foundation and conducted by a nine-member team led by a physician at the University of Massachusetts Medical School concluded that juveniles who are tried in adult criminal courts are far more likely than adult defendants to have serious impairment of their competency. They are less likely to understand that it may be to their advantage not to talk freely to the police during interrogation. The report concluded that "[s]tates should consider implementing policies and practices designed to ensure that young defendants' rights to a fair trial are protected." That might mean requiring competency evaluations before a juvenile is transferred to an adult court.[24]

Some statutes give adult criminal courts jurisdiction over juveniles who commit specified serious crimes, such as murder, but permit the adult criminal court to transfer the case to a juvenile court through a process known as *reverse certification*.

There are a number of reasons for and against certification or waiver. One of the strongest arguments in favor of waiver is that it sends a message to juveniles and thus serves as a deterrent. It also serves as notice to society that we are getting tough on juvenile crime. It can be argued, however, that this "get-tough" approach does not work but, rather, gives only the *appearance* of toughness and deterrence. If the system is too severe, police may not arrest; prosecutors may not prosecute or will charge lesser offenses; juries may not convict.

The efficacy of transferring juveniles to adult criminal courts has been questioned. One criminologist, who summarized recent research concerning whether juvenile waivers have a deterrent value, concluded that the studies do not permit strong conclusions and are inconsistent on the deterrence issue but that most of the research suggests that transferring juveniles to adult criminal courts from the jurisdiction of juvenile courts does not have a significant effect on preventing serious juvenile crimes. He did note, however, that such transfers might have a deterrent effect if juveniles were made aware of the consequences they would face if they commit crimes for which they might be tried in adult criminal courts. This research also found higher rates of recidivism among juveniles who were tried in adult courts as compared to those processed through juvenile courts.[25]

There is also an issue of the impact that trial in an adult criminal court has on a juvenile. A limited study of juveniles who were transferred to adult criminal courts, compared with similarly situated ones who were not transferred, found that the transferred juveniles were negatively impacted at sentencing.[26]

The Campaign for Youth Justice states that the organization is "dedicated to ending the practice of trying, sentencing, and incarcerating youth under the age of 18 in the adult criminal justice system."[27] There is some progress in that direction. As of October 1, 2018, New York no longer prosecutes 16-year-olds in adult criminal courts; beginning October 1, 2019, the state will no longer prosecute 17-year-olds in those courts. New York was one of only two states that prosecuted 16-year-olds as adults. With the new law, misdemeanors will be processed through family courts, while felonies will be processed in a new division of the criminal trial courts, a "youth part," and heard by judges trained in family law. After 30 days, those cases would be sent to family court unless prosecutors could prove extraordinary circumstances. Violent felonies can be moved to the adult criminal court if a weapon was used, the act resulted in significant physical injury to a victim, and the perpetrator engaged in criminal sexual conduct.[28]

In 2007, Connecticut ended its statutory requirement of automatically processing all alleged 16- and 17-year-old law violators in adult criminal courts. This legislative change, coupled with other reforms has, according to some experts, resulted in "a new consensus for progressive change in juvenile justice."[29]

For juveniles who are tried in adult criminal courts, the issue of how they are sentenced is significant. Capital punishment is not permitted and is discussed later in this chapter. Life without parole (LWOP) is another controversial issue. It is argued that juveniles who commit serious, especially violent crimes, should be punished as adults. But it is also considered by many professionals that most juveniles can be rehabilitated. Perhaps the major reason submitted for not sentencing juveniles to LWOP is the same reason for not executing them: They are, stated simply, *different*. The American Medical Association and the American Academy of Child and Adolescent Psychiatry submitted briefs to the U.S. Supreme Court prior to that Court's consideration of the issue of sentencing juveniles to LWOP in the case of *Graham v. Florida*. In their brief, these two groups stated as follows:

> The adolescent's mind works differently from ours. Parents know it. This Court has said it [in the case involving capital punishment, noted later in this chapter]. Legislatures all over the world have presumed it for decades or more. And scientific evidence now sheds light on how and why adolescent behavior differs from adult behavior. . . . [R]ecent advances in brain-imaging technology confirm that the very regions of the brain that are associated with voluntary behavior control and regulation of emotional response and impulsivity are structurally immature during adolescence. Studies have also revealed that these structural immaturities are consistent with age-related differences in both brain function and behavior.[30]

The 2010 U.S. Supreme Court decision concerning sentencing juveniles to LWOP is presented in Criminal Justice Systems Dilemma 12.1.

The U.S. Supreme Court followed that 2010 decision with two similar ones decided two years later. In 2012, the Court considered two cases involving teen defendants who were convicted of murder and sentenced to a mandatory life without parole sentence. The Court's decision was announced in *Miller v. Alabama*, which involved a 14-year-old male defendant who, with a friend, beat his neighbor and set fire to the victim's home (a trailer). Justice Elena Kagan wrote the opinion for the Court, noting that the mandatory sentence left the trial judge no discretion to decide whether a different punishment (e.g., life with the *possibility* of parole) would be more appropriate given the "lessened culpability" and greater "capacity for change" of juveniles. Justice Kagan stated the Court's holding succinctly, as follows:

> We therefore hold that mandatory life without parole for those under the age of 18 at the time of their crimes violates the Eighth Amendment's prohibition on "cruel and unusual punishment."[31]

Criminal Justice Systems Dilemma 12.1

Life Without Parole for Juveniles: Cruel and Unusual?

One of the greatest dilemmas faced by criminal justice systems is what to do with juveniles who commit serious crimes, especially crimes of violence. This focus features recent developments with regard to sentencing juveniles to life without parole (LWOP). Specifically, it deals with the issue of whether the practice constitutes cruel and unusual punishment in violation of the Eighth Amendment (see Appendix A).

Below is an excerpt from *Graham v. Florida*, decided the same day the Supreme Court dismissed a second case from Florida. *Sullivan v. Florida* involved Joe Harris Sullivan, who was 13 when he was arrested for allegedly sexually assaulting an elderly woman after he and two older co-defendants committed a burglary in her residence. Sullivan's attorney said that his client was one of only two teens nationwide who had been sentenced to LWOP for committing a crime other than homicide at the age of 13. The U.S. Supreme Court had agreed to review both Florida cases but dismissed Sullivan's case, stating that the decision to review it was "improvidently granted." The justices may have made that decision based on the fact that the *Graham* case applied more widely given his age, because there were some procedural issues with that case, or for any other reason.[1]

GRAHAM v. FLORIDA

560 U.S. 48 (2010), cases and citations omitted

The issue before the Court is whether the Constitution permits a juvenile offender to be sentenced to life in prison without parole for a nonhomicide crime. . . .

Petitioner is Terrance Jamar Graham. . . . Graham's parents were addicted to crack cocaine, and their drug use persisted in his early years. Graham was diagnosed with attention deficit hyperactivity disorder in elementary school. He began drinking alcohol and using tobacco at age 9 and smoked marijuana at age 13. . . . [When he was 16,] he and three other school-age youths attempted to rob a barbeque restaurant. . . . [He was arrested for attempted robbery].

Under Florida law, it is within a prosecutor's discretion whether to charge 16- and 17-year olds as adults or juveniles for most felony crimes. Graham's prosecutor elected to charge Graham as an adult. The charges against Graham were armed burglary with assault or battery, a first-degree felony carrying a maximum penalty of life imprisonment without the possibility of parole; and attempted armed robbery, a second-degree felony carrying a maximum penalty of 15 years' imprisonment.

[Graham pleaded guilty under a plea bargain and told the judge he intended to straighten out his life. Adjudication of guilt was withheld, and Graham was given two three- year probation terms to be served concurrently, with the first 12 months to be served in jail. He received credit for time already served in jail. Shortly after his release, he and two others were arrested for a home-invasion robbery involving forcible entry and a firearm. The victims were held for 30 minutes while the offenders ransacked the home and then barricaded the victims in a closet. Later that evening the offenders attempted another robbery; one offender was shot; Graham drove him and their accomplice to the hospital, left them there, and was apprehended by police as he drove away. When police signaled him to stop, Graham sped away. He crashed the car, tried to flee on foot, but was apprehended. Officers found three handguns in the car. For these crimes, including probation violation and a finding of guilt on the earlier deferred charge of armed burglary, Graham was sentenced to LWOP. The sentencing judge stated that no further juvenile sanctions were appropriate] and that the only thing I can do now is to try and protect and community from your actions. . . .

[The Court discussed the meaning of the Eighth Amendment's prohibition against cruel and unusual punishment.]

As compared to adults, juveniles have a "lack of maturity and an underdeveloped sense of responsibility"; they "are more vulnerable or susceptible to negative influences and outside pressures, including peer pressure"; and their characters are "not as well formed." These salient characteristics mean that "[i]t is difficult even for expert psychologists to differentiate between the juvenile offender whose crime reflects unfortunate yet transient immaturity, and the rare juvenile offender whose crime reflects irreparable corruption."

Accordingly, "juvenile offenders cannot with reliability be classified among the worst offenders." A juvenile is not absolved of responsibility for his action, but his transgression "is not as morally reprehensive as that of an adult." . . . [The Court referred to its recent decision in *Roper v. Simmons*—mentioned in the text and excerpted in the supplement—and saw no reason to reconsider its findings in that case. The Court referred to the *amici* brief cited in the text that refers to the lack of development of the teen brain.]

Juveniles are more capable of change than are adults, and their actions are less likely to be evidence of "irretrievably depraved character" than are the actions of adults. It remains that "[f]rom a moral standpoint it would be misguided to equate the failings of a minor with those of an adult, for a greater possibility exists that a minor's character deficiencies will be reformed."

[The Court refused the state's arguments concerning utilizing a case-by-case approach to deciding whether juveniles in cases of this nature should be sentenced to LWOP. The Court discussed in detail the philosophical bases for punishment: retribution, deterrence, incapacitation, and rehabilitation, rejecting the first three as reasons for imposing LWOP and noting that LWOP denies a juvenile a chance to rehabilitate. The Court also considered the lack of the use of LWOP for juveniles internationally. The Court then determined that LWOP for juveniles who commit a crime that does not involve homicide constitutes cruel and unusual punishment and thus violates the Eighth Amendment of the federal Constitution. Three justices dissented.]

---

1. *Sullivan v. Florida*, 560 U.S. 181 (2010), *cert. dismissed.*

In 2016, in *Montgomery v. Louisiana*, the U.S. Supreme Court held that the *Miller* case applies retroactively.[32]

Recent cases in Florida and other states have raised the question of whether the state may, in effect, impose life without parole by assessing such a long sentence that the youth would never have an opportunity to be released from prison. In 2012, the Florida Supreme Court accepted jurisdiction of another case involving the issue of *de facto* life without parole for juveniles. The First District Court of Appeal of Florida certified to the state's supreme court the question of whether the U.S. Supreme Court's decision in *Graham* prohibits a court from sentencing a 14-year-old to 70 years in prison upon conviction of attempted first-degree murder. Shimeek Gridine shot at the man he attempted to rob. The victim was not seriously wounded, but Gridine was tried as an adult and sentenced to 70 years without parole.[33]

In 2015, the Florida Supreme Court held that such a long sentence "does not provide a meaningful opportunity for future release." The state's highest court concluded as follows:

> Therefore, Gridine's prison sentence is unconstitutional in light of *Graham*. Accordingly, we answer the certified question in the affirmative, quash the decision on review, and remand this case to Gridine's sentencing court.[34]

JUVENILES IN ADULT JAILS AND PRISONS

Juveniles who are processed through adult criminal courts may be held in adult jails and incarcerated in adult prisons. The Juvenile Justice and Delinquency Prevention Act, passed by Congress in 1974 and amended in subsequent years, provides that funds be made available for juvenile justice and delinquency projects and programs to those states that comply with the statute's mandates. Among other provisions is the phasing out of juvenile detention in *adult* jails, but between 1994 and 1997 the number of youths under 18 who were held in jails increased by 35 percent. Their numbers began to decline, however, and by 2006, the population of juveniles held in adult facilities had decreased by 38 percent. Despite that decline, obviously the mandate has not been met: Juveniles are still detained in adult facilities, which has negative consequences.[35]

In December 2018, Congress passed and President Trump signed a bill to reauthorize and improve the Juvenile Justice and Delinquency Prevention Act, which had not been reauthorized since 2002. The new bipartisan legislation, though a federal bill, affects juvenile justice systems in states through funding. To accept federal funding under this bill, states must place limits on incarcerating juveniles for violations of status offenses; in general, not place juveniles in adult jails and prisons and separate them from adult inmates; and compile data on racial disparities and move toward a plan to address that issue. Treatment for mental health and substance abuse are addressed, and alternatives to incarceration are supported. The American Bar Association wanted more provisions but stated that the enacted legislation is a "critical step in the right direction" and represents "a national commitment to the rehabilitative purpose of the juvenile justice system."[36]

The federal restrictions regarding detaining juveniles prior to trial in adult facilities do not apply to incarcerating juveniles after they have been convicted in adult criminal courts. Officials are faced with housing these juveniles. If they are placed in the general population, they may be victimized by the adult offenders, but if they are isolated, they may develop mental issues or experience an exacerbation of already existing problems.

On its website in 2018, the Campaign for Youth Justice stated that on any given day, approximately 1,300 youths were in adult prisons and approximately 5,500 were held in adult jails. Youth of color were overrepresented in those data.[37]

In December 2018, attorneys for juveniles housed with adults in Michigan prisons argued their case before the Sixth Circuit. The case was on appeal from its dismissal by a district court judge in February 2018 based on the failure to exhaust administrative remedies before filing the suit. The class action suit represents at least "500 children ranging in age from 14-17 years" and details abuses these children have suffered by adults with whom they are incarcerated, including rape and other sexual assaults, the contracting of sexually transmitted diseases, and other alleged Eighth Amendment violations, including "increased punishment and degrading treatment through the use of tasers, solitary confinement and deprivation of rehabilitative programming and educational services." As of this writing, the Sixth Circuit had not rendered a decision.[38]

JUVENILES IN CORRECTIONAL FACILITIES

The placement of juveniles in correctional facilities is a relatively new practice. In the 1700s and early 1800s, it was thought that the family, the church, and other social institutions should handle juvenile delinquents. Jail was the only form of incarceration, and it was used primarily for detention pending trial. From 1790 to 1830, the traditional forms of social control began to break down as mobility and town sizes increased. Belief in sin as the cause of delinquency was replaced by a belief in community disorganization. A method was needed whereby juveniles could be put back into orderly lives. It was decided that the institution—the house of refuge, the well-ordered asylum patterned after the family structure—was the answer.

The institutional model was used for juveniles, adult criminals, elderly persons, the mentally challenged, orphans, unwed mothers, and vagrants. It was thought that by institutionalizing these persons their lives could become ordered as they were removed from the corruption of society. Life in the total institution was characterized by routine, head counts, and bells signaling the beginning and end of activities.[39]

By the 1850s, many people were admitting that custody was all the institutions offered. Problems such as overcrowding, lack of adequate staff, and heterogeneous populations led to the realization that institutionalization was not accomplishing its goal. The next concept for juveniles was the **training school**, typically built around a cottage system. It was thought that cottage parents would create a homelike atmosphere. Hard work, especially farm work, was emphasized.

In recent years, juvenile corrections have been characterized by overcrowding, shortage of staff, and a lack of resources, along with due process violations. The first nationwide investigation of juvenile institutions, published in 1993, disclosed that 75 percent of juveniles were housed in institutions that violated at least one standard relating to living space. Forty-seven percent lived in overcrowded institutions, up from 36 percent in 1987. Overcrowding was described as a "pervasive and serious problem across the nation."[40]

The study, mandated by Congress in 1988, found that only 27 percent of juvenile facilities met security standards. Only 25 percent of juveniles were in facilities that met standards for controlling suicidal behavior, and 11,000 youths committed more than 17,000 suicidal acts in a year, although only 10 were completed in 1990. The study disclosed that between 1987 and 1991 the proportion of confined juveniles who were minorities increased from 53 percent to 63 percent, with Hispanics increasing from 13 percent to 17 percent and African Americans from 37 percent to 44 percent.[41]

In a January 2018 publication, the Office of Juvenile Justice and Delinquency Prevention, reporting on the 2015 census, noted that the percentage of minorities in residential placement had risen to 69 percent, and most of those were black males. In terms of gender, females constituted 15 percent of youth in residential placement. Thirty-one percent of the juveniles were in private facilities. The report emphasized that the total number of youths in residential placement continued to decline, with nine in ten states cutting their rates by half or more between 2006 and 2015. The number of youths in residential placement facilities in 2015 was 48,043.[42]

In terms of overcrowding, the number of facilities housing juveniles that were over capacity in 2014 had declined to 4 percent from 8 percent in 2000.[43]

One final point to consider in evaluating juvenile facilities is the cost of detention/incarceration. In 2015, the Justice Policy Institute (JPI) published the results of its recent survey of the cost of confining juveniles. Based on data from 46 states, the JPI reported that the "sticker shock," as JPI called it, runs as high as $100,000 a year in 33 states and overall could cost taxpayers between $8 billion and $21 billion each year. The total cost, of course, depends on what one includes in the calculations. In addition to the actual costs of incarceration, the JPI included long-term costs, such as

- the cost of recidivism;
- the lost future earnings of confined youth;
- the lost future government tax revenue;
- additional Medicare and Medicaid spending; and
- the cost of sexual assault on confined youth.[44]

Juveniles may be confined in special facilities for youth offenders after they are processed through juvenile courts, but courts face special incarceration issues when juveniles are convicted and sentenced in adult criminal courts, especially when those sentences are lengthy.

Types of Institutions for Juveniles

Despite the earlier movement toward diverting juveniles from closed institutions (see **Supplement 12.7** for a discussion), today many juveniles who are under the care and custody of the state are confined in institutions or in traditional training schools. Detention centers and shelters are used to confine those who have been referred to juvenile courts and are awaiting disposition by those courts. These facilities are used for detaining juveniles who cannot be confined in their own homes. A child who is to be placed in a correctional institution may be held temporarily in a reception or diagnostic center, pending a decision concerning which institution would be the best placement for the child. The primary concern in this section is with the facilities in which the juveniles are placed for confinement after disposition of their cases: training schools, boot camps, and group homes.

Generally, the *training school*, which houses most confined juveniles, is the largest of the facilities. It was the first type of facility that was widely accepted for the confinement of juveniles, and it is the most secure. Some jurisdictions operate other types of facilities that are less secure, such as ranches, forestry camps, or farms. Most of these facilities are located in rural areas and permit greater contact with the community than the training school provides.

Boot camps have also been used to incarcerate juveniles. In the boot camp atmosphere, the offender participates in a strongly regimented daily routine of physical exercise, work, and discipline, which resembles military training. Many of the programs include rehabilitative measures, such as drug treatment and educational programs, but this method of incarcerating offenders has its critics, and most boot camps have been abolished.

Of the boot camps used to incarcerate juveniles, two examples stand out. First, in 2001, Tony Haynes, age 14, died in a privately owned and operated Arizona boot camp, the Buffalo Soldiers' Camp. It was alleged that Haynes was forced to stand for five hours in 116-degree heat and that he was dehydrated; he was then taken to a motel and put in a bathtub to cool off. In February 2002, the director of the camp, Charles F. Long II, age 56, was arrested on second-degree murder and child abuse charges. Several staffers were also charged in the boy's death. Troy A. Hutty, 29, a former corporal at the camp, was charged with manslaughter, pleaded guilty to negligent homicide, and was promised probation as he agreed to testify against Long.[45] In January 2005, Long was convicted of reckless manslaughter and sentenced to six years in prison. He was released in 2010.

The second example is from Florida. On January 6, 2006, Martin Lee Anderson, 14, died while being detained at a boot camp in Panama City. Anderson was admitted to the camp on a charge of grand theft after he was accused of stealing his grandmother's car and of violating his probationary terms. It was alleged that Anderson died as the result of being kicked by correctional officials after he stopped running during a drill, all of which was videotaped. Seven former correctional officers and a nurse were acquitted in this case, but the case led to the enactment of a statute, the Martin Lee Anderson Act of 2006, which eliminated boot camps and replaced them with juvenile detention centers that focus on education. With budget cuts in Florida, however, the last of those facilities was closed in 2008.[46]

The least physically secure facilities are *group homes*. Unlike *foster homes*, which are community-based facilities in which juveniles live with families, many group homes are small institutions. Most are operated by a staff, not a family. The cost per juvenile resident is twice as high for staff-operated group homes as for foster care. Group homes may be a poor substitute for foster care homes because they remove the positive influence of the family atmosphere.

The staff of many juvenile institutions attempts to make the facilities as homelike as possible. A campus-like environment or cottage setting, with a small number of juveniles housed in each building along with cottage or house parents, is typical. Despite these efforts, the architecture of many juvenile facilities reflects the premise that all who are confined there must face the same type of security as those few who need the more secure environment. Security is very important, but the facilities should not preclude opportunities for rehabilitation.

Legal Issues in Juvenile Facilities

Institutions for detaining juveniles have come under scrutiny by the courts. After complaints about Mississippi youth prisons and lawsuits filed by the Southern Poverty Law Center (SPLC), a civil rights organization headquartered in Mississippi, the Civil Rights Division of the U.S. Department of Justice (DOJ) began investigating some of that state's institutions that house juveniles. In 2003, the DOJ cited abuses in the Mississippi correctional system, charging the system with violating the constitutional rights of juveniles and failing to provide general and special education services at two institutions: the Oakley

Training School (which confined serious male offenders) and the Columbia Training School in Clarion (which confined both female and male juveniles). Among the findings were the following:

- The schools violated the juveniles' First Amendment rights by forcing them to engage in religious activities.
- The juveniles were subjected to unsafe living conditions and received inadequate treatment and care.
- Disciplinary practices included pole-shackling, the improper use and overuse of restraints and isolation, pepper spray, and staff assaults on juveniles.[47]

The report documented the following specific abuse cases:

- "A 13-year-old boy under suicide watch at Columbia was hog-tied face down with his hands and feet shackled together.
- Suicidal girls at Columbia were forced to undress and then were placed naked in a dark room for three days to a week, with only a hole in the floor as a bathroom.
- A girl at Columbia was sprayed with pepper spray for yelling at an employee during an exercise drill.
- Several girls at Columbia were forced to eat their own vomit if they threw up during an exercise."[48]

As a result of these findings, the state entered into a consent decree with DOJ regarding changes that it promised to make. In 2007, the SPLC sued the State of Mississippi over the conditions at the Columbia Training School. In early 2008, the state closed that prison and relocated the inmates. In November 2008, the SPLC called for the state to close the Oakley Training School, citing facts indicating the state's failure to make the changes required by its consent decree with DOJ. A SPLC spokesperson referred to the Oakley facility as a warehouse for which the state was spending $300 a day per child and not providing any treatment. Most of the juveniles incarcerated there, it was argued, could be treated effectively under supervision in the community for $23 a day. Court monitors who inspected the institution and filed a report in November 2008 found that the state was in substantial compliance with only 16 percent of the required changes. Among other findings, the report noted that 30 percent of the inmates who were referred for substance abuse treatment were not getting treatment. In 2009, a settlement agreement was reached concerning what the SPLC called "shockingly inhumane abuses of children" in a detention facility in Meridian, Mississippi, where reportedly children were kept in unsanitary cells for 23-24 hours a day.[49]

In 2012, the State of Mississippi settled a case filed by the SPLC in 2009 concerning brutal treatment of juveniles who were convicted in adult criminal courts and subsequently confined in the Walnut Grove Youth Correctional Facility, which was operated by the second-largest private prison corporation in the country, GEO Group, Inc. Among other provisions, the state must provide a variety of rehabilitative services for the boys and house them in a facility that uses utilizes juvenile justice rather than adult correctional facility standards. Greater protections against violent sexual abuse must be implemented and extensive solitary confinement will not be permitted.[50]

Another example is California, where then-governor Arnold Schwarzenegger signed a consent degree in November 2004 for a four-year plan to reform the state's youth correctional system. In particular, the agreement was to make the Herman G. Stark Youth Correctional Facility in Chino, California, the model juvenile facility. In 2007, the independent Office of the Inspector General issued a report noting that little had changed at Stark. Youth offenders remained in their cells for up to 22 hours a day; they were not participating in educational or training classes; abuses uncovered in previous years were still in existence; gang and racial fighting still existed; and the state was paying approximately $175,000 a year to house each inmate. Stark housed approximately 800 male offenders, including the most difficult and dangerous youth offenders. The inspector general called the facility a "recipe for tragedy."[51] On August 27, 2009, the California Department of Corrections and Rehabilitation announced that the Stark facility would be closed as a youth facility.[52]

In addition to a right to adequate living conditions, medical care, and so on, some lower courts have ruled that specific constitutional rights of adults must be extended to incarcerated juveniles. For example, the Sixth Circuit Court of Appeals held that the right to counsel applies to incarcerated juveniles when they raise claims involving other constitutional rights as well as for civil rights actions that relate to their incarceration. If the juveniles cannot afford counsel, the state must provide it for them in these cases. The issue arose in a class action suit in Tennessee and involved incarcerated youths who claimed that they were being denied access to courts.[53]

One of the most recent legal issues raised in juvenile corrections is that of solitary confinement. In a 2015 case involving issues raised by a death row inmate, U.S. Supreme Court Justice Anthony Kennedy used the case to comment on an issue that was not before the Court but that involved the inmate who was appealing: solitary confinement. Hector Ayala had spent the majority of his 25 years in prison in administrative segregation, which meant solitary confinement. Justice Kennedy noted that in all probability that meant that Ayala spent his time "in a windowless cell no larger than a typical parking spot for 23 hours a day; and in the one hour when he leaves it, he likely is allowed little or no opportunity for conversation or interaction with anyone." Justice Kennedy quoted the Court's decision in an 1890 case, noting that solitary confinement, even for inmates sentenced to death, bears "a further terror and peculiar mark of infamy." In terms of juveniles in solitary confinement, Justice Kennedy referred to Rikers Island inmate Kalief Browder, who was "held — but never tried — for stealing a backpack." Browder, a teenager, was in solitary for two of the three years he was held, and he committed suicide in the jail. Justice Kennedy cited scholarly research showing that solitary confinement is particularly harmful to juveniles as well as to mentally challenged persons. Justice Kennedy appeared to be asking someone to bring a case on whether or not solitary confinement is unconstitutional.[54]

At its annual meeting in August 2017, the American Bar Association adopted Resolution 112E, calling for policies and statutes banning the use of solitary confinement for any person under the age of 18. The ABA noted that although President Barack Obama and the U.S. Department of Justice had banned the use of solitary punishment of juveniles in federal facilities since 2016, the practice was in use in many state and local juvenile facilities.[55]

There were some significant developments on this front. For example, as part of a consent decree between the American Civil Liberties Union and the Illinois Department of Criminal Justice, Illinois made a significant move away from placing juveniles in custody in solitary confinement. In September 2014, New York City announced its plans to end the use of solitary confinement to punish teenagers confined in the Rikers Island complex.[56]

Illinois officials stated that the research was clear that persons with mental challenges, which includes most youth in custody, were psychologically damaged by placement in solitary confinement.[57] California and other states had enacted policies to reduce its use even among adult inmates, for example, in California as a result of a settlement in a legal case.[58] Finally, the First Step Act of 2018, discussed earlier and signed by President Trump in December 2018, contains provisions for eliminating solitary confinement as well as life without parole for juveniles but that statute only applies to federal institutions.[59]

An important legal issue concerning incarcerated juveniles is whether they have a *right* to treatment.

Treatment and Juvenile Corrections

Originally, special facilities were established to isolate juveniles from the harmful effects of society and from incarcerated adults. Later, with the development of juvenile courts, the treatment philosophy prevailed. During the past century, however, various commissions have pointed out the failure of juvenile corrections to provide adequate services and programs to enable the successful implementation of a treatment philosophy. As we have noted, in more recent years, courts have entered the picture, requiring some elements of due process in the adjudication of juveniles, changes in the disciplinary handling of institutionalized juveniles, and changes in the degree and kinds of services provided in those institutions.

The assignment of juveniles to special facilities for the purpose of treatment after they have been through proceedings that do not involve all elements of due process raises the critical issue of whether juveniles have a *constitutional* right to treatment. Recall that the original reason for not infusing the juvenile court with due process requirements was that, unlike adult offenders, juveniles were not being punished. They were being treated, and juvenile court judges acted in the best interests of the children. Thus, juveniles did not need due process requirements to protect them from governmental action.

The U.S. Supreme Court has discredited the practice of using the philosophy of rehabilitation to deny juveniles their basic constitutional rights, and it has acknowledged that rehabilitation has failed. However, the Court has also articulated its support for the retention of at least part of the *parens patriae* philosophy in juvenile proceedings while applying some but not all due process requirements. This has had a somewhat confusing result.

Scholars and many courts have taken the position that, under the doctrine of *parens patriae,* juveniles have given up some of their constitutional rights in order to be processed through a system that is based on treatment rather than punishment. Therefore, the state must provide that treatment or relinquish custody of the child. This position is based on cases involving the legal rights of confined mentally challenged persons.

The U.S. Supreme Court has not decided a case on the constitutional right to treatment for juveniles, although in *O'Connor v. Donaldson,* which involved the confinement of mentally challenged persons, the opinion of the Court *implied* that the justices might not hold that juveniles have a constitutional right to treatment.[60] However, recall the earlier discussions regarding federal requirements (as articulated by the DOJ) concerning mental health treatment and other issues in the Mississippi youth prisons. Finally, recall the earlier mention in this chapter of the December 2018 passage of the Juvenile Justice and Delinquency Reauthorization Act of 2018, which does place a priority on rehabilitation of juveniles both in and outside residential placement facilities. Whether reasonable programs will be funded remains an issue.

There is little question, however, that some forms of treatment should be provided for juveniles. Like adults, juveniles are entitled to reasonable medical care, and some medical problems might be even more critical for them than for adults.

JUVENILES IN THE COMMUNITY

The cost of incarcerating juveniles in state facilities is extremely high. The Justice Policy Institute (JPI) concluded that because most of the youths in custody are held for nonviolent rather than violent offenses, most of them "could be managed safely in the community through alternatives that cost substantially less than incarceration and could lower recidivism by up to 22 percent." Community supervision would also be much less expensive, "yielding up to $13 in benefits for every dollar spent."[61]

The Campaign for Youth Justice estimated that sending a juvenile to prison for 20 years could cost between $1.25 and $1.5 million; yearly costs in a juvenile facility were between $32,000 and $65,000. In contrast, early intervention and adequate care and treatment could save almost $5.7 million over the life of the offender.[62]

There are several ways to supervise juveniles within the community. We look first at individuals who are already in custody. They may be released from institutions and placed on parole, usually called **aftercare**. Historically, juveniles have had no right to early release, but most do not remain in confinement for long periods of time. Usually, they are released to aftercare, but if they violate the terms of that release, they may be returned to confinement.

The type of aftercare for juveniles is important. Aftercare should begin with a prerelease program while the juvenile is in confinement. There are two kinds of prerelease programs in juvenile institutions. In the first type, juveniles may be given furloughs or weekend passes to visit their families, a practice that permits gradual reentry into society. In the second type, juveniles may be moved to special cottages within the institution, where they live for a period of time with other inmates who are almost ready to be released and where special programs are provided to prepare them for that release. The length of the aftercare period depends on the needs of each juvenile.

Florida has reported a successful aftercare program for juveniles. The state began such programs in the 1990s. Eckerd Juvenile Justice Aftercare services, which have spread from Florida to North Carolina and Texas, claim a savings of millions over residential and detention centers as well as a reduction in recidivism, improvement of social skills, and improvement in mental health, along with youth and parental satisfaction. Eckerd ("one of the largest privately-funded nonprofit youth and family service organizations in the United States and a national leader that has given much-needed second chances to more than 100,000 children since 1968") provides the following services for the youth and their families both in their homes and in the communities in which they live:

- "Transition planning;
- Individualized assessment;
- Educational, vocational, and recreational planning;
- Crisis intervention;
- Community service;
- Counseling for adjustment and social skills building;
- Life Skills Training (an evidence-based intervention)."[63]

Another type of community care of juveniles is called *respite care*. Respite care programs, which exist in various jurisdictions throughout the country, are designed for runaways and their families. Under respite care, the children are given a break from their families and vice versa. A report on these programs states that some families actually lock their children out of their homes, practically begging the county or the state to take charge of children they have found to be incorrigible. Many of these children are not a threat to society, but they need a place to stay while problems with their families can, hopefully, be worked out. Respite care gives juvenile court judges an option for status offenders other than the potentially detrimental detention centers and jails. These programs provide a cooling-off period, followed by counseling for all involved parties. The goal is to reunite the child with his or her family as quickly as possible.[64]

Finally, juveniles may be placed on parole under supervision after confinement or placed on probation without confinement. Recall that probation is the most frequently used sanction for adults; the same is true for juveniles, and the same issues are raised. As with adults, the key issue with juveniles is whether serious offenders may be placed in the community without causing unreasonable harm to others. Concerns and legal issues regarding placing juvenile sex offenders in the community are discussed in **Supplement 12.8**.

JUVENILES AND CAPITAL PUNISHMENT

According to the Death Penalty Information Center (DPIC), between 1976 and 2005, when the U.S. Supreme Court held that executing persons for crimes committed when they were juveniles is unconstitutional, 22 persons in that category were executed.[65] At the end of 2004, 71 offenders, or 2 percent of the total death row population, were under the death sentence for murders they committed as juveniles. They were from 12 states, with Texas holding 40 percent of them. Two-thirds of the juvenile offenders were persons of color; all were males. Fifty percent of the victims were females; two-thirds were white.[66] A review of cases leading up to the 2005 decision is important for historical purposes.

The 1986 execution of James Terry Roach, then 25 but executed for a crime he committed when he was 16, raised the issue of whether capital punishment should be imposed on juveniles. In an earlier case, Monty Lee Eddings, who was 15 when he murdered an Oklahoma highway patrol officer who stopped him for a traffic violation, was successful in the appeal of his death sentence to the U.S. Supreme Court. Eddings's attorney argued that capital punishment for a crime committed while the offender was a juvenile constituted cruel and unusual punishment. The Supreme Court did not decide that issue but sent the case back for resentencing on the grounds that at the sentencing hearing the lower court did not consider mitigating circumstances. The trial court considered the mitigating circumstances and resentenced Eddings to death. Before his case reached the U.S. Supreme Court a second time, however, the Oklahoma Court of Criminal Appeals changed the sentence from death to life imprisonment.[67]

In 1985, the U.S. Supreme Court upheld the death sentence of a defendant who was 18 at the time he committed his capital crime.[68] In 1988, the Supreme Court decided *Thompson v. Oklahoma*, in which it reversed the capital sentence of William Wayne Thompson, who was 15 when he committed the crime for which he was given the death penalty. In *Thompson*, a majority of the Supreme Court agreed that the execution of an individual who was 15 at the time he committed a capital crime is cruel and unusual punishment despite the circumstances of the crime. In deciding the issue, the Supreme Court used the standard established in *Trop v. Dulles*, decided in 1958. The standard is "the evolving standards of decency that mark the progress of a maturing society."[69]

The U.S. Supreme Court's decision in *Thompson* banned capital punishment for youths who are under 16 when they commit a capital offense; however, it did not answer the question of whether capital punishment is cruel and unusual when imposed on youths between the ages of 16 and 18 at the time the capital murder is committed. The Supreme Court made this very clear in its opinion, noting that it had been asked to declare capital punishment unconstitutional for all youths under age 18:

> Our task today, however, is to decide the case before us; we do so by concluding that the Eighth and Fourteenth Amendments prohibit the execution of a person who was under sixteen years of age at the time of his or her offense.[70]

In 1989, the U.S. Supreme Court decided the cases of two other death row inmates who had committed murders while they were juveniles. One was 17 years and 4 months old when he raped and sodomized a 20-year-old woman repeatedly, before he killed her with a bullet in the front and another in the back of her head. The second juvenile was 16 years and 6 months of age when he killed a 26-year-old mother of two by multiple stab wounds in her chest. The U.S. Supreme Court held that capital punishment for these youths did not constitute cruel and unusual punishment.[71]

In 2002, the U.S. Supreme Court held that a national consensus had emerged that executing mentally challenged persons constitutes cruel and unusual punishment. Some legal scholars thought the reasoning might be extended to executing persons who committed murders when they were 16 or 17 years old. The U.S. Supreme Court declined to make that extension, as demonstrated by its refusal in October 2002 to review the case of Kevin Stanford, who has been on Kentucky's death row since 1982 for raping and murdering a 20-year-old gas station attendant when Stanford was 17. Stanford argued that there is an emerging consensus that juveniles who committed their crimes while under 18 years old should not be executed. When the U.S. Supreme Court refused to review Stanford's case, the dissenting justices issued an opinion stating that "[t]he practice of executing such offenders is a relic of the past and is inconsistent with evolving standards of decency in a civilized society. We should put an end to this shameful practice." The dissent noted that since its 1989 decision, five states had banned the execution of juveniles under age 18.[72]

In August 2002, when the U.S. Supreme Court declined to stay the execution of Toronto M. Patterson, who was 17 when he committed murder, three justices urged their colleagues to reconsider their decision regarding the execution of offenders who were 16 or 17 when they committed capital murder. Patterson was executed.[73]

In January 2003, the U.S. Supreme Court rejected the appeal of Scott A. Hain, 32, an Oklahoma death row inmate who committed murder when he was 17. Hain was executed in April 2003.[74] In October 2003, the Court refused to review the case of Nanon McKewn Williams, a Texas inmate who was on death row for a murder he committed when he was 17. Williams's attorney said that, had the case been reviewed, he had planned to argue by analogy to the Supreme Court's 2002 decision that capital punishment is unconstitutional in the case of the mentally challenged.[75]

In October 2004, the U.S. Supreme Court heard the case of Christopher Simmons, 27, who killed at age 17. In the case of *Roper v. Simmons*,[76] decided in 2005, the Court held that the execution of persons who committed their capital crimes when they were 16 or 17 is unconstitutional. The facts and an excerpt of the case are presented in **Supplement 12.9**.

JUVENILE AND ADULT CRIMINAL JUSTICE SYSTEMS: A BRIEF ASSESSMENT

Many issues face justice systems today. One of the most important was illustrated by a school shooting that occurred as this section was being reviewed for publication. On May 7, 2019, just three days before the semester was to end at Stem School in Highlands Ranch, Colorado, a male student entered an English class late, reportedly yelled, "Don't move," and started firing a hand gun. Kendrick Castillo, described as a "gentle teenager fascinated by cars and engineering," was shot dead when he lunged at the shooter. Eight other students were injured in the rampage. Students called Castillo a hero, as his brave act that resulted in his death gave the other students and the teacher a few seconds to dive for cover. Several male students then tackled the shooter, identified as 18-years old, and later arrested, along with a 16-year-old female student. The older student falls under the jurisdiction of the adult criminal court, but the arrest of the younger one raised the issue of whether we should continue to preserve juvenile justice systems or process her (and others) through adult criminal justice systems. Both alleged shooters were charged with first-degree murder, attempted murder, and assault.[77] Both were charged as adults.

Should judges have a choice or should waivers be mandatory if specific crimes, such as murder, are alleged? If we retain juvenile systems, how closely should they mirror adult criminal systems in structure and in procedure? Will crime rates be affected by changing the current systems? What types of treatment should be provided for juveniles who violate the criminal law? What should we do with those who violate social rules and commit so-called status crimes?

Significant changes have already been made or are in the process of being made within juvenile and adult criminal justice systems. Some, such as changes in sentencing statutes and policies, have been discussed in this text and its suppplement. Others will be initiated perhaps even before this text is published. As these changes are proposed, perhaps we should keep in mind the following passage from the 2000 presidential address at the annual meeting of the Academy of Criminal Justice Sciences. President Alida V. Merlo focused her address on juvenile justice, which she described as being at a crossroads between the "get-tough" punitive legislative approaches and the recent reductions in juvenile violence and the apparent softening of public attitudes toward juveniles. In her summary, Merlo stated the following:

> We can either continue to move toward more punitive juvenile justice policies, greater intolerance for adolescents, growing racism, more costly and more inhumane policies, and an ever-widening gulf between poor children and the rest of us, or we can blaze a new path. As teachers, scholars, researchers, students, and practitioners, we have the opportunity to infuse the system with a new kind of thinking—thinking that is informed by research, by the evaluation of programs, and by an understanding of the complex societal conditions that cannot be eliminated without substantial long-term investments.[78]

Merlo's statements were predictive of the view that some politicians, scholars, and members of the general public are taking today. Whether the change in attitude is due to a change of heart, budget crises, legal challenges, or all of these and other reasons, is not really material; the fact is that changes are occurring. It is a challenging period for juvenile justice systems in particular and criminal justice systems in general, and it is an exciting time to be studying and contemplating a career in these critical areas of our lives.

Summary

Juvenile justice systems held the highest hopes for success in rehabilitation, reformation, and reintegration, but they contained some of the greatest deprivations of constitutional rights. In the name of "the best interests of the child," the government took away liberty without due process of law. Under the guise of treatment and rehabilitation, not punishment, juvenile court systems swept into their clutches many who otherwise would not have been processed by court systems.

There is a need to treat juveniles differently than adults. There is a need to segregate them from adults in confinement. There is a need to offer them opportunities for improvement so that they can succeed in a competitive world. But those needs may not be met by violating juveniles' U.S. constitutional rights.

After an overview of juvenile justice systems, this chapter looked at the current data on juvenile offenders, noting in particular the issues of race and ethnicity and gender. The constitutional rights of juveniles were considered in some detail, with the chapter focusing first on the critical U.S. Supreme Court cases and looking in particular at the right to counsel, especially with regard to indigent juveniles.

This chapter then turned to an analysis of juvenile court organization and procedures. The discussion showed that, although not all procedural requirements of criminal courts have been applied to juveniles, many due process rights have been extended to them in juvenile courts. No longer is it sufficient to say that juveniles are not arrested; they are apprehended. They are not found guilty; they are adjudicated. They are not sentenced, but dispositions are made of their cases. The change in wording does not compensate for a lack of due process. In many respects, present-day adult criminal and juvenile court systems are similar, but states have some room to experiment in their juvenile systems. For example, trial by jury is not required by the U.S. Constitution but has been extended by statute to juvenile courts in some states. The role of attorneys in juvenile courts was also discussed.

Violent crimes appear to be committed by a few juveniles, but those violent few are responsible for a large percentage of the total crimes that juveniles commit. Concern with this violence and with recidivism has led some states to pass statutes giving adult criminal courts jurisdiction over juveniles who commit serious crimes. In other states, after a proper hearing, juvenile courts may waive jurisdiction over juveniles who are charged with serious crimes. Considerable attention was given to the processing of juveniles in adult criminal courts, including constitutional issues regarding this practice, the evaluation of waivers, and sentencing, with particular emphasis on life without parole and confining juveniles in adult facilities.

The next major focus of the chapter was on juveniles in correctional facilities. Juveniles have received differential treatment in corrections, too, although it is not at all clear that those differences are positive. Indefinite detention of juveniles under the guise that they are being treated when they are being detained without treatment has been held by courts to be inappropriate. Unfortunately, disillusionment with treatment and rehabilitation in many jurisdictions has resulted in a decreased emphasis on treatment, even in the case of juveniles. At the other extreme has been the position that institutionalization is bad for juveniles and therefore should be abandoned, with juveniles being cared for in community treatment facilities.

The execution of juveniles is one of the most controversial areas in juvenile court systems. The chapter noted the recent changes in the legal aspects of executing juveniles, including an excerpt in the supplement from the U.S. Supreme Court's holding on the issue.

The final section of this chapter consisted of a brief look at juvenile justice and criminal justice systems.

In conclusion, some scholars are questioning the wisdom and efficiency of retaining juvenile court systems if most of the procedures of adult court systems become a part of juvenile systems. Others note the unfairness of a system that is moving toward criminal court sentences without all of the elements of due process provided in those courts. One law professor stated the issue as follows:

> As juvenile courts' sentencing practices resemble increasingly those of their criminal counterparts, does any reason remain to maintain a separate court whose sole distinguishing characteristic is its persisting procedural deficiencies?[79]

It may be that the future of criminal justice is related to what we do with juvenile court systems. Certainly, this is an area to follow closely as the U.S. Supreme Court ponders and decides whether to continue the march toward greater due process and equal protection or to retract from that path to a more conservative interpretation of the U.S. Constitution.

Key Terms

adjudication 286
aftercare 302
certification 293
delinquency 286
detention 285
detention centers 285
disposition 286
intake decision 292
juvenile 284
juvenile court 285
juvenile delinquent 284
parens patriae 284
petition 285
status offense 284
training school 298
waiver 293

Study Questions

1. How were alleged juvenile offenders processed historically?
2. What events led to the emergence of juvenile courts in the United States?
3. What are the basic ways in which juvenile courts and adult criminal courts differ?
4. Briefly describe juvenile court procedures.
5. Do juveniles have a federal constitutional right to a trial by jury in juvenile court proceedings? Should they have this right?
6. Evaluate pretrial detention of juveniles.
7. What is the role of the police to juvenile offenders?
8. Define and discuss intake proceedings in juvenile systems.
9. Describe the role of the prosecutor and of the defense attorney in juvenile proceedings.
10. Discuss the disposition of a juvenile case and the appeals process.
11. Why are some juveniles tried in adult criminal courts, and how is this accomplished? Evaluate this policy.
12. Discuss and evaluate sentencing juveniles to life without parole (LWOP).
13. What are the results of confining juveniles in adult facilities? Have any recent changes been made in this practice?
14. Discuss some of the recent legal findings about juvenile institutions.
15. What is the current status of the capital punishment of juveniles?

Notes

1. Orman Ketcham, "The Unfulfilled Promise of the American Juvenile Courts," in *Justice for the Child*, ed. Margaret Keeney Rosenheim (New York: Free Press, 1962), p. 24.
2. See Alexander W. Pisciotta, "*Parens Patriae*, Treatment and Reform: The Case of the Western House of Refuge, 18491907," *New England Journal of Criminal and Civil Confinement* 10 (Winter 1984): 6586.
3. See Anthony Platt, *The Child Savers* (Chicago: University of Chicago Press, 1969).
4. John R. Sutton, "The Juvenile Court and Social Welfare: Dynamics of Progressive Reform," *Law and Society Review* 19(1) (1985): 142.
5. Federal Bureau of Investigation, *Uniform Crime Reports, Crime in the Unitd States, 2017* (September 2018), https://ucr.fbi.gov/crime-in-the-u.s./2017/crime-in-the-u.s.-2017/tables/table-41, accessed November 4, 2018.
6. The Sentencing Project, "Fact Sheet: Trends in U.S. Corrections—Youth," p. 6, https://www.sentenceproject.org, accessed November 3, 2018.
7. Christopher Hartney and Linh Vuong, National Council on Crime and Delinquency, *Created Equal: Racial and Ethnic Disparities in the US Criminal Justice System* (March 2009), p. 3, http://www.nccdglobal.org/, accessed January 2, 2015.
8. Linh Vuong and Fabiana Silva, National Council on Crime and Delinquency, Special Report, *Evaluating Federal Gang Bills* (December 1, 2008), p. 9, http://www.nccd.global.org/, accessed January 2, 2015.
9. Carl E. Pope and Howard N. Snyder, Office of Juvenile Justice and Delinquency Prevention, *Race as a Factor in Juvenile Arrests* (Washington, D.C.: U.S. Department of Justice, April 2003), pp. 1, 6.

10. "ABA Finds Right to Lawyer Is 'an Unfulfilled Promise,'" quoting *Maryland: An Assessment of Access to Counsel and Quality of Representation in Delinquency*, an 81-page report by the American Bar Association, pp. 2-3, cited in *Criminal Justice Newsletter* (November 17, 2003).
11. Justice Policy Institute, *Reducing Racial Disparities in Juvenile Detention* (February 1, 2002), http://www.justicepolicy.org/, accessed January 3, 2015.
12. Eli Hager, The Marshall Project, "Trump Appointee Changes Long-Standing Policies Regarding Racial Disparities in Youth Incarceration," reprinted in the *American Bar Association Journal* (September 25, 2018), http://www.abajournal.com, accessed September 26, 2018.
13. Juvenile Justice and Delinquency Prevention Act, USCS, Title 42, Section 5633 (2019).
14. National Council on Crime and Delinquency, "Fact Sheet: Girls in Juvenile Justice," http://www.nccdglobal.org/, accessed January 3, 2015.
15. *Changing the Status Quo for Status Offenders: New York State's Efforts to Support Troubled Teens*, Vera Institute of Justice, https://www.vera.org, accessed January 15, 2019.
16. "Adolescent Behavior Is Not a Crime," Vera Institute of Justice, https://www.vera.org/content/adolescent-behavior-not-crime, accessed January 15, 2019.
17. Sarah Hockenberry and Charles Puzzanchera, "Juvenile Court Statistics 2016" (August 2018), pp. 6, 12, 21, https://www.ojjdp.gov, accessed November 4, 2018.
18. *In re Gault*, 387 U.S. 1 (1967). See also *Lanes v. State*, 767 S.W.2d 789 (Tex. Crim. App. 1989), requiring probable cause to arrest a juvenile.
19. Campaign for Youth Justice, "Key Facts: Youth in the Justice System," p. 2, http://www.campaignforyouthjustice.org, accessed January 3, 2015.
20. *Schall v. Martin*, 467 U.S. 253, 265 (1984). The adult preventive detention case is *United States v. Salerno*, 481 U.S. 739 (1987).
21. Campaign for Youth Justice, "Key Facts: Youth in the Justice System," p. 3.
22. Sarah Hockenberry and Charles Puzzanchera, Office of Juvenile Justice and Delinquency Prevention, *Delinquency Cases Waived to Criminal Court, 2011* (December 2014), p. 2, http://www.ojjdp.gov/pubs/248410.pdf, accessed January 15, 2019.
23. Ibid., pp. 3-4.
24. *Juveniles' Competence to Stand Trial: A Comparison of Adolescents' and Adults' Capacities as Trial Defendants* (Philadelphia: MacArthur Foundation Research Network on Adolescent Development and Juvenile Justice, 2003), as cited in "Many Juveniles Lack Competence for Adult Court, Study Finds," *Criminal Justice Newsletter* (March 18, 2003), p. 5.
25. Richard E. Redding, Office of Juvenile Justice and Delinquency Prevention, *Juvenile Transfer Laws: An Effective Deterrent to Delinquency?* (June 2010), http://www.ncjrs.gov/pdffiles1/ojjdp/220595.pdf, accessed April 3, 2011.
26. Benjamin Steiner, "The Effects of Juvenile Transfer to Criminal Court on Incarceration Decisions," *Justice Quarterly* 26(1) (March 2009): 77-106.
27. Campaign for Youth Justice, "Mission and Goals," http://www.campaignforyouthjustice.org/about-us/mission-and-goals, accessed January 3, 2015.
28. For a discussion, see Lorelei Laird, "New York Raises Age of Adult Criminal Prosecution to 18," *American Bar Association Journal* (April 14, 2017), http://www.abajournal.com, accessed April 14, 2017.
29. Richard A. Mendel, Justice Policy Institute, "Juvenile Justice Reform in Connecticut: How Collaboration and Commitment Improved Outcomes for Youth" (February 27, 2013), http://www.justicepolicy.org, accessed May 5, 2015.
30. "Brief for the American Medical Association and the American Academy of Child and Adolescent Psychiatry as *Amici Curiae* in Support of Neither Party," submitted to the U.S. Supreme Court in the case of *Graham v. Florida* (July 23, 2009), pp. 2, 3. See also *Graham v. Florida*, 560 U.S. 48 (2010).
31. *Miller v. Alabama*, 567 U.S. 460 (2012).
32. *Montgomery v. Louisiana*, 136 S. Ct. 718 (2016).
33. *Gridine v. Florida*, 93 So. 3d 360 (Fla. Dist. Ct. App. 1st Dist. 2012), *review granted*, 103 So. 3d 139 (Fla. 2012), *quashed by in part, certified question answered by and remanded by*, 2015 Fla. LEXIS 532 (Fla. 2015).
34. *Gridine v. Florida*, 175 So. 3d 672 (Fla. 2015), *cert-denied, Florida v. Gridine*, 2016 U.S. LEXIS 1716 (March 2016).
35. Howard N. Snyder and Melissa Sickmund, Office of Juvenile Justice and Delinquency Prevention, *Juvenile Offenders and Victims: 1999 National Report* (Washington, D.C.: U.S. Department of Justice, September 1999), p. 208; Antoinette Davis et al., "The Declining Number of Youth in Custody in the Juvenile Justice System," National Council on Crime and Delinquency (August 2008), http://www.nccdglobal.org/sites/default/files/publication_pdf/focus-declining-youth-custody.pdf, accessed January 3, 2015. The statute is codified at USCS, Title 18, Section 5031 et seq. (2019).
36. Debra Cassens Weiss, American Bar Association, "ABA-Supported Juvenile Justice Bill with 'Rehabilitative Purpose' Passes Congress," *American Bar Association Journal* (December 14, 2018), http://www.abajournal.com, accessed December 14, 2018.
37. Campaign for Youth Justice, "Key Facts: Youth in the Justice System," www.campaignforyouthjustice.org/, accessed November 5, 2018.
38. Kevin Koeninger, *Courthouse News*, "Juveniles Housed with Adults Bring Claims to Sixth Circuit" (December 6, 2018), https://www.courthousenews.com/juveniles-housed-with-adults-bring-claims-to-sixth-circuit, accessed December 7, 2018. The suit is *Doe v. Snyder*, 2018 U.S. Dist. LEXIS 29255 (E.D. MI, So. Div. February 23, 2018).
39. See David J. Rothman, *The Discovery of the Asylum* (South Salem, NY: Criminal Justice Institute, 1988), pp. 50, 51.
40. "Crowding of Juvenile Facilities Is 'Pervasive,' Study Finds," *Criminal Justice Newsletter* 24 (April 15, 1993): 4.
41. Dale G. Parent et al., *Conditions of Confinement: Juvenile Detention and Corrections Facilities. Research Summary* (Washington, D.C.: U.S. Department of Justice, February 1994), p. 1. This publication is a summary of the congressionally mandated study, and it was prepared by Abt Associations, Inc., under a grant from the Office of Juvenile Justice and Delinquency, Office of Justice Programs, U.S. Department of Justice.
42. Sarah Hockenberry, Office of Juvenile Justice and Delinquency Prevention, "Juveniles in Residential Placement, 2015" (January 2018), p. 1, https://www.ojjdp.gov, accessed January 16, 2019.
43. Office of Juvenile Justice and Delinquency Prevention, Juvenile Residential Facility Census, Washington, D.C.: U.S. Census Bureau (producer), available on an undated pamphlet

distributed at the annual meeting of the American Society of Criminology, November 2018.

44. Justice Policy Institute, *Sticker Shock: Calculating the Full Price Tag for Youth Incarceration* (December 9, 2014), pp. 1, 3, www.justicepolicy.org/research8477, accessed May 9, 2019.
45. "Ex-Camp Worker Pleads Guilty," *Arizona Republic* (February 21, 2002), p. 1B.
46. "Cuts Force Last Youth Boot Camp to Close," *Orlando Sentinel* (Florida) (June 21, 2008), p. 3B; "U.S. Won't File Charges in Boot Camp Death," *Boston Globe* (April 17, 2010), p. 2; *The Consequences Aren't Minor: The Impact of Trying Youth as Adults and Strategies for Reform,* Campaign for Youth and Justice, http://www.campaignfor youthjustice.org/, pp. 1-16, accessed April 3, 2019. See also the Marvin Lee Anderson Act of 2006, 2006 Bill Text Fl. H.B. 5019 (2006).
47. "Abuse Cited at Mississippi Youth Correctional Education Centers," *Correctional Educational Bulletin* 6(12) (August 19, 2003): n.p.
48. Ibid.
49. Southern Poverty Law Center, http://www.splcenter.org/, accessed January 3, 2015.
50. Southern Poverty Law Center, "Groundbreaking Settlement in SPLC Case Protects Incarcerated Children from Abuse in Mississippi" (February 27, 2012), http://www.splcenter.org/, accessed January 3, 2015.
51. "Youth Facility in California Called 'Recipe for Tragedy,'" *Criminal Justice Newsletter* (March 1, 2007), p. 6.
52. California Department of Corrections and Rehabilitation, "Public and Employee Communications" (August 27, 2009), http://www.cdcr.ca.gov, accessed January 3, 2015.
53. *Shookoff v. Adams,* 750 F. Supp. 288 (M.D. Tenn. 1990), *aff'd John L. v. Adams,* 969 F.2d 228 (6th Cir. 1992). The U.S. Supreme Court case on which the decision relies concerns the right of adult offenders access to courts. See *Bounds v. Smith,* 430 U.S. 817 (1977).
54. Davis v. Ayala, 135 S. Ct. 2187 (2015), Justice Anthony Kennedy, concurring, case names omitted.
55. Debra Cassens Weiss, "ABA House Supports Money Bail System Reform, Ban on Solitary Confinement for Juveniles," *American Bar Association Journal* (August 14, 2017), http://www.abajournal.com, accessed August 29, 2018.
56. New York: "National Roundup: New York's Rikers Island to End Solitary Confinement for Teenagers," *Washington Post* (September 29, 2014), cited on the website of the Campaign for Youth Justice, http://www.campaignforyouthjustice.org, accessed January 4, 2015.
57. Duaa Eldeib, "Time Spent in Solitary Confinement Drops Dramatically in Illinois Youth Facilities," *American Bar Association Journal* (October 26, 2017), http://www.abajournal.com, accessed November 4, 2017.
58. See *Ashker v. Government of California,* 2018 U.S. Dist. LEXIS 134731 (U.S. Dist. Ct. N.D. Cal. 2018).
59. First Step Act of 2018, 115 S. 3649 (2018).
60. *O'Connor v. Donaldson,* 422 U.S. 563 (1975).
61. Justice Policy Institute, "The Cost of Confinement: Why Good Juvenile Justice Policies Make Good Fiscal Sense" (May 2009), http://www.justicepolicy.org, accessed January 4, 2015.
62. Campaign for Youth and Justice, "Key Facts," p. 5.
63. Jody Grutza, Reclaiming Futures, "Juvenile Justice Aftercare Program Shows Success in Florida and Beyond" (September 27, 2012), http://www.reclaimingfutures.org/aftercare-program, accessed May 6, 2015.
64. Eric Weingartner, Vera Institute of Justice, *"Respite Care: An Alternative to Foster Care for Status Offenders in New York City"* (June 30, 2002), https://www.vera.org/, accessed January 4, 2015.
65. Death Penalty Information Center, "Juveniles and the Death Penalty," http://www.deathpenaltyinfo.org/juveniles-and-death-penalty, accessed January 4, 2015.
66. Death Penalty Information Center, "Death Penalty for Juveniles Was Banned by the Supreme Court in 2005," http://www.deathpenaltyinfo.org/juvenile-offenders-who-were-death-row#streiboverview, accessed January 4, 2015.
67. *Eddings v. Oklahoma,* 455 U.S. 104 (1982).
68. *Baldwin v. Alabama,* 472 U.S. 372 (1985).
69. *Thompson v. Oklahoma,* 487 U.S. 815 (1988); *Trop v. Dulles,* 356 U.S. 86, 101 (1958) (plurality opinion).
70. *Thompson v. Oklahoma,* 487 U.S. 815 (1988).
71. *Stanford v. Kentucky,* 492 U.S. 361 (1989).
72. *Stanford v. Parker,* 2001 U.S. App. LEXIS 26419 (6th Cir. 2001), *cert. denied,* 537 U.S. 831 (2002). See also *Atkins v. Virginia,* 536 U.S. 304 (2002).
73. "3 Justices Call for Reviewing Death Sentences for Juveniles," *New York Times* (August 30, 2002), p. 1; *Patterson v. Cockrell,* 2002 U.S. App. LEXIS 6396 (5th Cir. 2002), *cert. denied,* 536 U.S. 967 (2002).
74. *Hain v. Mullin,* 852 P.2d 744 (Okla. Crim. App. 1993), *cert. denied,* 537 U.S. 1173 (2003).
75. "High Court Passes on Local Case: Activists Sought Ruling on Killers Younger than 18," *Houston Chronicle* (October 21, 2003), p. 17. The case is *Williams v. Texas,* 540 U.S. 969 (2003). See also *Atkins v. Virginia,* 536 U.S. 304 (2002).
76. *Roper v. Simmons,* 453 U.S. 551 (2005).
77. Julie Turkewitz et al., "Colorado School Shooting Victim Died Trying to Stop the Gunman," New York Times (May 8, 2019), https://www.nytimes.com, accessed May 10, 2019.
78. Alida V. Merlo, "Juvenile Justice at the Crossroads: Presidential Address to the Academy of Criminal Justice Sciences," *Justice Quarterly* 17(4) (December 2000): 639-661, quotation is on p. 657.
79. Barry C. Feld, "The Punitive Juvenile Court and the Quality of Procedural Justice: Disjunctions Between Rhetoric and Reality," *Crime & Delinquency* 36 (October 1989): 443.

Amendments to the United States Constitution

[The first ten amendments are referred to as the Bill of Rights. They were ratified on December 15, 1791. The ratification dates of the subsequent amendments are noted.]

Amendment I

Congress shall make no law respecting an establishment of religion, or prohibiting the free exercise thereof; or abridging the freedom of speech, or of the press; or the right of the people peaceably to assemble, and to petition the Government for a redress of grievances.

Amendment II

A well regulated Militia, being necessary to the security of a free State, the right of the people to keep and bear Arms, shall not be infringed.

Amendment III

No Soldier shall, in time of peace be quartered in any house, without the consent of the Owner, nor in time of war, but in a manner to be prescribed by law.

Amendment IV

The right of the people to be secure in their persons, houses, papers, and effects, against unreasonable searches and seizures, shall not be violated, and no Warrants shall issue, but upon probable cause, supported by Oath or affirmation, and particularly describing the place to be searched, and the persons or things to be seized.

Amendment V

No person shall be held to answer for a capital, or otherwise infamous crime, unless on a presentment or indictment of a Grand Jury, except in cases arising in the land or naval forces, or in the Militia, when in actual service in time of War or public danger; nor shall any person be subject for the same offence to be twice put in jeopardy of life or limb; nor shall be compelled in any criminal case to be a witness against himself, nor be deprived of life, liberty, or property, without due process of law; nor shall private property be taken for public use, without just compensation.

Amendment VI

In all criminal prosecutions, the accused shall enjoy the right to a speedy and public trial, by an impartial jury of the State and district wherein the crime shall have been committed, which district shall have been previously ascertained by law, and to be informed of the nature and cause of the accusation; to be confronted with the witnesses against him; to have compulsory process for obtaining witnesses in his favor, and to have the Assistance of Counsel for his defence.

Amendment VII

In Suits at common law, where the value in controversy shall exceed twenty dollars, the right of trial by jury shall be preserved, and no fact tried by a jury, shall be otherwise re-examined in any Court of the United States, than according to the rules of the common law.

Amendment VIII

Excessive bail shall not be required, nor excessive fines imposed, nor cruel and unusual punishments inflicted.

Amendment IX

The enumeration in the Constitution, of certain rights, shall not be construed to deny or disparage others retained by the people.

Amendment X

The powers not delegated to the United States by the Constitution, nor prohibited by it to the States, are reserved to the States respectively, or to the people.

Amendment XI [1795]

The Judicial power of the United States shall not be construed to extend to any suit in law or equity, commenced or prosecuted against one of the United States by Citizens of another State, or by Citizens or Subjects of any Foreign State.

Amendment XII [1804]

The Electors shall meet in their respective states and vote by ballot for President and Vice-President, one of whom, at least, shall not be an inhabitant of the same state with themselves; they shall name in their ballots the person voted for as President, and in distinct ballots the person voted for as Vice-President, and they shall make distinct lists of all persons voted for as President, and of all persons voted for as Vice-President, and of the number of votes for each, which lists they shall sign and certify, and transmit sealed to the seat of the government of the United States, directed to the President of the Senate; — the President of the Senate shall, in the presence of the Senate and House of Representatives, open all the certificates and the votes shall then be counted; — The person having the greatest number of votes for President, shall be the President, if such number be a majority of the whole number of Electors appointed; and if no person have such majority, then from the persons having the highest numbers not exceeding three on the list of those voted for as President, the House of Representatives shall choose immediately, by ballot, the President. But in choosing the President, the votes shall be taken by states, the representation from each state having one vote; a quorum for this purpose shall consist of a member or members from two-thirds of the states, and a majority of all the states shall be necessary to a choice. And if the House of Representatives shall not choose a President whenever the right of choice shall devolve upon them, before the fourth day of March next following, then the Vice-President shall act as President, as in case of the death or other constitutional disability of the President. — The person having the greatest number of votes as Vice-President, shall be the Vice-President, if such number be a majority of the whole number of Electors appointed, and if no person have a majority, then from the two highest numbers on the list, the Senate shall choose the Vice-President; a quorum for the purpose shall consist of two-thirds of the whole number of Senators, and a majority of the whole number shall be necessary to a choice. But no person constitutionally ineligible to the office of President shall be eligible to that of Vice-President of the United States.

Amendment XIII [1865]

Section 1. Neither slavery nor involuntary servitude, except as a punishment for crime whereof the party shall have been duly convicted, shall exist within the United States, or any place subject to their jurisdiction.

Section 2. Congress shall have the power to enforce this article by appropriate legislation.

Amendment XIV [1868]

Section 1. All persons born or naturalized in the United States, and subject to the jurisdiction thereof, are citizens of the United States and of the State wherein they reside. No State shall make or enforce any law which shall abridge the privileges or immunities of citizens of the United States; nor shall any State deprive any person of life, liberty, or property, without due process of law; nor deny to any person within its jurisdiction the equal protection of the laws.

Section 2. Representatives shall be apportioned among the several States according to their respective numbers, counting the whole number of persons in each State, excluding Indians not taxed. But when the right to vote at any election for the choice of electors for President and Vice-President of the United States, Representatives in Congress, the Executive and Judicial officers of a State, or the members of the Legislature thereof, is denied to any of the male inhabitants of such State, being twenty-one years of age, and citizens of the United States, or in any way abridged, except for participation in rebellion, or other crime, the basis of representation therein shall be reduced in the proportion which the number of such male citizens shall bear to the whole number of male citizens twenty-one years of age in such State.

Section 3. No person shall be a Senator or Representative in Congress, or elector of President and Vice-President, or hold any office, civil or military, under the United States, or under any State, who, having previously taken an oath, as a member of Congress, or as an officer of the United States, or as a member of any State legislature, or as an executive or judicial officer of any State, to support the Constitution of the United States, shall have engaged in insurrection or rebellion against the same, or given aid or comfort to the enemies thereof. But Congress may by a vote of two-thirds of each House, remove such disability.

Section 4. The validity of the public debt of the United States, authorized by law, including debts incurred for payment of pensions and bounties for services in suppressing insurrection or rebellion, shall not be questioned. But neither the United States nor any State shall assume or pay any debt or obligation incurred in aid of insurrection or rebellion against the United States, or any claim for the loss or emancipation of any slave; but all such debts, obligations and claims shall be held illegal and void.

Section 5. The Congress shall have the power to enforce, by appropriate legislation, the provisions of this article.

Amendment XV [1870]

Section 1. The right of citizens of the United States to vote shall not be denied or abridged by the United States or by any State on account of race, color, or previous condition of servitude.

Section 2. The Congress shall have power to enforce this article by appropriate legislation.

Amendment XVI [1913]

The Congress shall have power to lay and collect taxes on incomes, from whatever source derived, without apportionment among the several States, and without regard to any census or enumeration.

Amendment XVII [1913]

The Senate of the United States shall be composed of two Senators from each State, elected by the people thereof, for six years; and each Senator shall have one vote. The electors in each State shall have the qualifications requisite for electors of the most numerous branch of the State legislatures.

When vacancies happen in the representation of any State in the Senate, the executive authority of such State shall issue writs of election to fill such vacancies: Provided, That the legislature of any State may empower the executive thereof to make temporary appointments until the people fill the vacancies by election as the legislature may direct.

This amendment shall not be so construed as to affect the election or term of any Senator chosen before it becomes valid as part of the Constitution.

Amendment XVIII [1919]

Section 1. After one year from the ratification of this article the manufacture, sale, or transportation of intoxicating liquors within, the importation thereof into, or the exportation thereof from the United States and all territory subject to the jurisdiction thereof for beverage purposes is hereby prohibited.

Section 2. The Congress and the several States shall have concurrent power to enforce this article by appropriate legislation.

Section 3. This article shall be inoperative unless it shall have been ratified as an amendment to the Constitution by the legislatures of the several States, as provided by the Constitution, within seven years from the date of the submission hereof to the States by the Congress.

Amendment XIX [1920]

The right of citizens of the United States to vote shall not be denied or abridged by the United States or by any State on account of sex.

Congress shall have power to enforce this article by appropriate legislation.

Amendment XX [1933]

Section 1. The terms of the President and the Vice President shall end at noon on the 20th day of January, and the terms of Senators and Representatives at noon on the 3d day of January, of the years in which such terms would have ended if this article had not been ratified; and the terms of their successors shall then begin.

Section 2. The Congress shall assemble at least once in every year, and such meeting shall begin at noon on the 3d day of January, unless they shall by law appoint a different day.

Section 3. If, at the time fixed for the beginning of the term of the President, the President elect shall have died, the Vice President elect shall become President. If a President shall not have been chosen before the time fixed for the beginning of his term, or if the President elect shall have failed to qualify, then the Vice President elect shall act as President until a President shall have qualified; and the Congress may by law provide for the case wherein neither a President elect nor a Vice President shall have qualified, declaring who shall then act as President, or the manner in which one who is to act shall be selected, and such person shall act accordingly until a President or Vice President shall have qualified.

Section 4. The Congress may by law provide for the case of the death of any of the persons from whom the House of Representatives may choose a President whenever the right of choice shall have devolved upon them, and for the case of the death of any of the persons from whom the Senate may choose a Vice President whenever the right of choice shall have devolved upon them.

Section 5. Sections 1 and 2 shall take effect on the 15th day of October following the ratification of this article.

Section 6. This article shall be inoperative unless it shall have been ratified as an amendment to the Constitution by the legislatures of three-fourths of the several States within seven years from the date of its submission.

Amendment XXI [1933]

Section 1. The eighteenth article of amendment to the Constitution of the United States is hereby repealed.

Section 2. The transportation or importation into any State, Territory, or possession of the United States for delivery or use therein of intoxicating liquors, in violation of the laws thereof, is hereby prohibited.

Section 3. The article shall be inoperative unless it shall have been ratified as an amendment to the Constitution by conventions in the several States, as provided in the Constitution, within seven years from the date of the submission hereof to the States by the Congress.

Amendment XXII [1951]

Section 1. No person shall be elected to the office of the President more than twice, and no person who has held the office of President, or acted as President, for more than two years of a term to which some other person was elected President shall be elected to the office of President more than once. But this Article shall not apply to any person holding the office of President when this Article was proposed by Congress, and shall not prevent any person who may be holding the office of President, or acting as President, during the term within which this Article becomes operative from holding the office of President or acting as President during the remainder of such term.

Section 2. This article shall be inoperative unless it shall have been ratified as an amendment to the Constitution by the legislatures of three-fourths of the several States within seven years from the date of its submission to the States by the Congress.

Amendment XXIII [1961]

Section 1. The District constituting the seat of Government of the United States shall appoint in such manner as Congress may direct: A number of electors of President and Vice President equal to the whole number of Senators and Representatives in Congress to which the District would be entitled if it were a State, but in no event more than the least populous State; they shall be in addition to those appointed by the States, but they shall be considered, for the purposes of the election of President and Vice President, to be electors appointed by a State; and they shall meet in the District and perform such duties as provided by the twelfth article of amendment.

Section 2. The Congress shall have power to enforce this article by appropriate legislation.

Amendment XXIV [1964]

Section 1. The right of citizens of the United States to vote in any primary or other election for President or Vice President, for electors for President or Vice President, or for Senator or Representative in Congress, shall not be denied or abridged by the United States or any State by reason of failure to pay poll tax or other tax.

Section 2. The Congress shall have power to enforce this article by appropriate legislation.

Amendment XXV [1967]

Section 1. In case of the removal of the President from office or of his death or resignation, the Vice President shall become President.

Section 2. Whenever there is a vacancy in the office of the Vice President, the President shall nominate a Vice President who shall take office upon confirmation by a majority vote of both Houses of Congress.

Section 3. Whenever the President transmits to the President pro tempore of the Senate and the Speaker of the House of Representatives his written declaration that he is unable to discharge the powers and duties of his office, and until he transmits to them a written declaration to the contrary, such powers and duties shall be discharged by the Vice President as Acting President.

Section 4. Whenever the Vice President and a majority of either the principal officers of the executive departments or of such other body as Congress may by law provide, transmit to the President *pro tempore* of the Senate and the Speaker of the House of Representatives their written declaration that the President is unable to discharge the powers and duties of his office, the Vice President shall immediately assume the powers and duties of the office as Acting President. Thereafter, when the President transmits to the President *pro tempore* of the Senate and the Speaker of the House of Representatives his written declaration that no inability exists, he shall resume the powers and duties of his office unless the Vice President and a majority of either the principal officers of the executive department or of such other body as Congress may by law provide, transmit within four days to the President *pro tempore* of the Senate and the Speaker of the House of Representatives their written declaration that the President is unable to discharge the powers and duties of his office. Thereupon Congress shall decide the issue, assembling within forty-eight hours for that purpose if not in session. If the Congress, within twenty-one days after receipt of the latter written declaration, or, if Congress is not in session, within twenty-one days after Congress is required to assemble, determines by two-thirds vote of both Houses that the President is unable to discharge the powers and duties of his office, the Vice President shall continue to discharge the same as Acting President; otherwise, the President shall resume the powers and duties of his office.

Amendment XXVI [1971]

Section 1. The right of citizens of the United States, who are eighteen years of age or older, to vote shall not be denied or abridged by the United States or by any State on account of age.

Section 2. The Congress shall have power to enforce this article by appropriate legislation.

Amendment XXVII [1992]

No law, varying the compensation for the services of the Senators and Representatives, shall take effect, until an election of Representatives shall have intervened.

Appendix B

How to Read a Court Citation

State v. Blakely, 47 P.3d 149 (Wash. App. 2002), *review denied*, 62 P.3d 889 (Wash. App. 2003), *and cert. granted*, *Blakely v. Washington*, 540 U.S. 965 (2003), *and mot. granted*, 540 U.S. 1174 (2004), *and rev'd, remanded, Blakely v. Washington*, 542 U.S. 296 (2004), *reh'g denied*, 542 U.S. 961 (2004).

This case has several citations; some cases have many more and go on for years. Some actions occurred after this case was decided by the U.S. Supreme Court; those references to related proceedings are omitted here.

Original Citation

[*State v. Blakely*][1] [47][2] [P.3d][3] [149][4] [Wash. App.][5] [2002][6].

1. Name of original case
2. Volume number of reporter in which the original case is published
3. Abbreviation for the reporter and the series of that reporter (here Pacific Reporter, 3d series); see Abbreviations for Commonly Used Reporters for other reporter abbreviations.
4. Page in the reporter where the opinion begins
5. Court deciding the case (Washington Appellate)
6. Year decided

Additional Case History

[*review denied*, 62 P.3d 889 (Wash. App. 2003)][7], [*and cert. granted, Blakely v. Washington*, 540 U.S. 965 (2003)][8], [*and mot. granted*, 540 U.S. 1174 (2004)][9], [*and rev'd, remanded, Blakely v. Washington*, 542 U.S. 296 (2004)][10], [*reh'g denied*, 542 U.S. 961 (2004)][11]

7. The Washington Appellate Court refused to review the case again.
8. The U.S. Supreme Court agreed to review the case.
9. The U.S. Supreme Court granted a motion regarding the case.
10. The U.S. Supreme Court reversed and remanded the case to the lower court.
11. The U.S. Supreme Court denied another review of the case.

Abbreviations for Commonly Used Reporters for Court Cases

Decisions of the U.S. Supreme Court

S. Ct.: Supreme Court Reporter
U.S.: United States Reports

Decisions from Other Courts: A Selected List

A., A.2d: Atlantic Reporter, Atlantic Reporter Second Series
Cal. Rptr: California Reporter
F.2d: Federal Reporter Second Series
F.3d: Federal Reporter Third Series
F. Supp: Federal Supplement
N.Y.S.2d: New York Supplement Second Series
N.W., N.W.2d: North Western Reporter, North Western Reporter Second Series
N.E., N.E.2d: North Eastern Reporter, North Eastern Reporter Second Series
P., P.3d: Pacific Reporter, Pacific Reporter Third Series
S.E., S.E.2d: South Eastern Reporter, South Eastern Reporter Second Series

Definitions

Aff'd Affirmed; the appellate court agreed with the decision of the lower court.

Aff'd per curiam Affirmed by the court. The opinion is written by the court instead of by one of the judges; a decision affirmed but without a written opinion.

Aff'd sub nom. Affirmed under a different name; the case at the appellate level has a different name from that at the trial court level. A case might also be reversed *sub nom.*

Cert. denied *Certiorari* denied; the U.S. Supreme Court refused to hear and decide the case. Some state supreme courts use this terminology; others use *review denied* or a similar term.

Concurring opinion An opinion agreeing with the court's decision but offering different reasons.

Dismissed The court dismissed the case from legal proceedings, thus refusing to give further consideration to it.

Dissenting opinion An opinion disagreeing with the reasoning and result of the majority opinion.

Later proceeding Any number of issues could be decided in a subsequent proceeding.

Reh'g denied Rehearing denied; the court's refusal to rehear a case that it has previously decided.

Remanded The appellate court sent a case back to the lower court for further action, usually with instructions concerning errors made by that court.

Rev'd Reversed, overthrown, set aside, made void; the appellate court reversed the decision of the lower court.

Rev'd and remanded Reversed and remanded; the appellate court reversed the decision and sent the case back to the lower court for further action.

Vacated Abandoned, set aside, made void; the appellate court set aside the decision of the lower court.

Glossary

A

Acquittal Legal decision regarding the failure of the prosecution to prove the guilt of a defendant in a criminal trial.

Adjudication The process of decision making by a court; normally used to refer to juvenile proceedings. The term is also used to refer to rule enforcement by administrative agencies.

Administrative law Rules, regulations, and enforcements made by agencies to which power has been delegated by other branches of the government. Administrative agencies investigate and decide cases concerning potential violations of these rules.

Adversary system One of two primary systems for settling disputes in court. In a criminal case, the accused is presumed to be innocent. A defense attorney and a prosecuting attorney attempt to convince a judge or a jury of their versions of the case. *See also* **Inquisitory system**.

Aftercare The continued supervision of juveniles after they are released from a correctional facility; similar to the term *parole* in adult criminal court systems.

Aggravated assault Technically, an assault is a threat to commit a battery, but often the term is used to refer to a battery. Aggravated assault generally involves a battery inflicted by use of a deadly weapon.

Aggravating circumstances Circumstances that are above and beyond the elements required for the crime but that make the crime more serious; may be used in reference to many crimes, but the concept is critical in capital punishment cases, where it is required.

Anticipatory search warrant A warrant that is issued for a search at a particular place at a particular time *in the future*. It is based on evidence of a *triggering* event that gives probable cause to believe that the evidence, contraband, or fugitive will be at that place at that time.

Appeal The stage in a legal proceeding in which a higher court is asked to review a decision by a lower court or agency.

Appellant The losing party in a legal proceeding, who seeks a review of the decision by a higher appellate court, or an agency.

Appellee The winning party in a lower court, who argues on appeal against reversing a decision by a lower court or agency.

Arraignment A hearing before a judge, during which the defendant is identified, hears the formal reading of the charges, is read his or her legal rights, and may enter a plea to the charges.

Arrest A law enforcement act of taking a person into custody because the individual is suspected of having committed a crime or is a danger to him- or herself or to others.

Arson The willful and malicious burning of the structure of another with or without the intent to defraud. Burning of one's own property with the intent to defraud is included in some definitions. Many modern statutes carry a more severe penalty for the burning of a dwelling than of other real property.

Assigned counsel An attorney appointed by and paid for by the court to represent a defendant who does not have funds to retain a private attorney.

Attempt In criminal law, refers to an act that may be defined as involving a *substantial* step toward the commission of a crime, combined with the *intent* to commit that crime.

Attendant circumstances Facts surrounding a crime, which are considered to be a part of that crime and that must be proved beyond a reasonable doubt, along with the elements of the crime.

B

Baby Moses laws Provisions for protecting from prosecution persons who abandon newborn babies in ways that will protect those infants, such as leaving them in designated *safe places*.

Bail Money or property posted to guarantee that a defendant will appear for a legal proceeding, such as a trial, sentencing, or imprisonment. If the defendant does not appear, the court may require that the money or property be forfeited.

Beyond a reasonable doubt The standard of proof for evidence required for a conviction in an adult criminal court or processing in a juvenile court; a lack of uncertainty; the facts presented to the judge or jury are sufficient to lead a reasonable person to conclude without question that the accused committed the act(s) charged.

Bond A written document indicating that the defendant or his or her sureties assure the presence of that defendant at a criminal proceeding and that, if the defendant does not appear, the court may require that the security posted for the bond be forfeited.

Booking The official recording of the name, photograph, and fingerprints of a suspect, along with the offense charged and the name of the officer who made the arrest.

Bow Street Runners The mid-eighteenth-century system that gave the police powers of investigation and arrest to constables who were given some training and paid a portion of the fines in successfully prosecuted cases.

Bureau of Justice Statistics (BJS) A federal agency mandated by Congress to collect, analyze, and publish crime data based on surveys of the general population, who are questioned about crime victimizations.

Burglary The illegal or forcible entering of any enclosed structure with the intent to commit a crime, usually theft. Some jurisdictions require that the intent be to commit a felony rather than a less serious crime.

C

Capital punishment Punishment by death for those convicted of a capital crime.

Case law Court decisions constituting legally binding interpretations of written laws, rules, agency, or court decisions. *See also* **Common law**.

Causation In criminal law, the requirement that the act charged be the *cause* of the harmful consequence(s) at issue.

Certification The process used to remove juveniles from the jurisdiction of the juvenile court to that of the adult criminal court; also called *transfer* or *waiver*.

Child abuse The emotional, psychological, or physical abuse of a child by parents, other relatives, acquaintances, or strangers. Includes the use of actual children (in contrast to virtual children) in pornography.

Circumstantial evidence Evidence that may be inferred from a fact or a series of facts. *See also* **Direct evidence**.

Civil law Distinguished from criminal law as the law that pertains to private rights.

Civil rights Sometimes called *civil liberties*; all the natural rights guaranteed by the U.S. Constitution (or by individual state constitutions), such as free speech and the right to religious beliefs and practices; also the body of law concerning natural rights.

Classification In corrections, the assignment of new inmates to the housing, security status, and treatment programs under which they will serve. Hopefully, these assignments are made in terms of those that best fit the inmates' individual needs.

Commissary The correctional facility store (or program) as well as the incidental items sold to inmates; also an inmate's account, which is debited when an item is purchased, as inmates are not permitted to have money within correctional facilities.

Common law Broadly defined, the legal theory and law that originated in England and is also common in the United States. More specifically, common law consists of the guidelines, customs, traditions, and judicial decisions that courts use in decision making. It is contrasted with *constitutions* and *written laws*.

Community-based correction facility A treatment or other correctional program that emphasizes assimilation of offenders into the community. Instead of imprisonment, the offender may be put on probation or placed on work release, education release, or in a drug treatment program, or assigned to a halfway house. Any of these arrangements may be combined with a furlough or parole release plan.

Community work service Punishment assigning the offender to community service or work projects; may be combined with restitution or probation.

COMPSTAT A strategic management process acclaimed by numerous organizations as effective in crime reduction; utilizes computer technology and other modern management techniques to devise methods of fighting crime.

Concurrent sentence A sentence for more than one offense served at the same time. For example, if an offender receives a three-year prison term for robbery and a five-year prison term for assault, these sentences to be served concurrently, the total prison sentence is five years.

Concurring opinion A judge's written opinion agreeing with the result in a case but presenting other reasons for the decision or emphasizing some of the reasons stated by the court's opinion.

Consecutive sentence A term of imprisonment for more than one offense that must be served one following the other. Thus, if an offender receives a three-year term for robbery and a five-year term for assault, the defendant has an eight-year term.

Constable An officer of a municipal corporation who has duties similar to those of a *sheriff*, such as preserving the public peace, executing papers from the court, and maintaining the custody of juries.

Contempt of court An act (usually committed in violation of a court order or rule) considered as embarrassing, humiliating, or as undermining the power of the court; may be civil or criminal.

Continuance The adjournment of a trial or another legal proceeding until a later date.

Contraband Any item (such as weapons, alcohol, or other drugs), possession of which is illegal or violates prison rules.

Contract system System for providing defense attorneys in which a governmental agency contracts with a local bar association, a private law firm, or a private attorney, to provide legal services for indigent defendants.

Corporal punishment Physical punishment, such as beatings or whippings; such punishments are no longer legally permitted in U.S. correctional facilities.

Correctional officer (CO) A corrections employee with supervisory power over a suspect or convicted offender in custody.

Crime An illegal act of omission or commission that is punishable by the criminal law.

Crime rate The number of crimes per 100,000 population.

Crimes known to the police All serious criminal offenses that have been reported to the police for which the police have sufficient evidence to believe the crimes were committed.

Criminal A person found guilty of an act that violates the criminal law.

Criminal justice systems The entire system of criminal prevention, detection, apprehension, trial, sentencing, punishment, and parole, probation, or other forms of supervision within the community.

Criminal law Statutes defining acts so offensive that they threaten the well-being of the society and require that the accused be prosecuted by the government. Criminal laws also prescribe punishments that may be imposed on offenders.

Cross-examination The questioning of a court witness by adversary counsel after one attorney concludes the **direct examination**.

Cruel and unusual punishment The punishments prohibited by the Eighth Amendment to the U.S. Constitution, as interpreted by the courts. Some examples are torture, prison conditions that shock the conscience, excessively long sentences, and the death penalty for rape without murder.

Curtilage The enclosed ground and buildings immediately around a dwelling.

Custody Legal control over a person or property; physical responsibility for a person or thing.

Cybercrime A crime committed by use of the Internet.

Cyberstalking Stalking someone by use of the Internet. *See also* **Stalking**.

D

Date rape Forced sexual acts that occur during a social occasion. The alleged victim may have agreed to some intimacy but not to the activities defined in that jurisdiction as constituting the elements of rape.

Deadly force Force likely to cause serious bodily injury or death.

Defendant A person charged with a crime and against whom a criminal proceeding has begun or is pending.

Defense attorney The counsel for the defendant in a criminal proceeding, whose main function is to protect the legal rights of the accused.

Defenses Responses by the defendant in a criminal or civil case. They may consist only of a denial of the factual allegations of the prosecution (in a criminal case) or of the plaintiff (in a civil case). An *affirmative defense* occurs when the defense offers new factual allegations in an effort to negate the charges.

Delinquency *See* **Juvenile delinquent**.

Demonstrative evidence Real evidence; the kind of evidence that is apparent to the senses, in contrast to evidence presented by the testimony of other people.

De novo Literally, *anew*; *afresh*. A *trial de novo* is a case that is tried again, as if no decision had been previously rendered or, in case of a decision, no transcript was made. In some jurisdictions, the first appeal from a lower court may be a trial *de novo*. The term may also be used to refer to other proceedings, such as a *hearing de novo*.

Department of Homeland Security (DHS) The cabinet level department created after the 9/11 terrorist attacks; its creation constituted the most extensive federal government reorganization in 50 years; it combines 22 federal agencies and constitutes the third largest federal agency.

Deposition Oral testimony taken from the opposing party or a witness for the opposing party. Depositions are taken out of court but under oath. They are recorded verbatim, usually by a court reporter. Attorneys for both sides are present. Depositions may be used when the deposed is not able to appear in court. They may also be used to impeach the testimony of a witness in court.

Deprivation model A model of *prisonization* based on the belief that the prison subculture stems from the way inmates adapt to the severe psychological and physical losses imposed by imprisonment. *See also* **Importation model**.

Detention *See* **Pretrial detention**.

Detention centers Facilities for the temporary confinement of persons (such as juveniles) held in custody while awaiting court disposition.

Determinate sentence A sentence for a specific crime and determined by the legislature; the parole board, correctional officials, or a judge cannot make changes in the sentence length. In some jurisdictions, the trial judge may have the power to suspend the sentence or to impose probation rather than the legislatively specified prison term.

Deterrence A punishment philosophy based on the assumption that the acts of potential offenders can be prevented. *Individual deterrence* refers to the prevention of additional criminal acts by the specific individual being punished; *general deterrence* refers to the presumed effect that punishing one offender will have on other potential offenders.

Dicta Statements by a judge or justice that go beyond the facts of a case and are thus not part of the actual ruling of the court. These statements are not legally binding precedents for future court decisions, although they may be indicative of how that judge would vote in a particular case.

Directed verdict Upon a finding of insufficient evidence to convict a defendant, the judge may direct the jury to return a verdict of not guilty. The judge may not direct a verdict of guilty.

Direct evidence Evidence offered by witnesses who testify to what they saw, heard, tasted, smelled, or touched.

Direct examination The verbal examination in a court proceeding of a person who is testifying; it is conducted by the attorney who called that individual to testify. *See also* **Cross-examination**.

Discovery The process of revealing to opposing counsel the documents and other evidence that are intended for use in the forthcoming trial, along with a list of witnesses counsel proposes to call to testify.

Discretion In a criminal justice system, the authority to make decisions based on one's own judgment rather than on specified rules. The result may be inconsistent handling of offenders, as well as positive actions tailored to individual circumstances.

Disposition The final decision of a court in a criminal or juvenile proceeding to accept a guilty plea, to find the accused guilty or not guilty, or to terminate the proceedings against the accused.

Diversion The removal of the offender from the criminal proceeding before or after guilt is determined and disposition through other procedures, such as work release, drug treatment, or community service.

Domestic violence The causing of serious physical harm or the threatening of such harm to a member of one's family or household, including spouses, ex-spouses, parents, children, persons otherwise related by blood, persons living in the household, or persons who formerly lived there. May include relationships of persons who do not live together but who have had or currently have intimate relationships, such as courtship.

Due process The constitutional principle that a person should not be deprived of life, liberty, or property without reasonable and lawful procedures. Due process must be provided in any adult criminal proceeding, including postconviction procedures, such as prison disciplinary hearings or parole revocations. Many aspects of due process have been extended to juvenile court proceedings.

E

Elder abuse Violent, psychological, financial, negligent, and other types of abuse of elderly persons. The crime is frequently committed by family members and involves such acts as stealing Social Security checks, withholding food stamps, committing assault and battery, neglecting to provide food and medications, and so on. Fraud against the elderly committed by strangers appears to be an increasing type of elder abuse.

Equal protection All persons under like circumstances must receive essentially the same treatment in criminal justice systems; they may not be discriminated against because of race or ethnicity, gender, minority status, disability, nationality, religion, or sexual orientation. Not all jurisdictions recognize all of these categories.

Euthanasia Painlessly ending the life of another, often at that person's request, because the individual is suffering intense pain that cannot be controlled and is near death as the result of an incurable disease. It is considered to be an act of mercy and may be referred to as *mercy killing*. The practice is illegal in most jurisdictions. *See also* **Physician assisted suicide**.

Exclusionary rule Requirement that evidence secured as the result of illegal actions by law enforcement officers must be excluded from a legal proceeding, such as a trial.

Expert witness A person with extensive training or education in a particular field, such as medicine, who testifies at depositions or at trials concerning a critical issue of that case, such as what caused the death of the deceased.

F

Federal Bureau of Investigation (FBI) A U.S. federal agency established in 1908 and delegated the power to investigate alleged violations of federal laws (unless they are otherwise assigned to another agency). The FBI investigates alleged civil, criminal, and securities violations. Although the agency is a federal one, it can, when requested, assist local and state law enforcement agencies with their investigations.

Felony A serious offense, such as murder, armed robbery, or rape. Punishment ranges from execution to imprisonment in a state or federal institution but also includes probation, community work service, fines, and other less punitive sanctions, as well as a combination of these measures.

Felony probation A probationary term for an offender convicted of a felony, in contrast to a misdemeanor.

Fetal abuse The abusing of a fetus, which may or may not lead to its death. In some jurisdictions, a resulting death of the fetus may lead to legal culpability, such as a murder or a manslaughter charge.

Fine The payment of a sum of money to a court by a convicted defendant in addition to or instead of other punishment(s).

Fleeing felon rule The common law rule that permitted law enforcement officers to shoot at any fleeing felon. The rule has been modified to require circumstances involving (1) the threat of serious injury to or death of an officer or others; (2) the prevention of an escape if the suspect threatens the officer with a gun; or (3) the officer's having probable cause to believe that the suspect has committed or has threatened to commit serious bodily harm.

Frankpledge system In old English law, a system whereby the members of a *tithing* had corporate responsibility for the behavior of all members over 14 years old. Ten tithings formed a *hundred*, and hundreds were later combined to form *shires*, similar to counties, over which a sheriff had jurisdiction.

Frisk An action by a law enforcement officer, airport security officer, or a correctional officer in a penal setting, consisting of patting down or running one's hands quickly over a person's body to determine whether the individual has a weapon or other contraband. This is in contrast to a body search, which is a more careful and thorough examination of the person.

Furlough In corrections, an authorized, temporary leave from a prison or other penal facility in order to attend a funeral, visit family, attempt to secure employment, or engage in any other approved activity.

G

Good faith exception The provision that illegally obtained evidence will not be excluded from a subsequent trial or other legal proceeding if it can be shown that law enforcement officers secured the evidence in good faith, meaning that they had a reasonable belief that they were acting in accordance with the law.

Good-time credits Credit for hours or days awarded for an inmate's satisfactory behavior in prison and resulting in a reduction of prison time that must be served.

Grand jury A group of citizens, convened by legal authority, who evaluate evidence to ascertain whether a crime has been committed and whether there is sufficient evidence against the accused to justify prosecution. If so, the grand jury may return an *indictment.* In some jurisdictions, grand juries are empowered to conduct investigations into alleged criminal activities.

H

Halfway house A place of confinement, such as a prerelease center, used to prepare an inmate for his or her return from confinement to living in free society. A halfway house may also be used to confine convicted offenders rather than send them to prison.

Hands-off doctrine A policy that courts use to justify nonintervention in the daily administration of corrections agencies.

Hate crime As defined in the federal criminal code, a crime "that manifests evidence of prejudice based on race, religion, disability, sexual orientation, or ethnicity, including where appropriate the crimes of murder, non-negligent manslaughter, forcible rape, aggravated assault, simple assault, intimidation, arson, and destruction, damage or vandalism of property." Penalties may be enhanced when a crime is designated as a hate crime.

Hearsay evidence Evidence of which witnesses do not have personal knowledge but merely repeat what they have heard others say. Hearsay evidence must be excluded from a trial unless it meets one of the legally recognized exceptions to the hearsay rule.

House arrest A form of confinement, usually on probation or parole, in which the offender is permitted to live at home (or some other approved place) but is restricted in his or her movements to and from the area. A curfew may be imposed, and the offender may be subject to unannounced visits from a probation or parole officer. In some cases, electronic devices are used to monitor the person's location.

Humanitarianism In penal philosophy, the doctrine advocating the removal of harsh, severe, and painful conditions in penal institutions.

Hundred In English law, a combination of ten tithings as part of the Frankpledge system. *See also* **Tithing** and **Frankpledge system**.

I

Identity theft The stealing of an individual's Social Security number or other important information about his or her identity and using that information to commit crimes, such as removing funds from the victim's bank account or using the person's credit cards.

Importation model A model based on the assumption that the inmate subculture arises not only from internal prison experiences but also from external patterns of behavior that the inmates take into prison. *See also* **Deprivation model**.

Incapacitation A punishment theory usually implemented by imprisoning an offender to prevent the commission of any other crimes by that person. In some countries (and in earlier days in the United States), incapacitation involved mutilation, such as removing the hands of thieves and castrating sex offenders.

Incarceration Imprisonment in a jail, a prison, or another type of penal institution.

Indeterminate sentence A sentence to confinement without a definite term. Parole board members or other persons determine when the offender should be released.

Index offenses The FBI's *Uniform Crime Reports* previously listed the occurrences of the eight crimes considered most serious: murder and nonnegligent manslaughter, rape, robbery, aggravated assault, burglary, larceny-theft, motor vehicle theft, and arson as index offenses. In June 2004, the FBI discontinued publishing data according to index offenses because of the misrepresentation of crime in an area that can be caused by a very high (or low) volume or rate of crime of only one of these serious crimes in that area.

Indictment The written accusation of a grand jury, formally stating that probable cause exists to believe that the suspect committed a specified felony.

Inevitable discovery rule Evidence secured illegally by police will not be excluded from the suspect's trial, provided it can be shown that the evidence would have been discovered anyway under legal means.

Informant A person who gives information to law enforcement officials about a crime or planned criminal activity.

Information A formal written document used to charge a person with a specific offense. Prosecutors issue informations, in contrast to an *indictment* issued by a grand jury.

Initial appearance The first appearance of the accused before a magistrate; if the accused is detained in jail immediately after arrest, he or she must be taken quickly to a magistrate for the initial appearance. At that point, the magistrate decides whether there is probable cause to detain the suspect and, if so, tells the suspect of the charges and of his or her constitutional rights, including the right to an attorney.

Injunction. A remedy issued by a court to order a person or an agency to do something or stop doing something; based on a request by a party who petitions the court for the relief. There are several kinds of injunctions, including those that are preliminary (until a further hearing), partial, temporary, or permanent.

Inmates Convicted persons who are confined in jails, prisons, or other penal facilities.

Inquisitory system One of two primary systems for settling disputes in court, in which the defendant must prove his or her innocence, in contrast to the *adversary system*, which has a presumption of innocence, requiring the state (or federal prosecutors in federal cases) to prove the defendant's guilt beyond a reasonable doubt.

Intake decision In prosecution, the first review of a case by an official in the prosecutor's office. Weak cases may be weeded out at this stage; in juvenile courts, the reception of a juvenile against whom complaints have been made. The decision to dismiss or proceed with a case may be made at this stage.

Intensive probation supervision (IPS) Close and intensive supervision of probationers by probation officers, presumably with small caseloads.

INTERPOL A world police organization that was established for the purpose of cooperation among nations involved in common policing problems.

Interrogatories A set of questions given to a party thought to have pertinent information that may be used at a trial or other legal proceeding. The party completing the interrogatories must sign an oath that the statements are correct.

Intimate partner violence (IPV) Violence toward a current or former spouse, or other persons with whom one has had an intimate relationship; also referred to as *courtship violence*.

J

Jail A local, regional, or federal facility used to confine persons awaiting a legal proceeding, as well as those serving short sentences.

Jessica's Law A law requiring registration and other restrictions placed on sex offenders living in the community; named after Jessica Lunsford, a young Florida victim of a released sex offender living near her home.

Judge An elected or appointed officer who presides over a court of law; the final and neutral arbiter of law who is responsible for all activities within that court system. A judge's opinion may be subject to an appeal.

Judicial review The authority of an appellate court to review the decisions of lower courts and the executive and legislative branches of government within its jurisdiction in order to determine whether any of those acts are in violation of that jurisdiction's case, statutory, or constitutional law.

Jurisdiction The lawful exercise of authority; the area within which authority may be exercised, such as the geographical area within which a court, police force, etc., has legal authority to act. Courts may have *original jurisdiction* to hear a case; if more than one court has authority to hear the same case, those courts have *concurrent jurisdiction*. *Exclusive jurisdiction* means that only one court may hear the case. *Appellate jurisdiction* is the power of a court to hear a case on appeal.

Jury In a criminal case, a group of people who have sworn to listen to the evidence during a trial and to decide whether the defendant is guilty or not guilty. In some jurisdictions, after a conviction, a jury may also recommend or even determine the sentence.

Just deserts The belief that those who commit crimes should be punished for those crimes; also the amount or type of punishment a particular offender deserves.

Juvenile A young person under age for certain privileges, such as voting, drinking alcoholic beverages, or consenting to sexual acts. If accused of a criminal or juvenile offense, usually a juvenile is not tried by an adult criminal court but is processed in the juvenile court, although when serious crimes are alleged, in many jurisdictions, juveniles may be tried in adult criminal courts.

Juvenile court The court having jurisdiction over juveniles who are accused of delinquent acts or offenses or criminal acts or who are in need of supervision because they are allegedly being neglected or mistreated by their parents or other guardians.

Juvenile delinquent A person under legal age (the maximum age varies among the states from 16 to 21, but 18 is the most common) whom a juvenile court has determined to be incorrigible or in violation of a juvenile or a criminal statute.

K

Kidnapping Restricting the freedom of a victim against his or her will and removing that victim from one place to another. *See also* **Parental kidnapping**.

L

Larceny-theft The unlawful removal and taking away of someone else's property with the intention of keeping it permanently. Historically, small thefts were categorized as *petit larceny* and large thefts as *grand larceny*. Some modern theft laws do not distinguish between these two types of larceny-theft.

Law Enforcement Assistance Administration (LEAA) The agency, established by Congress in 1965, that provided funding for the development of police departments, police techniques, police education, and police training. It was abolished in 1982. Money for law enforcement education was provided through the Law Enforcement Education Program (LEEP).

Law Enforcement Education Program (LEEP) *See* **Law Enforcement Assistance Administration (LEAA)**.

Legal duty An obligation to another that is imposed by law, such as the duty of a parent to go to the rescue of his or her child.

Lesser included offense An offense that is less serious than the crime thought to have been committed by the suspect. It has some but not all of the elements of the suspected crime. For example, second-degree murder is a lesser included offense within murder, but premeditation, required for first-degree murder, is not an element of second-degree murder. Manslaughter is also a lesser included offense within murder.

Lineup A procedure in which a group of people are placed together in a line to permit the complainant or an eyewitness to the crime to view the persons in an attempt to identify the alleged offender.

M

Magistrate A judge in the lower courts of the state or federal court system. Usually, magistrates preside over arraignments, preliminary hearings, bail hearings, and minor offenses.

Mala in se Actions that are intrinsically immoral, such as murder, rape, and robbery.

Mala prohibita Actions, such as the possession of small amounts of marijuana, that are wrong because legislation prohibits them, although there may not be general agreement that they are wrong in themselves.

Mandatory sentence A sentence having a length imposed by the legislature, with no discretion given to the trial judge. If the defendant is convicted, the specified sentence must be imposed.

Manslaughter The unlawful killing of a human being by a person who lacks malice. Manslaughter may be *involuntary* (or *negligent*), the result of recklessness while committing an unlawful act (such as driving while intoxicated), or *voluntary*, an intentional killing committed in the heat of passion.

Marital rape Rape of one spouse by another. Not all jurisdictions recognize this act as a crime, although the number that do so is increasing.

Marshal A sworn law enforcement officer who performs the civil duties of the courts, such as the delivery of papers to begin civil proceedings. In some jurisdictions, marshals serve papers for the arrest of criminal suspects and escort inmates between jail and court or into the community when they are permitted to leave the jail or prison temporarily. Marshals may also transport offenders from one jurisdiction to another; escort fugitives from their places of capture to the jurisdictions in which they will be tried; provide security for designated persons; or fly on planes as an added security measure.

Megan's Law A law requiring sex offenders released from confinement to register with local law enforcement authorities when they move into a community. In some jurisdictions, the offenders are required only to notify law enforcement officers, but in others, they must notify all residents within a certain distance of their residences. Megan's Law is named after Megan Kanka, who was raped and murdered by a neighbor who lived across the street from her home and who was a released sex offender, as were his housemates.

Mens rea The required criminal intent of the accused at the time an alleged criminal act was committed.

***Miranda* warning** The rule, stemming from *Miranda v. Arizona*, that stipulates that anyone in custody for an offense that might result in a jail or prison term must be warned of certain rights before any questioning by law enforcement officials occurs. These rights include the right to remain silent, to be told that anything said can and will be held against the suspect, the right to counsel (which will be appointed if the suspect cannot afford to retain private counsel), and the right to cease talking at any time. If the warning is not given or is given and violated, any information obtained from the suspect may be inadmissible as evidence at trial. The defendant may waive these rights if this is done willingly and knowingly and with the legal capacity to make that decision.

Misdemeanor A less serious offense, punishable by a fine, probation, community work service, or a short jail term, in contrast to a felony, a more serious crime.

Mistrial A trial that is invalid and thus cannot stand. Judges may declare a mistrial for such reasons as an error on the part of the prosecution or the defense, the illness or death of any of the parties participating in the legal proceedings, jury tampering, or the jury's inability to reach a verdict within a reasonable period of time.

Mitigating circumstances Circumstances that do not justify or excuse a crime but that, because of justice and fairness, make the crime less reprehensible; they may be used to reduce a charge to a lesser offense, such as to reduce murder to manslaughter. Mitigating circumstances must be considered before the death penalty can be imposed. *See also* **Aggravating circumstances.**

Molly Maguires A powerful secret police organization in the 1870s in Pennsylvania.

Moot The term used to describe a controversy that has ended or evolved to the stage at which a court decision is no longer relevant or necessary as it would not have an impact on the legal rights of the parties before the court.

Motion A written document (or a verbal request) submitted to the court, asking for an order or a ruling.

Motor vehicle theft The stealing of a motor vehicle, in contrast to the stealing of a vehicle part or larceny-theft *from* a motor vehicle.

Murder The unlawful killing of another person with either express or implied malice aforethought. Some jurisdictions also include a fetus as a victim.

N

National Crime Victimization Survey (NCVS) Crime data collected by the Bureau of Justice Statistics (BJS) and based on surveys of people to determine who has been victimized by crime and the nature of that victimization.

National Incident-Based Reporting System (NIBRS) A reporting system used by the FBI in collecting crime data. In this system, a crime is viewed along with all of its components, including the type of victim, type of weapon, location of the crime, alcohol/drug influence, type of criminal activity, relationship of victim to offender, and residence of victims and arrestees, as well as a description of the property and its value.

Negligence In law, an act that a reasonable person would not do, or would not fail to do under similar circumstances. Liability for negligence does not require a criminal intent.

Nolo contendere Literally, "I will not contest it." In a criminal case, this plea has the legal effect of a guilty plea, but it cannot be used against the defendant in a civil action based on the same act. The plea might be used in a case involving a felony charge of driving while intoxicated. A guilty plea could be used as evidence of liability in a civil action of wrongful death filed by the family of a victim who died in the accident, whereas a *nolo* plea requires that the plaintiff in the civil action *prove* liability.

Nonnegligent manslaughter *See* **Manslaughter.**

Norms The rules or standards of behavior, shared by members of a social group, that define appropriate behavior.

O

Offenders Persons who have committed a criminal offense and either entered a guilty plea or have been adjudicated as guilty by a court of law.

Open prison A prison that makes use of the natural environment for security purposes. For example, the prison might be located on an island surrounded by treacherous waters, as in the case of Alcatraz, located in San Francisco Bay and once used as a maximum-security federal prison.

P

Pardon An act by a state governor or the U.S. president (in federal cases) that exempts a convicted offender from punishment or, in the case of those already serving terms, further punishment, and removes the legal consequences of the conviction. Pardons may also be granted after a person is released from prison. Pardons may be absolute or conditional; individual or granted to a group, or class, of offenders; and may be full or partial, in which case the pardon remits only part of the punishment or removes some of the legal disabilities resulting from the conviction.

Parens patriae Literally, "parent of the country"; the doctrine from English common law that was the basis for allowing the state to take over guardianship of a child. In the United States, the doctrine forms the basis for juvenile court jurisdiction. The doctrine presumes that the state acts in the best interests of the child.

Parental kidnapping The crime of **kidnapping** a child, committed by a parent who does not have the legal authority to take the child or who has not been granted permission to do so by the parent (or other person) who has legal custody or by the court.

Parole The status of an inmate who is released before the completion of his or her prison sentence. Usually, the parolee must be supervised in the community by a parole officer.

Parole board A panel that decides whether an inmate is released on parole from a prison before the expiration of his or her sentence. In some jurisdictions, the parole board makes recommendations but the governor makes the final decisions regarding parole release.

Parole officer A government employee who supervises and counsels inmates paroled to the community. He or she may have the power to recommend parole revocation or even to revoke parole when parolees violate the terms of their release.

Parole revocation The process of removing the parole status of an individual due to violations of parole conditions or for committing a new crime. The revocation, which requires due process, often results in returning the parolee to prison or some other confinement institution.

Penitentiary Historically, an institution intended to isolate convicted offenders from one another, giving them time to reflect on their bad acts and become penitent; later, synonymous with prison.

Peremptory challenge A challenge that may be used by the prosecution or the defense to exclude a potential juror from the jury panel without stating a reason for doing so. Each attorney gets a specified number of peremptory challenges. Peremptory challenges are distinguished from *challenges for cause*, which are unlimited and must be based on a reason for disqualification, such as a conflict of interest with the case.

Petition A formal document for filing an action with a criminal or juvenile court, requesting the court to grant a request, such as a petition for a new hearing.

Petit jury *Petit* literally means "small, minor, or inconsiderate"; a trial jury, in contrast to a *grand jury*. *See also* **Jury**.

Physician assisted suicide (PAS) An act by a physician that enables a patient to take his or her own life in a relatively painless way, such as by self-administering a sufficient amount of drugs prescribed by the physician and designed to end that individual's life.

Plain view doctrine The legal doctrine that permits a law enforcement officer who is legally searching a place for particular items to seize those items that are in plain view but not listed on the search warrant.

Plea bargaining Negotiations between the defense and the prosecution before or during the trial of a defendant. The process may result in reducing or dropping some charges or in a recommendation for leniency in exchange for a plea of guilty on another charge(s). Plea bargaining may also result in no changes in the charges or sentence recommendations. Any bargain reached by the attorneys must be approved by the judge.

Police An official authorized to enforce the law, provide services, and maintain order, using physical (including deadly) force if necessary.

Posse The rural police system in which the sheriff may call into action any number of citizens over a certain age if they are needed to assist in law enforcement.

Prejudicial errors Errors made during legal proceedings that substantially affect the rights of parties and thus may result in the reversal of a case.

Preliminary hearing An appearance before a lower court judge to determine whether there is sufficient evidence to submit the case to the grand jury or to the trial court. Preliminary hearings may include the bail decision.

Presentence investigation (PSI) An investigation of the background and characteristics of the defendant; it may include information that would not be admissible at the trial; it is presented to the court to be used in determining a sentence.

Presentment A document issued by a grand jury that states that probable cause exists to believe that the suspect committed the crime. Presentments are issued without the participation of the prosecutor. *See also* **Indictment**.

Presumption of innocence A cornerstone of the adversary system; provides that a defendant is innocent unless and until the prosecution proves guilt beyond a reasonable doubt, as determined by the decision maker, usually a jury.

Presumptive sentence The normal sentence is specified by statute for each offense; judges are permitted to deviate from that sentence but usually may do so only under specified circumstances or must give reasons for the deviation.

Pretextual stop A stop allegedly for a minor traffic offense but actually conducted as a pretense to look for a more serious offense, such as the possession of illegal drugs.

Pretrial detention The detention of a person in jail (or some other approved facility) between arrest and trial, either because the judge has refused bail or the defendant cannot meet the bail requirements. Generally, the purpose of detention is to assure the presence of the accused at trial. Defendants may also be detained because they are thought to present a danger to themselves, to others, or to both if they are released pending a trial or other judicial proceeding. Such detention is referred to as *preventive detention.*

Preventive detention *See* **Pretrial detention**.

***Prima facie* evidence** Evidence that, on its face, is sufficient to constitute a fact unless it is sufficiently refuted.

Prison A federal or state penal facility for detaining adult offenders (although juvenile offenders are also incarcerated in adult facilities on occasion) sentenced to a year or longer after conviction of crimes.

Prisonization The process of an inmate's becoming accustomed to the subculture of prison life.

Private security forces Persons employed privately instead of by the government to provide security from criminal activity.

Proactive In policing, preparing for, intervening in, or taking the initiative in finding criminals, in contrast to depending on the reports of others.

Probable cause In search warrant cases, a set of facts and circumstances that leads to the reasonable belief that the items sought are located in a particular place. In arrest cases, the facts and circumstances lead to the reasonable belief that the suspect has committed a crime.

Probation A type of sentence that permits a convicted offender to remain in the community, usually under the supervision of a probation officer, rather than be incarcerated. Also the part of the criminal justice system that is in charge of all aspects of probation.

Probation officer A government official responsible for writing the presentence reports on offenders; supervising probationers; reporting violations of probation conditions; and providing evidence of those violations.

Probation revocation The process of declaring that a sentenced offender violated the terms of probation and that probation will, as a result, be revoked or cancelled. If probation involved a suspended prison or jail sentence, the revocation may mean that the original sentence is invoked and the individual is sent to a prison, jail, or other penal facility.

Procedural law The body of law that provides the legal methods of procedures by which *substantive law* is enforced.

Property crimes Crimes aimed at property. Serious property crimes include larceny-theft, burglary, motor vehicle theft, and arson.

Pro se Literally, "on behalf of self"; acting as one's own attorney.

Prosecuting attorney A government official responsible for representing the state (or federal government) against an offender in criminal proceedings.

Prosecution The process that occurs when the state (or federal government) begins the formal process in a criminal case. The action is taken by a prosecuting attorney.

Public defender An attorney retained and paid for by the government to represent indigent defendants in criminal proceedings.

R

Racial profiling The reaction to persons based solely on their race or ethnicity.

Rape Historically, unlawful vaginal intercourse with a woman by threat or force and against her will. Unlawful intercourse is called *statutory rape* if the act is consensual but the alleged victim is under the age to which one may legally consent to sex. More recently, some rape statutes have been rewritten to include male victims and female perpetrators, as well as penetration of any body opening by any instrument (called *rape by instrumentation*), including but not limited to the male sexual organ. Recently, the FBI changed its reference from the use of the term *forcible rape* to *rape.*

Reactive In policing, depending on the reports of others to find criminal suspects and evidence of an alleged crime, rather than working proactively. It is important because police are not in a position to observe most criminal behavior.

Recidivism The process by offenders of committing additional crimes.

Recidivists Offenders who commit crimes repeatedly, especially those who do so after they are released from a term of confinement in a jail or a prison.

Recusal The removal of oneself from a proceeding, such as by a judge who has a conflict of interest in a case.

Reformatory An early correctional facility, which was less physically secure than prisons and in which the emphasis was on changing or reforming the offender. Today the term is normally used to refer to institutions for the confinement of juveniles who have been adjudicated in a juvenile court and ordered to serve time.

Rehabilitation A punishment philosophy based on a belief that the offender can and will change to a law-abiding person through treatment programs and facilities. Rehabilitation may be most likely to occur in community-based programs rather than during incarceration in penal institutions. The *rehabilitative ideal* is embodied in specific treatment facilities, such as those for substance abuse offenders, as well as by use of probation, parole, the indeterminate sentence, and the juvenile court.

Reintegration A punishment philosophy emphasizing the return of the offender to the community, so that employment, family ties, and education can be restored.

Restitution Punishment that requires an offender to repay the victim with services or money. This punishment may be imposed instead of or in addition to other punishment or fines and may be a requirement of probation or parole.

Retribution The philosophy that offenders should be given the punishment they deserve in light of the crime they committed, such as "an eye for an eye."

Right to counsel The right to be represented by an attorney at crucial stages in the criminal justice system. Indigent defendants have the right to counsel provided by the state (or, in the case of a federal offense, the federal government).

Robbery The use of force or fear to take personal property from the person of another against that person's will.

S

Sanction A penalty or punishment that is imposed on a person in order to enforce the law.

Search and seizure The examination of a person or a person's property and the taking of items that may be evidence of criminal activity; generally requires a search warrant. Unreasonable searches and seizures are prohibited by the U.S. Constitution.

Search warrant *See* **Warrant**.

Self-report data (SRD) Crime data collected by asking people to report about their criminal activity; usually conducted by use of anonymous questionnaires.

Sentence The punishment imposed by the court on a convicted offender.

Sentence disparity Inequalities and differences in sentencing as, for example, when people found guilty of the same crime receive sentences varying in length and type, without reasonable justification for those differences.

Sheriff The chief law enforcement officer in a county, usually chosen by popular election.

Shires *See* **Frankpledge system.**

Showup An identification procedure during a police investigation; it involves showing the alleged victim only one person rather than several, as in a *lineup*; the process is permitted only in extraordinary circumstances.

Silent system In penitentiaries, the historical practice of not permitting inmates to speak with one another. In some institutions, inmates communicated by use of sign language.

Social system The interrelationship of roles, acts, and statuses of people who make up the social structure; a social group or set of interacting persons or groups considered a unitary whole because it reflects the common values, social norms, and objectives of the individuals whom it comprises, even though the group is considered distinct from those individuals.

Stalking Defined by the National Violence Against Women Survey as "a course of conduct directed at a specific person that involves repeated visual or physical proximity, nonconsensual communication, or verbal, written or implied threats, or a combination thereof, that would cause a reasonable person fear." The word *repeated* means two or more times. Jurisdictional statutes may vary from this definition. *See also* **Cyberstalking**.

Stare decisis Literally, "let the decision stand." The doctrine that courts will abide by or adhere to the rulings of previous court decisions when deciding cases having substantially the same facts.

Status offense A class of crime that does not consist of proscribed action or inaction but, rather, of the personal condition or characteristic of the accused—for example, being a vagrant. In juvenile law, a variety of acts that would not be considered criminal if committed by an adult—for example, being insubordinate or truant, or running away from home.

Statute of limitations The time limit in which to file a charge for a crime or a civil action. The statute of limitations may differ from jurisdiction to jurisdiction but usually does not apply to murder charges, which may be brought at any time. Recently, some jurisdictions have removed or extended the statute of limitations for sexual abuse crimes.

Statutory law Law that the legislature has originated and passed by written enactment and that has been signed by the state's governor (or, in the case of federal law, by the president of the United States).

Statutory rape *See* **Rape**.

Subculture A group of significant size whose behavior differs significantly from the behavior of the dominant groups in society.

Subpoena A command, issued by a court, ordering a person to appear in court (or at another designated place) at a specified time and place for the purpose of giving testimony on a specified issue. Persons may be ordered to bring documents pertinent to the case; that order is called a *subpoena duces tecum*.

Substantive law Law that defines the elements of crimes and the punishments legally available for those acts. *See also* **Procedural law**.

Summons A formal document issued by the court to notify a person that his or her presence is required in court for a particular reason at a specified time and date.

T

Theft *See* **Larceny-theft**.

Three strikes and you're out Name of legislation enacted in recent years and designed to impose long sentences on persons who commit three or more serious crimes.

Tithing In English history, a system of ten families who had responsibility for the behavior of members over the age of 14. Tithings were also important in protecting the group from outsiders. *See also* **Frankpledge** and **Hundred**.

Training school A secure corrections facility for juveniles who are confined by juvenile court order.

Transportation Security Administration (TSA) A federal agency created by the Aviation and Transportation Security Act (ATSA), enacted two months after the 9/11 terrorist attacks. The TSA was developed to take over the security screening functions for all commercial flights in the United States.

Trial In criminal law, a court proceeding during which a judge, a jury, or both listen to the evidence as presented by the defense and the prosecution and determine whether the defendant is guilty beyond a reasonable doubt, or should be acquitted. *See also* **Mistrial**.

True bill The prosecutor's indictment returned with the approval of the grand jury. After hearing the prosecutor's evidence, the grand jury determines that the indictment is accurate; that is, it is a *true bill*.

Truth in sentencing The concept requiring that actual time served by offenders is closer to the time allocated for the sentence. Many jurisdictions established 85 percent as their goal, meaning that offenders could not be released for any reason until they served 85 percent of their sentences.

U

Uniform Crime Reports (UCR) Official crime data, collected and published by the Federal Bureau of Investigation (FBI) and based on *crimes known to the police*—crimes that are reported to or observed by the police and that the police have reason to believe were committed.

USA Patriot Act The Uniting and Strengthening America by Providing Appropriate Tools Required to Intercept and Obstruct Terrorism Act of 2001, enacted in response to the 9/11 terrorist attacks and subsequently amended.

V

Venue The location of a trial; a *change of venue* is the removal of a trial from the location where it would normally be held to another location, either to avoid public pressure or to obtain an impartial jury.

Victim compensation programs Plans for assisting crime victims in making social, emotional, and economic adjustments.

Victimology The discipline that studies the nature and causes of victimization, as well as programs for aiding victims and preventing victimization.

Vigilantism Literally, *watchman*; action by a person who is alert and on guard, cautious, suspicious, ready to take action to maintain and preserve peace; actions of citizens who take the law into their own hands in an effort to catch and punish criminals.

Violent crimes Crimes defined by the FBI's *Uniform Crime Reports* as serious crimes against a person. They include murder and nonnegligent manslaughter, robbery, rape, and aggravated assault.

Voir dire To speak the truth; the process of questioning prospective jurors to determine their qualifications and desirability for serving on a jury.

W

Waiver In criminal law, the giving up of one's legal rights, such as the right to counsel or to a jury trial. Waivers must be made knowingly and intelligently; that is, the defendant must understand what is being relinquished. In juvenile proceedings, juveniles may be waived to the jurisdiction of adult criminal courts. Some rights may not be waived.

Warden Historically, the chief administrative officer in a correctional facility, most generally a prison.

Warrant A court-issued document authorizing an officer to arrest a suspect or to search a person, personal property, or a place for specified reasons. A warrant should be issued only on a finding of probable cause.

Watch system A system charged with the duties of overseeing, patrolling, or guarding an area or a person. Watchmen were prominent in the early watch system of policing.

White collar crime The illegal actions of corporations or individuals, committed while pursuing their legitimate occupations. Examples are consumer fraud, bribery, and embezzlement.

Workhouse An English institution used to confine and punish offenders who were forced to work at unpleasant tasks. The term is used in some places today to refer to institutions that emphasize reformation or rehabilitation through work.

Work release The release of an inmate to attend school or to work outside the institution but requiring that person to return to the institution at specified times, such as at night.

Writ An order from a court. *See also* **Writ of *certiorari*.**

Writ of *certiorari* *Certiorari* literally means "to be informed of." A *writ* is an order from a court giving authority for an act to be done or ordering that it be done; a writ of *certiorari* is used by courts that have discretion to determine which cases they will hear. Today this writ is most commonly associated with the U.S. Supreme Court.

Case Index

Name Index

General Index

E

Q

R

Photo Credits

Chapter 1, page 4: Memorial in aftermath of Parkland shooting, AP photo/Wilfredo Lee; **14**: Man on cell phone, ©photka/Fotolia; **18**: Angel Raich, AP Photo/J. Scott Applewhite

Chapter 2, page 32: Mourner of James Byrd, Jr., AP Photo/David J. Phillip; **36**: Richard Guthrie, Ozier Muhammad/The New York Times/Redux

Chapter 3, page 51: London policeman, ©jerome DELAHAYE/Fotolia; **59**: U.S./Mexico Border Crossing, Omar Martinez/picture-alliance/dpa/AP Images; **66**: William Bratton, AP Photo/John Minchillo

Chapter 4, page 78: March in Washington D.C., 1053377672; **81**: Traffic policeman, ©mario beauregard/Fotolia; **83**: Policeman with suspect, ©Lisa F. Young/Fotolia

Chapter 5, page 113: Police officer funeral, 10067958a

Chapter 6, page 126: U.S. Capitol, ©anujakjaimook/Fotolia; **127**: Supreme Court, ©trekandphoto/Fotolia; **139**: Sonia Sotomayor, Steve Petteway, Collection of the Supreme Court of the United States

Chapter 7, page 146: Law school class, ©Monkey Business/Fotolia; **156**: Clarence Earl Gideon, Florida Department of Corrections/State Archives of Florida; **156**: Gideon's petition, Collection of the Supreme Court of the United States; **163**: Jerry Brown signing California Money Bail Reform Act, AP Photo/Rich Pedroncelli

Chapter 8, page 195: Michael Morton, AP Photo/Austin American-Statesman, Ricardo B. Brazziell

Chapter 9, page 205: Walnut Street jail, Library of Congress, 3a29866; **207**: Early New York prison at Auburn, New York State Archives; Education Dept. Division of Visual Instruction, Instructional lantern slides, circa 1856-1939, A3045-78, D47 ApS; **210**: Alcatraz, ©Alessandro Lai/Fotolia; **214**: Overcrowded prison, AP Photo/Rich Pedroncelli

Chapter 10, page 229: Correctional officer at Deuel Vocational Institute, AP Photo/Rich Pedroncelli; **239**: Female inmate, Laurie Mason Schroeder/The Morning Call via AP

Chapter 11, page 272: George W. Bush before signing Adam Walsh Child Protection and Safety Act, White House photo by Paul Morse

Chapter 12, page 298: Juvenile prisoner, ©Alexander Raths/Fotolia

Printed in the USA
CPSIA information can be obtained
at www.ICGtesting.com
LVHW020312060823
754369LV00006B/347

9 781543 800227